Uganda's Civil Society

History, Challenges, Prospects

Editors
John De Coninck, Arthur Larok

FOUNTAIN PUBLISHERS
www.fountainpublishers.co.ug

Fountain Publishers
P. O. Box 488
Kampala
E-mail: sales@fountainpublishers.co.ug
         publishing@fountainpublishers.co.ug
Website: www.fountainpublishers.co.ug

Distributed in Europe, North America and Australia by
African Books Collective Ltd (ABC),
P. O. Box 721
Oxford OXON OX1 9EN,
United Kingdom.
Tel: 44(0) 1865–726686, Fax: 44(0)1865–412 341.
E-mail: orders@africanbookscollective.com
abc@africanbookscollective.com
Website: www.africanbookscollective.com

© The National NGO Forum 2021
First published 2021

All rights reserved. No part of this publication may be reproduced, stored in a retrieval system or transmitted in any form or by any means electronic, mechanical, photocopying, recording or otherwise without the prior written permission of the publisher.

ISBN: 978–9970–19–601–2

Contents

Foreword .... *v*
Acknowledgments and Dedication .... *vii*

SECTION I: INTRODUCTION

Chapter 1 Uganda's Civil Society – An Overview of Issues. 1

SECTION II: UGANDA'S EVOLVING AND DIVERSE CIVIL SOCIETY

Chapter 2 Expanding 'Civil Society': Women and Political Space in Contemporary Uganda 13

Chapter 3 Contemporary Civil Society and the Democratisation Process in Uganda: A Preliminary Exploration 34

Chapter 4 "Find the Groups and you have Found the Poor?": Exploring the Dynamics of Community-based Organisations in Arua and Kabale 58

Chapter 5 Building Community Associations from the Inside or the Outside? Social Capital and Community Associations in Northern Uganda   79

Chapter 6 The Social Power of Religious Organisation and Civil Society: The Catholic Church in Uganda 106

Chapter 7 Traditional Leaders and Decentralisation 132

SECTION III: A VALUE-DRIVEN SECTOR?

Chapter 8 The State, Civil Society and Development Policy in Uganda: Where are we Coming From? 147

Chapter 9 "Webisanga Kabaka!" (You behave like a King!): Civil Society Leadership in Uganda 164

Chapter 10 Climbing the Credibility Ladder: Civil Society, Donor Support and the Accountability Challenge in Uganda 205

SECTION IV: CREATING IMPACT

Chapter 11 The Ambiguities of the 'Partnership' between Civil Society and the State in Uganda's AIDS Response During the 1990s and 2000s as Demonstrated in the Development of TASO 219

Chapter 12 Financial Inclusion Programming for Poor Women and Men in Uganda 239

Chapter 13 Civil Society Organisations and Local-Level Peace-building in Northern Uganda.. 250

Chapter 14 Civil Society and Land Use Policy in Uganda: The Mabira Forest Case.. 275

SECTION V: THE STATE AND CIVIL SOCIETY

Chapter 15 Ugandan Civil Society in the Policy Process: Challenging Orthodox Narratives 297

Chapter 16 Relations between Gender-focused NGOs, Advocacy Work, and Government: A Ugandan Case Study 312

Chapter 17 Protecting the Tree or Saving the Forest? A Political Analysis of the Legal Environment for NGOs in Uganda 325

Chapter 18 Developing a 'Civil' Society in Partial Democracies: In/civility and a Critical Public Sphere in Uganda and Singapore............ 339

SECTION VI: RESOURCING CIVIL SOCIETY'S GROWTH

Chapter 19 The Impact of Western Management Tools on Ugandan NGOs: Some Contextual Notes 367

Chapter 20 The Financial Sustainability of Ugandan NGOs: Are we no Better than Government? 379

Chapter 21 The Current Aid Architecture: Challenges for Civil Society Organisations in Uganda... 401

SECTION VII: CONCLUSIONS

Chapter 22 Uganda's Civil Society - Where do we go from here?........ 411

Index 420

Foreword

It is an honour to associate with this important book on Uganda's civil society. These pages trace the history and evolution of an important dimension of our country's make-up and identity, a story of political upheaval and instability, but also of inspiration demonstrated by the resilience of its people.

There is little doubt about the centrality of civil society, in all its forms, in our country. This volume comes at a time when Uganda has experienced perhaps the quickest pace of civil society growth anywhere in the world, although exact numbers are unknown, as no robust census has as yet taken place. Studies on specific sub-groups, such as community-based organisations (CBOs), non-governmental organisations (NGOs), savings and cooperatives societies, professional associations and others, however, suggest a strength that could be in the hundreds of thousands.

Has this growth been accompanied by sufficient research and reflection? After a decade as a civil society leader, I submit that collective thought leadership and consolidated knowledge about the sector are largely absent. Research might exist here and there, but a systematic collection that can shape narratives and action in a constructive way has so far been lacking. It is thus commonplace to hear a politician, public official, scholar, or citizen speak seemingly authoritatively about the role, impact, purpose, and position of "civil society", without recourse to empirical evidence, and at times in ways that distort its essence and track record. This book is thus timely: it presents us with a good launching pad into systematic research and inquiry into the phenomenon of civil society in Uganda and possibly beyond.

In an era of global governance shifts, these pages also remind us that it is time to look back in history and reflect on the foundational philosophy of the idea and practice of civil society. Uganda is at a critical juncture, and so is its civil society. As historians remind us, without a good understanding of where we are coming from, it is not always easy to appreciate the present and much more difficult to project the future. Our aspirations for this future, and the role of civil society therein, need to be understood and evaluated by a comprehensive understanding of the past. As several chapters in this book indicate, the role, leadership, impact and linkages with and within civil society have been longstanding questions of inquiry which we must keep researching into if we are to develop a truly value-driven and people-based civil society.

Any future volumes about civil society have this book as a reference point to build on, especially on themes that articles in this collection may not have covered in depth, including the economic value of Uganda's civil society, inter and intra relationships within and between diverse civil society groups, the impact of new technologies, or the emergence of new civic movements and their relationship with conventional civil society, as well as with political society. Civil society's capacity to adapt to urgent issues, including the looming climate crisis, and to unprecedented occurrences such as the Covid-19 pandemic will also probably continue to feature as important areas of inquiry.

The two editors of this important and timely book are not only long-standing civil society practitioners, but have also exhibited an unwavering commitment to building civil society thought and knowledge leadership in Uganda. It has been a privilege working with them through the years, in various spaces and capacities.

As global leaders are prompting us to question the values of generosity and justice, we, as civil society leaders, need to constantly query our sector's relevance and resilience. This book is an important resource to spark that discussion in and outside the sector.

Richard Ssewakiryanga
Former Executive Director
Uganda National NGO Forum

Acknowledgements and Dedication

We would like to express our gratitude to all those who journeyed with us along the eventful road that eventually led to the development of this volume. Putting together this collection of essays has not only reflected our respective experiences – challenging, exhilarating and sad at times – as our civil society evolved over the past 25 years, but it has also been informed by the views and encouragement of the many colleagues and friends that this journey has thankfully brought close to us.

Sadly, over the years, several have disappeared and this volume is dedicated to the memory of one of the posthumous contributors, Rosemary Adong Okech, a civil society pioneer of exemplary drive, integrity and commitment to social justice who tragically passed away while leading her organisation.

We thank all the contributors for allowing us to reprint their work, thus assembling an eclectic and hopefully stimulating volume. We also acknowledge Care International, the Centre for Basic Research (CBR) and the Community Development Resource Network (CDRN) for accepting to have their articles reproduced. These articles have not been altered, other than for minor corrections and where indicated.

We recognise and thank Mr. Richard Ssewakiryanga for accepting to write the preface for this book, and under whose leadership we entered into a partnership with the Uganda National NGO Forum to promote this publication. The Uganda National NGO Forum also provided much-needed financial support for the printing costs.

John De Coninck and Arthur Larok
Editors
Kampala, 2021

SECTION I
Introduction

1

Uganda's Civil Society – An Overview of Issues

John De Coninck

This volume has been compiled to meet several intents. The first is to promote appreciation and debate on the role of civil society in the development of our nation. This book thus seeks to provide elements of answers to several questions: Is the notion of 'civil society' helpful in understanding Uganda's history and useful in positing scenarios for the future? What does such a notion precisely mean in the local context? What has been the role of civil society over the years? Has it made a mark? What drives its development and how does it relate to the State? What are current challenges and how might these be addressed in the future?

Secondly, and on a practical note, the student of Uganda's civil society has hitherto been forced to seek information from an often poorly accessible range of sources, making an overview and analytical comparison of perspectives quite difficult. The editors' immediate intention is therefore to bring together a range of articles and essays, all focused on issues directly relevant to Uganda's civil society, its history, characteristics, challenges and prospects: a first home for a range of views, analyses and research outcomes – whether previously published or not.

The search for documents to include in these pages produced an unexpected wealth of material although, as the editors had to restrict their selection, this collection necessarily involved hard choices. We have, however, attempted to be as comprehensive as possible in the selection, while privileging articles that are critical and thought-provoking, in order to generate questioning and discussion.

Civil society in a changing global context

The questions raised above are not only relevant to Uganda's setting, as they also animate current debates about civil society across the continent and beyond. It is a truism that we are witnessing a worldwide period of rapid and far-reaching change, where global concerns and consequent shifts in power centres and alliances continuously take place. As a result, 'development', and the means to attain it, is being constantly re-evaluated. We now see analyses depicting an increasingly complex and fast-moving reality where globalisation simultaneously presents opportunities and exclusion for minorities and the poorest, where security concerns (rather than 'good governance') shape international policies, where shifts in power are harder to fathom and where global mechanisms (to keep our world intact and liveable) progressively take centre stage, then meet resistance. Perceptions of 'development' have indeed considerably evolved from the technology-driven and somewhat simplistic 'modernisation' drives of the 1960s and 1970s, as we now increasingly realise the need to widen our thinking to the issue of 'change' and especially of people-driven change.

It is a complex reality, taking us far from a time when 'non-state actors' were seen as efficient service providers, honest innovators, and advocators for change and accountability. We now see civil society organisations increasingly accepted as both a normal part of the ever more privatised service delivery apparatus in many countries, and as legitimate actors to influence local and global policy. What international conference, for instance, does not accommodate NGO perspectives or representatives?

In this context of global compacts and 'multi-stakeholder approaches', the notion of civil society, however, becomes increasingly subject to controversy. Where, for instance, does 'business' start and where does 'philanthropy' stop? Are civil society drives for poverty eradication only linked to market development? How do we interpret the phenomenal growth of civil society organisations, including NGOs with multi-billion dollar budgets? To whom are these organisations accountable? On our continent, are they the new missionaries, adjuncts to a form of self-seeking neo-colonialism, or should they be viewed as the efficient harbingers of equitable service delivery, or as promoters of democracy? And even: as donor support is re-directed and downsized, should we prepare for the demise of the African NGO as we know it?

Civil society in Uganda

In Uganda too, we appear to be moving away from the facile assumptions made about civil society organisations two decades or so ago: their strong value base, their seemingly unstoppable growth, their commitment to social justice and representation of the interests of the poor and disadvantaged; their autonomy from the State and their relative effectiveness in service delivery compared to government agencies; all these are now under scrutiny.

Civil society is indeed as diverse as it changes, reflecting Uganda's broader social and political trends; and linking with the State and the market in evolving ways. The numbers and influence of civil society organisations have grown very rapidly in the past 25 years, spurred in part by the onset of a political and social environment that unhesitatingly welcomed their presence at the time. And we see a growing voice in policy matters, reflecting a desire to hold government to account and to ensure effective service delivery.

This is at first glance. But let us step back: is the notion of civil society itself of relevance and of use in our local context? One school of thought advances the position that this is a Western-inspired liberal notion that must be re-conceptualised to be of relevance here. As two of the entries (by Aili Mari Tripp and Nyangabyaki Bazaara) in the second chapter of this volume point out, of especial issue here are two interconnected concerns: one relates to the identity and make-up of civil society itself, the other to its position vis-à-vis the State. Bazaara proposes a conceptualisation of civil society intimately linked to the promotion of democracy and his historical analysis shows how and why 'civil society organisations', including peasant cooperatives and trade unions, at times participate in civil society – when they promote democracy and attempt to hold the state to account – and at times do not, such as when focusing on service delivery and when co-opted by State institutions. Tripp echoes a criticism levelled at a Western-driven analysis that gives much prominence to a particular type of civil society organisation, namely the 'NGO', a form of organisation that is readily recognisable to Western lenses, often male-dominated, and in tune with a capitalist, private-sector driven construct of society, as opposed to other forms of associational life, such as community-based organisations.

It is indeed, by any measure, community-based organisations that engage a great many more Ugandans than other organisations. These are very different from the more vocal and visible NGOs, often more 'democratic' in their make-up, though very atomised. Some represent well-defined constituencies, others the interests of third parties. As the entry by the Community Development Resource Network on "Find the Groups and you have Found the Poor?" however reminds us, the widely held belief that the needs and interests of Uganda's poor are directly or indirectly represented through community-based organisations needs scrutiny, particularly since forming a group to take advantage of external benefits has become part of ordinary people's lives. Kristof Titeca and Thomas Vervisch also examine community-based organisations and test the proposition that the accumulation of social capital (through such groups and associations) provides the missing link to understanding democratic governance and economic development. Their conclusion is far more nuanced and, by distinguishing between bonding, bridging, and linking social capital in the context of community associations in northern Uganda, they show that social capital cannot be assumed to promote democratic practices, but rather stress the importance of autonomous organisational progress, characterised by an optimal combination of different forms of social capital that changes over time and context.

Ronald Kassimir also reminds us in this volume of the difficulties in using a Western-inspired "civil society" lens (as a force towards liberalisation and democratisation) when applied to civil society organisations whose capacities and ethos might not predispose them to press for political change. The article, which examines another dimension of civil society in Uganda, the Catholic Church, poses the question as to what kind of power civil society organisations possess, and argues that a key component of the answer lies in internal organisational dynamics. In this case, the Church lacks the kinds of linkages with its members to socialise them into new roles and values, while its leaders consider organisational sustainability as a priority that guides their political vision. This does not make the church any less of a member of civil society, Kassimir argues, but it does lend a risk-averse quality to its social and political roles.

Similar observations arise when Rebecca Mukyala-Makiika, in her article on another type of civil society formation - traditional cultural institutions - examines whether these can promote good governance through Uganda's decentralised system, given their considerable popular base, but despite their undemocratic foundations and their exclusion by law from engaging in partisan politics. Their popularity, however, makes them prey to all forms of political manoeuvres, leading to increased control by the State. While they can use their popular base to, say, mobilise resources, the author concludes by pointing out that their ability to perform will depend on their organisational strength and on their capacity to stand autonomously, not only in relationship to the State but also to other political groups in society.

What positioning vis-à-vis the state?

The relationship between State and civil society indeed provides a recurrent theme in this volume. This reflects the global discourse on the notion and roles of civil society in relation to democracy and often, in the African context, in restraining an omnipresent, autocratic State. As we have noted, 'civil society' remains in Western texts frequently defined in terms of its linkages with the State, with the nature of this relationship highlighting many of the supposed attributes of the sector (its democratic nature, its role as 'incubator' of democratic practice and organisational growth, and its role in 'countervailing' State power).

In Uganda, can we assume the existence of an effective civil society independent from the State and uniformly infused with pro-democracy values? Several articles show that these assumptions may at best be only partially valid. In her article, Karen Brock examines the participation of civil society organisations as actors in the poverty reduction policy process. The article discusses some of the assumptions and contradictions implicit in the application of external narratives about civil society to Uganda, such as being able to 'hold the State to account', 'eradicating poverty' or providing 'voice' for 'empowered citizens' and concludes that these hold true only to a limited extent. It suggests that civil society actors are largely reactive, responsive to resources offered for particular activities and functions. Such an analysis in the first instance encourages us to question the effectiveness of NGO-Government collaboration: Mary Ssonko in her study on relations between gender-focused NGOs, advocacy work and government, argues that a close relationship has kept NGOs visibly engaged and 'successful' but do not necessarily alter the status of poor women. On the other hand, Government can co-opt NGOs while appearing receptive to the concerns of civil society organisations in the presence of the international aid community, where it projects itself as generally espousing the precepts of 'good governance'.

Further, the Ugandan State is adopting a more activist stance. We see Government involvement in 'strategic' industries and 'strategic' infrastructure. A statist project appears to be emerging, and with this, the space for alternative voices and initiative is coming under threat, as exemplified by the restrictive features of the legislation to control NGOs and the long drawn out discussion on an NGO national policy, as shown in Arthur Larok's article "Protecting the Tree or Saving the Forest?". The anti-terrorism and media control legislation then also provide an opportunity to deflect demands for 'good governance' – for the sake of 'security' - and an opportunity to stifle voices of dissent, other than through carefully controlled procedural democracy, with its regular ballots and tolerated political parties.

NGOs are therefore frequently represented as 'trouble makers' by State officials, reflecting an ambivalent attitude by Government on what constitutes allowable advocacy activities for civil society organisations (especially when they 'stray' into what is considered the political arena). Self-censorship then ensues and many organisations see their relationship with the State as one of collaboration, rather than confrontation, with this approach viewed as a cause of achievement, if not celebration). David Hammett and Lucy Jackson's paper draws from the Ugandan and Singaporean contexts, where legislation has moved towards increased State control over civil society. The authors show how notions of civility and incivility are used to suppress or marginalise civil society, and how organisations respond by negotiating the fine line between being civil enough to avoid government intervention, while being uncivil enough to be able to push for change. Not only do such responses present challenges to liberal and pluralist models of civil society, which assume both the space for and ability of citizens to influence government, but they also allow for the deployment of a discourse of 'civility' which provides an effective tool for government control over civil society.

Control of civil society by the State apparatus is of course not a new phenomenon: under colonialism, civil society organisations were heavily controlled, especially the then all-important cooperative societies, to ensure the stability of the colonial order. John De Coninck, in his article on "The State, civil society and development policy in Uganda: where are we coming from?", argues that, since long before independence, civil society has been closely enmeshed with the State and the demarcation between 'civil society' and 'government' remains blurred till this day, making any understanding of civil society as somehow separate from the State precarious. Co-option by the State has translated itself not only into a concentration by organisations on the uncontroversial provision of social services, but also into limited self-awareness. Its fragmented and apolitical nature presents further hurdles for civil society to discharge its more recently acquired function of holding the State accountable, aggravated by the increasingly pervasive business ethics that characterise sub-contracting, thus diminishing any appetite for politically-oriented advocacy work.

What values and skills?

There indeed appears to be a growing crisis of legitimacy for NGOs (and civil society generally), a hiatus between rhetoric and practice and a loss of moral ground. Civil society organisations are then perceived as top-down organisations led by elites with autocratic tendencies. The issue of values, especially in relation to leadership, is tackled by Moses Isooba et al in their article "You behave like a king!" The authors outline the challenges facing NGO leaders in relation to change and show that NGO leadership is rarely associated with the desirability of this change, but as a way to derive social recognition and a position of privilege. Leaders indeed face a host of challenges preventing them from embracing transformation (intense personal family and social expectations; internalising demands for change management from different sources, the fear of failing at personal and social levels, and cultural strictures of many kinds). NGOs are also frequently being criticised for using an opaque and exclusive language of 'strategic plans', 'participation and local ownership' or 'harmonised approaches' and 'integrated community-based interventions' which mask a fundamental orientation towards their own survival in a competitive world, as exemplified by expensive vehicles and lavish lifestyles. This then makes it unsurprisingly difficult for NGOs to fight for the rights *of* others, and certainly *with* others.

Money also shapes identity, and it is in the light of the web of relationships described above that the nature and values that animate civil society may be understood. As Ugandans evolve in a society increasingly pervaded by corruption as the expected mode of survival, civil society is no exception: briefcase NGOs and Global Fund scandals point to severe shortcomings. In addition, civil society organisations are often asked to whom they are accountable and for all practical purposes it is to donors, driven by fixed-term projects, not grand designs. With growing scepticism about the ethics that animate civil society, disillusionment has crept in, as Larok outlines in his article on the accountability challenge facing NGOs. Some are unmasked as motivated by expediency or corrupt practices, responding to sometimes less-than-charitable donor interests, or more driven by their own survival needs than in contributing to a fairer society. Indeed, can civil society organisations hold the State accountable to the people without a strong sense of values and enhanced credibility in the eyes of all concerned parties? With the legitimacy of the sector questioned by public opinion and government alike, this has on the one hand provided justification for the State to tighten control on civil society organisations and, on the other, prompted the latter to develop self-regulating mechanisms and quality standards.

What roles does civil society then play in Uganda?

In spite of these challenges, evidence suggests that civil society organisations continue to have impact in diverse ways. How exactly? As harbingers of democracy? As popular greenhouses for community democracy and organisation? As sources of much-needed social capital? As service providers? As advocates? As intermediaries between people and State?

Chapter 4 – "Creating Impact" – attempts to provide elements of answers by presenting widely different experiences. The consequences of 'partnership' with State institutions by an NGO provide the focus to Eduard Grebe's article on The AIDS Support Organisation (TASO). The article shows that the government's reputation for good leadership in the fight against HIV/AIDS has not been as clear-cut as often assumed, as its "partnership approach" in fact prevented strong and critical civil society voices from emerging, while the harmful impact of a socially conservative agenda was not checked. This was reflected in TASO, which became one of the most important and effective providers of support in the fight against HIV/AIDS but was not commensurably able to influence policy.

At a practical service delivery level as well, NGOs can claim credit for several social welfare innovations. The article by CARE-Uganda charts the success of its Village Loan and Savings Associations (VSLA) methodology, initially primarily designed to enable illiterate and extremely poor rural women access financial services, but now serving literate and non-literate people in rural areas, market towns, and peri-urban areas. The article shows how the financial services provided have over time diversified and how CARE-Uganda has entered into partnerships with various commercial banks. The remarkable impact of the VLSA method has inspired many other organisations to adopt the approach and it is estimated that in Africa alone more than 11 million people are currently benefitting from this methodology. In Uganda, there are over 1 million members in some 35,000 Savings Groups/VSLAs.

On another front, Paul Omach examines the contribution of a wide range of organisations, faith-based and secular, in promoting peacebuilding in northern Uganda to end the decades-long insurgency, led by the Lord's Resistance Army. Omach reminds us that civil society organisations provided alternative narratives of the conflict, exposed brutalities against civilians by all parties, and fostered peacebuilding. The author shows how these organisations lobbied, facilitated negotiations, engaged in building cultures of peace, promoted reconciliation, sustained local livelihoods, and influenced peacebuilding interventions, all in spite of a national context that constrained their activities.

Finally, Patrick Hönig's piece focuses on the Save Mabira Forest campaign, often quoted as a rare example of successful civil society activism when faced with powerful business and political interests. The article provides a more nuanced analysis, showing that the campaign, while exhibiting a desire for environmental and social justice, also demonstrated an exclusionist agenda linked to identity politics. This illustrates the more ambiguous role played by civil society than is often assumed, when one focuses on what civil society organisations do, rather than what they are supposed to do.

The role of donors

As several texts in this volume indicate, the prominence of Western-inspired concepts related to civil society's existence and growth reflects the importance of another major set of institutional actors on the Uganda landscape, the donors.

These have been at the heart of the development of several segments of civil society for several decades, a support ostensibly motivated not only by a desire for improved service delivery and poverty reduction, but latterly also for a pluralist, democratic society with accountable government – assumed to be indispensable for 'development'. Over the years, however, the context for aid delivery has changed, including a growing accent on 'partnership' and on national ownership of development processes. For donors, whose power in Uganda has decreased in recent years (commensurably with their diminishing relative contribution to public finance), issues of global security and the commercial interests of Western capital increasingly supersede concerns for human rights and 'good governance'. Still, involvement with NGOs is seen as an important (though no longer central) dimension to their engagement in the country.

Despite this waning influence, donors remain crucial to NGOs, almost all of whom have remained entirely dependent on their financial and other forms of support. This has not only resulted in a frequent disconnect between NGOs and their constituencies (why raise funds locally, for instance?) but, as we have seen, has also accelerated the adoption by NGOs of rights-based approaches and a growing interest in holding government to account. Simultaneously, this has fostered the impression among Government and the general public that NGOs are foreign-driven and lacking in popular legitimacy.

One of the chapters (by Rosemary Adong) in this volume provides insights in the intricacies and 'living reality' of the relationships between Ugandan civil society organisations and their donors where "participation", "partnership", "lobbying and advocacy" and "gender" have become new buzzwords for development practice and inform these new development relationships, yet do not originate locally. The author attempts to trace the origin of these words, their local interpretation and the resulting practice by local organisations and 'capacity-building' agencies.

In his paper on the current aid architecture, John De Coninck examines the context of current debates on donor support for civil society organisations in Uganda. He discusses the challenges this represents, including a framework that reduces risk-taking, choice and diversity within civil society, reflecting the existence of an 'aid chain' linking donors to beneficiaries that distributes and codifies power to its various participants. It is also a framework informed by a vision of change that suits relatively simple recipes, especially politically-neutral "projects" and a linear, predictable donor-driven vision of development. The author argues that this results in NGOs increasingly being contract-, rather than vision-driven, seeking recognition to "beat the competition", at the expense of a sense of independent identity, sector-wide cohesion and local ownership. As NGOs work in an increasingly demanding environment, with growing competition for funds and recognition, they must demonstrate 'impact'. They are very action-driven, considering the delivery of output and sound financial accountability as what is expected from them.

Another aspect of the relationship with donors is that local NGOs are increasingly being required by donors and supporters not only to show that they are accountable, but also financially sustainable. In their article, Silvia Angey and Christina Nilsson explore attempts by NGOs at generating income and diversifying their resource base, such as through negotiating better donor terms, income generating activities, local fundraising, consultancy work, and engaging in micro-finance. The authors' research shows that, while some NGOs have showed an ability to attain at least a certain degree of financial sustainability, the many challenges faced include the restrictions imposed by legislation and ensuring that income generation does not steer the organisation away from its mission, as well as the small size of a middle class that might otherwise support local fundraising efforts.

To conclude

What can the foregoing discussion add to shaping our collective future? We have earlier suggested that the notion of civil society needs to evolve in tandem with our changing perspectives on the nature of development, from the more deterministic modes of the 1960s and 1970s, to the prescriptive models of the later decades (the years of structural and other adjustments), on to the more recent understanding of development as a change process understood by the people themselves – where they are no longer 'beneficiaries', but the designers and builders of their own future, encompassing the tangible 'livelihoods' dimensions of well-being, as well as its less practical dimensions, psychological, mental, even spiritual.

Citizens should indeed not be viewed as passive recipients of State diktats: it would be erroneous to assume the existence of a disempowered citizenry, only able to compose with the State through a web of patrimonial relationships. Recent developments, as the concluding chapter describes, suggest that we should not. Such an understanding then re-shapes the role of outsiders, of the development industry and of governmental authorities as catalysts rather than prime movers, leaving the centre of the stage to people, their organisations, their values and their ambitions.

What also emerges from the foregoing is that civil society cannot be a positive force for democracy and development – in Uganda and elsewhere – solely because it is civil society – civil society organisations can only make a change, not through the size of their membership or budgets, but through the convictions, values and expertise they encompass. Civil society will otherwise remain a mere collection of organisations – NGOs, trade unions, cooperatives, faith-based organisations, etc. - in a sector that remains fragmented, far from being a political community able to organise itself and to defend a set of common values vis-a-vis an increasingly omnipresent State and business elite. An institutionally-based conceptualisation of civil society should therefore not mask a potentially more significant understanding of civil society in terms of a set of values.

If ultimately the role of civil society is to make it possible for citizens to participate in shaping and taking control of their destinies, there is, however, little doubt that this is a steep agenda in Uganda's current context, as government's vision (and practice) becomes increasingly exclusive. The challenges are immense: can you partner with a State that oppresses? Can you hold the State accountable and safeguard civil rights, when there is reluctance to engage in the contested terrain of 'demanding accountability' for reasons of culture, fear and State admonition? Can civil society thrive as donor influence (and donors' protective "cover") wane, while financial flows abandon NGOs in favour of security–linked and other concerns?

In spite of this, we observe that civil society organisations are increasingly involved in policy issues, engaging government and donors on major choices. They have been meeting a degree of success in forging networks and alliances and the voice of civil society is starting to be more loudly heard on human rights and people's marginalisation. The signs are emerging of a new advocacy agenda, questioning a kind of development that amplifies unequal growth with other nations, as well as within the country, that is ecologically unsustainable while deepening poverty in the long run. A comprehensive alternative, value-based social project is however yet to emerge. This would require political commitment, engaging directly with power and forging a long-term, unified, sector-wide vision, based on deeply-held values. To these forward-looking themes, we turn in the concluding chapter of this volume.

SECTION II

Uganda's Evolving and Diverse Civil Society

2

Expanding 'Civil Society': Women and Political Space in Contemporary Uganda

Aili Mari Tripp[1]

Abstract

This essay argues that the notion of civil society needs to be expanded by widening the political space it occupies in order to provide a clear break from the gender-biased legacy that 'civil society' currently carries with it. It shows how notions of civil society based on Western liberal theory have been appropriated to describe aspects of African associational life in ways that have uncritically accepted a gendered public-private distinction which is problematic even in the Western context. Drawing on examples from Africa with a particular focus on Uganda, the author argues that popular definitions of civil society fail in several dimensions and suggests that only when we expand our understanding of the political can we fully appreciate the importance of struggles in which the protagonists are members of non-dominant sectors of society.

Notions of civil society based on Western liberal theory have been appropriated to describe aspects of African associational life in ways that have uncritically accepted a gendered public-private distinction that is problematic even in the Western context. Popular definitions of civil society fail along at least three dimensions that can be demonstrated by examining the struggles of women's organisations in Uganda.

First, the sharp separation of public-private does not appreciate the centrality of the family to civil society and to the public sphere. It tends to neglect the close connection between the private and public spheres. For example, family relations that prevent women from participating in associations and in politics have repercussions for the broader polity. Even when women engage in politics, they may face discrimination and marginalisation by people who think women's place is in the home. It makes little sense under these circumstances to separate politics from domestic life. The two spheres are also linked by laws that impinge on family relations. This is not to say that there is no

---

[1] Department of Political Science and Women's Studies Program, University of Wisconsin-Madison. Article reprinted from Kasfir, N. *Civil Society and Democracy in Africa: Critical Perspectives*, Cass (1998). Reprinted by permission of the publisher Taylor & Francis Ltd, http://www.tandfonline.com

distinction between the private and the public. But rather, as Anne Phillips suggests, there needs to be an uncoupling of these divisions from their gendered moorings, that is, the implicit association of women with the private sphere and men with the public.[2]

One consequence of the sharp public-private split is the failure to incorporate women adequately in the literature on civil society and the public arena in Africa. The narrow way in which civil society has often been defined makes it largely the domain of male middle-class, educated urbanites, leaving most women and peasants out of the picture. At the heart of the dilemma is the limited way in which politics and political space has been configured and understood.

Second, many civil society approaches ignore the salience of organisations that do not engage the state for policy change, especially local level organisations that may otherwise embody broader social change in institutions and political culture. Moreover, these organisations, especially at the local level, are critical to improving the quality of everyday life. For women, as the case study in this article shows, many of these seemingly small and insignificant organisations are important in challenging local practices that perpetuate women's subordination.

A third problematic approach to civil society focuses on values of civility and tolerance. Many civil society approaches cannot explain incivility caused by processes of social change. For example, in Uganda some women have found that when they fight to democratise the public sphere and open it up to women, others use violence and uncivil means to maintain the *status quo*. The assumptions of pluralist theory that a quietly negotiated consensus can be worked out is not always possible under such circumstances. Instead, it is necessary to disaggregate the causes of conflict and the perpetrators of incivility in order to evaluate the costs of social progress involved in adopting the kinds of institutional arrangements that can best create conditions of civility.

These and other problems with common conceptualisations of civil society impede analysis of important sectors of society and their political activities broadly defined. For this reason, the notion of civil society needs to be expanded by widening the political space that it occupies. Political spaces need to be seen as locations of contestation and accommodation over resources, influence and power. The argument of this article is that the expansion of political space in the notion of civil society provides a clear break from the gender-biased legacy that 'civil society' currently carries with it.

Public-private dichotomies

'Civil society' in western liberal thought

Western liberal thinking about civil society historically has, often unconsciously, defined civil society as the exclusive domain of men.[3] Civil society, according to John

---

2   Anne Phillips, *Engendering Democracy* (University Park, Pennsylvania, 1991).
3   Martha Ackelsberg and Mary Lyndon Shanley, 'Privacy, Publicity, and Power: A Feminist Rethinking of the Public-Private Distinction', in N.J. Hirschmann and C. DiStefano (eds.), *Revisioning the Political: Feminist Reconstructions of Traditional Concepts in Western Political Theory* (Boulder, 1996), 218; Carole Pateman, *The Disorder of Women* (Stanford, 1989), 118-40.

Keane, is not an unrestricted public sphere in which all citizens have equal access and ability to express their social interests, but rather a sphere which is dominated by male interests.[4]

For Western liberal thought, the theoretical basis for separating public and private spheres goes back to John Locke, who in his *Second Treatise* associated the public sphere with universal, impersonal and conventional criteria of achievement, interests, rights and equality. The private sphere, in contrast, was tied to the family, which was based on natural ties of sentiment and blood. The public sphere came to be associated with men, while the private sphere was the domain of women.[5] Since the time of Locke, liberal theory has separated the domestic realm, in which household relationships were seen as non-political and private, from the public sphere of civil society, which became perceived as the domain of men. While many contemporary theorists would include women's associations within civil society, they draw sharp lines between the public and private spheres in ways that reify the gendered construction of these spheres. What these theorists have failed to recognise is that the public - private boundaries themselves have been culturally, socially, juridically and politically constructed.[6]

Contrary to these implicit assumptions in liberal theory, however, public and private spheres are inextricably linked. One notable exception to these liberal assumptions was the theorist, John Stuart Mill, who, in his famous essay *The Subjection of Women*, argued that what goes on in the household reflects and affects the broader power configurations. He showed that women's political status can only be changed (for example, granting women the right to vote) if the patriarchal relations in the private sphere are transformed.[7] Among more contemporary theorists, Carole Pateman has similarly argued that the two spheres are inseparable, connected by a patriarchal structure. Moreover, the way women are included in public life is determined by women's position in the private sphere.[8] The public sphere is affected by gendered practices in the home. Women, for example, often find it difficult to participate in politics because the way private lives and work patterns inside and outside the home are structured leaves them with the heaviest responsibilities for child rearing and housework.[9]

When women have participated in public life, it has been not on their own terms, but rather in ways that are more in line with patriarchal beliefs and practices. Pateman concludes that women cannot participate fully in public life without changes in the private sphere. Thus, the family is at the heart of civil society, and not seen as irrelevant or separate from it.

---

4   John Keane, 'Introduction', in John Keane (ed.), *Civil Society and the State* (London and New York, 1988), 20.
5   Pateman, *The Disorder of Women*, 121.
6   Martha Ackelsberg and Mary Lyndon Shanley, 'Privacy, Publicity, and Power', 228; Susan Okin, *Women in Western Political Thought* (Princeton, 1979).
7   Pateman, *The Disorder of Women*, 129.
8   Ibid., 132.
9   Phillips, *Engendering Democracy*, 95 6, 100.

Although theoretically the private sphere is supposed to be a sphere free from the state's purview, laws are systematically enacted that regulate and shape domestic life,[10] once again dissolving the public—private dichotomy. Women's struggles over the rights of welfare mothers, domestic violence, sexual harassment and rape have often challenged those boundaries. Some struggles have sought to expand the boundaries of privacy (for example, abortion rights), while other struggles have sought to limit the rights to privacy (for example, domestic violence, child abuse).[11] Thus, there are ways in which the state needs to protect the privacy of the private realm, but there are also other ways in which the state needs to involve itself in the domestic sphere.

Liberal theory seeks to insulate the public sphere from the private sphere in all respects and protect the public sphere from the influences of the economy, the family and everyday life. It seeks to create a political order that is detached from and not influenced by social inequality rather than trying eliminate those inequalities.[12] It fails to recognise that inequalities, like gender subordination in the private realm, will be manifested in the public realm and thus provoke efforts to organise in response. An adequate notion of civil society must make room for the organisations engaged in these struggles.

Civil society and politics in Africa

Gendered notions of the public-private duality have been transported from liberal theory into contemporary discussions of civil society in Africa. One of the main consequences of this focus is to obliterate the relationship between the family and the public sphere. The second consequence is to minimise women's contributions in the public sphere.

The family and the public sphere

One way of looking at the relationship between the family and the public sphere is to examine the impact internal family politics has on who participates in politics and how. Many of the national-level struggles over access to resources and power are played out at the household level. In spite of their different objectives and scope, household conflicts are every bit as 'political' as struggles that 'engage' the state, but with consequences of differing scope. Women's subordination in the household impinges directly on civil society and on politics. In Uganda, one of the biggest obstacles to women's mobilisation has been men's objections to women's involvement in associational activities. Many men fear that women might gossip about them, that group activities will detract from women's housework, and that women will come in contact with other men or with new ideas. This has limited many women to organisations involving only women, but men have often found even these organisations threatening.

---

10 Ibid., 95.
11 Martha Ackelsberg and Mary Lyndon Shaisley, 'Privacy, Publicity, and Power', 220; Phillips, *Engendering Democracy,* 119,
12 Nancy Fraser, *Justice Interruptus: Critical Reflections on the 'Postsocialist' Condition* (New York and London, 1997), 79.

Similarly, women's political activity has often been curtailed by overbearing husbands. In the 1996 presidential elections there were reports throughout the country of incidents of intimidation and harassment by husbands who held different political views of wives who had voted for Yoweri Museveni. Some wives were killed, beaten, thrown out of homes, and some had their voter cards grabbed from them or destroyed.[13] The Alert Group of Uganda Women's Network (UWONET) appealed to Museveni and the Interim Electoral Commission (IEC) to stop these incidents of intimidation and harassment, which violated women's rights as well as their civil rights. Stephen Akabway, the Interim Electoral Commission Chairman, eventually appeared on TV and radio, and issued press statements warning husbands to stop harassing their wives over their voting choices.

Women politicians likewise face constraints from their families and from the public at large. Married women politicians often find it difficult to locate a constituency in which to run. If they run in the constituency where they were born, they are told to go to the constituency where they were married. When they run in their husband's constituency they are told "You came here to marry, not to rule".[14]

Women candidates have to project an image of absolute devotion to their husbands and family to a degree not required of men. In general, female candidates running in the 1996 parliamentary elections faced greater public ridicule than men. Some women candidates risked their marriages and faced public humiliation by their husbands. In one case a husband even nominated his wife's rival.[15] Similarly, in the 1994 Constituent Assembly race, many officials running the elections were openly hostile to women candidates.[16]

Not surprisingly, these same constraints are evident in local-level politics. Large numbers of women face opposition from spouses when they attend local council meetings. Local councils are part of a five-tiered governance structure, which begins at the village level, where it is made up of nine village elected representatives. In a study of local councils in Pallisa, Tabitha Mulyampiti found that the women who attended meetings tended to keep quiet. When they did speak, they felt that their concerns were inadequately addressed.[17] One Pallisa council member said that once all the men in her council decided that women should not bother attending the meetings since it interrupted their domestic chores and that men should attend on their behalf. Another Pallisa council member commented:

> We are still neglected by our fellow committee members, the men. Many of them still think that a woman's husband should decide on her behalf. The committee is also

---

13 David Musoke, 'Women Petition Museveni', *New Vision*, 18 May 1996.
14 Aili Mari Tripp, 'Women and Politics in Uganda: The Challenge of Associational Autonomy' (book manuscript, forthcoming).
15 Beatrice Mugambe, 'Are Women Afraid of Seeking Elective Office?', *Arise* (1996), 32-3.
16 Deborah Kasente, 'Women in the Constituent Assembly in Uganda', paper presented at public forum on 'African Women and Governance Seminar and Training Workshop', Entebbe, Uganda, 24-30 July 1994.
17 Tabitha Mulyampiti, 'Political Empowerment of Women in Uganda: Impact of Resistance Councils and Committees' (MA thesis, Women's Studies, Makerere University, Kampala, 1994).

dominated by men and usually when I talk, they think — before I can complete my sentence — that I am trying to oppose them. They have even stopped calling me to the meetings.

These attitudes carry over to the parliament, where there are many vocal women representatives. Loi Kageni Kiryapawo, NRC representative of Tororo, put it bluntly: 'In our case, when we are supposed to represent the interests of women, we are always shut down by the men. In most cases their reaction is negative and since they make up the majority of the House, their decisions are always paramount.'[18]

Yet another crucial constraint on women who were active in the local council system was the fact that men had more time to meet than women, who were saddled with domestic responsibilities. Women leaders complained that men scheduled meetings at times inconvenient for women, who had responsibility for domestic chores. Men also often came late to meetings, which meant they ended late, posing additional problems for women with children and suspicious husbands.

Clearly, the struggles within the domestic arena for the right to participate in organisations and in local and national politics are in and of themselves political struggles that demonstrate the inseparability and connectedness of the private and public spheres. The lack of freedom in the domestic sphere has everything to do with women's ability to participate in the public arena. By tying 'politics' so tightly to the public sphere in theoretical discussions, it becomes difficult to appreciate the inseparability of the public and private spheres and the intensely political nature of domestic conflicts over the right of women to participate in organisations, public fora and in elections.

Moreover, it makes it impossible to talk about other ways in which family politics is located in the public sphere. In Uganda, for example, as Mikael Karlstrom has pointed out, many Baganda find the system of socio-political organisation based on clans under royal rule to be a legitimate form of political expression, yet this is family politics being played out in the public sphere of the Buganda Lukiiko (parliament).[19] In this case, the sharp boundary between 'public' or 'private' spheres becomes absurd, highlighting once again the constructed nature of these two spheres.

Arenas of mobilisation

Not surprisingly, gender analysis is also largely absent from the debates on civil society. This has to do with the ways in which civil society, the public realm and politics are generally defined. There is a great deal of variability in the use of the concept of civil society. By most definitions, civil society is lodged between the state and the household. Moreover, civil society is seen as autonomous of the state, yet simultaneously engaging it. Some, like Jean-François Bayart, emphasise its confrontational nature to the state, while others see its role as mediating between state and society.[20]

---

18   'The Task Ahead for a Woman Legislator', *Arise*, 5 (1992), 16-17.
19   Mikael Karlstrom, 'Clans, Kings, Councils: Reflections on the Applicability of the Civil Society Concept to Contemporary Uganda', Paper presented at the thirty-eighth annual African Studies Association meeting, Orlando, Florida, 3-6 Nov. 1995.
20   Jean-François Bayart, 'Civil Society in Africa', in Patrick Chabal (ed.), *Political Domination in Africa*

One view distinguishes civil society from society because of its political functions.[21] Chazan, for example, argues that Africa has always relied heavily on organisations. However, the problem is how to identify and cultivate civil society out of the many existing forms of associational life.[22] Her definition narrows the notion of civil society even further to the section of society that 'interacts with the state, influences the state, and yet is distinct from the state'.[23] Thus, civil society tends to become identified with the activities of organisations that are formal, registered, middle class and urban-based. Nongovernmental organisations (NGOs), churches, human rights organisations, professional associations, and other such organisations gain salience.[24] These organisations, led by educated urbanites, are seen as capable of engaging the state in appropriate ways to bring about policy changes.

Another view sees a broader range of non-political associations as constituting civil society and makes a distinction between civil society and political society (for example, political parties). Unlike civil society, political society is involved in electoral contestation over state power.[25] Both definitions of civil society separate politics from society and most certainly from the family and the domestic realm. The first approach is unclear about what makes civil society political and the other tends to separate civil society from politics. Moreover, both definitions seem to embody a fairly narrow definition of what is political.

Chazan argues that most voluntary organisations in Africa do not meet her criteria for being included in civil society. These criteria include having "specific and well-defined objectives, participatory governing structures, discrete constituencies, activities that go beyond catering to the immediate interest of their members, and an ability to form alliances with other groups with quite different declared purposes". She implies that local organisations are often too inwardly oriented and not sufficiently concerned with affecting public policy to be of political importance. Hence the implication is that they fall out of civil society. As she puts it:

> Village communities, small-scale credit associations, and spiritualist cults are often inward-oriented, pointedly detached from the market and state, and more concerned with protecting themselves from outside interference than affecting public policy. By ignoring the government, they undermine its authority and thus cannot be considered part of the crucial 'missing middle'.[26]

(Cambridge, 1986); John Harbeson, 'Civil Society and Political Renaissance in Africa', in John Harbeson, Donald Rothchild and Naomi Chazan (eds.), *Civil Society and the State in Africa* (Boulder, 1994).

21 Larry Diamond, 'Toward Democratic Consolidation', *Journal of Democracy*, 5, 3 (1994), 5; Harbeson, *Civil Society*, 14.
22 Naomi Chazan, 'Africa's Democratic Challenge', *World Policy Journal* (1992), 279.
23 Ibid., 281.
24 Dwayne Woods, 'Civil Society in Europe and Africa: Limiting State Power through a Public Sphere', *African Studies Review*, 35, 2 (1992), 78; Naomi Chazan, 'Africa's Democratic Challenge', 287.
25 Michael Bratton, 'Civil Society and Political Transitions in Africa', in John Harbeson, Donald Rothchild and Naomi Chazan (eds.), *Civil Society and the State in Africa* (Boulder, 1994), 56.
26 Chazan, 'Africa's Democratic Challenge', 287.

One consequence of defining civil society in this way in Africa is that 'civil society' starts to look very much like 'male society'. Organisations like trade unions, co-operatives, human rights groups and national business associations that are frequently associated with civil society tend to be led by men. Even though women constitute the most active part of the membership of churches, they nevertheless are mainly led by middle-class educated men. By focusing on this narrow section of organisational life, not only are women, who run most local level organisations, written off the map, but most political activity which takes place at the local level is also deemed irrelevant.

Airbrushing women out of the picture

One consequence of the public-private dichotomy is to make women's involvement in the public sphere invisible. First, women are often simply airbrushed right out of the picture when discussing the more formal political spheres. Even though women usually make up at least half the electorate and are often among the most mobilised groups in society, this rarely earns them recognition as a sector worthy of specific attention in accounts of civil society and political mobilisation. From Mali to Kenya, Sierra Leone and Zaire, women have been at the forefront of protests against repressive regimes. In Niger, several thousand women protested against the exclusion of female delegates from the National Conference in 1991 when only one woman was included out of the original 68 delegates. In Sierra Leone, women were virtually the only societal group that openly resisted soldiers by organising mass demonstrations at a crucial juncture when the military was considering postponing the elections which had been scheduled for 26 February 1996.[27] In Nairobi's Uhuru Park in 1992, women confronted the police in demonstrations in support of political prisoners. In Mali, women were at the forefront of some of the most dramatic and bloody clashes between demonstrators and President Moussa Traoré's forces in 1991. Public ire grew in the face of the regime's murder of women and children demonstrators, resulting in events that led to the unfolding of a political transition. Rarely have these struggles been incorporated into literature on democratisation.[28] Studies of local politics, where one would expect greater attention to women's concerns, fare little better when it comes to gender analysis.

Second, even when women figure prominently in associational life and their mobilisation is discussed at great length, the gender dimension of their activities often remains unnoticed and unanalysed. Hence, an otherwise excellent article on business associations and politics in Benin and Togo recognises only in passing that the associations are made up entirely of women. Moreover, the piece does not explore the political and

---

27 Yusuf Bangura, 'The Concept of Policy Dialogue and Gendered Development: Understanding its Institutional and Ideological Constraints', Paper prepared for the United Nations Research Institute for Social Development and Centre for Policy Dialogue workshop, 'Working Towards a More Gender Equitable Macro-Economic Agenda', Rajendrapur, Bangladesh, 26-28 Nov. 1996, 29.

28 See, for example, John F. Clark and David E. Gardinier (eds.), *Political Reform in Francophone Africa* (Boulder, 1997); Michael Bratton and Nicolas van de Walle, *Democratic Experiments in Africa: Regime Transitions in Comparative Research* (Cambridge and New York, 1997); Marina Ottaway (ed.), *Democracy in Africa.' The Hard Road Ahead* (Boulder, CO, and London, 1997).

gendered implications of this sociological fact.[29] Another well-documented account of NGOs in Kenya, *The Two Faces of Civil Society* by Stephen Ndegwa, identifies the Green Belt Movement as standing out among NGOs in its persistence in challenging the state, but does not analyse what gender might have to do with this observation. Instead, Wangari Maathai's personal leadership acumen is used to explain the Green Belt Movement's uniqueness, resulting in only a partial explanation.[30] Another superb study of a landmark struggle between a Kenyan widow and her husband's clan over who had the right to bury the husband draws out the significance of the conflict for conceptions of modernity, tradition, ethnicity, class and being Luo. However, it scarcely mentions gender, one of the most salient dimensions of the struggle, nor does it interrogate how this particular identity clashed with other identities including clan, class and ethnicity.[31] More commonly, if women are absent from the conventional public realm, that absence is rarely noted, questioned or analysed.

Struggles for 'political space'

Yet politics is not the prerogative of political parties nor of an urban-based elite. Politics involves negotiations, accommodations, and struggles over access to resources, power and influence. It permeates social interactions and takes up 'political space'. According to Adrian Leftwich, "politics consists of all the activities of cooperation and conflict, within and between societies, whereby the human species goes about obtaining, using, producing and distributing resources in the course of the production and reproduction of its social and biological life".[32]

Thus, not all political conflict is about engaging the state. It may occur in a variety of political spaces, that is, in families, clans, churches, district development associations, market places, local self-help groups, and parent—teacher associations. By defining civil society narrowly and by sharply bifurcating the political from the domestic spheres, the organisational life of women in a country like Uganda is largely overlooked because women's political struggles (and some of those of men) are not limited to such narrowly defined 'public' arenas. In fact, as Joel Barkan has shown, most peasant farmers would also be dropped from view in the event that a narrow definition of the public was employed.[33] By broadening our notion of political space to incorporate the multiple locations of power contestation, our understanding of civil society must then necessarily be expanded.

Women's participation in politics in Uganda goes beyond electoral politics and the five-tiered local government councils to extensive participation in local-level multi-

---

29 John R. Heilbrunn, 'Commerce, Politics, and Business Associations in Benin and Togo', *Comparative Politics*, 29, 4 (1997), 473-92.
30 Stephen N. Ndegwa, *The Two Faces of Civil Society: NGOs and Politics in Africa* (West Hartford, CT, 1996), 97.
31 David William Cohen and ES. Atieno Odhiambo, *Burying SM: The Politics of Knowledge and the Sociology of Power in Africa*. Portsmouth, NH, and London, 1992).
32 Adrian Leftwich, *Redefining Politics* (London and New York, 1983), 11-12.
33 Joel Barkan, 'Resurrecting Modernization Theory and the Emergence of Civil Society in Kenya and Nigeria', in David E. Apter and Carl R. Rosberg (eds.), *Political Development and the New Realism in Sub-Saharan Africa* (Charlottesville and London, 1994), 110.

purpose organisations that are involved in a wide variety of activities that affect the welfare of the community in a practical way. Many women see their organisations as an alternative to the exclusions and marginalisation they face in more conventional political arenas, even in a country like Uganda that has sought to widen women's political participation under the National Resistance Movement (NRM) regime led by President Yoweri Museveni. By incorporating women's organisational strategies into our definition of the public, we begin to see women as political actors who are not simply relegated to the domestic sphere. We see women active in political spaces that may or may not involve the state.

Certainly there are important autonomous women's organisations in Uganda that engage the state around a wide variety of concerns. For example, the women's movement has pressurised the NRM to place women in key positions in the government as vice-president, ministers, permanent secretaries, cabinet members, district administrators, and in special commissions. Many women's organisations were instrumental in lobbying during the 1995 Constituent Assembly for a constitutional provision, which was eventually adopted, that would guarantee women one-third of the seats in local government.

However, even these organisations that have actively pressurised the government do not constantly engage the state. The emphasis on civil society 'engagement' does not situate societal organisations that intermittently do so.[34] Few organisations exist in a perpetual state of engagement and most engage only as the need arises. Moreover, as important as these intermediary organisations[35] are in addressing key concerns of women *vis-a-vis* the government, they are not the only public arenas in which women mobilise.

Broadening 'civil society'

Women tend to be involved in more localised multi-purpose organisations that do not constantly engage the state or lobby for policy changes, but are nevertheless important to the welfare of their members, their families and communities. Their participation is political in that it involves participating in public arenas and struggles over access to resources and power. Women's local struggles are also important because they have challenged local patronage networks, pushed for greater government and NGO accountability, sought to bridge ethnic and religious divisions in the community, and to make participatory structures in the community more inclusive to women and the poor.[36] Collective action at the intermediary level aimed at public policy change is clearly important and can have implications for the broader society. But, at the same

---

34 Michael W. Foley and Bob Edwards. 'The Paradox of Civil Society', *Journal of Democracy,* 7, 3(1996), 39.

35 Examples of such organisations include Action for Women in Development (ACFODE), Forum for Women in Development (FOWODE), Uganda Women's Network (UWONET), The Association of Uganda Women Lawyers (FIDA), National Association of Women's Organisations of Uganda (NAWOU), Pressure Group on Rape and Defilement, and Women's Global Network on Reproductive Rights.

36 Aili Mari Tripp, 'Women and Politics in Uganda: The Challenge of Associational Autonomy' (book manuscript, forthcoming).

time, widespread local-level changes are transformative in a profound but different way. Without these kinds of concrete changes in the daily practice of communities, the impact of changes at the national level are necessarily limited.

Because of the instability in the country under Amin and Obote II, it was not until the 1986 NRM takeover that women's organisations began to grow exponentially. According to my survey,[37] after 1986 urban women began to participate in large numbers in multi-purpose women's associations (usually with income generation at the core of their activities) and in credit and savings associations. Most organisations which had a membership of between 20 and 30 were involved in a combination of activities that ranged from producing handicrafts or other goods for sale to cultural activities (music, drama, dance), providing assistance to orphans or other people in need, cultivation, sports and involvement in community self-help initiatives of various kinds, for example, buildings, roads, wells, and assisting rural women's groups with their skills. The women's groups would switch emphasis on various activities as the needs of the members changed and as new opportunities presented themselves. Men were more likely to be in single-purpose organisations such as co-operatives, sports clubs and burial societies.

The multi-purpose organisations did not generally 'engage' the state unless provoked. Although their participation tended to cater to the needs of their members, they could under various circumstances become involved in local struggles over resources and power on issues that affected them. Given a broader understanding of 'civil society', many of their struggles were intensely political and significant when taken as a part of a broader movement of change. For example, in the course of my research I came across the following struggles involving women's organisations:

- A women's group in Jinja challenged local male authorities to let them establish and control a health clinic, fighting for the right of women to lead in community activities.
- In Kiyembe market in Kampala, a women's co-operative of 200 members fought to regain their market stalls after the town clerk had thrown half the women out of their stalls and brought in male vendors to replace them.
- An informal women's group in Kawaala, Kampala, were key actors in a community initiative that challenged the way in which the city council was implementing an infrastructure rehabilitation project funded by the World Bank. The residents drew up an alternative plan laying out new terms for community participation in the project.
- In Kamuli, one umbrella women's organisation representing 5,600 members struggled with and changed an undemocratic leadership and organisational structure.

---

37 I conducted a 1993 survey of 1,142 randomly selected citizens (80 per cent women) in Kampala, Mbale, Kabale and Luwero.

Struggles of these kinds revolving around women's concerns seemed fairly new in these communities and had sprung up partly as an unintended consequence of the NRM regime's encouragement of female mobilisation. The struggles involved concerns that had to do with the sustenance of the women and their families — issues that held great importance to their daily lives. In no way are such concerns trivial to those involved even if they do not add up to national policy concerns.

Moreover, these struggles reflected and fed into a groundswell of changing popular opinion regarding women's status. In spite of the continued limitations and obstacles women faced in the public arena, women felt that new political spaces had afforded them new possibilities for asserting their interests. When asked what was one of the biggest changes women had experienced since the NRM came to power, survey respondents overwhelmingly were of the opinion that the biggest changes had to do with women becoming active in politics and secondly that women could engage in any kind of occupation or business. Not surprisingly, other major changes that were identified had to do with women's 'increase in confidence', 'feeling liberated,' 'knowing they were of value', 'not being dependent on men', 'asking for their rights as women', and so on. As one respondent put it: "In the past women's position did not change even with education. Previously women were in teaching and nursing but not in other fields. But today educated women are holding ministerial posts." Another explained: "Previously it was difficult to see women in many different jobs, but they have come up. Women even used to say they would not do certain jobs, but now they are out there rearing animals and chickens, going to meetings, doing crafts. They are very active now. They even pay fees for their school going children." All of these perspectives reflect a changing national consciousness about the position of women, yet they arise out of individual experiences and are partially shaped by women's participation in associational life at the local level.

Difficulties in engaging the state

However, even well-organised urban associations have trouble engaging the state for a number of reasons. Although intermediary organisations can play important advocacy roles, often they do not meet with success because the state is incapable of responding. It does not make much sense to talk of advocacy when the government is cracking down on organisations and limiting their activities. This was the case when President Idi Amin, in the face of resistance from women's organisations, banned all women's associations in Uganda in 1978 except for his own creation, the National Council of Women. As a result, most national organisations either disappeared, kept a low profile or became temporarily dormant in this period.

In another instance, after Tito Okello came to power in a September 1985 coup, insecurity was at its height in Kampala: rape by the military was widespread and kidnapping of schoolgirls by soldiers was rampant. Women's organisations held a demonstration in Kampala in which over 2,000 women participated, calling for peace and protesting against the mistreatment of women by soldiers.[38] A group of women's organisations wrote to the Minister of Internal Affairs and to the Minister of Defence in October 1985 complaining of the treatment of women at road blocks. The women's organisations held a peace seminar and invited the Minister of Foreign Affairs and the commander of the army, General Bazilio Okello, to address them. At the seminar the General told the women that they deserved to be raped and blamed the army's looting on the women themselves. Women who attended this meeting were outraged that their reasonable demands were treated with such contempt.

The notion that the predatory regimes of Amin or Okello could have responded to the women's demands would have been absurd. It made little sense to talk of advocacy when the military was carrying out institutionalised crimes while blaming its victims. But even under the more benign authoritarian regime of Museveni, the conditions for effective lobbying may be absent. The state may simply not have the capacity or the will to respond to societal pressures. Many of the lobbying efforts of national women's organisations have met with little response from the government, not because of NRM opposition to the proposed changes, but because the regime has lacked the wherewithal and the commitment to respond. For example, the United Help for Widows and Orphans Association (UHWOA) had been fighting since 1993 without success to get the government to give proper attention to their concerns and the government has reneged on promises to provide pensions and subsistence money.

Similarly, women's efforts around rape, defilement and sexual harassment have come up against a wall on most occasions. Many women's organisations such as the Association of Uganda Women Lawyers (FIDA), Action for Development (ACFODE), National Association of Women's Organisations of Uganda (NAWOU), Uganda Muslim Women's Association and others - all under the rubric of the Pressure Group on Rape and Defilement - have tried to push the government to take stronger action on rape. They have protested the Ministry of Justice's foot dragging in providing for a family division in the Uganda courts to facilitate privacy and the speedy prosecution of sexual offenders. They have called on the Ministry of Internal Affairs to take rape and sexual abuse cases more seriously, demanding the establishment of a family desk at every police station to process cases of abuse. Likewise they have petitioned the Ministry of Local Government to educate members of the resistance councils and committees not to settle rape cases out of court, but to bring them to justice. There has been little if any response from the respective ministries to these concerted efforts.

Yet another example of government intransigence is the Domestic Relations Bill, which was drawn up by the Ministry of Women with the help of women's non-governmental organisations. This Bill has languished at the Ministry of Justice for years without action. Thus even active national organisations can fail in their efforts to engage a state that lacks the will or the capacity to act in a responsive way.

---

38 Maxine E. Ankrah, 'Conflict: The Experience of Ugandan Women in Revolution and Reconstruction' (unpublished paper, 1987), 15.

Incivility and social progress

Civil society approaches have also failed to reconcile their emphasis on civility with social change. Some theorists focus on the values of trust, reciprocity and civility that civil society is supposed to foster.[39] Civil society is assumed to be virtuous and civil, transcending particular interests, yet at the same time activated and engaged. Putnam, for example, argues that "Citizenship in a civic community is marked, first of all, by active participation in public affairs'. At the same time, 'virtuous citizens are helpful, respectful, and trustful toward one another, even when they differ on substance. The civic community is not likely to be blandly conflict-free, for its citizens have strong views on public issues, but they are tolerant of their opponents."[40]

This emphasis on tolerance overlooks the fact that democratisation, even in the West, has not come about without conflict and has often been spearheaded by groups organised along social cleavages, most notably class.[41] Some resolve this tension by imagining a monolithic civil society dancing to the same tune, sharing a single orientation. Within this perspective, civil society is based on solidarity and consensus, conformity and agreement.[42]

But such pluralistic approaches suggest that deep gender, class, racial and other such differences based on inequality can simply be wished away. They assume that struggles against authoritarianism and neopatrimonialism can always be waged simply by sitting down and peacefully hammering out a consensus. If the past is any predictor of the future, it would seem that conflict is often unavoidable in processes of social change, including processes that seek to open up the public sphere and to expand civil rights.

Women who want to participate in the public sphere in Uganda, whether it be in the economy or in a community project, have very often had to fight for that right. In spite of the women's efforts to find a peaceful solution, consensus is not always possible when changes of this magnitude are under way.

The fear of incivility and conflict thus tends to lump all conflict together without separating incivility that arises as a result of the process of social change from incivility that is a product of a breakdown in governance or an abuse of governance. It fails to distinguish between the various perpetrators of incivility and their motives. Some state-inspired violence is directed at protesters seeking regime change. There is also defensive violence engaged in by activists responding to attacks by a violent regime. Violence can be directed by dominant groups against less powerful groups or vice versa in periods of instability and change. Challenges to the *status quo* may evoke violent reactions

---

[39] Victor Azarya, 'Civil Society and Disengagement in Africa', in John Harbeson, Donald Rothchild and Naomi Chazan (eds), *Civil Society and the State in Africa* (Boulder, 1994); Ernest Gellner, *Conditions of Liberty: Civil Society and its Rivals* (London, 1994); Réné Lemarchand, 'Uncivil States and Civil Societies: How Illusion Became Reality', *Journal of Modern African Studies*, 30,2 (1092), 177-91; Edward Shils, 'The Virtue of Civil Society', *Government and Opposition*. 26, 1(1991), 3-20.
[40] Robert Putnam, *Making Democracy Work: Civic Traditions in Modern Italy* (Princeton, 1993), 889.
[41] Foley and Edwards, 'The Paradox of Civil Society', 46-7.
[42] Meadwell, in John A. Hall (ed.), *Civil Society: Theory, History, Comparison* (Cambridge. 1995), 193-4.

from those who seek to preserve their privilege. Civil society approaches generally do not delineate between struggles over what the rules should be and struggles over applying the rules. The former struggles can lead to enormous unrest, whereas the latter can usually be negotiated. Moreover, the fear of incivility fails to account for those institutional arrangements that can bring about more civil ways of dealing with differences.

Consider how much resistance and conflict was involved in one small effort Ugandan women made to involve themselves in a community project in a village near Jinja. In this case, the sources of incivility lay with those who were attempting to hold on to an older social configuration that excluded women's leadership. The example is offered to illustrate the problem with the way incivility is conceptualised and other central themes of this article.

Beauty is in the eye of the beholder women project

Ekikwenza Omubi ('Beauty is in the eye of the beholder') Women's Project[43] began to establish a parish health clinic which they intended to run. By 1993, 37 community-run health clinics had already been established in Jinja district compared with eight units in 1989. Two of these clinics were initiated by women's groups and these were the only two that resulted in local conflicts. Since the government was increasingly relinquishing control of the medical system to private and community initiatives, it had made modest sums of money available to the sub county administrative units to assist in the establishment of new clinics.

This women's group had determined that access to adequate health care was the community's main concern and had carried out a baseline survey of parish health needs with the help of a schoolteacher. Local male village leaders objected to their leadership of this initiative explicitly because they were women, poor and illiterate. The women, nevertheless, gained the backing of the Deputy District Medical Officer; the District Administrator, the County Chief, leaders of nearby villages who would be using the health unit, and most of the men and women in the village. However, they were unable to persuade the leaders in the local councils to support them. The women raised funds, collected donations of furniture for the health clinic, and even received financial support for their struggle from women's groups in towns over 100 miles away. The conflict became so intense that men threatened bloodshed if the women did not back down, while the women leaders said they would rather die than give up this project they had started. Since there was nothing monetary to gain from leadership of this health unit, leadership remained the key issue at stake. The headmaster of the village secondary school explained the conflict succinctly: "Women wanted to manage with men at the back, men want control with women at the back."

The health unit was built and operated successfully, largely due to the intervention of the Deputy District Medical Officer. He saw that his job was facilitated by the

---

43   The name of the association comes from the Lusoga proverb *'Ekikwenza omubi - omulungi takimanyha'*, which roughly translated means, when someone falls in love with an ugly one, the beautiful one keeps wondering why.

women's leadership of such health units because women were the individuals primarily responsible for the health of the household. Women paid the clinic fees, they took the children to the hospital and were the ones who attended health education seminars. Because of this he argued: "I call the women my fellow health workers. I have refused to recognise the male dominated management. I take cognizance of collective participation. Male domination at any one stage negates those objectives, for they are now used to subordinating women. They cannot envisage a change."

The group emerged out of a Mother's Union group within the Protestant Church of Uganda, the dominant denomination in the community. Although some of the members still belonged as individuals to the Mothers Union, they broke away in order to gain greater autonomy in their activities and to link up with Catholic and Muslim women who were involved with broader community concerns. Religious differences have played a major role in the country's turbulent history of the past two decades. The anti-sectarian principle behind the formation of the Ekikwenza Omubi is typical of the way in which women throughout the country are finding new bases for collective mobilisation primarily around common economic interests and around the provision of community services. It is especially significant in a country where religious and ethnic divisions continue to threaten the country's fragile stability. Thus the objectives of the group were not only to broaden women's participation in the life of the village but also to create broader forms of association based on tolerance of difference. However, the women's anti-sectarian posture became a source of conflict when the local council leaders attacked Gertrude Mbago, the leader of the women's group, for working with women of other religious persuasions. They cast aspersions on her by saying that she was a member of the Democratic Party, a party that is frequently associated with Catholicism in Uganda.

The issue of who had the right to control the clinic also had strong class dimensions. What especially irritated the male leaders was that Mbago, and most of the women in the women's group, were illiterate and poor. The headmaster of the primary school in the village said: "Would you like to be ruled by an illiterate person? It would be ridiculous to allow this woman to lead women around here who are educated. You see that woman is very bright and if she had formal education she could move mountains." The women in the group were small-holder farmers and were involved in small businesses. The group's leader, Mbago, was a trader in second-hand clothes and ran a restaurant that catered for workers at a nearby coffee factory. In contrast, the men opposing Mbago included high ranking civil servants, retired headmasters, wealthy farmers and businessmen. The men were educated, spoke English and some had even travelled abroad.

The local council leaders tried to split the organisation along class lines, telling the better-off women in Ekikwenza Omubi to leave the association and form another group because the lower class women were too difficult to deal with. The wealthier women formed a new group and the local council leaders tried at one point to get this new organisation to manage the clinic. But, interestingly, the wealthier women secretly continued to support Ekikwenza Omubi. They quietly reported to the Ekikwenza Omubi on what the local council leaders were up to. Gender interests proved in the end to be the overriding concern uniting the women in this struggle. In an ironic twist to the story, the wealthier women's own lack of economic status, according to Ekikwenza Omubi women, is what kept them from openly asserting their common gender interests independent of the influence of the local council leaders. For the poor women, it was their economic autonomy from men that had permitted their involvement.

Although Mbago recognised the limitations of her education, she did not believe this should prevent her from becoming involved in community affairs. Mbago responded to attacks on her lack of education, financial status and, most importantly, the fact that she was a woman:

> What do they [the local council leaders] mean when they say I am illiterate, and a woman then? Now me as a woman, I saw the problems of the lack of health facilities and I stood up. I did not even get a shilling from them [the village leaders], not one chair, not one table, nothing. They did not help with the baseline survey. Why should they now ask to take over? I will not allow anybody to lead me. I am still firm and I pray that it is over. It may mean that I die but I do not mind.

Her husband added: "Men just want to take over what is not theirs ... She is in line with government policy. All women have been called to wake up. That is why I have supported her and I even think the government will help the women."

One older woman, Rachel Katawera, put the gender-based conflict in historical perspective, explaining that lack of education had never been an obstacle to men's leadership in the past: "Men for long and in fact up to until now are desirous of keeping women under them. They reason like fools. Okay, Mbago did not go to school and even my father ... did not go to school. But he ruled [as county chief *saza*] and people respected him. My child, support Mbago. She has born an idea and I do not see why she should be discouraged."

In the course of the conflict, one of the issues that was debated was the meaning of 'community participation in development'. Everyone supported 'community participation', but, as it turned out, the village leaders and the women's group had very different understandings of what that meant in terms of leadership. They also differed on what kind of health unit should be built. The male leaders had wanted a large dispensary and some even proposed facilities that would provide better services than the main hospital in Jinja. The women designed a modest health centre that included an outpatient clinic and maternity unit, which they felt was feasible given available resources. Almost all the villagers interviewed were pleased with the services provided by the clinic, which had been serving up to 30 patients a day. But, to their dismay, the local council officials won the battle over the clinic. The new District Medical Officer succumbed to pressure from the local council leaders and decided to take the clinic away from the women. The clinic was closed down, leaving the community with no local health care provider. The District Medical Officer told the women to get a licence and open a private clinic without government assistance. But since the clinic had always been a non-profit operation the women opposed the District Medical Officer's suggestion.

Lessons from Ekikwenza Omubi

The Ekikwenza Omubi Women's Project is an organisation that reflects many of the unfolding changes in Uganda's associational life. To begin with, the story of Ekikwenza Omubi demonstrates the importance of the family to women's participation in the public arena. The husband of Gertrude Mbago was solidly behind her and justified his wife's involvement as a response to the government's encouragement of women to participate more broadly in society. The husband's critique of male domination and his praise of his wife's leadership skills made it easier for Gertrude Mbago to assume leadership of the organisation in the face of fierce resistance by local elders.

The story of Ekikwenza Omubi also challenges the view that only organisations of educated middle class elites have the wherewithal to build cross-cutting ties and operate outside of kinship networks. It is not possible *a priori* to categorise organisations without looking at the role they, in fact, play. So-called 'modern' registered urban middle class associations with their pajeros, fax machines and letterhead stationery may be infused with particularistic interests and lack the virtues of toleration, while small informal organisations like Ekikwenza Omubi may be horizontally structured to include a heterogeneous membership operating along strict guidelines to ensure accountability and the smooth operation of their organisation. This case study shows that where opportunities exist, small local women's groups are every bit as likely to form along cross-cutting lines (in this case multi-religious lines) as any group of middle-class highly educated women. Moreover, they demonstrated a conscious tolerance for diversity within their daily operations.

In fact, the new mobilisation of women in Uganda more generally goes beyond the close and even extended family. I found hardly any organisations in the four towns surveyed that were made up solely of members of the same ethnicity or religion, suggesting that women and even men are not mobilising simply along family or clan lines. In Kampala, for example, the Baganda constitute 64.5 per cent of the population, with smaller numbers of Banyankole, Basoga, Banyarwanda and numerous other ethnicities. At least 94 per cent of women and 86 per cent of men in organisations were involved in multi-ethnic associations. All, with the exception of the explicitly religious organisations, were of mixed religious backgrounds. Even in Kabale, which had the highest concentration of a single ethnicity (81.5 per cent said they were Bakiga), as many as 76 per cent of women were in groups that included multiple ethnicities (compared with 58 per cent of the men), As many as 73 per cent of women were in religiously mixed organisations, which meant that *none* of the non-religious women's organisations were made up of women of only one religious denomination.

The Jinja conflict was a significant political struggle even though it did not involve 'engaging the state'. As such, it demonstrates the importance of expanding political space for new actors. It is indicative of how far women have come in a short period of time to dare to take on the male village elders. As far back as people could remember, there never had been a struggle of this kind in this village in which women collectively challenged male authority. Even though the struggle was localised, it was an important part of broader changes that are occurring in the country. It vividly demonstrates that national-level declarations encouraging female participation mean little if they are not translated into the daily lives of people. These are highly important efforts to challenge, transform and democratise a male-dominated political culture.

Finally, the case study illustrates the difficulty many notions of civil society have in dealing with disorder. In this case, the women were threatened by the male elders in the community. As mentioned earlier, a process has been set in motion in Uganda by a regime that is encouraging female mobilisation, insisting on broad social transformations in gender relations. Those that have a stake in maintaining the *status quo* do not generally give up their power and privilege without mounting some opposition.

As it turned out, most of the local-level conflicts I studied in Uganda involved physical violence and intimidation on the part of the local council authorities, many of whom had more education and a higher income level than the women they were opposing. With the tacit approval, if not complicity, of the local council, the male vendors at Kiyembe in Kampala beat the market women who were demanding a return of the market stalls that had been removed from them by the Town Clerk and given to the young male vendors. These men threatened to kill and imprison the women. In another part of Kampala, in Kawaala, security forces and police were used consistently to intimidate residents at meetings called by the Kampala City Council and the local council leaders to discuss an infrastructural rehabilitation project. Sometimes the meetings resulted in outbreaks of violence. Women protested against the Kampala City Council infrastructural rehabilitation project quietly by not cleaning their compounds and by not burning their garbage when engineers came to try to start construction. In Jinja a women's group had started to raise fish to give to children in the community because many were suffering from *kwashiorkor* as a result of economic difficulties. When the group's leader went to Nairobi for training, the local council officials poisoned all the fish because they resented the initiative of women in the community. The women drained the pond and started again with the help of the Ministry of Agriculture.

Such conflicts demonstrate the lengths to which leaders will go in order to protect their vested interests, that is, resources and power. And yet it is difficult to see what the women in all these cases could have done differently in the interests of preserving civility, short of withdrawing their demands.

Conclusion

The concept of 'civil society' is a difficult one to employ not just because it is taken to mean so many different things by different people, but also because it can often obscure more than it reveals. Because of the way it is located in notions of the public - private divide, it brings with it all the gendered baggage that this dichotomy embodies. Not only does it obscure the gendered way in which the public - private dichotomy has been constructed, it also fails to appreciate the political nature of the private sphere. It obfuscates the close relationship between the private and public spheres, especially the way in which the constraints women face within the private sphere affect their participation in the public sphere. The dilemma is replicated in the appropriation of 'civil society' into the literature on African politics by giving salience to urban elite non-governmental organisations and associations that engage the state, thus leaving out of view most localised women's organisations and rural associations.

In order to expand civil society, it is therefore necessary to eliminate the sharp separation of distinct public and private spheres embodied in the current use of the concept of 'civil society'. All public spaces are sites for political contestation. They cannot be detached from the domestic sphere. Rather, civil society includes spaces that recognise the political character of conflicts within the private sphere and the way in which they affect the public sphere.

More importantly, there are multiple arenas for political action. The national state is not the only arena where important political struggles are waged. Women, in particular, are active in their own associations, which can become springboards for their involvement in diverse contests for resources and influence, sometimes involving the state, but often involving other societal actors. By privileging only struggles that involve the state at the national level as 'political', civil society approaches neglect important struggles at the local level.

Finally, those who define civil society in terms of its promotion of values of trust, reciprocity, tolerance and civility fail to explain how incivility can be avoided in periods of social change. Supporters of democracy cannot always count on leaders of authoritarian or totalitarian regimes to sit down patiently and work out their differences with them. Similarly, women seeking to expand female participation in the public arena cannot always expect to be received with open arms in an atmosphere of tolerance and civility, as the women in the Jinja village found when they started setting up a health clinic. Notions of civility need to be refined to account for different circumstances, different forms of conflict, different actors, objectives and institutional solutions.

While much of this critique has been directed at liberal notions of civil society and political space, I want to be clear that I am not advocating a civic republican notion of the public sphere, which emphasises "people reasoning together to promote a common good that transcends the mere sum of individual preferences."[44] As we saw in the case study, the male leaders and the women's group had very different ideas about what 'community participation' meant in terms of who would lead the effort to establish the health clinic and the extent to which the women would participate in the endeavour. They also had different objectives for the health clinic. Both sides felt they were promoting the 'common good', yet their visions of that common good were very much at odds with one another. Civic republicanism does not allow private interests to assert themselves in the political public sphere.[45] It assumes that the common good

---

44   Fraser, *Justice Interruptus*, 86.
45   Ibid., 87.

can be known in advance and that the conflict will necessarily result in a mutually acceptable outcome. As we saw in the Jinja case study, the outcome favoured the group of more economically powerful and politically influential village leaders. And yet the closing of the clinic hardly could be said to have benefited the community at large.

This article has broadened the notion of political space in order to expand the idea of civil society. It does not privilege associational 'engagement of the state' at the national level over other forms of more localised political activity in the way that 'civil society' does. Instead, there is a recognition of the complementarity and necessity of political reform along many dimensions that range from changes at the national level to changes in people's daily lives. Legislative and constitutional changes, for example, are irrelevant unless they are adhered to and legitimated by people in their day-to-day practices. With the lens of analysis so narrowly fixed on civil society's role in policy making and legislative change, we may miss important dynamics that are occurring within communities that can have broad implications when taken together as part of a more generalised phenomenon. Only when we broaden our understanding of the political at both the national and local levels can we fully appreciate the importance of struggles for resources, influence and power in which the protagonists are members of non-dominant sectors of society.

3

Contemporary Civil Society and the Democratisation Process in Uganda: A Preliminary Exploration

(with a focus on Cooperatives, Trade Unions and the Media)[1]

Nyangabyaki Bazaara

Abstract

Although Dr Bazaara's article was originally published as a Working Paper by the Centre of Basic Research in 2000, it remains of interest today on two counts. First, the author proposes a conceptualisation of civil society intimately linked to the promotion of democracy and his historical analysis shows how and why 'civil society organisations' at times participate in civil society – when they promote democracy and attempt to hold the state to account – and at times do not, such as when focusing on service delivery. The analysis is thus based on the belief that to grasp the nature of civil society in Uganda, there is a need to examine civil society as it 'is' and not as it 'ought' to be, as a historical phenomenon, not as a programme; as a process and not as a formal phenomenon robbed of movement and transformation.

Secondly, Dr. Bazaara's focus on organisations that have historically been active in Uganda (peasant co-operatives, trade unions, development\ welfare\ charity NGOs) remains of interest, especially since the work of the former is generally poorly documented. Like co-operatives, trade unions have had periods when they participated in civil society and others when they did not. Generally, it is the argument of this paper that in recent years, particularly after the NRM captured state power, there has been a proliferation of many non-state organisations and the decline of others. These mutations and permutations are yet to produce strong impulses in civil society.

---

1 Reprinted by kind permission of the Centre for Basic Research, Kampala. Originally published as CBR Working Paper 54, April 2000. The emphasis on Cooperatives, Trade Unions and the Media is the editors'.

Introduction

The very idea that people can be forced to be democratic and\ or free is quite startling. Freedom and liberation front autocratic rule as well as democracy and accountability cannot be decreed. They must have a social basis in which they arise, are nurtured and sustained.[2]

The faith in 'civil society' being a mechanism for enhancing democracy is now fairly well entrenched in Uganda, especially among the non-governmental organisations involved in lobbying and advocacy.[3] This faith has two origins. First, it stems from a legacy of the brutal dictatorship Uganda witnessed for several years, and the desire to forestall the re-emergence of such a scenario. Second, is the donor agenda of 'poverty and democratic governance' that is based on the assumption that one of the most important pre-requisites for poverty reduction is good governance. In turn, good governance can only be safeguarded by civil society.[4] Both sources of this 'faith' assume that civil society in Uganda is weak and in need of empowering. It is not surprising, therefore, that considerable amounts of foreign donor resources, the magnitude of which is unknown, have been poured into Uganda. The end result is supposed to be a strengthened civil society that has the capacity to advance democracy and block the horrendous dictatorships Uganda went through for more than two decades.[5]

However, this external support for civil society raises the question whether or not this empowerment is, indeed, strengthening civil society and, in turn, whether this civil society is buttressing democratic values and practices in Uganda. As Oloka-Onyango has observed, "whether or not they (donors) have facilitated the process of democratisation in the country is a complex question requiring a much more comprehensive analysis that examines issues from both qualitative and quantitative dimensions."[6] Many of the

---

2 John-Jean Barya. 'The New Political Conditionalities of Aid: An Independent View from Africa, *IDS Bulletin*, 24/1. 199: 17.
3 For example, Livingstone Sewanyana, a Director of one of the prominent human rights organisations posed the question: 'What kind of democracy do we want and how can we sustain it'?' He answered 'In part… in the case of Uganda …the answer… lies in the empowerment at civil society. See Livingstone Sewanyana, 'Democratisation and the Growth of Civil Society'. Kampala, Foundation for Human Rights Initiative. 1996. See also Juma Okuku, 'Non-Governmental Organisations (NGOs) and the Struggle for Democratic Governance: 'The Case of Uganda'. *Mawazo*, 7/2, December 1997.
4 Oloka-Onyango and Barya argue that civil society played a quite negligible or absolutely no role in processes of change that brought National Resistance Movement (NRM) to power. See Oloka-Onyango and J.J. Barya. 'Civil Society and the Political Economy of Foreign Aid in Uganda', *Democratisation*, 4/2, 1997.
5 This is not to say that donors did not support civil society organisations in the past. "What is remarkable about this period is that support is seen in the context of an agenda spearheaded by the World Bank and other multilateral donors, an agenda of poverty reduction and good governance." For an examination of aspects of the support for civil society organisations, see Julie Hearn, 'Foreign Political Aid, Democratisation and Civil Society in Uganda in the 1990s. Centre for Basic Research Working Paper No 53. Kampala, Centre for Basic Research. August 1999.
6 Oloka Onyango, 'Civil Society and the Place of Foreign Donors in Contemporary Uganda: A Review of the Literature and the Donor Policy Environment: paper presented at a Workshop of the Collaborative Partners on the Project 'Foreign Political Aid, Democratisation and Civil Society in

donors project civil society as simply being non-governmental organisations (NGOs).[7] This perspective commits two fatal errors. First, it does not realise that some NGOs do not qualify to be part of civil society.[8] Second, it leaves out other civil society actors whose role is in fact more decisive when it comes to the process of democratic opening.

For us to appreciate the role of foreign political aid, we need, as a preliminary step, to understand the empirical map of the organisations that have participated in civil society. The objective of this paper, then, is to make a preliminary map of the character of civil society in Uganda and to illustrate how its character and activities have been shaped by its dependence on foreign resources (foreign political aid). Our approach is to focus on civil society activities of organisations that have historically been active in Uganda, namely: peasant co-operatives, trade unions, development/welfare/charity NGOs, women organisations and human rights organisations. Although this does not necessarily exhaust all the organisations that are active in civil society, it nonetheless covers fairly substantive ground, and some tentative conclusions can be arrived at about the nature of civil society in Uganda and how it is changing as a result of foreign political aid. It is hoped that future research will build on this map.

It is the argument of this paper that in recent years, particularly after the NRM captured state power, there has been a proliferation of many non-state organisations and the decline of others. These mutations and permutations are yet to produce strong impulses in civil society. Not that civil society does not exist in Uganda; but from the evidence in our possession, existing civil society is yet to prove that it can hold the state accountable and also push for democratic governance. Foreign political aid has entered civil society circles in favour of certain sections that probably are not decisive in strengthening democracy.

The analysis and conclusions of this paper are based on materials collected through a library search[9] and interviews with a number of people knowledgeable on the non-state sector or parts of it.[10] The research was conducted as part of a collaborative effort

---

Africa', Johannesburg. 11-13 March 1998. p 20.

7 Julie Hearn has attempted to map out the kind of donors involved in providing political aid to some Ugandan civil society organisations (read NGOs). It is very clear that organisations that have received foreign political aid are NGOs. But to understand the potentialities of civil society in holding the state accountable we need to examine other types of civil society organisations and their role in the democratic process. (Julie Hearn, op.cit.) See also Nyangabyaki Bazaara and Kintu Nyago, 'Civil Society Empowerment and Poverty Reduction in Uganda: A Review Essay', Paper presented at the First Regional Meeting of the Civil Society Programme, organised by the Council for the Development of Social Science Research in Africa (CODESRIA). Dakar (Senegal) 14-15 April 1999 See also J. Oloka-Onvango. op.cit.

8 An organisation can be considered to be part of civil society if it engages the state. Civil society is a relationship between associational life and the state. Some NGOs do not engage the state and, therefore, cannot be considered to be part of civil society. As will he shown later in the paper, many of the NGOs in Uganda are poverty alleviation organisations that do not seek to challenge the status quo.

9 The libraries consulted include Centre for Basic Research, Makerere University Main Library, Department of Gender and Women Studies, Department of Political Science and Public Administration, Department of Economics, Foundation for Human Rights Initiative. Development Network of Indigenous Associations (DENIVA), and the network of Ugandan Researchers and Research Users (NURRU).

10 The following people were interviewed: Edward Ruhanga, Secretary for Research; Uganda Railway

between the Institute of Development Studies at Sussex (UK), University of Legon (Ghana), the Centre for Policy Studies (South Africa) and the Centre for Basic Research (Uganda) on the theme Foreign Political Aid, Civil Society and Democratisation.

Conceptualising civil society

To be able to discern the empirical manifestations of civil society in Uganda requires taking a position in the debate on how to conceptualise civil society. As is now well known, engagement with the concept elicits different meanings to different people at different times. In the case of Africa, this concept has been imported mainly from Western philosophical traditions. This has raised eyebrows as to the extent of its usefulness in capturing the empirical reality of the African situation. It is not surprising, therefore, that there is a strong call for unpacking the concept and operationalising it in concrete local realities.[11] Indeed, in many instances, the concept of civil society is conceived in universalistic or programmatic fashion. What civil society can or cannot do is determined *a priori*. In other words civil society is not seen as an historical phenomenon that is shaped by the peculiar social and political realities of the times.[12]

All writings on civil society in Uganda attempt to define it. The elementary definition is that civil society is composed of voluntary associations that occupy the space between the family and the state. In this regard the majority of commentators are in agreement that the following organisations have participated in civil society: non-governmental bodies, professional associations, trade unions, women and youth organisations, academic staff associations and cooperatives.[13] However, there are disagreements as to whether or not political parties should be considered as part and parcel of civil society. Mujaju, Sewanyana and Tukahebwa contend that political parties are also part of civil society.[14] Implied in this argument is the contention that democracy can be advanced through the existence of autonomous associations interacting with the state as well as

---

Workers Union (national level), Mr. Bisereko, Ministry of Justice, Prof J. Kwesiga, Executive Secretary, DENIVA, Mr. Kigenyi-Wansolo, Programme Officer, National Union of Disabled Persons of Uganda (NUDIPU), Mr. Zie Gariyo, Uganda Debt Network (UDN), Ms. Zam Zam Nagujja Executive Director Federation of Ugandan Women Lawyers (FIDA); Mr. Zedriga; Executive Secretary, National Non-Governmental Organisations Forum (NGO Forum); Ms. Peace Kyamureku Deputy, Secretary General, National Association of Women Organisations of Uganda (NAWOU); Ms. Hope Mwesigye, Director, Uganda Gender Resource Centre (UGRC); Mr. Onyango Obbo, Senior Editor, The Monitor Newspaper.

11 Oloka-Onyango and Barya, op.cit.
12 This is surprising because although usage of the concept is retraceable to Alexis de Tocqueville, the contemporary usage is in many instances at odds with his conceptualisation. Tocqueville anchored his analysis of democracy in actual historical process. This is why he was able to show the difference between civil societies in French and American democracies. See Henk E. S. Woldring, 'State and Civil Society in the Political Philosophy of Alexis de Tocqueville', *Voluntas*, 9/4. 1998.
13 See Akiiki B Mujaju. 'Civil Society in Uganda' (Paper Presented at a Conference on 'Civil Society Issues in Eastern Africa organised by the Centre for Basic Research Held at Fairway Hotel, Kampala, 12-14 December 1997): and Livingstone Sewanyana, 'Culture and Civil Society in Uganda' (Arusha Paper Presented to EASUM's Mini-Consultation on 'Culture and Civil Society, 27-29 November 1996). Godfrey B. Tukahebwa, 'The Role of District Councils in the Decentralisation Programme in Uganda', Department of Political Science Occasional Paper, Kampala: Makerere University, 1998.
14 See Mujaju, 1997. ibid; Sewanyana, 1996, ibid; and Tukahebwa, 1998, ibid.

political parties. But this raises questions as to the distinction between civil society and political society and what the relationship between the two should be.

In the concrete situation of Uganda, the conceptualisation of civil society and its likely impact on democratic processes has been greatly influenced by political realities. Among these realities, the most important, for our purposes, is the banning of political party activities by the National Resistance Movement (NRM). In response to that ban, a debate ensued about what true democracy in Uganda should be and what institutional framework is necessary to buttress it. On the one hand, there are those who see the sum and substance of democracy in Uganda as that of liberal democracy or the multiparty system.[15] On the other, there are those, particularly in the NRM, who see liberal democracy as being ill-suited for Uganda. They argue, to begin with, that multiparty democracy has had a bad history in Uganda because the parties collaborated with past dictatorships. Secondly, they argue that the socio-economic conditions necessary for multiparty democracy have not evolved as yet in Uganda. Y.K. Museveni, the President of Uganda, has argued in reference to the Constituent Assembly debate as follows:

> Another issue of importance in the CA debate was whether or not we should have political parties. We in the NRM argued that there are no healthy grounds for party polarisation in Uganda at this time because of the absence of social classes. In Western democracies, parties have usually been founded on some sort of class basis: parties for the middle class, parties for workers, and so on. On what basis would parties in Uganda be formed, since Ugandans are overwhelmingly of one class, peasants? The polarisation one is likely to get in Uganda and countries like it, is vertical polarisation tribe A will join party A, tribe B party B, and so on. This will be sectarian. What is crucial for Uganda now is for us to have a system that ensures democratic participation until such a time as we get, through economic development, especially industrialisation, the crystallisation of socio-economic groups upon which we can then base political parties.[16]

It is not surprising that in as far as the concept civil society is associated with democracy, its application in Uganda is enmeshed in the movement-multi-party democracy debate. While we agree that non-governmental organisations, professional associations, trade unions, women and youth organisations, academic staff associations and co-operatives have at one time or another participated in civil society in Uganda, we disagree that political parties should be included in the conceptualisation of the phenomenon of civil

---

15 The leader of one of the oldest parties in Uganda argued as follows: "...in the tradition of Uganda, democracy presupposes a multi-party system" This statement is quoted in Expedit Ddungu, 'Popular forms and the question of Democracy, the case of resistance councils in Uganda' in Mahmood Mamdani and Joe Oloka-Onyango (eds.), Uganda: Studies in Living Conditions, Popular Movements and Constitutionalism, Kampala: Centre for Basic Research, 1994: 368.

16 This argument raises a lot more questions than can possibly be dealt with here. First, it is not true that peasants are undifferentiated in Uganda. Second, this argument is reminiscent of those days when the likes of Nyerere defended one-party states on the pretext that political parties were divisive and diverted the energy of the people from development. Third, tribalism is not necessarily negative. There are instances when organising around a tribe can be progressive. Finally, after the devastating ethnic conflicts in the Balkans, the argument that Western countries cannot deteriorate into sectarian conflicts is questionable. See Yoweri Kaguta Museveni, *Sowing the Mustard Seed: The Struggle for Freedom and Democracy in Uganda*, London: Macmillan Publishers Ltd., 1997. p 195.

society. This is because political parties aspire to capture state power while civil society organisations do not and only influence policy in indirect ways. However, as many writings on civil society suggest, a relationship exists between non-state organisations active in civil society and political parties. In fact, political parties derive strength from such organisations and vice versa. The mere existence of civil society organisations without political parties may render the former impotent.

Oloka-Onyango and Barya advance another view related to the movement-multiparty debate. They argue that 'normal' political parties should not be considered as being part of civil society. However, in the context of Uganda, it is important to go beyond 'form' to examine 'substance'. They argue that the ban on political parties has robbed Ugandan political parties of their 'true' functions and reduced them to mere organisations that can rightly be considered as being part and parcel of civil society.[17] The same argument seems to have been advanced by F.W. Juuko who contends that Ugandan political parties have been giving birth to splinter groups that may turn out to be a foundation for a strong civil society although, of course, there is a possibility of such groups becoming anarchical.[18] To Juuko, political parties have been disintegrating because of the lack of internal democracy and their support for dictatorial regimes in the post-independence history of Uganda. As such, the historical political parties have done little to strengthen civil society.[19] He seems to suggest that the ban on parties is strengthening civil society and ushering in new forms of democracy.

The discussion over how to conceptualise civil society has also touched on the issue of what the relationship between civil society and the state should be. Mujaju contends that civil society is at 'bay' in Uganda. This conception has serious theoretical and empirical implications for understanding the relationship between the state and civil society organisations. First, it assumes that civil society organisations are a uniform phenomenon carrying out a coherent agenda and perpetually in conflict with the state. However, as Robert Fatton, Jr. has argued,

> Civil society is neither homogenous nor wholly emancipatory: in fact it is contradictory, exhibiting both democratic and despotic tendencies. Moreover it is conflict-ridden and prone to the devastating violence of multiple forms of particularisms. Civil society should therefore he analysed in the plural, rather than as a uniform and unitary political space.[20]

This is exactly what is taking place in Uganda: a process of shifting relationships between civil society organisations depending on the issues at stake. The dialectic of cooperation and devastating rivalry marks the operation of civil society organisations. Much of the discussion on civil society presumes that it has the inherent attributes

---

17 Oloka-Onyango and Barya. 1997. op.cit
18 F. W. Juuko. 'Political Parties, NGOs and Civil Society in Uganda' in Joseph Oloka-Onyango, Kivutha Kibwana, Chris Maina Peter (eds.), *Law and the Struggle for Democracy in East Africa*, Nairobi, Claripress Ltd, 1996, pp 192-193.
19 F.W. Juuko. ibid. 192
20 Robert Fatton Jr, 'Africa in the Age of Democratisation: the Civic Limitations of Civil society', *African Studies Review*, 38/2 September 1995: 93.

to defend democracy. However, in reality, not all-civil society organisations are in favour of democracy. Even, the extent to which those organisations whose mission is to advance democracy can do so is dependent on historically specific socio-political contexts.[21] Besides, it is erroneous to assume that uncivil organisations are necessarily anti-democratic.

The other issue that has animated the discussions on civil society is how to conceptualise the relationship between civil society and society at large. The basic argument is that the middle class controls the majority of civil society organisations in Uganda. These organisations cannot be expected to champion the interests of the majority of Ugandans who happen to be peasants and workers. Aili Mari Tripp argues that "The narrow way in which civil society organisations have often been defined makes it largely the domain of male middle class, educated urbanites, leaving most women and peasants out of the picture".[22] This has serious implications for the assumption that civil society will advance democracy, especially given the fact that donors have adopted a programmatic approach to civil society. This leaves out a number of civil society organisations that are not chosen to be empowered. For if democracy is also about resources and power, the support of a section of civil society and the neglect of another sidetracks the important process of negotiation and the arrival at a consensus with all parties involved. It may, in fact, lead to some organisations becoming uncivil.

Many of the writings portray the relationship between civil society organisations and the state as that of conflict.[23] This erroneous view has its origin partly in the assumption that the state is a neutral or monolithic set of institutions. In practice, we know that the state always intervenes in society in favour of some social groups to the disadvantage of others. This means that at all times the state co-opts (co-operates with) parts of civil society at the same time as it punishes others.[24] In the case of Uganda, this fact is demonstrated by the cosy relationship between the NRM regime and the Uganda Manufacturers Association, in contrast with the very uneasy relationship between the NRM and Trade Unions or with several non-governmental organisations. In addition,

---

21 In this paper we are referring to democracy in limited procedural sense as '... the freedom to form and join organisations, freedom of expression, right to vote, eligibility for public office, right of political information, free and fair elections, institutions for making government policies depend on votes and other expressions of preference'. See R. A. Dahl, 'Polyarchy, Participation and Opposition. New Haven: Yale University Press, 1971: 3.

22 Aili Mari Tripp, 'Expanding "Civil Society": Women and Political Space in Contemporary Uganda'. *Commonwealth and Comparative Politics*, 36/2, July 1998, p. 85.

23 I have not dealt with the issue of the nature of the Ugandan State and how it has been transformed not only by the NRM struggle but also by donors, some civil society organisations, or even society. Quite often the literature on civil society, including this study, does not deal with the issue of what ways the state is being transformed by forces of globalisalion, civil society or constitutionalism processes.

24 For a more elaborate treatment of the debate over how to conceptualise the sate-civil society relationships, see Mutahi G. Ngunyi, 'Building Democracy in Polarised Civil Society, the Transition to Multi-party Democracy in Kenya' in Joseph Oloka-Onyango, Kivutha Kibwana and Chris Maina Peter, op. cit. See also Timothy M. Shaw and Sandra J. Maclean, 'Civil Society and Political Economy in Contemporary Africa: What Prospects for Sustainable Democracy', *Journal of Contemporary African Studies*, 14/2 (1996).

we consider civil society in this paper to be as a process and not simply a catalogue of organisations. As Edmond J. Keller has noted:

> Civil society is not society writ-large, but only a sub-set of it. What defines civil society is its agenda. It is created when autonomous associations adopt and act upon a civic agenda. In that sense the manifestation of civil society tends to be situational and intermittent. These groups may not have been born as civic organisations, but they are moved by circumstances to engage in politics. They might demand constitutional reform, government accountability, their human and political rights, and an end to official corruption… in many cases, it [civil society] has been a decisive catalyst in regime change. However, the effectiveness of civil society in bringing about regime change is highly contingent, conditioned by other factors such as the relative strength of the incumbent regime, the role of external actors, the relative coherence of formal opposition groups, internal and external political and economic factors. Moreover even when it is crucial in bringing about regime change, civil society role is eclipsed in the aftermath. Because of its inchoate nature it is unable to play a direct role in policy formation, and only indirectly contributes to democratic consolidation. [25]

Let us sum up for this section. Our analysis is based on the belief that to grasp the nature of civil society in Uganda, there is need to examine civil society as it 'is' and not as it 'ought' to be, as a historical phenomenon, not as a programme; as a process and not as a formal phenomenon robbed of movement and transformation. As Mamdani has hinted, civil society needs to be understood "analytically, in its historical formation, and not programmatically, as an agenda for change".[26] We need to examine civil society in relation to the economy and to the wider processes of change. This means moving away from a historical, normative, essentialist or universalistic approaches to conceptualising civil society.

Against this background, we now turn to mapping out the nature of civil society as it has developed historically in Uganda. The idea is to indicate the strength of each civil society sector, whether or not it engages the state, in what manner and with what impact. We shall indicate the extent of foreign political aid support and the effect such support produces on processes of internal democracy and the ability to change policy or hold the state accountable, especially in the current epoch. In the following parts of the paper we look at cooperatives, trade unions, the media and non-governmental organisations of various characteristics (poverty alleviation, women and human rights organisations).

Peasant co-operatives

According to statistics from the Ministry of Co-operatives, there are 6,238 registered primary co-operative societies, 31 district unions, 6 national unions and the Uganda

---

25 Edmond J. Keller, 'Political Institutions, Agency and Contingent Compromise: Understanding Democratic Consolidation and Reversal in Africa', Working Paper of the University of California, Los Angeles, 1 November 1997.
26 Mahmood Mamdani, 'Indirect Rule, Civil Society and Ethnicity: The African Dilemma' Social Justice' 23/1-2, 1996 p 148

Co-operative Alliance (UCA) as an apex organisation for peasant co-operatives as of 1999.[27] In 1952, there were 278 registered co-operatives with 14,832 members.[28] In 1965, there were 1,825 primary societies and 31 district unions. In 1978, there were 3,054 societies and 41 unions.[29] Generally speaking, there has been a phenomenal growth of co-operatives since the 1950s. Does this growth imply enhanced strength of co-operatives to deal with the state and influence policy in their favour? Does this expansion in numbers mean that there was enthusiastic participation of the membership and hence democracy within the movement? What role does the cooperative movement play in policy formulation in contemporary Uganda? What foreign political aid have co-operatives received in recent years, and what has been its impact of the internal processes of cooperatives and their ability to contribute to the opening of democratic political space?

It should be noted here that we are dealing with peasant cooperatives. There are other co-operatives with a different social base such as merchants. An example of a merchant co-operative is the Kiyembe Co-operative Society.[30] The issues over which the peasant co-operatives have confronted the state are different from the issues over which merchant co-operatives have faced the state. We shall not deal with other categories of cooperatives because we need more empirical data to arrive at a reasonable conclusion as to their participation in civil society and their contribution to democracy in Uganda.

Peasant cooperatives have been undergoing internal changes and the manner in which they relate to the state since they were legally allowed to operate in 1946. Conceptually, this means that at certain points in history, co-operatives have participated in civil society and at other points they have not. The sources of these changes are multiple and require a historical treatment.

Historically, peasant co-operatives developed in response to the monopolisation of trade in agricultural products by immigrant European and Asian communities, as well as the low price the colonial state offered for peasant products. The high point arrived when the colonial government established the Coffee and Lint Marketing Boards, which were essentially a mechanism for siphoning off rural surpluses to prop up Britain's declining economy after World War II. For instance, an ideologue of the peasants complained bitterly in a local newspaper:

> We the growers are aggrieved to see that the Protectorate Government refuses to free our cotton for which we sweat. Probably the Government is so shy that it has been so far unwilling to inform us of the fact that we the producers are its labourers to whom it pays a wage or gift of shs.30 on every 100 lbs. Once again we implore the Government

---

27 Lameck Kibikyo, 'Civil Society Matrix showing their Activities and Types', Kampala, Centre for Basic Research (Mimeo), 1999.
28 Crawford Young, Neal P Sherman and Tim H. Rose. *Cooperatives and Development: Agricultural Politics in Ghana and Uganda*, Madison: The University of Wisconsin Press, 1981. p.60.
29 Ibid . p 66
30 For details about Kiyembe Co-operative Society, see Aili Mari Tripp. 'Local Women's Associations and Politics in Contemporary Uganda' in Holger, Bernt Hansen and Michael Twaddle (eds), *Developing Uganda*. Kampala: Fountain Publishers. 1998.

to understand that it has no right whatsoever to save for itself any money that would accrue to us from cotton.[31]

These grievances were partly responsible for the 1945 and 1949 uprisings that shook the then Uganda Protectorate. One of the demands of the rioters was that growers gin their own cotton and also sell their products directly wherever they liked.[32] The colonial state responded by effecting reforms that were meant to undermine the militancy of the nationalist movement and to bring the ship of the co-operative movement into a politically safe harbour. This it did by enacting the 1946 Co-operative Societies Ordinance. The effect of this ordinance was to diminish the autonomy of the co-operative societies. No co-operative society could operate without being registered by the Registrar of Societies, and state officials had the right to look into the finances of the cooperative societies to ensure that they were not being used for political purposes. From the mid-1950s, "never again would a co-operative be so politically significant as a protest vehicle acting on national policies."[33]

These reforms transformed the nature of co-operatives from being popularly based to essentially organisations for the elite.[34] This trend continued into the post-independence period. The question that arises is: why is it that the co-operative membership was unable to fight for their autonomy? Mamdani argues that for that to happen required a reform in the nature of the colonial state. This, however, did not come to pass in the post-colonial period. What changed in the colonial period was a simple de-racialisation (read Africanisation) of the state and not civil society. Africanisation, argues Mamdani, simultaneously unified as it fragmented.

> With independence the defence of racial privilege could no longer be in the language of racism. Confronted by a de-racialised state, racism not only receded into civil society, but also defended itself in the language of individual rights and institutional autonomy. To indigenous ears, the vocabulary of rights rang hollow, a lullaby for perpetuating racial privilege. Indigenous demands were formulated in the language of nationalism and social justice. The result was a breach between the discourse on rights and that on power: with the language of rights appearing as a fig leaf over privilege, and power as the guarantor of social justice and redress.[35]

It is not surprising, therefore, that the state continued to play a paternalist role or that it was essentially dictatorial. Significant to note is the ideology of developmentalism

---

31 Quoted in Mahmnood Mamdani. *Politics and Class Formation in Uganda*, New York: Monthly Review Press. 1976. p. 181
32 Uganda Protectorate. Report of the Commission of Inquiry into the Civil Disturbances in Uganda During April 1949, Entebbe: Government Printer.
33 Crawford Young. Neal P. Sherman and Tim H. Rose. op.cit., p. 74.
34 Stephen Bunker's analysis shows that in the post-independence period, Bugisu Co-operative Union continued to struggle for its autonomy and to sell its agricultural product – coffee – at prices of its own choice. The leadership being corrupt undermined this struggle and led to the state to intervene and to diminish the autonomy of cooperatives. See Stephen G. Bunker, *Peasants Against the State: the Politics of Market Control in Bugisu, Uganda, 1900-1983*; Urbana: University of Illinois Press, 1987.
35 Mahmood Mamdani, 'Indirect Rule, Civil Society and Ethnicity: The African Dilemma', *Social Justice* 23:1-2. 1996, p 49.

that saw the state as a very important actor in rural development. In this context, co-operatives became instruments for reaching the masses to make them grow export crops and to collect rural surpluses rather than for the advancement of the interests of the peasants. In addition, political parties saw co-operatives as one of the best mechanisms to generate votes. As a result, co-operatives, particularly in the 1960s, became divided along political party lines. Whereas in the 1950s co-operatives could fight for better prices for peasant agricultural products, in the 1960s higher prices were associated with the regime in power seeking electoral votes. For example, the first ruling party in post-independence Uganda, the Democratic Party, increased prices for coffee from 50 cents a pound to 60 cents a pound to woo the support of the coffee farmers and to ward off its rival, the Uganda People's Congress (UPC). Similarly, UPC increased the price of cotton in 1965 way above the world market price simply because the regime was trying to woo the support of the peasants.[36] These price hikes were temporary and actually ended as the world market prices began to decline in late 1960s.

The entry of politics in the operation of the cooperatives introduced conflicts that undermined their autonomy. The purpose of elections in co-operatives ceased to be about choosing individuals that would provide leadership but about the political party an individual was affiliated to. Studies made in the mid-1960s revealed that

> The cooperative had been an important instrument for reinforcement of the position of the 'big men' of the parish, for most of which cotton growing was only an ancillary activity. "The cooperative society was, therefore, less important as a means of improving agricultural production than as a means of access to cash that could be invested in non-agricultural enterprises. It was a political office in the local society that was valued jealously guarded by the Big Men and elders for its contacts with the power structure beyond the parish, its potential political clout, and its kickbacks.[37]

It is not surprising, therefore, the many of the first generation of political leadership originated from the co-operatives.[38]

However, the increase in factional conflicts in the co-operative leadership opened the way for embezzlement of co-operative funds, loss of accountability and democracy. Membership participation was on the wane by the end of the 1960s. J. Opio-Odongo concluded, for example, that since the 1950s there had been "a decline in member participation" in Lango Co-operative Union.[39]

---

36 See Nyangabyaki Bazaara, 'Agrarian Politics, Crisis and Reformism in Uganda, 1962-1996' PhD Dissertation: Queens University, 1997. pp. 111-113.
37 Crawford Young, Neil Sherman and Tim H. Rose, op.cit., p.68.
38 "In Bugisu, most politicians active either locally or nationally were associated with the Bugisu Co-operative Union. Mathias Ngobi, Minister of Agriculture and Co-operatives until his arrest in 1966, made his reputation as Manager of the Busoga Growers' Co-operative Union from 1958 to 1962, a period during which the union was remarkably successful. Felix Onama, Minister of Defence under Obote, attained visibility as the General Manager of the West Nile Co-operative Union from 1960 to 1962. George Magezi, who was a Minister from 1963 to 1966, was President of the most consistently effective co-operative union, the Bunyoro Co-operative Union from 1958 on." Ibid: p.61
39 Joe Martin Aldo Opio-Odongo, 'The Cotton Co-operative as an Institutional Innovation in Uganda', PhD Dissertation, Cornell University, 1978, p. 233.

To increasing factional fights and embezzlement of funds, the state responded not by encouraging more accountability and democratic practice within the co-operatives but by passing legislation that increased state control over co-operatives. As the Secretary of the Uganda Co-operative Alliance noted, the 1970 Co-operative and Peasant Societies Act, for example "deprives the co-operative movement of its autonomy" and called for its amendment "so that power can be returned to the co-operators".[40] Under the 1970 Act the state minister was given more powers to intervene in the affairs of cooperatives, including dismissal of the elected leaders of the co-operatives. The Minister of Co-operatives, Adoko Nekyon, exemplified the changed attitude of the state when, in 1967, he said the following:

> Democracy cannot work in a [co-operative] union. It can never work. If anybody is under illusion that democracy can be introduced in business, then he can take over from me even tomorrow morning. We are going to continue with dismissing of unions [leadership] that are not functioning properly. Any union I find has been working badly should assume in advance that it is already dismissed.[41]

Throughout the brutal dictatorship of Amin (1971-1979) the hand of the state remained strong. Typical of a military regime, the approach to co-operatives was militaristic. Since some of the leadership of the co-operatives had aligned themselves to the ruling political party, a number were killed while others were exiled. Fearful of confronting the military government, some peasants abandoned growing export crops or sold their crops outside the co-operative unions, in a parallel market that is popularly known as *magendo*. Even during the Obote II period, co-operatives were effectively unable to participate in policy-making. Again, the leadership was not accountable to the members: many co-operative unions did not hold Annual General Meetings. With a return to multi-party politics, co-operative leadership was divided along political party lines. The effect was that some unions splintered into factions. For example, in the first part of the 1980s, a group of individuals led a breakaway faction to create Kitara Co-operative Union from Bunyoro Growers Co-operative Union. As if this was not enough, the faith of the membership in the co-operatives was diminished by the inability of the co-operatives to pay members promptly. This arose partly from the eroded infrastructure of the co-operatives and the lack of crop finance. The infrastructure such as trucks and ginneries had broken down due to years of neglect and also because of the looting associated with the 1979 war and the civil war that followed between 1981-1986. These conflicts greatly weakened the co-operative movement.

The National Resistance Movement period (1986 to the present) has not been favourable for the co-operatives. First, in legal terms, the new Co-operative Act does not substantially return the initiative to the people to enforce accountability and democracy within the co-operatives.[42] Embezzlement of co-operative funds, for

---

40 Didas Bakunda. 'Call for Co-op Act Amendment', *New Vision*, 25 May 1989.
41 Uganda Government, *Hansard*, Vol. 68. 1967
42 For an elaborate analysis of the relationship between the State and the co-operatives, see Mahmood Mamdani, 'Pluralism and the Right of Association' in Mahmood Mamdani and Joe Oloka-Onyango (eds), *Uganda: Studies in Living Conditions, Popular Movements and Constitutionalism*, Kampala:

instance, has continued unabated.[43] The difference between past regimes and the NRM is that the NRM has refrained from involving itself in leadership squabbles within the movement. In that sense, the NRM has allowed some room for autonomy. However, the implementation of Structural Adjustment Programme policies has dealt a serious blow to co-operatives. The liberalisation component of these policies has exposed co-operatives to severe competition, thereby undermining their profitability. For instance, co-operatives used to enjoy the virtual monopoly of processing agricultural products. In the case of coffee, its role in processing coffee beans had by 1989 shrunk dramatically.

> Private coffee processors are capturing the coffee business in the country from the co-operative movement. Out of the total amount of coffee produced in Uganda, only 22% is handled by the co-operatives; the rest is channelled through private processors.[44]

In this context, the cooperative movement lacks the internal coherence to influence policy or even to carry out purely economic activities.

We have come across evidence that the co-operative movement has been receiving funds from foreign donors in recent years. However, cooperatives have acted as mere clearing ground for these funds. These include, the Luwero Triangle Project, the PL 480 programme and the Northern Uganda Co-operative Rehabilitation Project. The Swedish International Development Authority (SIDA) funded the Luwero Triangle Project (LTP) that covered the districts of Mpigi, Luweero and Mubende. The object of the funds was the rehabilitation of the co-operative marketing structure, namely building storage infrastructure and the provision of credit. The PL 480 was a programme that involved a donation of soya beans from the US government. The money generated was used, for instance, to provide credit to those growing soya beans. The Northern Uganda Co-operative Rehabilitation project aimed at constructing stores for primary societies, the purchase of vehicles, tool manufacture, etc, for the districts of Gulu, Lira, Apac, and Kitgum. The project was funded by SIDA.[45]

The question is: did this assist the co-operatives to become more internally democratic and to hold the state accountable? It must be noted from the onset that mere reconstruction of physical infrastructure cannot reintroduce accountability and participation within the co-operative movement. This is especially so in the context where trade liberalisation seems for the time being to be liberating the peasants from the 'big men and women' of local areas. These big people for a long time have used the cooperatives for their private accumulation and political advancement. They have in the past been responsible for late payments for peasant agricultural products or cheating. In a liberalised environment, peasants at least get their pay promptly. As long as the competition in trade does not deteriorate into the kind of monopoly witnessed

---

Centre for Basic Research and JEP, 1994.
43 For example, a government official "...called for more openness and democratisation of Co-operative Unions to solve the movement's perpetual problems of mismanagement and finance". See Dawin Dawa, 'Co-operatives Told to be Democratic', *New Vision*, 15 July 1992
44 'Cooperatives losing Coffee Business to Private Processors', Weekly Topic, 28 June 1989
45 Jossy R. Bibangambah, 'The co-operative Movement in Uganda's Transition to a free market Economy', *Yearbook of Co-operative Enterprise*, 1993.

in the 1920s up to the 1950s, co-operatives may not have real issues around which they can organise themselves better and also influence policy.

Whether or not foreign political aid to co-operatives in recent years has strengthened co-operatives requires more empirical research than was possible for the purposes of the present study. However, on the basis of the available evidence, one can conclude that foreign aid is mainly focused on poverty alleviation through the co-operatives rather than questioning the entire logic of exploitation and reproduction of poverty.

Foreign funds have a tendency to create conflicts within co-operative organisations and diminishing accountability of the leadership to the membership. It should be noted, however, that the gross amount of foreign funds to co-operatives is so dismal that it leaves out many cooperatives. As Oloka Onyango has observed, co-operatives together with trade unions are not popular with donors. Whether this is bad or good must be the subject of more detailed empirical research. In overall terms, it would seem from the evidence available to us, that participation of co-operatives in civil society has been dismal in recent years.

Trade unions

Trade unions are legally organised under the umbrella of the National Organisation of Trade Unions (NOTU). The affiliates, 17 in number, include the following: Uganda Railway Workers Union; Postal and Telecommunication Workers Union; Amalgamated, Transport and General Workers Union; National Union of Education Workers; Uganda Electricity Board Workers Union; Uganda Public Employees Union; National Union of Plantation and Agricultural Workers; Uganda Medical Workers Union; Uganda Civil Servants Union; National Union of Clerical, Technical Employees Union; Textile and Garment Workers Union; Printers and Journalists Union; Building and Construction Workers Union; Mines Union; Uganda Hotel Workers Union; Cooperative Movement Workers Union; and Beverages and Tobacco Workers Union. Uganda Medical Workers Union and Uganda Civil Servants are new unions registered in 1994. Until the 1993 Trade Unions Laws (Miscellaneous Amendment) Statute, the registration of unions was confined to the private sector. Governmental employees were prohibited from joining trade unions. We shall try to provide the reason why the state was willing to allow groups that were previously prohibited from joining unions to do so.

Like co-operatives, trade unions have had periods when they participated in civil society and others when they did not. Trade unions have been dependent on external political aid right from independence. This political aid was clearly associated with Cold War politics. Foreign funds have been at the heart of leadership wrangles, lack of accountability and democracy within trade unions. The changing economic and political environment, leading to weakened trade unions has exacerbated these problems. This is particularly so in the era of post-Cold War politics and structural adjustment policies. To appreciate the changing character of the trade union movement we need to analyse them within a historical context.

The development of trade unions in Uganda can rightly be traced to the Second World War years. Before that period, the working class was composed of seasonal migrants who would work for a short period and return to their home areas. Because of this, workers' resistance to exploitation took an individual rather than a collective form. Towards the beginning of the Second World War conditions for the formation of a relatively stable and skilled working class emerged. After the war, Britain encouraged a modicum of industrialisation as a way of solving its 'dollar" crisis.[46] This industrialisation led to the crystallisation of some form of a stable working class. Out of these developments emerged trade unions and hence strikes from 1938.[47]

The response of the colonial state to the workers' militancy in the post-World War II years was to put in place a plethora of rules and regulations essentially aimed at ensuring that trade unions would not become political but would remain economistic. One of the responses was the enacting of the 1952 Trade Unions Ordinance. This ordinance required that each trade union be compulsorily registered. Secondly, each trade union had to submit every change of rules in the constitution to the Registrar of Societies for approval. Thirdly, leaders of the unions had to have worked with a particular industry for a period of not less than three years. Fourthly, the Registrar of Trade Unions was empowered to oversee the union finances to ensure that these funds were not used for political activities.[48] Finally, the formation of general unions was disallowed.

Because the colonial state forbade the registration of general unions as a mechanism of fragmenting the working class, and because the trade union leadership was imbibed with doses of 'responsible unionism' by British trade union advisors, Ugandan trade unions were reduced to economistic organisations. In fact, they played little role in influencing the course of political events that led Uganda to independence.[49] Although unionisation increased in the post-colonial period with membership rising from 783 in 1952 to 178,868 members in 1970, trade unions nonetheless lost their autonomy and ability to champion an agenda that would protect their rights to strike and their freedom of speech.[50] There were a number of factors responsible for these developments. Firstly, the post-colonial government accused the working class of sabotaging UHURU by going on strike. Secondly, in its desire to attract foreign investors, the state went out of its way to minimise workers' strikes. The Minister of Labour argued as follows,

> Strikes and industrial unrest will earn a bad reputation for this country and... the consequences will be to deter investors from bringing industries here and will discourage these countries that might be willing to lend us money for development schemes from giving us assistance.[51]

---

46 See Mahmood Mamdani, *Politics and Class Formation in Uganda*, New York: Monthly Review Press 1976. p. 247-260
47 For an elaborate analysis, see John-Jean Baryaharwego, 'Law, State and Working Class Organisation in Uganda: 1962-1987, PhD Thesis, University of Warwick, 1990.
48 See Mahmood Mamdani, 'Pluralism and the Right of Association' op. cit., pp. 50-531.
49 The kind of education trade union leaders were exposed to "advanced a technocratic and economistic definition of trade unionism" See John-Jean B. Barya, 'Workers and the Law in Uganda.' Kampala CBR Publications, Working Paper No. 7. 1991
50 For the growth of unionism see Barya, op.cit., p. 104.
51 Uganda Government, The Trade Disputes (Arbitration and Settlement) Bill, Second Reading,

Facing pressure from the state, and ideologically divided into east and west camps, the trade union movement was weakened further. Even towards the end of the sixties, the formation of the Uganda Labour Congress (ULC), a trade union that was supposed to have united the various fragments of the trade union movement, did not alter the fact that it was operated as essentially an extension of the state. This was so much so that the UPC government could have the courage not only to expel foreign workers in 1968, but also to declare strikes illegal during the 1970 Nakivubo Pronouncements.

The increased control over the workers movement in the first decade of independence can be seen from the trends in workers strikes, with a peak of 161 strikes in 1962.[52] Immediately after independence the workers carried out many strikes. But from 1965 onwards, the numbers begin to dwindle because of the state's increased control over the trade union movement.[53] The period also coincides with the process of heightened state repression in the country.

The life and activities of trade unions in Uganda in the post-coup years has been interpreted in different ways. J.J. Barya believes that during the early years of Amin's rule trade unions actually regained their autonomy. According to Barya, this was because of three factors. One, the appointment of a minister who favoured trade unions autonomy. Two, the desperate attempt by the Amin regime to gain some legitimacy. And, three, the strikes of the 1971-1973 period.[54] This situation led to the amendments of a number of laws governing the unions. Decree no. 29 of 1973 restored the autonomy of trade unions in law. On the other hand, Mamdani contends that although the 1973 Decree appears to have restored the autonomy of trade unions, this did not change the general direction of state-trade union relationship, namely, administrative regulation and control.[55] The only difference, however, is that during the Amin period, a trade unions umbrella organisation, the National Organisation of Trade Unions (NOTU) was formed.

The ability of the trade unions to influence policy in their favour was further diminished by the 1972 Economic War that essentially led to the collapse of the industrial sector. As Asowa-Okwe noted,

>...as a result of the so-called economic war (1972-1973) during which Asians were expelled and the subsequent diplomatic and economic embargo from the west, Uganda's industrial base almost totally collapsed. This contributed both to weakening of trade unions (especially through a loss of membership) and the repressive industrial

---

Hansard, 9 July 1964, National Assembly Debates.
52 These figures are quoted in Barya, op.cit. p 104.
53 The UPC government would sometimes justify the curb on trade union activity as being necessary for development.
54 J. Barya, op.cit., p 197.
55 See Mahmood Mamdani. 'Pluralism and the Right of Association', in Mahmood Mamdani and Joe Oloka-Onyango (eds), op.cit., p. 532. J.J. Barya also qualified this in his subsequent contribution. "Although the 1973 Decree restored the autonomy of unions to the pre-1970 Act situation, the autonomy of unions after 1973 must be seen in relative terms. They were autonomous in terms of their operations but subject to specific controls and supervision by the state". See J. J. B. Barya, 'Workers and the Law in Uganda', op. cit. p.21.

relations regime practised by the employers (both soldiers and civilians) who took over these properties and expropriated from the departed Asians. More often than not the employers resorted to police and military force to resolve industrial conflicts or simply to suppress any workers' dissent.[56]

In the 1980s, the political situation remained hostile to workers. During the 1980 election, characterised by vote rigging and electoral fraud, workers did not support the UPC party that was later to ascend to power. For this reason, the UPC government viewed workers as belonging to the opposition. The UPC government adopted an anti-union and anti-workers' behaviour. Asowa-Okwe notes:

> It is in this context that we locate the government's violation of workers' freedom of association. This violation consisted of partisan political intervention, illegal intervention or an opportunistic use of the law and open repression.[57]

The most blatant violation of workers' rights was when the workers of the Lira Spinning Mill went on strike. This major strike in 1984,

> left a worker and a school girl in Lira Town College dead, killed by the UNLA [Uganda National Liberation Army] after the Industrial Minister ordered the army to intervene in an industrial strike.[58]

Besides a military solution to workers strikes, the UPC government greatly interfered in the internal affairs of the unions. The UPC government was concerned that trade unions could easily be used as front organisations for the forces opposed to its rule. It, therefore, tried as much as possible to influence activities of the trade unions to ensure that the leadership of the unions was sympathetic to government. In cases where the leadership was already pro-UPC, the UPC blocked fresh elections as required by the constitutions of the respective trade unions. For example, no delegates conference was held during Obote II because of the fear that individuals opposed to the UPC would be elected. At the same time, the crisis in the trade unions was intensified because of their dependence on external funds. It has been observed that leadership struggles were, in many instances, also encouraged and funded by foreign trade unions intent on furthering their own interests in Uganda's unions.[59] In the case of the Uganda Textile and General Workers' Union, the leadership was divided into two factions. One faction was sponsored by a foreign trade union thus making this faction more responsive to its foreign funders than to the union membership.[60]

Besides the political environment, the IMF/WB sponsored structural adjustment programmes, further undermined trade union viability. Not only were many industries

---

[56] Asowa-Okwe, An Evaluation of Trade Unions and Social Conditions of Industrial Workers in Uganda CBR Consultancy Report No 3, Kampala: Centre for Basic Research, 1999, p. 8.
[57] Ibid., p. 266
[58] Behind the Failure of Uganda's Textile Industry', *Forward* 9/2. (December 1987). See also Luke Akiki, 'Industrial Unrest in Uganda', Forward 6/2 (1984); Edward Rubanga, 'Workers' Control: The Struggle to Take over Mulco Textile Factory in Uganda', Kampala: CBR Publications, Working Paper No.19. 1992.
[59] J.J. B. Barya, 'Workers and the Law in Uganda'. op.cit.
[60] Ibid.

not operating - implying the existence of an industrial reserve army desperate to work for very low wages - but also the inflation spiral that accompanied government's over-expenditure constantly eroded the real value of wages. The effect was that during Obote II trade unions were extremely weak, a situation that bred a leadership that was not accountable to its membership. It is for this reason that workers' strikes of the period were organised outside the trade unions; they were wildcat strikes, an indicator that the workers did not trust the leadership to champion their interests.

During the NRA/NRM regime, i.e. from 1986 to the present, the workers' right to organise has generally been upheld to the extent that at one time workers could take over a factory and manage it for four months without the government using its coercive arms. As Rubanga noted in respect of the workers' take-over of MULCO Industry:

> Like the rest of the people workers at MULCO took advantage of democracy and freedom the NRA (National Resistance Army - NB) brought to Uganda in 1986. It cannot be imagined that under Amin or Obote II workers could be allowed/tolerated by the state to take over a factory whether state-owned or joint venture without state intervention.[61]

The irony, however, is that while the working class movement is enjoying more relative freedoms, it is in the same breath facing a crisis of survival. A number of factors account for this development.

First, the numbers organised in trade unions is declining because of the effect of down-sizing/retrenchment and the decline of certain traditional industries. For example, at the time of research the Mines Trade Union did not have the requisite numbers to continue to be registered. The textile industry used to have a labour force of 10,000. Today there are only 400, a number that is less than the statutory 1,000 members to remain registered with government. The Uganda Railway Workers Union (URWU) used to boast of a membership of 8,000. At the time of research, it had only 1,200 registered members. The Uganda Clerical and Technical Employees Union (UCTEU) lost its members in the restructuring and privatisation exercise at the behest of the IMF and World Bank. With the dissolution of the Coffee Marketing Board, a government parastatal that used to be in-charge of marketing Uganda coffee abroad, 3,000 workers were laid off. The union lost more workers in the banking sector because of restructuring mainly in the former government-owned Uganda Commercial Bank (UCB). UCB used to have one half of the members of the UCTEU.[62] The privatisation of many industries has also led to many workers losing jobs as the new owners get new employees who are not unionised.

Second, trade unions have been weakened by the IMF/World Bank-sponsored Structural Adjustment Programmes (SAPs), particularly their effect on the nature of industrialisation and market for those industries. In general, SAPs have undermined

---

61 Edward Rubanga. 'Workers Control: The Struggle to Take over Mulco Textile Factory in Uganda' Kampala: CBR Publications Working Paper No.19. 1992. p 30

62 The only expanding unions are those based in the plantation sector, especially the sugar industry. I am grateful to Edward Rubanga for much of the information on the current trends in the trade union movement.

the import-substitution type of industries established after World War II. SAPs were designed to undermine non-competitive industries and also to punish workers who were presumed to be enjoying high wage rates due to political action (strikes) rather than rates determined by the forces of supply and demand. The idea is that when there are more workers than the jobs available, employers can pay lower wages and boost their profits. However, employers cannot enjoy more profits because the market for Ugandan industries is narrow because of competition from cheap goods from the international market. The best example here is the textile industry. Nytil Picfare sells a pair of bed sheets for a single bed at shs. 40,000. The workers are paid on average shs. 30,000 per person (family) per month. The wages of the workers are lower than the pair of bed sheets they produce. Yet there are imported bed-sheets costing between shs. 3,000 and shs. 7,000. In other words, Nytil Picfare does not have either the local or the international markets for its products. It is no wonder that in the recent discussions on wages, the unions suggested shs. 65,000 per worker and the employers retorted that they would never make profit at that level.

> Employers were overwhelmingly concerned that a basic wage of U. shs. 65,000 would compel them to reduce the labour force, to afford the wages. Many others feared they would close, thus exacerbating the problem of unemployment.[63]

The employers argued that what was reasonable is Shs 25,000 (or US $ 25) per month. The point here is that when local industries are facing a shrinking market, the response is to further cheapen the price of labour or to lay off workers. The overall effect is that the unions are weakened. For example, the Uganda Railways laid off 3,000 workers and the unions did not raise a finger. Trade unions even failed to force employers to give workers terminal benefits. Retrenched workers have resorted to individual solutions - filing court cases against their former employers.

Third, trade unions have a problem of funds. Many trade unions used to get money from foreign trade unions. Donors were willing to provide those funds because of the Cold War. The character of a trade union was defined by the source of funds. For trade unions funded from the East, emphasis was on raising the consciousness of the general membership to resist exploitation. For the unions funded from the West, emphasis was on training the leadership in the skills to steer the membership from political (resistance) to 'responsible' unionism - technical and economistic unionism.

With the collapse of the Soviet Union and Eastern European governments, signalling the end of the Cold War, the supply of funds to Ugandan unions has dwindled. The East can no longer send funds; the Western unions have cut back on the funds they used to send partly because the Cold War ended, and partly because of the crisis of accountability within Ugandan unions. The little money they send is focused on taking the union leadership for training courses or seminars abroad. Two things have happened as a consequence. First, many trade unions - already facing dwindling numbers and hence reduced membership dues - do not have money to hold delegates conferences

---

63 Federation of Uganda Employers, 'Affordable and Sustainable Minimum Wage in Uganda From Employers' Perspective', Kampala, Federation of Uganda Employers, December. 1997.

where accountability is exercised by the members and where union members can crystallize strategies for influencing policy. The Uganda Electricity Board Union has only recently held its first delegates conference since 1980.[64] The Uganda Railway Workers Union is supposed to hold its delegate conference every five years but has been unable to do so since its last conference in 1991. The Uganda Textile Workers Union cannot hold its delegates conference because it does not even have the requisite (legal) number of members, besides not having the funds to organise a delegates' conference.

It is not surprising that the main theme of a workshop organised by National Organisation of Trade Unions of Uganda (NOTU), the Friedrich Ebert Foundation (FES) and International Confederation of Free Trade Unions held on 16-18 August 1999 at Mandela Sports Hotel, was the dwindling numbers of the trade unions' numerical strength. It was noted that trade unions membership was declining and that this translated into financial and legal difficulties - especially with regard to the registration requirement.

In the NOTU/FES workshop, it was proposed that those unions that do not have the requisite numbers should amalgamate. The assumption here is that this would increase the trade unions' political and economic clout. However, it would seem that the state would not welcome such a move as it would strengthen the workers. It will be recalled, that the colonial government legislated against general unions precisely to fragment the working class. It is in this context that we can place NRM's acceptance that medical workers and civil servants can form unions but not a general organisation. Besides the state, there were other obstacles to the amalgamation proposal. The leadership of the existing unions had vested interests not to amalgamate. Is it surprising that out of 17 General Secretaries only 4 turned up for the NOTU/FES workshop and yet this workshop was basically designed for unions General Secretaries?

It should be noted, however, that the current misfortunes of the union may be temporary, themselves to be reversed given the fact that trade unions are organised around concrete material interests with a popular membership. The deterioration of living conditions in the present context will become a basis for the reform of trade unions.

The media

Right from the outset it should be noted that the media is not a homogenous entity. It represents different social categories. In this sense, we can identify media for civil society and media for political parties. We can also identify the sensational media that does not advance democracy in any meaningful way. In this section, we consider two aspects of the media. First, is the kind of media in existence in Uganda, the extent we should consider it to be part and parcel of civil society. Second, we consider organisations of journalists and the extent to which they are contributing to a discussion of crucial issues of democracy.

---

64 I am grateful to Edward Rubanga for the information.

The media that champions issues of democracy presumes an environment in which civil society can freely organise and also express their views, in this case democracy. In the particular case of Uganda, there is the state control over the media while, at the same time, there is the general socio-economic conditions that promote or undermine the media.

For simplicity, we shall consider the media to be having two phases. The first phase is the post-independence era before the NRM assumed power. The second is the era of liberalisation of the media. In the first phase, we see clearly that the state controlled the media apart from a few independent newspapers such as the Luganda daily, Munno. Until the early 1990s, the state owned the radio, the TV and newspapers. Thus, throughout the post-independence period the media was circumscribed in the kind of issues it could tackle in order to extend democracy simply because journalists could not "bite the arm (government) that fed them". Private publishers were tightly monitored. In the late 1960s, an independently run magazine called Transition was banned because it dared criticise the UPC government on the manner it had handled constitutional issues. The Editor, Rajat Neogy, and a correspondent, Abu Mayanja, were imprisoned. In subsequent years, journalists have had a rough time being imprisoned and have even been killed.

Journalists formed the Uganda Journalist Association (UJA) in 1971 as a response to the threat they saw coming with the Amin regime. However, UJA was not effective because the leadership was at the same time drawn from journalists working for the government-owned paper, radio and TV. Journalists in the private media found it difficult to be members of an organisation run by those in government media which according to Zie Gariyo, "remained merely the official propaganda machine of the state".[65] UJA was useless and, in fact, several journalists such as James Bwogi were murdered.

During the NRM period, the media has had more space and many privately owned newspapers have mushroomed.[66] These papers have been at the forefront in exposing the violation of human rights and corruption. However, there are areas where the NRM government has not been very tolerant. These areas include the performance of the military in northern Uganda and the NRM's foreign policy in the region. On these issues, the NRM has imprisoned or committed to court many journalists. In line with its commitment to the rule of law, the NRM passed a new statute: The Press and Journalists Statute (6/1995). The aim of the statute is "to ensure the freedom of the

---

65 Zie Gariyo, 'The Media, Constitutionalism and Democracy in Uganda', Kampala: CBR Working Paper No. 32. 1993 p.43. See also Zie Gariyo. 'The Press and Democratic Struggles in Uganda 1900-1962', Kampala CBR Working Paper No. 24, 1992.

66 This is a contentious statement. To B.K. Twinomugisha-Shokoro, "The NRM government has tactfully allowed the registration and publication of newspapers, magazines and setting up of private radio and TV stations to effect this impression. In my view, however, the existence of so many newspapers circulating at a given time is not necessarily an indication that the media enjoys freedom. On the contrary, the NRM regime has put in place tools to curtail such freedom." See B.K. Twinomugisha-Shokoro', 'How Free is the Media in Uganda?' *East African Journal of Peace and Human Rights*, Vol. 4 No. 2, 1998. p.176.

press" and to establish a Media Council and the National Institute of Journalists of Uganda (NIJU). The Media Council is a regulatory body that deals with the conduct, standards and discipline of journalists. It is also supposed to arbitrate between the public and media and the state. The Media Council exercises disciplinary control and acts as a censorship body. The NIJU is supposed among other things to train journalists.

The Press and Journalists Statute raises serious issues of control. First, it has made it difficult for anyone wishing to practise journalism to join the profession. The requirement that someone must have a university degree is a serious obstacle. Even worse is the requirement that a journalist cannot practise the profession without having a valid practising certificate and his or her name recorded in the Register kept by the Media Council. Registration is usually a mechanism for excluding undesirable journalists. This gives the government room to deal with those journalists who step out of line on the basis of the laws of defamation, sedition, etc. The journalists' associations could as well handle some of the functions that have been given to the Media Council. These include maintaining professional standards and good relations with international journalists. But the government saw it fit to transfer these to a state-controlled body. The question is: what was the role of the journalists' bodies in the enactment of the 1995 Press and Journalists Statute?

The ability of the journalists to raise the awareness of the public on issues of democracy or human rights is circumscribed by the fact that most papers are published in English and also have limited circulation. This means that the bulk of Ugandan society does not have the chance to read the papers either because they are illiterate or they cannot afford to buy the newspapers.

The liberalisation of the print media has come with its costs. Because of competition, the cost of producing papers has risen for three reasons. First, papers have introduced colour thus increasing the volume of ink used. Secondly, they have expanded the range of topics they deal with. While an average paper used to be 16 pages, now it has to be at least 24 pages or more. Finally, papers never used to send journalists to cover functions outside the country. Because of the competition, more and more newspaper publishers have to send journalists to cover external events such as football matches. All this means the cost of producing newspapers has increased when the prices at which they sell are stagnant because of the general poverty of the people. This makes publishers worried about their survival. The net effect has been to turn to issues that appeal to readers but side-track serious issues of democracy.

A similar story can be found in the electronic media. The NRM liberalised the radio and TV services. Today there are more than 10 privately-owned FM radio stations and more than 4 privately-owned TV stations. Much of what they broadcast is pure entertainment. Apart from the Central Broadcasting Service (CBS) FM radio which tends to deal with political issues surrounding the Buganda monarchy, other radio stations are mainly commercial and the owners would not like to 'rock the boat'.

Regarding journalists' organisations and their role in civil society, it is true that they were involved in protesting some of the draconian aspects of the Press Bill.

However, journalists could not push far enough because they are politically divided along cleavages within Uganda society. Moreover, many are comfortable with the peace the NRM ushered in and, therefore do not want to antagonise the Movement. On the other hand, the NRM has used intimidation tactics that has pushed newspapers to practise self-censorship.[67] Thus apart from a few, many newspapers never discuss issues of civil and political rights, not to mention socio-economic rights.

Cleavages within the journalists' community have prevented the establishment of viable organisations to advance their interests or broader societal concerns. Indeed, it is precisely those cleavages that led to the collapse of the Uganda Journalists Association (UJA). At the same time, serious issues such as the undemocratic character of structural adjustment programmes are rarely addressed.

Conclusions

This paper is a product of a preliminary investigation into the character of civil society in Uganda and how it operates in the current epoch of foreign political aid and structural adjustment programmes. From the evidence in our possession, it is clear that the economic and political liberalisation and changes brought by the NRM have created space for the expansion of organisations with potential to operate in civil society. Taking advantage of these changes, donors have poured into Uganda resources meant to strengthen civil society. Unfortunately, donors have narrowly defined civil society as being NGOs, and the bulk of the aid go to NGOs.[68] Moreover, the dependence of NGOs on foreign resources has served to weaken them rather than strengthen them so that they can create more space for democratisation or even buttress democratic values. Many of them do not even practise democracy in their operations. Although they present themselves as being champions of the poor, in reality they serve to sweeten the bitter pill associated with the development of capitalism. Many of the NGOs in Uganda are simply charity/development service oriented, focusing on the apolitical poverty alleviation programmes. Their programmes alleviate but do not eradicate the pain of poverty. They rarely seek to influence policy and change it in ways that expand the space for democratic activity. NGOs cannot challenge the social and political power that reproduces poverty or oppression. This is because, they are not membership-based organisations, and they are philanthropic. NGOs in Uganda are still 'young', have a narrow social base and their activities are too narrowly spread to have any impact in terms of deepening the democratisation process.

Donors have not supported the old face of civil society such as co-operative societies and trade unions to a meaningful extent. This is not surprising because if they did, this would run counter to the neo-liberal agenda. Theoretically, the donors' denial of

---

67 For cases where journalists have been arrested or harassed see 'Human Rights Watch. Hostile Democracy: The Movement System and Political Repression in Uganda'. New York. *Human Rights Watch*, August 1999.

68 For an elaborate treatment of NGOs, see Susan Dicklitch. *The Elusive Promise of NGOs in Africa: Lessons from Uganda*, New York, St. Martin's Press inc., 1998.

support to such organisations may in itself serve as a catalyst for them to push the state to create some space for democracy. The problem is that the entire environment of structural adjustment undermines their ability to push for a democratic agenda. These drawbacks undermine the ability of the old face of civil society to play the kind of roles they played in the 1940s and 1950s creating space for democratisation in Uganda.

Finally, there are a number of issues that need theorising. The more particular one is what the role of civil society would be once dictatorship or democracy has been established. The other is theorising the state vis-à-vis not only civil society and the state but also the state and the rest of society. In real life we know that the state always intervenes in favour of certain groups to the exclusion of others. This much is very clear in the context of Uganda where the state has a warm relationship with the Uganda Manufacturers Association and is relatively hostile to the working class. This Ugandan State is a capitalist state mediating conflict in such a way that capitalist development is realised at a less political cost. The question is: what kind of civil society would this be that advances the rights of the downtrodden while at the same time allowing the development of capitalism?

4

"Find the Groups and you have Found the Poor?": Exploring the Dynamics of Community-based Organisations in Arua and Kabale[1]

Community Development Resource Network (CDRN), with Community Empowerment for Rural Development (CEFORD); Kabale District Farmers Association (KADIFA), CARE-Uganda

Abstract

This article contributes to the literature about the widely held belief that Uganda's poor people's needs and interests are directly or indirectly represented through community-based organisations. As more initiatives, both government and NGO-led, attempt to use this channel to reach the poor, the validity of this assumption is examined.

The research indicated that income generation was the most common function of the groups encountered. Many small economic groups were founded after an external intervention of one kind or another; others - self-help groups - were initiated by people themselves. Forming a group to take advantage of external benefits has become part of ordinary people's lives. Such groups may be said to exist in name only, being 'revived' when the possibility of an external benefit appears to be present. The research found that self-help groups usually include a high proportion of the poorer members of the community, compared to externally stimulated groups, in part because self-help groups tend to be beneficial to the poorer and because entry is usually not governed by complex and costly rules; the group functions as a 'loose' organisation bound by trust amongst its members. Externally-stimulated small economic groups on the other hand are usually dominated by the better-off members of the community. While they do include poorer members,

---

[1] This is a shortened version of a CDRN/CARE 2003 publication. The authors extend special thanks to the Participation Group of the Institute of Development Studies (IDS) at the University of Sussex, United Kingdom and Transform Africa for the financial and technical backstopping they provided to the research team. The technical support from John De Coninck, Tom Blomley, Uwe Korus, Simon Amajuru and Paddy Bahigwa, Rosie McGee and Karen Brock of IDS is gratefully acknowledged. Thanks are also extended to the district and sub-county authorities in Arua and Kabale.

such individuals are usually in the minority, excluded by high membership fees, social stigma and low self-esteem. There was a general lack of poorer people's participation in National Agricultural Advisory Services (NAADS) activities, because the groups that they belong to fail to comply with the set standards of legitimacy (registration and a focus on a commercial agricultural enterprise).

The authors conclude that the assumption 'find the groups and you have found the poor' is only partially correct. It may be more accurately rendered, as 'In some kinds of groups, you will find some kinds of poor people.'

Introduction

This research report is borne out of CDRN and CARE's endeavour to strengthen their support to civil society organisations in Uganda. "Find the groups and you have found the poor?", takes as its starting-point the widely-held belief that the needs and interests of poorer people are directly or indirectly represented through community-based organisations (CBOs), and that working with CBOs is therefore a route to poverty reduction. As more and more initiatives, both government- and NGO-led, attempt to use this channel to reach the poor, our research examined the validity of this dominant assumption.

The study was designed as applied research, using an iterative approach and involving local partner organisations, with the specific intention that the findings would inform the learning and practice of the implementing partners: CARE, CDRN, CEFORD, KADIFA, the United Batwa Development Organisation of Uganda and the Koboko United Women Association. In addition, the questions addressed by the research have a far broader relevance to development debates in Uganda.

"Find the groups and you have found the poor?" is an assumption which underpins the activities of a range of development actors, including national and international NGOs, in a variety of development processes. For many of NGOs, the provision of various kinds of support to community groups is undertaken on the premise that such groups include those who are most vulnerable, and are least likely to benefit from development efforts. There is also an understanding that if the capacity of such groups is strengthened, their members may be empowered to claim their social, economic and human rights. In addition, government efforts to deliver services through decentralised mechanisms are also increasingly focusing on CSOs, including those which are active at the community level. Perhaps the best contemporary example of this is the Government of Uganda's Plan for the Modernisation of Agriculture (PMA), which has the stated aim of reducing poverty through the commercialisation of agricultural production. Under the PMA, the privatisation of agricultural extension services is being implemented via the National Agricultural Advisory Services (NAADS).[2] An

---

2 NAADS is a Government of Uganda programme designed to develop a demand-driven, client oriented and farmer-led agricultural service delivery system particularly targeting the poor and the

inherent part of the NAADS process is the formation and registration of farmer's groups, which are supposed to channel the needs of farmers to a sub-county level umbrella organisation, the Farmers Forum, which in turn prioritises farmers' needs and oversees the contracting and provision of agricultural extension services (Master document of the NAADS Task Force and Joint Donor Groups, 2000).

Programmes like the PMA, and the activities of local and international NGOs, both use groups as an essential linkage in the distribution of resources for development to communities and poor people. At the community level, there is a rich array of forms of organised co-operation, through which people strive to achieve shared goals (Brock, McGee, Okech and Ssuuna, 2002; CDRN CBO research). These groups may have a sense of formality for those belonging to them, even if outsiders see them as informal; they may be legally registered, or they may exist outside the realms of the legal system. Anecdotal evidence tells us that, as Government retreats from some of its earlier areas of intervention and places a greater emphasis on the role of CSOs in service delivery, the number and density of both informal and formal groups at the local level is growing.

This research examined the dynamics of the range of groups that exist at the community level in Arua and Kabale districts, in the light of the assumption that collaboration with such groups by government and NGOs will result in enhanced access of services to poor people, and thus to poverty reduction. The basic question we used to challenge this assumption was: "What are the strengths and weaknesses of groups in representing the interests of the poorer members of a community?" For the purposes of this research we adopted a series of definitions of commonly used terms.

After setting the background to the four communities in which the research took place, this article outlines an overview of reasons for group formation, and a presentation of the perspectives of a range of development actors – government, NGO and private sector – about working with groups. *Section Two* outlines what kinds of groups exist in a given community; who are the poor and do groups represent their interests; the nature of the relationship between groups and external groups or institutions; and, if the poorer members of a community are not in groups, why not, and where are they? *Section Three* discusses our conclusions and their implications.

An overview of research sites, groups and external perspectives on group formation

The research was carried out in Arua and Kabale Districts. Two villages were selected in each of these districts, according to a range of criteria including livelihoods, isolation, density of groups, presence of marginalised groups, and language. This small number of sites allowed researchers to spend sufficient time in a community to ensure that findings are not superficial, and to examine in detail the diverse and sometimes conflicting

---

women. NAADS was born as a result of the failure of traditional extension approaches to bring about greater productivity and expansion of agriculture, despite costly Government interventions. (Master document of the NAADS Task Force and Joint Donor Groups, 2000).

perspectives that prevail when examining potentially controversial questions of social organisation.

Patterns of group density and type vary across these sites, for several reasons. Thus, Kamuhoko, located in a sub-county where there have been many NGO interventions over the years, had the highest density of groups across the four villages, many of them directly related to external interventions. Rondo, close to both a road and a town, also has a multiplicity of groups. Mindrabe groups demonstrate a range of types, which is very similar to that in Rondo, but are fewer in number, reflecting Mindrabe's relative isolation. In Rwamahano, very extreme physical isolation has resulted in a lack of links to external actors. The relatively small number of groups as compared to other sites has resulted into social exclusion. The Batwa, despised and discriminated against by their Bakiga neighbours, have formed self-help groups – for burial, and collective digging - which mirror those of the Bakiga.

The range of groups encountered in these villages was wide both in terms of function, and organisational structure. We discuss in detail the different functions of groups later, and whether function is a variable that shapes the ability of the group to represent poorer members of the community. The types of groups included local or indigenous groups (stretcher and burial groups, clan groups, collective digging groups) and externally stimulated groups by Government (e.g. NAADS groups); by International NGO (e.g. rotational credit groups); by Ugandan NGOs (e.g. Wwmen's income generating groups); by multilateral development organisations (e.g. income generating groups for refugees); and stimulated by Church or Mosque (e.g. youth groups, prayer groups).

One of the key findings of the research is that local or indigenous groups usually include a high proportion of the poorer members of the community amongst their members, and thus are representative of the poor in the proportional sense of representation. Externally stimulated groups, meanwhile, are far more exclusive in terms of their membership. They often exclude the poorer members of the community in a range of ways, which are discussed in more detail in the next section. Despite their being exclusive, interviews with some of the external actors who provide the stimulus to form groups reveal a range of perspectives, which agree on the positive aspects of group formation for development efforts and poverty reduction. Sub-county officials interviewed for the research for instance took the view that central government has instructed them to work through groups, especially in implementing various government programmes under production, community services, and health sectors (eg. PMA, FAL and CHAI programmes). Members of groups are the first beneficiaries of these government programmes. Central to their understanding of why groups contribute to poverty reduction is the government officials' idea that the trickle-down effect of government programmes is increased by working through groups as opposed to individuals, and that groups can be used in bottom-up participatory development planning to ensure that local government reflects the needs of the poor.

It is not just government officials who are working through groups. Civil society also uses groups to deliver their services. In interviews, CSO officers said that the motivation driving them to work with groups were their own institutional objectives of poverty reduction.

Government and NGOs seem to share the perception that working through groups brings benefits, especially providing a conduit to reach the needy/poor beneficiaries of their programmes/services. Both institutions go as far as sensitising people and actually encouraging the formation of more groups to work with. Government and NGOs whose goals are poverty eradication also believe that the groups represent the interests of poor people. These perspectives illustrate that the assumption 'find the groups and you have found the poor' is very much alive in the attitudes and strategies of external development actors, governmental and non-governmental, who are working in the districts and sub-counties where our research sites are located.

The strengths and weaknesses of groups in representing the poor

Contrary to the definition of groups adopted for this research, many respondents understood 'groups' to be formal, organised and structured, either registered at the sub-county or somehow recognised or connected to a more powerful external institution such as a church. In Rondo, for example, an elderly respondent said "groups" only arose after the 1979 war, when relief agencies came distributing food and relief and asking people to form groups to access these. Thus in Vurra, in common with the other sites, many people take 'group' to mean a formal entity constituted for the purposes of receiving and channelling benefits. Most respondents tended to overlook or ignore informal small, unregistered groups such as digging groups, unless prompted. This illustrates the degree to which formality and legitimacy are equated, and perhaps the extent to which local and indigenous groups are under-valued because they do not bring in outside benefits. This is of particular interest in the light of the finding that it is precisely those groups that are undervalued, which includes the highest proportions of poorer community members. This is resonant with another finding, discussed in greater detail below, that poverty and poor people continue to be associated with considerable social stigma.

Social support groups: Engozi, clan-based groups and 'family groups'

Engozi[3] groups were only found in the Kabale sites but, in Rwamahano and Kamuhoko, they were extremely important to local people. The functional root of Engozi is that of carrying the sick on stretchers to receive medical attention; one reason Engozi groups initially formed was the inaccessible terrain in much of the Kabale region. All villages in Kabale have an Engozi group, and the vast majority of households are members, encouraged by their own sense of the dangers of existing outside of this social support mechanism.

All Engozi groups are clustered around the hills where people live. Alongside every village Engozi group, which includes men and women, there is a parallel Engozi comprised of only women, which plays a supportive function to the village group. In

---

3   Engozi is a Rukiga (language spoken in Kabale) word, which refers to a woven basket where a patient is placed as they carry him/her to a health facility.

Rwamahano, all Bakiga villagers aged 18 years and above are members. Youths who are the new entrants are required to pay 6000/= but in the event of late expression of interest, such new entrants are charged 11,000/=. Women pay only 2500/=. The membership is charged annually. The Rwamahano Engozi has dual features: on the one hand, it is a social support system for mutual insurance, while on the other it is an informal group with strict socio-cultural rules, but without a formal constitution or legal registration. In Rwamahano, the Batwa have appreciated the significant role played by the Engozi and this, coupled by the exclusionary nature of the present Engozi, has led them to form their own Engozi groups, parallel with those of the Bakiga. As well as carrying the sick to medical attention, and burying the dead, some Bakiga Engozi operate a medical insurance scheme. Members create a pool of savings, which are lent out at a time of need to cover medical expenses. In such cases, every member contributes to the pool by ensuring regular monthly deposits ranging from shs. 200/= to shs. 1000/=. Male members of the group carry patients to health units and contribute labour in the event of burial in the village. The parallel women's Engozi plays a supplementary support role, such as cooking during the burial ceremony, and digging for the bereaved family.

Engozi groups have strong informal rules and regulations, which are binding to every member. These include payment of heavy fines in the event that a member fails to abide by the group's norms and values. Common offences include absenteeism from group activities and failure to procure Engozi permission before conducting a burial. Fines range from cash payment of 1,000/= to 10,000/=, depending on the gravity of the offence. The Engozi court may demand for a goat to be slaughtered, plus a pot full of local brew to reconcile with the offender. Historically, stubborn absentees were at times subjected to a public flogging as punishment, depending on how many times they had defaulted. The Bakiga community regards those who fail to maintain their membership and fulfil their obligations to Engozi as outcasts. Such people include migrant labourers who can no longer afford to come back home to attend burials, those who are too poor to contribute to the Engozi or those who for some reason prefer to live in a secluded existence, some of whom were reported to be of un-sound mind. Thus, the Bakiga Engozi is presented to outsiders as a group that is inclusionary, and at first appears to be so, with most households being members. However, the exclusion of the Batwa, and the fact that there are membership obligations which some are unable to meet exposes another side of the Engozi – its exclusionary nature.

By contrast, another type of social support group, the Biika or clan group, does not make any pretence at being inclusionary. Members predominantly belong to one family lineage, clan or sub-tribe. Married women are usually assimilated into clan groups of their husbands. They however revert back to their father's clan in case of broken marriage. Unmarried young women belong to clan groups of their fathers. Elderly clan members normally head these clan groups. These groups play a significant role in protecting the rights of clan members, and are in addition a social support mechanism. In the Arua sites, for example, clan groups try to ensure that all clan members have access to land; some also operate rotational saving and credit schemes. They help those who are too old to help themselves, and are under obligation to protect and take care of every member of the clan. In Kamuhoko, clan groups have been relatively successful in helping raise school fees for school children in the clan whose parents are too poor to afford them. The Bakiga clan groups in the Kabale sites also help with burials and funerals among clan members, bearing the primary obligation to support the bereaved family. It is in addition to this core support from the clan that the Engozi also makes a contribution. A family therefore receives support first from the clan-based inner circle, and then from the village-wide Engozi group.

A unique example of a clan group was encountered in Mindrabe village in Arua. Unlike the Bakiga clan groups, of Kabale, the Midia[4] clan Land Committee does not exist to provide social support, but to oversee the distribution of land. The Committee is made up of members of the Midia clan, only one of several clans resident in the village, but is nonetheless responsible for distributing land to all those who request it. Outsiders who wish to utilise land for any sort of project are required to go through this traditional land committee to access land on agreed terms and conditions, and several have successfully done so. Among the beneficiaries include the Koboko Youth Association, which has built a vocational youth education centre on land in Mindrabe village. It was however noted that this traditional committee is not operating in collaboration with government structures and has no links with the district land board and the official land tribunals instituted by government.

Another interesting variation on clan groups was encountered in Kamuhoko: the "family group." Although this category was outside the bracket of the research definition of groups, which requires membership from more than one household, it was so pronounced that it could not be over-looked. Such groups are a curious hybrid of clan-based groups, such as Engozi and Biika; self-help groups (discussed below); and groups which form in the hope of gaining external benefits.

The story of 'family groups' in Kamuhoko begins with the Rubango Association, formed by members of an extended family, and formally registered as a group in 1989. The primary objective of forming a group was to support one another, and to raise school fees. However, this group was also able to benefit from a local government programme in 2001. The success of the Rubango Association in gaining external benefits motivated other family groups to emerge with the hope of accessing government funds. In this case, however, the families were nuclear, rather than extended. One example of such a group, started by Fred Kamugisha, was formally registered in 2001. The group has 11 members who are Kamugisha's sons, daughters and wife; the husband is chairperson, the wife is vice-chairperson, and a son is secretary. Most family groups, like the Kamugishas, seem to have been formed in an attempt to organise the household around a selected agricultural enterprise – potatoes, passion fruit, chicken, mushrooms, or piggery. This reflects a major external stimulus: the expectation that the NAADS programme would

---

4   Midia clan is a big clan, it stretches over more than one sub-county. Midia is also used as a name of a sub-county.

bring agricultural handouts to groups, which are committed to commercial agriculture. Although they were able to register, they were not able to get the benefits by virtue of the fact that the group members are also members of the same household.

When the research team arrived in the village, however, there were high expectations that they might be bringing benefits to the community. Thus, when researchers initially asked about groups in the community, they were told of at least 20 'family groups'. Further probing revealed that most of these 'groups' existed in name only, and had been temporarily resurrected in the hope of obtaining external benefits.

The example of family groups reveals the ingenuity of adapting traditional ways of organising to provide basic security – around family, sub-clan or clan – to contemporary contexts, such as the provision of benefits to formally organised groups. Second, it reveals the lack of sensitisation around the PMA programme in Kamuhoko village; clearly, the desire to register formally to take advantage of the benefits of PMA would not have existed if households had been aware of the criteria, which make a group legitimate to register for PMA. Thirdly, it shows the extent to which forming a group to take advantage of external benefits has become part of ordinary people's lives, with groups, which exist in name only, 'revived' when the possibility of an external benefit appears to be present.

Small economic groups – self-help and external stimulation

Income generation is by far the most common function of the groups encountered in the research. There is a considerable diversity of small economic groups across the four villages. A significant distinction between them is their origin: the majority were founded after an external intervention of one kind or another. The minority, however, were initiated by people themselves. We have called these self-help groups.

Self-help groups in the four villages usually originate from a circle of friends or relatives of the same socio-economic class, who have a common interest. They emerge as a result of a need for co-operation among neighbouring families. Usually, self-help groups are composed of members within the boundary of a village. They do not focus on formalising the status of the group or building relationships with other groups or institutions. Groups of this kind are seldom registered, often not recognised by the community as "groups," and even get "forgotten" by authorities. In this study, self-help groups were found in all four sites, but were most common in Rwamahano where, as with the Engozi groups, Bakiga and Batwa form separate self-help groups.

The most common activity of self-help groups is collective agricultural labour, sometimes for cash payment, and sometimes to pool labour for work on members' own fields. Most such digging groups, however, also have a rotational savings aspect.

One example of a digging group is the Mukanyonko Tukore Group, in Rwamahano village, Kabale, started in 1996. The idea of forming this group was borrowed from a neighbouring village, which had rotational digging groups. The group started with 12 members and four years later they increased to 17 (10 men and 7 women). There is a committee of 6 people (2 women and 4 men) but the group makes decisions during general meetings. The main objective of the group is to sell their labour and get money for mutual benefits, by making fortnightly contributions of 200/=, selling their labour for digging and house construction, smearing and thatching, and carrying out farming activities on hired land and selling the produce jointly. The group also gives loans to its members out of the group fund. The group is run by a set of rules, some of which are written and others not. For example, late coming attracts a fine of 200/= and for absenteeism depending on the reason, the culprit pays between 700/= and 1000/= The group members have realised some benefits in working together. All members have been able to buy household utensils such as mattresses, cups and plates. The members feel that there has been unity created amongst the group members and there is solidarity between them. However, the group members mentioned the challenges they face include the fact that members are only able to make very small contributions. The isolation of the village means that there are few opportunities to increase their capital or diversify their activities.

Despite their informal status and absence of legal documents, self-help groups tend to be beneficial to the poorer sections of the community. Group benefits go directly to individual members of the group. Entry and exit is usually not governed by complex rules; the group functions as a 'loose' organisation bound by trust amongst its members.

Self-help groups were the most numerous type of group encountered during this study. In some locations, especially Kamuhoko, the number of such groups, mostly composed of women members, has increased tremendously in recent times. This reflects a very high rate of out-migration by men, who have left for a range of destinations to try and earn money. The women left behind gain solidarity, experiences and ideas from their membership of groups, as well as often being able to acquire household utensils such as saucepans, plates and mattresses.

While women dominated the membership of self-help groups in Kamuhoko, across the other three villages, self-help groups included both men and women. By contrast, however, externally-stimulated small economic groups are largely composed of women. Externally-stimulated small economic groups are also different from self-help groups because they are frequently channels for external funds, and they are often dealing with larger amounts of resources than the very small amounts which self-help groups rotate or earn. Another crucial difference is that while self-help groups are mostly composed of the poorer members of a community – which may result in social stigma being attached to the group - externally-stimulated groups are usually dominated by the better-off members of the community. While they do include poorer members, such individuals are usually in the minority, and tend to be ordinary group members rather than group leaders.

One example which provides an exception to the general tendencies of externally-stimulated groups is that of the Nazareti Apiary group in Rondo which, unlike most groups of this type, includes a majority of poorer community. The group was founded 1998. The founder member narrated the origins of the group

I had been in Ayelembe women's group that comprise mostly women in upper Rondo village. Therefore I wanted to mobilise our women to share these ideas and also organise our women to support each other ...When I went to Yoro to train women on improved cook stoves, I was given 2 hives with skilled instructions on how to run the apiary.

There are a number of variables which have contributed to this group developing in a way that represents well the poorer community members. First, the nature of the external stimulus that formed the group was that of a single individual whose own membership of a parish-level Women's Group sensitised her to different ways of working, which she wanted to replicate. Secondly, the Women's Group to which she originally belonged was itself successful and sustainable, having been able to gain access to a series of donor funding envelopes to continue its activities; it provided and continues to provide a model for the Nazareti Group. Thirdly, are the considerable formal and informal networks to which the group has access via an 'advisor'. Fourth, and perhaps most important, is the personal approach of the founder member towards creating and maintaining an inclusive environment for poorer members.

The experience of the Nazareti Apiary Group is significantly different from that of other externally-stimulated groups. Perhaps the clearest contrast comes in the case of groups which have been formed or formalised in order to register as beneficiaries from the NAADS programme. Working through groups is inherent to the structure of the NAADS programme; the programme provides its services via sub-county Farmers' Fora (FF), made up of 15 members, each representing groups from one parish. If groups are to benefit from the NAADS, they are required to register at the sub-county, paying a fee of 5000/=. With 80% of the NAADS money coming from donors and 8% from the central government, the district local government and sub-county each contribute 5%. The farmer groups have to provide counterpart funding of 2% of the sub-county NAADS budget.

While the NAADS programme is meant to reduce poverty by transforming the rural poor from subsistence farmers into commercial farmers, the structure of the programme excludes many of its own targets by the decision to work with groups. In the Arua sites, for example, most of the poorer members of communities do not belong to formal groups, and are not engaged in a commercial agricultural enterprise. Some existing groups are unable to meet the registration fee necessary to become a NAADS group. As the Arua District NAADS Coordinator observed, "NAADS works with only the active poor". The very poor farmers are not in groups as evidenced from well-being rankings. Some of the groups who would otherwise be potential beneficiaries are excluded for failure to pay the registration fee. In Rondo village many new groups sprung up in order to try and access the benefits they thought would come from NAADS, but were not successful; this was also the case in Muko sub-county. The Chairperson of Muko Farmers Forum observed that many farmers erroneously thought that groups would be able to access farm inputs or credit from NAADS. In both Rondo village and Muko sub-county, many groups declined as quickly has they had risen when farmers received sensitisation about the benefits which were actually on offer.

In the Arua sites, most of the groups already benefiting from NAADS are fairly well-established and stable, have historically received external support and were already formally registered at the sub-county. Well-being ranking in these communities showed that, with only one exception, groups which had successfully registered with NAADS were primarily composed of better-off members of the community.

In the Kabale sites, meanwhile, the story is very different. The NAADS progamme in Ikumba sub-county has yet to be implemented. In Muko sub-county, where the programme is being implemented, none of the residents of Rwamahano have any interaction with NAADS apart from two women who are in NAADS groups in their village of origin. The extreme isolation of the village contributes to this, as does the opinion of the Muko Farmers Forum chairperson, who believes that "the Batwa need separate interventions."

In the four research sites, the lack of poor people's participation in NAADS is not because they do not belong to groups, but rather because the groups that they belong to fail to comply with the standards of 'legitimacy' set by NAADS. In this case, the legitimacy of groups in the eyes of outsiders – formality, registration and a focus on a commercial agricultural enterprise – are the very things which militate against many poor people taking part in formally-constituted small economic groups because they have divergent interests and lack registration fees as well as information.

Faith-based groups

Members of faith-based groups mainly receive benefits in the form of spiritual well-being, their fundamental function being that of communal worship. Faith-based groups were not common compared to groups with other function, and were encountered only in the two Arua sites. They were most prominent in Rondo, where an active church in the neighbouring village of Ayelembe had stimulated the formation of a number of groups – a prayer group, a revival group and a youth group – which counted Rondo villagers amongst their members. In Mindrabe, a Moslem Youth Association combined worship and Islamic study with plans and hopes of accessing outside resources.

In addition to addressing the physical and psycho-social needs of members, faith-based groups also sometimes carry out income generating activities - but these activities usually tend to benefit the church or mosque, rather than individual members. Other groups – the Mother's Unions of Rondo and Mindrabe, associated with the Church of Uganda – undertake a range of activities which benefit the extremely poor members of their communities. These include visiting the sick and providing food to the destitute. The group also tried to educate villagers about the causes of HIV/AIDS. These activities are charitably motivated, reflecting the religious perspectives of the group members.

Who are the poorer people in the community?

To establish who the poorer community members are and the criteria by which the community members perceive poverty, the study employed well-being ranking analysis. This tool was applied during general community meetings as well as in meetings with selected groups. Adult village members attended the meetings generally mixed with poorer community members and the less poor. The very poorest were not well represented, as is often the case in such exercises (see for example, Narayan *et al* 2001). At the community meetings, men and women worked separately to rank all households in the village.

Contradictory views sometimes emerged. While some residents of all four research sites perceived the whole community to be poor, in Mindrabe, some participants reasoned that any person who had two hands could not be considered poor because (s)he had the potential to transform his or her life by engaging in income generating activities. The majority of residents were placed in the lower half of the well-being categories. Apart from a few exceptions, most women-headed households were ranked in the lower well-being categories. The exception to this were some widows in Kamuhoko, who were perceived to have greater decision-making power over resources – particularly access, ownership and control of land - which increased their well-being status.

The community members developed the criteria of poverty used in the ranking. The principal criteria identified in all four sites were inability to provide food for oneself and family; landlessness (or access to limited land); physical weakness (due to old age, sickness or disability) and lack of social support from offspring and extended family. Poverty was also described in a range of ways, from lack of basic means of survival, to social status and to attitude and laziness.

Such views reflect those found in many other qualitative studies of poverty (Narayan et al 2000, UPPAP) and reveal that being poor remains an experience of social stigma, and that negative stereotypes about poor people continue to abound. There is no clearer example of this negativity emerging from the research than perceptions of the Batwa of Rwamahano. The Batwa are despised by their Bakiga neighbours as being dirty, illiterate and extremely poor; in some cases, they are not even thought of as people. This seems, among other factors such as loss of their patrimony (forest), to be the underlying basis for extreme prejudice and social exclusion against the Batwa. During village meetings, they sat in their own group, separate from that of the Bakiga. The most vocal Mutwa participating in village meetings observed,

> Until recently, the Bakiga used to call us wild animals. We were not allowed to drink on the same cup with Bakiga in drinking places. They used to throw food at us like dogs.

Discussions with the Batwa themselves showed that they clearly perceive themselves as poor. As well as seeing this in terms of having no land, inadequate food, and a lack of good clothing, they also view their exclusion from political processes like local elections as an inherent part of their experience of poverty.

Men and women from the different sites had different perceptions of who the poor are. However, features of poverty also differ between the two districts; casual labouring for food, mentioned in Kamuhoko and Rwamahano, reflects the acute land shortage in Kabale district, and is therefore not mentioned in the Arua sites.

Do groups represent poorer community members?

For the purpose of this study, "representing the interests of the poor" is construed as being representative of the poorer members of the population (in terms of composition and proportional representation); addressing interests of the poor (either by providing for own members; or by redistributing benefits from group to poorer members of community) and advocating for the interests of the poor. The analysis of whether groups represent poorer community members was carried out by looking at key areas of group dynamics: membership requirements, group activities, benefit sharing, gender considerations, leadership opportunities, division of tasks and group sustainability.

In all sites it was established that entry into many groups is gained through the payment of membership fees, and the ability to perform group activities. The membership fees vary, depending on the interests and activities a group is involved in. Across sites, membership fees varied from 200/= to 10,000/=. While all formally constituted groups charge membership fees, it was also found that informal self-help groups sometimes have fees; rotational digging and savings groups charge the lowest membership fees.

A common finding across all sites was that on many occasions, poorer people are effectively excluded from group membership because they cannot meet membership fees; obviously, this is particularly true of formal groups charging higher membership fees. There are, however, also many examples, from both the Arua and Kabale sites, where groups are able to approach membership fees with a degree of flexibility which allows poorer people to become members. Self-help groups in many cases accept aspiring members who do not have money but can contribute labour that is equated to the required membership fees. Some groups have stretched their support to the poor who cannot afford to pay membership fees at one go, by allowing them to pay in instalments.

Admission to certain groups is based on speciality. For instance, in bee-keeping groups, one has got to be a bee-keeper, and in the traditional healers' group one has to be knowledgeable in herbs and treatment. Whether poor or better off, if one had the expertise, they would belong to the specialised groups. Some groups, however, exclude poorer members of the community simply because of the activity in which they engage. People with disabilities, the terminally ill, and the elderly among other poorer members of the community are usually not in position to be members of groups that are engaged in energy-demanding activities. Brewing associations, carpentry groups, sand mining associations and brick-making associations are some of the groups where the elderly and other physically weak persons would not participate.

In Engozi groups, with virtually obligatory membership, all categories of members are obliged to participate in mainstream group activities, regardless of weakness or advanced age. Unlike the case of membership fees, no concessional arrangements are offered to widows, the weak or elderly, despite the fact that their status makes it harder for them than for other members to meet the group's activity requirements. This could be interpreted as an apparently inclusive group, which whilst embracing all households in membership, fails to concede that different group members may need different treatment.

Every group has rules and regulations; some are written down, some are not. Many rules are designed to enforce members' commitment to group activities. Failure to abide by these rules and regulations results into punishments that take the form of payment of fines, suspension or excommunication from the group. Again, the Engozi groups provide an extreme example of what can be an inconsiderate and inflexible system. Here, failure to abide by the rules and regulations may sometimes cost the defaulter eviction from the village, as was the case with a very poor woman in Kamuhoko village who had a miscarriage and buried the fetus without permission:

> They demanded that I leave the village or I sell my piece of land to pay a fine… we declined to sell the land…we have five children to take care of… we were excommunicated from the village Engozi group and we joined another one in the neighbouring village.

Across the groups encountered in the research, when a group compared men and women, the men usually took most of the leadership roles; but the vast majority of members were women. There were two notable exceptions. Money-handling positions, such as the treasury posts, were often given to women because they are considered as being more "trustworthy" than the men. Second, in Midia village, many groups had women leaders, who had themselves started the groups. This is a reflection of the degree to which the gendered approach of external actors has been able to push women forward through affirmative action, and a long period of favourable external funding for women's groups.

Many of the groups interviewed had leadership structures with defined positions such as the chairperson, vice chairperson, secretary and treasurer. Even some informal groups, such as the family groups of Kamuhoko discussed above, mirrored this classic structure of formally constituted groups. Across all sites, however, most of the leaders of formal groups are normally from the relatively better-off well-being categories, whilst individuals from the lower categories mostly participate in groups as ordinary members. Although it was mentioned by various groups that all the group members, including ordinary members, take decisions, we observed during discussions that those in the relatively better-off categories made most of the contributions. When researchers offered space to the "silent" members to speak out their opinions, they often were unable to do so in public. In their own Focus Group Discussions, however, they spoke out; suggesting that their silence may have been due to intimidation and an inferiority complex. This seems to suggest that, despite first impressions of egalitarianism, there are strong hierarchies in place around decision-making in groups, and that these do not favour the poorer members. Although members elect their leaders, it was also found that founding members tend to be re-elected over and over again.

However, as discussed above, the poor have more control over those small economic groups, which they have initiated themselves. Many members of such groups confirmed having benefited from these, particularly by enabling them to buy household items on a rotation basis. While the poor in these groups control leadership and 'own' the groups themselves, the benefits they are controlling are relatively minor in contrast to those groups where leadership is dominated by local elites.

This study also established that poorer people's interests are less represented in groups that have larger formality requirements, with high membership fees. Such requirements at once effectively exclude poorer community members. Further, it is very often this formal legitimacy that allows a group to qualify for external benefits designed to reduce poverty.

Relationship between groups and external institutions

Group formation

As we suggested in the introduction, one of the main defining features of a group is whether or not its formation was due to an external stimulus. This can be development or relief interventions, which create or use groups to channel resources to communities. In the sites of Rondo, Midia and Kamuhoko, external NGOs as well as government programmes, particularly NAADS and the Community Action Programme (CAP),[5] have influenced the formation of groups. CAP was particularly influential in the Arua sites, and worked through groups to provide agricultural extension to increase the incomes of communities; similarly, NAADS provides advisory services to farmers through groups.

As discussed above, many people in the research sites formed groups in response to NAADS. We however note a subtle distinction here about the types of external stimulus that cause group formation. The majority of such groups were however based on incorrect *perceptions* of what it would provide. In this case there is no *direct* relationship between the local and the external group; but an *indirect* relationship, mediated by rumour and misinformation, which causes groups to form. The research found that these groups simply fall away once correct information is provided, but this does not mean that their formation is without effect. The whole process can be extremely demoralising for those who formed the group in the hope of receiving benefits, and it illustrates a profound degree of dependency on external assistance.

External NGOs have also influenced group formation through the implementation of their programmes in a range of ways. For example, InterAid initiated formation of groups, such as the Asunga Nursery Group, in Midia, and had a programme of tree planting in Koboko County, which encouraged and financially supported the formation of groups. In Kamuhoko site, CARE also influenced the formation of groups, such as Kamuhoko/Kigarama Mushroom Growers, for the provision of agricultural advice. There were numerous examples of groups which had formed to take advantage of specific NGO interventions, but which were not sustainable, and collapsed quickly at the end of programmes. Those which had managed to survive had usually gone on to access a new form of external NGO programme funding.

---

5   A closed programme, formerly in West Nile and under the Prime Minister's office.

Group activities

External actors often dictate the activities that a group carries out, directly or indirectly. Such groups implement the activities in the hope of continued support from the external institutions. Asunga Nursery group in Midia for instance planted trees because that was the priority of InterAid that was providing the financial, material and non-material support. InterAid defined this priority after the West Nile region experienced a massive influx of Sudanese refugees in the early 1990s who were temporarily settled in transit camps. The refugees caused deforestation by cutting trees for shelter construction and wood fuel. At the time of resettling the refugees in camps, UNHCR had an obligation to ensure that trees were replanted in these areas. InterAid, working on their behalf, took the responsibility of tree planting. Many groups were formed in the process, but those in our research site failed as soon as InterAid withdrew. This experience suggests that in cases where an external agent dictates group activities according to its own analysis, which is not owned by the group, it will not survive the withdrawal of the external support.

It is therefore quite exceptional for externally-stimulated groups to provide long-term, sustained support to poorer people. Where the external stimulus is for relief – as in the case of refugee groups – or for a particular development activity dictated by the external actor, the resulting group may well include poor people and benefit them for a brief period, but is unlikely to survive the external intervention. This will only be the case, however, if the external actor has a specific goal of reaching the poorer members of the community; and many do not, arguing that it is the 'economically active poor' who provide the only route to poverty reduction in the wider community.

On the rare occasions where an externally-stimulated group – like the Nazareti Apiary Group discussed earlier – manages both to survive beyond the withdrawal of the external intervention, and continue to count poorer people amongst its membership – it is often due to a particular combination of factors. These include the presence of a particularly strong leader; the existence of a relatively dense network of intermediary organisations through which new sources of external funding might be sourced; and a reasonably solid financial foundation built up through initial group activities. There is also a largely unquantifiable and unpredictable factor of adaptability to changing circumstances, and the will of the members to hold the group together.

Such a finding presents a familiar challenge to external actors: how to ensure that their interventions are sustainable. As many studies have shown (see for example James 2003, CDRN/SNV 2003), it is the internal dynamics of a group, which will determine its continued success or failure; this is as true of small community-based organisations as it is of large companies. As James notes:

> some aid project documents appear to believe that we can construct organisations, a folly tantamount to believing that we can construct an ear of corn or a living flower by placing cells on top of each other. (2003:1)

This study suggests that groups which are constructed in this manner almost inevitably collapse.

If the poorer community members are not in groups, why not, and where are they?

Many of the formal, externally-stimulated groups encountered include limited numbers of poor people amongst their members. Self-help groups, meanwhile, are in fact a coping mechanism of poorer community members. A substantial proportion of poorer community members are not in groups at all.

Why are many poorer people not in groups?

Even at village level there exists a strong class barrier between the better off and the poorer community members. The village "middle class" perceives the poor as being "bad hearted", naturally lazy, uncooperative and have no initiative to engage in group activities. The marginalised and excluded, such as the Batwa, those of unsound mind and the destitute, are sometimes feared, thought to be surrounded by mysterious powers and bad omens. This generates fear and resentment from others, preventing any meaningful interaction, including group membership.

Better off community members reasoned that the poor were poorly informed about the usefulness of being in a group, with limited mobility and little exposure to ideas from other areas, and therefore lack the inspiration. There was, however, no evidence of any organised community effort to provide the necessary sensitisation and inspiration to poorer community members. Whereas the poor may indeed be unwashed, or fail to exhibit the expected etiquette, the better off have often responded by using this predicament as an excuse to put up high walls of discrimination and social exclusion against the poor, with no sign of sympathy for them or any attempt to help them out. The perception that the poor do not know about the benefits of being in groups is misguided, as some of those outside groups were very clear about such benefits. One such noted that:

> If I were able, I would be in a group because through groups, members are able to buy plates, saucepans and even pay school fees up to higher levels of education. All this is possible because the group allows pooling of resources, if we are many we can contribute 10,000 shillings to so and so, but if I am alone, I will get 1000 shillings and spend it on soap and that's it.

Many poor people however do have attitudes and make choices that inhibit them from joining groups. Given the daily struggles of survival such as casual labouring for food and money as well as other basic necessities of living, the opportunity cost of spending time in a group is prohibitive. Some poor perceive groups as time wasting. Group benefits are usually long term, while the poor use survival strategies that deliver short-term benefits. The poor are also well aware of what the better off think about them. This erodes their esteem and confidence, which keeps them away from groups and gatherings, leaving them in an information shadow. They hardly get information about groups - a vicious circle! Further, many poor people fear to join groups because they feel those in groups are well-off:

> How can you stay with those who are OK? They will laugh at you and back-bite you. Some rich educated group members are too confident, they show off, and do not listen to poor people. Even if you talk they ignore you!

Active discrimination is also evident in the matter of physical bodily limitations such as disability or weakness. The chairperson of Asunga Nursery in Midia, for example, reported that the group admits people with disability as members. They are assigned appropriate activities such as making polyethylene pots for seedlings, which is manageable by the weak and disabled. This kind of sympathy and inclusion was not widely evident among the rest of the groups encountered.

Many groups are rooted in the clan and extended family; and for some, the main basis for group formation was strong neighbourhood linkages and long-term foundation of mutual trust. Such groups tend to lock out "foreigners" - newcomers to the village and ethnic minorities who do not belong to the dominant tribes and clans in the area.

Apart from exclusion mechanisms, which prevent the poor from joining groups, some group leaders misuse the group assets at the expense of benefits for all the members. Respondents in Rondo and Midrabe called this corruption by group leaders. Poorer people said that they preferred to spend their strength in an activity that can give them tangible benefits instead of "supporting" corrupt group leaders. Empty promises by the "angels of mercy" who do not fulfil their pledges to these groups are also a factor in discouraging the poor from joining groups. This appeared to be relatively common with the formal and externally instigated groups, which promise – or appear to promise – many benefits.

How do the poor cope outside groups?

Groups are usually governed by the principle of mutual sharing of costs and benefits, not charity. The weak, sickly, very old and severely disabled do not fit, but our study revealed that there are other unorganised mechanisms which attempt to provide a safety net for this category of the poor. Clan and family systems, sympathetic neighbourhood, faith-based support networks and other incidental events help the poor to survive beyond their means outside groups. This may include approaching existing groups for support, which does not necessarily involve membership. Poorer community members, for example, have used the land committee in Koboko (discussed above) as a survival mechanism of accessing land.

Some poor people survive on relatives within their clans who give them mainly food. The NAADS coordinator Midia sub-county remarked: "...they have a village culture of sympathy where villagers will somehow assist such people." Between the Lugbara and the Kakwa, the culture of sharing and the extended family system are prominent, although support to the extended family members is limited to the provision of basic necessities such as food. Apart from depending on relatives or clans mates, some very poor people survive on their children. This is common with the elderly. In all sites, children are seen as a source of social security.

Whilst collective digging for cash payment may be seen as a group activity, individual digging – or other agricultural activities such as chasing away vermin - for payment in food is one of the survival mechanisms for the poor, particularly the Batwa. One Mutwa woman remarked that: "…If I don't go to dig for someone in exchange for food, I will die in the house," implying that her only survival mechanism is this casual labouring. The Batwa also work for the forest officers such as selling their forest products. In return, the Batwa are allowed to go to the forest (their ancestral land) to pick bamboo and other products such as honey and firewood. This situation represents an extreme irony of exploitation, in which the Batwa are forced to engage because they have no alternative means of sustaining their livelihood. An extreme strategy of last resort is also begging.

Some very poor people depend on church systems or faith-based groups for their survival. For example, in Rondo and Midrabe, the Mothers Union does help very poor members of the community, usually the sick and the elderly, by providing them with food and other basic necessities of life. Similarly, in Kamuhoko, the Church of Uganda contributed to building a house for a widow of a former church pastor and still provides her with basic support such as paying school fees for some of her children.

Some of the poorer people not in groups engage in excessive drinking to "forget" their problems and this leads instead to more poverty because the limited money is spent on alcohol while reducing their capacity to engage in productive activities.

Conclusions and recommendations

We find that the assumption 'find the groups and you have found the poor' is only partially correct. It may be more accurately rendered as 'In some kinds of groups, you will find some kinds of poor people.'

Many poor people themselves perceive groups as an avenue for reducing their poverty. According to the poor, groups do this in two ways: by providing a means to work together in self-help groups, and through tapping external benefits. This and other evidence suggests that *some* groups are an important avenue for reaching *some* poorer people – especially small, informal self-help groups, and some types of externally-stimulated groups. Small, informal self-help groups belong to poor people. If poorer members of society are to be directly targeted by poverty alleviation programmes, they may be reached by working with these. However, what poor people value about these groups are their lack of exclusionary mechanisms and their sense of ownership.

Direct interventions to work with these groups should therefore be approached with extreme caution, to minimise the risk of destroying their identity or agenda, for instance through the use a practical, bottom-up and genuinely participatory approach, to provide support according to expressed needs, perhaps in small incremental packages over time, which would match their absorption capacity. A second option would be to 'leave them as is', recognising the tendency of most development interventions to impose external agendas on existing structures.

As some types of externally-stimulated groups exclude the poor, while some include them, development actors should be encouraged to take a more critical perspective on their work with groups and their promotion of group formation, to find out whether they are supporting groups, which include or exclude the poor; and thereby strengthen their support to inclusive groups.

Some of the poorest people are not in groups, but could join if mechanisms of exclusion were tackled and changes made. These mechanisms include membership fees, affirmative action for women (which results in the exclusion of men), ethnic or neighbourhood-based discrimination, rigid savings amounts and payment schedules, 'information shadows' and hostile attitudes towards the poor. NGOs could therefore encourage and/or institute flexibility in group membership fees as one of their working guidelines. Government could, especially in the case of NAADS, make provision for flexibility in the payment of membership group registration, and co-funding by groups. Government and development partners could recognise and appreciate that, for information dissemination to have an impact, it should be repetitive and take a multi-media approach. This is resource consuming and requires adequate budget attention.

Other poor people, meanwhile, are unlikely to become part of groups, whatever happens. These are the destitute and chronically poor – the very old, the very weak, the landless, the chronically sick, the homeless, the ethnic minorities. These cannot access resources through groups, and frequently experience extreme social exclusion. Government therefore needs to create new mechanisms, supplementary to existing channels, for these people. The PEAP review process, which aims to reduce chronic poverty by 2017, needs to take this into account.

Bibliography

Brock, K., McGee, R., Adong, R., Ssuuna, J. (2003), "Poverty Knowledge and Policy Processes in Uganda: Case Studies from Bushenyi, Lira and Tororo Districts".

Community Development Resource Network, SNV (2003) "Do not run faster than the ball: From development programme to local NGO. The CFORD story in Uganda".

Glasius, M. (2001), "Civil Society: A very brief history" Civil Society Briefing No.1 London: Centre for Civil Society, LSE.

Hulme, D. and Edwards, M., (eds.) (1994), *NGOs, States and Donors. Too Close for Comfort?*, London: Macmillan.

Isooba, M. et al. (2002), "Assessment and Analysis of Civil Society Organisations operating at Local, District and National levels on Issues of Environmental Rights and Natural Resource Management." Kampala: CDRN, mimeo.

Master document of the NAADS Task Force and Joint Donor Groups, (2000) Ministry of Agriculture, Animal Industry and Fisheries, Government of Uganda.

Narayan, D. et al. (2000), *Voices of the Poor. Can Anyone Hear Us?*, World Bank.

Narayan, D. et al. (2000), *Voices of the Poor. Crying Out for Change*, World Bank.

Thomas, A. (1992), *Non-Governmental Organisations and the Limits to Empowerment*, Oxford.

Uganda Participatory Poverty Assessment Process (2000), "Deepening the Understanding of Poverty", Ministry of Finance, Planning and Economic Development, Government of Uganda.

Uganda Participatory Poverty Assessment Project (2000), "Learning from the poor", Ministry of Finance, Planning and Economic Development, Government of Uganda, Kampala

Van Rooy, A., (ed.) (1998), "Civil Society and the Aid Industry: The Politics and Promise", London: Earthscan.

Wvyts, M., Mackintosh, M., and Hewitt, T., (eds), (1992), *Development Policy and Public Action*, Oxford: OUP.

5

Building Community Associations from the Inside or the Outside? Social Capital and Community Associations in Northern Uganda[1]

Kristof Titeca,[2] Thomas Vervisch[3]

Abstract

Social capital does not always promote democratic practices, but has different effects at different points. This dynamic is well characterised by a distinction between bonding, bridging, and linking social capital. This is analysed through an examination of three community associations in Northern Uganda. In particular, it is shown how linking social capital can negatively impact the association in general, and democratic governance in particular, if not accompanied by sufficient bonding, and bridging social capital.

Introduction

Social capital refers to the networks, and norms that enable people to act collectively. Proponents of social capital theory have argued that the accumulation of social capital is the missing link to understanding democratic governance, and economic development. The distinction between bonding, bridging, and linking social capital has brought the analysis of social capital, and these expected outcomes a step further. While bonding social capital is based on exclusive solidarity between "people like us," the bridging

---

[1] Reprinted (with minor changes) from World Development 36(11), Titeca, K., Vervisch T. 'The dynamics of social capital and community associations in Uganda: linking capital and its consequences', pp.2205-2222, 2008, with permission from Elsevier.

[2] Research Foundation – Flanders, Institute of Development Policy and Management, University of Antwerp. Kristof.Titeca@ua.ac.be. Thomas Vervisch: Associated member Conflict Research Group, Ghent University, Belgium

[3] The authors would like to thank the anonymous reviewers of the journal *World Development* for valuable comments, and suggestions on an earlier version of the paper. Kristof Titeca's research was financed by the Centre for Third World Studies/Conflict Research Group, Ghent University (with whom he was affiliated during the research for this article) and the "Fonds voor Wetenschappelijk Onderzoek" as part of his Ph.D. research.

form of social capital refers to more inclusive solidarity between people of different backgrounds. Bonding social capital is more or less labelled as "the first step" in the process of creating social capital, but it is the bridging form of social capital that is highly relevant in relation to the outcomes of democratic governance, and economic progress. More recently, emphasis has been made on the linking form of social capital, that is the accumulation of linking ties with formal institutions, and individuals in positions of power. The underlying idea is that "there is an optimal dynamic balance of bonding, bridging, and linking social capital, which simultaneously facilitates democratic governance, economic efficiency, and widely-dispersed human welfare, capabilities, and functionings" (Szreter 2002, p. 580). Community organisations take a central role in this discussion, as they are labelled the main "building blocks" to creating new stocks of social capital. This article challenges the assumptions about the positive outcomes of linking social capital through an examination of Ugandan community associations. It argues that linking social capital can negatively impact the association in general, and democratic governance in particular, if not accompanied by bonding, and bridging social capital. Rather than automatically leading to positive outcomes, linking social capital can also lead to the disorganisation of the groups.

The first part of this article elaborates a theoretical framework on social capital, and community associations. It is argued how community associations are characterised by different, and dynamic combinations of different forms of social capital which impact the democratic character of these associations. The second part of this paper analyses these theoretical premises through three ethnographic case studies of community associations in West Nile, Uganda. In the final section, we draw some conclusions regarding the impact of linking capital on democratic practices in community associations. On a more general level, it offers conclusions on the role of external interventions in the creation of social capital.

Community associations, democracy, and social capital

Social capital, and community associations

One of the consequences of the rise of the social capital debate in the middle of the nineties was the increased interest in community organisations. This was in particular in response to the work of Robert Putnam, who defines social capital as "the features of social life - networks, norms, and trust - that enable participants to act together more effectively to pursue shared objectives" (1995, p. 664–665)[4] Putnam equates social capital with horizontal organisations, or more specific with "networks of civic engagement," hence the link between the social capital, and civil society debate. These organisations are labelled as the main "building blocks" in which new stocks of social capital occur. Grassroots involvement in community organisations with face-to-face relationships lead above all to the "real" social capital (Szreter,2002). Even

---

[4] The conceptual history of social capital does not start in the middle of the nineties, but it was the work of Robert Putnam that brought the whole discussion to the forefront. For a conceptual history of social capital, see the useful article of Farr (2004).

Putnam himself admits that social capital, and these community associations are so interconnected that it is sometimes difficult to see which is the chicken, and which the is egg (Putnam, 2000: 152). Community organisations are therefore defined as an excellent playground for democracy, through the social capital they embody, and the democratic values they promote (Putnam, 1993).

This social capital debate has led to the promotion of community associations in the implementation of development activities in developing countries. The World Bank's Social Capital Initiative has highlighted the importance of this debate for developing countries (Grootaert & van Bastelaer, 2001). The papers produced through this initiative consider the relevance of community organisations, and the social capital they represent for a broad spectrum of development interventions such as access to credit, service delivery, natural resource management, and community-based development (Bebbington & Carrol, 2000; Isham & Kähkönen, 1999; Kähkönen, 1999; Krishna & Uphoff, 1999; Pantoja, 2000; Pargal et al., 1999; Reid & Salmen, 2000; Sorensen, 2000; van Bastelaer, 2000). What is common for this broad field of development interventions is the assumption that these organisations facilitate democratic governance at the local level. Members learn to create, change, bargain, and control the institutional settings of their organisation. These internal institutions are necessary to deter free riders, to cut the costs of membership, and more in general, to increase organisational efficiency (Ostrom, 1990; Patterson, 2003). This process of developing the internal "rules of the game" also facilitates participation, and accountability, and as such creates local institutions in which democratic governance is practiced (Esman & Uphoff,1984; Putnam, 1993).

Bonding, bridging, and linking capital

In the past ten years, the distinction between bonding, bridging, and linking social capital has brought the analysis of social capital a step further by questioning "how social networks differ from one another in ways that are relevant to their consequences" (Putnam 2004, p.668–669). Gittell and Vidal (1998) were the first to explicitly use the concepts of bonding, and bridging social capital. While bonding social capital is based on exclusive solidarity between "people like us," and only helps people to "get by," the bridging form of social capital refers to more inclusive solidarity between people of different backgrounds, and helps people to "get ahead" (Briggs, 1998).

In terms of democratic governance, the bridging form is more productive than the bonding form of social capital. Bonding social capital has an important downside, as it can lead to more exclusive forms of solidarity based on kinship, class, ethnicity, religion, and so on (Portes & Landolt, 1996, 2000; Portes, 1998). High stocks of bonding social capital can therefore lead to the exclusion of several groups in society, and even to conflicts between these groups (Colletta & Cullen, 2000). As bridging social capital connects people with different social backgrounds it has the capacity to span these social gaps, and enhance more inclusive forms of solidarity (Putnam, 1995, 2000). These cross-cutting networks traverse social gaps, and therefore, increase contact with various other people, supporting tolerance, and preventing groups from becoming inward focused (Paxton, 2002).

More recently, the work of Woolcock (1998), and Szreter (2002) introduced the concept of linking social capital to further refine the conceptual framework. Where bridging, and bonding social capital are mainly horizontal metaphors, the linking form refers to networks that connect people across explicit vertical power differentials. Szreter and Woolcock (2004, p. 6) gave the following explanation: "We would define linking social capital as norms of respect, and networks of trusting relationships between people who are interacting across explicit, formal or institutionalized power, or authority gradients in society." According to the authors, examples of linking social capital are in the first place related to accessing bankers, law enforcement officers, social workers, health care providers, NGO officials, politicians, and the public administration in general. As such, the key function of this linking form of social capital is the capacity to leverage resources, information, and ideas from these formal institutions (Woolcock, 2002).

By focusing on bonding, and bridging social capital as horizontal metaphors, it must not be forgotten that poverty also has a vertical dimension. It has been widely shown that poverty is about powerlessness and social exclusion: a lack of ties with political elites, and people in power to influence those formal institutions, and policies which influence, and enhance the lives of the poor (Bebbington, 1999; Cleaver, 2005; Fox, 1996; Heller, 1996; Prakash, 2002; World Bank, 2000). Linking social capital refers to this specific capacity of engaging power structures. Linking social capital is therefore clearly linked with democratic governance, as it brings in issues of power, and politics, and refers in, particular, to the quality of the relationship between communities, and their representatives (Szreter, 2002).

Bonding, bridging, and linking social capital in community associations: basic arguments

This literature on bonding, bridging, and linking social capital formulates some basic arguments with regard to which community associations will succeed in becoming local democratic institutions, and which not. By focusing on these arguments, we shift our focus from the community to the associational level as our level of analysis.

Firstly, bonding social capital is labelled as "the first step," as all community organisations start within their own community. Strong bonding ties provide the foundation for trusting, and reciprocal relationships between the members, and as such, facilitate cooperation, and coordination within the organisation (Saegert, Thompson, & Warren, 2001). Secondly, without additional bridging ties, these community organisations can create local institutions that are closed, hostile to others, or even corrupt (Portes, 1998). Building networks between a diversity of local institutions within the same community, and enhancing links with other communities will lead toward more open, and democratic local institutions which can speak for the whole community, as it can bring together neighboring communities which in the past were divided because of different interests, and identities (Saegert et al., 2001). Finally, these organisations need to create linking social capital. As such, they will learn to promote community interests in formal institutions, to participate in public policy, and to hold accountable their officials. Szreter (2002) referred back to the British trade unions of the 19th century, which evolved from sectional, and apolitical (bonding) toward more inclusive (bridging) organisations before finally receiving the linking social capital that turned them into an accepted partner of the formal institutions. On a general level, these different steps overlap with the three roles that Browns (1991) pointed out when looking at the efficacy of organisations in sustainable development: the ability to maintain local effort, the ability to create bridging ties to other organisations, and the ability to influence politics through vertical ties. To summarise, the social capital literature argues that community organisations need to transform bonding into bridging ties as to "reach out," and create linking ties as to "scale up" the impact of the organisation (Woolcock, 2002). This view therefore entails the implicit assumptions that firstly, groups or organisations should have all three types of social capital, and secondly, that there is a linear progression from bonding to bridging to linking social capital. Only in these circumstances will organisations reach the optimal dynamic balance of bonding, bridging, and linking social capital, and contribute to democracy, and development.

In the past, considerable efforts have been made to nuance the positive outcomes of social capital by pointing out its downsides (Colletta & Cullen, 2000; Portes & Landolt, 1996, 2000; Portes, 1998). As already mentioned, this critique was in the first place a critique of the downside of bonding social capital, redefining the positive outcomes of social capital more specifically as the outcomes of bridging social capital (Putnam, 1995, 2000). Much less is known about the possible negative aspects of the linking form of social capital, which is what this article aims to address. It specifically seeks to analyse how linking social capital can negatively affect the functioning of community organisations in developing countries. In another context, Putnam (1993) has made considerable efforts to explain the difference between "bad" vertical patron–client networks that are integrated in the "amoral familism" present in the south of Italy, and 'good' horizontal civic networks which, according to Putnam, explain the working of democracy in northern Italy. In general, vertical networks spanning power disparities are mainly used by the powerful to control the powerless. Therefore, Putnam (2004) proposes to distinguish between "responsive," and "unresponsive" linking social capital. The "unresponsive" form can lead toward nepotism, corruption, and suppression, while responsive linking social capital has the potential to nourish respectful, and trusting ties between communities, and their representatives within formal institutions (Szreter & Woolcock, 2004).

This chapter aims to spark this debate by challenging assumptions about the positive outcomes of "linking social capital" through an examination of Ugandan community associations. In particular, it argues how linking social capital can negatively impact the democratic character of these organisations, if not accompanied by bonding, and bridging social capital. We define democracy procedurally, as a decision-making process in which participation and accountability are two key aspects (Patterson, 1998). The internal democratic character of the organisation refers to the effective participation of the members in the internal decision-making process, and if, and how they can hold their leaders accountable, while the external democratic spill-over effects refer to the extent to which the association is participating in broader community policies, and discussions, and the extent to which the association is playing a role in holding community leaders accountable. In this sense, both the private, and public side of social capital are being analysed.

Both community associations and social capital are defined as context specific, and dynamic, in that the contribution which different organisations make to different forms of social capital varies by context, and over time (De Silva, Harpham, Huttly, Bartolini, & Penny, 2007). Consequently, the democratic character of these community organisations cannot be explained by one particular form of social capital at one particular moment, but rather by the optimal, and dynamic combinations of different forms of social capital that change by context, and over time (Prakash, 2002; Szreter, 2002; Woolcock & Narayan, 2000).

To capture these different combinations, and their dynamic character we present detailed accounts of three community associations in the West Nile region in northern Uganda. Through their life histories we show how they built bonding, bridging, and linking social capital, and highlight the role linking social capital plays in the functioning of these organisations. We stress that social capital is a process issue, and that before measuring its impact one has to understand the causes, and mechanisms of how social capital is created (Dudwick, Kuehnast, Nyhan Jones, & Woolcock, 2006). These case studies are therefore an ethnographic supplement leading to a deeper understanding of what the abundance of quantitative surveys on social capital try to measure. The distinction between bonding, bridging, and linking social capital proves to be a relevant framework for guiding research on social capital, and community organisations. In particular, it is shown how linking social capital can negatively impact the association in general and democratic governance in particular, if not accompanied by sufficient bonding, and bridging social capital.

Case studies

These findings are based on three case studies of community associations in the direct vicinity of Arua town in Arua district in Uganda.[5] Arua is situated in the West Nile region in North Western Uganda. The town, and its surrounding peri-urban centres have about 85,000 inhabitants. Ethnographic data in the community associations were gathered through formal, and informal interviews, and observations.[6] The case of the OPEC boys demonstrates how strong bonding, and bridging social capital can lead

---

5   The OPEC boys are located in the town, and on the outskirts of the town, while VUPEG, and CARYM are located outside of the town.
6   Fieldwork, funded by the Research Foundation – Flanders (FWO), was conducted from October to December 2005.

to a democratic, and powerful form of linking capital, whereas the cases of VUPEG, and CARYM show how linking capital can have detrimental effects on the democratic practices of the organisation.[7]

The OPEC boys[8]

The OPEC boys are a group of men who started their activities by smuggling fuel from the Democratic Republic of Congo (DRC) to Arua town in Uganda, where they sell it. They are named after the coalition of oil-producing countries, and are about 300 - 400 men strong.

The origins of the OPEC boys can be traced to the period in exile during the first half of the eighties. With the overthrow of the brutal dictatorship of Idi Amin, Obote's Uganda National Liberation Army (UNLA) occupied the West Nile region, and committed many brutalities in revenge for the atrocities of the Amin regime. Most of the population fled into exile in Congo, and Sudan in late 1979, and the early 1980s. During this period in exile, a few young men had started selling transit fuel from Kinshasa and Kampala. When they returned to their home areas, they had no education, or assets. Because of the strategic location near to the Congo, and Sudan, they became active in the illegal trans-border fuel trade, which was tapped from transit tankers, or bought in the DRC. This was especially the case for the Aringa, a Muslim sub-group of the Lugbara. When they came back from exile (from 1983 onwards), their home area, Aringa county, was still plagued by armed conflicts. As a result, many Aringa came to settle within Arua town. Many were uneducated, unskilled, and without any assets. This group of "unanchored" Aringa youth became the core group of the OPEC boys: numerous Aringa young men were drawn into the trans-border fuel trade. As there was much demand for fuel, they soon became very successful. There was also no petrol station in the area, which made the local government authorities tolerate them. Moreover, rebel groups were still plaguing West Nile, drawing on the same "unanchored, uneducated, and disaffected former soldiers, and youth" (Gersony 1997: 77) as the OPEC boys: if these young men had not been active in the fuel trade, they could easily have been drawn into criminal activities, or even another rebel movement.

Because of their success, they were soon joined by young men from neighbouring districts, and other ethnic groups, such as the Aivu, or the Terrego. Moreover, they soon expanded into other activities, and even started their own construction firm. Some OPEC boys stopped selling fuel and started working in this construction firm, which was headed by engineers who were unemployed but educated brothers of the OPEC boys. Because of this rapid growth, the organisation became divided in several sub-groups (both within town, and the surrounding villages), but remained with an

---

[7] The three organisations were selected because they had strongly varying linkages with external actors when coming into being. They are therefore ideally suited for providing deeper insights in the key-theme of this article, that is, the effects of linking capital on the association.

[8] This section describes the history of the OPEC boys up to the late nineties. Different dynamics came into play after this period, when their leaders were arrested, which had a profound impact on the organisation of the movement. For an elaborate description of the OPEC boys (in French) see Titeca (2006), and Lecoutere and Titeca (2007).

overall OPEC boys structure ("OPEC Arua"). All of these groups (both the overarching organisation, and the sub-groups) have a formal structure with a chairperson, assisted by a vice-chairperson, treasurer, etc., which conduct meetings on a regular basis. This formal structure was one of the factors contributing to greater trust among the different members, and member groups: these meetings were not only used to take "formal" business decisions, but also to solve conflicts among the different members, organise community work, and so on. Moreover, through these meetings, intangible benefits were provided to the members such as support for members with financial problems (e.g., contributing to hospital costs, or school fees) or assisting members with deaths in their family.

The OPEC boys are therefore not only seen as economic actors, they are also seen as social actors which are respected by the wider local population. Much of this has to do with the fact that the OPEC boys regularly represent issues of the wider community to the local government. For example, when the market authorities decided to introduce a tax for small restaurants at the market ground, the OPEC boys played a crucial role in representing the interests of the women running these restaurants. These women felt the tax was far too high, but the district threatened to confiscate their utilities if they refused to pay. The women informed the overall OPEC boys' leadership about their problem. The OPEC boys held a general meeting (with all the sub-groups) to discuss the issue, after which it was decided to be a genuine complaint, as it was seen as a deliberate attempt by the government to "strangle people's livelihood, and push them into poverty."[9] The OPEC boys leadership went to the market authorities, who in turn refused to talk with them. After this, the OPEC boys went to the district authorities, where they presented their complaint, and threatened further action such as creating chaos in town, or stopping fuel sales.[10] The tax was subsequently abolished. This example illustrates how the OPEC boys represent the interests of other groups, and thus form bridging capital with other groups within society, through which they are able to influence the local government. On their own, without the support of the OPEC boys, these market women do not have much impact on the local government. The government is not dependent on them (as they are on the fuel of the OPEC boys), and they are not organised into groups with a strict leadership structure. This latter factor proved to be crucial in linking up with the district, as the leaders of the OPEC boys have always been in close contact with the district authorities. As a result, the district leadership does listen to these women with the support of the OPEC boys. Also in other cases, the OPEC boys acted as intermediary between urban groups (such as the motorcycle, or bicycle taxi groups, the carwash groups, and other small businesses), and the local government. This did not only happen when these groups' interests overlapped with their own interests. It rather reflects the strong feelings of solidarity between all

---

9   Interview OPEC boy October 19, 2005.
10 The OPEC boys were more effective with the district authorities than with the market authorities because the former are essentially responsible for the provision of peace, and security in the district, which makes them most vulnerable to the demands of this potentially dangerous group of unemployed young men. The fact that the OPEC boys are able to form a rebel group therefore is a reason for the district authorities to listen to the OPEC boys, not for the market authorities.

the urban marginalised groups, including the OPEC boys, who all regard themselves as "survivors." It can therefore be argued that the OPEC boys are representing the interests of marginalised sections of society, and inducing political participation, as the local government, and the urban community negotiate about certain issues.[11]

The OPEC boys started out of bonding social capital between a group of Aringa young men who were trying to survive in exile, and in the difficult circumstances of their return. As their activities proved to be very successful, they were joined by many other unemployed young men from other ethnic groups, who even came from surrounding districts. As these unemployed young men had little other possibilities for employment and were making a good income with the OPEC boys, it was very much in their interest to make the group function well. To deal with this expansion in members, and activities, formal structures were introduced to facilitate the cooperation between the different sub-groups, and individual members. This entailed an increased participation through regular meetings, in which representatives of the sub-groups attended the general meetings of OPEC Arua. Through these meetings, decisions were made about the conduct of individual members, the allocation of resources, and the representation of wider community interests to the local government. The effect of this expanding bridging capital for the OPEC boys was what Putnam it envisaged it to be: networks of trust, and reciprocity were built in the wider community, in which the local authorities were held accountable (Putnam, 1993). Crucial in this evolution of the organisation was their charismatic leader, K.[12]. K. started smuggling goods at a young age while in exile, and back in Arua, he was among the first to start smuggling fuel. Through his expertise, contacts, and charisma, he was strongly respected, and soon became the founder of the actual OPEC boys. He was the most important factor in introducing a strong discipline among the members, setting up the organisational structure, expanding to the other businesses, and attracting members from other ethnic groups (K. himself is a Terrego, a non-Aringa), and districts. Under his leadership, the OPEC boys were also providing different services to the wider urban community: on a regular basis, they were cleaning the streets, providing transport for funerals, and acting as a community vigilante. Because of these community services, K., and the OPEC boys were highly respected among the wider population.[13] In other words, K. proved to be an important factor in building both the bonding, and bridging capital of the OPEC boys.

Additional factors facilitating the formation of social capital are the general feelings of marginalisation in West Nile (Leopold, 2005). The local population feels they are being betrayed, and neglected by the current Museveni government, and see the OPEC boys as 'sons of the soil' who are taking their rights into their own hands by creating

---

11 For a similar Ugandan case of the influence of urban informal groups on local processes of governance, cf. Titeca (2009).
12 This paper wants to analyse particular processes, rather than personalities, no real names were used in this paper.
13 For a detailed discussion of this respect by the wider population, cf. Titeca (2006), p. 152–156.

employment in the face of strong neglect by the national government (Titeca, 2006, Titeca and De Herdt 2010). This does not only create a feeling of reciprocity, and solidarity within the wider population in the West Nile, but also within the OPEC boys, who strongly identify with "being an OPEC boy while being neglected by the government."[14] These already existing feelings of trust among the OPEC boys are further enhanced by the illegal nature of the OPEC boys' activities, for the simple reason that their illicit smuggling activities (including the income derived from these activities) need higher degrees of trust, and reciprocity than legal activities (Skaperdas 2001, p. 184–187). This is both the case internally among the OPEC boys,[15] and externally in their relationship with the wider population, which informs them about the movement of the government authorities, and helps them hiding.

This bridging capital - in the sense that relationships are established with other urban marginalised groups, and the wider population, but especially the fact that the OPEC boys provide employment to a vast group of "unanchored, and uneducated young men" - in turn gives the OPEC boys linking social capital. The local government realises that, although the OPEC boys perform illicit activities, they provide employment to a large group of unemployed marginalised, and therefore potentially dangerous, young men. In the recent history of rebel movements in Northern Uganda in general, and West Nile in particular (cf. Leopold, 2005), they could easily be drawn into criminality, or even rebellion. The OPEC boys even provide order to this marginalised group, as they use their structures to regulate the (mis)behaviour of their members: misconduct is punished after consultation among the subgroup executive, which decides on the specific penalty. For example, during the field research cases of fighting were penalised either through financial, or physical punishments (with strokes of the cane). Alternatively, in case of any complaints, the local government contacts the overall OPEC boys leadership, who in turn contacts the sub-group leadership, who discipline the culprit.

The local government therefore prefers to tolerate, and even support the OPEC boys, and their illicit smuggling activities. It provides them with financial incentives, or state-sponsored development initiatives: they helped several OPEC boys sub-groups to officially register as a Community-Based Organisation, which enabled them to access the World Bank-sponsored Northern Ugandan Social Action Fund (which essentially aims to build social capital). With these funds, some of the subgroups have started small-scale projects such as poultry farming. The local government also helped them to win tenders, for example, to clean the market, or hospital, and politicians have negotiated jobs for them with major infrastructure works in the area. Moreover, in this privileged position, the OPEC boys act as an intermediary between urban marginalised

---

14 Interview OPEC boy November 02, Arua, Uganda 2005.
15 Titeca and De Herdt (2010) show how the cross-border trade in West Nile is regulated by a number of 'practical norms' which guide behaviour of both traders and state officials. The OPEC boys are part of this dynamic: they have strict guidelines on the behaviour within the association. Similarly, information about suppliers, and smuggling routes is based on trust.

groups, and the local government (as demonstrated above in the case of the market women).

The specific bridging capital of the OPEC boys enabled them access to the local government authorities, in the sense that the local government authorities tolerated them, and had an advantage in supporting them. In this context, the synergy (Evans, 1996a, 1996b) between local government and the OPEC boys enabled the latter to further "scale up" their association: it helped them to diversify their activities, and register as a Community-Based Organisation, as well as gaining access to the World Bank (NUSAF) funding.

Vurra patriotic entertainers group (VUPEG)

"Vurra patriotic entertainers group," or VUPEG is an association registered as a Community Based Organisation (CBO), Non-Governmental Organisation (NGO), and cooperative alliance, based in a sub-county of Arua district. At the start, its objectives were purely political: it was founded by a politician of the area, who had been a minister since 1991. More specifically, the organisation was founded in support of his 1996 (national) elections campaign. Under the clear chairmanship of its chairman (hereafter referred to as "the Chairman") the association, consisting of 22 (male) of his staunchest supporters, was doing entertainment throughout the sub-county in support of the candidature of the minister. The minister was clearly encouraging this, as he was providing the association with financial assistance. As the Constitution puts it "VUPEG was founded at the start of the 1996 electoral process for the purpose of giving Patriotic Education to the people of VURA through traditional media-songs, plays, folk stories, and dance. It was blessed, and supported straight at the start by [the minister]"[16]. After the re-election of the minister, VUPEG expected him to further contribute to the association: their keen support in organising entertainment activities for the minister can for the most part be explained out of the hope to receive some benefits from the minister, to get a "share of the cake".[17] If not direct material, or logistical benefits, at least some indirect benefits, in linking them up with national or international donors. None of these proved the case. Instead the minister mainly encouraged them to go their own way in becoming a development organisation, and to write project proposals to this extent.

In other words, the organisation did not start out of bonding social capital, but out of linking social capital: there was no associational form of solidarity, and cooperation to 'get by', but rather an association (under the clear leadership of one-man) which wanted to develop itself through linking up to the 'local big man'. This linking social capital did, however, not bring them much benefit, as the VUPEG members were disappointed in the limited support of the minister. At this point, many of the original members left the organisation, because they had expected clear material benefits, and were not really interested in the new developmental orientation of the association.

16　VUPEG constitution, unpublished, 1998, p. 1.
17　VUPEG is in this no exception, as this is a very common phenomenon in rural Uganda – many similar organisations were encountered during the field research.

They were, however, replaced by new members from the wider community, who were more interested in the developmental activities of the organisation.

With the help of a few educated members who joined the organisation, a democratic structure was set up (with a board, general meeting, elections, etc.) and the organisation registered itself as a Community Based Organisation, and Non-Governmental Organisation.

Also development proposals were written, which proved to be successful. From 1999 to 2001, VUPEG received funds from the Poverty Alleviation Programme (PAP), a governmental poverty-reduction programme for a microfinance scheme. The organisation further expanded, and soon became an umbrella organisation under which many Community-Based Organisations registered, and participated in the activities.[18] Its principal activity became a cassava-multiplication programme, supported by local intermediary organisations (which in turn receive funding from a range of international donors such as GTZ). This cassava-multiplication proved very successful, to the extent that VUPEG staff became hired by certain local government authorities to act as an agricultural trainer. In other words, 'reaching out' to new members with other, developmental, and non-political, motivations reduced the exclusive political character of the organisation. Also the fact that VUPEG became an umbrella organisation increased the inclusion of other groups in society. This brought bridging capital with strong positive effects: development partners were found, democratic structures were installed, and other organisations within the wider community shared in the benefits.

After its first attempt to create linking capital during the 1996 elections, the association tried this again during the 2001 parliamentary elections in which they started supporting another candidate. This support was the individual (undemocratic) decision of the Chairman, who decided this candidate would be the most beneficial option for the association. The Chairman and some other key members started acting as his local campaign agent, once more hoping on direct benefits for the association. However, this candidate was not elected. As VUPEG had been openly campaigning against this elected candidate, the relationship between VUPEG and the elected politician were not really amicable. This also affected the relationship with the sub-county authorities:[19] as the majority of the sub-county authorities (as the LCIII chairman, and councillors) were strong supporters of the elected candidate, they had a negative attitude toward VUPEG, which they perceived to be connected with opposition politics, with no other motive as obstructing the work of the sub-county, and the elected candidate. According to VUPEG, "[the elected candidate] has no other objective than to fulfil the personal needs of the sub-county councillors,"[20] while the sub-county authorities claim the accusations of VUPEG are a simple result of their powerlessness, frustration, and low level of education.

---

18 In 2005, VUPEG had a total of 1,560 members, and 68 Community-Based Organisations (CBOs) in 9 parishes.
19 Under Ugandan decentralisation, a system of five "layers" of local government is introduced: district (LC V), county (LC IV), sub-county (LCIII), parish (LC II), village (LC I).
20 Interview VUPEG staff member, November 02, 2005.

As a result of this generally bad relationship, VUPEG claims that the sub-county authorities consistently try to sabotage their activities by not giving out information about programmes they could access, and ignoring their capacities as agricultural trainers. While VUPEG staff was at one point being hired as agricultural experts by the district offices, they are not currently being hired, or approached by their own sub-county,[21] which instead is hiring trainers from other sub-counties.

Throughout its history, VUPEG has continuously been trying to link itself to local politicians, in the hope of attracting certain benefits. This was particularly the initiative of the Chairman, who argued that "the organisation has a political background. And therefore, we will never leave our engagement in politics".[22] This linking capital did not prove very productive, as the particular politicians either did not get elected, or lost interest in the association. Instead of bringing material benefits, it led to negative relations with the local sub-county authorities with harmful effects for the development of the organisation. From a social capital perspective, it does not really matter if the sub-county authorities were really "boycotting" the organisation, or not; what does matter is that there was definitely no synergetic effects taking place between the organisation, and the local government. This linking capital also negatively affected the internal democracy in the association: As the Chairman was both the founding member, and above all the person responsible for connecting VUPEG with the outside world, linking the association with politicians, and donor organisations, this gradually led to a situation where he was considered the principal owner of the association, both by himself, and the majority of the members. This led to several instances where he was misusing his power position. One problem was that he occasionally took money from the organisation's account without informing the treasurer. Although financial issues should be handled by the treasurer, the Chairman refused to accept this. For example, at one point, money was taken to buy stationery for the association, but only a limited amount of money was accounted for. There were also other problems on an organisational level: According to the constitution of the organisation, the general assembly has to meet every year. During this meeting, general elections are held, in which the board, and executive committee members are re-elected. However, the Chairman - as the chairman of the board - resisted a general assembly as he did not want his power position to be challenged. Most of the members did not want to challenge the Chairman about this. On the one hand, he refused to respond to these allegations, as "he just starts shouting at people demanding accountability!"[23] On the other hand, members did not want to challenge his position, as he was the initiator of the organisation, and as he was controlling access to the outside contacts (donors, and politicians).

---

21 Four staff members act as trainers of the NAADS offices of the district offices, and are hired by two other sub-county authorities, for example, to give trainings on bee-keeping.
22 Interview Chairman, 23 April 2007.
23 Interview member VUPEG, 17 October 2005.

The transformation of VUPEG into a dictatorial one-man organisation had a double effect: on the one hand, it meant that certain members became less interested in the organisation. The accountant, for example, refused to work any longer directly with the Chairman.[24] On the other hand, it led to a polarisation within the organisation. The Chairman had certain members on his side, who often accompanied him on his field trips; while a few other - more educated - members allied themselves around Dr. Ray.[25] Dr. Ray is the most educated member of the organisation - he is a veterinary doctor - and most often consulted whenever a 'difficult' issue arises. The whole situation led to strong tensions between Dr. Ray, and the Chairman. For example, when Dr. Ray was writing project proposals (he was the only member with a university degree), the other members felt left out, and had the feeling he was using project proposals in order to plot against them. Dr. Ray, however, took the forefront in leading the opposition against the dictatorial behaviour of the Chairman. After the Chairman had misappropriated 60,000 Ugandan shillings, Dr. Ray forced the Chairman to hold a general meeting, where finally a vote of no confidence was cast. In the meeting, the Chairman was downgraded to vice-chairperson. Nevertheless, when the newly elected chairperson had to move to another district two months later (for professional reasons), the Chairman became chairperson again. The members unanimously judged that the Chairman had been punished enough by being a vice-chairperson; and could therefore take up his older position again.

In other words, even if he had been acting wrongly, he is still seen as the only legitimate leader of the organisation. As a member comments "He might have acted wrongly, but he is providing the organisation with funds!."[26] In this situation, linking capital gave one personality the power to dominate the organisation, leading to a general malfunctioning of the organisation. Although formal democratic structures were introduced, it became no 'playground for democracy', rather a playground for the 'gatekeeper' (Bierschenk, Chauveau & De Sardan, 2000) to the higher-level institutions, negatively affecting general accountability, participation, and transparency. This particular relation between VUPEG and the higher-level institutions is therefore in line with Putnam's 'unresponsive' form of linking capital, fostering corruption, and nepotism rather than 'scaling up' the impact of the organisation (Putnam, 2004; Szreter & Woolcock, 2004).

Catholic, agricultural, and rural youth movement (CARYM) Arua

The Catholic, Agricultural, and Rural Youth Movement (CARYM) is a Catholic Church founded lay people's organisation. Its activities are embedded in the structures of the Catholic Dioceses, and its main aim is "to develop the abilities of rural youth for self-

---

24 Although this affected the interest of the members, and the related level of activity of the organisation, it did not affect the overall membership as such: none of the membership organisations pulled out.
25 Dr Ray originates from the village where VUPEG is based. He did not join from the beginning (as he was studying outside of Arua), but joined the association around 1998. He had started a business in animal drugs around that time, and he felt that the VUPEG membership might be beneficial for his business.
26 Interview VUPEG member, November 28, 2005.

reliance, and the improvement of the living conditions in the villages,"[27] and its main target-group the non-school going youth. Its main office is in Kampala, and it has 15 local branches over Uganda. CARYM Arua started in July 2002. This was mainly in cooperation with the young, and dynamic manager of the Dioceses youth centre, Michael, who had been very active in the local Dioceses structures: he started as a chapel youth leader, had several other functions in the Dioceses, and was finally appointed youth centre coordinator. In this position, he is the person with overall responsibility for the youth centre, and of all organisations working in the youth centre, among which CARYM is the most important.

Twenty-six motivated members were selected among the catholic youth from the different Diocesan parishes. (In fact, no selection had to take place as there was space for 30 members, and only 26 candidates turned up.) Also an executive was elected, along with a coordinator. The coordinator, which is the only paid position in the organisation, runs the daily activities of the organisation; while Michael (as the youth centre coordinator) remains financially responsible for the organisation, and reports back to the local Dioceses, and the national CARYM offices in Kampala. All these rules were laid down in a detailed constitution.

CARYM's main activities are twofold: on the one hand projects, and training in the field of sustainable agriculture, and on the other hand a "dairy cow" project, in which cows are passed on to the different members through a rotational scheme. To this extent, CARYM Kampala gave the individual members of CARYM Arua a training course in sustainable agriculture, a dairy cow, a bicycle, and farm tools. In return, the individual members had to pass on knowledge from their training on sustainable agriculture to the members of their community. According to the Constitution, and the rules of agreement with CARYM Kampala, the CARYM Arua coordinator has to monitor the activities of the individual members in their local communities, and report back to the national CARYM office. In this sense, the CARYM project aims at introducing a culture of participant, and responsible citizens, not only within the organisation, but also in the wider community, through passing on the training.

As the support of CARYM Kampala is only temporary (four years), it strongly encourages its member organisations to look for other donors in support of their activities. CARYM Arua proved to be fairly successful in this. It has been contracted by GTZ (German development agency) as trainers in food, and nutrition schemes in the refugee camps in the area; and World Vision donated a carpentry workshop to the organisation. Within CARYM, these successes are mainly attributed to Michael, who has been active in the church structures for a long time, and has many contacts through his position as a youth centre coordinator. Moreover, he was the one who established the links with CARYM Kampala, and the other donor organisations. This linking social capital gave Michael strong respect within the organisation, but inversely affected participation, accountability, and general group communication: for example, CARYM has to submit a monthly report to the national CARYM office, in which they

---

27 "CARYM constitution", unpublished, p.1.

describe their monthly activities. The coordinator has to submit these to Michael, who has to forward them to CARYM Kampala. The problem is not in the writing of the report, but in the fact that the report is forwarded to Michael, who does not forward it to the national office. As the coordinator explains

> Communication with the national office is quite difficult for us. There is a gap for us members. We do not communicate many times. We communicate through [Michael]. But me, as a coordinator, I do not. Because we need to respect the hierarchy! (...) We are supposed to report monthly to the national office. But it is a bit difficult internally. We as members sit, and handwrite these reports. We then give it to [Michael], who should type it, and send it to the national office. But we do not get feedback from him if it is sent, or not. [Michael] should send our report together with a financial report that he writes. But he forgets. We ask him, but no clear answer is given. He will say the youth secretary is too busy. No one else can assist us. We are yet to find a proper solution for this.[28]

Because of the strong respect for Michael, members do not dare to confront him, nor do they have the capacity to consult anyone else on this, because Michael is controlling all the outside contacts of the organisation. Even when the national CARYM coordinator came to monitor CARYM Arua's activities, and urgently requested them to send monthly reports, this did not change this attitude. "As [Michael] was in contact with the national office, he must be knowing what is best for us,"[29] was the comment of the secretary.

As a result, reports were never sent. Moreover, the CARYM coordinator stopped monitoring the activities of the individual members in the different parishes, and individual members stopped reporting on their activities. In this general context, members did not feel obliged to give further training to their community members. Throughout the interviews, members emphasised how they no longer felt encouraged to organise the time-consuming training courses without the direct support and knowledge of the executive. It was found that the 26 members on average trained three people from their community, while at least 10 people per person was the figure agreed with the national office.

The CARYM executive also proved to be unaware of the financial status of CARYM: no one knew the actual budget of CARYM, how much money was, and could still be spent. As the coordinator comments

> We do not know where the money comes from, if it is money from the national office, or where. [Michael] gives us a broad figure, but we have no clue of what it is spent on. Last time I asked, but he told me that he first was going to update the old data, and then give accountability to me. But up to today, he has not done this.[30]

In other words, the members do not dare to confront Michael. Also meetings proved to be problematic. Although they initially were having a monthly executive CARYM meeting, and a general CARYM meeting every two months - as was laid out in the

---

28 Interview CARYM coordinator, November 21, 2005.
29 Interview CARYM secretary, November 08, 2005.
30 Interview coordinator, October 23, 2005.

constitution - CARYM meetings soon proved to be very rare.[31] According to the CARYM members, this is mainly because Michael hardly has time left for meetings: through his status as educated 'gatekeeper,' linking the organisation to external actor, Michael not only obtained political power within the organisation, but also in the wider local political field: he was elected as a village chairman, an elected member of the local School Management Committee, and a frequently asked master of ceremony for fundraising activities. In other words, Michael had been accumulating more and more power through his outside contacts ('linking capital'), which allowed him to increasingly neglect formal rules within the association regarding democratic procedures, participation, and accountability. This also had an effect on the bonding capital of the association. Whereas members initially had some form of bonding capital through the meetings, and trainings, they started becoming less, and less involved with the organisation as a whole: members no longer met as an 'organisation,' had no impact, or input in it, and therefore slowly lost contact with the association. The organisation became more, and more a collection of individuals (instead of an association united by social capital), being only left with the material aspects of their membership, such as the dairy cows. They no longer felt involved with the association.

Although this process reduced the function of the executive to almost purely ceremonial, this was nevertheless perceived as legitimate by both the executive, and the individual members. During many interviews, and observations, it was emphasised how the development of CARYM would not be possible without the involvement of Michael, who was often described as the "father"[32] of the association. He had been involved with the Dioceses for a long time; he had a higher educational level; but most importantly, he has been linking them to the different developmental actors. Thanks to his efforts, they had received several benefits from CARYM, a carpentry workshop from World Vision, and some extra employment for GTZ - all of which had proved impossible without Michael. As a result of his efforts, members did not dare, or did not want, to confront Michael on issues such as lack of transparency, accountability, and participation.

Concluding, we can say that linking capital was the basic form of social capital in CARYM: it was the national CARYM office, in cooperation with the local church authorities, which formed the association. As such, the association is in a continuous relationship with the higher-level CARYM offices, and has to provide reports, attend training courses, write proposals, etc. Through this relationship "resources, information, and ideas" (Woolcock, 2002) are received, which indeed have positive effects on the organisation: knowledge was received, and (in the initial stages of the association) passed on to the wider community. No 'synergy' was formed with the local government, but a good cooperation was in place with the international donors

---

31 Browsing through the minutes of the general CARYM meetings, the authors indeed saw this tendency reflected: in the initial six months of the movement, four meetings were held (July 01, 2004; October 03, 2004; November 06, 2004; December 23, 2004) whereas in the following 12 months only one meeting was held (October 29, 2005).
32 For example, interview with CARYM members on October 25, 2005, and November 21, 2005.

which were present in the area. However, the fact that linking capital was the only source of social capital soon proved to be problematic for the organisation: the leader, Michael, bases his authority on his links with higher-level formal institutions, and is effectively controlling all access, both to the national CARYM authorities, the local church authorities, and other donors (GTZ, and World Vision). Just as with VUPEG, this authority proved detrimental to the democratic development of the organisation.

These findings strongly contradict earlier research on faith-based organisations (FBOs) (Cnaan, Boddie, Handy, Yancey, & Schneider, 2002; Greely, 1997), which argues how strong social ties are developed through religious participation, and that religion as a basis for bonding creates "deeper, broader, and more sustaining relationships" (Lockhart 2005: 57). Through the creation of this religiously based bonding capital, FBOs are considered less corrupt, more participatory, more transparent, and so on. They are considered true "agents of transformation" (Clark, 2007: 77), which are more effective, and trustworthy (Silverman, 2002) than secular organisations.[33] The case of CARYM, however, shows that these 'stronger' bonding ties never came into existence, and how CARYM is not less corrupt, participatory, and transparent. On the contrary: from the beginning of the association, the important status of Michael within the local church hierarchy proved to be an important factor in hindering democratic processes within the organisation. Michael's lack of transparency, and authoritarian tendencies were easily accepted as he had always been strongly embedded within the local religious structures, and negatively affected the initial processes of participation, and accountability (e.g., the organisation of meetings). This process is similar to the conclusions from other empirical studies of African civil society groups (Barkan, McNulty, & Ayeni, 1991; Bierschenk et al., 2000; Fatton, 1995; Mohan, 2002; Patterson, 1998, 2003; Platteau & Gaspart, 2003), which describe how the links of certain leading members with powerful outside actors such as the state, or donors negatively affect the internal dynamics of groups. As Patterson (1998, p. 427) states, this "results in limited participation, skewed communication between members, and leaders, and leaders who are not accountable for their actions," which is exactly what happened with CARYM.

The case of CARYM also contradicts earlier findings on the more holistic approach of faith-based programmes. As Cnaan et al. argue: "The congregational approach to service differs from that of the professional care in that it is holistic: contact with those being served does not end when the problem disappears" (2002: 291). In other words, through their holistic approach, faith-based programmes have a more long-term commitment to their clients than secular programmes (Monsma & Soper 2003, p. 25). This was definitely not the case for CARYM: in a follow-up visit in early, 2007, the

---

33 These findings are also reflected in the policies of multilateral donors (cf. Belshaw, Calderisi, & Sugden, 2001; Marshall & Marsh, 2003; Marshall & Keough, 2004) for whom FBOs are seen as the right actors which are able to mobilise the moral energy of the faith communities in support of the Millennium Development Goals (Clark, 2007: 77). FBOs also play an important role in policy implementation in the US (Bartkowski & Regis, 2003; Monsma & Mounts, 2002).

association had virtually collapsed. As the funding from the national office had ended, the association's activities had totally stopped - CARYM Arua only existed on paper.

Conclusion

Social capital does not always promote democratic practices, but has different effects at different points. This dynamic is well characterised by a distinction between bonding, bridging, and linking social capital. In this article, three associations were described which throughout their history have developed different kinds of social capital. Three conclusions can be drawn from these case studies. Firstly, linking capital can result in a centralisation of power in the hands of the gatekeeper, negatively affecting the internal, and external democratic character of the organisation. VUPEG, and CARYM came into existence because of links to higher-level institutions, respectively, politicians, and church institutions. In both organisations, a 'development broker,' or 'gatekeeper' was regulating access to flows of information, and resources. This gatekeeper neglected all democratic procedures, but he was seen as legitimate by the individual members. This is similar to what Platteau writes about elite capture in a community-based association in West Africa

> In a context where the ability to deal with external resources of funding is concentrated in a small elite group, the bargaining strength of common people is inevitable limited, hence their ready acceptance of highly asymmetric patterns of the distribution of programme benefits. If the intervention of the elite results in an improvement in the predicament of the poor, however small that improvement, the latter tend to be thankful to their leaders: the outcome represents a Pareto improvement over the previous situation, and this is what matters after all. (Platteau 2004: 227).

Even in the instances where individuals, and groups from the wider community joined the association - and therefore introduce bridging capital - this was moulded into undemocratic patterns of power, and legitimacy. For instance, VUPEG attracted individual educated members from the wider community, and became an umbrella organisation with many community associations. It soon became clear that there was an embezzlement of funds by the Chairman, and neglect of other democratic practices. In spite of the bridging capital, it took a long time for any action to be taken, which did not prove very effective, as the Chairman soon regained his old position. In spite of his undemocratic, and corrupt practices, the Chairman therefore never lost his legitimacy.

Secondly, this first point brings us to a much larger conclusion, namely that the larger context in which CBOs operate has a profound impact on their internal dynamics. This stands in stark contrast with much of the reasoning of the social capital literature, which seems to assume that CBOs operate within a vacuum. Our case studies demonstrate how CBOs are bound by institutions, and norms in their environment, which have a strong impact on organisational outcomes, and the behaviour of individuals within the organisation (North, 1990). This corresponds with insights from the literature on new institutionalism, which emphasise the examination of rules, norms, and processes in analysing organisations: any attempt at understanding organisations has to be understood in the larger context, as formal, or informal procedures, routines, norms, and conventions do have an impact on the internal dynamics of associations[34] (Powell & Di Maggio, 1991). These institutions are not always functional with regard to achieving the organisation's goals, which Campbell (1998) (quoted in: Hall & Taylor, 1996, p. 949) described as a 'logic of social appropriateness' instead of a 'logic of instrumentality.'

The same can be argued with regard to social capital, as larger norms and institutions do shape the building of social capital in these associations. This is well reflected in our discussion on the role of the gatekeeper in CBOs, a position which is to a great extent influenced by larger norms, and institutions. Within CARYM, Michael's privileged position is to a great extent embedded in larger social hierarchies, but in particular in his role within a respected local organisation, that is, the church. This religious role acts as a strong basis of power, and legitimacy, which allows asymmetric patterns of distribution to occur within the organisation. Our findings therefore provide an important correction with regard to the assumptions about faith-based organisations, and development, as they point out how embeddedness into wider religious structures can act as a legitimating force for corruption, and undemocratic practices. A similar dynamic can be seen within VUPEG: the Chairman also bases his authority on his role in the local religious structures, but even more so on his connection to the local political sphere. This provides him with the necessary power, and legitimacy within the organisation (or at least a substantial part of this organisation).

Similarly, the specific context of a lack of access to resources has a profound impact on the formation of social capital in all three of the associations. Within VUPEG, and CARYM, this poverty, and underdevelopment makes the member rely on linking capital at all costs - even if it involves corruption on the part of the gatekeepers. Members do not necessarily care much about bonding capital, as their main preoccupation is access to resources. The OPEC boys have the same concern, but in slightly different circumstances, and with the opposite effect: in their specific situation, linking capital was initially absent. Members therefore had all advantage in making the organisation effective, that is, they had to have strong bonding capital in order to gain access to resources. This factor, in combination with their larger social, and political circumstances (e.g., feelings of political, and social marginalization), also had a profound impact on the efficient formation of bridging, and linking capital, something which has been described in detail above.

This brings us at our third conclusion: the case of the OPEC boys shows how linking capital can produce positive results when firmly embedded in bonding, and bridging capital. Whereas VUPEG, and CARYM came into existence through higher-level initiatives, the OPEC boys originated as a community initiative to "get by". This bonding social capital gradually expanded through bridging ties with the wider community, in which many young men joined their association, and in which the

---

[34] For a more detailed empirical study on how institutions affect internal dynamics in organisations, cf. Patterson (2003).

OPEC boys represented the interests of other groups. The combination of bonding and bridging finally led to linking ties with the local government, in which this particular synergy further helped the organisation to develop itself. In this sense, bonding, and bridging capital guides the behaviour of the association in linking up with higher-level institutions, and can act as a break on potentially undemocratic practices. For example, a chairperson of one of the OPEC sub-groups was, in 2004 immediately fined, and sacked from his position when he was found to be embezzling funds from the association's account. In this process of transforming from a small-scale survival initiative to a larger-scale association, democratic practices became part of the organisation. Instead of being imposed by a higher-level institution, these participatory and accountable structures arose out of need, and are embedded in the practices of the organisation.

From a theoretical point of view, these conclusions provide empirical insights with regard to the two assumptions that organisations follow a linear progression from bonding to bridging to linking social capital; and that the optimal balance in the end should include all three forms of social capital.

First of all, our cases question the progression assumption. As the cases of CARYM, and VUPEG clearly demonstrate, it is implausible that all community-based organisations always progress from bonding to bridging to linking social capital. On the contrary, it is shown how community-based organisations can be heavily dependent on linking capital for their development: from the beginning, they are created through higher-level institutions as the church, political parties, NGOs, international donors, and so on. However, our case studies do support the fact that only a progression from bonding to bridging to linking social capital seems to give the expected positive results of furthering development, and democracy. At least it is clear that community-based organisations need to be embedded in locally produced bonding, and afterwards bridging social capital, as was the case with the OPEC boys. Only then the effects of linking social capital were positive and some form of democratic governance was achieved within the organisation. This was not the case for VUPEG, and CARYM, which followed another path of social capital formation.

Secondly, our conclusions also question the normative assumption that associations should have all types of social capital in the end. An interesting question in this regard is if organisations can specialise in one type of social capital over another. The CARYM members, for example, do not care much about the association's lack of bonding capital, as the linking capital provides them with strong benefits. Then, the question is, if bonding, or bridging social capital is really needed? In the short-term they do not, as the members receive their benefits anyhow through the 'gatekeeper.' However, in the long-term, the absence of bonding, and/or bridging capital gives the association many difficulties such as authoritarian tendencies, and corruption. The rich literature on empirical studies of African civil society groups (cf. Barkan et al., 1991; Bierschenk et al., 2000; Fatton, 1995; Mohan, 2002; Patterson, 1998, 2003; Platteau & Gaspart, 2003) demonstrates how links with the state, and donors have a strong impact on the internal dynamics of these groups. As our case studies demonstrate, strong bonding, and bridging capital is needed in order to have efficient linking capital within these community associations. Specialisation in the linking type of social capital seems only plausible when organisations move away from the local level. Bebbington and Carrol (2000), for example, described how federations become specialised 'gatekeepers' for the coffee producers toward external power structures such as the international coffee market, and the state. Such extra community organisations (De Silva et al., 2007) act as intermediaries, which connect communities with national organisations, government, and the broader civil society. As these organisations no longer have to take into consideration specific community issues, they can go beyond this community level, and focus on linking capital. This is not possible for community-based associations, as strong social bonds are the very 'nature' of their organisation. They should present specific community issues, and therefore need to be embedded in their communities. As the OPEC Boys demonstrate, the bonding type of social capital has to be the very foundation of a community-based organisation in order to allow the bridging, and linking types to effectively increase the impact of the organisation.

This brings us to a more general policy conclusion about the role of external interventions in the creation of social capital. Social capital is seen as a missing link to development, and democratic governance, and external development interventions are requested to "create social capital that increases the voice, and economic opportunities of the poor" (World Bank 2000: 129–130). Supporting community associations in order to build this social capital is therefore becoming a standard donor strategy. Our case studies suggest that external interventions can not only create, or 'scale up' the impact of social capital OPEC), but social capital can also be negatively affected by them (VUPEG, and especially CARYM). External interventions can confuse the optimal combination of different forms of social capital within an association, by abruptly creating a high stock of linking social capital, bringing new resources, ideas, and information to the association. Although this can be very useful, too often the association does not possess sufficient bonding, and bridging social capital to handle this externally induced linking social capital.

In their article on community-driven development, Platteau and Gaspart (2003) cited Tilly (1985) from whom they learnt that African states received their legitimacy from the outside world, not as a result of an endogenous bargaining process between rulers, and ruled. Platteau, and Gaspart point to a similar conclusion for many African rural communities. By disbursing considerable amounts of money, and resources, external development interventions enable local leaders to build up outside legitimacy, and as a consequence, prevent the autonomous evolution of community leadership on a total accountability vis-a-vis the community members (Platteau & Gaspart 2003: 1700). Our article argues that the same analysis is valid at the associational level. In terms of social capital dynamics, when externally induced linking social capital is not embedded in more locally produced dynamics of bonding, and bridging social capital, it can prevent the autonomous evolution of accountability between the leaders, and the members of the association. This indicates the importance of an autonomous organisational dynamic progress, characterised by an optimal combination of different forms of social capital that changes over time, and context. When linking social capital is introduced without sufficiently embedded bonding, and bridging social capital, this can negatively affect the development of the organisation. External interventions in support of social capital formation should be aware of this dynamic process, in order to not negatively affect it.

References

Barkan, J. D., McNulty, M. L., & Ayeni, M. A. O. (1991). "Hometown" voluntary associations, local development, and the emergence of civil society in Western Nigeria. *The Journal of Modern African Studies*, 29(3), 457–480.

Bartkowski, J. P., & Regis, H. A. (2003). *Charitable Choices: Religion, race, and Poverty in the Post-welfare Era*. New York: New York University Press.

Bebbington, A. (1999). 'Capitals and capabilities: A framework for analyzing peasant viability, rural livelihoods and poverty.' *World Development*, 27(12), 2021–2044.

Bebbington, A., & Carrol, T. (2000). Induced social capital and federations of the rural poor. Social Capital Initiative 'Working Paper No. 19. Washington, DC: World Bank, Social Development Department'.

Belshaw, A., Calderisi, R., & Sugden, C. (Eds.) (2001). *Faith in development: Partnership between the World Bank and the churches in Africa*. Washington, DC and Oxford: Regnum Books and World Bank

Bierschenk, T., Chauveau, J. -P., & De Sardan, J. P. (2000). *Courtiers en développement: les villages africains en quête des projets*. Paris: Karthala

Briggs, X. de Souza (1998). 'Brown kids in white suburbs: Housing mobility and the multiple faces of social capital'. *'Housing Policy Debate*, 9(1), 177–221.

Brown, L. D. (1991). 'Bridging organisations and sustainable development'. *Human Relations*, 44(8), 807–831.

Campbell, J. L. (1998). 'Institutional analysis and the role of ideas in political economy'. *Theory and Society*, 27, 377–409.

Clarke, G. (2007). 'Agents of transformation? donors, faith-based organisations and international development'. *Third World Quarterly*, 28(1), 77–96.

Cleaver, F. (2005). 'The inequality of social capital and the reproduction of chronic poverty'. *World Development*, 33(6), 893–906.

Cnaan, R. A., Boddie, S. C., Handy, F., Yancey, C., & Schneider, R. (2002). *The Invisible Caring hand: American congregations and the provision of welfare*. New York: New York University Press.

Colletta, N. J., & Cullen, M. L. (2000). 'The Nexus between violent conflict, social capital and social cohesion: Case studies from Cambodia and Rwanda. Social Capital Initiative'. Working Paper No. 23. Washington, DC: World Bank, Social Development Department.

De Silva, M. J., Harpham, T., Huttly, S. R., Bartolini, M., & Penny, M. E. (2007). 'Understanding sources and types of social capital in Peru'. *Community Development Journal*, 42(1), 19–30.

Dudwick, N., Kuehnast, K., Nyhan Jones, V., & Woolcock, M. (2006). *Analyzing social capital in context. A guide to using qualitative methods and data*. Washington DC: World Bank.

Esman, M., & Uphoff, N. (1984). *Local organisations: Intermediaries in rural development*. Ithaca, NY: Cornell University Press.

Evans, P. (1996a). 'Introduction: Development strategies across the public–private divide'. *World Development*, 24(6), 1033–1037.

Evans, P. (1996b). 'Government action, social capital and development: Reviewing the evidence on synergy'. *World Development*, 24(6), 1119–1132.

Farr, J. (2004). 'Social capital: A conceptual history'. *Political Theory*, 32(1), 6–33.

Fatton, R. (1995). Africa in the age of democratisation: The civic limitations of civil society. African Studies Review, 38(2), 67–99.

Fox, J. (1996). 'How does civil society thicken? The political construction of social capital in rural Mexico'. *World Development*, 24(6), 1089–1103.

Gersony, R. (1997). 'The anguish of Northern Uganda. Kampala'. Submitted to the US Embassy, Kampala and USAID Mission, August.

Gittell, R., & Vidal, A. (1998). *Community organizing: Building social capital as a development Strategy.* Thousand Oaks, CA: Sage.

Greely, A. (1997). 'Coleman revisited, religious structures as a source of social capital'. *American Behavioral Scientist*, 40(5), 587–594.

Grootaert, C., & van Bastelaer, T. (2001). 'Understanding and measuring social capital: A synthesis of findings and recommendations from the social capital initiative. Social Capital Initiative'. Working Paper No. 24. Washington, DC: World Bank, Social Development Department.

Hall, P., & Taylor, R. (1996). 'Political science and the three new institutionalisms'. *Political Studies*, XILV, 936–957.

Heller, P. (1996). 'Social capital as a product of class mobilisation and state intervention: Industrial workers in Kerala, India'. *World Development*, 24(6), 1055–1071.

Isham, J., & Ka"hko"nen, S. (1999). 'What determines the effectiveness of community-based water projects? Evidence from Central Java, Indonesia on demand responsiveness, service rules, and social capital'. Social Capital Initiative Working Paper No. 14. Washington, DC: World Bank, Social Development Department.

Kähkönen, S. (1999). 'Does social capital matter in water and sanitation delivery? A review of literature. Social Capital Initiative'. Working Paper No. 9. Washington, DC: World Bank, Social Development Department.

Krishna, A., & Uphoff, N. (1999). 'Mapping and measuring social capital: A conceptual and empirical study of collective action for conserving and developing watersheds in Rajasthan, India'. Social Capital Initiative Working Paper No. 13. Washington, DC: World Bank, Social Development Department.

Lecoutere, E., & Titeca, K. (2007). 'The Opec Boys and the political economy of smuggling in Northern Uganda'. HICN Working Papers 36, Households in Conflict Network.

Leopold, M. (2005). *Inside West Nile*. Oxford: James Currey.

Lockhart, W. (2005). 'Building bridges and bonds: Generating social capital in secular and faith-based poverty-to-work program'. *Sociology of Religion*, 66, 45–60.

Marshall, K., & Keough, L. (Eds.) (2004). *Mind, heart and soul in the fight against poverty.* Washington, DC: World Bank.

Marshall, K., & Marsh, R. (Eds.) (2003). *Millennium challenges for development and faith institutions.* Washington, DC: World Bank.

Mohan, G. (2002). 'The disappointments of civil society: The politics of NGO intervention in northern Ghana'. *Political Geography*, 21, 125–154.

Monsma, S. V., & Soper, J. (2003). *What works: Comparing the effectiveness of welfare-to work programs in Los Angeles.* Philadelphia: Center for Research on Religion and Urban Civil Society, University of Pennsylvania.

Monsma, S. V., & Mounts, C. M. (2002). *Working faith: How religious organisations provide welfare-to-work services*. Philadelphia: Center on Research on Religion and Urban Civil Society, University of Pennsylvania.

North, D. (1990). *Institutions, institutional change and economic performance*. New York: Cambridge University Press.

Ostrom, E. (1990). *Governing the commons: The evolution of institutions for collective action*. Cambridge: Cambridge University Press.

Pantoja, E. (2000). 'Exploring the concept of social capital and its relevance for communitybased development: The case of coal mining areas in Orissa, India'. Social Capital Initiative Working Paper No. 18. Washington, DC: World Bank, Social Development Department.

Pargal, S., Huq, M., & Gilligan, D. (1999). 'Social capital in solid waste management: Evidence from Dhaka, Bangladesh'. Social Capital Initiative Working Paper No. 16. Washington, DC: World Bank, Social Development Department.

Patterson, A. S. (1998). 'A reappraisal of democracy in civil society: Evidence from rural Senegal'. *The Journal of Modern African Studies*, 36(3), 423–441.

Patterson, A. S. (2003). 'Power inequalities and the institutions of Senegalese development organisations'. *African Studies Review*, 46(3), 35–41.

Paxton, P. (2002). 'Social capital and democracy: An interdependent relationship'. *American Sociological Review*, 67(2), 254–277.

Platteau, J. P. (2004). 'Monitoring elite capture in community-driven development'. *Development and Change*, 35(2), 223–246.

Platteau, J. P., & Gaspart, F. (2003). 'The risk of resource misappropriation in communitydriven development'. *World Development*, 31(10), 1687–1703.

Portes, A. (1998). 'Social capital: Its origins and applications in modern sociology'. *Annual Review of Sociology*, 24, 1–24.

Portes, A., & Landolt, P. (1996). 'The downside of social capital'. *The American Prospect*, 26, 18–22.

Portes, A., & Landolt, P. (2000). 'Social capital: Promise and pitfalls of its role in development'. *Journal of Latin American Studies*, 32(2), 529–547.

Powell, W., & Di Maggio, P. (Eds.) (1991). *The new institutionalism in organisational analysis*. Chicago and London: The University of Chicago Press.

Prakash, S. (2002). *Social capital and the rural poor: What can civil actors and policies do? In Social capital and poverty reduction. Which role for the civil society organisations and the state?* (pp. 45–57). Paris: United Nations Educational, Scientific and Cultural Organisation (UNESCO).

Putnam, R. D. (1993). *Making democracy work: Civic traditions in modern Italy*. Princeton: Princeton University Press.

Putnam, R. D. (1995). 'Tuning in, tuning out: The strange disappearance of social capital in America'. *Political Science and Politics*, 28(4), 664–683.

Putnam, R. D. (2000). *Bowling alone. The collapse and revival of American community*. New York: Simon and Schuster.

Putnam, R. D. (2004). 'Commentary: "Health by association", some comments'. *International Journal of Epidemiology*, 33(4), 667–671.

Reid, C., & Salmen, L. (2000). 'Understanding social capital. Agricultural extension in Mali: Trust and social cohesion'. Social Capital Initiative Working Paper No. 22. Washington, DC: World Bank, Social Development Department.

Saegert, S., Thompson, J., & Warren, M. (Eds.) (2001). *Social capital and poor communities*. New York: Russen Sage Foundation.

Silverman, R. M. (2002). 'Vying for the urban poor: Charitable organisations, faith-based social capital, and racial reconciliation in a Deep South City'. *Sociological Inquiry*, 72(1), 151–165.

Skaperdas, S. (2001). 'The political economy *of organised crime: Providing protection when the state does not'. Economics of Governance*, 2, 173–202.

Sorensen, C. (2000). 'Social capital and rural development: A discussion of issues'. Social Capital Initiative Working Paper No. 10. Washington, DC: World Bank, Social Development Department.

Szreter, S. (2002). 'The state of social capital: Bringing back in power, politics, and history'. *Theory and Society*, 31(5), 573–621.

Szreter, S. & Woolcock, M. (2004). 'Health by association? Social capital, social theory, and the political economy of public health'. *International Journal of Epidemiology*, 33, 1–18.

Tilly, C. (1985). 'War making and state making as organised crime'. In P. Evans, D. Rueschemeyer, & T. Skocpol (Eds.), *Bringing the state back* in (pp. 169–191). Cambridge: Cambridge University Press.

Titeca, K. (2006). 'Les OPEC Boys en Ouganda, Trafiquants de Petrole et Acteurs Politiques'. *Politique Africaine*, 103, 143–159.

Titeca, K. (2009). 'The 'Masai' and Miraa: public authority, vigilance and criminality in a Ugandan border town'. *Journal of Modern African Studies* 47(2): 219- 317.

Titeca, K., & De Herdt, T. (2010). 'Regulation and cross-border trade: the importance of practical norms in West Nile, North Western Uganda'. *Africa*, 80(4).

Van Bastelaer, T. (2000). 'Does social capital facilitate the poor's access to credit? A review of the microeconomic literature'. Social Capital Initiative Working Paper No. 8. Washington, DC: World Bank, Social Development Department.

Woolcock, M. (1998). Social capital and economic development: Toward a theoretical synthesis and policy framework. *Theory and Society*, 27(2), 151–208.

Woolcock, M. (2002). *Social capital in theory and practice: Reducing poverty by building partnerships between states, markets and civil society.* In Social capital and poverty reduction. Which role for the civil society organisations and the state? pp. 20–44). Paris: United Nations Educational, Scientific and Cultural Organisation (UNESCO).

Woolcock, M., & Narayan, D. (2000). 'Social capital: Implications for development theory, research, and policy'. *The World Bank Research Observer*, 15(2), 225–249.

World Bank (2000). *World development Report* 2000/ 2001. New York: Oxford University Press.

6

The Social Power of Religious Organisation and Civil Society: The Catholic Church in Uganda[1]

Ronald Kassimir

Abstract

The socio-political role of civil society organisations depends in large part on their internal organisational resources and capabilities. Current work in the social sciences often focuses on the critical importance of civil society in explaining liberalisation and democratisation in Africa and other parts of the developing world. While authors taking this perspective would not deny that the power resources and internal dynamics of the organisations making up civil society influence their effectiveness, more systematic attention needs to be paid to such factors. Otherwise, analysis will continue to make presumptions about social organisations that, however 'civil', lack the capacity to effect political change. In this paper, the author uses the example of a Ugandan religious organisation to address this issue, specifying the kind of power and influence that the Catholic Church possesses in Uganda, and exploring to what extent its social power correlates with the assumptions of conventional civil society approaches.

This article poses the question of what kind of power civil society organisations possess, and argues that a key component of the answer lies in internal organisational dynamics. Scholarship that privileges the place of civil society in understanding political transitions, in Africa and elsewhere, is now pervasive in the social sciences, and donor agencies are actively seeking to strengthen civil societies on the continent. While none of the proponents of civil society actors deeply condition their political possibilities, it is striking that such considerations enter into these approaches in an unsystematic manner (when they enter into them at all). This is not only a matter of putting the

---

[1] Reprinted from Kasfir, N. *Civil Society and Democracy in Africa: Critical Perspectives*, Cass (1998) by permission of the publisher Taylor & Francis Ltd, http://www.tandfonline.com. The author wishes to thank Irving Leonard Markovitz, Aili Mari Tripp, Roger Tangri, and especially Nelson Kasfir for their comments.

theoretical cart before the empirical horse, although it is clear that we lack a great deal of knowledge about civil organisations in Africa[2]. Without a way of theorising about the social power of organisations, scholars and donors may bet on the wrong horses, that is, focus on those organisations that, however, 'civil', lack the capacity to effect political change.

Civil society organisations are often defined on an *a priori* basis, that is, scholars identify them with categories taken from other (typically Western) societies. Alternatively, these organisations are identified by what their leaders say they are or claim to be in support of, rather than in terms of what they do and for what purposes. When these self-identifications and claims conform to standard conceptualisations of 'civil' organisations, their socio-political role is often presumed independently of an analysis of the social power of these organisations. To the degree that civil society is invoked as an independent variable in explaining democratisation and democratic consolidation in Africa, the failure systematically to incorporate the power resources of social organisations into the analysis greatly limits the claims of the civil society approach.[3] The consequences of ignoring organisational capacities are, it is argued, both the perpetuation of an inflated sense of the political efficacy of empirical 'civil societies' and the rendering of 'civil society' as a weak analytical tool, indeed, it is worth asking why we should expect civil society, or any organisation that is part of it, to play an assigned role.

Below, I use the example of a Ugandan religious organisation to address this question. One observer has written of "the immense influence that the Christian churches have over the majority of the population in Uganda".[4] In the analysis that follows, I specify *what kind of influence the churches* have in Ugandan society and politics, and explore to what extent this influence correlates with the *a priori* assumptions of civil society approaches.

When applied to Africa, civil society approaches tend to focus on normative dimensions, while the social power of organisations is either assumed, ignored or treated as exogenous to its role in making civil society effective. For example, by insisting that civil society organisations are those that promote participatory values and a sense of political efficacy among their members or by stressing how they relate to the state

---

2 One author rightly states that there is "a wide gap existing between theory and Concrete investigation. That is, little empirical work has been undertaken by the champions of 'civil society' to substantiate or elaborate their theoretical assertions". M.G. Ngunyi, 'Religious Institutions and Political Liberalisation in Kenya', in P. Gibbon (ed.), *Markets, Civil Society and Democracy in Kenya* (Uppsala, Nordiska Afrikainstitutet, 1995), 122.

3 In is superb study of the political orientation and organisational power of NOGs in Kenya, S.N. Ndegwa "treats civil society actions as the dependent variables that need to be explained rather than as the causal variables of political reforms", *The Two Faces of Civil Society: NGOs and Politics in Africa* (West Hartford, CT: Kumarian Press, 1996), 110, emphasis in original.

4 J. M. Waliggo, 'The Role of Christian Churches in the Democratisation Process in Uganda 1980-1993', in P. Gifford (ed.), *The Christian churches and the Democratisation of Africa* (Leiden: E.J. Brill, 1995), 224.

- that is, that they engage the state but are autonomous from it[5] - these approaches divert attention from the politics going on inside organisations that contribute to their potential for political influence. But until we know what organisations can and cannot do - that is, what kind of power they hold - we can say little about their capacity to contribute to political change.[6] Here I argue that a focus on capacity, and especially *internal organisational dynamics*, can provide a handle for grasping the power of social organisations. By internal dynamics, I mean the relationships among organisational leaders as they attempt to define and purse the goals of their organisation, and between them and their members or followers.

Without understanding the social power of civil society organisations, and especially their internal politics, the invocation of civil society as an analytical tool will continue to be asserted rather than demonstrated. Foley and Edwards have identified two basic variants of the civil society approach that make strong claims on behalf of the power of civil society. What they label 'Civil Society I' is associated with neo-Tocquevillian approaches and focuses on the "ability of associational life in general and of the habits of association in particular to foster patterns of civility in the actions of citizens in a democratic polity".[7] Viewed from the lens of social power, I call this the power of organisational leaders to socialise members by instilling participatory norms and a sense of efficacy in social and political life. What Foley and Edwards label 'Civil Society II' construes "civil society as a sphere of action that is independent of the state and that is capable - precisely for this reason - of energising resistance to a tyrannical regime".[8] There is no necessary reason to privilege opposition in this version (though many civil society approaches do this). Thus, one could also include as possible action support for democratic regimes and/or an insistence on their accountability. Viewed through the lens of social power, I call this the power of organisational leaders to mobilise members to promote political change.

Foley and Edwards, in their critique, emphasise the contradictions between these two versions of civil society. I would add that, in practice, many conventional civil society approaches combine them through suggesting that socialisation may be necessary for mobilisation, that is, that norms and a sense of empowerment transform actors' identities and interests in ways that affect the nature and direction of mobilisation. Here, I will concentrate on mobilisation, incorporating the issue of socialisation when it influences the former. The broader point is that civil society approaches put

---

5   For typical cases, see J.W. Harbeson, 'Civil Society and Political Renaissance in Africa', in J.W. Harbeson, D. Rothchild and N. Chazan (eds.), *Civil Society and the State in Africa* (Boulder, CO: Lynne Rienner, 1994).1-29, L. Diamond, 'Rethinking Civil Society: Toward Democratic Consolidation', *Journal of Democracy*, 5, 3 (1994), 4-17; and N. Chazan, 'Africa's Democratic. Challenge', *World Policy Journal*, 9, 2 (1992), 279-308.

6   See Ndegwa's savvy discussion of the 'organisational power' of NGOs in *The Two Faces of Civil Society*, chapters 2 and 6, and M. Bratton's analysis of the relationship between organisational autonomy and organisational capacity in 'Peasant-State Relations in Postcolonial Africa: Patterns of Engagement and Disengagement', in J.S. Migdal, V. Shue and A. Kohli (eds.), *State Power and Social Forces Domination and Transformation in the Third World* (Cambridge: Cambridge University Press, 1994), 231-54.

7   M.W. Foley and B. Edwards, 'The Paradox of Civil Society', *Journal of Democracy*, 5, 3 (1996), 39.

8   Ibid., 39.

mobilisation and socialisation at centre-stage, but their *a priori* lens lacks the tools for analysing these processes. By looking at civil organisations through the lens of social power and the ways in which internal organisational dynamics affect capacities for mobilisation and socialisation, I demonstrate the limits of putting current efforts at political reform in Africa in the frame of civil society.

The Roman Catholic Church in Uganda provides a revealing case study for exploring the power of an organisation to mobilise and socialise. The church is not a 'typical' example of a civil organisation, nor is Uganda typical of the contexts within which social organisations operate. Rather, the case demonstrates that a focus on organisational capacities, viewed through the lens of social power, has broad applicability to understand social organisations and the efficacy of civil society in the trajectory of political transitions on the continent.

Catholicism, civil society and organisational dynamics

One reason to focus on organisational capacities is that it offers a picture of what churches do 'on the ground'. This picture provides a means of assessing the predominant, although not unanimous[9], view that African Christian churches are 'naturally' leading organisations in civil society and the democratisation process, destined to play out a role resembling the one attributed to Poland's Catholic Church in the 1980s. This *a priori* optimism for Christian churches in Africa tends to conflate the political stance of religious organisations with their political efficacy, and their relative autonomy from the state with their capacities to effect change.[10] Much of this confusion among the optimists is tied to the claims made by church officials regarding their own position, and thus the place of the organisation they lead, in political, social and moral reform. The Kenyan Catholic Church has declared itself the 'conscience of society',[11] while the Ugandan Catholic hierarchy dons the mantle of the "moral conscience of the nation" and proclaims that "the saving Gospel of Jesus Christ is the *most effective instrument* for a fundamental change of the human person and human society".[12] However, whatever the intentions or degree of sincerity of these religious leaders, it is clear that they cannot through the act of public discourse, will themselves into becoming the exemplars of civil society. Without the organisational capacities to take on the declared

---

9 For example, J. Haynes, *Religion and Politics in Africa* (London: Zed Books, 1996), chapter 4.
10 Examples of this optimism can be found in some of the essays in P. Gifford (ed.), *The Christian Churches and the Democratisation of Africa* (Leiden: E.J. Brill, 1995); and H. Assefa and G. Wachira (eds.), *Peacemaking and Democratisation in Africa: Theoretical Perspectives and Church Initiatives* (Nairobi: East African Educational Publishers, 1996).
11 This is the title of a recently published collection of the pastoral letters of the Kenyan Episcopal conference: R. Mejia, S.J (ed.), *The Conscience of Society: The Social Teaching of the Catholic Bishops of Kenya (Nairobi: Pauline Publications Africa*, (1995), Interestingly, the title is taken from a speech given by Jomo Kenyatta to a gathering of East African Catholic Bishops in 1976: 'The Church is the conscience of society, and today society needs a conscience. Do not be afraid to speak.'
12 Catholic Bishops of Uganda, *With a New Heart and a New Spirit* (Kisubi, UG: St. Paul Publications-Africa. 1986), 69, 10.

role of a leading institution, such pronouncements may only have the effect of creating expectations that are not met.[13]

Thus, scholarly discussions of the role of the African Christian Churches in political reform tend to parallel the bold assertions of church leaders. Several examples can be found in the most detailed volume to date that describes this role. The editor, Paul Gifford, argues in his introduction that, while past accounts of African churches and politics construed religious organisations as passive or reactive, in the recent work "the direction of influences to be traced has now been reversed; it is less how the churches have responded to political developments, than how they are helping to shape them".[14] While creating analytical space for the agency of the churches is laudatory, this orientation risks making the same mistake as older approaches, that is, privileging one particular perspective. It also mirrors the same *a priori* assumptions of civil society approaches by deciding in advance that civil organisations are principally independent variables, and assigning them a role rather than analysing it.

While subscribing to the view that democratisation efforts on the continent constitute Africa's 'second liberation', Gifford is cognisant that there have been serious obstacles to the extension and consolidation of democratic rule. He adds that "if any real change is to be effected the contribution of the churches is therefore even more critical than ever".[15] Such a formulation tends toward tautology. If democratisation succeeds, it is in large part due to the churches. If it fails or stalls, then the churches are needed more than ever. There is no room here for a scenario in which the churches' role is marginal, or where their inactivity is constructive for democratic rule. The point is not that the churches do not have a significant role. Rather, it is that this role cannot be assumed *a priori*.

Finally, the optimistic view endorses the image of a natural connection between civil society and democratisation, within which the churches are inserted:

> From this perspective of civil society, it is obvious why churches are seen as so important to Africa's democratisation. In so many one-party states, the churches were the greatest single element of civil society. The contribution of the churches to Africa's democratisation and the ways in which this contribution could be increased have become important areas of study.[16]

If this is the case, it is incumbent to show the precise *mechanisms* through which churches take a major position in civil society. However, not all church mechanisms for intervening in the democratisation process provide evidence of its 'civil' nature or qualities, at least if the concept of civil society is to have any specificity and avoid tautology. In other words, the intervention of churches on behalf of political reform is not necessarily through their location in civil society. In addition, churches are complex

---

13 At a 1993 conference of East African religious leaders, Gifford reports that 'some delegates actually argued that church was Africa's "only hope for social change". P. Gifford, 'Introduction: Democratisation and the Churches', in Clifford (ed.), *The Christian Churches and the Democratisation of Africa*, 9.
14 Ibid., 11, emphasis in original.
15 Ibid., 13.
16 Ibid., 8.

organisations with complex goals. A democratic political vision may be seen as a means to some other end - be it the protection or extension of institutional privileges or social justice for the masses - as well as an end in itself. It is thus crucial to see how organisations act to defend themselves as institutions in order to understand their capacities to play effective roles in confronting states and promoting democracy.

Religious institutions, and the Catholic Church in particular, have a diverse repertoire of mechanisms, only some of which are related to their 'civil' nature - as conceptualised by civil society approaches, these are neo-Tocquevillian socialisation and political mobilisation. But churches have other ways of intervening in the public sphere that need not rely on these 'civil' mechanisms: the participation of church leaders in elite social networks, formal and informal diplomacy, service provision and development projects. Even official church discourse addressing public matters would be a dimension of its 'civil' role only if these pronouncements are connected to socialisation and mobilisation capacities. Indeed, all of these mechanisms have been part of the church's repertoire for centuries, long before the emergence of civil societies in continental Europe.[17] None of them require the participation of the laity in order to be effective, although they may imply that, if the church does not achieve its ends or is threatened, a broader activation of the laity may ensue.

Civil society approaches can only bring specificity to the concept, and make an argument about its efficacy in political change, by demonstrating that the leaders of civil organisations connect with their members and the wider public via the mechanisms of socialisation and mobilisation. Only once it is established that these capacities are present does it make sense to worry about whether these organisations influence politics and the public sphere in 'civil' ways - that is, promote 'civil' values through 'civil' means in pursuit of 'civil' ends. In this regard, Gifford notes an important paradox in the present role of African churches. It has been the mainline Protestant and Catholic churches that have been most closely involved in political reform efforts on the continent, while African independent churches and newly established Pentecostal churches have tended to be either quiescent or supportive of recalcitrant authoritarian regimes. Yet it is the latter churches that demonstrate an ability to socialise their members into a new sense of personal and social efficacy under trying conditions, and, on occasion, to mobilise them for both religious and other purposes. Gifford writes that "*in theory* there is no reason why the mainline churches should not play such a role; but in practice it seems that the newer Pentecostal churches have been able to achieve these ends in a way that the mainline churches have not".[18] Ironically, the African churches that evince the neo-Toquevillian attributes seen as the *sine qua non* of a 'civil' organisation in some approaches are the ones least disposed to support, and organise on behalf of, democratisation. At the same time, the mainline churches have rarely done so through the civil mechanisms of socialisation and mobilisation. A clear example is the role of Catholic bishops as titular heads of national conferences in West Africa.[19] This has

---

17 S. Kalyvas, *The Rise of Christian Democracy in Europe* (Ithaca. NJ: Cornell University Press, 1996).
18 Gifford, 'Introduction', 6, my emphasis.
19 See Haynes, *Religion and Politics in Africa*; Gifford, 'Introduction'; and P. Gifford, 'Some Recent

occurred through the long-standing church mechanisms of diplomacy and arbitration that do not require, and in fact did not involve, the mobilisation of members.

Of course, *in theory* there are reasons why the mainline churches do not play their assigned role. The problem is that the relevant theories lie outside the civil society approach. Concepts in organisation theory and the sociology of religion, especially the distinction between churches and sects, require an analysis of internal organisational dynamics that do not fit easily with *a priori* assumptions. In an instructive analysis of the Kenyan case where the mainline Christian churches did have some success in mobilising and socialising members against the Moi regime, while independent and evangelical churches rallied to its support, Ngunyi shows how divergent church histories, internal modes of authority, intra-church conflict and organisational interests account both for religious mobilisation and the diverse purposes to which it is directed. Rather than construing the mainline churches as acting out their assigned role in civil society and the others as pathological deviants, he provides a far richer and empirically grounded analysis. For the mainline churches, Ngunyi argues that the protection of once privileged status, ethnic sympathies, state manipulation and support for lay empowerment and participation intertwine in explaining their challenge to the political *status quo*.[20]

Since the coming to power in 1989 of the National Resistance Movement (NRM) headed by Yoweri Museveni, the role of Uganda's Catholic church has been quite different from its sister church in neighbouring Kenya. On the one hand, the Ugandan church appears to have acted in ways consistent with the expectation of civil society approaches. Preaching and making formal pronouncements supportive of everything from democracy, clean and accountable government, human rights, women's rights and personal security, it has used its access to substantial donor aid to engage in an array of development projects, and encouraged church members to participate in the constitution-making process, elections, and serving in the local council system introduced by the NRM.

On the other hand, it is very difficult to measure the effectiveness of church leaders' statements, since they often coincide with the NRM's own political discourse. In many ways, church officials have had close and collaborative relations with the regime.[21]

Developments in African Christianity', *African Affairs*, 93 (1994), 513—34.

20 Ngunyi, 'Religious Institutions and Political Liberalisation in Kenya'. The role of churches in Kenya has attracted much attention from scholars. See A.C. Abuom, 'The Churches' Involvement in the Democratisation Process in Kenya', in H. Assefa and G. Wachira (eds), *Peacemaking and Democratisation in Africa: Theoretical Perspectives and Church initiatives* (Nairobi: East African Educational Publishers, 1996), 93-116; M. Bratton, 'Civil Society and Political Transitions in Africa', in Harbeson, Rothchild and Chazan (eds.), *Civil Society and the State in Africa*, 51-81; G. Sabar-Friedman, 'Church and State in Kenya, 1986-1992: The Churches' Involvement in the "Game of Change", *African Affairs*, 96(1997), 25-52; and D. Throup, '"Render unto Caesar the Things that are Caesar's": The Politics of Church-State Conflict in Kenya, 1978-1990', in H.B. Hansen and M. Twaddle (eds.), *Religion and Politics in East Africa: The Period Since Independence* (London: James Currey, 1995), 143-76.

21 R. Kassimir, 'Ambiguous Institution: The Catholic Church and Uganda's Reconstruction in the First Five Years of the NRM', in Leonardo Villalon and Philip Huxtable (eds.), *The African State at a Critical Juncture* (Boulder, CO: Lynne Rienner, 1998).

Moreover, it is striking that, on many of the most critical issues facing Uganda, the church has been relatively silent. It has not taken part in public debates regarding the acceptance of structural adjustment packages and economic reform in general, nor on other issues like land reform and the occasional arrest of journalists. On the controversial decision by the government to impose a value-added tax, which was protested against vigorously by local business people, the church did enter the debate, but only to oppose the tax's application to foreign donations.[22] Until 1996, it made little effort to press the NRM to seek a peaceful negotiation to the unending rebellion in northern Uganda. Even the government-run newspaper labelled the church's intervention as long "overdue".[23] The church's peace and justice programme, which was to establish offices across the country, has been moribund in most dioceses.

Thus, church leaders have played a strikingly ambiguous role in Ugandan civil society. I will examine this role by gauging the church's capacity for mobilisation and socialisation in several different arenas. First, I examine the fluctuating and divided position of church officials on what is perhaps Uganda's most contentious political issue, whether to maintain the no-party movement system of the NRM or return to a multi-party system. As support for and action on behalf of the latter is an important component of what a civil society organisation is 'supposed' to do, the church's role is hard to grasp via a civil society approach. A focus on internal organisational dynamics, the legacy of the church's past experience in political mobilisation and its present capacities provides a better angle from which to explain its current ambivalence toward multi-party competition.

Catholic organisation and political mobilisation

In Uganda, the connection between religious organisations and political mobilisation has been dominated by a rather unusual phenomenon in African politics: the rise of political parties whose base of support is rooted (or perceived to be rooted) in religious identities with the active intervention of church officials. This section analyses the role of Catholic Church leaders in partisan mobilisation, the relationship between church officials and lay leaders of the 'Catholic party', and the church's broader position in the debate on multi-party politics in Uganda under the NRM.

In 1989, a public statement by a group of Catholic Church leaders signalled a surprising shift in Ugandan politics that goes against the expectations of conventional notions of civil society. Only three years earlier, in the first pastoral letter issued by the Uganda Episcopal Conference after the capture of state power by the NRM, Uganda's Catholic bishops declared that "a multi-party system of government is an expression of the fundamental freedom of assembly and association guaranteed by our National Constitution".[24] The NRM came to power determined to replace the multi-party

---

22 *Uganda News Bulletin*, Aug. 26, 1997.
23 *New Vision*, June 18, 1996.
24 *With a New Heart and a New Spirit*, 77. Elsewhere in this document, the bishops wrote that "the leaders of the church, represented by the hierarchy and the clergy, will not identify themselves with any particular political grouping", 68.

system which had characterised periods of civilian rule in Uganda's post-colonial history with a 'movement system', that is, non-party politics. It promptly banned party activity, especially during elections, although it allowed existing parties to maintain headquarters, hold private meetings and publish newspapers.

In 1989, as the NRM was initiating an elaborate process to construct a new constitution, the bishops issued a pastoral letter which dropped their insistence on the appropriate party system: "As to the concrete question of what form of government Uganda should adopt, we must state clearly that the church does not advocate any one form."[25]

This shift of the official church's political vision to, in effect, neutrality regarding the question of parties in Uganda is momentous not only because of its past advocacy of multi-partyism, but also because of past ties between Catholic religious identity and one of Uganda's leading political parties-the Democratic party (DP) – whose support was seen as predominantly Ugandan Catholic. From 1986 up to the present, the DP has been in the forefront in demanding that a multi-party system be included in the new constitution. But in this it failed. Uganda's new constitution, which took force in October 1995, continues the no-party movement system of the NRM for five more years, after which a referendum on the future of party competition will be held.

The logic of conventional civil society approaches suggests a contradictory account of this watershed event. On the one hand, the church's abandonment of support for multi-partyism could be interpreted as problematic for freedom of association in civil society and prospects for democratisation. On the other hand, the church's abandonment of the DP's position could be understood as the de-linking of a 'primordial' political identity (that is, Catholicism) and its institutional representative (that is, the church) from the political arena, a positive development for civil society.[26] Looking at the shift in the church's position through the lens of social power, and particularly the organisation's mobilisational capacity, provides a richer interpretation - one that takes full account of intra-organisational dynamics, in particular, the relationship between church officials and lay elites. However, the church's role in Ugandan political mobilisation must also be viewed historically. It has often been asserted that church leaders were the primary agents of the mobilisation of lay Catholics in support of the DP. But a more nuanced reading of the party's history shows that efforts to mobilise Catholics by church leaders were not straightforward, or even central. Lay elites and activists were, in fact, the central actors in the formation and expansion of the party. Church officials were

---

25 Catholic Bishops of Uganda, *Towards a New National Constitution* (Kisubi, UG: Marianum Press. 1989), 19. They continued: "The Church does not censure any government, *of whatever form*, provided that the whole governmental system is constituted in such a way that it is able to guarantee the common good, that is the respect of human rights and the welfare, both spiritual and material, of the citizens", 20, my emphasis.

26 For aim argument against seeing religious identity in Uganda as 'primordial', see R. Kassimir, 'Catholics and Political Identity in Toro', in Hansen and Twaddle (eds.), *Religion and Politics in East Africa*, 120-40.

certainly allies of the laity, but never controlled the party. In fact, church leaders and party activists sometimes clashed; their interests intersected but were never identical.

The particular kind of religious pluralism that prevailed in Uganda prepared the way for the association of religious identities with parties. Under British colonial rule, the Anglican Church, despite its smaller membership compared with the Catholics, operated in many ways as a de facto established church, especially in the kingdom areas in the south and west of the protectorate. Lay Catholics, and especially elite Catholics, experienced discrimination in public sector employment and in access to other forms of patronage under indirect rule native governments. This situation of Anglican privilege, and the grievance it engendered among Catholic clergy and laity, was the raw material used by DP leaders to mould a political support base.

The DP was launched in the mid-1950s as a response to court politics in the Buganda kingdom, where a leading catholic chief was denied the prime ministership through backstage dealings by Protestant politicians and the Buganda king. Catholic chiefs and other elite Catholic Baganda organised the DP in response to this incident on the presumption that, with the Buganda parliament (*lukiiko*) ostensibly moving towards direct elections, they could take through the ballot box what was being denied them by established mechanisms of patron-client politics, which favoured Anglicans.

Catholics elites in other districts in the protectorate, experiencing similar discrimination in their local governments, soon opened DP branches. By the late 1950s, the DP existed as a relatively decentralised party that began developing national-level structures as Uganda moved towards independence. Its building blocks were disgruntled elites who tapped into lay associations established by the missionaries under the rubric of Catholic Action, the primary mode of lay organisation developed by the church in Europe after World War I. They also reached out to Catholic professional organisations, especially the Catholic Teachers Guild.

To varying degrees, and with varying levels of openness, church officials supported the party through sermons, publications, and backstage exhortation.[27] At the time of the DP's formation, the church unambiguously applauded it: "There is a new political association of Catholics in formation, and it is received with enthusiasm in all Catholic quarters,…it will be called the 'Democratic party' and will allow non-Catholics to join."[28]

As nationalist activity increased in the latter half of the 1950s, the church urged voters to support parties that guaranteed religious freedom and especially the rights of parents to choose the form of their children's education. The latter was a thinly disguised code for continued church control over their schools, which the DP supported. Connected to this was an attack on parties seen as communist or as 'fellow travellers'- a label applied to the populist Uganda National Congress (the first Ugandan political

---

[27] For the only detailed case study. See A.G.G. Gingyera-Pincywa, *Issues in Pre-Independence Politics in Uganda: A Case Study on the Contribution of Religion to Political Debate in Uganda in the Decade 1952-62* (Kampala: East African Literature Bureau, 1976).

[28] Uganda National Council of Catholic Action, *Memorandum on the Situation of the Catholic Mission in the Uganda Protectorate* (1956), 7.

party) and its successor, the Uganda People's Congress (UPC). As the leadership of these parties was predominantly Protestant, Catholic Church officials denounced these parties both as serving Protestant interests and as Communist-influenced.[29]

Many Ugandan Catholics, whether or not taking the communist accusation seriously, did perceive the UPC as a party controlled by Protestants, just as many Protestants had come to see the DP as a Catholic party.[30] Elite Catholics surely saw the UPC's goal, in part, as maintaining the system of Protestant privilege in most of Uganda's districts. DP leaders seemed to be largely successful, though varying from district to district, in mobilising ordinary Catholic voters. However, no exit polls exist that would confirm Catholic voting support for the DP in any election. In effect, elite Catholics established a potential alternate network of patron-client ties to the existing system from which many Catholics were shut out. It is certainly plausible that loyalty to the church influenced ordinary Catholics to support the DP, although this claim lacks solid evidence. In most cases it can be more persuasively hypothesised that this was secondary to the motivation that the interest of Catholics was best served by ending the system of Protestant privilege.

Thus, to the degree that the DP gained the support of ordinary Catholics, it was able to overcome the fluidity of Catholic social identity through constructing a sense of common political interest.[31] The existence of a political organisation founded by elite Catholics helped to 'create' a Catholic political identity and interest as much as a pre-existing interest led in some natural way to the formation of the party.[32] This interest was defined and mobilised by lay party leaders; the role of church officials, while present, was clearly secondary.

The DP's association with Catholicism is complicated by its putative ties to Christian Democracy. Some observers, such as Colin Leys, have argued, without offering any direct evidence, that the party's name was shortened from Christian Democracy Party.[33] The DP's 1984 official history, while playing down such connections and arguing against the claims that the DP was a 'confessional' party, hardly helps its own case since

---

29 'The Protestant approach to life, in Uganda, and its tendency to consider Protestantism as a step-stone [sic] to wealth, social superiority and power, is not alien to the spread of radicalist ideas', Uganda National Council of Catholic Action, *Memorandum*, 63.

30 The acronyms for the two parties were popularly satirised as religious emblems. DP became *Dini ya Papa*, (Swahili for 'Religion at the Pope') while UPC became United Protestants of Canterbury.

31 See Kassimir, 'Catholics and Political Identity'. In a sense, this is reverse of Latin's case study of the Yoruba, where fairly well-defined and relatively stable notions at Anglican and Muslim identity did not evolve into a sense of common political interest and organisation. See D.D. Latin, *Hegemony and Culture: Politics and Religious Change Among the Yoruba*, Chicago, IL: University of Chicago Press, 1986).

32 Kalyvas discusses a similar process of Catholic political identity formation in nineteenth-century Europe in *The Rise of Christian Democracy*, chapter 1.

33 "[T]he fact that it was originally to have been called the Christian Democratic Party indicates the analogy with European Democratic parties which guided the thinking of the founders of the DP." C. Leys, *Politicians and Policies. An Essay on Politics in Acholi, Uganda 1962-5* (Nairobi: East African Publishing House, 1967), 5-6. Even if the first past of this claim is true, it is not proof that Christian Democracy 'guided the thinking' of the DP's founders.

the volume was edited by a staff member of Christian Democratic International, was published in Rome, and includes photographs of party president Paul Ssemogerere with various European Christian Democratic party leaders and Pope John Paul II.[34]

The image of the DP as a Christian Democratic Party in the European mode, while valid in some respects, obscures as much as it reveals, at least to the degree that it implies that support is based upon socialisation into a Catholic political vision rather than a form of machine politics.[35] Unlike Christian Democracy in Western Europe (as well as Latin America), the DP was formed as a response to discrimination against Catholics in public sector employment and their treatment at the hands of Protestant chiefs, not in opposition to class-based secular movements (liberalism, Marxism) seeking to expunge the church and religious faith from the political arena. European and Latin American parties, in their origins, had more overt Catholic content regarding ideology, social values and safeguarding the status of the church. In the DP's political discourse, the only overt pro-church position was its support for continued church control over education. In general, the DP's raison d'être was far more the social mobility of lay Catholics than the promotion of a Christian world view or the protection of church privileges.

Church leaders seem to have been far more attached to the ideals of Christian Democracy than party activists. The most important point is that a distinction can be made between church support for the party and church control over its ideology and politics.[36] As Gingyera-Pincywa documents, the discourse on Christian Democracy that emerged in Uganda in the late 1950s was produced and disseminated by the church, not DP leaders. He also notes that in most instances the DP's policies were not easily distinguishable from the UPC, and in fact the DP promoted some policies not in accord with the tenets of Christian Democracy as it had been explicated by the church. Rather than supporting a party infused with Christian Democratic principles, the church was attempting to bring the DP, formed largely for other reasons, to these

---

34 See R Muscat (ed.), *A Short History of the Democratic Party 1954-1984* (Rome: Foundation for African Development, 1984). To make matters more complicated, the volume was ghost-written by a Makerere University History Professor who is a Protestant DP supporter.

35 In his landmark study of Christian Democracy, Michael P. Fogarty identified the DP as a Christian Democratic movement, noting in a new preface to his book "the victory in the Uganda elections of 1961 of the Democratic Party, of primarily Catholic inspiration and with encouragement front the clergy and Catholic Action," *Christian Democracy in Western Europe, 1820-1953* (Westport, CT: Greenwood Press. 1957, 1974), xxvi. It is also true that over the years the DP has received advice and financial support from international Christian Democratic organisations, and particularly parties in Germany and Italy. Of course, these parties, and especially the latter, have become better known for machine rather than ideological politics.

36 Michael Twaddle writes: "But had the DP really been established quite so firmly as a confessional party on the European Christian Democratic model in the early 1950s, one would expect more philosophical underpinning than just a few unfriendly remarks by one expatriate priest and just one pastoral letter ostensibly designed more to protect Catholic interests in schools than to foster the development of any one political party" 'Was the Democratic Party of Uganda Purely Confessional Party?', in Edward Fashole-Luke et al (eds.), *Christianity in Independent Africa* (Bloomington, IN: Indiana University Press, 1978, 260.

principles.[37] Church support was not the same as church control, and its relationship with the party was a marriage of intersecting rather than identical interests. Once formed, the DP consistently pursued its own agenda and, while remaining respectful to the institution, rarely took the church's priorities as its priorities.

Even this respectfulness had its limits, as two brief examples will illustrate. When the UPC, in coalition with the Buganda-based and Protestant-dominated Kabaka Yekka Party, emerged victorious over DP in Uganda's 1962 independence election, it brought to power a government largely controlled by Protestants, exactly what the DP and the church had feared. In 1964, the UPC government announced a drastic nationalisation of church schools. While this affected both Anglican and Catholic institutions, it was protested against with much greater vehemence by the Catholic Church, not only because of its traditional concerns with autonomy and control over the socialisation of the laity, but because church leaders surmised (correctly, as it turned out) that Anglicans would, in many instances, be appointed as heads of Catholic schools. However, the degree of social protest against the nationalisation was quite muted among the laity and the DP.[38] Indeed, at the very moment when the Catholic Church was under its greatest threat since the early missionary period, large numbers of DP parliamentarians were crossing the floor to join the UPC.

The following year, a row developed between the bishop of the Catholic Diocese of Fort Portal and local DP leaders in Toro, largely because the latter accused the Bishop of not standing by them in their battle against the UPC-dominated local government. The bishop ended the affair by dissolving the Toro Catholic council, which the local administration had accused of being a DP front allied with a rebellion in the southern part of the kingdom. Apparently, church leaders in Toro could not accept an organised group of lay members claiming to represent Catholics who "were constantly undermining Diocesan authority and causing friction in the diocese", thus disturbing "the peace of the church".[39]

Thus, Catholic Church leaders by the mid-1960s could literally not win for losing. When the church was under threat (the school issue), the supposedly Catholic DP not only attempted a meagre defence, but many of its leading members joined the party that implemented the policy. On the other side, lay Catholic leaders and DP loyalists in Toro were trying to pull church leaders closer to their cause, producing internal divisions and ultimately the decommissioning of the leading lay association in Fort

---

37 At times, the church appeared to believe that the DP was already a Christian Democratic party. Thus, Gingyera-Pincywa is correct in referring to this as "wishful thinking or an attempt to read into the Party's policy something it did not have". *Issues in Pre-independence Politics*, 205.

38 Kathleen G. Lockard writes that most teachers, including Catholics, welcomed the nationalisation. "In general the teachers felt that their own self-interest lay more on the side at government control, since the churches as employers had traditionally demanded high standards of Christian morality of their teachers, particularly on the question of monogamous marriage." 'Religion and Political Development in Uganda 1962-1972' (Ph.D. Dissertation University of Wisconsin-Madison. 1974), 336.

39 *Annual Report, Lay Apostolate in Fort Portal Diocese*, 1966. A new association, set up to take the place of the Toro Catholic Council, contained within its constitution: "no Catholic Association can be tolerated or allowed in a Diocese if its aims and actions as well as its procedures disturb the peace of the Church" For more details, see Kassimir, 'Catholics and Political Identity'.

Portal Diocese. Although this need not signify that church leaders had begun to regret their support for the DP, it does echo the dangers seen by late nineteenth-century European church leaders in lay mobilisation.[40] Once lay leaders gained some autonomy from the institution, and a base of support outside church channels, they developed interests of their own - their support for the church when it was under threat was not guaranteed, and a tendency to make representative claims on behalf of Catholics challenged the church's hegemony.

By 1966, Uganda first moved towards a one-party state under the UPC and then almost a decade of authoritarianism following the military coup led by Idi Amin. These devastating political conditions almost eliminated the DP's existence until 1979, when Amin was ousted by the Tanzanian army in alliance with Ugandan dissident groups. The party re-surfaced to contest the 1980 post-Amin election of that year as an organisation that still maintained roots in the lay Catholic community, but that had also taken on a regional cast as many Protestant Baganda and other Protestant southerners flocked to the DP to prevent the return of UPC.[41] Church leaders, who had made the institution available as a refuge for members during the Amin years but mostly avoided voicing public critique and opposition[42] again supported the DP in this election, although less overtly than in the late 1950s and early 1960s, and with less unanimity. It is difficult to tell whether this support occurred because it saw the DP as a Catholic party, or because there was no alternative to preventing a UPC victory. Given what was now a more diverse social base for the DP, and the past experience described above, the latter seems more plausible.

Milton Obote and the UPC returned to power in the 1980 election, which most observers and many Ugandans believe would have been won by DP were it not for massive vote-rigging on behalf of the UPC. The rigging was the ostensible motivation for Museveni and his colleagues to start their guerrilla war. The war may have sown the seeds for a further gap between the church and the party. Even in the 1980 elections, some Catholic priests in Western Uganda had forged connections to Museveni's fledging Uganda Patriotic Movement party (UPM), which fared poorly in the 1980 elections.

---

40 See Kalyvas, *The Rise of Christian Democracy*, Chapters 1 and 2.

41 In his autobiography, Yoweri Museveni claims that this caused consternation for older DP leaders who felt that the influx would dilute its ability to pursue Catholic elite interests: "Frightened by the new members, the old Catholic originals [of DP] starting talking of themselves as the only legitimate *members of the party, banasangwaawo, and referring to the newcomers as upstarts."* Sowing the Mustard Seed: The Struggle for Freedom and Democracy in Uganda* (London: Macmillan Publishers, 1997), 118. This is echoed even today by the Mobilisers Group, which emerged from within the party in the early 1990s to criticise the DP leadership's occasional alliances with the NRM and to purify it back to its roots (although it never framed the matter as Catholic roots).

42 M. Louise Pirouet remarks that, under Amin, "The churches found themselves dragged, against their will, into becoming foci of opposition, until eventually they became feared by those in power". 'Religion in Uganda under Amin', *Journal of Religion in Africa*, 11, (1980), 13. This is notably different from the pro-active stance taken by the mainline Kenyan churches in opposition to Moi, making it remarkable that Sabar-Friedman would state that in relation to the Kenyan churches "It is interesting to note that, although significantly different in (their) historical background and [their] political affiliation, both the Anglican and Roman Catholic Churches of Uganda have taken upon themselves a similar role" under Amin and Obote. 'Church and State in Kenya', 29.

During the guerrilla struggle in Toro, not only lay members, but some priests as well, supported and even joined the NRA. When Obote was overthrown in a military coup by northern army officers in 1985, the DP agreed to support the coup leaders. Even though these officers were Catholics, many southern Catholics (priests and laity) who were otherwise DP sympathisers saw this move as a sell-out. When the NRM defeated the military regime six months later, church connections with DP varied greatly across regions: fairly strong in the north (now seen as threatened and ripe for retribution under a southern-dominated NRM), mixed in Buganda and weakest in most parts of the west.

This is the historical trajectory within which to situate the church's turnaround from openly supporting a return to a multi-party system to neutrality. In 1990, one year after the bishops' declaration of neutrality, an all-Uganda meeting of priests to discuss the constitutional debate produced a formal recommendation in support of a multi-party system.[43] This opinion was far from unanimous, however. In Fort Portal Diocese, many priests supported the no-party movement system, with younger priests especially hostile to a return to multi-party competition. Fort Portal's bishop at the time, the late Serapio Magambo, had referred to "cheap party politics" as one of Uganda's many ills.[44] Elsewhere he pronounced:

And now what a pack of lies we hear, that religion divides people. If it divides people, what do politics and economics do? No, religion as a bond between God and his people unites people… It is religionism or the use of religion for selfish political or economic ends that divides people. It had better be banned from Uganda.[45]

Magambo was both defending the church against attacks made by NRM radicals on its past political role while accepting, in principle, the NRM's opposition to the politicisation of religious identities so strongly connected with political parties. In reviewing memoranda submitted to the constitutional commission by religious bodies, John Waliggo, a Catholic priest and the commission's secretary, reported a general lack of consensus on the multi-party issue.

> On issues which were quite controversial throughout the country, the memoranda from the religious bodies were also sharply divided. Such issues included citizenship, the death penalty, and the nature of the political system, the form of government, the electoral system, the traditional rulers and the national language. This was one indication that the gap between the institutional church and the members, the people of God, was becoming narrower in this democratisation process.[46]

---

43 *New Vision*, Aug.6, 1990.
44 Bishop S.B. Magambo, *The Life and Mission of Lay People in Uganda* (Kisubi, UG: Marianum Press, 1988), 9.
45 Bishop S.B. Magambo. 'A Critique of Ugandan Christian Education', in *Proceedings of the Catholic Teacher Guild Seminar* (Kinyamasika, Fort Portal Diocese, 3-12 Dec. 1988), 12, my emphasis.
46 Waliggo. 'The Role of Christian Churches', 220. Although he does not say so explicitly, Waliggo clearly implies (in ways that are consistent with my own observations) that these divisions were as pervasive within churches as they were across them. In an editorial, the independent newspaper *The Monitor* stated that during the 1996 presidential elections, "The Churches must face the fact that they failed to set the moral tone for the campaigns … in the last 16 years, the Church has often seemed at sea; with sections of it hob-nobbing with the regime of the day and abandoning their duty to fight for justice, and only a few tenacious ones speaking out against wrong. At the beginning of this year, both the

By declining to provide unambiguous support for the DP, or even the more neutral goal of a return to multi-partyism, church leaders implicitly endorsed the position of the NRM's anti-sectarian policy and reflected the views of many (but not all) lay members that the politicisation of religious identities, and the role of the church in it, was inappropriate, 'un-civil' behaviour.[47] Ironically, this end was to be achieved, at least in the frame of civil society approaches, by decidedly 'un-civil' means - the banning of political parties. For the church, the old problem of lay members claiming to represent Catholics in the political arena was solved, at least for the moment.[48] However, church leaders were now reflecting the actual and diverse views of its members in their neutral public stance, rather than simply asserting their power to represent members' interests as they had typically done in the past.

Thus, the shift signalled that church leaders had abandoned past goals of political socialisation on the principles of Christian Democracy and the mobilisation of distinctly Catholic political interests. As I have argued, church officials were always more ambivalent about such mobilisation than has commonly been acknowledged, and less central to it than has often been asserted.

Lay organisation, socialisation, and social action

The question then arises of what other kinds of socialisation and mobilisation is the Catholic Church capable of affecting that could be coded as civil society practice? Waliggo, Uganda's leading Catholic intellectual and the church's most open advocate of elements of liberation theology, writes that

> given the immense influence that the Christian churches have over the majority of the population in Uganda it is evident that they have not done enough to mobilise women, youth, workers, children and farmers to stand up to defend their rights. Yet tangible democracy can only be attained through organising such powerful sections of society to be promoters and defenders of democratic governance.[49]

This section will provide answers to why the churches (and in this case, the Catholic Church) "have not done enough to mobilise" these social groups, or to engage in consciousness-raising forms of socialisation,[50] by analysing the kind of influence that the churches have over Ugandans.

---

main Churches, the Catholic and Protestant, and the Islamic leadership split in factions supporting the main presidential candidates". 31 December 1996. However, it should be noted that during the campaign, the Catholic Archbishop of Kampala, Cardinal Emmanuel Wamala, publicly criticised the behaviour of candidates and irregularities in the electoral system, an intervention denounced by some NRM supporters although not by Museveni himself. Still, the Cardinal's statements did not endorse the opposition or its stance of returning Uganda to a multi-party system.

47   This both in spite of, and because of, the fact that religion did emerge as the basis for political rivalry during several elections under the NRM, mostly in the two southwestern districts of Kabale and Bushenyi.

48   It should be added that there is little evidence that the DP would explicitly play the Catholic card if it was allowed to compete openly. The question is more whether old alignments would re-constitute themselves under a multi-party system that would replay the old Catholic - Protestant divide.

49   Waliggo, 'The Role of Christian Churches', 224.

50   Indeed, there is a strong sense, both among more conservative clergy and populists like Waliggo, that education - whether consciousness-raising or the more traditional forms of evangelism - leads directly

Church-based organisations, of course, do not exist only or even primarily to act directly in the political arena. Lay associations have been established by the Ugandan church to assist in its pastoral and evangelical mission, and to socialise the laity into the values and beliefs of the faith, and obedience to the clergy. In principle, these groups could be called upon to mobilise in defence of the church when under threat by external forces, or internal schisms. More ambitiously, they might enter the public sphere with an explicitly Christian agenda, not in the sense of practicing interest group politics, as with the DP,[51] but to imbue 'civil society' with Catholic values. The majority of these associations were created by Catholic missionaries in Uganda under the umbrella of Catholic Action, meaning that they were to be tightly controlled by the clerical hierarchy. In a social context where most Catholics, especially in rural areas, have limited contact with the institution's official representatives, mobilised Catholic Action groups were intended to supplement catechetical training, sustain the laity in the absence of regular access to the sacraments, and serve as a shield against 'backsliding'.

While associations like the Legion of Mary apparently flourished in the past, in recent years they have become stagnant, and virtually ignored by young Catholics and most males. Older groups such as the Legion reproduce themselves, but their composition is largely older women whose piety and good works are appreciated by others who rarely join their ranks.[52] Whatever their past capacity for socialisation, groups formed on the principles of Catholic Action only touch a minority of Catholics.

The majority of church members regularly violate many of the faith's norms and doctrinal rules, obviously a situation not unique to Uganda. This is largely a function of the Catholic Church's inclusionary membership criteria. The act of baptism, along with confirmation after training in the basic doctrines of the Catholic faith, are the only essential requirements for Catholic membership. These inclusionary criteria vastly expand the range of possible orientations to formal doctrine that do not contradict membership. In this sense the Catholic Church is like a 'family', whose sons and daughters remain members no matter how loyal or prodigal their actions become. Under such an organisational principle, the relevant question is less into what values most Catholics are being socialised than under what conditions any kind of socialisation is possible.

The church both creates the conditions for multiple interpretations of Catholic identity through its inclusionary criteria, and then defines this reality as a problem in need of solution. Church leaders across Africa recognised that their control over most of their nominal members was tenuous, and in the 1970s instituted a new priority in lay organisation: Small Christian Communities (SCCs). SCCs were modelled, in

---

to mobilisation and is thus the main mechanism to be employed in order to achieve it. In the sentence that immediately follows his call to organise the social groups he mentions, Waliggo writes: "Civic and political education cannot be left to government agencies alone", privileging education as the primary tool for mobilisation. 'The Role of Christian Churches', 224.

51 For an account of religious identities as interest groups in Uganda see D.M, Mudoola, Religion, Ethnicity and Politics in Uganda (Kampala: Fountain Publishers, 1996).
52 See Kassimir, 'Catholics and Political Identity', and R. Kassimir, 'The Politics of Popular Catholicism in Uganda', in T. Spear and I. Kimambo (eds.), African Expressions of Christianity (forthcoming).

theory, on the base communities which had begun to take hold in Latin American, and which in some cases became the organisational locus of liberation theology. The idea was that lay Catholics needed to take more responsibility for their own socialisation through bible-reading, prayer and self-help groups based on residence. In the spirit of the second Vatican Council of 1962-65, the grip of the institution was to be loosened by the mobilisation of SCCs, with the goal of instilling a sense of efficacy and empowerment in members' spiritual lives, which might then spill over into more social and political pursuits (as in parts of Latin America, where members took part in oppositional social movements against authoritarian regimes). SCCs were to be vehicles of a Christianisation, evangelisation and socialisation from below, rather than from the top down. A recent report of the Association of Members of Episcopal Conferences of East and Central Africa (AMECEA) states that SCCs

> make a great contribution to the much needed decentralisation of power in the church. They are schools of leadership, where Catholics who are often afraid to chair a meeting or speak in public, learn self-confidence and basic leadership skills. In the long run, this experience may prove to be the most important contribution of the church to the process of democratisation of society.[53]

Thus, the church imagines SCCs in the way that de Tocqueville described Protestant congregations in nineteenth-century America and Putnam depicts the choral societies of northern Italy.[54] SCCs were to be schools in the 'art of association', and in the development of values, skills and self-confidence that nurtures democracy and civil society from below.

However, the bulk of the AMECEA report is a remarkably frank exposition on the limits of SCCs, indicating that, after 20 years of experimentation, the results have been uniformly meagre across Eastern and Central Africa. Almost all of what it has to say rings true for Uganda, based on my research carried out from 1989 to 1991. Like other churches in the region, the Ugandan church unambiguously endorsed SCCs as an organisational innovation designed for a new kind of lay socialisation and mobilisation. However, in discussions with clergy and lay members in Fort Portal, most combined an almost ritualised approval of the need for SCCs with a sense that it was a 'flavour of the month' without a genuine commitment to its aims. In a paper on SCCs presented at Fort Portal Diocese's Synod in 1989, the author (a lay person) reported that SCCs have failed to take hold in the Diocese, and those that started up disbanded rather quickly. He asks: "Why would we have to think of SCCs at this material time when we are holding this synod? Is it because the church says we ought to have them or is it because Christ's faithful in this diocese deem it necessary to have SCC?"[55]

---

53 'Small Christian Communities: 20 Years Later', *AMECEA Documentation Service*, 472 (1997), 15.
54 R.D. Putnam with R. Leonardi and R.Y. Nanetti, *Making Democracy Work: Civic Traditions in Modern Italy* (Princeton, NJ: Princeton University Press. 1993).
55 J. Aduta, 'The Laity and Small Christian Communities', Fort Portal Synod, Position Paper No.7, (1989), 2.

There have been a few exceptions. In the Diocese of Fort Portal, sections of Butiiti parish had several very active SCCs, holding prayer meetings and engaging in a variety of self-help projects. The parish priest of Butiiti, an American of the Holy Cross Mission order, played a key role in nurturing these groups and pushed very hard for these areas to be made into a separate parish.[56] It is no coincidence that a rare occasion of the flourishing of SCCs occurred under the guidance of a relative outsider who is more autonomous from the diocesan hierarchy and less threatened by the potential autonomy of these groups than local clergy. The same pattern was evident in Latin America, where base communities were often mobilised by members of religious orders, often foreign, outside the immediate control of the diocesan hierarchy.[57]

Four aspects of SCCs are most pertinent to our discussion. First, SCCs in Uganda were not structured as voluntary organisations, but as the lowest branch of the church's territorial administrative system to which all Catholics living in a village, or a portion of a village demarcated by a hill or valley, belonged. The AMECEA report states that many SCCs "have started out on a wrong basis: as purely administrative sub-divisions of existing outstations". Elsewhere, the authors observe that SCCs tend to see themselves "as an administrative unit rather than as a community of life".[58]

Second, the hope that SCCs might prove to be the key mechanism for the engagement of Catholics in the public sphere has been a misplaced one. "The huge political, economic and social problems of the continent (which the Bishops analysed so clearly during the African synod) have not become the concern of the average SCCs."[59] Thus, even where SCCs may have contributed to a deeper evangelisation, this has not translated into 'Christian' action in the public arena. In 1986, Uganda's bishops noted this situation regarding Catholic youth, which has changed little in the ensuing decade: "In this mission [for the youth] the church is facing grave difficulties. Many young people fail to see the relevance of the gospel message in their lives, and even those who are faithful to Sunday prayers, are failing to take up their responsibility in the social, economic and political fields with a Christian identity."[60]

Third, the neo-Tocquevillian goal of SCCs as schools for the growth of participatory values in an institution dominated by hierarchical structures has been difficult to realise. While the leaders of SCCs are elected, "the election process does not guarantee a participatory leadership style; leaders of SCCs can be very directive even authoritarian, copying…what they have seen in the parish priest or in politics!"[61] Rather than

---

56 He finally succeeded in 1994. When the parish of Kyarusozi was elected by the bishop who "officially handed it over to the congregation of the Holy Cross". Reported in Pact Bulletin [a publication of Fort Portal Diocese], October 1994.
57 See J. Burdick. 'Looking for God in Brazil' *The Progressive Church in Urban Brazil's Religious Arena* (Berkeley, CA: University of California Press, 1993): D.H. Levine, Popular Voices in Latin American Catholicism (Princeton, NJ: Princeton University Press, 1992); and C. Smith, *The Emergence of Liberation Theology: Radical Religion and Social Movement Theory* (Chicago, IL: University of Chicago Press, 1991).
58 'Small Christian Communities', 16, 14.
59 Ibid., II.
60 *With a New Heart and a New Spirit*, 57, my emphasis.
61 'Small Christian Communities', 14.

transforming the patrimonial relationships and styles predominant in Uganda's public sphere, SCCs may be prone to capture by a patrimonial logic, an observation made by several writers on NGOs in general.[62]

Finally, and as implied in the above comment from the report, priests themselves have not been easily reconciled to SCCs, which require them to shift "from being the organiser of everything to being the animator and facilitator".

> One of the major problems of the Church…is that on one hand the SCCs has [*sic*] become the pastoral option of the Church, on the other hand priests and seminarians are still largely training in the traditional image of priesthood and feel ill at ease and not competent in the role of animator. It is often not their fault as they have never been trained for it.[63]

Indeed, while SCCs are envisioned as looser components of the church system than lay associations established as Catholic Action, they were never intended to act independently of clerical leadership and monitoring. In their 1986 pastoral letter, the Uganda bishops wrote with regard to SCCs that "when we come on pastoral visitation we shall be happy to see the progress made by these groups".[64] Here again, the reluctance of church leaders to grant autonomy to lay associations produces an outcome conducive neither to mobilisation nor socialisation. The authors of the AMECEA report are sociologically astute on this point, and are worth quoting at length.

> Hierarchy is part of the self-understanding of the Catholic Church which the Vatican Council counterbalanced with the concept of the church as people of God and of collegiality, a balance that is not easily maintained. The same balance is needed in the formation of SCCs… If they do not have sufficient autonomy, their life can be stifled by too much control from the centre. If they are not embedded into structures and the life of the larger parish, they can take on a sectarian character.[65]

Thus, SCCs have not proved to be efficacious vehicles for socialisation or mobilisation within Catholic networks. In Uganda, most Catholics have not been socialised into obedience. Indeed, SCCs were intended to counter disobedience by fostering a greater sense of individual and community responsibility within the normative framework of Catholic doctrine. Nor have most lay members, although inactive in SCCs, abandoned the church. Instead, they maintain a partial loyalty, grounded in a partial acceptance of doctrine and a periodic reliance on the church as a means of social support. They strategically accept the trappings of institutional paternalism while seeking other forums for participation. These arenas have expanded greatly since 1986, when the NRM introduced the system of local councils. Many Catholics who are active in church organisations also participate in this evolving experiment in local democracy, but rarely with the agenda of advancing Catholic interests or christianising the public sphere. While Catholics are socially and politically active, especially at the local level,

---

62   See, for example, A, Fowler. 'The Role of NGOs in Changing State-Society Relations: Perspectives from Eastern and Southern Africa', *Development Policy Review*, 9, 1 (1991).
63   'Small Christian Communities', 15.
64   *With a New Heart and A New Spirit*, 52.
65   'Small Christian Communities, 17.

socialisation and mobilisation has largely occurred outside official church organisations, networks and world views.

To make the case for 'civil society' as the central analytical tool for understanding political change, proponents of this view must demonstrate the capacity of civil organisations for mobilisation and socialisation. However, in spite of the ostensible "immense influence that the Christian churches have over the majority of the population of Uganda", [66] at least in the case of the Catholic Church, this has not translated into such capacities. If a 'civil organisation' with as pervasive a social presence as the church is constrained in this regard, this should give pause to granting explanatory power to other organisations, or to civil society more generally. However, the argument offered here, focusing on the social power of the Ugandan church leaders, does not maintain that Catholics do not mobilise *as Catholics* in contemporary Uganda. Rather, when this mobilisation occurs, it is typically outside the formal channels the church establishes to link officials with lay members, and for purposes that are unrecognisable by conventional civil society approaches.

The use of the term 'sectarian' in the above quote from the AMECEA report is not meant in the metaphorical sense, popularised by the NRM in Uganda, of political mobilisation along 'primordial' identifications, but in the more traditional sense of religious mobilisation outside the control of the church that incorporates heterodox religious practices. Ironically, while the figurative sectarianism of religious identities and institutions has been a relatively infrequent occurrence in post-1986 Uganda, literal 'sectarianism' within the church has been a growing phenomenon.

Perhaps not coincidentally, the increasingly moribund trajectory of old and new Catholic lay organisations has been accompanied by a dramatic increase in the expression of popular religious beliefs and practices in Uganda, and the public and organised nature of these expressions.[67] Many of these practices encompass popular concerns with witchcraft and spirit possession. Such concerns are prominent across Africa in the 1990s. As Monga colourfully notes: "The idea of being possessed traverses all social classes, all 'tribes'. Exorcism, as a result, is a booming business."[68]

It is certainly booming in contemporary Uganda, and Catholics are major participants. Lay members do mobilise for spiritual purposes, but often do so outside church structures, or use formally recognised associations for purposes radically different from their stated objectives. Church policy has been either to ignore or suppress such movements, both because of their perceived heterodox practices and because they validate a lay religious charisma independent of the church.[69] Thus, for the most part, church leaders have been unable or unable or unwilling to harness this energy, further limiting it as an organisational locus for mobilisation. More recently, however, they

---

66   Waliggo, 'The Role of Christian Churches', 224.
67   Kassimir, 'The Politics of Popular Catholicism'.
68   C. Monga, *The Anthropology of Anger: Civil Society and Democracy in Africa* (Boulder. CO: Lynne Rienner, 1996), 140.
69   Kassimir, 'The Politics of Popular Catholicism'.

have given more consideration to co-optation strategies in order to establish a deeper linkage to popular concerns.

What do exorcism and witchcraft have to do with civil society? Primarily, the answer is that effective and accountable leadership is connected in popular conceptions with the maintenance of order, and witchcraft is perceived as one source of disorder in all of rural, and much of urban Uganda.[70] Witchcraft is also linked to unfair advantage in the accumulation of wealth and power, although perhaps less so in Uganda than in other African societies.[71] Indeed, it would not be too much of an exaggeration to say that popular notions of 'civility' are informed by the control of witchcraft and other manifestations of evil spirits and the devil.[72] When state institutions and important social organisations like the mainline churches do not take a leading role in this control, popular movements may emerge to carry it out.

One way to gauge the church's potential for accommodation with popular religiosity is to contrast two recent examples from Western Uganda. First is the case of Dosteo Bisaaka and his exorcism movement in Western Uganda. A former Catholic catechist, Bisaaka's movement swept the region in the late 1980s until it was banned by the government in 1991. Part of the reason for the banning was pressure on the NRM by the Western dioceses of Fort Portal and Hoima, which had lost thousands of followers to the movement. One could interpret the church's response to this group as markedly 'un-civil' in that, although Bisaaka was accused of counselling group members not to seek modern medical care, the NRM's ostensible reason for its banning, the principal reason for the church's opposition was that Bisaaka was engaging in direct competition for members and publicly denouncing the church as irrelevant. Bisaaka followers whom I interviewed in 1991 argued that they were being denied freedom of religion, which the church should be upholding. In a sense, both the church and the NRM regime demonstrated their power to define organisations as 'legitimate'- in this case a 'legitimate' religion - and thus a legitimate member of civil society.

---

70 While not discussing witchcraft, Mikael Karlstrom makes a very persuasive case for the connection between local conceptions of civility with order, and even hierarchy, in Buganda. 'Imaging Democracy: Political Culture and Democratisation in Buganda', *Africa*, 66, 4 (1996), 485—505.

71 See P. Geschiere, *The Modernity of Witchcraft: Politics and the Occult in Postcolonial Africa* (Charlottesville, VA: University of Virginia Press. 1997).

72 Thus, while Fatton is correct in bringing concerns about witchcraft into the discussion of civil society, he misses the connection between witchcraft eradication and popular notions of what might be called civility, focusing instead on the allegedly 'obscurantist' nature of such practices. "Witchcraft and counter-witchcraft rituals are deeply embedded in the private practices of daily existence: they are personal remedies to the overwhelming presence of evil, and they pervade civil society with a supernatural aura. Civil society is thus not all enlightenment; it is also the domain of profoundly inegalitarian and obscurantist institutions and lifestyles. Nor does its opposition to the state automatically spell freedom, as 'witches' – self-seeking predatory rulers and aspirants – can easily subvert it into corrupt and cruel ends." R. Fatton, 'Africa in the Age of Democratisation: The Civic Limitations of Civil Society', *African Studies Review*, 38, 2 (1995), 76-7. I cannot imagine anyone who believes in the 'reality' of witchcraft disagreeing with this last sentence, but it confuses the point, which is that it is 'witch-cleansing' that can spell freedom, or, at minimum, order.

However, by the mid-1990s, the banning order was rescinded, and Bisaaka and his followers openly began to practice once again. In June 1997, the group threw a birthday party for their leader in his home *saza* (county) of Buyaga in Kibaale district. *The New Vision* reported that the event "caused a temporary standstill... when schools and some government departments closed to celebrate the local prophet's birthday." In addition, the NRM-appointed Resident District Commissioner of Kibaale was reported to having thanked Bisaaka "for having solved the witchcraft problem that had bedevilled Bunyoro Kitara Kingdom but more particularly Buyaga county which had become a no-go area".[73]

The second example of popular religious mobilisation took place within the Catholic Church, where similar remedies for spirit possession and protection against witchcraft were sought. A once relatively inactive lay association in Fort Portal Diocese dedicated to the Uganda martyrs - *ekitebe ky' bakaiso* or Uganda Martyrs Guild - began performing exorcisms and casting out evil spirits in 1991. At first, the Diocese reacted cautiously, inviting the group to hold its sessions in the diocesan meeting hall and sending priests to observe whether the group's practices were in accord with church doctrine. But over the next few years, and not long after the arrival of a new bishop, the church became more open to the group. According to the guild's president, Lawrence Kasaija, the diocese formally recognised the group in 1995, with guild leaders taking an oath of fidelity to the church and promising to stop their activities should the church re-consider its ruling.[74] Several priests have joined the movement, which now has thousands of members and conducts witch-finding operations across the Toro region and elsewhere in the country. Opinions about the group are not unanimous. Other diocesan priests are deeply opposed to the point of refusing to allow guild members to operate in their parishes. One priest stated: "These things just don't happen. It is either the work of a trickster or of mentally unbalanced people"[75] But, as a regional Catholic magazine article put it: "The sale of rosaries has shot up, the prayers are firmly biblical in content and both the reception of the sacraments and the reading of the Bible have vastly increased. Who wants to quarrel with a movement of this kind!"[76]

The Martyrs Guild movement may be accomplishing many of the goals that other church lay associations are unable to, but in a very different way from that which the church officials would have preferred, or even imagined. This is a movement begun by a layman who works as an equal with supportive priests in fighting evil. In the process, what the church had typically viewed as heterodox practices are being re-defined as 'Catholic', enabled by the tradition of exorcism within the church that had been largely ignored until now.[77]

---

73 *New Vision*, 17 June, 1997. In interviews conducted in June 1997, several church leaders stated that Bisaaka had forged ties with the NRM and that some of the regime's officials were now followers his movement.
74 Interview with Kasaija, 1 July 1997.
75 In Fr. Raphael, 'Driving Away Evil Spirits', Leadership, 357 (1996), 17.
76 Ibid.
77 "The Guild is and remains an official movement of the Diocese and, as is usual in the Catholic Church in such

One obvious, and complementary, interpretation of the church's a typical co-optation of the movement is to counter the influence of Bisaaka (who had explicitly stated that Christianity had been superseded by the arrival of his movement), as well as the growing number of Protestant Pentecostal churches in Uganda that have begun to attract Catholics. But it is worth considering who is being co-opted here: the guild or the church? The church's willingness to recognise lay charisma, and its compromise with popular notions of spiritual power, might imply a new capacity for mobilisation. To the degree that conceptions of accountability and justice are connected to the control of witchcraft, the church's engagement with popular religiosity may also evolve into augmenting the social power of the church in local 'civil' society, although here civil means something very different than in standard civil society approaches.

Of course, accountability and justice are certainly not defined at the local level solely in terms of the control of witchcraft. If the church's popularity and mobilisational capacity increases as a result of its compromise with popular religious concerns, it will have to contend with both the 'un-civil' vigilantism that such movements sometimes practice, as well as how such concerns connect with more material dimensions of governance and political participation. Local notions of 'the civil' are themselves fraught with multiple and contradictory definitions, something typically missed in most civil society approaches. But the larger point of this section is to suggest that without some kind of mobilisational capacity linking leaders to followers, the church's socio-political practice is not captured by a civil society framework for analysis. A focus on the social power of the church is a more effective analytical framework for understanding its actual practice, as well as its purposes.

Conclusion

This article has argued that an understanding of the role of social organisations in civil society is presupposed by an account of the capacities of civil organisations to act in the public sphere. Civil society approaches themselves see socialisation and mobilisation as two central 'actions' that civil organisations take in confronting or engaging the state. Without empirical verification for the capacity of organisations to socialise or mobilise, the justification for analysing them through the lens of civil society is weak. I have demonstrated the serious obstacles which the Ugandan Catholic Church leaders face with regard to the socialisation and mobilisation of its members, and thus the limits of a civil society approach in accounting for its role in Ugandan society and politics.

Of course, this does not mean that all African social organisations, or even all religious organisations, lack these capacities. Rather, I argue that we must first view organisations through the lens of social power to grasp their political influence, rather than an *a priori* determination to place them under the rubric of civil society. In examining the role of the Ugandan Catholic Church in political, social and religious

---

circumstances, no official pronouncement is made on the out-of-the ordinary side-shows of the movement as long as what they teach is not heretical". Note that the danger is what is taught, not what is practised. Ibid.

mobilisation, the church lacks the kinds of linkages with its members that foster such mobilisation and the mechanisms for socialising members into new values and roles. Church officials' ambivalence toward mobilisation is both a cause and consequence of their actual capacities. In general, Catholic leaders view the reproduction of the institution not only as a priority that guides their political vision, but as the necessary condition for the organisation's action in realising this vision. This does not make the church any less of a member of civil society. It does, however, lend a distinct risk-averse quality to its socio-political role, reinforces its 'logic of maintenance', [78] and gives doubt to the utility of a civil society approach in accounting for its capacity to effect change.

Uganda is both a difficult and an important case for thinking about the role of civil society actors, both the churches and other organisations, because whether it is in a 'phase' of democratisation or of democratic consolidation is an issue debated both by scholars and Ugandans themselves.[79] Clearly, the current political system under the NRM falls short of the definition of democracy commonly accepted by civil society approaches, with critics pointing not only to the unfair electoral advantages of the NRM in a no-party system, but also to restrictions on associational rights in civil society itself.[80] An ambiguous outcome has emerged where opposition parties promote multi-partyism but not broader reforms in associational life, while most civil society organisations have not taken sides on the multi-party question. This situation has been to the advantage of the NRM regime, which has proved to be quite adept at manipulating it by presenting the image that Uganda is already in a phase of democratic consolidation. This raises another kind of critique of civil society, approaches not discussed here - that is, the way in which party structures, state policies and the broader political context shape the structure and direction of civil society.[81]

In linking the issue of consolidation to the role of civil society, it is apparent that once the political situation has moved from, or at least is defined as other than, a simple matter of opposition to authoritarian rule, the question of how civil society actor's work within a system is a thorny one. For religious organisations, Archbishop Desmond Tutu has described the conundrum of once-activist churches in post-apartheid South Africa with great eloquence: "we knew what we were against, and we opposed that fairly effectively. It is not nearly so easy to say what we are for and so we

---

[78] The term is from J.A. Coleman, 'Raison d'Eglise: Organisational imperatives of the Church to the Political Order', in J.K. Hadden and A. Shape (eds.), *Secularisation and Fundamentalism Reconsidered: Religion and the Political Order* Volume III (New York: Paragon House. 1989).

[79] Michael Bratton and Nicolas van de Walle have coded Uganda as a 'blocked' and 'managed' political transition in their recent comparative study: *Democratic Experiments in Africa: Regime Transitions in Comparative Perspective* (Cambridge: Cambridge University Press, 1997).

[80] See M. Mamdani. 'Pluralism and the Right of Association', in M. Mamdani and J.Oloka-Onyango (eds), Uganda' *Studies in Living Conditions, Popular Movements, and Constitutionalism* (Vienna: JEP Books, 1994), 519-63. Mamdani points out that the NRM did not create these restrictions, which have been in place since the colonial period, but have not acted to remove them.

[81] See Ndegwa, *The Two Faces of Civil Society,* and Foley and Edwards, 'The Paradox of Civil Society'.

appear to be dithering, not quite knowing where we want to go nor how to get there."[82] For once-activist Catholic churches under authoritarian rule, in the shift to ostensibly liberal democracies in Eastern Europe and Latin America, their role has also become decidedly more ambiguous: the Polish church has taken strong public stances, and used its political clout, in favour of 'illiberal' causes, while the Latin American churches, if not exactly retreating from the public sphere, have had difficulty defining their role in a more open political context.[83] This implies that the kind of organisational capacities conducive to mounting an effective challenge to authoritarian regimes may not be equally propitious in the consolidation of democracies or of civil societies.

The Ugandan Catholic Church has been on a different trajectory; whether it is able to move from its role as a refuge under political chaos to an effective socio-political actor in a new political situation remains to be seen. In the 11 years since the rise of the NRM, the results have been ambiguous at best, and many church leaders, while proclaiming the important place of the church in civil society, have been ambivalent in practice about 'how to get there', scholars must systematically consider organisational capacities and internal organisational politics to see how civil society actors got to the place they currently occupy.

To repeat, the point here is not that the Ugandan church lacks social power or that it has no political influence. Rather, the kind of power that the church possesses, and the mechanisms it deploys to achieve influence, are not best understood through the lens of civil society. In Uganda's political struggles not only to identify the appropriate institutions of democratic rule, but to define the content of democracy itself, the church may have a role to play. But by asserting a leading role without the capacity to play it, church leaders run the risk of building up expectations which cannot be met. Civil society proponents, by conflating the power of a normative idea with an analytical tool, run a similar risk.

---

82 D. Tutu, 'Identity Crisis', in Paul Gifford (ed), *The Christian Churches and the Democratisation of Africa* (Leiden: E.J. Brill, 1995), 96, my emphasis.
83 For the latter, see C.A. Drogus, 'Review Article: The Rise and Decline of Liberation Theology: Churches, Faith, and Political Change in Latin America; *Comparative Politics*, 27, 4(1995). 465-77.

7

Traditional Leaders and Decentralisation[1]

Rebecca Mukyala-Makiika

Abstract

Recent decades have seen an increase in the number of ethnic and communal movements demanding cultural and collective rights. This partly resulted in the government restoring traditional leaders in 1993, the same year decentralisation was launched. The author examines whether traditional leaders and institutions can promote good governance through decentralisation in Uganda, despite the fact that they themselves are undemocratically constituted.

While noting that traditional leaders symbolise culture and collective rights and that, given their popular legitimacy, traditional leaders can be agents of social and political stability, the author highlights the scepticism surrounding their particularistic tendencies, their intolerant tendencies and their organisational weaknesses, illustrated, among others, by their limited autonomy vis-à-vis the state. Further, traditional leaders are not supposed to participate in partisan politics, but their popularity makes them prey to all forms of political manoeuvres by opportunistic politicians. The effect of the thin boundary between culture and politics has also seen the transformation of the concept of culture into an ideology to control traditional leaders by the state. Within the drive for decentralisation, other issues of contention include the lack of agreement on the powers to be devolved, and the institutions to which power is being devolved.

Nevertheless, traditional leaders have tried to initiate development projects at the local level to back up the decentralisation policy. They can use their popular base to give legitimacy to the local leadership and to mobilise resources. They can also be countervailing forces against the state at both national and local levels. They can above all stimulate participation in decision-making. The author, however, concludes by pointing out that their ability to perform all these duties will depend on their organisational strength and their ability to stand autonomously not only in relationship to the state but also to other political groups in society. Besides, the distinction between

---

[1] This article originally appeared in Nsibambi, A. (1998), *Decentralisation and Civil Society in Uganda: The Quest for Good Governance*. Fountain Publishers: Kampala

what constitutes culture and what is politics significantly limits their range of activities. Accordingly, traditional leaders must learn to walk the tight rope in order to survive in the minefield of democratic politics.

The 1980s and the 1990s have been a watershed of two important developments in Uganda. On the one hand, there is increasing pressure for democratisation. Several groups, both at the domestic scene and at the international level, have been demanding for increased citizen participation in the decision-making and implementation processes at various levels of government. On the other hand, there is an increase in the number ethic and communal movements demanding cultural and collective rights. Partly as a result of the above pressures and partly as a result of an ideological conviction of the need to empower local communities to take charge of their destinies through local institutions of self-governance and resource mobilisation, the NRM government embarked on the policy of decentralisation in 1993.

The objectives of the decentralisation policy, among other things, were to transfer political, administrative, financial and planning powers from the centre of local government councils; to promote popular participation, empower local people to make their own decisions and to enhance accountability and responsibility (Local Government Act, 1997).

As a recognition of the role traditional leaders played in the liberation struggles against Obote and Lutwa between 1981-1985[2], and in the interests of reconciliation and redressing historical wrongs, and also as a result of pressure from several groups in Buganda such as *Kirimutu*, and *Abazukulu ba Kintu* (grandchildren of Kintu) as well as a strategy to ensure support for the Movement System during the CA elections, the government restored traditional leaders in 1993, the same year decentralisation was launched. Subsequently, traditional institutions were enshrined in the 1995 constitution.

The resurgence of ethnicity and cultural rights' movements in general and the restoration of traditional leaders in particular, at a time when there are efforts towards increasing people's participation in the decision-making and policy implementation processes through decentralisation, raises a number of questions. What is the interface between traditional authorities and decentralisation? To what extent can traditional leaders and institutions promote good governance through decentralisation in Uganda? Will traditional leaders use their popular legitimacy to enhance popular participation and development at the level or will they inhibit it? In short, can traditional leaders be agents of the democratisation process in Uganda, despite the fact that they themselves are undemocratically constituted? This chapter addresses these questions in order to indicate areas of compatibility as well as conflict potentialities between traditional and elected leaders both at local and national levels.

---

2   Princes Elizabeth Bagaya of Toro is credited for linking the NRM to Chief Abiola of Nigeria who donated 200,000 dollars to the liberation struggle, while the *Kabaka* of Buganda visited the war zone in 1985, a factor which boosted the morale of the guerrilla fighters.

The theoretical debates backdrop

The debate as to whether traditional leaders enhance decentralisation or inhibit it has been a subject of debate amongst a number of scholars (Nsibambi, 1995; Byanyima, 1991; Kasozi, 1994; Kayunga, 1995). This debate revolves around a number of issues. People in favour of traditional leaders argue that Uganda is a multicultural state with poly-ethnic regions. Its cultural diversity was a result of forced colonial incorporation of previously self-governing, territorially homogenous cultures in to one political entity. Cultural diversity in its poly-ethnic regions arose from individual and family migration. In the context of this cultural diversity, two things become significant. First, power is dispersed from the centre to the local areas in a manner that recognizes this cultural diversity. In short, if decentralisation policy in a multi-ethnic state is to succeed, administrative boundaries should coincide with cultural boundaries. Secondly in the context of culture diversity, cultural right should be part of the democratisation process. In case of Uganda, restoration of traditional leaders was intended to preserve and promote cultural and collective rights.

It has also been argued that if decentralisation is to enhance democracy, it should take into account why previous democratisation processes have failed in Africa. Cultural theorists have argued that one of the major problems facing democracy builders in Africa is the failure to recognise the diverse historical and cultural dimensions of the continent (Carlos Lopez, 1996:141). The universalisation of the democratic model is absurd in much as it assumes that codes of morality and political conduct must be identical.

Thirdly, if decentralisation is to promote economic development, it should equally take stock of why previous projects have failed to transform Africa economically. Like in the case of democracy, the development theorists and practitioners ignored the cultural variable and the value of indigenous knowledge. Traditional leaders are seen either as custodians of this indigenous knowledge or as its symbols in which case these leaders can be used as one of the pillars of local government (Hoek, V.D.,1988; Othiambo Anedi, 1993; Duane Swany,1996). Since traditional leaders symbolise culture and collective rights, the goals of democracy and economic development enshrined in decentralisation can only be realised with their active involvement in local governance. Besides the above arguments, traditional leaders are believed to be essential for decentralisation, democracy and development in other ways. There is a strong relationship between social stability and decentralisation. Instability always gives the central government an excuse to intervene in the local affairs of communities. The more the central government intervenes at the local level, the less powers it will delegate. Social and political stability, on the other hand, can make local communities acquire powers and responsibilities which they can use to transform themselves into autonomous entities even if there was no formal delegation of power (Kayunga, 1995:246). Given their popular legitimacy, traditional leaders can be agents of social and political stability both at the local and national levels. Where it is difficult to establish civil society on the basis of social classes in the Marxian sense, or on the basis of other occupational social categories, cultural distinctiveness may constitute the base for the organisation of self-help projects at the local level. Civil society grassroots organisations and other community associations may constitute themselves as ready-made points of departure (Doornbos, 1991). The hierarchical nature of organisation is one of the traditional leaders' key resources.[3] They facilitate community participation in development projects in particular and the decision-making at whatever level of government.

There is a lot of scepticism, however, on the role traditional leaders can play in either promoting democracy or development at the local level. Ordinarily group-differential rights for minority cultures inhibit the development of shared identity necessary for stable social order. Traditional leaders encourage people to focus on their differences other than what unites as human beings. Traditional leaders and other collective rights make people more conscious of group rights/ differences, and more resentful of other groups (Kymlick, 1995, p.4). In local polyethnic communities, this can be a cause for social disorder which can easily slow down the process of development. Social disorder will lead to state intervention in local matters thus endangering the entire process of decentralisation.

Secondly, traditional leaders are symbols of collective and cultural rights. Collective cultural rights pose a number of problems to the process of decentralisation if its ultimate objective is to ensure democracy and popular participation at the local level. Whereas citizenship is based on individual rights, collective rights empower a particular community to limit the liberty of its own members in the name of group solidarity of cultural purity.

Thirdly, as organs of civil society, traditional institutions have been subjected to a number of criticisms. According to Habermas, identity formation, ethnicity, and religious and linguistic movements are a matter of the private sphere. They are prior to participation or rational and critical debate by individuals in the public sphere. Whereas civil society is a realm of civility, bargaining, rationality, compromise, accommodation, negotiations, and tolerance, traditional movements are soul-rousing, calling for sacrifice, feelings of exaltations, hatred, and intolerance which may eventually lead to social polarisation and threaten to demolish the public sphere (Neera Chandhoke,1995, p.245).

How useful are traditional leaders in decentralisation?

Whatever opportunism and pessimism surrounding the role of traditional leaders, their ability to enhance decentralisation and probably promote popular participation and economic development at the local level of governance will depend on their organisational strength by which we mean the degree of their autonomy from the state both in material and functional form; the amount of resources needed to carry

---

3   Buganda's traditional authority is very hierarchical. On the top is the king (*Kabaka*). Below him is the *Lukiiko*, followed respectively to the smallest social unit (the family) in the following order: *Kiika, Essiga, Omutuba, Olunyiriri, Olugya,* and *Nyumba* (homestead).

out whatever project at the local level and the political support they enjoy both from their subjects and other stakeholders in Uganda's political process; the level of internal cohesion within the traditional institutions and, lastly, the reciprocal and reinforcing linkages between traditional institutions (Bratton and Van de Walle, 1993).

Organisational autonomy

Theories of civil society presuppose that if an organisation has to act as a countervailing force against the state, it must itself be de-linked from it in organisational terms (Michael Bratton, 1989). What this means is that state structures should not coincide with structures of traditional authority and the traditional leadership should be kept out of state responsibilities.

In Buganda, this organisational de-linkage has been achieved by invoking an old tradition of "the king does not work" (*Kabaka takola*). According to this tradition, all "Princes and Princesses of the Drum"(*Abalangira b'engoma*) are not supposed to occupy any political or public office[4]. This tradition has in effect kept most royal Baganda from any significant political office. On the negative side, this tradition goes against the individual rights of these princes that is the right to work and associate with any political group of their choice. On the positive side, however, it safeguards the autonomy of traditional institutions and limits the extent to which the state can use them to extend its own hegemony.

In Toro, however, the situation is different. Kaboyo, the late king of Toro was Uganda's ambassador before becoming a king. The historical linkage with the powers that be significantly undermined the autonomy of Toro's traditional institutions. Upon his death the linkage between the state and Toro kingdom was formalised by the appointment of President Museveni as one of the *Omujwara Kondo* (guardian) of the young king.

Financial autonomy

One of the biggest problems facing traditional institutions and leaders is a narrow resource base. According to the 1995 constitution, no person is compelled to pay allegiance or contribute to the cost of maintaining a traditional leader. Besides, traditional leaders are not allowed to exercise any administrative, legislative or executive powers of government at whatever level (The Uganda Constitution, 1995, Article 246). What this mean in practice is that they cannot levy taxes on their subjects. Their sustenance depends on rent derived from cultural sites, rent from markets but on the land belonging to the king, donations from external sources and voluntary contribution from the subject, both in kind and in the form of labour. Perhaps the central government should give financial assistance to traditional institutions in order to ensure their viability.

There are three problems associated with voluntarism as a source of income. First, since the amount to be contributed is uncertain, planning is extremely difficult.

---

[4] The "Princes of the Drum" are the children of the king born while he is still in possession of the royal drum (*Mujaguzo*), that is, after the assumption of kingship.

Secondly, it is very difficult to hold traditional leaders accountable. A number of their activities tend to be done in an informal manner. There is no forum to discuss funds generated from cultural sites such as the *Kabaka*'s markets or other money-generating activities such as the collections during *bika* football competitions. Since most actors, within the traditional institutions are not elected, even if there was a misappropriation of funds, it is very difficult to hold anybody accountable. The biggest problem is the competition between the central government and the traditional authorities for 'cleanliness'. Traditional institutions are supposed to be the 'true' representatives of the African tradition, a tradition of equality untainted by the forces of globalisation. Because of this romanticised approach to Africa's past, and, therefore, to the institutions which symbolise that past, there is a danger of hiding several malpractices in resource utilisation under the guise of maintaining the image of traditional institutions.

However, traditional institutions can easily be personalised by one or a few people who contribute most to their sustenance. The king becomes a subject of his subjects. In Toro, for example, the *Omuhikirwa* (prime minister) is so central to the economic life of the kingdom to the extent that it is difficult to imagine its survival without his generous financial contribution, at least for the moment. The *Voice of Toro* is by and large his brainchild and a product of his financial clout. Apart from making the king a subject of his subjects, it becomes difficult to change such a leader even when there is evidence of wrongdoing.

Organisational cohesion

Another important factor which determines an organisation's capacity to contribute towards social transformation at whatever level and to act as a countervailing force against the state is the degree of internal cohesion. Internal cohesion has two dimensions. First, the cultural values which these traditional institutions seek to symbolise should be accepted by the majority of the members. Secondly, traditional leaders should be enjoying popular legitimacy.

In Uganda there are several problems which limit traditional institutions' ability to be internally cohesive. First, due to internal migrations, all former kingdoms in Uganda are now polyethnic. As early as 1931, for example, Mbale County was composed of 14 major ethnic groups, out of which the Bagwere were 36.1%, Banyole, 17.3%, Bagisu, 14.8%, Iteso, 14.1% and Baganda 8.3%. In Isingiro County, in the former Ankole kingdom, there were 7 major ethnic groups: Banyankore constituting 82.6%, while the Baganda were the second largest ethnic group (4.8%).[5] By 1959, Mutuba subdivision, Kyagwe County, East Mengo was composed of 34 major ethnic groups with the Baganda constituting only 32.1%.[6]

The social transformation of the kingdoms from homogeneous to multicultural entities raises the following questions. Is it possible to create administrative boundaries at the local level which coincide with ethnic boundaries? Should citizenship or the right to participate at the local level be determined by one's nationality or one's contribution

---

5   Uganda protectorate, The Native Population of Uganda, 1931.
6   Uganda, General African Census 1959: Tribal Analysis, East African Statistical Department. 10 May 1959, p.206.

to the development of the local communities concerned? How do you protect the culture of the major ethnic group without endangering the cultures of the minorities in the kingdom areas?

Unfortunately, no institutional arrangements have been put in place in any of the kingdoms or other local communities to safeguard minority ethnic groups, the *banamawanga* (foreigners). The only legal provision to protect minorities at the local level is the constitutional provision which makes support for traditional leaders at the local level voluntary. At one time there was a proposal for special representation of minority ethnic groups in Buganda in the *Lukiiko*. This was vehemently rejected. Increasingly, citizenship is being constructed around nationality. Whatever the level of assimilation within ethnic groups at the local level, there are several attempts to exclude some people from participating in local affairs in the name of culture. For example, it is assumed that no outsider should be allowed to participate in the *binyomo* (brown ants) rituals.

The danger, however, is that the cultural argument has been extended beyond the true cultural values of any local community. With personnel powers devolved to local communities as a result of decentralisation, people are increasingly being recruited on the basis of their nationality rather than individual merit. These developments are extremely dangerous given the poly-ethnic nature of our local communities.

Even within the same cultural group, traditional institutions are facing several internal conflicts relating to leadership. In Busoga, the position of *Kyabazinga* (traditional leader of Busoga) is being contested by three personalities, each of them invoking a lot of historical and traditional arguments to back up his claim.[7] In Bunyoro, the issue of who is the traditional leader of Bunyoro was resolved in the courts of law between the current *Omukama* (king) and his brother. In Toro, family feuds after the death of Kaboyo have significantly undermined the legitimacy of the kingdom. In Buganda, social pressure was to be invoked to stop prince Kimera's attacks on the *Kabaka*. In Teso, attempts to get a traditional leader, the *Emorimor*, have come to naught because of internal disagreements by interested parties.

The powers of traditional leaders and their political legitimacy is largely dependent on the various myths which are constructed around them. One of these myths is that *Kabaka tasobya* (the king never does any wrong). Feuds of the above nature will certainly undermine the myths surrounding traditional leaders. This in effect will erode their much cherished political resource that is political legitimacy.

Relationship between traditional institutions with popularly elected leaders at the local level

The introduction of traditional leaders has created two forms of authority at the local levels of governance.[8] One form of authority consists of people who derive their right

---

7   The three claimants are Henry Wako Muloki, prince Eriakesi Ngobi Kobe Kiregyeya and Mzee Daudi Kidubuka Wakoli. Muloki is the recognised *Kyabazinga* of Busoga.

8   The Cabinet line-up of Buganda includes Attorney-General, Advisor and Strategic Planning; Finance, Commerce and Industries; Royal Tombs, Buganda Heritage Centre, Traditional Sites, Buganda Museum, Tourism and Sports; Works, Traditional Communal Work, Maintenance and Rehabilitation

to govern from the fact that they were elected by universal suffrage. Another category comprises those who derive their right to govern from inheritance and tradition. The former category looks at people as a collection of individuals each with a specific set of rights. The latter looks at people as a cultural unit with a set of collective rights. Two major forms of conflict are bound to emerge as a result of these forms of authority at the local level. One of them is the competition for resources. Both popularly elected local authorities and traditional leaders need a significant amount of resources to enhance their programmes aimed at enhancing their legitimacy. In Hoima, for example, the popularly elected council was uneasy with the return of Bunyoro's property to the *Omukama* on the ground that it was paid for by the tax payers' money. In Buganda, whether public land in Buganda should be managed by Mengo on behalf of the *Kabaka* or by the popularly elected district councils has been a source of major controversy. Another conflict emerging from this dual form of authority at the local level relates to the issue of representation. Whenever there is a controversial issue affecting the local community, a conflict has always arisen as to who should speak for the people. Members of parliament and elected officials or local councillors claim the right to speak for the people because they carry the people's mandate. Members of the *Lukiiko* claim that, since the issues under discussion have got a "cultural component", the "custodians of people's culture", that is the traditional institutions such as the *Lukiiko* in Buganda and *Rukurato* in Toro are the rightful spokesmen of local communities. On several occasions this has led to conflicts between traditional institutions and people's representatives at various levels of government. For example, there were instances of conflict between the Buganda caucus in the Constituent Assembly (CA) and the *Lukiiko* on the question of federalism during the constitution-making exercise.

Collective versus individual rights

Theories of civil society and collective action assume that resistance at individual level is pre-political, primordial and rudimentary (Neera Chanhoke, 1995:250). Individual rights have to be gathered into collective projects on the basis of shared interests. Associational life is, therefore, the sphere where the individual is encouraged to articulate resistance against state oppression. People, whose views are opposed to the 'mainstream' position of the local communities, are not tolerated. In the struggle for federalism, for instance, people who had [offered] views on how federalism in Buganda could be brought about, were either thrown out of the *Lukiiko* or pressurised to resign. Those outside the *Lukiiko* were automatically 'denationalised' and attempts were made to redefine the constitution of a 'true' Muganda. Such attempts to deny or ostracise dissenting voices their identity could in the long-run have a bearing on the durability of traditional institutions.

---

of Buganda Public Buildings, Women Affairs and Community Development; Local Government Secretary General, Protocol, Public Relations and Functions; Culture, Traditional and Luganda Language; Information, Broadcasting, Akiika Embuga Newspaper and Publications; Education; Health; Agriculture, Animal Industry and Fisheries; Economic Planning, BUCADEF and other economic companies: and Youth and Cabinet Secretary.

Politics of traditional institutions

According to the 1995 constitution, traditional leaders are not supposed to participate in partisan politics. But their popularity makes them prey to all forms of political manoeuvres by opportunistic politicians. As mentioned earlier, one of the objectives of the restoration of traditional rulers in their cultural capacity was to ensure the victory for the Movement during the 1994 CA elections (Oloka-Onyango, 1997). Nevertheless, the opposition has also discovered their political value. During the CA the mutipartyists tried to form an alliance with supporters of federalism and traditional institutions but this failed because, for some federalists like Besweri Mulondo, an alliance with UPC was out of the question. Localised social movements alliances are normally born out of necessity. People come together because they believe that localised struggles cannot succeed against state power on their own (Neera Chandhoke, 1995:210). The contradiction with alliances, however, is that in an attempt to create a common position, they bring together groups with divergent opinions on issues, priorities, concepts of power and empowerment, etc. In the alliance, each group not only struggles for autonomy but it also strives to establish itself as the dominant force. In the process, the alliance itself either suppresses other subordinate groups or assigns them a supportive role (Kayunga, 1997).

The above phenomenon has greatly affected traditional institutions. Recognising their political potential, especially in Buganda, the multipartyists have penetrated these institutions and are using them in multiparty struggles against the NRM. Sometimes, as was the case with the Land Bill, the traditional institutions had, in alliance with the multipartyists, wanted a postponement of the debate, not necessarily because they wanted the people to be more educated about it but because they wanted to use the land Bill controversy to erode the NRM popular base in Buganda. In short, the struggle for multipartyism has become the most dominant issue in the alliance between the traditional leaders in some parts of the country. The genuine demands of traditional leaders are merely supportive or residual.

The implication of competition for hegemony between multipartyism and the genuine demands of the traditional institutions is that whereas the Buganda traditional leaders have succeeded in maintaining an autonomy vis-à-vis the state, they have lost it to other forces in society. And as long as they are perceived as agents of political opposition, it becomes very difficult for the state to give them more powers at the local level.

The fallacy of the "culture" and "politics" dichotomy

The condition for the return of traditional leaders was that they remain within the realm of culture outside the political arena (Museveni, 1998). This means that traditional leaders have to constantly grapple with the problem of drawing a distinction between what constitutes culture and what constitutes politics. Culture can be defined as the composition of those ideas, values and habits which people share in common (Jacobs, 1992). Culture symbolises religion, language, literature, art, customs, laws, social organisation, technical production, economic exchange, and philosophy (Lategan and

Baker, 1996:121). This broad definition makes it very difficult to draw a boundary between culture and politics. Basically, the way people govern themselves has got a cultural component. Yet governance lies within the realm of politics. Even rights, such as the freedom to choose, have a cultural component because people's choices may be affected by structural factors which include culture. Though language lies within the sphere of culture, it may acquire political value when it is used as an instrument in political campaigns as was the case with the 1998 Kampala local council elections.

The effect of the thin boundary between culture and politics has been the transformation of the concept of culture into an ideology to control traditional leaders by whatever political forces. When the president appointed one of the *Kabaka*'s sisters a cabinet minister, culture was invoked to block it, out of fear that it would bring the institution closer to the state and compromise its autonomy. The argument was that royals do not participate in politics. Whereas most people's cultural patterns are constructed around land relations, when the opposition and traditional institutions, including the *Kabaka*, tried to make some demands in the name of culture, the response of the state was that land was a political issue and traditional leaders should keep out of it. Culture has acquired political overtones. When traditional leaders participate in activities which are supportive of the state but which weaken the opposition, that is culture. When they participate in activities which are seen to undermine the state but strengthen the opposition, that is politics.

Since culture is not static, it would be risky to organise the political system around something which is always changing. There is also a question of which culture is to be protected or safeguarded? Some of the opponents of the cultural institutions argue that traditional leaders are not demanding the return to the pre-colonial order but foreign cultural traditions which have been internalised. Some of the traditional leaders such as the *Kyabazinga* of Busoga were created by the colonialists whose objective was not to protect people's tradition but to streamline colonial administration. In Ankole, the area of jurisdiction which the *Omugabe* claims far exceeds the pre-colonial Nkore kingdom (Karugire, 1980). In Buganda, the *mailo* land system significantly contradicts the pre-colonial land system in which land was communally held. In fact, from 1908 up to the late 1940s there was a *Bataka* movement agitating against the unfair distribution of land in Buganda in accordance with the 1900 Buganda Agreement. This colonial pattern, however, seems to have been internalised and it is being paraded as cultural tradition. The implication of this amorphous distinction between culture and politics is that it is difficult to know exactly what role traditional leaders are supposed to perform at the local level.

Gender and the traditional authorities

One of the significant innovations in decentralisation is the empowerment of women, hitherto denied political rights due to cultural and economic factors. Due to the patriarchal nature of our societies, traditional authorities are, by and large, the domain of men. All the 52 clans of Buganda are headed by men. So are 126 clans of the Baruli. *Abataka* (clan) councils in Uganda, which are very important organs of traditional authorities, are, therefore, male-dominated (Mukyala, 1992). If traditional institutions have to play a role which is not significantly contradictory to decentralisation, they must go beyond their culture and try to redress the gender imbalance in their midst.[9]

Issues of contention and their political implications

People's ability to participate in local politics depends on a number of factors. One significant factor is the legitimacy of the political institutions through which they exercise the right of participation and the rules and procedures for the exercise of this right. In the context of decentralisation, it is important that there is agreement on the powers to be devolved, and the institutions to which power is being devolved (traditional or popularly elected officials). Much as decentralisation is in its fifth year of implementation, there is no consensus on the above issues.

Perhaps one would argue that the biggest contradictions between traditional institutions and supporters of decentralisation, especially in Buganda, is the failure to determine the level at which popular power should be located. Whereas there was a general agreement on the type of powers to be transferred to the local areas, there was no agreement on the level at which these powers should be delegated. According to the supporters of decentralisation, if the policy is to lead to popular participation and people's empowerment to hold leaders accountable, the power should be as close as possible to the people. The nearer power is to the people, the more empowered they are in determining the course of their destiny (Karuhanga, 1994:54). The state insisted that the basic unit of the decentralisation should be as small as possible. The district and the sub-county were, therefore, seen as the ideal levels which can promote people's empowerment at the local level.

In Buganda some supporters of the traditional institutions insisted that power be delegated to Mengo. It was argued that the unit to which the powers should be given should be large enough to ensure economic viability. For Buganda in particular, Mengo was seen as the ideal location for local power. From Mengo power was to be delegated to the 20 *sazas* (counties) which originally constituted Buganda kingdom.

The second source of controversy is the character of the local units. Whereas the state was pushing for mono-ethnic decentralisation in which administrative units are not constructed around ethnic or communal boundaries, supporters of traditional leaders have often pushed for poly-ethnic decentralisation in which administrative and cultural boundaries at the local level coincide. People who enjoy linguistic or any form of ethnic commonality should be organised into a single local government within a federal arrangement.

Lastly, the powers of traditional leaders at the local level are still subject to controversy. Whereas the constitutional provision is that traditional leaders should not participate in partisan politics and should not engage in any administrative

---

9   Buganda's Cabinet constituted on 15th April 1996 has only four women out of an executive of 34 members. Even this level of representation is a replica of national politics; it does not go a long way in redressing the gender imbalances in our society.

responsibilities, supporters of traditional leaders argue that they should be given more powers. Even if the power was to be that of titular head of the local communities, they should be empowered to assent to all local government legislation before coming into force as by-laws.

The existence of the above issues of controversy relating to traditional leaders in the context of decentralisation has two major implications. First, people's participation in decision-making, resource mobilisation and project implementation at the local level depends on the degree of popular commitment to self-improvements. Unresolved issues of local nature undermine this will with significant implications for the intensity and nature of participation. Secondly, the existence of issues of controversy empowers the opposition against the state. That is why it has been very easy for the Democratic Party to use the traditional institutions in Buganda, particularly the *Lukiiko*, in its struggles against the NRM government.

Traditional leaders and development

The above problems notwithstanding, traditional leaders have tried to initiate development projects at the local level to back up the decentralisation policy. In Buganda, the Cultural Development Foundation (BUCADEF) has been initiated to implement the *Kabaka*'s vision of "The New African Village by the year 2000" (NAV 2000). NAV 2000 aims at radically and massively improving the quality of lives of the people in Buganda by the year 2000. This aim, which looks over-optimistic, is to be realised by blending progressive traditional management practices with modern managerial styles for the realisation of sustainable individual and collective development. NAV 2000 intends to organise the whole population in Buganda into viable development-geared organisations at the local level. Through these organisations and through the application of the renowned traditional cultural practices, the people will be mobilised, trained, guided, and facilitated to exploit their development potential.

Overall NAV2000 is an integrated programme that will tackle a range of issues concerning health, hygiene, population control, farming methods and practices, attitudes towards work, marketing, small scale enterprise development, illiteracy, community self-help attitudes, food security, financial management and business attitude development. In various districts of Buganda, scholarships aimed at promoting education have been promised in the name of the *Kabaka*. Development associations will be formed at the sub-county (local council III) levels. These local level organisations are the social points of the decentralisation policy.

In Bunyoro, under the supervision of the *Omukama*, the Bunyoro Youth Association (BYA) is mobilising resources for the promotion of education in the three districts of Masindi, Kibale and Hoima. And in Busoga, the *Kyabazinga* recently launched the Busoga University Fund to ensure the establishment of Busoga University.

Another important development is that two private radio stations, *Central Broadcasting Service* (CBS) and *Voice of Toro* have been set up in Buganda and Toro respectively. Two newspapers are also linked to traditional leaders in one way or another.

These are Njuba Times (Buganda), and Kodhyeyo (Busoga). If these radio stations are not used to sow seeds of ethnic division, they can be agents of creating popular awareness at the local level plus information gathering and dissemination. They also facilitate citizen's participation in the debates on local and national issues. Information at the local level is vital in the planning process, it is also important in the fight against corruption amongst local and national leaders. This will ensure political and economic accountability, a factor which is essential for the success of any decentralisation policy.

Conclusion

Traditional leaders can be very important factors in decentralisation. They can use their popular base to give legitimacy to the local leadership. They can use their popular base to mobilise resources at the local level to supplement the necessary revenue for local government. They can also be countervailing forces against the state at both national and local levels. They can above all stimulate participation in decision-making at various levels through both the print media and electronics media. Their ability to perform all these duties, however, will depend on their organisational strength, that is the resources (cultural, political and economic) at their disposal, and their ability to stand autonomously not only in relationship to the state but also to other political groups in society which may wish to exploit the popularity of traditional institutions for political reasons. Besides, the distinction between what constitutes culture and what is politics significantly limits the range of activities. Accordingly, traditional leaders must learn to walk the tight rope in order to survive in the minefield of democratic politics.

SECTION III
A Values-Driven Sector?

8

The State, Civil Society and Development Policy in Uganda: Where are we Coming From?[1]

John De Coninck

Abstract

The author presents a historical analysis of the evolution of the state and civil society to reflect on current notions of development, on development policy and on the main actors shaping it. While civil society organisations played an important role in the independence struggle, he argues that they were swiftly co-opted by the state and, from 1986, concentrated on the uncontroversial provision of social services. From long before independence, 'civil society' has been closely enmeshed with the state and the demarcation between 'civil society' and 'government' remains blurred. After 1986, an era of growth for civil society organisations was fuelled by the availability of donor funding, but in the late 1990s, the role of the state was revisited, prompting donors and others to foist upon civil society a new role, that of holding government 'accountable'. This may not be easy, given civil society's limited self-awareness, its fragmented and apolitical nature and, more specifically, its nurturing in an environment where its existence has been seen as supportive to the ruling order. Further, the sector is increasingly pervaded by the business ethics that characterise sub-contracting.

This explains the absence of conflict between state and civil society and why civil society organisations have such difficulty in meeting donors' expectations with regard to holding government to account. It is growing donors' influence that lies in the adoption of messages that, given government's and NGOs' dependence on foreign funding, have quickly become akin to conditionality: 'participation', 'good governance' and 'poverty reduction'. 'Participation' thus co-exists with highly restricted forms of accountability and its rhetoric is used to legitimise various situations and systems. Simultaneously, the international agenda has stressed the privatisation of development and its technocratic nature. 'Development' has become epitomised by successful private endeavour. This has been applied to the development industry itself: consultants and NGOs promote business plans and a vision of development that rests on the ability of the individual Ugandan to surmount, essentially alone, the considerable challenges she faces.

---

[1] Reprinted from K. Brock, R. McGee and J. Gaventa (eds.), Unpacking Policy – Knowledge, Actors and Spaces in Poverty Reduction in Uganda and Niger, Fountain Publishers, Kampala, 2004.

Introduction

In recent years Uganda has been held up as a leading example of poverty reduction policy bearing fruit in sub-Saharan Africa. Government, we are often told, working hand-in-hand with a committed international community, can be credited with a measurable reduction in the number of poor people in the country, against many odds. To what extent and why has this been possible? The premise of this chapter is that a historical perspective on the context in which this success has emerged offers insights into the nature and limitations of that success, as well as throwing into relief the technocratic and usually imported discourse in which poverty reduction statements and analysis are often couched.

When we attempt to trace the origins of the current development policy environment and of some of the assumptions that guide it, there indeed appears to be much continuity between what we see today, and the events and thoughts that have characterised the Uganda polity in colonial times and throughout the first decades of its post-colonial existence. We start by looking at some of the key events and institutional actors that shaped this recent history and policy arena.

The roots of a hegemonic State and an emerging Civil Society: 1920-1986

It is often recalled that, at the time of independence in 1962, Uganda was viewed as one of the more promising emerging states in sub-Saharan Africa. This optimism was informed by the country's natural resources endowment, the way these resources had been harnessed during the colonial era and, most especially, how these had allowed for the existence of relatively well-developed and efficient services provided and managed by an omnipresent State.[2]

Uganda's mode of insertion into the international economy had been determined by the 1920s and has remained a constant for most of the subsequent period. Decisions made by the colonial authorities eighty years ago indeed continue to shape the country's socio-economic landscape. This mode of insertion informed a 'development policy' essentially framed to service the needs of an export-oriented economy based on peasant agriculture, as opposed to the settler or plantation economies in neighbouring states. The focus was thus the construction of the necessary regulatory framework, which was also demarcated along racial lines.[3] It included control over labour supply, through tax measures and the promotion of cash cropping in selected parts of the country, as well as a land policy guided by the creation of a private land market, from which

---

[2] Thus, from 1963 to 1970, economic growth averaged 6% p.a. and Uganda had the fourth highest GDP per capita in sub-Saharan; gross primary school enrolment was 67% (De Coninck J., 1992, Evaluating the Impact of NGOs in rural Poverty Alleviation – Uganda Country Study, ODI Working Paper 51, ODI: London). This central position of the State had nevertheless allowed for the development of a business sector, based on a few plantations as well as a few industries, in part controlled by a community of Asian origin.

[3] Ugandans were initially excluded from business and trade, to the benefit of an Asian commercial community of small traders and export processors.

foreigners were excluded. It also comprised the regulation of trade and marketing through minimum pricing mechanisms, marketing boards and licensing regulations, and control over business enterprises (initially export crop processing).[4] The basis of a smallholder peasant economy had thus been firmly established well before World War Two.

While the State was seen as the main provider of services needed to make this possible, a measured development of what were much later to be described as 'civil society organisations'[5] had been encouraged by the colonial authorities. The State, however, extended its regulatory arm into this arena as well, forging a symbiotic relationship with civil society, whose characteristics are still much in evidence today. Of the institutions making up civil society in the colonial era, perhaps the most important were the co-operatives of export crop growers, initially established by the Buganda middle peasantry in the 1930s. While officially sanctioned, these were placed under statutory authority immediately after World War Two. Similarly, trade unions came under state control, with nationwide unions banned in 1952 and others placed under the tutelage of a new Labour Department.

'Civil society' additionally comprised mission-established hospitals and educational establishments - the first actors to engage in social service delivery -, as well as other charitable institutions, such as the Uganda Red Cross and Asian-inspired philanthropic organisations. While the colonial state welcomed the former into public service delivery roles, the product of these institutions threatened its current form. Mission secondary schools, for instance, bred young men and a few young women who questioned the legitimacy of the colonial order. More broadly, this highly regulated and racially-divided environment did not go unchallenged. Emergent trade associations and militant co-operatives increasingly engaged in political activism, while trade unions were amongst the first organised groupings to openly confront the economic edifice, and thus the basis of colonial rule.[6]

The colonial authorities responded by guardedly opening certain doors and shaping the environment that Uganda inherited at independence. Co-operatives, for instance, were assisted to acquire cotton ginneries, heretofore the preserve of Asian and European business concerns. A parastatal, the Uganda Development Corporation (UDC), was established to make selective investments in the industrial sector and African participation in trade was promoted.

In an attempt to ensure the development of a middle class with a stake in the 'system', a delicate relationship was thus created with civil society institutions, some of which were later to give rise to pre-Independence political parties. This provided

---

4   At the same time, the 1929 Colonial Development Act established an aid fund, the precursor of DFID. In Uganda's case, initiatives eligible for assistance included agricultural research and extension, transport and communications, water supplies and public health among others.
5   Loosely described here as autonomous or semi-autonomous non-government organisations of citizens, beyond the family, situated outside the State, but not necessarily in confrontation with it (See Bayart J-F., 1986, "Civil Society in Africa", in Chabal, p (ed), *Political domination in Africa; reflections on the Limits of Power*. CUP: Cambridge p. 111).
6   Mamdani M., 1976, *Politics and Class formation in Uganda*, London: Heinemann, p. 181.

the backbone for Uganda's transition towards an independent state, with the Buganda monarch at its first head, uneasily co-existing with an elected Prime Minister, Milton Obote.

At the outset of independence, little changed. Fundamental policy shifts were precluded by the unstable balance within the political structures of the country, which a ruling bureaucratic elite only managed to alter in 1966.[7] The State became increasingly militarised and re-affirmed its central position in Uganda's political economy. Colonial 'development policy' was initially maintained in the form of five-year development plans, whose main planks were the expansion of export production, import substitution and infrastructural development - a true mirror of dominant development discourses outside Uganda. The State continued to service an export-oriented economy based on smallholders, encouraged to become 'progressive farmers' with secure land rights.[8]

But development policy in the 1960s also emphasised the direct promotion of the private sector, mainly through partnerships between UDC and Indian capital, as well as the promotion of indigenous business interests.[9] This reflected an all-important 'Africanisation' drive, a conscious effort by the state to displace the dominant Asian interests, notably through monopolistic marketing boards. Despite accelerating towards the end of the decade, this drive ultimately failed, and its failure heralded Amin's coup in 1971. The late 1960s were marked by lower export prices, growing capital outflows and increased reliance on IMF loans. Time was bought to avert crisis. The ascendancy of a bureaucratic elite was further advanced by State involvement in new areas, concretised by Obote's 'Move to the Left' and 'Common Man's Charter' (1969), reminiscent of neighbouring Tanzania's Ujamaa and 'Arusha declaration'. Much of the manufacturing sector was henceforth monopolised by the state and parastatal corporations proliferated.

Simultaneously, the co-operative movement - the largest segment of 'organised civil society' - was further expanded (loans were granted by Government to acquire crop processing facilities, for instance) and bureaucratised,[10] with the distinctions between 'civil society' and 'business' and between 'civil society' and 'state' both becoming more blurred. The second largest organised segment within civil society remained the trade unions. These were also increasingly controlled: reflecting the government strategy

---

7   The power of the Buganda kingdom (and of chiefs and middle peasants associated with it) was swept away that year when Obote's armed forces, led by Gen. Idi Amin, invaded the palace and forced its King into exile. The post-independence federal constitution was replaced by a unitary one in 1967.

8   The parallels with the current Programme for Modernisation of Agriculture (PMA) and the Land Act are striking... A central (and extremely expensive) element of this policy was a Tractor Hire Scheme launched in the early 1950s but greatly expanded in the mid-1960s.

9   The World Bank, in one its first activities in Uganda, for instance, supported an entity called African Business Promotion Ltd with, amongst others, training schemes and credit guarantees for small traders. Other efforts included the establishment of a Management Training Centre (a joint project by Government and the ILO) and extension services. For a discussion of these various initiatives, see De Coninck J., 1980, *Artisans and Petty Producers in Uganda*, D. Phil dissertation, Mimeo, University of Sussex: Brighton. Here again, the parallel with contemporary policy is striking: the equivalents of ABP Ltd, currently consist of various donor-funded private sector promotion schemes.

10 See Brett E.A., 1970, "Problems of Cooperative development in Uganda", UNSRID, Geneva.

of 'African Socialism', unions came under the direct supervision of the Department of Labour, while import substitution, though reflected in growing industrial GDP, resulted in fewer people employed in manufacturing. The emasculation of trade unions culminated in the expulsion of the more militant workers of Kenyan origin, and the banning of strike action, also in the name of 'socialism', in 1970.

The growing role of the State challenged civil society in other ways too.[11] Political parties were eventually banned, mission schools were integrated within the state system (1970 Education Act); and other forms of political dissent, often associated with the traditional kingdoms, were severely controlled. Civil society was confined to operating in more 'traditional fields' ('charity', health delivery) and sustained in doing so by the early interventions of 'charity'-oriented international NGOs, with Save the Children-UK from 1956 and OXFAM a few years later.

The parlous state of the economy, marked by high inflation, scarcities, the growing international and internal isolation of the regime, its failure to co-opt the Buganda elite, and the continuous dominance of Asians in trade, all contributed to Amin's military take-over in 1971. On paper, 'development policy' continued to be generated as before. Uganda's last 5-year Development Plan, while signed by Amin, was a legacy of the previous regime. A growing gap between 'policy on paper' and 'real policy' was, however, soon to be become evident. In 1972, the President declared an 'Economic War' and the Asian community was forcefully evicted. Over the ensuing years, as public resources were plundered in an increasingly ad hoc and unregulated fashion, and further contracted as a result of the Asian expulsion, contradictions deepened. The state apparatus itself – so central until then – was reduced to its repressive form. Its ability to offer services to the population considerably diminished and, while any form of dissent as could be orchestrated by civil society was banned, it was the churches and church-linked organisations which played an increasing role in filling widening gaps in the provision of social services.[12]

Further isolated by the terror it unleashed and largely dependent on a mercenary army, Amin's regime saw its economic base shrink as its mainstay, the small peasants, retreated further and further into subsistence agriculture or engaged in production for export on a thriving black market. By 1980, real GDP per capita was only 62% of that in 1971, and the collapse of the industrial sector and the end of crop subsidies further eroded the influence of two historic pillars of civil society, the trade unions and the cooperatives.[13] The heightened use of repression eventually led to the regime's downfall.

---

11 Bayart 1986, op.cit, p. 112.
12 The Churches also played an increasingly important behind-the-scenes political role, leading to State repression, symbolised by the murder of the Anglican archbishop Janani Luwum in 1977. Similarly, the leadership of the co-operative movement was decimated and all non-governmental media outlawed. Asian-founded charities did not survive the community's physical removal.
13 Livingstone I. 1998, "Developing industry in Uganda in the 1990's" in Hansen, H.B. & M. Twaddle (eds), *Developing Uganda*, Kampala: Fountain

After 500,000 deaths, Milton Obote returned to power in 1980 and with him the semblance of a democratic order.[14]

The arrival of two new entrants signalled Uganda's brief return to international respectability and confidence. International NGOs started large-scale relief operations, with their most high-profile intervention in famine stricken Karamoja in the early 1980s. International donor agencies also made their presence felt in Uganda for the first time, in the guise that is now familiar, with IMF- and WB-led Stabilisation and Structural Adjustment Programmes. Experiments with these characterised development policy in the period 1981-1985, foisted upon a government constantly struggling for survival. Superficially, there were initial 'successes': inflation was brought under control, exports resumed, admittedly from a very low base, and credits started flowing into the country.

Obote had inherited a state whose survival was initially only possible thanks to the presence of foreign (Tanzanian) troops. Less than a year later, Yoweri Museveni, contesting the validity of the 1980 general elections widely regarded as fraudulent, launched a guerrilla war that increasingly captured the government's attention. Economic policy acquired a surreal quality, with unexpected consequences. As the recently arrived IMF and World Bank advisors barricaded themselves indoors during nights of widespread gunfire in the capital, the black market and currency speculation flourished, and the army, under-resourced, deeply divided and undisciplined, ultimately proved unable to sustain the regime.

A circuitous journey: The NRM era (1986 to date)

In spite of this turmoil and isolation, Uganda's policy trajectory had followed a pattern not unlike that witnessed in other sub-Saharan countries, from an all-encompassing State at the helm of the economy, to a repositioning of its role through Structural Adjustment. In the initial post-independence period, the policy process was firmly in the hands of a semi-autonomous state bureaucracy. This directly benefited from its involvement in the economy, through the multiplication of parastatal entities, the imposition of taxes on export production, or the co-option of the co-operative movement.

Some aspects of this trajectory were, however, specific to Uganda. From the mid-1970s, the state had withered to a condition of near collapse, with very limited capacity to implement any kind of government policy, whether of a structural adjustment or any other nature. Further, chaos only allowed a truncated form of civil society to emerge, much weaker than in other parts of East Africa at the time. Young, cowed, and used to close State supervision, it emerged either politicised (the Churches), moribund (the Trade unions), banned (the 'traditional kingdoms') or complacent with its cosy, non-confrontational relationship with the State (development organisations, mostly expatriate-managed and dominated by high-profile international relief NGOs).

---

14 Growing repression necessitated the creation of an external enemy, Tanzania, which eventually led to Uganda's invasion by Tanzanian forces and their capture of Kampala in 1979. After three short-lived transition governments, Obote returned to power in December 1980, after general elections, widely regarded as fraudulent and the first to be held since 1962.

When Yoweri Museveni came to power, re-establishing the ascendancy of the State was imperative.[15] This was first to be achieved through the extension of the Resistance Council (RC) structure - originally put in place in areas of the country 'liberated'by Museveni's guerrilla army – to all parts of the national territory and in firm reaction to the autocratic practices of the earlier regimes.[16]

Secondly, a political system was put in place that was meant to be inclusive of all factions that had made up Uganda's political landscape in the previous decades, under the umbrella of the National Resistance Movement. As an NRM-linked author notes,

> The concept "movement" most fully conveys what was needed and what happened. (...) A society which was oppressed by the state, but which also lacked "motion" because of centuries-old stagnation needed a cataclysmic push, a national coalition of democratic, political and social forces to spark the process of revolutionary change.[17]

And thirdly, the State re-asserted its presence in the economic sphere. For a while, there was a complete break with the earlier economic orthodoxy: barter trade was, for instance, initiated to exchange primary products for road construction and technical assistance, the national currency was *revalued*, and marketing of scarce commodities was organised by the State through the RCs.

This period of reconstruction provided space for the emergence of indigenous civil society organisations, symbolised by the creation of an umbrella organisation, DENIVA.[18] With social service delivery still beyond the capacity of government and with donor funding to NGOs in Uganda no longer compromised by political instability, a 'laissez-faire' attitude by Government towards NGOs characterised the late 1980s and early 1990s, so long as there was no 'political' agenda.[19] Simultaneously, the relative peace that prevailed in many parts of the country after 1986 encouraged people to build their own local community-based organisations, including many types of voluntary associations, self-help farmers' groups, and parents-teachers' associations.

This era of growth for civil society organisations, with most engaged in service delivery, accelerated as the World Bank and other donors forced fiscal orthodoxy upon Government. Seen as ideologically preferable to state delivery, CSOs were considered

---

15 Collier P. & S. Pradhan, 1998, "Economic Aspects of the Transition from Civil War" in Hansen, H.B. & M. Twaddle (eds.), *Developing Uganda*, Kampala: Fountain, p. 20.
16 The RCs were a pyramidal structure of local committees from village to district levels, later re-named Local Councils. "Grassroots democracy" through RCs took the form of resolution of disputes, provision of security and the all-important distribution of sugar and other essential commodities to local residents.
17 Kabwegyere T., 2000, "Civil Society and Democratic Transition in Uganda since 1986" in Mugaju, J., and J. Oloka-Onyango, *No-Party Democracy in Uganda, Myths and Realities*, Kampala: Fountain
18 The Development Network of Indigenous Voluntary Associations, established in 1988, immediately after a group of NGO workers and academics attended a conference in Sudan.
19 This also arose out of pragmatic considerations. While the 1989 NGO Registration Act, administered by the Ministry of Internal Affairs, called for close supervision of NGOs, the capacity to do so has been absent (De Coninck, 2000: 15).

'less corrupt and closer to the people'.[20] [21] This was the heyday of NGOs. Generously funded, they could act with impunity and without reference to government policies. Government functionaries viewed the resources flows benefiting these stalwarts with a good measure of envy and even cynicism.[22] This era also established two important dimensions of 'civil society' in Uganda: firstly, the lasting association - even equation - of 'civil society' with NGOs, while its other components, trade unions and co-operatives, were being undermined by structural adjustment, liberalisation and retrenchment; and secondly, the tendency for NGO growth to be driven by the availability of donor funding rather than providing a direct answer to specific locally-rooted social or political imperatives.

The failure of the initial experiments with a 'command economy', in part due to the collapse of the Soviet bloc, had led the government to revert to the policy context that had been pioneered during the Obote II regime. Structural adjustment, privatisation, and liberalisation had again become the order of the day. This was concretised in the 1987 Economic Recovery Programme (ERP). Aimed at macro-economic stability and infrastructure rehabilitation, with extensive external financing, the ERP entailed a substantial review of the role of the state in the economic sphere. A pro-poor agenda appeared for the first time, and with it an explicit role for civil society: "A distinctive feature of the policy [was] its heavy reliance on NGOs and community-based rural organisations (the resistance councils) which are well placed to supplement the government's capacity to implement projects directed at the poor" (Twaddle & Hansen 1998: 9).

Nevertheless, as the State reasserted itself, the democratic flourishing of the early years was slowly supplanted by a more exclusive vision of its role. Resistance Councils were turned into bureaucratised and salaried Local Councils and were complemented by various other local structures.[23] The long arm of the state could be felt in all the country's villages through councils that increasingly acted as transmission belts for the policies and edicts originating in Kampala. Further, a new Constitution, deferring the re-introduction of party politics and entrenching the 'Movement system', was adopted by Parliament in 1995 and crowned by presidential and parliamentary elections the following year, stamping the NRM imprimatur for another five years.

---

20 From 160 registered NGOs in 1986, their number grew to over 600 in 1990 and 3500 in 2000 (De Coninck, 1992; Tulya-Muhika, S., 2002, *Notes for presentation of Preliminary Findings,* Uganda NGO Sector survey 2002, mimeo 2002).
21 Clayton A., 1998, NGOs *and Decentralised Government in Africa,* Occasional Paper 18, INTRAC: Oxford, p.11.
22 In 1992-3, for instance, expenditure by NGOs in Uganda was estimated at US$ 125 million, almost equivalent to the World Bank's contribution to the Rehabilitation and Development Plan that year (Dicklitch S., 1998, "Indigenous NGOs and Political Participation" in Hansen, H.B. & Twaddle, M., (eds), *Developing Uganda,* Kampala: Fountain, p. 148. The term 'briefcase NGO' also emerged at the time to characterise shady undertakings masquerading as NGOs.
23 Movement committees, Youth councils, Women's councils, Organisations of people with disabilities. Local councillors at certain levels became eligible for stipends.

The 1990s saw a number of policy undertakings, some of a pioneering nature on the continent. In 1990, a Programme for the Alleviation of Poverty and Social Costs of Adjustment (PAPSCA) was launched which was among the first World Bank Social Funds and pioneered direct funding through NGOs. The government started a micro-credit scheme in 1995 and universal primary education was announced a year later. In 1997, a wide-ranging Decentralisation Act was passed, entailing the devolution of responsibility for political, financial and administrative affairs, to districts and sub-counties, with locally elected representatives and extension staff responsible towards directly elected district councils. This was made possible in part by a regular increase in international assistance provided to the Government[24] and by a decentralisation process that allowed donors to target their assistance through the 'adoption' of particular districts.

It was also during this period that the role of the state was revisited. The 1997 World Development Report[25] and the DFID White Paper 'Eliminating World Poverty'[26], for instance, questioned the minimalist view that had so far prevailed. Donor influence and familiarity, the nascent decentralisation context and growing concerns with 'poverty reduction' continued to make Uganda fertile ground to test new approaches. The focus was now on an expanding local government apparatus and on the central authorities' attempt to eradicate poverty through a new policy initiative, the Poverty Eradication Action Plan (1997).

Within civil society, the bonanza years for NGOs were over. The latitude for their involvement in service delivery was narrowing while donors were reconsidering the funding of such activities through NGOs. The larger NGOs, with their burgeoning bureaucracies, were confronted by the new and difficult challenge of downsizing and the need to explore new funding mechanisms, especially sub-contracting or, less frequently, state grants. At the political level, the emergence of a relatively well-resourced corporatist State also led to the redefinition of the political space that civil society would be allowed to occupy. A new NGO Bill was drafted, placing civil society organisations under strict supervision by the Ministry of Internal Affairs.[27]

But this new vision has not gone unchallenged. The NRM has been in uninterrupted power since 1986. While the vested interests of an entrenched elite have deepened, protected by the increasing militarisation of public life, resistance is assuming a number of different forms. On the one hand, although relatively inexperienced and poorly organised, some elements in civil society have been increasingly vocal in their

---

24 Donor aid has continued to increase – from 9.1% of GDP, for instance, in 1998/9 to 13% in 2001/2. Uganda was also the first country worldwide to benefit (from 1997 onwards) from the HIPC initiative. This has not prevented Uganda's debt stock from continuing to rise from 62% of GDP in 19989 to 70% in 2002/2 (Ministry of Finance, Uganda Government, 2003, Ministry of Finance, Planning and Economic Development, Background to the Budget 2002/2003, Kampala).

25 World Bank, 1997, World Development Report 1997: The State in a Changing World. World Bank: Washington DC.

26 HMG, 1997, 'Eliminating World Poverty: The Challenge for the 21st Century. White Paper on International Development'. HMSO: London.

27 At the time of writing, this Bill has been withdrawn from the parliamentary timetable to allow for further consultations with civil society organisations and other parties.

questioning of Government policy. The Churches have denounced the perpetuation of violence in the North, the Uganda Debt Network (UDN) has taken an active stance against corruption in public life, the Uganda Joint Christian Council has denounced electoral irregularities, the *Monitor* newspaper has taken an independent political stance on many issues. Secondly, the electorate increasingly uses its power at local levels to express frustrations by recalling local council officials, or at least needs to be cowed into voting 'wisely'. Thirdly, donors have more frequently and more openly expressed disquiet at the 'slow nature of progress towards democratic governance'.[28] And finally, armed opposition has shown resilience in several parts of the country, in part reflecting local feelings of exclusion from the mainstream political processes and the accompanying rewards.

Where are we now? The persistence of poverty – and the new wisdom

From 1988, Uganda complied with World Bank prescriptions, the regime gained in acceptability (illustrated by its accolade of belonging to the 'New Leadership in Africa'), and positive indicators provided succour and legitimacy to the international recipe for development. The experiment had been shown to succeed. Uganda came to epitomise success, the showcase of orthodox development practice on the continent.

As the 1990s proceeded, this vision proved increasingly problematic. The figures were not so glowing after all. If the percentage of the population under the poverty line had indeed declined,[29] this was not the case in the northern part of the country and persistent critics, including some in the tripartite government-donor-NGO partnership Uganda Participatory Poverty assessment (UPPAP), were questioning the validity of the data. GDP growth was showing signs of slowing down and, in the all-important agriculture sector, was barely keeping pace with population growth. State revenues were stagnant,[30] military expenditure was growing, as was the external stock of debt. The high dependence on donors showed every sign of persisting and local savings rates were failing to grow. Further, earnings from the main export crop, coffee, declined by 70% in dollar terms between 1998/9 and 2001/2.[31]

Independent Uganda inherited a foreign-inspired notion of a State that, while symbolising the new nation, from 1966, in reality quickly proved unable to discharge even its most basic responsibility of territorial integrity. As elsewhere in Africa, the state had preceded the nation.[32] Further, after the first few post-independence years, much of the post-colonial period was marked by its contraction and the increased use of violence to ensure compliance by the local population.

---

28 See, for instance, NGO Forum, 2001.
29 From 56% in 1992 to 35% in 2000 (Ministry of Finance, Planning and Economic Development, Uganda Poverty Status Report, 2003, Kampala, p. 164)
30 The fiscal deficit widened from 6.7% of GDP in 1997-8 to 12.7% in 2001-2 (Ministry of Finance, Background to the Budget, 2002-3).
31 Uganda Poverty Status Report (2003:14).
32 Chabal, quoted in Clayton, op. cit, p. 9.

With the advent of the NRM, supported by keen donors, Uganda has undergone the introduction and consolidation of a pervasive Local Council structure, decentralised governance and the re-affirmation of the role of the state in service provision, albeit using resources mostly provided by 'development partners'. Far from the State withering away, the reverse has occurred, sometimes surreptitiously, and the numbers of people depending on the State's continued existence has grown rapidly.

Nevertheless, the contemporary Ugandan state remains fragile. Its assertion of power is not unchallenged country-wide, and still depends on a well-resourced repressive apparatus and access to foreign resources. Its prominence on the institutional landscape, as the 'weak Leviathan',[33] reflects the relative weakness of other actors, rather than its inherent strength.

This relative weakness has prompted donors and others to foist upon civil society (mainly, as noted above, NGOs) a new role, that of holding government 'accountable'. From cheap and honest service deliverers, NGOs are now to become agents for democratisation. This expectation emerges in a context where civil society, by playing this 'accountability' role, could lend legitimacy to the regime – a potentially useful function now that donors have become more vocal in demanding progress towards multi-party democratic forms of governance. An author close to the NRM notes:

> The multiplicity of diverse civil society organisations and their growing participation and assertiveness clearly proves that no-party democracy is by no means a negation of pluralism. As civil society gains influence to shape public policy, political leaders will be compelled to be more accountable and transparent.[34]

If civil society is given the opportunity to play the role of political parties, whether ascribed by Government or by donors, can it take up the challenge? This may not be easy, given its immaturity, its limited self-awareness, its fragmented and apolitical nature and, more specifically, its nurturing in an environment where its existence has been seen as supportive to the ruling order. While civil society organisations played an important role in the independence struggle, we have seen that they were swiftly co-opted by the state and, from 1986, concentrated on the uncontroversial provision of social services. In any case, from long before independence, 'civil society' has been closely enmeshed with the state. The demarcation between 'civil society' and 'government' thus remains blurred: individuals, for instance, move seemingly effortlessly from one to the other, as indeed they move to the employ of donors. Further, working for a recognised NGO, often 'middle-class' and 'urban' in its cultural orientation especially where an international NGO is concerned, remains a prized social achievement, accompanied by what many consider a luxurious lifestyle.

Many CSOs, as we shall see later, appear to be preoccupied with accountability to their donors and their own self-perpetuation, rather than with accountability to their would-be constituencies. The sector is increasingly pervaded by the business ethics

---

33 Bratton M., 1989, Beyond the State: Civil Society and Associational in Africa, in *World Politics*, 41, p. 410.
34 Kabwegyere, op. cit, pp.107-8.

that characterise sub-contracting.[35] Further, the persistence of peasant agriculture and of an atomised social life makes bridging the gap between NGOs and their would-be local constituencies problematic, while the many community-based organisations also operate in a heavily regulated environment.

The foregoing helps us appreciate the absence of conflict between state and civil society. According to a recent study on the relationship between CSOs and local governments,[36] CSO representatives sought to collaborate more closely with government, in the form of co-operation on specific projects, rather than to develop an independent stance on, say, local planning mechanisms, or the political rather than technical dimensions of project implementation. Further, competition for funds and contracts *among* NGOs fosters atomisation, disunity and a greater distance from common social agendas. Civil society, therefore, does not much threaten the space currently occupied by the political elite: quite the contrary, it can be seen to provide it with the legitimacy that allows its perpetuation.[37]

This might explain why civil society organisations have such difficulty in meeting donors' expectations with regard to holding government to account. While exceptions do exist, as with UDN, they mostly occur at central level, where the local contradictions, such as with the demands of sub-contracting, are least intense. Nevertheless, as the daily *Monitor* noted:

> There is a lot of irony (...). Most independent human rights groups (...) have shunned the activist role which directly campaigns against violations and chosen show activities, like seminars and workshops (...) They fudge or claim they are 'working quietly behind the scenes.[38]

International NGOs, meanwhile, have also had to adapt. The resources at their disposal made this process easier than for many local NGOs, but they have had to contend with a donor environment that increasingly questioned their 'operational' role in the country, often said to have created 'islands of excellence'. Many have re-invented

---

35 See Community Development Resource Network, "Thoughts on Civil Society in Uganda", CDRN: Kampala, 2003. Similarly, the engagement of CSOs in national development programmes has been mainly scrutinised from a technocratic perspective (Uganda Participatory Development Network, 2002, "Adventure or Joint Venture? CSO participation in national government programmes: experiences and challenges", Kampala, 2002).

36 Community Development Resource Network, 2001, "A study of relationships between Civil Society and Local Government in Northern Uganda", mimeo, CDRN: Kampala.

37 Where such conflict develops, the State intervenes with vigour. An apex organisation for NGOs, the NGO Forum, was refused registration in 1998 when first created, much as in colonial times nation-wide Trade Unions were banned. Police were called to disband its meetings in 1999. The Monitor newspaper was banned for a week in 2002 for 'publishing false news'. Popular political debates aired on FM stations (*ebimeeza*) have been prohibited by the Minister of Information and the stations themselves were banned for some time. NGOs are thus allowed as "facilitators of NRM objectives, not alternative sources of power", just as political parties are allowed to exist, not to act (Dicklitch, op.cit. p. 152).

38 Cited in Bazaara N, 2000, "Contemporary Civil Society and the Democratisation Process in Uganda: A Preliminary Exploration", Centre for Basic Research, Working Paper 54, CBR: Kampala.

themselves as 'capacity-builders' for local NGOs and local government and/or focused on an 'advocacy agenda'.

But international NGOs are also donors in their own right. Many of the challenges faced by CSOs reflect the growing influence of donors since the late 1980s. One illustration of this lies in the adoption of messages that, given government's and NGOs' dependence on foreign funding, have quickly become akin to conditionality and have resulted in a *de facto* donor monopoly on ideas underpinning development policy-making.

Donor funding in Uganda has, for instance, coincided with an increased acceptance of the need for 'participation' in the development process. This has manifested itself, in the first instance, in the need for 'consultations' whenever development policy has to be defined. Many 'development actors' are consulted, including prominent NGOs. A recent study indicates that these selective invitations are in turn used by Government and donors to stamp a seal of approval on particular partners[39] and that such 'consultations' are sometimes seen to provide a legitimisation of what is often considered a screen for cosmetic change.[40]

Secondly, participation has been extolled in 'development field practice'. Here again, Uganda has provided a conducive experimentation ground, with an explosion in the use of Participatory Rapid Appraisal (PRA) and related approaches in a wide range of situations in the early 1990's. Villagers have been known to ask the (often white) development worker: "Which type of map would you like us to draw? A resource map? A social map?" PRA has found its way into community development work, official government guidelines for local councils (Uganda Government 2002) and the development-speak of any self-respecting government functionary in Kampala and in the districts. As PRA has become an explicit condition for funding, one-day PRA courses can easily be organised by the burgeoning consultancy companies in the capital. So long as a certificate is issued, practice matters little.

'Poverty reduction' is another illustration. As we have noted, tackling poverty did not immediately appear as a stated goal of Government policy. However, from about 1992, when Government finally succeeded in stabilising the economy, poverty reduction provided an increasingly important rationale for the regime's existence, with solid prompting from the donor community. The elaboration of such policy was initially seen as the sole prerogative of the state and its 'development partners', the donors, drawing on their own information and without recourse to CSOs. Donors have since become the key actors in attaching legitimacy to subsequent policy initiatives for poverty reduction. First amongst these initiatives has been the Poverty Eradication Action Plan (PEAP), the local equivalent of the Poverty Reduction Strategy Paper (PRSP). Intended as a 'broadly owned' policy initiative, the PEAP nonetheless appears

---

39 Lister S. & W. Nyamugasira, 2001, "A Study on the involvement of Civil Society in Policy Dialogue and Advocacy, Lessons learnt on their Engagement in Policy Advocacy, and Future Direction", mimeo, DFID
40 UPDNet, op.cit.; Porter D. and M. Onyach-Olaa, 1999, 'Inclusive Planning and allocation for Rural Services', *Development in practice*, Vol 9, Nos 1 & 2, February 1999.

to have mainly provided a medium for negotiations between donors and Government, rather than a collective, national initiative to focus efforts for national development. Secondly, the much-hailed UPPAP, while promoting the 'voices of the poor' as part of the now-accepted consensus around poverty as a multifaceted phenomenon, has been much centralised among selected ministries, donors and a few CSOs in Kampala.[41]

For different reasons, the discourse of 'gender' also found a fertile environment. The new regime, having antecedents as a guerrilla organisation with women soldiers and women representatives on its clandestine Resistance Councils, had availed space for women's voices to be heard. Building on this opportunity, after 1986 a small, educated elite fostered affirmative action for women in a number of fora, including women representatives in Parliament. Simultaneously, however, 'gender' became a catchword of many donor-inspired interventions. Gender officers proliferated in development agencies, and the elaboration of a 'gender policy' became another hurdle to be overcome by whichever local organisation was seeking donor funding, to accompany the strategic plan or log frame.

'Advocacy', 'governance' and 'accountability' have also been much bandied about. The accountability agenda has been most visible within debates on decentralisation, 'grassroots democracy' and the role of CSOs. With regard to the former, donors have been enthusiastic supporters of the decentralisation process, in part perhaps because decentralisation has afforded them a technical blueprint solution and a legitimisation of their support to a regime which might appear less than 'democratic' to their home public. The Government has not been slow to recognise this, as it provided *it* with internal justification too. Kabwegyere notes:

> The involvement of millions of people directly or through their representatives in discussing public affairs at all levels of the LC system has certainly done a lot more to enhance the process of democratisation than was ever achieved under multiparty politics.[42]

But the reality is somewhat different. The decentralisation drive has done much to reinforce local power-holders. We have also seen that the decentralisation process has allowed the state to re-legitimise itself and reaffirm its primary role in service delivery, with considerable resources now being channelled to the local level. Central government has recognised some of the risks involved: developing accountability in the districts remains a priority and the Ministry of Local Government continues to play a key supervisory role.

This accountability channel currently appears to be much more important than any played by CSOs, although, as noted, donors have placed much emphasis on the necessity of civil society developing its voice in this respect. As Chabal noted some years ago:

---

41 The PEAP and UPPAP have also been instrumental in providing the two windows of opportunity that heralded participation of civil society in the national policy process with regard to poverty reduction.
42 Kabwegyere, op.cit, p. 103.

In situations where formal institutions of political representation – elections, political parties, legislatures – have been emasculated by executive monopoly, accountability comes to 'depend almost entirely on the ability of civil society to curb the hegemony of the state'.[43]

Development in the local context

While Uganda's development experience is often hailed as the epitome of 'participatory development', the poor still feel disenfranchised. How does this relate to the context described above?

We must first recall the pervasive and long-standing autocratic environment in which the attempts at 'participatory development' are situated. In the period under review, for instance, it is only in the last few years that people have been provided with opportunities to have their voices heard. Arguably, for some, the last genuine elections were held in 1962. Since then, it is mainly the LC structure (rather than civil society organisations) that has provided this channel to the population. But this is not a straightforward channel. Belonging to this structure is, in the first instance, mandatory for every citizen and exclusive of other options. 'Participation' must therefore be exercised within a single and all-encompassing political perimeter. With the years, as noted, this structure has been increasingly used by the State for its own purpose: the population has been pressed into its age-old cultural mould of 'the chief commands', nurtured in school establishments where the teacher is *always* right. The LC structures are therefore increasingly rarely used other than as transmission belts for central decision-making, while often providing convenient spaces for the powerful to dictate at local level. LCs have been assimilated into a local culture in which accountability must defer to seniority and power, and in spaces where clientelism is the accepted mechanism for resource allocation.

The application of an array of participatory methodologies mentioned above seems to have made relatively limited impact on the power relationships shaping these structures. While bottom-up planning is everywhere the order of the day, much has been stripped of its intent as a methodology for facilitating social change and reduced to a set of slavishly applied steps and methods. Here also, a set of 'participatory' techniques has been appropriated within a cultural context and political practice where participation and representation often remain elusive.[44]

Linked to the above is the painfully slow progress towards an 'accountable state', to use an imported phrase. In spite of the presence of the multitude of local councils listed above, situated moreover in a highly decentralised context, local power-holders continually seem to 'get away with it'. Corruption has become an accepted way of life and is reminiscent of earlier regimes. The powerful who do not 'eat'[45] are branded

---

43 Chabal, cited by Bratton 1989, p 416.
44 As Midgley noted elsewhere: "The State supports community participation for ulterior motives, for purposes of political and social control (…) to reduce the costs of programmes (and) to neutralise spontaneous participatory activities" (quoted in Dicklich, op.cit, p.152).
45 The locally accepted term for using public resources for personal gain.

fools rather than those who do 'eat' being branded social deviants. Suspect deals are applauded and semi-legitimate activities proliferate. It is no wonder, therefore, that international league tables continue to place Uganda amongst the most corrupt countries. At a more general level, the state, by clearly indicating which topics are open for discussion and which are not (defence expenditure, for instance), has also set boundaries beyond which participation is not applicable and, in so doing, has reinforced what local communities have learnt from their history, the history of a non-accountable colonial and post-colonial state. 'Participation' thus co-exists with highly restricted forms of accountability and its rhetoric is used to legitimise various situations and systems.[46]

Limited accountability is not the sole prerogative of Government and local councils, however. As we have mentioned, civil society organisations have also found it difficult to develop their own mechanisms to be answerable to those they profess to serve. Even where membership organisations are concerned, members are often resigned to seeing their leadership amass power, resources or other privileges with impunity. Further, many civil society organisations uneasily combine 'philanthropic' objectives, for donor consumption, with economic advancement objectives for their membership and leadership. Must not donors' liberal expectations of CSOs acting as standard bearers for accountability therefore be re-evaluated?

The paradox described above highlights the deepening legitimacy gap which the NRM regime currently has to confront. Inclusiveness and grassroots democracy increasingly seem to lack substance, while demands for 'opening up' the political system proliferate in different quarters: the urban population, elements of the press, sections of the intelligentsia and, importantly, donors who find justifying their on-going support to their respective public opinions ever more difficult.[47]

Within this context, the poverty reduction agenda assumes a new urgency. Faced with growing disillusionment, the regime is under increasing pressure to demonstrate that the Movement system delivers. While advances are undeniable and while many, particularly in the rural areas, acknowledge the gains made by Government in providing desperately needed social and physical infrastructure, many of these gains are being eroded by high population growth and rapid environmental destruction. Regional disparity is also persisting, with large areas of the North, still wracked by civil unrest, lagging way behind the rest of the country. This regional imbalance reflects the antecedents of the Ugandan state, a creation, as noted above, of colonial convenience. The Movement, in spite of its inclusive character, is still struggling with overcoming the fractious nature of this state. While national unity remains a costly[48] and time-

---

46 Thus, whatever its original intent, UPPAP was not conducted with a view to rendering accountability to the local poor.
47 See NGO Forum, 2001, "Uganda: The Economy, Poverty and Governance. Summary Report of the Consultative Group Meeting held at Kampala International Conference Centre, May 14-17, 2001", mimeo.
48 Thus in 2002/3, several ministries found their budgets cut overnight to accommodate additional defence spending, the latter exceeding its budgetary allocation by 16% three quarters of the way through the financial year.

consuming effort, ethnicity has persisted as a commonly held explanation for patterns of resource allocation at macro and micro levels. The State is widely perceived to be dominated by one group, whose interests it primarily serves, at the expense of others.

By the time Yoweri Museveni's band of guerrillas captured the State, a persuasive rhetoric of self-reliant development had become established (National Resistance Movement 1986). The early years of the new regime created a climate favourable to the discourse on 'participatory development' and saw active steps being taken to put this into practice. With time, a deepening chasm appears to have developed between rhetoric and reality. Both local and international influences account for this. Within Uganda, we have noted how the regime has successfully adopted a discourse of 'bottom-up development' not only to promote local governance, but also to cloak its sustained grip on power. This has been possible thanks to the conjunction of institutions with relatively poor accountability mechanisms: local councils and other state institutions; dependent civil society organisations and donors with a stake in the success of their Uganda enterprise.

Simultaneously, the international agenda has stressed the *privatisation* of development and its *technocratic* nature. Here again, Uganda has provided fertile soil. Beginning as a social movement, 'development' has become epitomised by successful private endeavour. This has been applied to the development industry itself: consultants and NGOs (themselves increasingly turned into commercial enterprises), promote business plans and a vision of development that rests on the ability of the individual Ugandan to surmount, essentially alone, the considerable challenges she faces.

9

"Webisanga Kabaka!" (You behave like a King!): Civil Society Leadership in Uganda[1]

Moses Isooba, Betsy Mboizi, Ida Kusiima

Abstract

With the recent growth in Civil Society Organisations (CSOs) in Uganda, this young sector has pointed towards a need for 'leadership development'. Several 'capacity-building' organisations implement leadership development programmes. This study examines Ugandan NGO leadership within a framework that envisages such leadership as the product of an amalgam of traditional (autocratic, high power distance) and modern (often assumed to be charismatic, visionary, participatory) values, recognising that leadership behaviour is also contingent on the environment in which the leader operates. It defines successful leadership as the ability to remain essentially true to one's organisational mission amidst an ever-changing environment.

The authors outline the challenges facing NGO leaders in relation to change, and why and how leaders develop, learn and change. They show that NGO leadership, while rarely associated with the desirability of change, is not only understood as a position of vision and authority, but also as a relationship between leaders and followers. It is a way to derive social recognition, a position of privilege. Leaders face a number of challenges and blockages preventing them from embracing change (intense personal family and social expectations; internalising demands to change management from different sources, the fear of failing at personal and social levels, cultural strictures of many kinds). Women leaders struggle with these and additional gender related challenges while leaders of faith-based organisations grapple with other issues. Against this, there are incentives for change, such as determination to succeed, pressure from staff and donors, and 'crucible' experiences.

Successful leaders are seen as those with a determination to lead against all odds, those consciously embracing change as necessary and part of learning, those adept at leading people internally and externally to the NGO, and those emerging from a particular set of family circumstances, including supportive networks.

---

1   This is a shortened version of a paper issued by the Community Development Resource Network in 2005. Reprinted by kind permission.

Against this background, capacity builders need to design personalised approaches to organisation development interventions, to desist from the routine of westernised and textbook models of Organisational Development, and emphasise the real life experiences of the leaders, the cultural context in which they operate and a clear set of values, cultural and/or spiritual.

Introduction

Leadership and civil society organisations

Effective leadership is increasingly viewed by development actors as one of the most critical components in the development of civil society in Africa. At first glance, the problems of poverty, disease and conflict indeed seem so great that extra-ordinary leadership is needed to address them (James and Mullins 2004). Although it is increasingly acknowledged that leaders are the key to organisational change and that personal change is essential to any such change, the fact that human change is a complex and intensely personal process is often overlooked. Understanding what affects leaders in African CSOs (Civil Society Organisations) and what causes or prevents leaders from changing their leadership behaviour is therefore important – both for NGO leaders and for CSO capacity-building organisations, so that they may in time improve their organisational and leadership development programmes.

CSO leaders on the African continent face an enormous challenge: fulfilling their organisation's vision while at the same time steering their organisation through a complex and ever-changing society characterised by poverty, disease and conflict. Constant changes in the social and political environment, stakeholder demands as well as donor policies and priorities command leaders to widen their perspectives and draw on new ideas and different ways of thinking. In addition, in much of our region,

> Many NGOs are still led by founding leaders. As they grow and develop, such NGOs naturally hit a 'pioneer crisis' as they are forced to develop more formal structures and systems as well as a shift in leadership styles to maintain their performance. Structures and systems are much easier to change than styles of leadership. The essential entrepreneurial qualities required to set up an organisation from inception are not the same ones as needed to lead a much larger organisation. Either the leader is able to change his/her own way of leading or eventually the leader has to change. (James, 2002)

Why this study?

Given the above, the need for leadership development within African CSOs is gaining prominence. Thus, a number of 'capacity building' organisations have implemented leadership development programmes. We need to understand much better the challenges facing civil society leaders in the different cultures and contexts in which they lead. We need to understand much better why and how leaders develop, learn and change. We need to stand back from our relentless capacity-building activity to reflect and learn to improve our practice by understanding better what makes leaders change. Specifically, our study in Uganda was thus being undertaken to provide an in-depth understanding of NGO leadership in a Uganda context; the pressures and demands facing NGO leaders; the incentives and sources of the impetus for change; the sanctions and risks to leaders of changing and/or not changing and the implications for OD (organisational development) and leadership development.

This article is divided into seven sections. The second reviews civil society, leadership and other contextual issues relevant to our research in Uganda. In the third, we delve into the findings, starting with documenting the local perceptions of leadership, followed by challenges and blockages to leadership and change in section four. The fifth section outlines incentives to change and conclusions are offered in chapter six. The seventh and final chapter examines the implications of our findings for organisational development work.

Leadership in the literature

There is a large body of literature on leadership issues, although much of this focuses on the corporate sector and only a few studies have attempted to explore leadership in an African context, let alone an African civil society context. In much of this literature, leadership is identified as a critical element for organisational effectiveness. There is also an emphasis on the importance of personal traits and individual behaviour in determining who is an effective leader. The bulk of this research seeks to establish the personal and psychological qualities of specific leaders, their style and behaviour (Adair; Kotter; Zaccaro & Klimoski, cited in Kakabadse & Kakabadse, 1999). This has also included studies into their physical appearance, intellectual ability, personality and inter-personal skills. More recently, researchers have focused on such attributes as charisma, visioning, and the ability to promote learning.

The leadership literature offers other suggestions as to the personal characteristics of an effective and successful leader: a blend of extreme personal humility with intense professional will (Collins 2001), a high level of 'people skills' and the ability to promote and share a clear vision, to communicate effectively and to motivate (Kakabadse & Kakabadse 1999), the ability to be in touch with both the inner and outer world and to manipulate the world and bend it towards one's own ends (Kaplan 2002), and the ability to continue learning in life (Bennis & Thomas 2002). Other leadership studies carried out by Blunt & Jones (1992) focus on the leader's ability to strike an appropriate balance between leadership and management.

Leaders are not leaders in a vacuum: they exist within a very influential context. Leadership style and behaviour is therefore contingent on the circumstances and environment in which the leader operates. Such a contingent approach suggests that leadership behaviour is affected by e.g. culture, tradition, legal and political frameworks, and organisational culture (Schein, cited in James, 2004). Other authors, such as Bennis & Thomas (2002), focus on the way leaders are shaped by the era in which they live and the way crucibles (defining transformational experiences) shape a leader's values, character and capacities.

Attempts have also been made to trace some of the cultural traits shaping and influencing leaders and organisational culture (Hofstede 1994). Hofstede's study shows that East African societies generally have a high 'power distance', whereby leaders are found to be autocratic or paternalistic and employees are dependent on and afraid to disagree with them. Another characteristic of societies in East Africa is their collectivistic nature. A determining aspect of a collectivist society is said to be the extended family and growing up as part of a group. It is noted that people who grow up being dependent on a group are usually often dependent on power figures. The extended family notion is often transplanted in the workplace and the feeling of mutual obligations of protection in exchange for loyalty is prevalent and poor performers are seldom discarded (Hofstede, 1994). Another consequence of the collectivistic nature of East African societies is the widely recognised obligation of African managers to networks of kin and ethnic affiliates (James 2004; Blunt & Jones 1992; Kenya NGO Council 2001; Hofstede 1994). Growing up as part of a group, knowing that the group is the only secure protection against hardship, leads to a perception of owing lifelong loyalty to the group. Thus, the 'followership' of an organisation and how freely they attribute leadership authority is increasingly recognised as having an important role in the behaviour and success of a leader.

As well as facing the challenge of working in a high power distance and collectivist environment, female leaders are also faced with another set of pressures. In terms of gender roles in East African societies, men are supposed to be more concerned with achievements outside the home and to be assertive, competitive and tough. Women are supposed to be more concerned with taking care of the home, of the children, and of people in general – to take the gentle roles (Hofstede 1994). Consequently, Kakabadse and Kakabadse (1999) note that the expected gender roles prescribed to women affects female leaders in various ways, including prejudice, promotion opportunities, harassment, lower salary, and family pressure.

Religion is another very influential, though contentious and complex, factor for leadership in African societies. It has been noted that religious experience is the most pervasive and fundamental collective experience of African people (Mgibi in James 2004). There is therefore a spiritual dimension of leadership, whether it is considered as simply your inner-self or something outside of yourself (God).

Leadership in society is as old as mankind himself and there have been leaders and followers before the advent of organised civil society. In Africa, clans and later tribes were all organised around a key figure who would play the leadership function of providing direction and problem solving. In the African perspective, the Leader was/is perceived as a 'life-long chief', addressing every problem, and knowing it all. There was a 'followership dependence' with followers dependent on their leader for representation of their views to the outsider and to take care of their interests (Tosh, 1978). Some writers argue that until recently, 'stateless' societies without any clear political leadership prevailed in some parts of East Africa. In such societies, every person was as good as his/her neighbour and nobody assumed any special position of leadership (Tosh,

1978). In other parts of our region, however, African kingdoms developed sovereign political entities headed by a single leader who delegated authority to representatives in charge of the territorial units into which the kingdom was subdivided. All had a "divine king" who enjoyed special supernatural powers. The king was the kingdom and he owned all the land and the people all belonged to him. Such traditional leaders gave their leadership a semblance of sacredness.

Recent analyses of the state in Africa are also of relevance to our understanding of leadership issues, even though we focus on leadership of non-state organisations.[2] Of particular interest is the notion of the 'neopatrimonial' state, which emerges from "the incorporation of patrimonial logic into bureaucratic institutions" (Bratton and van de Walle 1997: 62), because it is characterised by the personalisation of power, whereby all positions of political power are held by virtue of the ruler's patronage, and based on ties of personal, nepotistic, ethnic or regional loyalty. The treatment of public office, and access to the resources that public office gives access to, is seen as a means to personal and communal gain, rather than as a means of pursuing a broader public good. The geographical extension of power is also via networks of 'clients', at every level. Inclusion within this patronage system becomes the main source of accumulation and security. This form of politics has been linked to Africa's general economic 'stagnation' and failure to 'develop' since independence, "in part because the arbitrary nature of personalised decision-making within a presidentialist system creates instability and is also, along with clientelism, highly susceptible to corruption."[3]

While both the personal and professional leadership characteristics mentioned above could apply to a leader in any sector, the Kenya NGO Council (2001) has identified five crucial factors for effective NGO leadership: (i) The individual's self-awareness (motivation, values, self-knowledge and competencies); (ii) The ability to deal with followers (including staff, Board of Directors, beneficiaries, family, clan etc.); (iii) The ability to continuously assess organisational health and adapt to changing context; (iv) The ability to understand the donor scene and (v) The ability to balance the politics of NGO space. One of the major external influential factors on NGO leadership is donors. Most NGOs in the region depend heavily on external donor funding and managing donor relations and economic resources is therefore considered one of the keys to successful NGOs (Kenya NGO Council, 2001). In relation to this, Kaplan (2002) notes that NGO practitioners are faced with demands for over-hasty timeframes, short-term projects and quick results and this does not allow time for reflection and development of visions, which are crucial parts of the leadership learning process.

Juggling these influential factors is demanding and justification for leadership development is therefore not in doubt. Several studies by African NGO members of the International Forum on Capacity-Building have confirmed the need to focus capacity-building efforts on leadership development (IFCB 1998, 2001, cited in James, 2004),

---

2   For a more detailed exposition, see also Hickey (2003).
3   Hickey (2003:30).

moving away from an earlier emphasis of capacity-building programmes on staff training. As the difficulties of integrating learning back into an unchanged organisation are better appreciated, there has been an increasing emphasis on complementing such training with organisation-wide OD efforts. It is now being increasingly recognised that for organisations to change and build their capacity, leaders themselves have to change (James 2002). Furthermore, commitment of leadership to change is synonymous with their commitment to their own personal change. Where leaders did not change their attitudes or behaviour on a personal level, the organisations failed to change as a result. Many CSO capacity-building organisations in the region, such as CDRN, have thus re-designed their capacity-building interventions to include leadership development.

Our theoretical framework and research process

From the literature, we see a difference between leadership as understood from a 'traditional context' and leadership as understood and shaped by the corporate sector. Are we witnessing a hybrid of the American corporate sector type of leadership and traditional leadership, all heavily influenced by the Eurocentric leadership tradition? We thus propose to examine NGO leadership in Uganda within a framework that envisages such leadership as a product of an amalgam of (i) traditional (autocratic, power distance type) and (ii) modern leadership (often assumed to be charismatic, visionary, participatory), (iii) recognising that leadership style and behaviour is also contingent on the circumstances and environment in which the leader operates.

Our study also takes as point of departure the fact that as organisational development actors, organisational change is hinged on the ability of the NGO leader to change and his/her ability to successfully operationalise the organisation's mission. Because leadership is a critical element for organisational effectiveness, leaders need to change attitudes or behaviour on a personal level for organisations to change. We also assume that organisations that have been successful in keeping their mission in focus have had effective leaders. However, this needs to be complemented by an ability to adapt organisations' need to change to remain relevant in an ever-changing world. Change is thus an integral part of organisational survival and growth.

Our research is being undertaken collaboratively and regionally by three organisations in Kenya, Malawi and Uganda, in order to contrast the cultural and other contextual differences between these countries. For too long, Africa has been stereotyped as a homogenous continent with blueprint solutions applied. There is thus a need to compare and contrast research findings, while those findings that may have a more universal significance may offer the potential for replication in other counties.

In-depth interviews were held with key CSO leaders and key informants (capacity building practitioners and donors). While the choice of less than 20 NGO leaders as respondents is not statistically significant, extensive interviews provide insights into the NGO leadership and change process. This choice was largely based on our knowledge of the leaders drawn from both former and current CDRN partners, as well as 'non-partners'. Some we considered "successful", others not so successful, (fulfilling our definition of 'successful leadership' – See section below). We also chose leaders from both faith-based and secular organisations, and from rural and urban areas, with activities covering service delivery and policy advocacy. Some were founder leaders, others second (or later) generation leaders; 11 were men and 5 women.

Only top executives of the organisations were interviewed, as resources did not allow for interviews with 'followers'. This led to two limitations in our work. First, we assumed that by only talking to a leader, we were able to find out if such a leader is successful or not from the interviewer's perspective. Similarly, an interaction with the organisation for a much longer time would have told us more about the leader than a one-off interview. Secondly, we assumed that leadership is vested in the 'chief executive': this may not necessarily be the case in all organisations, such as those that have tried to espouse a collegiate management style, or where the leader has recently assumed his/her position and for that matter faces a different set of challenges while settling in. Another challenge encountered during this study has been to link leadership to change. It proved difficult for our respondents to make any such linkage immediately; our questions were opening up new areas for reflection, for both newly-installed leaders, as well as for their more seasoned NGO colleagues. Despite these limitations, we feel that our findings are of relevance to NGOs in the country. Our sample, though small, reflected different but typical NGOs throughout the country and our information has been complemented by other key informants, as well as a practice of OD work at CDRN over the years. This gives us a measure of confidence as to the applicability of our research findings to the wider national context.

The context: Leadership and civil society in Uganda

Our research is situated in a context[4] where Uganda's successes in absolute poverty reduction have been widely acknowledged. With much donor support, Government has steered Uganda's economic recovery from the collapse of the 1970s and early 1980s. This has been concretised in Uganda's main policy framework, the Poverty Eradication Action Plan which spells out Government intentions and actions for poverty reduction, with a view to reducing absolute poverty to less than 10% by 2017. Despite these gains, Uganda remains amongst the poorest countries in the world, with 85% of the population engaged in small-scale subsistence farming, furthermore heavily afflicted since the 1980s by the AIDS pandemic. A significant number of people in Uganda remain poor and amongst these, many live well below the poverty line for many years. This persistent and widespread poverty, as the subsequent sections attempt to highlight, has proved to be a crucial contextual dimension for our work.

Many of the current manifestations of CSOs and their leaders reflect Uganda's civil society's experiences in the past eight decades, going back to the colonial era. While the colonial State was the main provider of social services within the overall design of an export-oriented economy based on small–holder agricultural producers, a measured

---

4   This summary draws from De Coninck (2004B).

(though highly regulated) development of CSOs was nonetheless encouraged. The state forged a relationship with civil society, whose characteristics are still in great part evident today. After World War II, trade associations and co-operatives increasingly engaged in political activism, while trade unionists were amongst the first to openly confront the economic edifice, and thus the basis of colonial rule (Mamdani 1976: 181). After independence, a militarised state occupied a central position in Uganda's political economy and the peasant cooperative societies and trade unions were taken over by the Government and bureaucratised. "CSOs were challenged in other ways too: mission schools were integrated within the state system; political parties were eventually banned and other forms of political dissent curtailed. The 1970s were characterised by Idi Amin's repressive regime and "[By 1986, therefore…] chaos had only allowed a truncated form of civil society to emerge, much weaker than in some other parts of East Africa at the time." [5]

The 1990s witnessed a very rapid growth in the numbers of CSOs, largely because many donors preferred to channel their financial support to the CSOs which were considered "less corrupt, more efficient and closer to the community". This era of growth saw most NGOs engaged in service delivery. It also established two important dimensions of 'civil society': the lasting association – even equation – of 'civil society' with NGOs, while its other historical components, trade unions and co-operatives, were being undermined by structural adjustment, liberalisation and retrenchment; and secondly, the tendency for NGO growth to be driven by the availability of donor funding at least as much as by the need to provide an answer to specific locally-rooted social or economic imperatives.

> Equally importantly, this was also the time when NGOs established their position at the apex of social desirability. Working for a recognised NGO, often 'middle-class' and 'urban' in its cultural and political orientation, especially where an international NGO is concerned, became a prized social achievement, accompanied by what many consider a luxurious lifestyle, rather than a commitment to an alternative societal vision.[6]

The NRM government has been in power since 1986 and is currently seeking a constitutional amendment to award itself another 5 years. This has bred some resistance within civil society ranging from being muted to openly challenging the government and questioning government policy. Churches and other civil society organisations have taken a stand on this and other contentious issues. This has also bred a relationship of growing suspicion and mistrust between the state and civil society. NGOs have been branded a 'security threat' and government is in the process of finalising the NGO Amendment Bill 2000 which is intended to keep all CSOs on a short leash and constrain their activities.

---

5   De Coninck (2004A: 4).
6   Ibid. The term 'briefcase NGO' also emerged at the time to characterise shady undertakings masquerading as NGOs.

Civil society: Contemporary characteristics

Many of these historical trends continue to shape Uganda's civil society. Three contemporary dimensions are worth highlighting at this point.[7] First, growth continues to characterise CSOs at both local and national levels. There were 4,700 registered NGOs in 2003 (Barr, 2003), with most of this growth accounted for by local organisations (92% of all organisations registered in 2000) (Wallace, 2004). Dependence on donors also continues to be much in evidence, although it is a minority (but dominant) group of NGOs that have direct access to such sources. This dependence (in part a knock-on effect from the GOU's own dependence on external finance) has meant that fundraising is a major activity for many CSOs and has translated itself into an acceptance of donor conditionalities, beyond the specific conditions associated with funding flows. More fundamentally, perhaps, "(...) the poverty discourse is in itself largely conditioned by the adoption of messages that, given government's and NGOs' dependence on foreign funding, have quickly become akin to conditionality and have resulted in a de facto donor monopoly on ideas underpinning an accepted vision of development and development policy-making."[8]

Secondly, this growth, often a result of external stimuli, is reflected in the somewhat thin roots of CBOs (and especially NGOs).[9] The sector is also fluid: NGOs come and go, some are not registered, and many change activities.[10] "Many CSOs thus appear to be preoccupied with accountability to their donors and their own self-perpetuation, rather than with accountability to their would-be constituencies."[11] NGOs and CBOs are also part of a very diverse and fragmented sector. Competition for various donors' funds, contracts and recognition *among* NGOs fosters self-interest, disunity, distrust (Wallace, 2004), and a greater distance from common social agenda. The demarcation between 'civil society' and 'government' remains blurred: individuals, for instance, move from one to the other. The Government's vision of CSOs focuses on both service delivery and this is translated into invitations extended to selected CSOs, such as invitations to tender for contracts or invitations to take part in policy fora. Many donors have also foisted upon civil society (mainly NGOs) the role of holding government 'accountable.'

The CSO response to this situation has often been ad hoc, with many NGOs becoming 'multi-purpose'. CSOs then undergo a crisis of identity, as a locally rooted vision often contradicts an imported agenda. Thus, the shift towards 'advocacy' creates a situation for CSOs "which does not necessarily find its origins in Uganda culture, or sit comfortably with contemporary politics and its emphasis on consensus" (CDRN/NGO Forum, 2003). There is widespread resistance to engage with other political

---

7   This section is summarised from De Coninck (2004A).
8   De Coninck (2004A:6)
9   Many NGOs, even in the districts, are urban-based or urban-oriented. One fifth of registered NGOs are located in Kampala (Barr et al, 2003).
10 Barr et al (2003) estimate that between 15% and 30% of registered NGOs are actually in operation.
11 De Coninck (2004A: 6).

processes beyond official invitations and, in most cases, advocacy work is hesitant and reactive.

Leadership in local organisations: Social roots and political realities

If we now turn our eyes to 'traditional' or socially rooted notions of leadership in the specific context of Uganda, we must first acknowledge the cultural diversity that characterizes the country. Leadership styles to an extent reflect this cultural diversity, with a distinction between the northern and southern parts of the country. In what has remained the lesser developed part of Uganda (the North), cultural traditions reflect patterns of dispersed authority, as opposed to the more centralised traditional kingdoms of Southern Uganda, institutions that have recently been allowed to resurrect as 'cultural institutions' by the current government, after years of proscription.

In spite of its 'peasant agriculture' orientation, colonial rule further enhanced non-accountable 'top down authority patterns that have continued to find their expression in many facets of national life today. Whether it is the youngster towards his/her father, the school-going child towards the teacher, the adult towards the parish or sub-county chief (titles still in use today), or the junior civil servant emulating the norms of his/her British predecessor, authority is generally acknowledged to be in the hands of 'untouchables'.

The arrival of the NRM government with its 'resistance council' structure (later re-named local councils) and its emphasis of decentralised governance reflected a profound attempt to change these mental patterns which, the new government argued, had allowed fascism to take root in Uganda soon after independence and well beyond Amin's regime. Mamdani summarises the NRM's political project thus:

> Reforms were aimed at ensuring that local participation in governance could occur on the basis of equitable forms participatory citizenship, rather than the asymmetrical reciprocity of clientelism and divisive politics of ethnicity that so often provides the mobilising logic of patronage politics in Africa.[12]

Are these attempts producing a lasting change in leadership patterns? Some observers argue that caution should be exercised. In a recent study on policy making and implementation in Uganda, Brock and others[13] argue that, although the institutional channels exist through which the poor can participate, some key groups remain excluded, while inclusion itself does little to guarantee influence within decision-making areas. More generally, there is a growing body of evidence to suggest that neopatrimonial political practice is regaining prominence in Uganda. As one observer notes, "In a sense, the Movement's political project of replacing ethnic politics and patrimonialism with accountable governance and citizenship has faltered if not entirely failed."[14]

---

12   Mamdani, quoted in Hickey (2003:30)
13   Brock et al (2004)
14   Hickey (2003:30)

Leadership characteristics in Uganda's NGOs

If the NGO sector is young, ephemeral and to a large extent characterised by founders still in leadership positions, a lack of focus and questionable stability, what is the implication of this for NGO leaders? While the sudden blossoming of the CSO sector in part reflects opportunities and freedom afforded by political change, in part a desire for betterment of living conditions, many individuals have also turned to creating CSOs as a means of self-employment. CSOs thus have in effect taken on a dual mandate: that of ensuring the leader's/founder's own personal survival (and that of their extended families) as well as that of alleviating poverty in their respective communities[15] (De Coninck, 2004).

The Uganda CSO sector is, however, also a thriving hotbed of talent and ingenuity. This is possible because of the relative ease of entry into the sector where NGO 'social entrepreneurs' rise to the many challenges faced by the country, putting their experience and expertise to the service of public development. NGO leaders come from a variety of sources - public service, private sector, retired and retrenched professionals and demobilised army officers – and bring to the sector a wide range of skills and experiences. This ease of entry has in turn led to a degree of scepticism among civil society observers and - occasionally - within its own ranks too. Among the all-powerful donors that are close to the NGO sector, this scepticism can sometimes be expressed in strong terms. Thus, one of our key informants exclaimed:

> We want to see that the grants we give benefit the poor (...) So we want to see an organisation where the poor are truly the beneficiaries. But often the beneficiaries do not know what is going on. So that's the leadership you have in the NGO sector! There is a lack of transparency and commitment to the cause.

This state of affairs can be explained in different ways. Some see leaders selfish, self-seeking, poorly skilled but, more generally, the lack of a strong value system often echoes: "My problem is with the values behind the formation of NGOs. Most people see NGOs as another job, another means for survival. Where is the poor man? When you come out with a policy brief, whose policy brief is it?" These comments can lead to a rather cynical view of NGO leadership – and a view that seems to be slowly gaining ground. For some, therefore, 'successful' NGO leaders are described as manipulative, skilful in managing their Board and staff, able to discern the latest donor interests and good at 'donor speak'.

In spite of this growing scepticism and 'credibility gap', a good leader in an NGO nevertheless remains arguably its most precious resource, more valuable and scarcer than finance or equipment. According to a recent report to the Government on NGOs (Barr et al, 2003), NGO leaders in Uganda are very well-educated with over 84% possessing a tertiary or university degree; most NGO leaders are "middle-class", with "only" 30% having "poor parents." Most directors are married and with a large number

---

15 Barr et al (2003) also note that NGO leaders are entrepreneurial individuals with multiple occupations, such farming, trade or other business interests.

of dependants and, in 12% of the NGOs surveyed, the Director's spouse is also a staff member. Leaders are well connected locally, well-travelled both regionally and internationally. Many NGO leaders thus constitute a quasi-elite: it is to them that we now turn, first to examine their views on leadership and 'success'.

Local perceptions of leadership

For the purpose of this study, we defined successful leadership as the ability to remain essentially true to one's organisational mission amidst an ever-changing environment.[16] Good leadership entails seeking to develop a clear vision and mission for an organisation, as well as carrying out planning and other management functions that determine the goals needed to achieve the vision and mission, as well as their realisation.

Some of our respondents found it difficult to describe leadership in the NGO sector, let alone successful leadership. This was especially the case for those leaders who preferred to 'work from the background', or 'behind curtains.' One explained that leadership in the NGO sector is not well-defined, because, "there are many actors who contribute to it, all not in a very clear way" while another described her understanding of NGO leadership as "…an abstract thing. These are things that you do without thinking deeply about." With multiple ongoing OD interventions and numerous workshops, however, leaders have attained various leadership skills. This, coupled with the current discourses on leadership and participation and the heavy influence of both management and euro-centric leadership literature, has created an uncomfortable hybrid of imported and local perceptions of leadership. Nevertheless most of our respondents included in their definition of NGO leadership words such as 'heading', 'vision', 'relationship', 'recognition', 'representing', 'a calling', 'influencing' and 'management'. We develop this understanding below.

Leadership as 'visionary'

Most of our respondents understood leadership to be a position where one takes the lead and others follow. The leader is presumed to be the pathfinder, the discoverer of new ways of doing things, and thus the provider of guidance and strategic direction. Some of our respondents used the word "visionary" to describe this perception. One interviewee felt that leadership inspired with vision is the factor that determines who becomes the leader, and who the followers are. Commenting on the inadequacy of leadership training workshops, he noted: "So it's much more about inspiration. The person with the inspiration becomes the leader." The visionary leader should also be charged with the responsibility of making it 'contagious', so that the rest of the stakeholders to the organisation share it. One of our respondents thus kept mentioning the importance of a leader's creativity and how this should be shared: "Challenge when you have a team. Have the best way to market your ideas." The position of leadership, where the rest of the stakeholders in the organisation look to the leader for guidance, calls on the leader to have to 'go first' or be in front. The leader has to be the pace-setter

---

16 This may require an element of mission updating or "re-engineering", depending on the circumstances.

and example, s/he is often admired, sometimes to the extent that s/he feels a moral obligation to be of the utmost integrity: "The people sing your glory."

Leadership as 'the head'

We have seen that the NGO leader in Uganda has been groomed in a society where leadership is modelled on hierarchical norms. The titles which CSO leaders assume, such as Chief Executive Officer or Executive Director, point to a leader at the pinnacle of decision-making and recall the 'chiefdom' of old times. The leader is then looked up to as the fountain of wisdom, blessed with special knowledge on a vast range of subjects. It is the person with the highest rank or authority, ultimately answerable and in some cases even the main person associated with the organisation. Thus, one interviewee observed "As a leader, you are responsible for the actions of others... failures and successes, even calamities. You're responsible for lack of organisational growth because you're the one with the vision and innovation to facilitate people and utilise their potential." Some respondents, especially from the donor community were weary of leaders who seemed to personalise an organisation often, they felt, for their own recognition and other benefit. One of them said: "We want to see a leadership that involves staff to the extent that if the leader her/himself is not there, the organisation will not collapse. The organisation must not be for the benefit of one person." Another leader expressed the same sentiments when he recalled hard times: "As a leader, even when things are hard, you have to keep a straight face, otherwise people will say '*Awoireku amaadhi*' (S/he has lost stamina)". When leadership is seen as 'the head', in some cases, this notion is taken to mean that leadership is/has to be autocratic. Thus leadership is then viewed hierarchically, with the status of authority ranging from the lowest to the highest, each successive rank representing the increased importance of the position. One leader emphasised the importance of the cultural context, when he exclaimed: "The Church takes a lion's share of guilt in that the Bishop is infallible plus all those below in the structure." The leader is also a problem solver for the organisation. In one organisation, the staff referred to their Director as their mother who knew everything, solved their problems and was a "candle" for the organisation. One leader also explained that leadership is about making difficult decisions about the future.

All this required special facilities and privileges: in some of the organisations we visited, the leader had access to privileged information, in others a personal secretary was available, and in others; the biggest filing cabinet was located in his/her office. Some leaders indeed felt that they had to be 'in the lead' and ensure a sizeable power distance from their followers. This could take the form of autocratic behaviour which only allowed a very limited level of staff participation in the organisation, if any. As one explained, *"...Culturally, people expect a leader to be in the lead and not asking people. If we ask people, they will start to wonder whether we are really leaders because they believe that a leader should know all the answers."* In such a situation, decision-making is non-participatory, centralised and staff development appears to be minimal. Matters are worse when, as a result, the leader finds him/herself on a different wavelength from that of the staff, as was described by one of the interviewees, when mentioning all-important donor trends:

> The leader will often know about shifts in the development agenda of donors, because leaders are the ones who get invited for donor meetings. But staff often do not know: they get overwhelmed when leaders initiate changes to accommodate these trends because they do not fully understand. Many therefore feel threatened by change and can act as a blockage – they feel their leader is not consistent.

Maintaining a power distance may also mean remaining remote from the staff and unconcerned about them in other ways. One interviewee explained:

> For a long time, I didn't know where staff were living. Some people brought it up in the staff meeting and suggested that we make a list of addresses and telephone numbers but I thought 'why is that necessary?' I think this way of relating to staff is brought by my upbringing and the management theory I read. When you open up you raise expectations – 'can you help me support my sick aunt?' etc…

Leadership as 'relationship'

Some respondents defined leadership in terms of a relationship with a group of followers. This called for 'leadership with a human face' which some felt echoed the prescriptions of African culture, with its networks of kinship and friendship, far reaching familial ties, spiritual dimension, and mutual solidarity. This encouraged leaders to perceive their role as having to support such relationships of friendship for their followers, to adopt "people-centred leadership styles and even to inform their basic values and interpretation of issues:

> Leadership is people-orientated: keeping people's spirits up, maintenance of relationships, making sure people feel part of the group. (…) Leadership is a relationship with the led and the environment and as you go along you see what is not working. Then you adopt and take on new approaches. You must take an interest in your staff, creating bonds (…) There are certain cultural values, e.g. welcoming strangers, respecting others the way they are – these were teachings from my father around the fireplace.

In some cases, a successful leader was seen as the *leader of a family*, with contented followers, under the benevolent gaze of the 'father figure' or 'mother figure'. One of the leaders thus informed us that the staff called him *'Mzee'* (male elder) which, he thought, was wonderful. The women leaders we talked to introduced another dimension to leadership: providing comfort; playing the 'motherly' function. "To be a leader is about being someone others rely on to take them forward, comfort them, and confirm things to them when they are in doubtful situations". Women leaders bring to the organisation their own particular mix of skills learnt at home in the managing of domestic and family life. These, our respondents called "female attributes" and others took these attributes to mean a 'soft' leadership style and/or the use of effective inter-personal skills as a leadership tool. One of the female leaders described her vision as a leader as encompassing both the staff and the work of the organisation: "It is about sharing the vision, creating ownership and wanting people to excel and be self-driven. It is about the ability to guide others and manage other resources." She described the key to leadership as the relationship with and understanding other people: "It is what I get out of it at a personal level."

Some leaders recognised that sharing organisational vision and mission requires a relationship of mutual support between the leader and staff, and between them all and their various development partners. Thus, the leader should ideally be open with staff and the partners of the organisation (as a way of expressing guidance and commitment to their best interests). One interviewee referred to one of the aspects of leadership as transparency, which he explained to mean personal integrity, honesty and trustworthiness. "If someone entrusts you with money for orphans, the money must go to orphans. Some leaders resist meetings because they then have to be transparent."

Finally, some leaders also defined their relationships with staff as being informed by a spiritual dimension: "For me religion is the most important factor in leadership. The Christian value of tolerance and forgiving behaviour is important. I hear a voice saying 'Don't dismiss this person'. The Spirit of God is the most important influencing factor." Another leader from a faith-based organisation similarly shared: "People are made in the image of God and everybody has been given competencies which they must be given a chance to bring out". Another respondent mentioned that it was when she got 'saved' that she became more accommodative and accepting of others as a leader.

Leadership as 'privilege'

When assuming a leadership position - whether within an NGO or elsewhere - people become more aware of the leader, professionally and socially, as one who counts. Positions of leadership had a way of improving one's stature and importance in society, displaying ability and achievement. One leader mentioned that for many others in the CSO sector, what keeps them going is "… a personal ambition, one needs to be recognised." One such example was a respondent who mentioned that the personal reward for her was: 'Recognition. I want to do wonders, and feel happy at the end of the day." She would also like to be a development worker of international stature: "I would like to change global life in three to four years. To satisfy my curiosity and self-actualise…."

Some of our respondents mentioned that leadership often changes a person's class and status. The leader is rich, drives the most expensive car with his/her children attending a private school. In some cases one could tell who the leader is without any formal introduction, although this can lead to ambivalent feelings: "A leader of an NGO is really unfortunate because the notion is that a leader is rich and privileged. Immediately you step into leadership, then people say, you have 'fallen into things' - literally meaning you are bound to be rich." Leaders of NGOs are thought to have high status in society and are generally expected to relate with those of same status, for example politicians. "Why do you drive your car like a minister and you don't interact with them?" High social status among CSO leaders could lead to considerable scepticism when an NGO was seen as a leader's 'personal cash cow' or when leaders award themselves very high salaries. One of our respondents decried: "There is no difference between NGO and political leadership, it's a way of making money". Another interviewee recalled that when he was in charge of a project with much money, some people expected him to be corrupt, and they thought he was foolish not to use any of the project finances for personal gain. The high-sounding titles of NGO leaders mentioned above, and the expensive cars that often go with them, are also seen as status symbols that reflected the high social rank of the incumbent. This affects leaders in that they have to bow to societal pressures: "The urge to contribute money is so much – this is expected of a leader".

Leadership as 'proxy'

Some leaders whose organisations were either heavily donor-driven or part of a church structure, felt they existed merely to meet the agenda of others – donors, church. Although most of the leaders mentioned that they had particular goals and missions for their organisations, some expressed the hopeless situation in which they found their organisations, as well as themselves as leaders. It was as though their organisations had been formed to meet the donors' agenda, and they existed as 'proxy leaders' to champion the formers' interests: "Donor-driven agenda; donor projects, donor goal. A leader is driven by what he/she must have achieved at the end of a project and only concentrates on that." "The minor changes have been internally driven and that leaves me feeling very frustrated." This could be encouraged by donor behaviour, as one recognised: "Sometimes donors build personal relationships with one person within an organisation and if that person leaves, the funding tap is closed. Donors are also individual persons, trust and relationships matter."

Another group of leaders who intimated feelings of being chosen to carry out certain duties and yet with very limited discretionary power, were leaders in organisations that are part of a Church structure. As one explained,

> My faith and the values of my organisation as a faith-based organisation matter very much (...) these two are so linked, and Christ himself is part of these values. My work should have uniqueness in working for other people. We must be different from NGOs[17] and government. We need to work with the stewardship of someone who's been delegated. I regard myself as a vehicle of transparency and accountability. Money doesn't matter. Even if I was transferred elsewhere, I would bloom.

Leadership as 'calling'

This sentiment mostly emanated from the leaders of Church-linked organisations, who perceived their leadership as a divine calling, reflecting God's call to serve the people. This may also have an effect on the vision and values of such leaders; the vision that they have for their organisations is already foreseen by God, and the work of these leaders

---

17 In Uganda, many faith-based organisations are development arms of a Church diocese and not legally registered as NGOs.

is to bring it to pass through undertaking missions and goals that they then decide on. Thus, when asked about his vision for the organisation, one such leader replied:

> A leader comes with a certain set of values; I am a priest and that gives me certain values, including to get people to appreciate the fact that there is a power somewhere that demands a certain quality of life. My vision is that there should be equitable distribution of resources so people can attain a certain quality of life. This is also the mission of Christ and the government.

Leadership as 'management'

Some respondents saw management and leadership as two similar aspects of work, since the leader exercises a management function, with leaders oscillating between the two. This may also reflect the route taken by many of our respondents to leadership position, after assuming managers' roles. While occupying leadership positions, some continue falling back into their earlier management roles, with the day-to-day tasks taking prominence. Such a situation also prevails where organisations have a small staff complement and where leaders view their leadership positions as being task orientated, i.e. about getting a piece of work done: "...there must be a situation, a reason, a purpose and a task as well as a group of people that require leadership to keep track and ensure that the task is accomplished." Interestingly, almost all the leaders of faith-based organisations defined leadership to mean creating a conducive relationship with staff to be able to get the job done.

Any need for change?

While the leadership literature puts great emphasis on the need for leaders to change, it is interesting to note that when asked to describe effective and successful leadership only a small minority of respondents explicitly mentioned "change" as part of leadership qualities. Indirectly, a few respondents made reference to a change dimension of leadership by explaining that a successful leader must be willing to experiment and be willing and able to take up challenges and opportunities. Thus, one interviewee stated that one of the qualities of effective and successful leadership is the ability to rediscover oneself. And, at another point, "Change is all about anticipation - *obutebeda kwavunza omugogo.*" It seemed that the donor voice was louder with regard to the need for change: too seldom, organisations "evolve from a situation around one person who is passionate (often the founder), to a leadership that grows, (...) where the organisation feel they own the vision, identify themselves with the organisation which is possible with a leadership that involves staff to the extent that if a leader her/himself is not there, the organisation will not collapse."

But these were far from unanimous cries. Why is change apparently overlooked as an important part of leadership by leaders themselves? Several factors may explain this. While leaders may not consciously reflect on the need for change or may not consider change a necessary part of leadership, they may not be conscious about the link between organisational change and personal change, or emerge from a government background where long-term planning is prominent and dynamic change may not be valued. They may be influenced by local cultural notions of leadership that underline static power structures or see change as threatening, and do not recognise any need to undergo processes of renewal. It is not part of how people see their role in society. They may also reflect the history of the civil society sector in Uganda, where leaders have managed to survive, and have kept accessing donor funding without having to go through any personal or organisational change or simply, they may lack exposure: leaders may not know any better, or any different.

Pressures and blockages to change facing CSO leaders

We can now turn to a more detailed description of the pressures and blockages that appear to prevent our NGO leaders from experiencing and desiring change.

Pressures and blockages facing leaders

Change is a complex and intensely personal process. It involves shaking up one's comfort zone; the comfort taken in doing what one believes one does well and in the way one has always done it. It is in this comfort zone that the blockages for change are found, in turn reflecting a variety of pressures. Resistance to change does not, however, necessarily reflect opposition to it, but rather a kind of unconscious personal immunity to change caused by what has been referred to as 'competing commitments' (Kegan & Lahey, 2001). Thus, leaders may unconsciously resist change, for instance, to avoid conflicts, failure or tougher assignments. Our interviews indicate that leaders find it difficult to identify blockages to change themselves, most likely because unconscious competing commitments indeed exist. Clearly identifying and eventually overcoming blockages to change is further complicated by the fact that they intertwine: committing oneself to a transformational change process therefore involves confronting a number of blockages all at once. The interviews nevertheless revealed a number of pressures and blockages that are both internal to the person and his/her organisation and of a more external, environmental nature.

First, NGO leaders are faced with much pressure from their extended families to fulfil expectations of financial support, expectations that accrue from the mere fact that they head organisations and are thought to have 'arrived'. They for instance carry the burden of meeting the costs of education for many family members, the transport costs to family functions because they have cars, covering health bills etc.: "Working in one's area of origin can 'bog one down' because one is so close to one's relatives and constantly will be approached to provide financial support". NGO leaders are often times also expected to extend the use of office facilities to their spouses and family members. Use of an office vehicle to take children to school, do weekend shopping or go to the rural areas to attend funerals and other functions becomes the norm. But the family can further encroach into the 'professional space': spouses of NGO leaders can sometimes become directly involved in the organisation by providing professional support to the leaders: "I get professional support from my wife, she is a qualified Development Worker and she tells me what she sees in other organisations and in this way I get influenced and inspired." In other cases, the family contributes resources to the organisation: "I and my wife contributed land and other resources to the organisations in its stages of infancy." Beyond immediate relatives, the NGO leader is expected to provide to extended family and kin through patronage and other forms of largesse. The leader is expected to belong to a privileged class and thus have access to vital information about jobs and scholarship opportunities. "School fees, diseases, deaths, cultural pressures – this all weighs you down"; "Patience…when you have deadlines it can be so irritating when people have their own problems and come with them." The leader therefore finds him/herself in an intricate web of family and work relationships, making a clear distinction between family and organisation sometimes illusory.

Social expectations revolve around adherence to values, to being a role model as a 'success story': "As a leader people will put you on a pedestal. I'm a role model". This can take a variety of forms: even the dress code of the NGO leader, a tie and jacket for the man and elegant designer or 'ethnic' clothing for the woman are expected. By extension, family members (even extended family members) will be expected to dress smartly. NGO leaders are also expected to have well-furnished offices, 'of course' homes and driving the latest car model in the capital, and to adhere to the social habits of the well-to-do. If these social pressures and expectations of patronage have major psychological consequences on the leaders, they also find themselves 'lifted' to a social class which they have difficulty to distance themselves from:

> When I started driving a Prado Vehicle, the Town Clerk expected that I should join their drinking club. On many evenings, I was expected to join them and when I didn't, I was labelled as being arrogant. I feared that once I join that club, I might find it difficult to come down and thus be true to myself.

Secondly, the cultural context and value system within which NGO leaders find themselves can act as an important source of resistance to change. As outlined earlier, the context of kingdoms and village chiefs within which leaders have been raised and groomed positions the leader at the apex, knowledgeable and a fountain of wisdom. Kings, village chiefs and clan leaders were born in families where leadership was bestowed according to heredity rather than ability: change then becomes a threat to the entire leadership system and the values that underpin it. Because this perception of leadership is determined by culture and instilled into leaders as a value, it becomes difficult to challenge. A leader who attempts to distance him/herself from this context to embrace other leadership styles, for instance, may find him/herself torn between two value bases, and eventually settle for 'the devil that he/she knows'. One leader commented on the 'futility' of the whole process of trying to change and concluded:

> [Personal growth] is one of my weakest points. We all come from different backgrounds and we carry this with us, unconsciously. I was brought up in a certain way and got an idea of the ideal worker… we carry our value systems with us in work situations. At some point I felt I was being pushed in all directions and decided to back out.

One of our respondents, also a 'cultural leader' mentioned that his style of leadership is rooted in tradition: "As a cultural clan leader, I am the custodian of privileged information. I am the link between the present and the past. I am a leader because I belong to a certain lineage and this cannot be questioned. This therefore enables me to take unilateral decisions".

Third, balancing 'leadership' and 'management' proves a challenge for many NGO leaders. They suffer from decision-making and information that is centralised in their person and thus find themselves simultaneously shouldering the dual role of problem solving on a day-to-day basis and direction giving. In many organisations, lack of management experience amongst staff means that leaders are more involved in operational and administrative functions. Donors also apply pressure for timely delivery of outputs as per agreed 'logical frameworks' and checklists of indicators. Funders then tacitly shape leaders to become implementers of projects, with their short-term horizons. This calls for a brand of 'leader' who can provide a 'quick-fix' for a 'quick-win', with little emphasis on personal or organisational change. Reflection is a crucial part of the change process; not seeing change as a necessary part of successful leadership constitutes a major blockage for change. Yet finding time for reflection appears to be difficult. One respondent, when asked what is hindering him from preparing for change, replied: "We are too busy with the day-to-day running of the organisation for daily survival, e.g. report writing."

Fourth, relatively recent demands for participatory decision-making pose a new kind of challenge for NGO leaders, who are constantly exposed to the notion of participation through numerous capacity-building events and training cycles. Most of the leaders we interviewed explained that they have embraced a participatory style of leadership, although evidence from other sources (OD practitioners) would suggest that most are, in fact, still grappling with how to fully actualise this paradigm shift. "Some situations force you to dictate but I think I am between autocratic, dictatorship and participatory. I use a different style depending on the circumstances." The previous section showed that the perception of NGOs as 'a family unit' creates a situation where leaders are looked at as 'father or mother figures'. This creates further pressure: if leaders are not found to be sympathetic of the followers' problems, they are considered to be insensitive. Managing the 'power distance' thus becomes especially challenging:

> Leadership can isolate you. The staff becomes suspicious of you and you become more cautious. You may have to visit this staff at home instead of talking at the office, and even then you pray that no one is going to see you, because then they may begin suspecting all sorts of things. How do you jig the power of distance? How can you as a leader be separate yet be part of them? How can you be part without necessarily creating familiarity?

Fifth, some of the leaders interviewed made special reference to dysfunctional Boards. Some NGOs have Boards of Directors with relatively undefined roles, others have Board members who are 'hands-on' and inexperienced in playing their prescribed oversight and fiduciary responsibility. While some Boards function without distinct roles and responsibilities, they do not have complete independence from management processes and rarely do they oversee and support the leader. In some instances founder members constitute themselves into an Executive Committee to handle both management and policy functions. This lack of support from Board members was noted by some leaders, such as one who stated that "One of the constraints to leadership of NGOs is constantly changing boards, many of whom lack experience in the NGO world." Our 'capacity-building' informant also noted: "Boards need to be developed to support and challenge the leaders (not only praising them)."

Sixth is the fear of the unknown and of failing. For some leaders, the fear of change is linked to the apprehension of losing a position or a job. In a poor country like Uganda, working in an NGO represents for many a source of employment rather than a contribution to relieve poverty 'out there'. Employment security for Ugandan leaders is further underscored by the fact that many are faced with the challenge of supporting an ever-increasing extended family. An inevitable part of leadership is seen as the challenge of handling mistakes and failures. While people may have a propensity to directly identify themselves with success, shouldering the responsibility for failures, including colleagues' failures, as 'the face' of the organisation can be difficult for the NGO leader. Thus, being in a leadership position can be a lonely experience when organisational problems occur. One respondent explained:

> As a leader, you are responsible for poor organisational growth because you're the one with the vision and innovation to facilitate people and utilise their potential... If it is a success story, you share with all people. But if it is failure, you carry it yourself. In real life, that's how it is.

Finally, a Ugandan NGO leader is faced with increasingly competitive priorities from 'the outside.' These can take the form of having to beat off and 'outwit' competitors (usually other NGO leaders) for dwindling donor support. When asked whether the changes in his organisation were internally or externally instigated, one interviewee emphasised: "Unfortunately, the major changes have been driven by donors and government and this is reflected in our structure, type of staff, etc." As donors also increasingly call upon NGOs to be financially sustainable, many leaders are more preoccupied with soliciting funding than strategic thinking and upholding the vision and mission of the organisations. It is not uncommon to find CSO leaders who are not wedded to their organisation's missions because they keep being swayed in the search for funding opportunities. This is further manifested in situations where a CSO has both a business arm and a social agenda. Many donors are now also calling upon leaders of different organisations to undertake collaborative initiatives for greater impact. This presents a difficult situation to leaders whose coping strategy for managing competitive pressures is to be introverts.

Challenges of women leaders

While all leaders face challenges, some proved particular to the female leaders we interviewed. Society's notions about leadership and gender act as a barrier to change, given that traditional gender norms and divisions of labour attach particular identities and expectations to men and women. The latter fall under the category of the led. The upbringing of girls emphasises submission to male authority, first to fathers, uncles and brothers and later to their husbands. Men, on the other hand, are supposed to be more concerned with achievements outside the home and to be assertive, competitive and tough. To change calls into question deeply held beliefs we have long closely espoused, perhaps since childhood.

A respondent narrated how this affected her ability to perform as a leader. Having been admitted to university to do law, her father asked: "which man will ever accept your judgment?" Although she achieved her later ambitions as an NGO leader, this statement still rings in her ears. Later, in marriage, her husband became a major de-motivator by reminding her that she was "a mere woman" and relating any failure to the fact that women were incapable of doing any better. Most women respondents thus began their careers with a need for constant assurance regarding their performance and professional ability, to help counteract negative cultural 're-enforcements' and help build their confidence: "I desperately need approval, negative feedback destroys me... When an opportunity for a big post came, my supervisor and colleague had to push me into applying." Another respondent said that organisations are male entities and whenever women assume leadership in such organisations, there is an inherent struggle to acquire male attributes. This, if not properly measured and regulated, tends to be "overdone."

In these circumstances, it is not surprising that our respondents felt that women leaders have not been fully accepted by society. There was for instance only one specific comment on women's skills need. It was felt that since the women are not expected to lead, they grow without learning leadership skills. When accepted, however, they are expected to be motherly leaders and not just leaders. "There is a lot of social pressure and social expectations vis-à-vis work," said one female respondent. When a woman does well, she is labelled a 'man' an expression applied to women activists. *"Kyakula ssajja"* (she is manly), people will say of assertive women leaders. And when becoming adept at 'donor speak', males will resent the confidence they elicit in these powerful circles.

Our respondents also mentioned that women are expected to be morally upright, a condition which men are not so rigorously subjected to. Some women respondents felt that it is advisable to keep a good distance, by expressing fear of the limelight. "The men masquerade but pull down whatever you say." "Our male counterparts in the CSO sector look at us with lots of doubts." "In the end we get many media attacks."

In the view of some, in an effort to prove their ability, women managers can overreact. Some respondents expressed with unease that staff expect them to be motherly in the office. Women leaders felt burdened by this expectation and found this 'exploitative': "I have an urge to excel in what I do and this has nothing to do with being a man or a woman but about doing a job – but maybe I have lost a bit of my femininity." Another reaction was to become so humble as to undermine their confidence and underestimate their professional abilities, sometimes at the risk of missing a job opportunity.

Women identified utmost moral standards and distancing themselves from others as coping strategies: "Morality is vital because our male counterparts think women have to work twice as hard in order to be half as good" and one male respondent noticed:

> Female leaders are good and professional for as long as they divorce themselves from the 'woman factor'. They are meticulous and do not get excited over issues too quickly like their male counterparts. This quality makes them a special brand of leaders.

The impact of HIV/AIDS

While the HIV/AIDS pandemic still poses a major threat in Sub-Saharan Africa, it is interesting to note that none of our respondents mentioned this when asked what challenges they face in their leadership, until specifically asked about the impact of HIV/AIDS, at which point all the respondents explained how their organisations and they themselves had been affected by the disease. In the first place, the respondents explained that loss of key staff from AIDS and consequent high staff turnover manifest itself as major challenges for NGO leaders due to loss of key skills through sickness and death. But HIV/AIDS also affects the very heart of an organisation – issues that deal with organisational culture, values, and relationships; and has a detrimental effect on morale and motivation (James and Mullin, 2004). Two of our respondents shared: "[Our loss] has also created a need because so many need support and we're not able to respond – that somehow renders the organisation irrelevant." There also seemed to be a fear of opening a 'Pandora's box': when failing to put mechanisms in place to deal with HIV/AIDS issues at the work place, some leaders felt that their organisations would not have enough resources to 'effectively' deal with the situation, and thus essentially ignored it.

Challenges of founder leaders

Discussion with our respondents revealed that founder leaders are in many instances impervious to change as a result of fear for the unknown. They appear to have found it quite difficult to 'hand over their mission', which may be due to a conviction that they still have much to contribute, a lack of trust in others' ability to carry out their vision or a dearth of attractive alternatives. This might also be fear of losing 'their thing' (which they started). Nevertheless, while the Ugandan NGO sector has been characterised as having a strong presence of rather rigid founder Directors, changes are taking place. Thus, one of our interviewees, after being "too" supervisory and autocratic in his leadership style, shared: "At some point I started to be concerned with what happens when I'm gone. I realised that I have to share my skills and think of sustainability.'

Some of the founders interviewed thus displayed an ambiguous attitude to the ultimate leadership change. One respondent for instance talked at great length about the tendency of political leaders to cling to power, while at the same time arguing that leaders in the NGO sector must be given ample time in their leadership positions.

Challenges of church leaders

Three of the leaders in faith-based organisations explained how working within the framework of the church structures poses a challenge to their leadership. These were seen as rigid in terms of policies and the reluctance with which new ideas and initiatives are embraced by the senior clergy. Churches are often characterised by hierarchical structures that do not lend themselves easily to participatory methods or approaches. Thus, leaders of faith-based organisations often find themselves constrained or even controlled by the Bishops to whom they refer. One respondent noted that "We are a church organisation, we do community development and we struggle with the dual entity. Struggling with oneself and what the priests want. Pressure from the priests and their unnecessary demands..."

Beyond structural issues, respondents mentioned that the culture of the church is rooted in obedience and submission. Leaders of faith-based organisations thus find difficulty in bringing forth any change and this is further complicated by the politics of power within the church where the clergy are often said to be in a continuous struggle to rise to senior positions.

> I am boxed in the church thinking and how people perceive the church. This Church thinking and behaviour may not match the new developmental approaches and thinking. I have discovered by the grace of God that if the senior team was given space and authority to engage in independent work, we would move faster.

Coping with such rigidities within church-based organisations, according to our respondents, is easier for leaders who themselves belong to the clergy (very rarely does one find female leaders heading church-based organisations) than for lay leaders. A respondent belonging to the latter group related a number of clashes with his bishop and expressed his frustration: "My church does not want to change, it is conservative."

Leadership and change

We noted above that most of the leaders we interviewed did not explicitly mention change as part of successful leadership. When asked to identify a positive change in their leadership behaviour in a real and lasting way, our respondents could, however, identify change in their leadership style and behaviour. Three main types of changes were mentioned.

First was a more participatory leadership (normally as a cascade of events), involving shared leadership with some degree of participation and inclusion of staff in decision-making as well as recognising and nurturing staff's potential. In this case, the development dogma dictating participation and empowerment appears to have been accepted as a legitimate leadership style within the NGO sector. Some described their change as a substantial change in behaviour or perception, such as this leader of a church-related organisation: "Now I encourage people more to initiate things themselves. I'm more open with a participatory leadership style. Before, I thought I had power over people (staff, colleagues). Now I've come to understand that the power we have is power to and power with." Others described this type of change or part-change as minor adjustments:

> Before, I wanted things done at all costs. I didn't bother much about people. But I realised that work is done by people, not machines. I don't know what happened but now I spend more time sitting and discussing with staff.

In contrast, some of our respondents (especially those from the donor community) stated that the belief in and practice of 'participation' in NGOs is imaginary. NGO leaders find themselves falling back into the autocratic leadership style in which they were nurtured and with which they are very familiar:

> My view is that many leaders don't change. They may camouflage initially like during courting, but the real them will come out thereafter. They may continually depict 'change' in public and amongst donors but once back in their organisations, they then fall back into their comfort zones of the old self.

The last change observed related to leaders recognising and embracing their leadership position. This was more prominent for female leaders and was described as the female leader fighting off traditional gender roles and society's expectations as to how a woman should behave. One respondent described how she used to feel tied by her family's expectations of her fulfilling her role as a woman, including not attending higher education and nurturing her ailing mother, leading o a need for constant approval and assurance in all work related matters. Reduction in family obligations as a result of her mother's death and a spiritual experience led this respondent to feel more confident, courageous and 'look at things in a wider perspective as a leader', to the extent of founding her own NGO.

A few founders have also decided to step down. As noted in the previous section, however, this change can be somewhat ambiguous, in part because it is often prompted by donor pressure or the dictates of Western management practice (rather than an inner belief in the necessity for change), but also because some founder leaders who have 'stepped down' have retained a strong presence in their organisations.

Incentives for change

Increased competition for donor funds compels NGOs to be at the forefront of a competitive struggle by constantly changing and adapting to shifting circumstances, which puts NGO leaders under pressure to change their approaches and perceptions. At the same time, employment security is also paramount because many leaders shoulder the responsibility of providing for an extended family. Thus, if the leader is faced with pressure to change, e.g. from staff or Board, job security may be an incentive for change. Indeed, a few respondents noted that the consequences of not changing would most likely have been losing their job: "If I hadn't changed I think I would have been transferred or in worst case lost my job." Another interviewee had come to her organisation at a time when four leaders before her had failed to lead the NGO satisfactorily. Having come from a Government position where autocratic leadership was prevalent, and being determined not to fail, she felt compelled to adapt a more participatory behaviour. One leader mentioned the need for change within himself as necessary after reflecting on why he had been chosen in the first place: "At the end you're willing to sacrifice everything to see a desired change. That's when the values and results or achievements drive you…"

The internalisation of participatory leadership as the legitimate style within the NGO sector has also led to expectations of how a leader should behave and relate with followers. We have noted above that, for several respondents, the relationship with staff and supporters is an indispensable aspect of leadership. Followers' expectations and demands for change can therefore constitute a great impetus for change. This feature was especially prominent among female leaders, some of whom even tended to describe staff as "a family". Followers' expectations also emerge in this respondent's narrative: "When I was young, I was cheerful and stubborn but when I became a headmistress I learned to be calm and reflective because nobody expects a headmistress to be impulsive and go and hug you."

Donors and the power they hold to advocate for the adoption of current development management doctrine have a major influence on NGO leaders. Although none of the respondents described donors as playing a direct role in pressurising them for a change in their leadership style, the fact that all the respondents noted they had changed to adopt a more participatory leadership style appear to indicate that the Eurocentric management values that donors prescribe are influencing NGO leaders in Uganda to a large extent. Donors also support leaders to attend various training cycles where concepts such as participation, transparency and empowerment are promoted. Some are clear about the need for change in the CSO sector. Much of this was expressed in terms of change in the leaders' value system, so that grants "really benefit the poor": we recall our donor informant exclaiming earlier: "(…) that's the leadership you have in the NGO sector! There is lack of transparency and commitment to the cause." But how deep-seated is this change? Might donor power be responsible for the public show of NGO leaders as embracing participation and gender concepts, while the actual practice might be different? As a respondent herself said: "The patriarchal notion is so entrenched that it prevents some leaders from changing. Many leaders do not truly believe in concepts such as gender but will pretend in public."

We have also seen that female leaders face special challenges to gain recognition as leaders. Some of our male respondents argued that female leaders measure themselves and are measured by others against a male standard and therefore feel they constantly have to prove themselves, while others characterised many female leaders as having a tendency to be 'motherly'.

A number of respondents also linked change to a certain event or happening: "Although change is most often gradual, it sometimes happens with a bang." Thus, several of the leaders interviewed explained how a bad experience had led them to change their leadership style and the way they related with followers. Perhaps more importantly, it is at a deeper personal level that change is mentioned. Thus sickness and death of family members were cited as shaping the leader's thinking, especially during the earlier part of their lives. "My mum's death freed me. God set me up in my thinking from the time my mother died". When HIV/AIDS strikes in the family of the leader, it can trigger change within the leader and ultimately the organisation. One leader explained

> We have had 2 staff affected, we granted them some money and they were asked to leave when they could no longer work 100%. Later I lost 2 sisters and then I realised how badly they had been treated at their former workplaces. Immediately I saw the need to change the policies of my NGO and thus be proactive in preventing the spread of HIV. From January, we are setting up a fund to support staff with HIV/AIDS.

Several respondents also found participation in various OD and other training events an impetus for change. This was usually brought about by being involved in a personalised process where self-searching and reflection was emphasised. Having such an opportunity was crucial given a cultural context and educational system where people are not encouraged to question themselves or others and where the teacher is considered as knowing it all while the learner is ignorant: "I realised I was too fast, being a good listener – trying to understand the person behind, being tolerant and understanding people better, sharing with each other (including giving staff confidence to share), making everybody feel valued. Another leader described attending a 'self-determination' workshop as being an eye-opener. The workshop made her reflect on her own leadership behaviour. Yet another said: "I went for a PRA training last year and now I use it in all my work, even at organisational level." Travelling was also mentioned by some of our respondents as an incentive for change. Travel gives the NGO leaders a chance to learn from other leaders and they are then challenged to change: "Whenever I travel, I see how things are done and when I come back I want to put in practice these new learnings."

Finally, some of the NGO leaders we interviewed mentioned that they experience a heavy burden of work. This may, among others, be a result of fulfilling donor obligations of timely delivery of outputs, accountability and narrative reports. This is also borne out of the desire to keep ahead of other NGO leaders in the cut-throat competition for donor resources. This burden of work forces one to change, as one leader put it: "If your management style is to do it yourself, then it is burdensome."

What facilitates change?

Change is a complex process; it not only involves certain incentives, but also requires the leader to react to these incentives. A leader may experience an incentive (key) to change but not actually initiate any change. What, then, make leaders actually use the key and initiate a change? A number of such facilitating aspects have been identified; these 'facilitators' proved to be highly individual and not all were needed to initiate change.

First, successes, mistakes and failures and the way leaders reflect and make meaning out of events is a crucial part of the change process. Kouzes & Posner (2002) have identified a number of ways in which leaders learn, including learning by trial and error, by reading, by confronting themselves on what they are worrying about, and by bouncing hopes and fears off someone they trust. Our interviews indicate that women leaders tend to learn by reading and confronting themselves whereas male leaders mentioned learning by doing and accessing others as important learning mechanisms. One woman leader we met said that the hunger for knowledge had made her a successful leader; she recalled that it was when she went back to school, in recent years, that she was able to rediscover her potential. She felt aware of the need to become someone who would embrace all that she could be, "To satisfy my curiosity and self actualise." As she spoke, she felt the need to keep learning and to harness more of her potential.

Another trait that seemed consistent with the leaders who mentioned the need for change was the fact that they were critical of the current development thinking in the country. For example, one said that he saw some issues lacking in understanding development, and this transformed his thinking.

While it is argued in much of the leadership literature that an essential skill of leadership is the ability to continue learning in life and to make meaning out of events and experiences, true transformational learning is however only likely to take place when the leader learns and at the same time prompts others to learn, leading to concurrent individual and organisational learning. Thus, the leader being able to share the vision of the new direction or leadership style becomes crucial. One respondent explained how he had shared learnings from OD events with staff and how this, in his opinion, had led to less resistance from staff to the changes implemented. Another interviewee echoed: "There is nothing as useful as sharing with and learning from others."

For all the respondents, faith or what some called 'an inner voice' or 'conscience', played an important role in facilitating the change. A spiritual dimension was recognised as very important in supporting the change process by giving the leader the inner strength to carry out work according to his/her beliefs: "My faith in God and knowing that there is someone to see me through has enabled me to read the signs well so that I can know when it is time to leave an organisation."

Age also gives confidence through a lifetime of experiences. It often also gives of feeling that one has less to lose. With such confidence, change appears less threatening. Two respondents explained how age had changed their perception of leadership: "I have become softer with age. For me work is no longer about making a career. It's more about sharing my experiences and empowering young people and my staff." "When I was young I wanted to do everything. Now I know that I can do only so much."

While much of the Eurocentric leadership literature focuses on identifying the personal traits of effective leaders, our research indicates that effectiveness of African leaders depends on much more than personality; such as ability to handle outsiders' expectations. Our findings however also suggest that for some respondents, their personal traits played a significant role in facilitating change. These traits include being principled, self-determined to learn and change and not wanting to be tied down in a certain position. One leader of a Catholic faith-based organisation for instance had on a number of occasions gone against church policies to implement changes within the organisation (e.g. hiring female Protestant staff). This required both determination and self-confidence. For a number of respondents, gaining respect and recognition for the work they do was another personal trait acting as an important motivational factor for change. Three of the leaders we interviewed noted that the prospect of gaining recognition and respect for the way they lead their organisations is important for them. Another noted that implementing a change in the way he relates to staff had given him confidence: "Those who used to see me as a 'nobody' now respect me." Two others made reference to themselves as role models, which to them entails living by their value system.

Although leadership authors such as Kouzes & Posner (2002) argue that "if people are going to do their best, they must be internally motivated," a number of our respondents explained that external support from e.g. family (especially spouses), mentors and people believing in you is important in terms to give courage to carry through change. Much of the leadership literature (e.g. Kakabadse & Kakabadse; Bennis & Thomas; Kenya NGO Council) also shows how leaders gain support by making an effort to effectively communicate their vision to make it shared and by facilitating others to learn. "My Board was a supportive factor because they appreciated what I was doing." "If you don't get enough support from your family, you get a problem. Because people want to know if you're leading your home well. Thus this affects the change." Respondents were also noted to actively seek support from staff for the change. When asked how he implemented change, one leader answered: "Every training or workshop I've attended I've made sure to pass on the skills and knowledge to the staff. In this way individual learning are turned into organisational learning and it's not difficult to implement the change."

Some respondents also seem to derive indirect support from their family circumstances. Thus, one interviewee noted that seeing her mother strong and never breaking down despite hardship has inspired her to never give up and always push herself. Another explained how her constant rivalling with her brother had developed in her an attitude of always excelling.

The nature of change

What, then, can we comment on, as far as the nature of change among those NGO leaders we met? Three key characteristics seem to be emerging: one is that change demands self-determination and commitment. Leaders who change are found to be self-determined to learn and internalise this learning but also to create an environment for organisational learning through sharing experiences and common reflections. Change needs real commitment and a determination to face blockages, otherwise change will remain at the knowledge or intent level. How committed the leader is to change thus determines how far the change will be carried out. And the more conscious the leader is of the need to change, the clearer the path ahead. Some NGO leaders also enrol for leadership training courses in order to acquire the desired change for themselves and their organisation.

Secondly, although some leaders may experience a particular incident and are able to link this incident with their change, most respondents found it difficult to identify one crucible that immediately led to a dramatic change in their leadership behaviour. This indicates that for most leaders, change is a gradual process linked to a series of events, trainings, exposures, sharing of experiences, mentoring etc. that is reflected upon and internalised. Thus, a leader for whom reflection is an integrated part of leadership seems to turn small crucibles into learnings that are part of a continuous process. In this way, leaders build commitment to change and renewal through a process of learning from mistakes as well as a process of incremental improvements and small wins.

Third, while a few of the leaders interviewed have gone through a transformational type of change, most respondents seem to be struggling to translate knowledge and a willingness to change into actual practice. All the leaders mentioned having moved in the direction towards a participatory leadership style but still mention feeling the need to juggle with other leadership styles. This partial change may reflect the fact that some leaders have embarked on a change process but have competing commitments, or unconscious blockages preventing them from fully changing. Some CSO leaders also come from a government background and find their understanding of leadership challenged once in the CSO sector where they struggle to adapt to the expectations of participation. Finally, 'participation' often remains an external phenomenon that may be embraced because it is fashionable, rather than because it is truly believed in. This supports the view that, for many leaders, change is a slow process. They find themselves in a change process, which occurs within Uganda's young NGO sector, where the need for transformational change may not be felt as urgently as in countries where the sector has been well established for decades.

Conclusions - *"Obutebeda kwavunza ekigogo" (A banana tree which does not grow is a dead one)*

The importance of context

Much of what is emerging from our interviews appears to have a strong "Ugandan flavour". This to an extent validates one of our initial assumptions, about the specificity of context, and underlines the need for this research in the first place, with companion pieces in Kenya and in Malawi. In Uganda, 'context' means a very young NGO sector (therefore still dominated by founder leaders), growing fast, but dependent on donors, with limited social roots, facing a growing crisis of legitimacy amongst sections of the public, including all-powerful funding circles. It is also a sector that cannot draw from a strong tradition of independent and critical thought, but is close to an all-encompassing 'Movement system', which is itself facing turbulent times as the political landscape is changing with a planned transition to multi-party politics. And it is a sector embedded in a cultural context that continues to value a form of leadership (usually male) that places less emphasis on accountability mechanisms than clientelist networks.

But this context is not static: NGO 'succession' issues, with each passing year, become more widely broached and donors are strongly encouraging NGOs to adopt standardised management tools and practices, while a 'privatised' form of donor assistance is engulfing NGOs, especially at the district level. As political changes loom, there is much concern about a slide to 'neopatrimonialism'; and some NGOs are timidly venturing into issues of accountability and democratic governance. The impact of HIV/AIDS is also becoming increasingly difficult to ignore in the workplace and NGOs bear as much of this as other organisations in Uganda.

How is successful leadership perceived?

For the fieldwork, we developed our own definition of successful leadership (this had much to do with adapting to a changing environment, while remaining essentially true to or carefully renewing one's organisational mission). To what extent was this view shared by our respondents? How did *they* define a successful leader?

For several respondents, it proved *difficult to articulate a definition* of successful leadership and benchmarks proved difficult to elicit. However, certain elements of successful leadership emerged: on the one hand, leadership was felt to be beyond a job, beyond fulfilling a management function: it had to do with fulfilling a vision (being part of that vision), having determination and being *committed to a cause* (often guided by faith, and often a religious faith). This may require sheer *hard work*. But there was also an important personal dimension, beyond the social agenda: *being recognised* was mentioned by several respondents[18], having a measure of freedom, as well as having a successful career (especially when leaders are relatively young), and being the *head* of an organisation, with the privileges and responsibilities of a *role model*. This does not preclude a *management dimension* to leadership: thus, several interviewees mentioned an ability to surmount organisational challenges (a "difficult" board; a rigid church). Using a mix of autocratic, democratic, participatory approaches to managing, a successful leader was seen as *the leader of a family*[19], with contented followers. The focus on staff, on making people valued and sharing leadership, on being a good listener was strongest amongst female respondents.

The notion of change (foreseeing changes, dealing with competition, managing change, innovations, etc.) thus does not appear very prominently in the way our respondents think about successful leadership. Local perceptions are somewhat *un-strategic* although *vision* is stressed.

Who are the successful leaders?

Who, then, are the successful leaders? What characteristics do they display? First, is a *determination to lead*, against many odds. This determination is usually informed by a commitment to a cause, a faith. This, however, needs to be tempered by a good understanding of the environment and its changes ("multi-faceted, multi-alternative

---

18   This could include social recognition, recognition of one's ideas, of one's contribution to a cause.
19   We return to this important dimension later.

understanding and thinking"). Successful leaders have been able to steer their organisations, to register results and growth within a changing context (even if this element does not appear prominently in their own perception of success). Linked to this is attitude towards change: *embracing change* as a conscious decision, as necessary and exhilarating, positively acknowledging and learning from one's mistakes and driving change rather than being a victim of it appeared to define the most successful leaders we met. While a few of the leaders interviewed have gone through a transformational type of change, most respondents seem to be struggling to translate knowledge and a willingness to change into actual practice. Change is thus often a gradual process that is not linked to any specific event but a series of events, trainings, exposures, mentoring etc. that is reflected upon and internalised. Change also needs real commitment and a determination to face blockages, otherwise it remains at the knowledge or intent level. Level of commitment to change will directly inform how far change will be carried.

Visionary leadership alone, however, is not enough: in the Ugandan context, leaders also have to be managers, and especially *managers of people,* supporting Board members. Managing people in our context can be summarised as *creating a functional family,* as well as successfully playing the "power distance game": not allowing colleagues to be over-familiar, keeping the personal separate, while nurturing the organisational family as the head of the unit, the head of the "village". Achieving the right "mix" between visionary leadership and managing resources (including human resources) is thus vital, and constantly adjusting this mix in the light of changing circumstances.

Third is an ability to *manage external pressures* (donors are especially important, but also social pressures, and those of followers/members). Our respondents gave us many examples of intensifying pressures as they consolidated their leadership position, from payment of school fees for an ever expanding list of kin to political pressures of every kind. A fine line had to be drawn between acceding to these pressures, being recognised as the source of support (and benefiting from such acknowledgement), while not succumbing to these pressures.

In the end, of course, there is the ability to *surmount blockages to change.* Most prominent is *the fear of failing:* this can take several forms: the fear of not being a competent role model at all times; a concentration on the day-to-day as an escape route, including an inability to create space for reflection, or even to concentrate on managing at the expense of leading. But fear is not only at the personal level: there is a *fear of public opinion,* of people's judgements; even the fear of *political retribution* (in Uganda, if you dissent you often become the foe). In church-related development structures, there was a fear expressed of the church hierarchy. For women, a fear was also expressed of not conforming to traditional societal expectations with regard to women's roles. Many of our respondents are *not reflective:* they often mentioned they were "too busy" with the day-to-day tasks to have any time for reflection. *Bowing to social pressures,* can also be a block, which can also take several forms: time to be spent on relatives when you have deadlines to meet; the enormous pressures of working in one's local area; not managing high expectations of contributions. *Resistance within the organisation,* arising out of either established structures or the staff themselves was also mentioned. But we were constantly reminded that *culture and values* are extremely important to understand blockage to change: the NGO leader is groomed and situated in a patriarchal "I know it all" culture, where traditionally leadership is in one's hands often because of heredity and clientelism, rather than other forms of ability. Change then becomes threatening to the entire leadership system and the values that sustain it. Distancing oneself from this becomes perilous, especially for women.

So what does it take to become a successful leader?

Several factors emerge as contributing to successful leadership, to effectively translate personal change into organisational change. The first is *the willingness to learn* that is facilitated by a process of reflection, and trial and error. This personality trait is apparent in leaders with the self awareness and the courage to stand back and look at themselves from new perspectives or points of reference. These could be gleaned from the literature, from travel, from other people, from further studies, and most commonly from trials and errors in a wide variety of situations. Perspectives generally change with time and age, and for those leaders who are ready to 'travel in time'. What matters here is pro-activeness to change themselves and aspects of their leadership, evidenced by curiosity, and a conscious decision to learn and change values or behaviour, to put ideas into action.

Family circumstances appear as especially important: the personality of one's father or mother was mentioned by several respondents (where either was seen as playing a role model) and for women, competition for recognition as girls vis-à-vis boys. For women, having a father that "provided space", a strong-willed mother or grandmother, were crucial. Support from one's immediate family was also mentioned, as well as family expectations (pay-back for education expenses). Family responsibilities, especially at an early age, appeared to prepare people for leadership positions: having to look after bed-ridden relatives, orphans, other pressures: "make you grow up." Such early experiences build one's self-confidence and *determination to succeed*, which is also connected with what several respondents called an *"inner voice"*, or "faith", a voice that says "don't' give up" even (again!) "the voice of my mother…"

Meeting social expectations of a leader, of leadership is also important: "You need the credibility", as well as effective support networks. Support from for example boards, friends, and family (as indicated above) is essential in that it means social approval: first an encouragement, then a reward for taking the 'risk' of changing. For a leader, meeting social expectations is as important ("You need the credibility") as effective support networks. These reinforce each other and create a cycle of 'expectations and rewards'.

Several respondents also mentioned training events as having shaped their leadership qualities. These however, were *not* management training courses, but inspirational and sharing events meant to develop participants' self-determination or the availability of a mentor, confidant and/or coach. But, to be effective, such training events must focus on leaders with the willingness to change in the first place. Most respondents did not mention a defining experience or *crucible* that forged their leadership qualities, although a *series of moments* emerged for some, provided they were turned into successful learning points (most often the death of one's mother or father, forcing upon one new responsibilities, or an inspirational experience "becoming saved").

The particular views and challenges of women leaders

Women placed much emphasis on people development during our interviews. For them, successful leadership had much to do with making people feel valued, with enabling colleagues to carry the organisation. Female respondents often mentioned a thirst for knowledge as a driving force. Part of this learning was also seen as moving on from one leadership position to another (whereas men found such transition more threatening). Because of the gender inequalities from which women suffer, our female respondents often mentioned the need for social approval to keep them going ("I desperately need approval") and the need for being *morally upright* in all circumstances (men are not subjected to the same scrutiny). For some women, however, there is a persistent deep-seated lack of self-confidence, a continued *fear of the limelight* and a tendency to downplay achievements.

Leadership also appeared to be for women a particularly lonely experience, hindered by social prescriptions, by family obligations (such as caring for AIDS patients). As a result, some female respondents can become, we were told, aggressive in their pursuit for recognition and success. Part of the learning for women leaders was overcoming this, achieving a kind of plenitude. Perhaps not surprisingly, many men mentioned "aggressive women leaders, especially when dealing with male subordinates."

A leadership crisis?

Some respondents talked to us in terms of a "leadership crisis". What does such a "crisis" consist of? Where does it come from? From a youthful sector, expanding very fast, faced with the challenges of an equally rapidly changing environment (which also explains why leadership is so critical to successful organisations) or a hands-on Board of Directors? This is a challenge that the readers of management literature will be familiar with.

But is there a deeper *point of tension*? Is there a clash between the management ethos of the increasingly corporatised NGO sector with the local cultural environment? The importance of *personal experiences* and the *local cultural context* indeed feature prominently in our findings. Are successful NGO leaders thus not the product of the amalgam of forces described in the earlier part of this report? We find these to be of immense importance in shaping them, and in particular note that NGO leaders remain the product of the local environment rather than of any Western management tradition: we thus seem far from the bureaucratised management precepts that currently dominate notions of the voluntary sector in the West. While our leaders do not always identify how and why they have undergone change, within the Ugandan context, change is vital for success. So our leaders *do* undergo change, although this is rarely the product of management training.

This last point reminds us that, to bring this study to a meaningful conclusion, we need to draw lessons for our "capacity building" practice. Two of our respondents themselves challenged capacity builders to make research part of their work: we now must examine the implications of this study for us, 'capacity builders'.

Implications for OD and leadership development

There has been a growing need for capacity building services especially in the field of Organisational Development in Uganda. Some of the pressure has originated from Northern donors while some stems from an internal realisation of capacity gaps within NGOs themselves, which may in turn reflect a growing competition for both funding and community mandate. Our respondents however broadly felt that the support given in the past has not resulted in much change; some even found it irrelevant or insufficient. One staff from a donor organisation said that workshops have become the fashion for capacity builders. Currently, capacity building support often focuses on management training, with an emphasis on knowledge/content. Our respondents had attended many of these training events, but translating knowledge into skills and practice remained a big challenge.

The major capacity needs that were identified included the concept of managing staff and boards, building a team, ensuring shared leadership and managing leaders' social demands. Only three of our respondents had attended OD-type processes that left a lasting impression on them: "What really set off the change was attending an OD training especially leadership training." "I moved from fixation to analysis and reflection. The workshop (The self-determination workshop) made me reflect on my leadership behaviour". "I changed from being an autocratic leader to a participatory leader."

All our respondents expressed a need for capacity building, although to varying degrees. This demand seemed to emanate from the fact that organisational business in terms of its identity and work depends mostly on the leader. Most of our respondents did not have role models to copy from and as such leadership was seen as a struggle. Furthermore those in the neighbourhood are not necessarily exemplary! And what is "exemplary"? NGO leaders do not have agreed values and norms as to how business should be conducted; some draw experiences from working as civil servants, a very different context from NGO sector work. As one of our respondents further said: "We need to tap the experience of successful leaders, not that of OD books."

Making OD and leadership development personalised

Most respondents had much experience in their management role but much less in a leadership role. It was observed that even courses that are advertised as "leadership training" end up teaching managerial skills. Hence much need was expressed in the area of leadership skills development, but processes need to move several steps away from generalisation of participants' needs and standardisation of content to recognising and supporting individuals during the process. A respondent thus exclaimed: "We should be given space to reflect on what we have learnt throughout the years (...) Please help me discover myself." Such a process would include: (i) *Conquering leaders' fears:* Leaders wear a persona that makes onlookers admire them. Beneath this, however, is a fountain of fears rooted in personality, character and experience that block them from challenging the status quo and venturing into the unknown. Leaders thus experience superiority and inferiority complexes that also act as blockages to change. OD practitioners should focus their efforts on finding out in depth the causes of resistance to change and address them at a personal level; (ii) *Challenging leaders to think differently:* Our respondents felt that as leaders they think in a fixed way, and do not reflect or analyse issues. This widespread problem is embedded in our education system which does not encourage questioning. This can result in limited sharing of information across an organisation, as one respondent put it: "Leaders are not keeping staff abreast with changes happening in the environment and this makes staff overwhelmed or insecure." (iii) *Creating a conducive learning environment:* Linked to this, the learning environment can frequently become threatening, especially when facilitators use much development jargon to appear educated. Do we create reflection and learning time for individuals and groups during OD processes? Should we not engage in more backstopping counselling and guidance for those who need it? Facilitators were accused of assuming that participants are empty cups that need to be filled up. The facilitators were further challenged to understand the nature of work leaders are involved in so that the support is appropriate: "Do not wait to see your participants in Kampala workshops. Find them in the field, observe them at staff meetings, and interact with their staff. After that you can offer coaching"; (iv) *Culturally appropriate approaches:* Effective learning needs to be culturally informed since the culture of most leaders, as of all of us, impacts on the way they think and behave. Western literature does not say much about pressures from the extended family in relation to leadership, but draws from a context where there is total separation of work and family demands. We don't read of integrity in an environment where corruption is the norm. How do we deal with inexperienced youthful Board of Directors who are products of the various environmental forces we have discussed above? We thus need to study the culture of a particular leader so as to know better where s/he comes from when s/he chooses to embrace or to shun a particular learning or change; and (v) *Incorporating research for quality work*: Our support should therefore be based on properly researched knowledge and needs. We thus need to undertake much further research on OD work to keep relevant and appropriate.

Our practice: further challenges

Many processes that organisational leaders are taken through during workshops tend to be 'academic' in nature and rarely cause change in organisations. Secondly, in most organisations learning has not been institutionalised. Capacity builders thus need to ensure that they spread organisational learning by running more in-house sessions that involve individuals or sections of staff. Our support must therefore be seen as geared towards supporting the leader as part of a wider team in the organisation.

Secondly, we have noted that women leaders need to overcome different types of fears, derived from society's perceptions of their roles. Fear of making mistakes can hinder freedom to learn. It is important that constant support is offered until they have developed enough confidence in themselves. One female respondent told us: "Find out what makes this person fear. Especially for women... facilitate that person to identify where the barrier came from, whether during their childhood or at home with the husband." As we prepare groups to undertake assignments it may be important to create women's space alone at times.

Third, managing boards featured prominently as a gap in the respondents' practice. NGO boards in Uganda display several age-related problems, including little experience in understanding the environment NGOs work in and they emerge from different value systems, some of it which may not fit in the NGO sector. The need to have board members trained or coached about their role was thus widely expressed. Skills weaknesses centred on ability to interpret financial issues, translating the vision of the organisation and human resource management. 'Managing people' was also given prominence: building a team, ensuring shared ownership of leadership of an organisation, helping colleagues to manage social demands: all appear as areas of need for 'capacity-building'.

But skills are not enough. Respondents stressed the need for OD support informed by a clear set of values which could be cultural or spiritual: "In Uganda today, it is hard to find people with passion against injustice. We need to address the lack of accountability, responsibility, and care. People seem to have no values (...)." Talking about values is of course difficult: we have seen many leaders starting NGOs for selfish (usually financial) reasons and people's perceptions of leaders are often of individualistic individuals without depth. Suggestions for capacity builders included the need to draw examples from leaders outside this country. Examining realties in other places may influence the way business is run here. This could further be strengthened by long term exchange visits, apprenticeship/ attachment, well planned sharing of information, experiences, practice and rewarding outstanding NGO leaders; such were all possibilities at our disposal.

There is also a pool of existing male and female NGO leaders who are starting to feel *lost and useless*. These have in the past contributed to the vibrancy of organisations while they were in the positions of leadership. After handing over office to new directors they are however, considered as outsiders and disappearing from the NGO scene. These former leaders start to regret the decisions they took. A desire was thus expressed for a forum where they can access a talking partner who can prompt and reflect on challenges. These leaders could also be 'up-graded' to another level as counsellors and mentors supporting young leaders. This raises questions as to how much leaders prepare for exit. Does anyone help leaders talk about an exit strategy and prepare psychologically for this exit?

We saw that, in a number of cases, the boundaries between organisation and family appeared blurred. Further, leaders often draw their work motivation from relationships, rather than tasks at hand. Many times organisations are run as families whereby the leader behaves as a husband and the rest are either wives or children. This has different implications, including gender implications. We need to be transformative in our OD work and try to facilitate organisations to escape from such situations, that domesticate staff hinder them from achieving their development goals.

While relationships are important, they must be balanced with task orientation. Processes to support this could include staff exposure to develop self-confidence and ownership of the decisions they take, to prepare them to take risks and face challenges, be adaptable; to analyse their culture and consider 'cultural reengineering'; to manage psycho-social insecurity; to think outside the box, challenge assumptions and beliefs; to develop and discuss new principles and finally work within an agreed framework. The manager must be helped to speak to his or her heart (and not the head as is usually the case). The facilitator will need to invest in building an atmosphere of trust.

Some respondents mentioned that the leadership role isolates them from the public. How can we assist leaders to live 'true lives'? Much of this behaviour is dictated by the cultural expectations of leaders, and we know that culture is not changing at the same pace as development demands. But lack of change can easily render the leader irrelevant. A successful leader must be helped to work with ease in this dichotomy through constant analysis of the environment, reflection and learning. Secondly, the leader can be helped to replace a spirit of competition with cooperation, whenever possible, by looking at other leaders as a resource and support that can be tapped. This can for instance be done by developing support programmes that target managers from a given thematic area across organisations.

Most leaders of Ugandan NGOs have not appreciated the impact of HIV/AIDS within their organisations and in their work; its understanding is currently often confined to the personal/family sphere. It is at this point that it has become an impetus for change. There is therefore an opportunity for capacity builders to bring this reality home in organisations by sharing other peoples' experiences, and thus touching the values of leaders who are evading this devastating situation, to be able to respond to this local and global threat.

We have also seen that NGOs leaders are increasingly addressing the goals of financial providers, rather than their organisation's mission. Respondents generally recognised having been heavily influenced by donors. Donors need to keep in mind that organisations, many of which have been formed for survival of the funders and/ or other members, may not refuse to join capacity building programmes, in a bid to access donor funds. We should also be conscious of 'cosmetic change' in some of the partners that we facilitate, in a bid to please donors, such as working on strategic plans, but never implementing them!

What implications for us, 'capacity – builders'?

It seems clear that a key aspect of OD work needs to focus on leadership development given its pivotal role in NGOs in Uganda. Such leadership development needs demand diverse skills in strategic thinking, continuous learning for change based on in-house support, developmental counselling, etc. Yet, are we making the assumption that capacity builders are all experts in everything? Is it possible that there are certain levels of masquerading within the 'OD fraternity'? The challenge is for capacity builders to sharpen their skills in all organisational matters or call for help where needed. We need to develop quality control for our practice. Research is important to help us establish whether capacity building processes and activities are responding to real organisational needs.

Capacity builders can get stuck on generalities, forgetting that participants are there in their individual capacities. A learning process must therefore be planned in a way that meets both general (or group) and individuals' objectives. Facilitators need to sharpen their skills to enable them 'whistle while brushing their teeth'. This demands creativity in the planning of OD processes. But do we have the capacity and courage to do this? Capacity builders need to think of new and varying interventions during the time of organisational assessment. While we are part of a culture that puts more emphasis on relationships than tasks, current development thinking will render us irrelevant if we do not change or balance the two. The facilitators must support the process of re-engineering culture we mentioned above.

Finally, and importantly, capacity builders will do well with a thorough understanding of the gender implications of our work, given the patriarchal context we operate within. The research results indicated minimal gender understanding and practice among both leaders and capacity builders. Capacity builders have their own gender biases to overcome as well, yet they are required to facilitate gender sensitive change process. But this needs to be undertaken in full cognisance of the cultural context, since gender is all too often 'decampaigned' for being a foreign concept, and thus go beyond the application of imported tools and frameworks.

Bibliography

Barr A., Fafchamps M, and Owens T. (2003) "Non-Governmental Organisations in Uganda: A report to the Government of Uganda".

Bennis, W. and Thomas, R. (2002). *Geeks and Geezers: How Era, Values, and Defining Moments Shape Leaders*. Harvard Business Press.

Bratton, M. and N. van de Walle (1997). 'Neopatrimonial Rule in Africa'. In Bratton, M. and N. van de Walle, *Democratic Experiments in Africa: Regime Transitions in Comparative Perspective* (Cambridge University Press).

Brock, K., McGee, R., Gaventa, J. (2004). *Unpacking policy: Knowledge, actors and spaces in Poverty Reduction in Uganda and Nigeria*, Kampala: Fountain.

Blunt, P. and Jones, M.L (1992): *Managing Organisations in Africa*. Berlin and New York: Walter de Gruyter.

CDRN (2002). "Annual Report for 2001", Kampala.

CDRN/NGO Forum (2003). "Getting it Right: Poverty Knowledge and Policy Processes: What role for CSOs?", mimeo, Kampala.

Collins, J. (2001). "Level 5 Leadership: The Triumph of Humility and Fierce Resolve". *Harvard Business Review*.

De Coninck, J. (2004A). "Politics is (best) left to the Politicians – Civil Society in a period of political transition in Uganda: challenges and prospects. CDRN Civil Society Reviews", Comments and Reports Paper No. 5

De Coninck, J (2004B), "Chronic Poverty in Uganda, Synthesis report for the Chronic Poverty Research Centre", Mimeo, Kampala.

Dicklitch S., (1998). "Indigenous NGOs and Political Participation" in Hansen, H.B. & Twaddle, M., (eds), *Developing Uganda*, Kampala: Fountain.

Hickey, S. (2003). "The Politics of Staying Poor in Uganda", Paper prepared for the International Conference on 'Staying Poor: Chronic Poverty and Development Policy', Mimeo, IDPM, University of Manchester.

Hofstede, G. (1994). "Cultures and Organisations: Software of the Mind – Intercultural Cooperation and its Importance for Survival". The Association for Management Education and Development.

James, R. (2004). "Leaders Changing Inside-Out: What Causes Leaders to Change Behaviour? Cases from Malawian Civil Society". The International NGO Training and Research Centre INTRAC Occasional Papers Series No: 43.

James, R. and Mullins, D. (2004, June). "Supporting NGO Partners affected by HIV/AIDS". *Development in Practice*, Volume 14, Number 4

James, R. (2002). "People and Change: Exploring Capacity-Building in NGOS". *INTRAC NGO Management & Policy Series*, No.15

Kakabadse, A. and Kakabadse, N. (1999). *Essence of Leadership*. London: International Thomson Business Press.

Kaplan, A. (2002). "Development Practitioners and Social Process: Artists of the Invisible"

Kenya NGO Council (2001, October): A Guide to Being a Successful NGO Leader. *NGO Leadership Development Series*, No.3.

Kenya NGO Council (2001, September). "A Guide to Good Governance of NGOs". *NGO Leadership Development Series*, No. 1.

Kegan, R., Lahey, L, (2001). *How the Way we Talk can Change the Way we Work*, San Francisco: Jossey-Bass.

Kouzes, J. Posner, B. (2002), *Leadership: The Challenge*, San Francisco: Jossey-Bass.

Lister, S., Nyamugasira, W. (2001). "A study on the involvement of civil society in policy dialogue and advocacy, lessons learnt on their engagement in policy advocacy and future direction", produced for DFID, Uganda, mimeo.

Mamdami, M. (1976). *Politics and class formation in Uganda*, London: Heinemann.

Tosh J. (1978). *Clan Leaders and Colonial Chiefs in Lango: The Political History of an East African Stateless Society c.1800-1939*, Oxford Studies in African Affairs.

Wallace, T (2004), "The Impact and implications of rational Management tools on NGO partnership and practice", mimeo, Kampala.

10

Climbing the Credibility Ladder: Civil Society, Donor Support and the Accountability Challenge in Uganda

Arthur Larok[1]

Abstract

To hold others - e.g. the State - accountable, civil society organisations must be accountable themselves. The author examines the notion of accountability and applies it to the Ugandan context, charting the evolution of NGOs through the years and outlining the multiple rationales for the 'accountability agenda'. Ugandan NGOs face several challenges in being accountable, whether to those people they work for or work with, or towards their donors or indeed within themselves.

Although some examples of best practices are outlined, the author argues that a long-term collective effort is needed to make NGOs truly accountable. This must include further analysis of the social, economic and political constraints that impede accountability by NGOs, and possible remedial measures, including the necessary recalibrating of power imbalances in accountability relations. Above all, leadership that provides the moral high-ground to question convention and act in exemplary ways is required.

Introduction

Funding for civil society strengthening has become a vital part of the aid industry in the last two decades. Virtually every donor agency[2] has had a civil society support programme or at least asserts that civil society is critical for its activities, in what has been described as a move to "keep up with the Jones" (Van Rooy, 1998:54). This paper recognises that there is a multitude of reasons explaining keen support by development

---

[1] At the time of writing this article, Arthur Larok was the Country Director of ActionAid Uganda. He wishes to thank the Norwegian Agency for Development for the opportunity to share these reflections. The final paper greatly benefited from insightful comments and difficult questions asked by participants at the seminar held in Kampala on 12 March 2013. Errors and omissions remain the author's responsibility.

[2] In this paper, this largely refers to bi-lateral and multi-lateral aid donors or intermediary agencies, including co-financing agencies, such as international NGOs that provide funding to local civil society groups.

agencies for civil society, especially in the south, but one which takes centre stage in this essay, is the idea that civil society can be supported to 'hold government accountable' as part of the broader development project.

To be able to do this though, one must assume that CSOs are themselves accountable. This essay engages with the accountability question amongst a dominant sub-group within civil society, the NGOs. While inferences and reflections are made on civil society as a wider phenomenon, the underlying focus is drawn from the author's work experience, knowledge and research amongst NGOs. It is argued in the main that NGOs have an incomplete understanding of accountability and thus suffer deficits in practice. Only a few can therefore occupy the moral high-ground, as institutions to engage with the broader accountability struggle with the State. We can however draw lessons from the few that have the moral authority.

Civil Society and its rise to 'prominence'

Despite the growth of a cottage industry among political and other theorists about the notion of civil society and what it represents, its precise meaning remains elusive (White, 1994; Brock, 2002; Van Rooy, 1998, Oloka, 1998). Different interpretations make it conceptually and practically fluid (Oloka, 1998). While some attempt to distinguish civil from political society (White, 1994, 1996), others forcefully argue that political society and its actors (like political parties) must be part of it (Mujagu, in Oloka, ibid). Various definitions vaguely describe civil society as the whole of humanity once government and for-profit firms are excised, covering all those organisations that fill in the spaces between the family, the state and the market (White, Van Rooy, Oloka). Some analysts like Bradley maintain that the vagueness in the term is part of its appeal. Said he, "...having to define all things is actually part of our problem and over reliance on scientific categorisation" (Bradely, in Van Rooy, 1998: 56). Others, however, insist that if we allow civil society to be theoretically impoverished, to suit all political tastes, to exist as a residual category once all other slices of human life are drawn away, then it deserves abandonment (Fierlbeck, in Van Rooy, 1998:29 and Van Rooy: 199). In other words, civil society ought to be an observable reality.

Most definitions of civil society are couched in an ideal and positive tone; portraying it as what it ought to be, rather than what it is. In this paper, civil society is used to refer to those organisations populating the associational realm between the State and family which are not primarily driven by the desire to make profit or the quest to capture power. Instead they claim, albeit through *civilised*[3] means, to represent the collective interests of those of their members or sections of the citizenry, who for various reasons are considered to be better articulated through them. They include trade unions, NGOs (and NGO networks), faith-based organisations, professional associations, community-based organisations and some sections of the media. This definition attempts to de-link

---

3   The virtues of civility denote 'polite' and refined behaviour and treating others with respect and tolerance; acting civilly toward one another, care about families and fellow citizens. The emphasis on the word civil is to distinguish unpopular groups like Al Qaeda, the LRA, etc which by the definition occupy the civil society space.

from civil society the 'for-profit' private enterprises, political parties and groups that may be 'uncivil' but still populate the space described by White above.

Uganda's Civil Society in historical perspective

Civil society is a growing phenomenon in Uganda, with its growth often driven by external factors, including government initiatives, decentralisation and donor funding (De Coninck, 2004:2). The nature, composition and prominence of groups populating the civil society space have also been changing over time. In the pre-independence period where a measured development of what today is referred to as civil society was encouraged by the colonial government, key players on the civil society scene included producer and export cooperatives, trade unions and other social movements (ibid:52). After independence, the dominant group - cooperatives - were co-opted by the State and some formed the nucleus of state enterprises in the late 1960s. In the 1970s during Idi Amin's dictatorship, independent civic and civil action was severely curtailed but the students' movement remained formidable. There was a reincarnation of civil society in the 80s mainly in the form of international NGOs to fill gaps created by government failure and abuse in the 1970s and early 1980s.

It was, however, during the NRM rule that today's dominant form of civil society (NGOs) proliferated. The growth of this sub-group was prodigious; from about 160 in 1986 to 3,500 in 2000, to 4,700 in 2003 and about 5,500 by the end of 2005 (De Coninck; 2004; Oloka, 2006). The latest statistics from the NGO Registration Board puts the number in excess of 10,000. As in other parts of Africa, this NGO boom was and still is aided by donor funding (Nadia & Robrecht, 2002:28).

Why do donors support civil society? Accountability and more!

The reasons for increased donor interest in civil society strengthening are varied, in some cases even contradictory. This paper discerns at least three broad explanations; the neo-liberal rationale, the dissatisfaction with the performance of the state and finally the political liberalisation and policy engagement rationale.

These rationales, while inter-linked, each emphasise slightly different realities. According to the neo-liberal school, donor interest and support to civil society is part of a bigger project to promote Western capitalism driven by the neo-liberal agenda. Support to civil society is seen as necessary for the creation of the pre-conditions for the success of market-based economies. It is suggested[4] that, in the quest to support models for liberalised economies, donors were aware of the necessary social pre-requisites required for the market to work, and this was absent in many countries. The questions were therefore: who trains citizens in the values necessary for entrepreneurialism? How does one interest people in opening markets and curbing governments? The answer was to encourage associational life: civil society was projected as a form of social capital necessary for market functioning and its role as advocate for such reforms in pursuit of the capitalist dream was underlined (Van Rooy, 1998:36; Oloka, 1998:3).

---

4   For a more extended discussion of this theory, refer to a collection of several donor views including USAID, FES, Inter-American Foundation, etc. in Van Rooy, 1998

Another rationale was premised on the perceived State failure to deliver development. Donor attention to the phenomenon of civil society was in this case seen to reflect concern with the State-centric notion of governance which emerged as a major pre-occupation of post-war donor policies (Oloka, 1998:2; Amutabi, 2006:31-32). As criticisms of governments mounted, many turned to the concept of civil society to identify possible sources of political, economic and social renewal. In Uganda, numerous large donor supported projects through NGOs in the late 1980s and early 1990s ranging from tackling HIV/AIDS, providing education and health services in hard to reach areas, to assisting military demobilisation and poverty alleviation programmes, could be viewed in this light. Where a regime was viewed as corrupt, patrimonial and incapable of delivering services, an alternative had to be found. This argument presupposes a strong link between good governance, accountability and development, and promotes the idea that NGOs are more accountable than governments.

A third rationale for donor support to civil society is closely linked to the changing role of the State and the discourse on governance that emerged in the 1990s. The evolving role of the State, from development leadership in the 1970s, to its downsizing in the 1980s during the structural adjustment era, and its reincarnation in the 1990s had implications for donor support to civil society. In the 1980s, civil society - mainly international NGOs and their local partners – received considerable amounts of aid money in the form of projects. NGOs were viewed as gap fillers for a State that had been conditioned to downsize and retreat. Government played an 'absentee' role in an era dominated by project support. However, when it became apparent that recipient governments owned neither development projects nor their outcomes, a sudden shift to 'bring back' the State was made and policy-based lending and budget support were next in vogue.

For civil society, and in particular for NGOs, the heydays were over, or it was at least time for another switch in roles. Discourses shifted from statements on the role and efficiency of NGOs in service delivery to claims that CSOs could hold government to account by creating a demand side to efficient service delivery (Lister & Nyamugasira). Governance programmes became the major (if not dominant) focus of donor agencies with emphasis on human rights, democratisation, capacity building, institutional strengthening, transparency, accountability, and policy engagement (Oloka, 1998).

Accountability: Meaning and practice

It has become fashionable to debate about accountability and the need to hold agencies accountable. This underscores the continuing concern for checks and oversight, for surveillance and institutional constraints on the exercise of power. Schedler (1999), however, observes that accountability represents an under-explored concept whose precise meaning remains evasive; boundaries fuzzy and internal structures confusing. Two faces of accountability have nevertheless been suggested: on the one hand is answerability - the obligation by public officials to inform and explain their actions - and on the other, enforcement, which relates to the capacity of accounting agencies to impose sanctions on power holders who have violated their public duties (Schedler,

1999:14). Accountability is used here to mean a situation where a public agency or official is held responsible and bears consequences for actions or inaction on a duty they are expected to perform in the public interest. Accountability thus describes rights and responsibilities that exist between people and institutions that affect their lives (IDS).[5]

In other words, accountability is a relationship of power. When accountability systems function, citizens can make demands on powerful institutions, State and non-State alike, and to ensure that those demands are met. It presupposes at least three ways of redressing abusive power: subjecting power to the threats of sanctions; obliging it to be exercised in transparent ways; and forcing it to justify its acts. As Schedler (1999:15) emphasises, accounting persons, whether in government or in civil society, should not only tell what they have done and why, but bear the consequences. The exercise of accountability that exposes misdeeds but does not impose material consequences is seen as weak, diminished and or window dressing, rather than as a real restraint on power (Shedler ibid:16; Robinson, 2006:11).

Uganda's accountability dilemmas

Given this discussion, what are the accountability dilemmas in Uganda? It seems, first, that citizens appear weaker than the State and are thus unable to hold it accountable as an institution. The typical Ugandan is said to be 15 years old, dependent (the dependency ratio in Uganda is 12:1), poor and trying to survive at best. The blurring of boundaries between accountability institutions and a resurgent imperial presidency account for a rather poor performance of key State institutions. Accountability is, however, not just a relationship of power, but also one of trust. The latter is in short supply in Uganda and there is a near breakdown of trust among many government agencies and leaders alike. While Ugandans pay direct and indirect taxes, they see little in return in terms of service delivery: it could be argued that the cost paid for bad roads, poor public health facilities, poor quality education and agricultural extension, all make up for double taxation. When Ugandans resort to mob-justice, it suggests that they do not trust law and order institutions. Even when one government agency appears to be acting against another, this is perceived as unsustainable selective justice or a political witch-hunt.

In the case of civil society, given the discussion so far, what does accountability mean? What does an NGO that is accountable look like? Who should NGOs be accountable to and for what?

NGO credibility gaps and a heavy reliance on donor finance creating *'trusteeships'*

Shedler (1999) argues that agents of accountability, such as CSOs, should be open and subject themselves to a second order of accountability. The question as to who CSOs are accountable to in their work is controversial. Should CSOs be accountable to Government, to donors or to citizens? If it is to government as Hegel (1821, cited in Van Rooy, 1998:10) suggests, then a key rationale for accountability is undermined. The

---

5   Making Accountability Count, *IDS Briefing*, Issue 33, November 2006.

tendency for CSOs to account upward to donors has been criticised and government is often wary of such an accountability orientation. While it is reasonable to argue that NGOs should be accountable to all the above actors, depending on their specific situation, it is important to emphasise the need for CSO downward accountability to citizens. In Uganda, however, NGOs have been accused of being pre-occupied with accountability to donors and with their self-perpetuation, rather than to their-would be constituencies (De Coninck, 2002:63). As elsewhere in the world, many NGOs have weak linkages to the grassroots (Ottaway, 2000) and sometimes actually prey on their purported constituency. In 2006 for instance, several NGOs were implicated in a major corruption scandal involving the misuse of Global Funds meant for the control of HIV/AIDS, malaria and tuberculosis, a scandal that greatly dented their image.[6]

NGOs have themselves acknowledged that there could be some 'wolves' among the sheep and are trying to address this through an NGO Quality Assurance Certification Mechanism. In some cases, NGOs are accused of reproducing the same injustices and ways of work as they accuse the State of perpetrating.

Apart from compliance to legal or administrative requirements which the State often fault NGOs on, do ordinary citizens have a say over what NGOs activities and methods? As in the case of the unaccountable State mentioned above, there is very little that ordinary citizens can do about NGOs. As recently as 2018 and 2019, there has been a joint commitment by donors and NGOs to tackle accusations of collusion and kick-backs among NGO and donor staff. Lessons will hopefully be learnt from this renewed attention to accountability.

Blurred boundaries between civil society and the State

Identifying an 'NGO sector' is complicated by the blurred boundaries with the State, mostly because of a frequently changing donor aid architecture (Lister & Nyamugasira, 2003) which has conditioned some CSOs to become service delivery agents for the State, while many functions ascribed to CSOs, particularly those of holding government accountable, rest on the assumption that civil society has a separate identity (Brock, 2002:98) and sees this as its role. This may, however, not be the case in Uganda (De Coninck, 2004; Brock 2002:97). The common view of civil society as an autonomous space, standing in parallel to the State indeed needs rethinking, while recognising the critical role played by the latter in constituting civil society itself (IDS, CFS-2005:4) and where civil society support and activism is largely an offshoot of a broader donor-state affair. In Uganda, and especially within the decentralised system of governance, the same individuals often wear different hats; sometimes as public officials and simultaneously as patrons of civil society organisations.

Is civil society then any different from a generally discredited State? Two anecdotes illustrate this question: in Kampala suburbs, adverts for office spaces to let often

---

6   Corruption scandals among NGOs, including accountability-oriented ones remain a major concern to-date with intricate allegations of collusion between NGOs and donors.

mention "office space available, suitable for NGOs, Banks or Government". Secondly, while on a research trip in North-Western Uganda, an NGO team narrated visiting a household earlier met by government researchers. An elderly resident sceptically asked what the second team was now wanting, given that both teams were dressed alike, came in similar vehicles and asked the same questions. Perceptions of NGOs are thus constructed.

Leadership challenges and transition failures

One of Uganda's important governance and accountability challenges concerns leadership, a challenge most acutely faced by civil society organisations. Without leadership that exudes a different culture from what we see in the public arena and in the private market place, it may be illusory to expect CSOs to offer hope for Uganda. Civil society organisations themselves must demonstrate their ability to handle differently the social ills that undermine the State, with leadership longevity and the supremacy of the 'big men' (and women) who want to stay in power in perpetuity. Yet, while NGOs join the chorus to campaign for the restoration of presidential term limits, the 'founder syndrome' prevails in many NGOs. In the same way as the President believes he hunted and killed his animal and therefore must feast to the end, many NGO leaders appear unable to confront life outside the organisations they help found or, if they do transit, this is often partial, with a detrimental lasting influence on 'their' organisation.

Another challenge related to the lack of transparency and accountability in the way NGOs conduct business concerns corruption and discrimination along gender, tribe, region and religion categories, in turn linked to the resulting NGO belief systems and convictions. CSO workers have indeed been accused of being careerists, lacking conviction and being "just workers". A perception has in consequence developed that, along a few radical and altruistic NGO leaders, most look at themselves as workers taking the opportunity of available jobs in the sector and earning a comfortable living. Whether or not they serve the larger societal good is not part of their primary agenda; they are risk averse and generally partake of status quo, qualities that do not meet the needs of the times.

Best practices

Despite these challenges, several best practices must be noted, if only in the hope that some impulses within civil society may offer answers to the key accountability questions of the day. They represent attempts by many civil society organisations to 'climb the credibility ladder'.

The NGO Quality Assurance Certification Mechanism (QuAM) is a voluntary self-governance initiative by and for NGOs. Initiated by the Uganda National NGO Forum and DENIVA, two of Uganda's largest NGO networks, the QuAM outlines 59 standards and indicators of ethical conduct and responsible behaviour expected of publicly accountable NGOs. The 59 indicators allow NGOs to progress from 'start-up', 'improvement' to 'standards of excellence'. Acquiring any of these standards attracts recommendations for further improvement, as NGOs grow in governance voluntarily rather than assume 'a larger than life' posture simply to impress. Although the voluntary nature of the QuAM has been seen by some as its weakness, it is its most important attribute, for if the QuAM were made compulsory and enforced by the State, it could easily become a 'policing instrument' incurring the risks of backlash, such as forgeries, to be compliant. An important feedback aspect of the QuAM is its public vetting system that requires any NGO seeking accreditation to subject itself to its 'public', when questions are asked about the value an NGO offers to its constituencies or the 'communities' it services.

A related instrument and best practice is one developed by some international NGOs in 2005 that defines certain principles to guide their work, including respect for universal principles, such as independence from politics, responsible advocacy, effective programmes and non-discrimination. NGOs that subject themselves to such commitments certainly take a bold step to open, stand up and be counted.

Transparency boards are used by a few governments, especially at Local Government levels, and by several NGOs. These are open spaces where critical information about the organisation and its work is displayed. In the case of ActionAid Uganda, for instance, information shared includes summaries of its work in the locality, information about budgets and what financial allocation has been made and to whom, for accountability purposes. Values, mission and working principles are also shared, to enable ordinary people ask questions about how ActionAid adheres to these principles in practice.

Indicating the source of grants where this does not infringe the rules of the cooperating parties also presents an opportunity and can respond to claims that NGO are agents of foreign interests. Local governments have also started displaying information on budgetary allocations. While much more must be done beyond this type of information sharing and being transparent, this provides an opportunity to build knowledge that can provide a basis for accountability.

Effective governing Boards must also be mentioned. Many NGOs claim to have oversight boards, but their effectiveness is often doubtful. An effective board is meant to question, challenge, advise and sometimes draw on the technical expertise of its members to offer solutions to organisational challenges. Effective boards are also custodians of the mission of the organisation and finally, they are accountable to other organs such as general assemblies, depending on the nature of the organisation. Organisations are less transparent, less innovative and less accountable to different clients without effective boards. Yet, in many cases, boards are viewed as bodies that take out more than they give to NGOs, especially when they are docile 'secretariat projects' or when they interfere in minute management issues. An effective board, able to professionally hold management accountable thus remains an important organ for accountability and a best practice.

Term limits and succession planning. Whenever a discussion on term limits surfaces, especially in Uganda, the temptation is to quickly think about executive term limits for the position of President, infamously removed from the Constitution in 2005 before it was even tested. The principle, however, and this applies to NGOs as well, is about putting the institution before individuals and ensuring the existence of mechanisms, at least to guard against perpetual holding of posts by individuals. The 'founder syndrome' has been mentioned: term limits, as practiced by some organisations, must be about managing succession and building capacity in public voluntary organisations.

Organisations such as the Uganda National NGO Forum, the Uganda Joint Christian Council and others have previously emphasised that the tenure of their chief executives are clearly defined in their constitutions, and most importantly respected. Many other NGOs, especially international ones or those that are part of global entities such as ActionAid, often have defined time periods for contracting chief executives, thus ensuring regular leadership changes. Such practice encourages succession planning, saves the organisation from being held hostage by leaders and enables capacity to be systematically built. Conversely many organisations that suffer from the founder syndrome fail to outlive the strong personalities that form them. Setting term limits is thus a best practise to learn from.

Confronting governmental corruption. Many NGOs have dared to stand up by questioning government's commitment to deal with runaway corruption. By so doing, they open themselves to more public scrutiny than others. By participating actively in the anti-corruption campaign, these are conditioned to 'clean their own house'. Conscious and authentic involvement in the fight against corruption has proven a powerful incentive to start the fight within the organisation to provide the necessary moral authority to question others. Such best practice is supported by the Uganda Constitution that makes it a duty of every citizen 'to combat corruption and misuse or wastage of public property'.

Conclusions

In attempting to engage with the notion of accountability conceptually and practically, especially as it relates to civil society organisations and NGOs, understanding accountability as stemming from a relationship of power and trust and as manifested in the two dimensions of answerability and enforceability provides a useful starting point. In reviewing practical challenges towards fulfilling an accountability agenda, the constraint that agents meant to demand accountability in the Ugandan context meet is that they are mostly dependent for their survival and for access to critical services on those they are supposed to hold accountable. Power relations are thus skewed in ways that undermine accountability whether by the State or civil society.

Further, there are grave internal accountability challenges within institutions of State and civil society alike, that have progressively led to a breakdown in trust and to the rise of calculative and transactional relationships between those meant to hold institutions accountable and the institutions or leaders themselves.

Nevertheless, best accountability practices are emerging and present some hope from civil society. Whether or not these practices can deliver beyond the impulses that they currently respond to, calls for collective action within civil society. This could lead to a further analysis of the social, economic and political constraints that impede accountability by NGOs, and possible remedial measures, including the necessary recalibrating of power imbalances in accountability relations. Another area of query concerns costs: how can accountability be made affordable, focusing on both the process and procedural levels, as well as on results and outcomes?

This calls for moral leadership to be nurtured to steer above the murky waters that civil society currently finds itself in. A leadership that will provide the moral highground to question convention and act in exemplary ways.

References and Further Reading

Abdelrahman M. (2004). *Civil Society Exposed: The Politics of NGOs in Egypt*, London & New York: Tauris Academic Studies.

Amutabi, M. (2006). *The NGO Factor in Africa: The Case of Arrested Development in Kenya*. New York and London: Routledge Series.

Brock, K. (2002). Ugandan Civil Society in Policy Processes: Challenging Orthodox Narratives. In Brock, K, McGee, R & John Gaventa, J (Eds) *Unpacking Policy: Knowledge, Actors and Spaces in Poverty Reduction in Uganda and Nigeria*, Kampala: Fountain Publishers.

De Coninck, J. (2002). "The State, Civil Society and Development: Where are we coming from?" In Brock, K, McGee, R & Gaventa, J. (Eds) *Unpacking Policy; Knowledge, Actors and Spaces in Poverty Reduction in Uganda & Nigeria*, Kampala: Fountain Publishers.

De Coninck, J. (2004). "Politics is [best] left to Politicians", Civil Society in a Period of Political Transition in Uganda: Challenges and Prospects". CDRN Paper No.5, 2004.

IDS (2006). *Signposts to more Effective States: Responding to Governance Challenges in Developing Countries*. Center for Future States, IDS, UK.

Igoe, J. (2003). "Scaling Up Civil Society: Donor Money, NGOs and the Pastoralist Land Rights Movement in Tanzania". In *Development and Change*, Vol.34, No.5, (863 – 886).

Katsui, H. & Wamai, R. (Eds), (2006). *Civil Society Reconsidered: A critical look at NGOs in Development Practice*. Helsinki: University of Helsinki, Institute of Development Studies.

Larok, Arthur (2012). "The Civil Society Leadership Challenge in Uganda". A brief synopsis prepared for an NGO Leader's Retreat convened by the Uganda National NGO Forum, Hotel Africana, December 2012.

Larok, Arthur (2012). "The Role of Civil Society in a Changing Political Context: Reflections from Uganda". A Paper for a Seminar on Civil Society Trends & Political Engagement - MS TCDC, Arusha.

Lister, S. & Nyamugasira, W. (2003). "Design Contradictions in the New Architecture of Aid? Reflections from Uganda on the role of Civil Society Organisations". In *Development Policy Review*, 2003, 21 (1): 93-106.

Molenears, N. & Renard, R. (2002). "Strengthening Civil Society from the Outside? Donor Driven Consultations and Participation". In *PRSPs: The Bolivian Case*, IDPM, Belgium.

NGO Forum & Deniva (2006). "The Narrowing Space for NGO Operations in Uganda: An Analysis of the implications of the 2006 NGO Act".

Oloka Onyango J. (1997). "Civil Society and the Place of Foreign Donors in Contemporary Uganda: A Review of the Literature and the Donor Policy Environment".

Ottaway, Marina (2000). "Social Movements, Professionalization of Reform and Democracy in Africa". In Ottaway, M. & Carothers, T (Eds), *Funding Virtue: Civil Society Aid and Democracy Promotion*, Washington DC: Carnegie Endowment for International Peace.

Sabatini, A. (2002). "Who do International Donors Support in the name of Civil Society?" In *Development in Practice*, Vol.12, No. 1, February 2002, Pp 7-20.

Schedler, A. (1999). "Conceptualizing Accountability". In Schedler, A. (ed), *The Self-Restraining State: Power and Accountability in New Democracies*, London: Lynne Reiner.

Van Rooy & Robinson, Mark (1998). "Out of the Ivory Tower: Civil Society and the Aid System". In Rooy Van Alison (Ed), *Civil Society and the Aid Industry*, London: Earthscan.

Van Rooy (1998). "All Roads lead to Rome: Why bother about Civil Society?" In Rooy Van Alison (ed), Civil Society and the Aid Industry, London: Earthscan.

White, Gordon (1996). "Civil Society, Democratisation and Development". In Luckham, R & White, G (eds), *Democratisation in the South: The Jagged Wave*, pp 176- 218. Manchester and New York: Manchester University Press.

http://www.ingoaccountabilitycharter.org/wpcms/wp-content/uploads/INGO Accountability-Charter.pdf.

SECTION IV
Creating Impact

11

The Ambiguities of the 'Partnership' between Civil Society and the State in Uganda's AIDS Response During the 1990s and 2000s as Demonstrated in the Development of TASO[1]

Eduard Grebe[2]

Abstract

This article critically investigates state-civil society relations in the Ugandan AIDS response by tracing the history of Uganda's 'multisectoral' and 'partnership' approaches, particularly as it pertains to The AIDS Support Organisation (TASO). It finds that the Ugandan government's reputation for good leadership on AIDS is more ambiguous than commonly supposed, and that the much-vaunted 'partnership' approach has not enabled strong critical civil society voices to emerge or prevented the harmful impact of a socially conservative agenda. By the 1990s, TASO had become the most important provider of medical and psychosocial support services to HIV/AIDS patients, but was less effective in influencing policy or holding the state accountable (because the political context prevented a more activist stance). The effectiveness of civil society has been constrained by an authoritarian political culture and institutions that discourage vocal criticism. Despite these limitations, however, state-civil society partnership did contribute to the emergence of a relatively effective coalition for action against HIV/AIDS. Donors were essential in encouraging the emergence of this coalition.

---

[1] Reprinted from Global Public Health, Global Public Health, 11:4, 496-512, 2016, by permission of the publisher Taylor & Francis Ltd, http://www.tandfonline.com.

[2] South African Centre for Epidemiological Modelling and Analysis (SACEMA), Stellenbosch University, Stellenbosch, South Africa; and Centre for Social Science Research, University of Cape Town, Cape Town, South Africa, 8 May 2015. The author gratefully acknowledges financial support from the Developmental Leadership Program (see www.dlprog.org), which made the fieldwork for this study possible. Useful comments were received from the late Dr Adrian Leftwich and substantial comments on various drafts from Prof Nicoli Nattrass. The author also wishes to acknowledge the very useful advice and criticism received from three anonymous reviewers for this journal.

Introduction

Uganda experienced one of the earliest large-scale HIV epidemics in Sub-Saharan Africa, but gained a reputation for a highly effective response and strong political leadership on HIV/AIDS during the 1990s and 2000s. It is often cited as a model for addressing HIV/AIDS in resource-poor settings (Youde, 2007, p. 1). The energetic and 'hands-on' leadership of President Yoweri Museveni, appropriate public policy and the supportive approach adopted by the state towards civil society responses are seen as critical success factors.

The Ugandan government adopted a 'partnership approach,' with effective and relatively well-resourced civil society organisations – most prominently The AIDS Support Organisation (TASO) – thereby helping to compensate for weak state capacity in the health sector. The relationship between the state, donors and civil society during the period under review is widely perceived as highly productive. This paper explores some of the ambiguities in the 'partnership' between the state and civil society through the lens of TASO's growth and development in the context of a supportive yet relatively authoritarian state.

The research draws on an extensive series of interviews with leaders in civil society organisations, government officials, donor representatives and healthcare workers in Uganda[3]. The fieldwork was conducted in October 2008 for the purposes of a comparative analysis of 'AIDS response coalitions' in South Africa and Uganda.[4] In addition, documentary records and secondary literature informed the research. While the interviews were conducted some years before the production of this paper, the data remains useful for the purposes of a historical analysis of state-civil society partnership in the Ugandan AIDS response. A limitation of this research is that very few participants in faith-based and religious organisations were interviewed, and consequently the role of these groups and initiatives may be under-represented.

The analysis presented here acknowledges the progressive dimensions of AIDS policy under Museveni, but highlights also the constraints that Uganda's autocratic regime brought to bear on civil society. Whereas civil society in South Africa, Thailand and Brazil played an important role in holding governments to account both in the formulation and implementation of policy (e.g. Nunn, Dickman, Nattrass, Cornwall & Gruskin 2012; Nattrass 2014), the most important civil society organisation in Uganda, TASO, kept to a narrower, service-oriented mandate. (This contrasts sharply with the approach adopted, for example, by explicitly activist organisations such as South Africa's Treatment Action Campaign, see, e.g. Grebe, 2011). Uganda's state-civil society partnership in the 1990s and 2000s contributed to the emergence of an effective 'AIDS response coalition', but precisely because it emerged in the context of limited freedom of civil society to mobilise politically, it was complicated and ambiguous in its outcomes. The AIDS response coalition in Uganda certainly helped

---

3   Many more interviews were conducted than are directly cited in text, but also contributed to the development of the arguments presented here.
4   The research was conducted under the auspices of the Developmental Leadership Program.

facilitate prevention messaging and the rollout of treatment, yet the absence of strong and independent political mobilisation on AIDS meant that civil society was unable to counter Museveni's subsequent lack of commitment (and sometimes outright opposition) to condom promotion and related leadership failures. Donors had an important role in the emergence of the 'AIDS response coalition' described here, but may also unwittingly have undermined the emergence of an independent civil society voice.

It is a commonplace assertion in the international AIDS policy arena that 'leadership' on AIDS is critical to curbing HIV transmission and implementing AIDS treatment programmes. For example, an early collection of prevention 'best practice' case studies by UNAIDS argued that "Political action and leadership is clearly needed to set the direction for a national response" (UNAIDS, 1998, p. 6). This argument is perhaps most closely associated with former UNAIDS Executive Director, Peter Piot (see Piot & Coll-Seck, 2001; Piot, 2012). The notion of 'AIDS leadership' is, however, complex and under-theorised (Grebe, 2012). It is primarily used in the sense of 'political commitment' from national political leaders (see for example Bor, 2007), but is also used to refer to the ability of leaders to mobilise society-wide collective efforts (Piot and Coll-Seck, 2001). It has also been theorised and analysed in other ways, for example by combining measures of 'political commitment' and measures of state expenditure on AIDS (Dionne, 2011) and the difficulties of measuring 'political commitment' have been acknowledged (see Fox, 2011; Goldberg et al., 2012). The impact of regime type and constraints on political leaders have also been explored (Justesen, 2012; Fox, 2014). However, these theoretical and methodological difficulties are not analysed in detail here and for the purposes of this article 'leadership on AIDS' is conceptualised as building 'coalitions'[5] for effective responses to AIDS that involve state and civil society leadership (Grebe, 2012, pp. 13-24), in line with Piot and Coll-Seck (2001). This article focuses on the role of a 'partnership approach' in mobilising an effective AIDS response coalition.

State leadership and the making of an 'African success story'

In the late 1970s, North Western Tanzania and Southern Uganda probably constituted the epicentre of the African HIV epidemic (Epstein, 2007). By the mid-1980s many communities were being ravaged by the disease locally known as 'slim' (O'Manique, 2004; Thornton, 2008). The situation was exacerbated by the insecurity and social upheaval of a bloody civil war lasting from 1981 to 1986 that contributed to widespread fear and confusion and rendered any systematic state response nearly impossible.

By the time Museveni's National Resistance Army took power in January 1986, AIDS constituted a public health crisis that could also threaten economic reconstruction and

---

5 For purposes of this article, 'coalitions' simply refer to society-wide collective action that involves a wide range of actors from different sectors (e.g. government agencies, NGOs, faith-based organisations and churches, international donors, etc.). A more theoretically developed concept of coalitions is beyond the scope of this article, but interested readers are referred to Yashar (1997) and Leftwich & Hogg (2007) and, for application to the field of HIV/AIDS, Grebe (2012).

even the stability of the new regime.[6] The Museveni government started responding meaningfully to HIV shortly after coming to power. Prevention campaigns involved the President himself speaking openly about the risks of contracting HIV through sex and featured the slogans 'love faithfully' and 'zero grazing' (partner reduction), with little to no condom promotion (Allen and Heald, 2004, p. 1148). A subcommittee that had been set up by the second Obote government was upgraded to the National Committee for the Prevention of AIDS (NCPA) in October 1986 and a World Health Organisation mission to Uganda in January 1987 helped draw up a short-term intervention plan and a medium-term (five-year) action plan. These plans formed the basis of the Aids Control Programme (the first in Africa) and a donor conference in May 1987. The President made a number of high-profile speeches in which he drew attention to AIDS, and in December 1988 he unambiguously declared AIDS a major national priority, calling for an all-out public education campaign. This openness and willingness to tackle the issue of HIV and risky stood in sharp contrast to most African governments at the time (P. Piot, personal communication, December 20, 2010).[7]

But Uganda's status as a 'poster boy' for good governmental leadership on AIDS and Museveni's reputation as an exceptional African leader were probably cemented when it became apparent in the mid-1990s that HIV prevalence had started to decline, turning Uganda into the first African HIV prevention 'success story'. What exactly led to the decline in HIV prevalence is uncertain, and there has been considerable debate among scholars about the relative importance of different factors (see, for example, Gray, Serwadda, Kigozi, Nalugoda & Wawer, 2006; Green, Halperin, Nantulya & Hogle, 2006; Merson, 2006; Kirby 2008; Thornton, 2008; Atzori et al., 2009). It seems clear that changes in sexual behaviour – in particular reductions in the number of sexual partners – played a significant role (Stoneburner & Low-Beer, 2004; Low-Beer & Stoneburner, 2004; Kirby 2008). This is usually attributed to a combination of the 'natural' peaking of the epidemic and the prevention campaigns, while Thornton (2008, p. 33) emphasises the effects of the configuration of sexual networks on HIV trends and Epstein (2007, p. 160) argues that the many small community-based AIDS groups that were founded during the 1980s and early 1990s deserve much of the credit for changing sexual norms.

Initially, it was widely believed that the decline in HIV prevalence indicated that the Ugandan government's prevention campaigns had been immensely successful, resulting in the apparently radical behaviour changes that would explain declining

---

6   It has, in fact, been argued that Museveni – whose power base was the army – was shocked to discover that significant numbers of soldiers were HIV-positive. Museveni himself has recounted an incident where a significant proportion of Ugandan army officers sent to Cuba for training tested positive for HIV and Cuban President Fidel Castro personally informed Museveni of the problem (Garbus & Marseille, 2003, cited in Ostergard & Barcello, 2005; De Waal, 2006, p. 97). This is not to suggest that Museveni's personal leadership on AIDS was purely aimed at securing his regime; at most it shows this may have played a role.

7   Piot (2012, p. 175) also describes then-Ugandan Health Minister Ruhakana Rugunda's speech at the 1987 World Health Assembly as a 'lone voice' calling on his peers to face the reality of AIDS on the African continent.

HIV prevalence (e.g. UNAIDS, 1998; 2001). However, it has become clear that HIV incidence peaked well before Museveni came to power. Largely consistent with Stoneburner and Low-Beer's (2004) estimates, data (based on the author's estimates) shows a peak in estimated total new adult infections in 1983 and in adult population prevalence in 1988. Other estimates put the peak in incidence as late as 1987 (Kirby, 2008). The peak in incidence is partially explained by the natural evolution of the epidemics, but an unusually steep decline in incidence occurred (see, e.g., Kirby 2008), likely involved significant behaviour change. The exact timing of the behaviour changes that would help explain the steep decline incidence remain uncertain, but it is likely that (1) significant behaviour change took place before Museveni came to power and prevention started in earnest and also that (2) declines were especially deep and rapid in Uganda during the late 1980s and early 1990s, possibly as a result of the efforts at community level and those of civil society as well as those of Museveni and his government.

The estimates reported above were produced using UNAIDS's Epidemiological Projection Package (UNAIDS, 2011) and HIV surveillance data from Ugandan antenatal clinics, with adult HIV prevalence estimates calibrated using national seroprevalence survey data from the Uganda HIV/AIDS Sero-Behavioural Survey 2004-2005 (Ministry of Health [Uganda] and ORC Macro, 2006). The full set of estimates produced by the model show that AIDS deaths continued to rise until 1995, and the fall in the HIV prevalence rate is explained by demographic changes and deaths exceeding new HIV infections. (The model is reported fully in Grebe, 2012). It is thus possible that large-scale behaviour change resulted at least in part from the visibility of illness and death (both of which had started to increase markedly by the early 1980s) and community-based norm adjustment, and were to some degree enhanced by the partner reduction campaigns of the late 1980s. The degree to which these campaigns alone were the central drivers of Uganda's 'prevention success' is questionable, but the Ugandan government does deserve substantial credit for having tackled the epidemic head-on, speaking openly about the ways in which HIV could be contracted and making HIV prevention a major priority. It also successfully engaged donors and attracted significant resources that made possible the substantial and sustained response during the 1990s and 2000s.

While the Ugandan state took the lead in HIV prevention, it could draw on existing home-grown prevention responses from community groups, including in the rural areas at the epicentre of the epidemic (see Epstein, 2007). By 1988 it was seeking to integrate the efforts of government and civil society (including NGOs, faith-based and community-based organisations), eventually resulting in the 'multi-sectoral approach' of the 1990s (Thornton, 2008, p. 131). It possessed extremely limited capacity to provide health services (there were few hospitals and even fewer that had the resources to provide high quality services). AIDS services in Uganda were pioneered by civil society, including by church-run hospitals and later (most prominently) by TASO, which was founded in 1987. The government embraced and encouraged these efforts.

TASO founder Noerine Kaleeba describes being brought into high-level policy-making and says that the 'terrain had been set' for civil society to respond to AIDS (personal communication, October 16, 2008).

The government provided leadership in two important ways: (1) by ensuring AIDS featured prominently on the national agenda, and (2) by building partnerships with civil society on prevention and care, and coordinating the work of a diverse set of actors, first through the NCPA and later through the national AIDS Control Programme. Uganda's 'multi-sectoral approach' – including its failings – will be discussed in greater detail in the sections that follow.

By the mid-2000s, Uganda was performing significantly better than most of its peers in the provision of antiretroviral treatment, even if this progress was largely funded by donors and implemented by civil society organisations like TASO. Using a cross-country multivariate regression analysis, Nattrass (2008) shows that Uganda achieved a higher coverage of highly active antiretroviral treatment (HAART) than one might expect given its level of development, external resources, social characteristics and burden of disease.[8] She speculates that this may be related to Uganda's strong 'political leadership'.

TASO's birth and development from volunteer network to professional service delivery organisation

In early 1987, a group of 16 men and women (the majority of whom were HIV-positive) started meeting informally to share experiences and support one another in coping with the impact of HIV/AIDS on their lives (Ssebanja, 2007, p. 1). Most were HIV-positive or had loved ones who were ill with or had died from AIDS. This included Noerine Kaleeba, the group's leader, whose husband Christopher had died of AIDS shortly before.[9] As the group grew it formalised its structure and programme of 'living positively'. Kaleeba, a charismatic and energetic individual, was principal of the School of Physiotherapy at Mulago Hospital and became TASO's first director. She cites as motivation for the founding of TASO "a feeling of anger and frustration at the stigma and isolation of people with HIV and … the fact that families were abandoning their loved ones" (personal communication, October 16, 2008).

Medical services for AIDS patients were extremely limited. Dr Elly Katabira, a physician who had come across AIDS while working in Britain, was shocked to find large numbers of AIDS patients in Mulago Hospital when he returned to Kampala in 1986. He set up an outpatient clinic in late 1986 and opposed proposals for a segregated

---

8   Essentially, her cross-country regression analyses show that Uganda performed better than its peers when controlling for relevant factors.
9   The previous year, she had visited Christopher in England where he had become ill and been diagnosed with AIDS. In a remarkable interview for the PBS documentary 'The Age of AIDS', she describes how she travelled to Geneva to meet Jonathan Mann, director of the WHO's Global Programme on AIDS (see Cran & Simone, 2006; Barker & Simone, 2006). Her relationship with Mann would later prove valuable as TASO sought to mobilise international support. She brought Christopher back to Uganda, where he died in January 1987.

inpatient ward.[10] In 1987, Katabira had been put in touch with the fledgling TASO and became a key figure in their integration of social support and community-based services with medical services. At the time no life-saving treatment for HIV/AIDS was available, and the founders were responding primarily to the human tragedy caused by widespread stigma and discrimination, both within the healthcare system and the wider community, which condemned patients to lonely and undignified deaths. They strove to enable patients to "die with dignity" (P. Ssebanja, personal communication, 15 October, 2008).

TASO reached out to communities by visiting neighbourhoods to identify patients and running training workshops on caring for the ill at home. The group tackled stigma and discrimination by talking openly about AIDS and even the then-chairman of the AIDS Control Programme attended one of its AIDS sensitisation workshops (Ssebanja, 2007, p. 17). The rapidly expanding organisation obtained office and counselling space at Mulago hospital, helped set up an HIV testing service and day-care clinic in Masaka and provided advice to healthcare workers. Initially the focus was on providing counselling and psychosocial support, but increasingly the organisation responded to the weakness of the Ugandan healthcare system by providing medical services itself. By 2008, TASO operated 11 service centres throughout the country, employed over 1,000 staff and administered Uganda's largest antiretroviral treatment programme.

TASO's founders relied heavily on pre-existing interpersonal networks to build the movement. Personal friends and acquaintances, especially those formed within the Mulago teaching hospital, formed the core of the young organisation (Ssebanja, 2007). The group quickly attracted like-minded individuals and created links with outside actors. These included donors and charities (ActionAid was an important early supporter), AIDS activists and AIDS service organisations in other countries like the UK-based Terrence Higgins Trust, from whom it obtained support and information. It is notable that Kaleeba and several other founders were educated professionals with significant social capital, comfortable in elite circles and able to hold their own among policymakers. The importance of personal ties during early movement-building is confirmed by frequent references to a 'family spirit' in the recollections of founders (personal communication, N. Kaleeba, 16 October, 2008; P. Ssebanja, 15 October, 2008). Dense interpersonal networks characterised by relationships of trust, domestic and transnational elite networks – including what Keck & Sikkink, 1998, term 'activist networks' and interlinkages with professional and governmental networks – and deliberately constructed partnerships enabled TASO to mobilise support and gain influence. This 'network of influence' (see Grebe, 2012) acted as the scaffolding by means of which a coalition for an effective policy and programmatic response to AIDS could be built in Uganda.

---

10 Dr Katabira opposed segregating AIDS patients because he worried that it would exacerbate stigma and discrimination by marking AIDS as a "deadly and shameful disease." He also worried that a service outside the mainstream would not be sustainable (E. Katabira, personal communication, 14 October, 2008).

But movements and the broader coalitions they form rarely remain static. As will be shown in the next section, TASO's development was shaped by the demands of its institutional context, including limited political space for activism. It was able to adapt to its circumstances and cope with an influx of resources and the intensifying demands of large-scale service delivery in part by formalising its structure and operations. Its leaders decided early on to build formal systems (personal communication, N. Kaleeba, 16 October, 2008): the organisation appointed professional managers and donors like USAID invested heavily in the development of its technical capacity and managerial systems (personal communication, E. Ayers, 29 October, 2008). These choices enabled it to become a highly successful service delivery organisation. But precisely because it was involved in such an important partnership with government, TASO had very limited space or incentive to adopt a more critical stance towards other aspects of Uganda's AIDS strategy. This is lamented by some of Uganda's most prominent activists, like the International HIV/AIDS Alliance's Milly Katana:

> [TASO] has lost the crowd. ...TASO is riding on the back of its history... Of course it's the biggest – outsiders trust it, value it, they give them more money and they are expanding services, which is great. But to me that doesn't mean that they are leaders (Personal communication, M. Katana, October 24, 2008).

Tensions between civil society organisations are probably inevitable, especially where they may be competing for the same pool of donor funding. However, Katana is putting her finger on a widespread concern within Ugandan civil society that its biggest star, TASO, had achieved much in its partnership with government but that this partnership had come at the cost of lessened civil society capacity (at least from the largest and most prominent organisation attracting the most funding) to criticise government where necessary, to hold it to account on its commitments, and to show greater leadership in Uganda's AIDS response.

Uganda's multi-sectoral partnership approach and the impact of donors

The Ugandan government realised that HIV required a society-wide response, and this is most clearly expressed in its efforts to encourage civil society through a 'multi-sectoral' approach. This included civil society representation at the institutional level in the ACP and later the Uganda AIDS Commission. In the late 1980s, the country had just emerged from a long period of economic mismanagement and war that had decimated its infrastructure and economy. As AIDS patients placed growing strain on its weak health system, the government turned to both domestic and international 'partners' for assistance. TASO was not an overtly activist movement representing AIDS patients and hence embracing it would have seemed a low-risk strategy. TASO was provided with facilities at Mulago hospital (and later at hospitals throughout the country) and Noerine Kaleeba was appointed to the committee in charge of the AIDS Control Programme, apparently at the behest of President Museveni himself.

Putzel (2004, p. 26) attributes the willingness of the Museveni regime to tackle AIDS head-on to several factors, including that it listened to medical experts, a desire to "put the epidemic beyond partisan politics' and a 'firm coalition behind the President's HIV/AIDS campaign". But other literature and interviews with key informants suggest two further critical factors: First, HIV/AIDS in the military represented a very real threat to the new government's power base (De Waal, 2006). Second, the new NRM government was heavily reliant on donors and needed to legitimate itself in the eyes of both the international community and the Ugandan public. Tumushabe (2006, p. 8) has argued that the Ugandan 'success story' on HIV/AIDS became a critical 'approval and marketing issue' for the government. But that the Museveni government did play a strong and relatively inclusive leadership role is beyond question.

While a sense of partnership characterised the relationship with civil society from early on, there were distinct constraints and ambiguities. Political space for civil society activism was severely constrained: political and civil rights were (and remain) weak[11] and, despite the reintroduction of competitive elections, the political system is best described as a form of 'electoral authoritarianism' (see Van de Walle, 2013) characterised by patronage-based 'neopatrimonialist rule' (Rubongoya, 2007), presidential and party dominance (Mwenda, 2007; Golooba-Mutebi & Hickey, 2013) and intolerance towards political opposition.[12] TASO's focus on delivering services to those with HIV reflects the clear need to step in where the state was unable to provide the required services. But the constraints imposed by the prevailing 'political opportunity structure' also made it far less likely that TASO would opt for more vocal criticism or engage in politicised mobilisation of patients (see also Scholte, 2004, p. 229).

Indeed, several Ugandan AIDS activists and civil society leaders have argued that TASO generally failed to lead in civil society and, in particular, failed to support efforts to 'hold government to account' especially over its opposition to condoms (personal communication, M. Katana, October 24, 2008; B. Were, October 30, 2008). In contrast with more militant activists, TASO leaders displayed a general unwillingness to acknowledge conflict with government or serious failures in governmental leadership during interviews. Some intimated that open criticism would undermine TASO's partnership with the Ugandan government and consequently threaten service delivery (which is predicated on access to hospital infrastructure, etc.). An unwillingness to risk its partnership (and therefore service delivery) makes perfect sense from the point of view of TASO's leadership. Their extreme caution and nervousness in addressing the

---

11 Freedom House political rights and civil liberties ratings for Uganda varied between 4 and 6 over the period 1986 to 1995. Ratings are on a 7-point scale with 1 representing most free and 7 least free. Uganda was classified as "partly free" throughout the period (Freedom House, 2014).

12 For example, after Museveni's former physician Kizza Besigye ran for president in 2001, Museveni's campaign was characterised by open violence and intimidation, with Besigye fleeing into exile after the election. After the February 2011 elections, during which Museveni again defeated Besigye, brutal state repression met peaceful 'walk to work' protests over fuel prices, in which several people died and Besigye was arrested so violently that he had to be hospitalised in Kenya (Izama & Wilkerson, 2011, p. 64-65). More recently, the elected mayor of Kampala (from an opposition party) was arrested repeatedly.

issue nevertheless suggests that the Uganda's 'openness' and 'partnership approach' is more fraught and ambiguous than commonly supposed.

A number of respondents indicated that President Museveni seemed to have 'withdrawn' from the struggle in the mid-2000s, while others worried about shifts towards less progressive government policy on AIDS. Developments causing widespread concern included increased hostility to condom promotion, a proposed law that would criminalise deliberate HIV transmission and, some years after the fieldwork conducted for this study, the promulgation of the discriminatory Anti-Homosexuality Act.

A 'puritanical' and socially conservative agenda was not new in Uganda, even in the period under review in this paper, and elements of may have been present even in the early discourse on HIV/AIDS from Museveni and his government. De Waal (2006, pp. 98-105) argues that the lauded 'ABC' message ('Abstain, Be faithful, use Condoms) that the Ugandan government adopted[13] had *always* been a mixed and inconsistent one, often tailored so as to please or avoid offending specific audiences (i.e., according to De Waal the socially conservative agenda predated the anti-condom messaging of the Bush PEPFAR era during the 2000s – see below). On numerous occasions the president attacked condom promotion, especially to young people. The first lady, Janet Museveni (an outspoken 'born-again' Christian), has been particularly vigorous in her condemnation of condom promotion, telling an audience in the United States that "giving young people condoms is tantamount to giving them a license to go out and be promiscuous; it leads to certain death" (Museveni, 2004).

In the mid-2000s, the United States became (by far) the largest funder of Uganda's AIDS efforts (including by funding TASO's treatment and other services) through the President's Emergency Plan for AIDS Relief (PEPFAR). As an initiative of the Bush Administration, it came encumbered with policies rooted in a conservative religious agenda (such as reservation of funds for faith-based groups and for abstinence-based prevention programmes). As Epstein (2007, pp. 185-201) shows, this conservative religious agenda found fertile ground in certain sections of Ugandan society, in particular a number of conservative church groups and the first lady, who led a backlash against condom promotion programmes. By 2008, this constituted a significant worry for civil society leaders, including the former director of TASO, Dr Alex Coutinho, who obliquely criticised the Museveni government by referring to its approach as "anti-condoms and a little bit pro-abstinence" and argued that Museveni had to be brought back to the forefront of HIV prevention efforts (personal communication, October 14, 2008).

The Anti-Homosexuality Bill referred to earlier was introduced by Member of Parliament David Bahati in October 2009 as a private member's Bill. While same-sex relationships were already criminalised in Uganda (dating from British colonial rule), the Bill would exacerbate repression and discrimination by introducing two new offences, 'the offence of homosexuality' carrying a penalty of life imprisonment and

---

13 The 'ABC' prevention messages came later than the early 'home-grown' messaging undertook by Museveni himself in the late 1980s, which focused on 'zero grazing' etc.

'aggravated homosexuality' (defined to include homosexual acts with a minor or by a person who is HIV-positive), which would carry the death penalty. Despite strong condemnation from various quarters, including Ugandan lesbian, gay, bisexual and transgender activists and international human rights organisations, the Bill received substantial support from the Ugandan public and in the Ugandan media. Criticism of it was framed as 'Western interference' and as a battle over Uganda's moral self-determination (Sadgrove et al., 2012, p. 105). The Bill and the wave of homophobic sentiment expressed in the wake of its introduction seem to have tapped into a stridently socially and sexually conservative agenda in Uganda, which enjoys both public support and has powerful backers in the Museveni regime. The Bill was eventually passed (in slightly less draconian form, which dropped the death penalty provisions) in late 2013 and signed into law in February 2014, to widespread international condemnation.

It appears that again TASO was again placed in an invidious position, in which it had to maintain its partnership with the state – preventing open criticism, including of the Anti-Homosexuality Act – despite the severe impact the latter would have on its ability to deliver services to LGBTI people at high risk of HIV infection. In an online TASO blog, these carefully chosen words seems to embody the ambiguity of its position:

> While as TASO workers we understand our duties and obligation to serve everyone, we work (and have to abide by the laws) in a country where our traditions as Africans deny us the ability to talk about sex and sexuality openly ... And while the rest of Uganda is finally facing the reality of homosexuality, to TASO it is not new. But like I said, our clients are simply that, clients (Matovu, 2014).

Human Rights Watch reports that TASO was forced to suspend its 'Moonlight Clinics' – which provided services aimed at MSM and other vulnerable groups – in the wake of the promulgation of the Act, showing how a religiously-inspired socially conservative agenda supported by a repressive state impacts even on service delivery by non-activist organisations:

> Two community-based organisations that provided HIV testing, condoms, and lubricant to men who have sex with men (MSM) closed their doors after the Bill became law. They have reinitiated some services, but no longer receive drop-in clients. TASO, Uganda's largest HIV/AIDS organisation, has suspended its "Moonlight Clinics," through which it conducted outreach to MSM and other vulnerable groups, offering them HIV testing and education (HRW, 2014).

Praise for Uganda's relatively open and enabling attitude to civil society, and its 'partnership approach', must therefore be tempered by acknowledgement of the authoritarian tendencies of the Museveni regime, a cowed civil society and prevention policies undermined by a socially conservative agenda (both domestic, and for a time driven by the Bush Administration's conditions attached to PEPFAR funding).

The body charged with coordinating the AIDS response, Uganda's AIDS Commission (UAC), is in some sense a replacement for the former AIDS Control Programme, but like with other countries that became recipients of large numbers of grants (to the state, NGOs, etc.), donors instigated the creation of a coordinating body in the 1990s. However, it is important to recognise that while UAC is independent of the Ministry of Health and districts (which manage the public health system), it is by no means independent of executive control. It is widely seen as being under the control of and serving the interests of the Museveni government, mainly something that disturbed smaller civil society organisations who perceived its consultative processes as not giving them real influence over priority-setting at the highest level.

The UAC exercises its coordination role through a Partnership Forum (an annual meeting of stakeholders from all sectors) and a Partnership Committee, which meets regularly and takes day-to-day decisions, including on resource allocation. The Partnership Committee also acts as the Country Coordinating Mechanism for the Global Fund and controls a joint Civil Society Fund (often referred to as a 'basket fund'), through which pooled donor contributions are disbursed to civil society organisations. The exact origins of this fund are not clear from the interviews conducted for this research, but appears to be the result of an agreement reached between the Government of Uganda and donors to harmonise and coordinate the extremely fractured and uncoordinated funding provision by a large number of funders to a large number of civil society organisations.

Sectors are organised into 'self-coordinating entities' that are supposed to develop joint policy positions and present these to the Partnership Committee on behalf of their constituencies. While there are twelve such entities, the primary function of the partnership mechanism is to coordinate the work of international, domestic and faith-based civil society organisations, donors and government. At the district level there exists a similar set of structures known as the District AIDS Coordination Committees, with representation from the political leadership of the district, government departments, local civil society organisations, the private sector and people living with HIV/AIDS.

The Director General of the UAC at the time of the fieldwork for this study (Dr David Apuuli) argued that these structures were uniquely able to foster cooperation and coordination in the HIV/AIDS response because the Ugandan government is compelled by law to meet and come to joint decisions with donors, civil society and other stakeholders (personal communication, 21 October, 2008). Despite these consultative structures, neither the UAC nor its partnership mechanism is independent of the Executive. All commissioners are appointed by President Museveni, its Director General was described by some independent civil society leaders as highly protective of the President's interests and the UAC was described by some as ineffective in discharging its coordination function (personal communication, M. Katana, 24 October, 2008; B. Were, 30 October, 2008; L. Mworeko, 14 October, 2008). The creation of the Civil Society Fund was widely perceived as an attempt by the Museveni government to gain control over donor funds for civil society in order to deny resources to organisations critical of the government, a fact that activist Beatrice Were argued was central to the UAC's failings (personal communication, October 30, 2008).

The UAC therefore embodies a similar ambiguity to that identified earlier in the role of TASO. In order to effectively coordinate the Ugandan AIDS response, it needs to exercise significant control, may necessarily have to embody Presidential leadership, and structural conditions prevent it from becoming a forum where 'partners' (including CSOs and donors) express strong criticism of the Museveni Government or its policies. Certainly the more independent civil society informants described doing so within the consultative structures of the UAC as risking being side-lined, including losing access to funding through the Civil Society Fund. Executive control can therefore be seen as both necessary for effective coordination, but also as serving to discourage strong independent civil society of the kind that can hold government accountable, despite substantial civil society representation in UAC structures.

The unwillingness of large civil society organisations like TASO to openly criticise the government, the UAC or their major donors (most significantly PEPFAR) in interviews seems to confirm that the fears of the more outspoken activists were not entirely unfounded. Most donor funding for civil society flows (both via the CCM, other state bodies and directly) to service-delivery-oriented rather than critical activist-oriented organisations. That the bulk of funding goes to service provision is appropriate (given the cost of providing services), but if critical civil society voices are left marginalised and under-funded, it cannot be expected that government (and donors and the rest of civil society) will be sufficiently 'held accountable'.

Donors have substantial influence on policies and programmes in countries that are heavily dependent on foreign aid (Mayhew, 2002). This was particularly true in Uganda at the time of this research, where the majority of spending on AIDS-related programmes was financed externally and even state agencies like the Uganda AIDS Commission and programmes in the Ministry of Health relied for the bulk of their funding on foreign donors. Over the period 2003/4 to 2008/9, external financing accounted for 84-98% of HIV/AIDS expenditure (Lule & Haacker, 2012, p. 250). TASO was the major provider of medical services to HIV/AIDS patients, including the vast majority of antiretroviral therapy, and obtains almost all of its funding from international donors.

The influence of donors may serve to broker effective AIDS response coalitions or to inhibit their formation. Their clout in Uganda has allowed donors to support and strengthen an inclusive partnership approach and for an enabling environment that would allow civil society to participate effectively in the AIDS response, particularly in service provision. But paradoxically, donors may also have helped to inhibit the development of a vocal and independent civil society sector capable of exerting pressure on the state and holding it accountable (principally by failing to adequately fund critical and independent civil society). There is therefore also a certain ambiguity in the role of donors in the Ugandan AIDS response.

The influence of donors is felt in a number of ways: through direct conditionalities imposed on the receiving state and choices over which programmes and organisations to fund, but also more subtly through the competition over resources between the state and civil society as well as within civil society. The clout of donors is demonstrated by the resolution of a disagreement between TASO and the government over who was to provide the bulk of antiretroviral therapy, which was decided in TASO's favour largely because this was the preference of PEPFAR (personal communication, A. Coutinho, 14 October, 2008). This particular resolution makes sense, given TASO's greater capacity to deliver services, but does demonstrate that donors have substantial power owing to their control of the purse strings.

In situations where civil society is not well-developed or the political culture and institutions inhibit openness and broad participation in policy formulation and implementation, the potential for donors to broker inclusive coalitions is particularly significant. Keck and Sikkink (1998) describe a 'boomerang pattern' of influence, in which civil society organisations can obtain leverage over the state even where direct channels between it and the state are blocked. International allies (usually Northern NGOs, but sometimes intergovernmental organisations or donors) can bring pressure to bear from outside, either directly or via Northern states. De Waal (2006, pp. 58-59) argues that this pattern is responsible for much of the success of AIDS activism in Africa, where domestic activists have been able to exploit transnational networks comprising international NGOs, intergovernmental organisations (including those of the UN system such as UNAIDS) and, crucially, donor governments as a means of leverage over their own governments. Some respondents questioned donors' commitment to exerting their influence over the Ugandan government to prevent harmful policies. The Ugandan state's lack of capacity in the late 1980s, and its resulting dependence on donors and civil society organisations to provide public services, was arguably a major factor in its adoption of a partnership approach, but the progressive leadership of the Museveni government must also be acknowledged.

The fieldwork conducted for this article points to significant risks associated with powerful donors, despite their undeniably important role. Donors may dominate the agenda, may inhibit open engagement and limit the ability of domestic actors to build 'locally-appropriate coalitions'. The Bush Administration used financial assistance to advance a particular ideological agenda in alliance with sections of the domestic elite. Some society leaders (particularly those with an activist orientation and not involved in service provision) reported that donors were overly concerned with maintaining their partnership with the state, and consequently failed to support, and even undermined, the development of an independent and critical civil society sector.

Conclusion

While serious conceptual and analytical difficulties attach to the notion of leadership (not addressed in detail in this article), effective 'AIDS leadership' can be usefully described as *the mobilisation of coalitions around AIDS prevention and treatment*. A broad coalition that includes civil society, the state and the international community has certainly helped Uganda to mobilise one of the more effective AIDS responses in

Africa. It has performed admirably, particularly in rolling out antiretroviral treatment during the 2000s.

The choices of individuals, including political leaders like Museveni and civil society leaders like Kaleeba, were arguably as important as broader institutional factors in shaping the Ugandan AIDS response. 'Networks of influence' stand at the nexus of agency and structure, and is a useful concept for thinking about the processes involved in building coalitions for an inclusive and vigorous response. But the history of TASO also demonstrates how political and institutional context – including the lack of openness in the political system and the need for the state, donors and civil society to cooperate in order to deliver services – shaped the choices of individuals and constrained opportunities for accountability-oriented coalition-building. The reasons for the ambiguities in the 'partnership' between the state and civil society organisations like TASO (great success in service provision coupled with failure to act as a critical voice or 'hold government accountable'), appear to be the consequence largely of rational choices made within the context of these structural conditions.

This research demonstrates that while state-civil society partnerships – undergirded by effective civil society organisations, a supportive state and donor pressure – can help establish effective AIDS response coalitions. However, enhancing state accountability under authoritarian and semi-authoritarian regimes remains a substantial challenge.

References

Allen, T. & Heald, S. (2004). 'HIV/AIDS Policy in Africa: What has worked in Uganda and what has failed in Botswana?' *Journal of International Development*, 16, 1141-1154.doi:10.1002/jid.1168.

Atzori, C., Bonfanti, P., Carenzi, L. & Rizzardini, G. (2009). 'Efficacy Evidences in Prevention of HIV Infection in Developing Countries. A Critical Appraisal from Population-Based Studies'. *Journal of Medicine and the Person*, 7, 70–76. doi:10.1007/s12682-009-0019-9

Barker, G. (Writer, Producer & Director), & Simone, R. (Writer). (2006). 'The Age of AIDS: Part Two [Television Documentary]'. United States: PBS.

Bor, J. (2007). 'The Political Economy of AIDS Leadership in Developing Countries: An Exploratory Analysis'. *Social Science & Medicine*, 64, 1585–1599. doi:10.1016/j.socscimed.2006.12.005.

Cran, W. (Writer, Producer & Director), & Simone, R. (Writer). (2006). 'The Age of AIDS: Part One [Television Documentary]'. United States: PBS.

De Waal, A. (2006). *AIDS and Power: Why There Is No Political Crisis – yet.* London; Zed Books.

Dionne, K.Y. (2011). 'The Role of Executive Time Horizons in State Response to AIDS in Africa. Comparative Political Studies', Online First. doi: doi:10.1177/0010414010381074

Epstein, H. (2007). *The Invisible Cure: Africa, the West and the Fight Against AIDS*. London: Viking.

Fox, A.M. (2014). 'South African AIDS activism and global health politics'. *Global Public Health*, 9, 121-123. doi: 10.1080/17441692.2014.881526.

Fox, A.M., Goldberg, A.B. Gore, R.J. & Bärnighausen, T. (2011). 'Conceptual and methodological challenges to measuring political commitment to respond to HIV'. *Journal of the International* AIDS Society, 14. doi:10.1186/1758-2652-14-S2-S5.

Freedom House (2014). 'Freedom in the World: Country ratings and status, FIW 1973-2014 [Excel spreadsheet]'. Retrieved from http://www.freedomhouse.org/report-types/freedomworld#. UzRM0YUo5x.

Goldberg, A.B., Fox, A.M., Gore, R.J. & Bärnighausen, T. (2012). 'Indicators of political commitment to respond to HIV'. *Sexually Transmitted Infections*, 88, e1. doi: 10.1136/sextrans-2011-050221.

Golooba-Mutebi, F. & Hickey, S. (2013). 'Investigating the links between political settlements and inclusive development in Uganda: towards a research agenda' (ESID Working Paper No. 20). Effective States and Inclusive Development Research Centre, University of Manchester, Manchester.

Gray, R. H., Serwadda, D., Kigozi, G., Nalugoda, F. & Wawer, M. J. (2006). 'Uganda's HIV Prevention Success: The Role of Sexual Behavior Change and the National Response'. Commentary on Green et al. (2006). AIDS and Behavior 10, 347-350. doi:10.1007/s10461-006-9074-x.

Grebe, E. (2009). 'Leaders, Networks and Coalitions in the AIDS response: A comparison between Uganda and South Africa', (Research Paper 03). York: Developmental Leadership Program.

Grebe, E. (2011). 'The Treatment Action Campaign's Struggle for AIDS Treatment in South Africa: Coalition-Building Through Networks'. *Journal of Southern African Studies*, 37, 849-868. doi:10.1080/03057070.2011.608271.

Grebe, E. (2012). 'Civil Society Leadership in the Struggle for AIDS Treatment in South Africa and Uganda' (Unpublished doctoral dissertation). University of Cape Town, Cape Town.

Green, E. C, Halperin, D. T., Nantulya, V. & Hogle, J. A. (2006). 'Uganda's HIV Prevention Success: the Role of Sexual Behavior Change and the National Response'. *AIDS and Behavior*, 10, 335-350. doi:10.1007/s10461-006-9073-y.

HRW (2014). 'Uganda: Anti-Homosexuality Act's Heavy Toll: Discriminatory Law Prompts Arrests, Attacks, Evictions, Flight'. Nairobi: *Human Rights Watch*. (May 15, 2014). Retrieved from http://www.hrw.org/news/2014/05/14/uganda-anti-homosexuality-act-sheavy-toll.

Izama, A., & Wilkerson, M. (2011). 'Uganda: Museveni's Triumph and Weakness'. *Journal of Democracy*, 22, 64-78. doi:10.1353/jod.2011.0044.

Justesen, M.K. (2012). 'Democracy, dictatorship, and disease: Political regimes and HIV/AIDS'. *European Journal of Political Economy*, 28, 373–389. doi: 10.1016/j. ejpoleco.2012.02.001.

Keck, M. E., & Sikkink, K. (1998). *Activists Beyond Borders: advocacy Networks in International Politics*. New York, NY: Cornell University Press.

Kirby, D. (2008). 'Changes in sexual behaviour leading to the decline in the prevalence of HIV in Uganda: confirmation from multiple sources of evidence'. *Sexually Transmitted Infections*, 84(Suppl II), ii35-ii41. doi:10.1136/sti.2008.029892.

Leftwich, A. & Hogg, S. (2007). 'The Case for Leadership and the Primacy of Politics in Building Effective States, Institutions and Governance for Sustainable Growth and Social Development' (Background Paper 1). York: Developmental Leadership Program.

Low-Beer, D. & Stoneburner, R. (2004). 'Uganda and the Challenge of HIV/AIDS'. In N. K. Poku & A. Whiteside (Eds.), *The Political Economy of AIDS in Africa* (pp. 165-190). Aldershot: Ashgate.

Lule, E. & Haacker, M. (2012). 'The Fiscal Dimension of HIV/AIDS in Botswana, South Africa, Swaziland, and Uganda'. Washington, DC: The World Bank. doi:10.1596/978-0-8213-8807-5.

Matovu, S. (2014). 'TASO work and the newly signed law against Homosexuality in Uganda'. TASO Blog post (February 27, 2014). Retrieved from http://tasoonline.blogspot.com/2014/02/taso-work-and-newly-signed-law-against.html.

Mayhew, S. H. (2002). 'Donor Dealings: The Impact of International Donor Aid on Sexual and Reproductive Health Services'. *International Family Planning Perspectives*, 28, 220. doi:10.2307/3088225.

Merson, M. (2006). 'Uganda's HIV/AIDS Epidemic: Guest Editorial'. *AIDS and Behavior*, 10, 333-334. doi:10.1007/s10461-006-9120-8.

Ministry of Health [Uganda], & ORC Macro. (2006). 'HIV/AIDS Sero-Behavioural Survey 2004-05'. Calverton, MD: ORC Macro. Retrieved from http://pdf.usaid.gov/pdf_docs/PNADG508.pdf.

Museveni, J. K. (2004). 'The AIDS Pandemic: Saving the Next Generation'. Speech presented at 'Common Ground: A Shared Vision for Health', Washington, DC, 17 June 2004. Retrieved from http://Catholiceducation.org/articles/sexuality/se0106.html.

Nattrass, N. (2008). 'Are Country Reputations for Good and Bad Leadership on AIDS Deserved? An Exploratory Quantitative Analysis'. *Journal of Public Health*, 30, 398-406. doi:10.1093/pubmed/fdn075.

Nattrass, N. 2014. 'Millennium Development Goal 6: AIDS and the International Health Agenda', in *Journal of Human Development and Capabilities*, vol.15, Number 2-3: 232-246.

Nunn, A., Dickman, S., Nattrass, N., Cornwall, A. & Gruskin, S. (2012). 'The impacts of AIDS movements on the policy responses to HIV/AIDS in Brazil and South Africa: A comparative analysis'. *Global Public Health*, 7, 1031-1044. doi:10.1080/17441692.201 2.736681.

O'Manique, C. (2004). *Neoliberalism and AIDS Crisis in Sub-Saharan Africa*. Oxford: Oxford University Press.

Ostergard, R. L. & Barcello, C. (2005). 'Personalist Regimes and the Insecurity Dilemma: Prioritizing AIDS as a National Security Threat in Uganda'. In A. S. Patterson (Ed.), '*The African State and the AIDS Crisis* (pp. 155-170). Aldershot: Ashgate.

Piot, P. & Coll-Seck, A. M. (2001). 'International Response to the HIV/AIDS Epidemic: Planning for Success'. Bulletin of the World Health Organisation, 79, 1106-1112.

Piot, P. (2012). '*No Time to Lose: A Life in Pursuit of Deadly Viruses*' [Kindle version]. New York, NY: W.W. Norton.

Putzel, J. (2004). 'The Politics of Action on AIDS: A Case Study of Uganda'. *Public Administration and Development*, 24, 19-30. doi:10.1002/pad.306.

Rubongoya, J. B. (2007). *Regime Hegemony in Museveni's Uganda: Pax Musevenica*. New York, NY: Palgrave MacMillan.

Sadgrove, J., Vanderbeck, R. M., Andersson, J., Valentine, G. & Ward, K. (2012). 'Morality Plays and Money Matters: towards a Situated Understanding of the Politics of Homosexuality in Uganda'. *The Journal of Modern African Studies*, 50, 103-129. doi:10.1017/S0022278X11000620.

Scholte, J. A. (2004). 'Civil Society and Democratically Accountable Global Governance'. *Government and Opposition*, 39, 211-233.

Smith, R. A. & Siplon, P. D. (2006). Drugs into Bodies: Global AIDS Treatment Activism. Westport, CT: Praeger.

Ssebanja, P. (2007). *The Story of TASO*. London: ActionAid.

Stoneburner, R. L. & Low-Beer, D. (2004). 'Population-Level HIV Declines and Behavioral Risk Avoidance in Uganda'. *Science*, 304, 714-718. doi:10.1126/science.1093166.

Thornton, R. J. (2008). *Unimagined Community: Sex, Networks, and AIDS in Uganda and South Africa*. Berkeley, CA: University of California Press.

Tumushabe, J. (2006). 'The Politics of HIV/AIDS in Uganda' (Social Policy and Development Programme Paper 28). Geneva: United Nations Research Institute for Social Development. Retrieved from http://www.unrisd.org/unrisd/website/document. 49ca53f80256b4f005ef245/86cb69d103fcf94ec125723000380c60/\$FILE/tumushabe-pp.pdf.

UNAIDS. (1998). 'A Measure of Success in Uganda: The Value of Monitoring Both HIV Prevalence and Sexual Behaviour (UNAIDS Best Practice Collection)'. Geneva: Joint United Nations Programme on HIV/AIDS. Retrieved from http://data.unaids.org/ Publications/irc-pub04/value_monitoring_uganda_en.pdf.

UNAIDS. (2001). 'HIV Prevention Needs and Successes: a Tale of Three Countries. An Update on HIV Prevention Success in Senegal, Thailand and Uganda' (UNAIDS Best Practice Collection). Geneva: Joint United Nations Programme on HIV/AIDS. Retrieved from http://data.unaids.org/publications/IRC-pub02/jc535-hi_en.pdf.

UNAIDS. (2011). 'Spectrum/EPP 2011 [Computer software]. Geneva: Joint United Nations Programme on HIV/AIDS'. Retrieved from http://www.unaids.org/en/dataanalysis/tools/spectrumepp2011/.

Van de Walle, N. (2013). 'Electoral Authoritarianism and Multi-party Politics'. In N. Cheeseman, D. Anderson & A. Scheibler (Eds.), *Routledge Handbook of African Politics* (pp. 227-237). Abingdon: Routledge.

Yashar, D. (1997). *Demanding Democracy: Reform and Reaction in Costa Rica and Guatemala, 1870s–1950s*. Stanford, CA: Stanford University Press.

Youde, J. R. (2007). 'Ideology's Role in AIDS Policies in South Africa and Uganda'. *Global Health Governance*, I(1). Retrieved from http://blogs.shu.edu/ghg/files/2011/10/Youde_Ideology\%E2\%80\%99s-Role-in-AIDS-Policies-in-Uganda-and-South-Africa_Spring-2007.pdf.

Key informant interviews cited in the text

Apuuli, David, 21 October 2008, Kampala, Uganda.
Ayers, Elize, 29 October 2008, Kampala, Uganda.
Coutinho, Alex, 14 October 2008, Kampala, Uganda.
Kaleeba, Noerine, 16 October 2008, Masaka, Uganda.
Katabira, Elly, 14 October 2008, Kampala, Uganda.
Katana, Milly, 24 October 2008, Kampala, Uganda.
Mworeko, Lilian, 14 October 2008, Kampala, Uganda.
Piot, Peter, 20 December 2010, telephonic.
Ssebanja, Peter, 15 October 2008, Kampala, Uganda.
Were, Beatrice, 30 October 2008, Kampala, Uganda. 18.

12

Financial Inclusion Programming for Poor Women and Men in Uganda

CARE International in Uganda[1]

Abstract

CARE International in Uganda has worked in financial inclusion programming for the past 20 years. This paper outlines its experiences, some of the innovations that have been introduced over the years and the lessons learnt from this practice. The paper focuses on the Village Savings and Loans Association methodology, initially designed primarily for illiterate and extremely poor rural women to access financial services, but now serving both literate and illiterate populations in rural areas, market towns, and peri-urban areas. There are now more than one million members of such associations. Additional interventions have included financial education, business skills development, value chain development, and the development of group-based micro insurance products, including funeral coverage and health insurance. CARE Uganda has also entered into partnerships with various commercial banks, and have more recently linked savings groups to these institutions using mobile technology. Preliminary experience shows that digitalised financial services are potentially one of the easiest means for the rural poor to access the formal financial sector, thus bringing about a virtuous cycle of rising household incomes, improved health, better education and greater participation in the affairs of their communities.

CARE in Uganda

CARE's work in Uganda dates back to 1969. Now with a staff of approximately 150, CARE works in several regions of the country. Its long-term development programmes seek to address the key drivers of poverty and social injustice, namely prevailing gender

---

1 Authored by Sylvia Kaawe, Programme Manager, Melch Natukunda, Initiative Manager, Women and Youth Financial Inclusion Programme Team (with technical input from Grace Majara, CARE USA) April 2020

inequality and gender-based violence, poor governance leading to depletion of the natural resource base and limited citizen engagement and conflict.

While CARE primarily measures the impact of its work in the lives of women and girls (who on average represent over 75% of our programme participants), we also work deliberately with men and boys, both as change agents for greater gender equality and also as beneficiaries in their own right. CARE also works through strategic partnership with a wide range of civil society organisations, the private sector - including financial institutions - and government agencies. CARE's financial inclusion programming traces its roots to the late 1990s, with the introduction of the Village Savings and Loans Association methodology, as a driver for the rural and urban poor to access financial services.

Village Savings and Loan Associations (VSLAs)

The VSLA model was first developed by CARE International in 1991 in Niger, where a simple saving mechanism enabled poor women in rural areas to access large amounts of loan capital. In Uganda, the methodology was introduced in 1998 in the West Nile region, based on the Niger experiences.

Village Savings and Loans is a savings-based financial service, which facilitates the development of unregulated and usually informal group members' savings for their loan capital, with no external liabilities to any lending institution. VSLAs are self-selected, community based, and require little to no infrastructure to form. Groups of 15 to 30 people (usually about 75% women) meet on a weekly or bi-weekly basis to save into a common fund. This fund is used to support loans within the savings group as needed, with the loan interest used to provide a return on the invested savings. At the end of a set cycle (typically 9-12 months), the savings, with accumulated interest, are 'shared out' amongst the group members and a new cycle begins.

The VSLA approach addresses both supply and demand constraints that limit savings with financial institutions, thus overcoming factors such as poverty, low education, financial illiteracy and informal sector economic activity, coupled with distance, cost, poor service, safety concerns and lack of trust associated with formal financial institutions. VSLAs are also an important safety net for members who often decide to have both a 'social fund' for interest free loans in case of shocks and a 'productive' fund for investments in businesses and income generating activities.

Designed primarily for illiterate and extremely poor rural women, the methodology has matured over the years to serve both literate and illiterate populations in rural areas, market towns, peri-urban settlements and urban slums. To-date CARE-founded VSLAs serve more than seven million people, (of which 75% of are women), in 26 African countries. The remarkable impact of VLSA has inspired many other organisations to adopt the approach and it is estimated that in Africa alone more than 11 million people are currently benefitting from this methodology. In Uganda, there are over one million members in more than 35,000 Saving Groups/VSLAs.

Utilising the VSLA model, CARE has managed to reach all categories of rural people including the very poor and the extremely vulnerable, by challenging their capacity to break the vicious circle of poverty on their own. The strength behind the VSLA methodology is that members are enabled to decide their own destiny: in contrast with many other aid initiatives, the VSLA approach is self-managed and owned by members themselves. Furthermore, the VSLAs replicate themselves.

Over the years, CARE has continued to innovate and to adapt the methodology to accommodate different expectations and has become a platform for linking with other development outcomes. The VSLA model now offers a range of basic financial services created in order to bring about a virtuous cycle of rising household incomes, improved health, better education and greater participation in the communities and nations. CARE has used VSLAs as real engines for economic development as well as for social protection.

The VSLA methodology is also designed to ensure that women have equal and increased control over financial resources and access to financial services. This means that in addition to building financial skills and capabilities to manage financial resources and actively use relevant financial services and products, CARE, through the VSLA methodology, simultaneously increases women's voice and decision-making power within households and supports them to claim their economic rights at community and national levels. This includes advocating for policies and regulations that enable equal access to financial inclusion for women and men.

Access to and control over resources allows women to invest in businesses, and evidence from our work shows that women who participate in village savings and loan programmes are twice as likely to start and sustain a business than women who do not participate. Access to and use of financial services also provides a platform for women to engage in broader productive value chains, either as entrepreneurs or as paid workers. CARE also believes that VSLAs offer a real opportunity to maximise social protection investments in Uganda while having the potential of offering a graduation strategy and reducing lifelong dependence of households on social protection.

Overall, several benefits of the VSLAs have therefore emerged. The approach is savings-led with no external liabilities, hence promoting a fast personal savings growth. VSLA members have embraced the culture of savings, as the obligation to save some money in the weekly cash box encourages members to look for ways of making an income so that they can take off some money to save. VSLA operations are simple with a high level of transparency hence easy to build trust. VSLAs are also highly sustainable – once established, groups have almost no operating costs and groups easily self-replicate; the VSLA survival rate is high (99%). The welfare fund collected at every weekly meeting helps in meeting members' emergency needs Groups can act as platforms for accessing other financial institutions and services – pilot efforts have proven that VSLAs are more trustworthy clients and, finally, VSLAs provide social capital to members

Linkages to banking and digital solutions

CARE's learning experience appreciates that innovation is key to addressing the VSLA needs and has a long history of matching the progressive needs of groups as they go along the pathway of financial inclusion. Additional gap filling interventions have included; financial education, business skills development through training, mentoring and coaching, value chain development, enterprise skills development for the youth, brick and mortar banking and micro insurance products.

The financial landscape of Uganda is formulated under four tiers (commercial banks, credit institutions, micro-deposit institutions (MDIs), and unregulated tier-four institutions). However, the Tier 4 Act mandates the Uganda Microfinance Regulatory Authority (UMRA) to register groups (where VSLAs are categorised) through District Community Development Officers (DCDOs) and to maintain an up-to-date registry. This registration provides a mechanism to better understand the groups, as well as opportunities to avail additional services and linkages to the formal financial sector. This has also enabled VSLAs to benefit from on-going government interventions, such as the "Project for Financial Inclusion in Rural Areas of Uganda". As such, mature groups that have been operational for three years or more have benefited from group capacity strengthening interventions, such as linkages to formal banks, specialised training in financial literacy and entrepreneurship skills development.

CARE Uganda entered into partnerships with various commercial banks (e.g. Barclays, Postbank, Centenary Bank, Bank of Africa) and Mobile Network Operators to facilitate access to formal financial products for VSLA members. CARE's Bank Linkages model and digital financial solutions (electronic keys, digitalised E-wallets) increase the range of financial products and services available to VSLA members (e.g. zero-cost VSLA groups' savings accounts, credit facilities and loans at affordable rates, overdrafts, etc.), strengthen their financial security (reduced risk of theft of cash box, growing entrepreneurial aspirations of members) and addresses problems of transactional interface and distance to financial access points.

Across Uganda, CARE has so far linked over 2,569 VSLAs to formal financial institutions (952 using digitalised services and over 1,617 linked for ordinary savings and credit products with the bank). The linkage banking model and products are jointly developed with our banking partners and consumer protection is at the heart of our research and product development efforts.

The linkage model envisages a move from financial exclusion, to informal financial inclusion, then onto formal financial inclusion through five major steps: (1) identify the most financially excluded; (2) organise into groups and build capacity (group processes, financial literary, livelihood trainings; (3) access to financial services (group-based financial transactions, simple products); (4) co-design of demand-driven saving products, processes and delivery channels; and (5) co-design of demand-driven credit products, processes and delivery channels.

The model rests on seven linkage principles: (1) groups are linked, not individuals; (2) the linkage is demand driven, not supply driven; (3) core principles of the VSLA methodology are upheld; (4) the emphasis on member savings is maintained; (5) member savings are not held as collateral; (6) only mature groups are linked and (7) a conservative savings to credit ratio is maintained.

Despite the breakthrough in linkages to formal financial services, there are still challenges both at VSLA and bank levels. At VSLA level, there is a lack of long-term savings options; banks may be inflexible to allow larger savings, they are not amenable to the seasonal cash flow of rural households; and low fund security. The perceived commercial bank challenges include lack of savings products for the poor; geographic distances to where the VSLAs are; increased operational costs and risks; and inappropriate delivery channels. Thus, on the one hand, there are poor people who can save but face barriers in keeping their savings somewhere safe, as well as in accessing more sophisticated financial services. On the other hand, there are institutions which struggle to offer financial services to the bottom of the pyramid market segment but have limited success due to cost, distance and regulatory challenges. The main challenge is to solve this paradox by bringing the two categories (the bottom of the pyramid poor and the formal banking institutions) through innovative solutions, scale-up and advocacy.

Such advocacy can build on a strong business case for VSLA linkages, as there is a fit with the commercial banks' expansion strategies – accessing a new market segment of entry-level banking customers. The VSLA customers come with limited risks, considering that linkages target mature groups that have mastered the art of self-management, and of savings and credit transaction management. Secondly, VSLAs/groups are regular and reliable savers and, in the case of taking loans, they have a 95% repayment rate record, thanks to the financial literacy training they get as part of the linkage package. The linkage process also gives commercial banks a chance to develop and test new products which they can scale-up. From a Corporate Social Responsibility (CSR) point of view, there is also a good fit with the Commercial Bank values, while brand profile can be raised, trust can be built and other key stakeholders influenced. In some cases, the link also offers opportunities for employee engagement. Once linked into the formal financial sector, VSLA members/clients increase their savings (thus increased institutional liquidity) and others begin accessing additional products such as loans, which can be invested in their businesses, generating higher returns.

How have partnerships worked for CARE's linkage process?

The innovations described above have been a success partly because of strong partnerships with VSLAs and banks. In practice, partnership in this case means working together on the design of demand driven savings products, joint compliance, joint training manual development, joint roll-out of training and product, and complementary monitoring. In this way, partners are able to achieve sustainable win-win solutions and scale-up efforts too. CARE's role as an NGO is to identify mature VSLAs whose members form populations that for-profit institutions have not been able to reach or have little incentive to target. CARE also facilitates dialogue between various stakeholders and builds trust between the populations we serve and the formal financial institutions that would like to serve them. Finally, CARE promotes innovation by identifying and sharing needs that have not been met by existing commercial bank products.

Such partnerships have met with success because of a shared vision, objectives and respect each other's unique skills, trust and open communication, the adherence to common agreed principles. They also need to be supported at the highest level of management from each organisation as well as at the local staff level, for success to be registered.

A case of linkages to digitalised sub-wallets for increased financial empowerment of women

Our pilots have shown that it is possible to link savings groups to formal financial institutions using mobile technology. This is a promising start, but there is an urgent need to do more to develop these pilots and bring them to scale. There are 2.5 billion people globally who are financially excluded, hence a potential large entry-level banking market that requires nurturing through more partnerships with the private sector and sharing our model to encourage others to adopt it.

Funded by the Bill and Melinda Gates Foundation, the digitalised sub-wallets intervention is being implemented in partnership with a research team from Oxford University and Post Bank Uganda Ltd. The main aim is to test an innovative approach to improving women's equitable influence over household financial decisions by utilising mobile money sub-wallets specifically targeting women's priority needs and using household financial planning modules targeting gender and intergenerational conflict resolution.

The research focus of the project is expected by June 2020 and will generate high-quality evidence about the marginal impact of each of the interventions. The main entry platform for this study was CARE's existing/mature VSLA groups in line with the above mentioned linkage model.

Preliminary experience shows that digitalised financial services are potentially one of the easiest means for the rural poor to access the formal financial sector. However, women have lower adoption rates for digital technology, including mobile banking, compared to men. This is due to untailored products and services of so-called 'gender blind' institutions that do not recognise the specific needs of women and girls. In addition, social norms in Uganda's traditional patriarchal society prevent women from fully exploring their potential. Women in a household often have less decision-making power than the men, whether it is the husband, the in-laws or other male relatives.

The intervention currently being implemented in Bushenyi and Rubirizi targets men, women, and adolescent boys and girls. In total, the digitalised sub-wallets intervention is expected to reach 4,182 direct beneficiaries (all women and girls) and around 180,862 indirect beneficiaries (all women and girls).

By January 2020, 1,014 individual accounts had been opened with Post Bank. Increased digital sub wallet usage had resulted in 56.8% improved deposits/credits higher than debits/withdrawals (87.2% of the transactions were made by female with Ugx 89,808,757 ($24,605); and 13% being male at a transaction volume of Ugx 30,200,170 ($8,274). A functional Post Bank Service centre was also launched at

Ishaka (Bushenyi District) in September 2019, aimed at bringing banking services closer to VSLA members, considering that the nearest Post Bank branch is in Mbarara - over 60kms away.

In relation to handling gender and intergenerational conflict mitigation, CARE promotes the Household Dialogue Model whose sessions are focused on addressing the gender and social norms that affect women's autonomy and ability to make financial decisions, especially regarding their own savings. Ultimately households are required to jointly develop and implement their financial plans and are mostly linked to the digital sub-wallets of the group members. Implementing partner staff (community-based facilitators) conduct dialogue sessions using CARE's gender-transformative curriculum, developed specifically for the digital sub-wallet project. The specific purpose of these household dialogue sessions is to create a space for household members to freely express their views and create harmony for improved collaboration; to guide household members in the development and implementation of their joint financial goals and plans; and to create a space for household members to discuss and reflect on gender norms and power dynamics related to household decision-making. By January 2020, a total of 256 households had completed all the dialogue sessions and had set household financial plans.

Key lessons learnt included ensuring adequate focus on combating gender norms as key in implementing both digital sub-wallets and households dialogues; adapting to incorporate complicated cases and including polygamous households on the household dialogue agenda; and designing and deploying new mobile money solutions (sub-wallets) that address women's needs related to access and optimum utilisation of the services.

Other life-changing models that CARE has anchored onto VSLA programming

Youth-Skilling Pathway (YSP) Model. The Youth Skilling Pathways is a self-sustaining model promoted by CARE and developed in response to the identified employability and financial security needs among youth aged 15-25 years. These are economically disadvantaged youth out of school with little access to productive economic resources. The model responds to the common problems of youth in Uganda, which include lack of employable skills, and little or no access to productive resources like land and capital. The existing programmes on employment in the informal sector and agriculture generally lack focus; they have gaps in any apprenticeship schemes; and over-emphasise experience in the job market. There are significant negative cultural attitudes affecting the employment of both male and female youth, such as gender discrimination and dislike by the youth for low-paid work, especially in agriculture. These attitudes have contributed to rural-urban youth migration expecting to find work in the urban centres. These centres now increasingly have an overabundance of unskilled and unemployed youth, which is associated with redundancy and involvement in risky behaviours such as sex trade, drug abuse and crime.

This initiative therefore integrates the individual youth's development of technical skills with linkages to financial services and training. The financial education, soft and technical skills and VSLA participation helps prepare them as a ready-to-work and economic development-oriented young adult. The process consists of structured, short-term, supervised placements of youth that are focused around particular enterprises. In the trades, these youths are trained in basic vocational skills of their choice that are relevant to overcoming vulnerability for themselves and their households. The participating youth learn skills while working in a micro or small enterprise alongside a mentor who is a craftsperson/artisan. Their on-the-job learning is supplemented by classroom sessions on soft skills, financial education and VSLA methodology.

So far, the Youth Skilling Pathway model has been implemented for over four years (2011 to 2015) in several districts. In this time period, the model has been reviewed and has gradually incorporated a bank linkages element. Assessment and monitoring tools have been developed and applied to track and report on the performance of the model, including an apprenticeship register and apprenticeship tracer tool. Over the past four years, a total of 2,625 youths were enrolled; and 2,486 graduated youth are subsequently applying the knowledge and skills acquired through their training in an employment relationship or as self-employed young entrepreneurs. A total of 1,656 youth were employed by the artisan/mentors while 830 started their own IGAs or small scale enterprises. These outcomes are tracked every six months after graduation.

The comprehensive skilling approach imparts soft skills that trigger purposeful living with clear goals, and appropriate behaviour that is fundamental for youth employability and avails the participating youth with alternative means to attain entrepreneurial growth. It has proven very empowering for girls, enabling them to resist early marriages and sexual exploitation and to become more assertive in making sound life decisions and designing their destiny thanks to the life skills modules that form an integral part of the model. The model has been very instrumental in addressing drivers of poverty such as gender inequality, social exclusion, and unequal rights to access to resources and services. This is evidenced by the percentage of girl youth participants able to become employed, access critical services and start earning as a result of its implementation.

Progress of the model has been closely monitored by the Ministry of Gender Labour and Social Development with whom CARE partnered and has been valued as an appropriate response to youth employment problems. Plans are underway to advocate for its recognition and adoption by the Ministry of Education and Sports and linking it with official certification. Currently, certification is only done by the individual Civil Society Organisations promoting the model (AVSI, TPO and CARE International in Uganda, and 20 local partner NGOs that include APROCEL, COVOID, The Salvation Army and COMVIS)

A 2015 study showed that graduated youth earn on average UGX 56,926 per month as a result of the training. The study further showed a reduction in the vulnerability levels for the households whose youth acquired the promoted skills, going down from a vulnerability rating of 63.3% to 45.7%. Unlike other apprenticeship models that depend on external financial and material handouts from the promoter, the CARE model is focussed on providing youth with financial education, savings and credit knowledge, and entrepreneurial skills. It also links/mobilises youth into VSLAs to ensure their self-financing and thus making the approach more sustainable. This is because the skills imparted during the training improve youth employability and personal relationships (through increased self-esteem, self-confidence, increased negotiation capacity, knowledge of one's rights, etc), which in turn enable them to smoothly transit from the learning phase to the self- or formal employment stage.

As the monitoring and assessment data reveal, the model has proven relevant to the targeted youth. For example, in assessments of the participating youth, 41% (of which 71% are female) reported starting their own small scale enterprises as a result of the knowledge and skills gained. The main businesses included salon and hair dressing, tailoring, and bicycle and motorcycle repairs. The local implementing partner organisations are carrying forward the model and this is expected to enhance its sustainability. The implementation of the model has proven cost-effective, given the average training costs of UGX 300,000 per youth for a period of four to six months, depending on the type of enterprise/business. Considering the average monthly income of UGX 56,926 earned by the youth and the IGAs being sustained over a period of two years, the model is an affordable, quick and sustainable response to youth financial inclusion, economic empowerment and employability. The more capital intensive businesses, such as carpentry and tailoring, however, proved beyond the reach of youth, as they are not able to afford the start-up tool kits quickly compared to less expensive trades. Therefore, at least a one-year internship phase for skill perfection and savings accumulation to enable youth procure necessary start-up kits is recommended for such enterprises.

The Micro-Insurance Model: Besides savings and credit management, the VSLA methodology promotes a Social /Welfare Fund that acts as an insurance fund at group level. Group members internally collect savings to finance unanticipated emergencies and social obligations. These emergencies include sickness, fires, accidents, funeral costs, and urgent scholastic materials. Group members collect the social fund separately from the savings/loanable funds and on-lend to members as either interest-free loans or grants, as stipulated in the group internal rules and regulations. Usually interest free loans are lent and returned to the group within a period of two weeks to allow other members a chance to borrow in a bid to promote equity among group members.

CARE's experience has showed that any shock like drought, loss of harvest, ill health, and death are likely to have a profound and adverse impact on the livelihood options of already poor and vulnerable households. This is mainly due to their limited resilience and capacity to absorb or cope with such shocks. As Uganda's national poverty profile has a female face, reflecting the predominant gender inequality, to mitigate the effects of economic shocks, especially for poor and vulnerable women, micro-insurance was promoted.

In 2009, CARE Uganda began to work with Micro Ensure, a multinational insurance intermediary owned by Opportunity International, to design an appropriate funeral insurance product that was tailored to the most common need of the savings group members by that time. Groups could take out an insurance against unforeseen funeral expenses covering six people per member household including the VSLA member, one spouse and up to four children. The main lesson learnt from this initiative was that micro-insurance turned out to provide an effective protection for low income people against specific risks, in exchange for regular premium payments proportionate to the likelihood and costs of the risks involved. The target population for micro-insurance products is generally the persons ignored by mainstream commercial or social insurance schemes, i.e., vulnerable households, and for CARE, these are typically members of VSLA groups. Micro-insurance products are characterised by low premium, low cap and low coverage limits and are sold as part of a typical risk pooling and marketing arrangement.

The principal micro-insurance products to date are funeral coverage and health insurance. The micro-insurance model observes and adheres to the industry approved micro-insurance principles by using a group approach rather than individuals to minimise costs and spread risks. Households headed by widows and young mothers are particularly vulnerable to asset depletion and impoverishment with any disasters and shocks. For example, after the loss of a loved one or close relative especially the husband, the wife of the deceased is expected to take care of the burial arrangements but without any powers to make decisions about selling productive assets.

The funeral insurance product had the following features: a premium payment of UGX 35,000 for a period of one year covering a total of six people within the household between the age of three months and 65 years. On death of a spouse or the person who paid for the insurance, a total of UGX 500,000 and, in the case of a child, a total of UGX 300,000 was paid out. The health insurance product had a premium payment of UGX 80,000 covering four household members, with a supplemental charge of UGX 20,000 for each additional member beyond the first four. The benefits include screening, Out Patient Department (OPD) services and hospitalisation.

The micro-insurance products are promoted through Implementing Partner Organisations to reach scale and minimise costs to ensure provision of affordable products. The product is usually introduced and adapted to the welfare /social fund concept embedded within the VSLA methodology. CARE's key role is to engage with insurance companies, conduct rapid assessments to establish women and youth's insurance needs and guide product development and delivery channels to ensure relevance and suitability to the vulnerable households. For the promoted products, CARE has partnered with Jubilee Insurance and Integrated Community Based Initiative (ICOBI). Work is guided by a mutually signed MOU for smooth implementation. CARE and Jubilee Insurance have conducted intensive financial education to partner staff on what insurance is and how it works. Project staff are also oriented on products with a focus on why a particular product is to be used and how, and when to sell it among VSLA members.

This model has helped the VSLA members' households to absorb and manage shocks and asset loss resulting from ill-health and funerals. Cumulatively, since 2012 to date over 2,000 VSLA members have been registered as consumers for the different micro-insurance products. The model has proved sustainable as the beneficiary households have continued transacting with the insurance companies even after the supporting initiatives have ended.

Future financial inclusion programming

CARE is currently examining possible future initiatives. These include refocusing on strengthening the existing VSLAs by promoting critical interventions that provide solutions for the day-to-day challenges of targeted communities. The additional interventions include food security and nutrition, climate smart agriculture and resilience capacity building, increasing agricultural production and promoting value chains, market access and market linkage with key public/private sector players. There also needs to be a deliberate focus on gender transformation and conflict sensitivity in all proposed interventions and activities.

Secondly, CARE envisages promoting VSLA as an entry point to implement specialised skills and knowledge through the Farmer Field Business School model (specialised training on production, climate resilient agriculture and selected value chains).

In addition, we plan for the continued promotion of linkages to formal financial services providers for managing savings and loan growth needs and promoting affordable and user friendly financial products to the bottom of the pyramid category of the population where VSLA members largely belong.

CARE will also promote user-friendly, affordable and innovative technologies that can impact common problems of the population, including affordable and fast formal financial services technologies, agricultural and business skills development extension services, access to inputs and market opportunities, labour, and agricultural training.

CARE will continue its engagement and advocacy at various national and international fora i.e the Uganda National Inter Institutional Committee on consumer protection; the national Self Help Group Sub Committee, Global SEEP Network and World Bank on critical issues related to financial inclusion promotion in Uganda. Finally, it will integrate its programmatic approaches to other CARE Uganda programmes to strengthen synergies and complementarity across programmes and as well as to consolidate the impact of our work.

13

Civil Society Organisations and Local-Level Peacebuilding in Northern Uganda[1]

Paul Omach

Abstract

This paper examines the contribution of civil society, notably religious and faith-based groups, traditional institutions, non-governmental organisations (NGOs), human rights groups, and community-based self-help groups, in promoting local-level peacebuilding in northern Uganda. Civil society groups in northern Uganda provided alternative narratives of the conflict, exposed brutalities against civilians, and ideas of peacebuilding. They lobbied, facilitated negotiations, engaged in building cultures of peace, promoted reconciliation, sustained livelihoods at the local level, and influenced outside peacebuilding interventions. However, the national context constrained their activities. This article is based on research and consultancy materials, personal observation, official and unofficial documents from the government, international organisations, intergovernmental agencies, and NGOs, newspaper reports, and scholarly publications.

Introduction

The aim of this paper is to examine the nature and contribution of civil society organisations (CSOs) in promoting local level peacebuilding in northern Uganda. The experience of northern Uganda highlights the challenge of peacebuilding in a situation of multiple conflicts at various levels, national and local. Civil society peacebuilding activities at the local level highlight Boulding's assertion that cultures of peace survive in small pockets and spaces even in the most violent of conflicts (Ramsbotham et al., 2005: 217). CSOs in northern Uganda provided a link between the local, national, and international actors and ideas. They provided alternative local narratives of the conflict, emphasising brutalities against civilians and community demands for peace.

---

[1] Reprinted by kind permission from *Journal of Asian and African Studies*, Vol 51, Issue 1, 2016; SAGE Publications Ltd.

CSOs provided leadership, championed popular mobilisation for peace, and influenced outside peacebuilding intervention in northern Uganda. However, the national context constrained civil society peacebuilding activities.

The conflict in northern Uganda involved successive insurgent groups who fought against the government of Uganda from 1986 to 2006. The insurgents comprised soldiers and supporters of the previous regimes the National Resistance Army (NRA), led by Yoweri Museveni, had fought against and defeated during the five years of insurgency before coming to power. At the time the NRA came to power, the Ugandan state had collapsed. State-inspired violence, human rights abuses, and lawlessness were endemic, especially in southern Uganda, where the NRA derived its support. The legitimacy of the NRA government therefore rested on its promise and commitment to restore peace and provide security of life and property, the rule of law, and democratic governance (National Resistance Movement, 1986).

The leadership of the NRA constructed a narrative of the conflict in northern Uganda to suit the interests of legitimising its rule and military approach to conflicts. It presented the conflict in northern Uganda as an attempt by 'criminals' and people responsible for human rights abuses, and the collapse of the Ugandan state, to regain power. These 'criminals' must be defeated using military means, the narrative ran. In contrast, the leadership presented the NRA as a 'disciplined', 'pro-people army', which has restored security, rule of law, and respect for human rights, has reversed state collapse, and has made Uganda an attractive haven for foreign investment (Museveni, 1987a). Western donor states, multilateral agencies, and scholarly works recycled this narrative, and supported the military approach adopted by the government (Dolan, 2006: 28). They were content to treat the conflict as an "isolated situation of political instability" (United Nations Office for the Coordination of Humanitarian Affairs, 2000, para. 10). International NGOs also accepted the government's narrative and were careful not to 'overstep their boundary' by engaging in Uganda's domestic politics (Dolan and Hovil, 2006: 6). International NGOs, such as *Associazione Voluntary per il Servizio International* (AVSI), the Norwegian Refugee Council, Oxfam, CARE, and World Vision, which intervened in northern Uganda, restricted their activities to 'working in conflict' delivering humanitarian assistance. They supported local civil society groups in sustaining livelihoods and rebuilding local economies.

National CSOs were polarised, reflecting the regional north–south and ethnic divides and lack of national integration that are at the root of the conflict. The national media for instance recycled the argument that insurgent groups in northern Uganda lack a political agenda, while religious and faith-based organisations, NGOs and human rights organisations outside northern Uganda maintained a conspicuous silence and in some cases openly supported the government's military approach. Alternative narratives emphasising the humanitarian consequences of the military approaches and popular demands for a peaceful approach were ignored, or suppressed.

Civil society groups in northern Uganda comprising religious organisations such as the Justice and Peace Commission of the Catholic Church, the Anglican Church of

Uganda, the Acholi Religious Leaders Peace Initiative (ARLPI), traditional authorities, especially through the institution of *Ker Kal Kwaro Acholi*, and community-based organisations courageously advanced the cause of peacebuilding. They turned around the perceptions of the conflict towards peace, leading to increased engagement in peacebuilding in northern Uganda by multilateral agencies, and international and national NGOs (Dolan and Hovil, 2006). In May 2002, the Civil Society Organisation for Peace in Northern Uganda (CSOPNU), a 'loose' coalition of national and international civil society advocating for 'just and lasting peace' in northern Uganda, was established.

This article is an analysis of the role of civil society in local-level peacebuilding in northern Uganda. It offers an in-depth study on civil society peacebuilding activities in the Acholi sub-region, the epicentre of the conflict and civil society peacebuilding activities. The article relies on official reports and newsletters from CSOs, the district local government, government of Uganda, and intergovernmental agencies. These reports offer information on the conflict situation and peacebuilding interventions. The author has also used information on various aspects of the conflict in northern Uganda, which was personally collected during earlier research as well as personal observation of the conflict over the years. The study has also relied on secondary material from scholarly articles in journals and books.

CSOs and peacebuilding

Civil society is a historically variable concept whose appeal Kumar (1993) observes, is its many levels and layers of meaning. In classical usage, civil society was synonymous with the state. The modern idea of civil society is of a sphere distinct from the state (Carothers, 1999–2000; Kaldor, 2003; Kumar, 1993). For the purpose of this study, civil society constitutes the arena or sphere of un-coerced collective action around shared interests, purposes, and values. It is an intermediate arena between the state, private sector, or market and the family (Paffenholf and Spurk 2006). Civil society is an arena that provides space for diverse societal values and interests to interact, debate, and seek to influence society and the political process. CSOs consist of the wide array of non-governmental and not-for-profit organisations and groups that exist within the civil society arena. They include non-governmental organisations (NGOs), faith-based groups, human rights groups, trade unions, and ethnic based associations, among others. CSOs and groups express the interests and values of their members and respect for some ethical considerations. They recognise the importance of respecting human rights and promoting compromise, dialogue, and economic and social integration. They promote social and political spaces for dialogue and constrain arbitrary exercise of state power. They interact with the state and the environment defined by the state shapes them.

As Paris (2004) observes, from Alexis de Tocqueville to the present, scholars have emphasised the role of civil society in consolidating democracy. The legacy of democratic struggles in Eastern Europe and Latin America in the 1970s and 1980s enhanced this benign view of civil society. Civil society nurtures trust and reciprocity and fosters tolerance for diversity (Diamond, 1999; Putman, 1993). These are important for preventing conflict. Civil society monitors and checks the state in the exercise of power, promotes political participation, creates alternative channels for the articulation of and representation of interests, and promotes favourable conditions for market economic reforms. Harberson (1994: 2) and colleagues, in the edited volume *Civil Society and the State in Africa*, reflect this thinking: "We consider the possibility that civil society holds a key to understanding and addressing effectively the political and socio-economic crises in Africa and elsewhere", they wrote. Lewis (2002), however, questioned the usefulness of the concept civil society to Africa. Lewis argued that civil society is a Western concept bounded by a cultural and political setting.

In the 1990s, scholarly and policy works emphasised the positive contribution of civil society in democratisation and peacebuilding (Paffenholf and Spurk, 2006; World Bank, 2006). Civil societies increase trust and social cohesion, fill the void left by the state, and carry out functions such as providing services, protection of citizens, reintegration of ex-combatants and displaced persons, advocacy, and creating awareness and promoting reconciliation. Much of the interest in civil society is a result of the dominance of the neo-liberal paradigm and its emphasis on limited role for the state, and privatised delivery of social services (Lewis, 2002).

Other scholarly works caution against an overly positive view of the role of civil society in promoting democracy and peacebuilding (Bayart, 1986). Carothers (1999–2000) dismisses the notion that civil society "consists only of noble causes and earnest, well-intentioned actors." Carothers observes that "civil society everywhere is a bewildering array of the good, the bad, and the outright bizarre". Similarly, Chambers and Kopstein (2001) raise the need to ask the question, what type of civil society promotes democracy. They argue that there are both 'good and bad civil society'. Bad civil society is particularistic. It contains the elements of good civil society but only between members of a particular group. Bad civil society spreads the opposite of the virtues of good civil society, prejudice, hatred and extremism, to members of outside groups. Belloni (2008: 186–187) argues that even in consolidated democracies, "civil society is a vague and general concept, which can be filled with different contents – ranging from democratic to undemocratic actors and from peaceful to violent agents".

Paris (2004), drawing on Chambers and Kopstein, decries the focus of liberal peace approach to peacebuilding on 'quantity' rather than the "specific qualities of civil society". Paris (2004: 151–178) argues that the liberal approach to peacebuilding under looks the 'pathologies of liberalisation': the problem of 'bad' civil society, the 'behaviour of opportunistic conflict entrepreneurs', the 'destructive societal competitions' elections might generate, the role of saboteurs disguised as democrats, and 'the disruptive and conflict-inducing effects of economic liberalisation'. In neo-patrimonial and ethnically fragmented societies with strong national and group identities, some groups may condone human rights violations, and even accept neo-patrimonial relations. Conflict-torn societies are often highly polarised. CSOs are likely to reflect such polarisation.

They may differ in response to conflict. Some are likely to be sectarian, ignore human rights violations, support violent pursuit of conflict or be complicit in maintaining silence. Orjuela (2005) presented the case of a struggle by geographically and ethnically divided civil society in Sri Lanka, in favour of and against a negotiated settlement to the violent conflict.

Donais (2009) criticises the liberal peacebuilding approach for requiring local actors to "take ownership over a largely predetermined vision". The liberal peace approach, Donais argues, is full of tension between external imposition and local ownership. Donais contrasts this with the 'communitarian' approaches in which local actors design, manage and implement peacebuilding processes. The communitarian approach emphasises the roles of tradition and social context in determining particular visions of peacebuilding. It favours peacebuilding from below based on the conflict transformation approach that takes a positive view on the role of civil society in peacebuilding (Lederach, 1995).

Peacebuilding from below is linked to Lederach's idea of indigenous empowerment, which suggests that conflict transformation must include respect for and promotion of cultural resources in a given setting, and seeing the setting and people not as the 'problem' but as the 'answer' (Lederach, 1995: 212). The idea "echoes Elise Boulding's insight that cultures of peace can survive in small pockets and spaces even in the most violent of conflicts"(Ramsbotham et al., 2005: 217).

The conflict transformation approach to peacebuilding views states as multidimensional, comprising multiple political arenas at different levels, local, regional, and central (Manning, 2003: 26). The approach describes conflict-affected societies as a triangle with three levels. At the apex is the top military and political leadership; the middle, leadership comprising political, religious, business sectors; the third level is the grassroots. At this level are the majority of the population, internally displaced persons, local leaders, community-based organisations, and local NGOs. The conflict transformation approach requires coordination of peacebuilding at all levels. Most intra-state conflicts have roots in local issues and play out in local settings. Embedded cultures and economies of violence at the local level often provide serious challenges to settlements reached at the national level. Most often, local conflicts and issues are left unresolved by settlements arrived at the centre, requiring a reworking of the settlements at the local level. Neglect of the local level undermines consolidation of peace (Manning, 2003). Understanding of structures, attitudes, relationships, and behaviours that will erode cultures of violence and promote peace at the local level needs to underpin settlements reached at national level. This requires involvement of local actors and identifying and cultivating knowledge, cultures, and resources that promote peace. Put differently, effective and sustainable peace entails empowering communities torn by conflict. While acknowledging the importance of local understandings and cultural practices in peacebuilding, Schaefer (2010) cautions that local practices are heterogeneous and some local practices are not "necessarily compatible with the aims of working towards a less violent society".

The conflict transformation approach to peacebuilding has opened the space for CSOs in peacebuilding. CSOs have emerged to fill the gap left by weak and collapsed states. Multilateral and bilateral agencies have turned to CSOs in supporting peacebuilding. The Carnegie Commission on Preventing Deadly Conflicts (1997) underlined the importance of CSOs. Likewise, in 2005, the United Nations outlined the political contribution of a vibrant civil society in conflict prevention as well as in peaceful settlement of disputes. The local level approach to peacebuilding has however gone beyond looking at the role of CSOs as merely filling gaps left by weak states by implementing externally designed peacebuilding programmes. It emphasises respect for local norms and practices which local CSOs represent.

The nature of CSOs in Uganda

CSOs in Uganda are a diverse category. The Development Network of Indigenous Associations (DENIVA), a national apex organisation for CSOs in Uganda, defines CSOs in the Ugandan context as "organisations, organised groups, and individuals that come together voluntarily to pursue those interests, values, and purposes usually termed the "common group"". These include NGOs, community groups, labour unions, professional associations, faith-based organisations, parts of academia, and the media (DENIVA, 2006: 22). There is a long tradition of associational life in rural communities in Uganda. Grassroots organisations, mostly rural or village community-based mutual self-help groups, have historically been involved in livelihood-promoting activities such as improving agricultural production, operating rotating credit and loan schemes facilities, and offering funeral services. However, most grassroots groups emerged in the 1970s and 1980s as a response to the economic crises and state failure. They emerged to fill the void left by the state in the provision of social services. Grassroots associations include ethnic associations and faith-based groups, which were already in place during colonial rule. These categories of civil society are mainly involved in social services delivery. Their non-engagement in political advocacy is partly due to the country's history of authoritarianism and repressive rule (DENIVA, 2006). Another category comprising trade unions and cooperative associations were weakened through co-optation by the state and subsequently liberalisation of the economy under the structural adjustment programmes of the 1980s and 1990s (Bazaara, 2004).

The more formal and recent category of CSOs are NGOs, network organisations, and professional associations. These have proliferated since the late 1980s and 1990s with structural adjustment and good governance programmes. Through a process of social engineering, international donors have sought to create NGOs as part of civil society development (Dicklitch, 2001: 31; Hearn, 1999). International donors viewed NGOs as alternatives to the state to fill the void in the delivery of social services. From the 1990s, donors and governments assigned NGOs the role of ensuring accountability in implementation of poverty reduction policies and programmes. The role of CSOs became that of 'partnership' with the state (Hearn, 2001; Muhumuza, 2010).

The context of authoritarian rule and economic crisis has had a bearing on the functioning of CSOs in Uganda. It has resulted in a situation whereby most CSOs focus on service delivery and limit their activities to specific geographical areas. This is the case with self-help and community-based associations that were in existence before independence and the various civil society groups that emerged in response to the economic crisis of the 1970s and 1980s, and those of the 1990s. CSOs which emerged in the 1990s 'are urban-based', with headquarters in the capital Kampala (Dicklitch, 2001). They were formed by elites who discovered CSOs as a lucrative source of income from donors. These CSOs are influenced by donor agenda and ideology. This partly explains why civil society groups in Uganda began to change their orientation towards peace toward the end of the 1990s, when donor policy on the conflict was changing towards peaceful approaches. In addition, the Ugandan elite tend to be influenced by ethnic and political divisions that are endemic in Uganda. Activities of organisations run by the elite are susceptible to effects of political and ethnic divisions. Such a factor cannot be ruled out in explaining initial responses of national CSOs to the conflict in northern Uganda. Comparisons exist in Sri Lanka (Orjuela, 2005)

In addition, few CSOs in Uganda engage in political activism and advocacy because the government of Uganda is intolerant of involvement of CSOs in 'political' activities. CSOs perceived to be engaging in political activities are often threatened with de-registration (Bazaara, 2004; Dicklitch, 1998: 4; Muhumuza, 2010: 11). Most CSOs in Uganda are regulated by the NGO Act. Since 1989, it has been a legal requirement for all NGOs operating in Uganda to register with the NGO Registration Board in the Ministry of Internal Affairs. The initial registration is renewable after one year (NGO Registration Act 1989; NGO Registration (Amendment Act, 2006). The law is authoritarian and aims to control CSOs. Intolerance by the government of involvement of CSOs in 'political' activities has constrained advocacy work of human rights organisations. CSOs which have civic orientation prefer to play safe, through self-censorship or toeing the government line. This political context has influenced the role of civil society in peacebuilding.

The context and NRA government narrative of the conflict

The conflict in northern Uganda erupted in 1986, a few months after the National Resistance Army (NRA) led by Yoweri Museveni came to power after five years of guerrilla war against the government of Uganda. At the heart of the conflict is "lack of sufficient national integration" between the constituent ethnic, religious, and regional elements of the country (Omara-Otunnu, 1995). Since independence, continual struggles for political control and violent conflicts have bedevilled Uganda. State violence, coercion, and use security forces have been a dominant means of political control and retaining power. This was manifested in 1966 when Prime Minister Milton Obote suspended the constitution and replaced it with an interim one that centralised power in the presidency, which he ascended to, after deposing and exiling his predecessor Edward Mutesa. Obote's reliance on the military gave the army a taste of power. In 1971, the army, under the leadership of Idi Amin, assumed direct political power. Amin's rule was characterised by state violence, intimidation, and coercion. It resulted in social dislocation, institutional decay, and collapse.

When Amin was overthrown in April 1979, by a combined force of Tanzanian Peoples Defence Force and Ugandan guerrillas, violence and disorder escalated, as different groups struggled for political control (Decalo, 1990). The controversial elections of December 1980 that returned Milton Obote to power and the decision by Yoweri Museveni to launch a guerrilla war against the government compounded the situation. In July 1985, Milton Obote was ousted in a military coup led by General Tito Okello. Six months later in January 1986, NRA guerrillas led by Yoweri Museveni ousted the military government of Tito Okello. At the time, violence, lawlessness, banditry, and insecurity were rampant. The military government had lost control and rival armed groups controlled the capital city and other spaces.

To legitimise its insurgency and rule, the leadership of the NRA constructed a narrative of Uganda's political history portraying Ugandans as victims of the state. The leadership of the NRA argued that it was legitimate for Ugandans to use armed force to resist and overthrow the state. They presented the NRA as an ally of the people of Uganda in their struggle against the state, and the NRA insurgency as a 'second liberation' aimed at dismantling the state and reconstructing it along democratic and national framework'. President Yoweri Museveni referred to capture of power by the NRA as a "fundamental change" in the politics of the country (Museveni, 1992: 21; National Resistance Movement, 1986).

However, the NRA narrative did not find resonance throughout the country. The NRA insurgency had polarised the country along the regional and ethnic north–south or Nilotic–Bantu divide (Low, 1988; Omara-Otunnu, 1995). The NRA and the other rebel armies allied to it drew their support from among Bantu ethnic groups from the south, while people from northern Uganda dominated the government army the NRA deposed from power. The capture of state power by the NRA in January 1986 generated fear in northern Uganda.

When the NRA reached northern Uganda, the behaviour of NRA soldiers, who acted more like conquerors than the liberators they claimed to be, compounded existing fear and mistrust of intentions of the NRA. Units within the NRA engaged in harassment, robberies, and cold-blooded murders. The NRA rounded up former soldiers and took them to 'politicisation camps'. They tortured and tied those they arrested during operations to round-up former soldiers in the notorious 'three piece' or *Kandoya* fashion (ACORD-Gulu, 1997; Legum, 1986–1987; Pirouet, 1991; Republic of Uganda, 1997). The *Kandoya* fashion entails tying a person's arms tightly at the elbows behind the back. The method paralyses the limbs and damages internal organs. The government blamed this on undisciplined elements integrated into the NRA from UFM and FEDEMO (Amaza, 1998: 150; Behrend, 1998: 108–109; Republic of Uganda, 1997).

Relations between the army and the population deteriorated, as did security. People began to take up arms and to attack NRA soldiers. When in August 1986 former government soldiers who had reorganised under the banner of the Uganda Peoples Democratic Army (UPDA) attacked NRA positions in Gulu and Kitgum districts in Acholi, they found a receptive environment in which to operate. The attack provided organisational coherence to a hitherto uncoordinated resistance. Within a few months, the conflict spread to Lango and Teso. The conflict has gone through different phases, involving various rebel groups. The most devastating phase of the conflict was between 1988 and 2006, when the Lord's Resistance Army (LRA) emerged as the main rebel group (Behrend, 1998; Gersony, 1997).

Given the factionalism in the country, narratives of the conflict in northern Uganda became a major political tool. The leadership of the NRA portrayed the conflict as the result of "rear-guard actions of the defeated, moribund, sectarian, and neo-colonial elements" (Museveni, 1987a). NRA leader Yoweri Museveni criminalised insurgents, presenting them as "elements that have caused untold suffering to the people of Uganda, violated human rights, murdered people, destroyed the economy, and violated the sovereignty of the people of Uganda" (Museveni, 1987a). He argued that insurgents were fighting due to the fear of prosecution for crimes they had committed during the tenure of past regimes, and the desire to regain power in order to enjoy the concomitant benefits that go with it. He declared: "Fighting and annihilating these elements is a justified cause". The government variously portrayed the conflict in northern Uganda as the manifestation of 'primitivism', 'backwardness', and inability to cope with 'modern times' (Gingyera-Pinycwa, 1993: 130–131).

The NRA dismissed criticism of human rights abuses arising from the military approach. It labelled advocates for peaceful approaches to the conflict as "proponents of Uganda's backwardness and misery" (Museveni, 1987b). President Yoweri Museveni referred to exiled Bishop Benoni Ogwal of the Anglican Diocese of northern Uganda who had criticised the NRA for committing atrocities against civilians, as a liar "before man and God"; a person "whose past are tainted with crime or with collaboration with crime" (Legum, 1986-87; B468–469). Critics of the government's military approach and human rights violations were threatened and intimidated.

In the 1990s, the conduct of the LRA, which had emerged as the main rebel group, gave some credence to the official narrative of the NRA government of portraying rebels as criminals and terrorists who lack a political agenda, and should be defeated using a military approach. By the time the LRA emerged as the main rebel group, support among the civilian population had diminished (Branch, 2007). The LRA interpreted this to mean the civilian population in Acholi had switched support to the government. It turned its violence against suspected collaborators and supporters of the government, attacking communities, destroying homes, committing abductions, murders, mutilation, rape and looting. The organisation relied on abduction and forcible recruitment, especially of children and youth, to fill its rank. UNICEF (2004) put the number of children abducted at 25,000. The LRA initiated abductees into its ranks by forcing them to kill their own relatives, family members and other abductees, especially those it caught trying to escape. LRA commanders forced abducted girls into sexual slavery, turning them into 'wives' (Human Rights Watch, 2003). Besides, violence targeted against civilians, the LRA did not present a credible political agenda.

The government further portrayed the LRA as a proxy of the Islamist fundamentalist regime in Sudan, and presented itself as a victim of Islamic fundamentalism and international terrorism. By 1994, the LRA was receiving support from Sudan, in retaliation for Uganda's support for the Sudan People's Liberation Army (SPLA), which had been fighting against Sudan since 1983. By presenting itself as a victim of Islamic fundamentalism, Uganda sought to count on support of the United States, which considered Sudan a 'rogue' state and the Islamist regime in Sudan an international threat. The United States provided military support to Uganda and in December 2001 branded the LRA a terrorist group (US Department of State, 2001). Western academics such as Gersony (1997), Van Acker (2004), and Prunier (2004), among others, recycled the narrative of the LRA as a proxy, lacking a political agenda.

Civil society response differed, reflecting the polarisation of Ugandan society, geographic, regional, and ethnic. Other than local CSOs in northern Uganda who championed the cause of peace, others ignored, were indifferent, or openly supported the government's military approaches. The minister for pacification of northern Uganda observed that a 'let them suffer' attitude prevailed amongst those who viewed the conflict as a "God-given opportunity to repay the devil its due" (Bigombe, 1994). The national media, for instance, recycled the narrative that rebels had no political agenda.

The dubious moral standing of the LRA aside, criminalisation of the group delegitimised and painted them as a group without any merit, and not worthy to engage in dialogue with, and contributed to militarising the conflict. Criminalisation of rebel groups is based on the dubious distinction between 'old' and 'new civil wars', where new wars are viewed as criminal, depoliticised, and predatory, while old civil wars are political, even noble (Kalyvas, 2001).

CSOs and peacebuilding in northern Uganda

Civil society groups in northern Uganda played an important role in turning the perceptions of the conflict in northern Uganda towards peace. They championed the cause of human rights, provided leadership, and mobilised the local constituency around demands for the peaceful resolution of the conflict. They engaged in advocacy, facilitated contacts between rebel fighters and the government, and promoted reconciliation between rebels and the community. They organised workshops, issued statements, and facilitated the formation of peace clubs to change community attitudes, build a culture of peace, and foster reconciliation.

The most notable civil society groups involved in peacebuilding in the Acholi sub-region were the ARLPI, an interdenominational peace initiative comprising the Anglican Church of Uganda, Catholic Church, and Moslems, and Justice and Peace

Commission of the Catholic Church. *Ker Kal Kwaro Acholi*, the cultural institution of traditional leaders and Human Rights Focus, a local NGO based in Gulu district. Others included local NGOs such as Gulu Save the Children Organisation (GUSCO), Kitgum Concerned Women's Association (KICWA), and Gulu Hope for Peace, which carried out counselling and facilitated reintegration of abducted persons who escaped from rebel captivity. Community-based and self-help associations engaged in socio-economic activities to alleviate human suffering and rebuild local economies and livelihoods. International NGOs, including those that were not present in the north, provided support to the local civil society groups.

Political advocacy and mobilisation

As early as 1987, Acholi elders, chiefs, and civil and religious leaders had begun to make efforts to promote a negotiated end to the conflict. At the time, Acholi elders, chiefs, and civil leaders operated under a loosely organised association known as 'Council of Elders'. Religious leaders engaged in peacebuilding through the dioceses and organisations of the different denominations: Gulu diocese in the case of the Catholic Church and the diocese of Northern Uganda in the case of the Anglican Church of Uganda. By then, disenchantment with disruption caused by the conflict had begun to develop, leading to the emergence of a peace constituency. Between 1987 and 1988, Acholi elders and civil and religious leaders appealed to and facilitated the surrender of rebels. A council of elders established a reception and transit centre at the presidential lodge in Gulu town and received rebels who surrendered (Simonse, 1998). The role of elders was vital in instilling confidence in rebels who were distrustful of the NRA. At the time, the government had put in place a presidential pardon to encourage rebels to surrender and an amnesty offering immunity from prosecution for treason, theft, and torture to rebels who surrendered and renounced insurgency. Acholi elders and civil leaders facilitated negotiations between the fighting forces by acting as intermediaries. The negotiations resulted in the 1988 UPDA–NRA peace agreement that Lieutenant Colonel Angelo Okello of the UPDA and President Museveni signed and the Catholic bishop of Gulu diocese, Cypriano Kihangire, witnessed (Lamwaka, 1996; Omach, 2011: 284–285). A section of the UPDA, about 3,000 soldiers with 80% of the leadership, surrendered and the government integrated them into the army and resettled others into civilian life. A section loyal to the overall leader of the group, Brigadier Odong Latek, refused to surrender (Woodward, 1991: 182–183). The group loyal to Brigadier Odong Latek joined Joseph Kony's rebel group and formed the Uganda Christian Democratic Army, later renamed the Lord's Resistance Army (LRA) (Lamwaka, 1996; Omach, 2011).

Despite the setback, Acholi elders did not give up efforts at facilitating contacts between rebels of the LRA and the government. In 1993, they were instrumental in facilitating contacts between the minister of state in charge of the 'pacification of the north', Betty Bigombe and LRA commanders. The military command in the northern town of Gulu offered safe passage for peace emissaries to deliver messages to and from the LRA. A ceasefire was agreed upon, and negotiations were held between

LRA representatives and a delegation from the Uganda government comprising Betty Bigombe and commanders from the army's 4th division in Gulu. Clan elder and religious leaders from Acholi attended the negotiations. The negotiations raised hopes for a peaceful end to the conflict. The hope for peace was shattered when President Museveni gave an ultimatum to the LRA to surrender within seven days or face military action. The president accused the LRA of dishonesty and lack of good faith. He argued that the LRA was using the negotiations to replenish its fighters through recruitment and that it was negotiating with the government of Sudan for military assistance. The president ruled out further talks with the LRA (Omach, 2011; Pain, 1997: 20–21). In April 1995, Uganda broke off diplomatic relations with Sudan, alleging that Sudan was supporting dissident groups in Uganda including the LRA (Prunier, 2004).

The Ugandan army renewed military operations against the LRA. The LRA retaliated by attacking, abducting, mutilating, and killing civilians. The LRA massacred civilians in Atiak in April 1995, Sudanese refugees in Acol-pii camp in 1996, and civilians in Palabek in January 1997 (Amnesty International, 1997; Gersony, 1997; Republic of Uganda, 1997). The government army responded by forcing the population into camps, ostensibly to protect them (Amnesty International, 1999; Gersony, 1997). The United States, which had declared Sudan a rogue state and a threat to security by sponsoring Islamist fundamentalism, provided military assistance to the Ugandan government (*Africa Confidential* 1996: 1).

The government's inclination towards military approaches to the conflict did not destroy the resolve of CSOs to change perceptions towards peace. In February 1996, Acholi elders and chiefs constituted a cultural institution, *Ker Kal Kwaro Acholi*, to offer leadership in Acholi and effect popular mobilisation. This was aimed at reversing the destruction of political organisation and leadership in Acholi, which had been brought about by LRA violence and the government's repression, intimidation, and arrests. Lack of political organisation and destruction of leadership has been a contributory factor in prolonging the conflict (Branch, 2005: 5). *Ker Kal Kwaro Acholi* worked closely with religious leaders in Acholi, who in February 1998 formally inaugurated the ARLPI, an interdenominational peace initiative comprising the Anglican Church, Catholic Church, and Moslems. The formal inauguration of ARLPI was a significant development, which manifested inter-religious coexistence in a country where religion has been politically divisive and a source of conflict. The ARLPI is an example of what Carothers (1999–2000) and Chambers and Kopstein (2001) refer to as 'good civil society'. The inauguration of ARLPI was equally significant because religious groups have influence within Ugandan society. They are trusted and confided in, especially in times of crisis, when trust in the state has eroded. Religious groups operate as a 'trust'. Unlike NGOs, religious organisations are not controlled by the authoritarian NGO Act, which affords them greater freedom of action, without fear of threats of deregistration. They are in a better position to act as the voice of the voiceless.

Together with NGOs such as Human Rights Focus, the ARLPI and *Ker Kal Kwaro Acholi* carried out mobilisation to build consensus for peace at the local, national, and international levels. They organised peace rallies and training workshops, and produced newsletters and research publications highlighting the plight of civilians in the conflict zones. In 1996, an interfaith group of the Anglican Church of Uganda, the Catholic Church, and Moslems in Gulu organised peace-training workshops and the first public prayer for peace. In August 1997, a group comprising officials of the Anglican Church of Uganda, Catholics, and Muslim leaders organised a peace rally in Kitgum during which they asked the LRA to stop violence against civilians and called on the government to seek a peaceful end to the conflict (Rodriguez, 2002: 58–59).

By 1997, the call by civil society groups in northern Uganda for peaceful resolution of the conflict began to have resonance among groups in other parts of Uganda. A national consensus for peaceful resolution of conflicts began to emerge. Civil society groups and individuals outside northern Uganda began calling on the government to initiate dialogue to resolve conflicts in the country. In October 1997, religious leaders organised a peace rally in Kampala, while the president of the Uganda Law Society, when addressing judicial officials at the opening of the 1998 law year, reiterated the call for a peaceful end to conflicts in Uganda (Kimuli, 1998: 8).

More significantly, in 1997 the Parliament of Uganda extracted a concession from the government to discuss the conflict in northern Uganda. A new parliament had been elected in 1996. During the campaign preceding the election, voters in the conflict-riddled north expressed their frustration with the continuing conflict. Paul Ssemogerere, the presidential candidate who expressed intention to end the conflict through peaceful means, received massive endorsement from voters in the region (Gingyera-Pinycwa and Obong-Oula, 2003). Although Museveni, who favoured a military approach to the conflict, won the elections and was sworn in as president, the election generated optimism of transition to democracy. A progressive and democratic constitution had come into force in 1995. Among others, the new constitution granted the legislature power, with a two-thirds majority, to override the president's refusal to assent to legislation. Of particular interest, the constitution granted parliament power to appoint select committees to investigate specific problems. The sixth parliament exploited this provision to set up a committee to investigate the conflict in northern Uganda. The provision that the president could only dissolve parliament when its five-year term is complete provided parliament the autonomy and protection to act (Constitution of Republic of Uganda 1995, Chapter 6). There was thus euphoria of the dawn of a new and democratic era. However, the Parliamentary Sessional Committee on Defence and Internal Affairs charged with looking into the insurgency ruled out peace talks with the rebels, and instead recommended a military solution. A minority report of two members recommended peace talks. The report was a rebuff to the emerging peace movement (Republic of Uganda, 1997).

CSOs refocused their activities towards the international arena. The ARLPI lobbied the international community to put pressure on the government to negotiate with the LRA and to make concessions for peace. This was important because of the influence of Western donors on the political leadership in Uganda. In April 1997, representatives of

NGOs operating in northern Uganda, civil leaders, *Ker Kal Kwaro Acholi*, and religious leaders attended a civic forum, *Kacoke Madit* in London. The forum called on the government to initiate dialogue with all parties concerned to produce a lasting and durable peace (Pain, 1997). Civil society lobbied the United Nations, governments, and civil society groups in the United States, United Kingdom, the European Union, and Scandinavian countries. They highlighted the plight of children in northern Uganda such as those who walked long distances in search of safety and spent the night on the streets of Gulu town. In July 2003, religious leaders and other members of CSOs held overnight prayers and slept on the streets with the children.

In 2001, the ARLPI released a report, *Let My People Go: The Forgotten Plight of People in the Displaced Camps in Acholi*, and in 2002 Human Rights Focus published *Between Two Fires: The Plight of Internally Displaced Persons in northern Uganda*. In 2003, ARLPI published, *War of Words* (ARLPI, 2003), which criticised the role of the national media in the conflict, for presenting the LRA as an organisation not worth talking to and thereby supporting a military solution. The ARLPI argued that the national media, like the military, were engaged in the war in northern Uganda.

The emerging consensus towards peace was manifested in the formation in May 2002, of a 'loose' alliance of Civil Society Organisations for Peace in Northern Uganda (COSPNU). The alliance was instrumental in drawing international attention to the conflict and humanitarian crisis in northern Uganda and in convincing the government of Uganda to pass the Amnesty Act (2000) and developing a policy on internal displacement. In April 2004, the UN Under-secretary General for Humanitarian Affairs and Emergency Relief Coordinator Jan Egeland briefed the Security Council on the humanitarian situation in northern Uganda. Among other things, the Security Council stressed the importance of "exploring all peaceful avenues to resolve the conflict, including through creating a climate in which solutions based on dialogue might be found" (United Nations Security Council, 2004). Protection activities by international NGOs increased dramatically thereafter (Dolan, 2008). The lobbying by civil society also contributed to peace talks in Juba between the government of Uganda and the LRA in July 2006. In August 2008, the two sides signed a landmark Cessation of Hostilities Agreement. Since then, there has been stability in northern Uganda.

By insisting that government negotiate with and offer amnesty to the LRA, civil society in northern Uganda, especially community groups, elders, chiefs, clan leaders, and religious groups in effect rejected the official narrative of the conflict. This portrays the LRA as a group without merit and makes it immoral to engage with them in any way. Civil society understood the complexity of the conflict. They viewed LRA combatants as victims and perpetrators, or 'complex political perpetrators' (Baines, 2009), whom society failed to protect from abduction and conscription into the rebel group. Even those who joined 'voluntarily' might have done so because of lack of alternatives because of the socio-economic situation they found themselves living under. The ARLPI and elders made it clear that 'no one went to the bush willingly'.

This is a view one develops after 'seeing the suffering', and transcending government propaganda on the reality in northern Uganda (Armstrong, 2008).

Peace education and mediation

Even as ARLPI, *Ker Kal Kwaro Acholi*, and COSPNU lobbied government to offer amnesty for rebels and negotiate a peaceful end to the conflict, these civil society groups were also aware of the challenges of implementing amnesty and peace settlement at the local level. The conflict was so violent and was waged largely at the local level. Civilians suffered massive injuries at the hands of the LRA. The LRA mutilated, abducted, raped, and tortured (Branch, 2005; Human Rights Watch, 2005). This generated bitterness, tensions, and multiple conflicts at the local level. This is reflected in abuses using such labels as '*dwog paco*' meaning 'returnees', and 'killers' that formerly abducted persons are called and refusal to associate with them (Justice and Reconciliation Project, 2008: 5–6). This posed real dangers that any peace reached at the national level would falter when it came to implementation at the local level.

To address these challenges, the ARLPI, Justice and Peace Commission, Human Rights Focus, and *Ker Kal Kwaro Acholi* carried out peace education and conflict mediation activities. Human Rights Focus particularly carries out peacebuilding through promoting a culture of respect for human rights. It carries out human rights awareness to change the culture of violence. The organisation established human rights clubs and programmes in post-primary schools in the Acholi sub-region. Likewise, ARPLI together with Justice and Peace Commission recruited and trained volunteer peace animators. The volunteer peace animators are based at the sub-counties where they work with local religious leaders, council leaders, NGOs and other civil groups to promote and facilitate participatory dialogue and promote the culture of non-violence (Justice and Peace Commission of Archdiocese of Gulu, July 2007). *Ker Kal Kwaro Acholi* and the Acholi Religious Leaders Peace Initiative have been involved in mediating conflicts within communities, between ex-combatants and the community, formerly abducted persons, and clans. With increasing cases on land conflicts since the beginning of return of displaced persons to the villages, clan leaders and chiefs have been playing vital roles in resolving land conflicts.

Psychosocial support/counselling

To promote the reintegration of former combatants and abducted persons, CSOs such as GUSCO, the Kitgum Concerned Women's Association (KICWA), Caritas Gulu, and World Vision International offered psychosocial support. The conflict in northern Uganda traumatised both victims and perpetrators of violence. Those abducted by LRA rebels either participated in killings or witnessed them. According to Acholi tradition, the vengeful spirits of the dead or *cen* are likely to possess people who participate in killings, witness them, or encounter murder scenes. Those possessed by vengeful spirits of the dead are likely to be disturbed. They may be aggressive or show signs of withdrawal. Society shuns contact with such persons. Thus, they need cleansing to free them from evil spell and facilitate their acceptance into the community (Harlacher et al., 2006).

The CSOs mentioned above undertook measures to offer counselling services to people who escaped from captivity and LRA combatants who surrendered. In 1996, GUSCO, an initiative of civil leaders started to counsel and give psychosocial care to abducted children who escaped from the LRA or are rescued by the army. The children were kept in a reception centre for a period of between one and three months depending on their trauma experience. Caritas initiated similar programmes to provide psychological support in 1999. Other NGOs like World Vision International and Kitgum Concerned Women's Association (KICWA) operated reception centres providing counselling from trauma. In 2002, it created a reception centre for formerly abducted persons in Pajule, Pader district, to promote rehabilitation and reintegration into community.

Those the community received direct from captivity underwent elaborate traditional rituals to address the psychological effects of killing and facilitate their reintegration into the community. To promote individual and community healing and to facilitate reintegration, Caritas provided support to local communities to carry out traditional cleansing rituals. Caritas conducted research to get a better understanding of cultural processes and documented its findings: *Traditional Ways of Coping in Acholi* (2006).

Demobilisation and reintegration

In the absence of formal demobilisation and reintegration process, traditional leaders, chiefs, elders and clan leaders under their umbrella group *Ker Kal Kwaro* and the Acholi Religious Leaders Peace Initiative promoted the reintegration of former LRA combatants. They made sustained efforts to fight the stigmatisation of former LRA and facilitate their reintegration into society by promoting traditional and religious reconciliation processes at the grassroots and community levels. They discouraged society from using terms like 'returnees', 'formerly abducted children', and 'child mothers' because of the negative connotation and because it traumatises. They encouraged the community to forgive and reconcile with those who have returned from the LRA and now live amongst them. On their part, former LRA combatants were encouraged to confess to their clan elders whatever crimes they might have committed while they were engaged in the LRA insurgency, ask for forgiveness and undergo traditional cleansing rituals (Baines, 2009). They considered this as vital for encouraging other members of the LRA to surrender, thereby contributing to ending the conflict.

Clan and family heads also initiated traditional reintegration and reconciliation processes on their own accord. These ceremonies are initiated within clans after processes of counselling, truth telling, acknowledgement and symbolic compensation and rituals. *Ker Kal Kwaro Acholi* has also performed reconciliation and reintegration rites on a larger scale. International donors such as the United States Agency for International Development (USAID) facilitated some of these processes. The rituals include the ceremony of welcoming and cleansing returnees, which entail stepping on egg ('*nyono tong gweno*'), washing away tears ('*lwoko pig wang*') and cleansing ('*moyo kum*'). The ritual of re-establishing relations and reconciliation is '*mato oput*'. The ritual of cleansing areas where killing took place is '*moyo piny*'. The ritual involves burial of the bones and remains of those dead left unburied. The aim of this is to make peace with the dead and to facilitate reintegration of communities back to the villages after many years of displacement in camps.

Socio-economic and livelihood support

To address socio-economic problems and poverty, NGOs, community-based organisations, and self-help groups stepped in to fill the gaps created by weak state capacity and neglect. Some community-based organisations and self-help groups emerged spontaneously in response to the dire socio-economic situation, while others were established at the instigation of NGOs, the local and civil leadership to serve as implementing partners for donor, NGOs and government programmes. As Omona (2008) observed, the names of these grassroots organisations are highly value-laden, reflecting the socio-economic contexts. Example includes among others names such as *Lacan makwo twero toko lalonyo*, meaning a poor person who is alive has the potential to become rich; *Can deg nyap*, meaning poverty does not entertain laziness; and *Bedo dano tek*, meaning it is difficult to be a human being. These civil society groups engaged in promoting economic empowerment, income generation and food security. For example, ACORD in partnership with a local NGO, People's Voices for Peace set up micro-finance projects to support adults who escaped from LRA captivity, female victims of rape, widows and single mothers (Oywa, 1998). Another local NGO, Gulu Hope for Peace, with the assistance of *Jamii Ya Kupatanisha (JYAK)*, a Kampala-based NGO, provided vocational training for formerly abducted persons. The ARLPI lobbied and mobilised funding to establish the Acholi Education Initiative (AEI) to cater for education needs of children (Ochola, 2004).

Civil society groups also supported the district health services in responding to health issues such as the problem of HIV/AIDS. Gulu Catholic diocese, the Protestant church, ACORD, Gulu Community-Based Health Care Association, and youth groups, among others, supported in providing testing and counselling services, support, and care services for persons living with HIV/AIDS, and health education (Republic of Uganda, 2002: 25).

District local governments coordinated peacebuilding activities carried out by civil society actors, international donor and humanitarian agencies. This is vital to streamline civil society activities within district plans. The Joint Forum for Peace (JFP) in Kitgum district and the District Reconciliation and Peace Team (DRPT) in Gulu district were a result of such coordination efforts. These bodies provided opportunity for peacebuilding actors to share experiences and coordinate their efforts at a higher level. They have been vital in coordination of local reconciliation and rehabilitation as well as mediation efforts to resolve land conflicts, which have become endemic with resettlement into villages since the closure of camps (Interview with Clerk to Council Gulu, 2011).

Criticism of CSO intervention

Despite the noble intentions, CSOs had shortcomings. Their psychosocial support programmes raised ethical concerns. Keeping those who returned from LRA captivity at reception centres for some months was a traumatic experience. At the centres, counsellors, some with questionable skills, added injury to traumatised children by asking questions like "while you were in the bush, did you kill anybody?" (Interview with Community Development Officer Gulu, 2011). The centres were akin to a zoo, visited by researchers and humanitarian workers interested in learning about the LRA. Ironically, the centres not only served to draw international attention to the humanitarian crisis in the north, the government of Uganda found them useful for demonising the LRA (Dolan, 2002). In this way, civil society was complicit in the use of children as pawns in the politics of the conflict.

The counselling centres treated former LRA rebels as if they were a group of people with uniform 'bush experience' (Justice and Reconciliation Project, 2008). The centres overlooked the fact that former LRA returnees occupied different roles and ranks, and that some joined 'voluntarily' while LRA rebels abducted others. The centres also did not address the unique needs of boys and girls. The centres provided Western or 'modern' methods of counselling, which are inadequate in a situation where children who receive counselling later settle in a dislocated and traumatised society. Thus, on leaving counselling centres former LRA combatants and abductees underwent traditional cleansing once they returned to their families. The centres did not cater for the large number of formerly abducted persons and former LRA combatants returned direct to the community without going through trauma centres.

There have also been concerns about commercialisation of traditional rituals by NGOs and donors. The reconciliation programme of *Mato oput* for instance, was in a number of cases conducted with funding from donors and Western media widely covering it. It was more or less like acting 'traditional' justice rituals for the Western media. It is questionable whether members of the community attached meaning to processes carried out by NGOs. Additionally, traditional institutions are weak. They were re-established with the support of the government and donors during the 1990s to provide leadership, but also as an instrument to control the population. The youth especially do not take them seriously. Their dependence on the government for assistance such as the role of the government in constructing houses for them as part of the resettlement programme under the Peace, Recovery and Development Plan for northern Uganda (PRDP) has raised concern over their independence. Some people in Acholi cynically refer to them as "the government's chiefs" (Interview with an Administrative Officer Gulu, 2011).

Promotion of reconciliation at the local level has also been done in isolation of national processes. This is not in conformity with the conflict transformation approach, which emphasises coordination of national and local level peacebuilding. The conflict in northern Uganda is rooted in national politics. It is not a 'northern' or 'Acholi' problem as it has sometimes been presented in 'official discourse'.

Socio-economic and livelihood support intervention, have also been localised and micro in nature. These interventions only focused on symptoms, not the structural roots of socio-economic problems of poverty. They do not address the broad issue of governance and the situation that creates poverty, deprivation and conflicts in Uganda. Local level peacebuilding activities by CSOs need to complement rather than substitute national processes.

Challenges faced by CSOs

The national context provided the most immediate and formidable challenge to civil society involvement in peacebuilding. Civil society groups have had to contend with the government's intolerance of their involvement in political activism and advocacy. Government officials regarded groups advocating for a negotiated solution to conflict with intense suspicion (Rodriguez, 2002: 58–59). It accused CSOs of engaging in activism and advocacy, of overstepping their boundary by involving in politics and threatened to ban their activities. The brutal nature of the LRA rebels and inability to present a coherent political agenda worsened the situation. It made it very difficult to advocate for negotiation with them. According to Carlos Rodriguez, a renowned peace activist in northern Uganda, the government nearly banned the first interfaith public prayer for peace which was held in Gulu town in 1996. Political activism and advocacy for peace was risky and at times the consequences were tragic. In June 1996, two elders Okot Ogony and Olanya Lagony were killed while on a mission to meet LRA leaders (Gersony, 1997: 53–54). In August 2002 the Ugandan army attacked and held captive three priests, Fr. Carlos Rodriguez Locormoi of the Justice Peace Commission/Acholi Religious Leaders Peace Initiative, Fr. Tarcisio Pazzaglia and Fr. Julius Albanese of the Missionary News agency, who was on a visit to the north. The priests were meeting LRA rebels (Justice and Peace Commission of Archdiocese of Gulu, 5 August 2002). The army accused the priests of not obtaining permission from the relevant authorities, a charge the chairperson of the Acholi Religious Leaders Peace Initiative Archbishop John Baptist Odama denied (Justice and Peace Commission of Archdiocese of Gulu, 5 August 2002; ARLPI *Monitor* (Kampala), 3 September 2002:4). These incidences highlight the challenges civil society actors operating in a repressive environment face.

Inclination towards a military approach to the conflict, on the part of the government and rebel groups, especially the LRA, provided an obstacle to peaceful resolution of the conflict. There was little trust between the government and rebels. Each side wanted the other to surrender at the negotiating table. Consequently, peace negotiations tended to be accompanied by intense military campaigns and inflammatory statements. Peace processes tended to falter, and where agreements have been signed, there was little effort at implementation. Unfortunately, CSOs often lacked capacity to guarantee implementation, as was evidenced in 1988 with the agreement between government and UPDA rebels, which the Catholic diocese of Gulu had mediated.

Conclusion

Civil society actors have contributed to peacebuilding at the local level though a number of inter-related measures. Civil society actors have carried out advocacy and lobbying of fighting forces to negotiate, and the international community to put pressure on fighting forces to negotiate. They carried out activities aimed at creating awareness about the plight of civilians, changing public opinion and a building culture of peace, promoting reconciliation, sustaining livelihoods and rebuilding local economies. These measures target peacebuilding at the both upper or national level, and local level. This is because the national and local levels are interlinked. Peace at either level has effects on the other.

They engaged in peacebuilding in a challenging context of a state that does not accept alternative political views. The Ugandan state favours a military approach to conflict and is intolerant of any opinion to the contrary. The violent and brutal nature of the LRA and its failure to present a coherent political agenda led to their criminalisation by the governments of Uganda and the United States and labelling them a 'terrorist' organisation. This made it morally repugnant and politically unacceptable to engage them through peacebuilding activities. Civil society in northern Uganda defied this label and pursued the cause of peace. Their decision was based on the realisation that conflicts are complex and even the worst perpetrators of violence may at the same time be victims. To criminalise and preclude any peaceful engagement with them is not a useful option. Engagement with the LRA has contributed to a measure of peace since 2006, something a military option has failed to bring.

Civil society contribution to peace is important, but is not a substitute for the role of the state. The two must complement each other. Civil society peacebuilding activities such as those aimed at building local economies and improving livelihoods are merely sedative, unless efforts are made to redress the structural roots. Engagement by the state is therefore vital. Lack of commitment and repression by the state constrains and undermines civil society activities. To counter a repressive environment, civil society actors must employ collective advocacy to mobilise consensus for peacebuilding. Lobbying international actors contributes to putting pressure on the state to negotiate and compromise to build peace. Civil society activities require popular support and legitimacy from the grassroots. By its nature, many civil society groups in Uganda are often organisations of the urban and educated elite.

References

ACORD-Gulu (1997). 'A Survey of Causes, Effects and Impact of Armed Conflict in Gulu District. Report, ACORD-Gulu', April. Google Scholar.

Africa Confidential (1996) 'Arms against a sea of troubles'. *Africa Confidential*, 37 (23): 1. Google Scholar.

Amaza, O. (1998). *Museveni's Long March: From Guerrilla to Statesman*. Kampala: Fountain Publishers. Google Scholar.

Amnesty International (1997). 'Breaking God's Commands: the Destruction of Childhood by the Lord's Resistance Army'. Report no. AFR/01/97. London: Amnesty International. Google Scholar.

Amnesty International (1999). 'Breaking the Circle: Protecting Human Rights in the Northern War Zone'. Report no. AFR 59/01/99. London: Amnesty International. Google Scholar.

Armstrong, K (2008). 'Seeing the Suffering" in Northern Uganda: the Impact of a Human Rights Approach to Humanitarianism'. *Canadian Journal of African Studies*, 42(1): 1–32. Google Scholar.

ARLPI (2001). 'Let My People Go! The Forgotten Plight of the People in the Displaced Camps in Acholi. Gulu District, Uganda: ARLPI'. Google Scholar.

ARLPI (2002). 'Press Release. *Monitor (Kampala), 3 September, p.4. Google Scholar.

ARLPI (2003). 'War of Words. Gulu District', Uganda: ARLPI'. Google Scholar.

Baines, E. K. (2009). 'Complex Political Perpetrators: Reflection on Dominic Ongwen'. *Journal of Modern African Studies*, 47 (2): 163–191. Google Scholar, Cross-reference.

Bayart, J-F (1986). 'Civil Society in Africa'. In: Chabal, P (ed) *Political Domination in Africa: Reflections on the Limits of Power*. New York: Cambridge University Press. Google Scholar, Cross-reference.

Bazaara, N. (2004). 'The Role of Civil Society in Democratic Process in Uganda'. In: Mushi, SS, Mukandala, R. S., Yahya-Othman, S. (eds) *Democracy and Social Transformation in East Africa*. Dar es Salaam: Research and Education for Democracy in Tanzania, pp.104– 130. Google Scholar.

Behrend, H. (1998). 'War in Northern Uganda: the Holy Spirit Movements of Alice Lakwena, Severino Lukoya and Joseph Kony 1986–1997'. In: Clapham, C. (ed) *African Guerrillas*. Oxford, Kampala, Bloomington and Indianapolis: James Currey, Fountain Publishers and Indiana University Press, pp.107–118. Google Scholar.

Belloni, R. (2008). 'Civil Society in War to Democracy Transitions'. In: Jarstad, AK, Sisk, TD (eds) *From War to Democracy: Dilemmas of Peacebuilding*. Cambridge: Cambridge University Press, pp.182–210. Google Scholar, Cross-reference.

Bigombe, B. (1994). 'The Northern Question in Ugandan Politics'. Paper presented at a public seminar at the Sheraton Hotel, Kampala, 2 December 1994. Google Scholar.

Branch, A. (2005). 'Neither Peace nor Justice: Political Violence and the Peasantry in Northern Uganda, 1986–1998'. *African Studies Quarterly* 8(2): 1–31. Google Scholar.

Branch, A. (2007). 'Uganda's Civil War and the Politics of ICC Intervention'. *Ethics and International Affairs*, 21 (2): 179–198. Google Scholar, Cross-reference.

Carnegie Commission on Preventing Deadly Conflict. (1997) *Preventing Deadly Conflict*. New York: Carnegie Corporation. Google Scholar.

Carothers, T. (1999–2000). 'Civil Society. Foreign Policy' (Winter): 18–29. Google Scholar, Cross-reference.

Chambers, S, Kopstein, J. (2001). 'Bad Civil Society'. *Political Theory,* 29(6): 837–865. Google Scholar, Link.

Decalo, S. (1990). *Coups and Army Rule in Africa: Motivations and Constraints.* 2nd ed. New Haven and London: Yale University Press. Google Scholar.

DENIVA (2006). Civil Society in Uganda: At the Cross Roads? CIVICUS Civil Society Index Project'. Google Scholar.

Diamond, L. (1999). 'Towards Democratic Consolidation'. In: Diamond, L, Platter, M.F. (eds) *The Global Resurgence of Democracy.* Baltimore and London: John Hopkins University Press, pp.227–240. Google Scholar.

Dicklitch, S. (1998). *The Elusive Promise of NGOs in Africa: Lessons from Uganda.* New York: St. Martins. Google Scholar, Cross-reference.

Dicklitch, S. (2001). 'NGOs and Democratisation in Transitional Societies: Lessons from Uganda'. *International Politics* 38 (March): 27–45. Google Scholar, Cross-reference.

Dolan, C. (2002). *Which Children Count? The Politics of Children's Rights in Northern Uganda.* London: Conciliation Resources. Google Scholar.

Dolan, C. (2006). 'Uganda Strategic Conflict Analysis'. SIDA. Google Scholar.

Dolan, C. (2008). 'Is the PRDP a Three-Legged Table? Challenges for NGOs in Moving from Humanitarian and Short Term Interventions to Longer Term approaches in Light of the PRDP and Conflict Setting'. Speech at NGO Seminar for Scandinavian Based International NGOs in Kampala, Uganda, 10 April 2008. Google Scholar.

Dolan, C., Hovil, L. (2006). *Humanitarian Protection in Uganda: a Trojan Horse?* London: Humanitarian Policy Group, Overseas Development Institute. Google Scholar.

Donais, T. (2009). 'Empowerment or Imposition? Dilemmas of Local Ownership in Post-Conflict Peacebuilding Process'. *Peace and Change* 34(1): 3–6. Google Scholar, Cross reference.

Gersony, R. (1997). 'The Anguish of Northern Uganda. Results of a Field-Based Assessment of the Civil Conflicts in Northern Uganda'. Submitted to United States Embassy, USAID Mission Kampala, August. Google Scholar.

Gingyera-Pinycwa, A.G.G. (1993). 'Conflicting Fingers within the Iron Fist of National Unity'. In: Anyang, NP (ed) *Arms and Daggers in the Heart of Africa: Studies on Internal Conflicts.* Nairobi: Academy Science Publishers, pp.103–131. Google Scholar.

Gingyera-Pinycwa, A.G.G., Obong-Oula, Q. (2003). 'The Political "Moods" of Northern Uganda, 1986–96: A Study of Presidential and Parliamentary Elections'. In: Makara, S, Tukahebwa, G.B., Byarugaba, F.E. (eds) *Voting for Democracy in Uganda: Issues in Recent Elections.* Kampala: LDC Publishers, pp.56–89. Google Scholar.

Haberson, J.W. (1994). 'Civil Society and Political Renaissance in Africa'. In: Haberson, W. J, Rothchild, D, Chazan, N. (eds) *Civil Society and State in Africa.* Boulder and London: Lynne Rienner, pp.1–29. Google Scholar.

Harlacher, T., Okot, F.X., Obonyo, C.A. (2006). 'Traditional Ways of Coping in Acholi: Cultural Provisions for Reconciliation and Healing From War. Caritas Gulu Archdiocese'. Google Scholar.

Hearn, J. (1999). 'Foreign Aid, Democratisation and Civil Society in Africa: A Study of South Africa, Ghana and Uganda'. IDS Discussion Paper 368, March. Google Scholar.

Hearn, J. (2001). 'The "Uses and Abuses" of Civil Society in Africa'. *Review of African Political Economy,* 28(87): 43–53. Google Scholar, Cross-reference.

Human Rights Focus (2002). 'Between two Fires: the Plight of Internally Displaced Persons in Northern Uganda. Gulu District, Uganda': *Human Rights Focus.* Google Scholar.

Human Rights Watch (2003). 'Abducted and Abused: Renewed War in Northern Uganda. Report', *Human Rights Watch,*15, (12A) June. Google Scholar.

Human Rights Watch (2005). 'Uprooted and Forgotten: Impunity and Human Rights Abuses in Northern Uganda'. *Report* 17, Human Rights Watch, 12 September. Google Scholar.

Justice and Peace Commission of Archdiocese of Gulu (2002) 'The Arrest ('Capture') of Fathers Tarcicio, Julius and Carlos Rodriguez'. *Justice and Peace News.* 2, 5 (August).Google Scholar.

Justice and Peace Commission of Archdiocese of Gulu. (2007). 'Situation of Human Rights in Mid-northern Uganda. *Justice and Peace News.* 7, 21 (July): 10–11. Google Scholar.

Justice and Reconciliation Project (2008). 'With or Without Peace: Disarmament, Demobilisation and Reintegration in Uganda'. *Field Notes* No. 6, February. Google Scholar.

Kaldor, M. (2003). *Civil Society and Accountability. Journal of Human Development,* 4(1): 5–27. Google Scholar, Cross-reference.

Kalyvas, S. (2001). "New" and "Old" Wars: A Valid Distinction? *World Politics,* 54(1): 99–118. Google Scholar, Cross-reference.

Kimuli, E. (1998). 'Lawyers urge quick end to Kony War'. *New Vision* (Kampala), 14 January: 8. Google Scholar.

Kumar, K. (1993), 'Civil Society: An Inquiry into the Usefulness of an Historical Term'. *The British Journal of Sociology,* 44(3): 375–395. Google Scholar, Cross-reference.

Lamwaka, C. (1996). 'The Civil War and Peace Process in Uganda'. MA Dissertation, University of Bradford, UK. Google Scholar.

Lederach, J. (1995). *Preparing for Peace: Conflict Transformation Across Cultures.* New York: Syracuse University Press. Google Scholar.

Legum, C, ed. (1986–1987). *Africa Contemporary Record* 19: B468–B469; Google Scholar

Lewis, D. (2002). 'Civil Society in African Contexts: Reflections on the Usefulness of a Concept'. *Development and Change* 33(4): 569–586. Google Scholar, Cross-reference.

Low, D.A. (1988) 'The Dislocated Polity'. In: Hansen, H.B., Twaddle, M (eds) *Uganda Now: Between Decay and Development,* London, Athens and Nairobi: James Currey, Ohio University Press and Heinemann Kenya, pp.36–53. Google Scholar.

Manning, C. (2003). 'Local Level Challenges to Post-Conflict Peacebuilding'. *International Peacekeeping'*, 10(3): 25–43. Google Scholar, Cross-reference.

Muhumuza, W. (2010). State-Society Partnership in Poverty Reduction in Uganda. *Eastern Africa Social Science Research Review,* XXVI(1): 1–21. Google Scholar, Cross-reference.

Museveni, Y. (1987a). 'Speech on the Opening of the National Resistance Council Session'. Kampala, Uganda, 7 April. Google Scholar.

Museveni, Y. (1987b). 'Address to the Nation on the Anniversary of Uganda's independence'. Kampala, Uganda, 9 October. Google Scholar.

Museveni, Y. (1992), *What is Africa's Problem?* Kampala: NRM Publications. Google Scholar

National Resistance Movement. (1986), *Ten Point Programme of the NRM.* Kampala: NRM Publications. Google Scholar.

Ochola, M.B. (2004). 'Hope in the Storm: Experience of ARLPI in Conflict Resolution of Northern Uganda Armed Conflict'. Paper presented at the Swedish seminar on northern Uganda organised by the Mission Church of Uppsala, 15 April. Google Scholar.

Omach, P. (2011). 'Understanding Obstacles to Peace in Northern Uganda: Actors, their Interests and Strategies'. In: Baregu, M (ed) *Understanding Obstacles to Peace: Actors, Interests, and Strategies in Africa's Great Lakes Region*. Kampala: Fountain Publishers, pp.271–306. Google Scholar.

Omara-Otunnu, A. (1995). 'The Dynamics of Conflicts in Uganda'. In: Furley, O (ed) *Conflict in Africa*. London: Tauris Publishers. Google Scholar.

Omona, J. (2008). 'Civil Society Intervention in the War-Torn Gulu District in Northern Uganda: Policy Implications for Social Service Delivery'. *Journal of Civil Society*, 4(2): 131–148 Google Scholar, Cross-reference.

Orjuela, C. (2005). 'Civil Society in Civil War: The Case of Sri Lanka'. *Civil War*, 7(2): 120–137. Google Scholar, Cross-reference.

Oywa, R. (1998). 'Removing Obstacles to Peace: The Limitations of Building Peace through Local Level Humanitarian/Economic Development Activities. Address to Kacoke Madit 98', London, 17–19 July 1998. Google Scholar.

Paffenholf, T. Spurk, C. (2006). 'Civil Society Engagement and Peacebuilding. 'Social Development Paper no. 36. Washington, DC: World Bank. Google Scholar.

Pain, D. (1997). 'The Bending of Spears: Producing Consensus for Peace and Development in Northern Uganda'. Report Commissioned by International Alert in partnership with Kacoke Madit, London. Google Scholar.

Paris, R. (2004). *At War's End: Building Peace After Civil War*. Cambridge: Cambridge University Press. Google Scholar, Cross-reference.

Pirouet, M. L. (1991). 'Human Rights Issues in Museveni's Uganda'. In: Hansen, H.B., Twaddle, M (eds) *Changing Uganda*. London, Kampala, Athens and Nairobi: James Currey, Fountain Press, Ohio University Press and Heinemann Kenya, pp.197–209. Google Scholar.

Prunier, G. (2004). 'Rebel Movements and Proxy Warfare: Uganda, Sudan and the Congo 1986–99'. *African Affairs*, 103(412): 359–383. Google Scholar, Cross-reference.

Putman, R. (1993). *Making Democracy Work: Civic Traditions in Modern Italy*. Princeton, NJ: Princeton University Press. Google Scholar.

Ramsbotham, O. Woodhouse, T., Miall, H. (2005). *Contemporary Conflict Resolution: the Prevention, Management and Transformation of Dea*dly *Conflicts*. 2nd ed. Cambridge: Polity. Google Scholar.

Republic of Uganda (1997). 'Report of the Parliamentary Committee on Defense and Internal Affairs on the War in Northern Uganda'. Kampala: Republic of Uganda. Google Scholar.

Rodriguez, C. (2002). 'Acholi Civil Society Initiatives: The Role of the Religious Leaders'. In: Okello, L (ed) *Protracted Conflict, Elusive Peace: Initiatives to End the Violence in Northern Uganda*'. London: Conciliation Resources, pp.58–59. Google Scholar.

Schaefer, C. (2010). 'Local Practices and Normative Frameworks in Peacebuilding'. *International Peacekeeping* 4(17): 499-514. Google Scholar, Cross-reference.

Simonse, S. (1998). 'Steps Towards Peace and Reconciliation in Northern Uganda: An Analysis of Initiatives to End Armed Conflict Between the Government and the Lord's Resistance Army 1987–1998'. Report of a Consultancy Commissioned by Pax Christi Netherlands, The Hague. Google Scholar.

UNICEF (2004). *The State of the World's Children*. Oxford: Oxford University Press. Google Scholar.

United Nations Office for the Coordination of Humanitarian Affairs (UN OCHA) (2000). 'OCHA Senior Advisor on IDPs, Internal Displacement in Uganda: A Review of UN Strategic Coordination, 7 October'. In: *Uganda: Donor Underestimation of Crisis Hinders Response Beyond Adhoc Relief Interventions (2001)*. Global IDP Project. Available at: http://www.idpproject.org. Google Scholar.

United Nations Security Council (2004). 'Press Statement on Northern Uganda by Security Council President', SC/8057 AFR/900. Available at: http://www.un.org/News/Press/docs/2004/sc8057. Google Scholar.

US Department of State (2001). 'Statement on the Designation of the 39 Organisations on the USA Patriot's Act's 'Terrorist Exclusion List'. Available at: http://www.fas.org/irp/world/para/dos120-601.html (accessed on 15 November 2012). Google Scholar.

Van Acker, F. (2004). 'Uganda and the Lord's Resistance Army: The New Order No One Ordered'. *African Affairs*, 103(412): 335–357. Google Scholar, Cross-reference.

World Bank (2006). 'Civil Society and Peacebuilding: Potential, Limitations and Critical Factors', Report No. 36445-GLB, December. Washington, DC: World Bank. Google Scholar.

Woodward, P. (1991). 'Uganda and Southern Sudan 1986–9: New Regimes and Peripheral Politics'. In: Hansen, HB, Twaddle, M (eds) *Changing Uganda: The Dilemmas of Structural Adjustment and Revolutionary Change*. London, Kampala, Athens and Nairobi: James Currey, Fountain Press, Ohio University Press and Heinemann Kenya, pp.178–196. Google Scholar.

14

Civil Society and Land Use Policy in Uganda: The Mabira Forest Case[1]

Patrick Hönig

Abstract

Over the past few years, the Ugandan government has repeatedly initiated proceedings to clear one-fourth of the Mabira natural forest reserve in central Uganda and give the land to a sugar company controlled by a transnational business conglomerate. Each time the government took steps to execute the Mabira project, civil society groups organised large-scale protests that pressurised the government into shelving its plans. The Save Mabira Forest campaign has been widely cited as an example of how sustained protests by civil society groups serve as a corrective of democratic deficits in decision-making processes pertaining to the commons and as a deterrent to profit-driven business schemes hatched in collusion with carefree or corrupt bureaucrats and politicians. However, an in-depth analysis of the campaign suggests that ecological and social justice concerns are mixed up with identity politics and exclusionist agendas. Examining the complex web of interactions between state, big business and civil society in Uganda, this paper sheds light on the multi-layered and often ambiguous role played by non-governmental organisations in post-conflict societies of sub-Saharan Africa.

There is a growing consensus that policy-making on the use of the commons – land, air and water – requires a careful calibration of environmental, developmental and political concerns. However, as Polack and others (2013: 1-7) have noted, large-scale acquisition of land by transnational companies operating in Africa continues to occur with "minimal consultation and transparency". There are significant research gaps in the way long-term effects of land allotment for agro-industrial use are assessed, which in turn leads to less stringent risk assessment. Authors such as Muna Ndulo (2011) have convincingly shown that the adoption of neoliberal policies in aid-dependent

---

[1] Reprinted by kind permission from *Africa Spectrum*, 49, 2/2014, 53-77., German Institute of Global and Area Studies, Institute of African Affairs in co-operation with the Dag Hammarskjöld Foundation Uppsala and Hamburg University Press.

countries of sub-Saharan Africa has created a political climate that allows corporations to push through their agendas, sometimes even at the cost of violating legal standards and human rights. At the same time, there is growing recognition that civil society groups in sub-Saharan Africa have started to assert themselves at the policy-making level and fill a governance void left by states prepared to delegate their responsibilities (Opoku-Mensah, 2008). Against that background, governance of the commons has become an important area in which opposing interests play out and clash.

Pointing to governance as the core problem of dealing with the commons, Elinor Ostrom (1990: 8-18) observes that there is a wide spectrum of opinions. On one side, analysts have argued that effective management of the commons requires long-term strategies that private actors adapting to ever-changing market conditions are ill-equipped to bring to fruition. Ostrom notes that this school of thought sees no alternative to state institutions applying coercive force in governing the commons. Meanwhile, those at the other end of the spectrum claim that it is necessary to eliminate all public control and establish unconditional property rights regimes over divisible common pool resources such as land. The ramifications of the various positions, including Ostrum's own viewpoint that builds on the notion that "many solutions exist to cope with many different problems", will need to be discussed elsewhere. For the purposes of this paper, it will suffice to note that there has been considerable research into developing models of governance in areas of limited statehood, centring on the structural and political conditions in which power is generated and decisions are formed (Risse, 2011). Academic writing has moved beyond binaries pitting state against non-state actors.

Using the Save Mabira Forest (SMF) campaign in Uganda as a case study, this paper seeks to make an empirical contribution to the largely theoretical discussion about the nature of the state and civil society in sub-Saharan Africa and the processes of political decision-making. It will (a) present an account of the Mabira Forest project and the rationale behind it; (b) describe the components and triggers of the Save Mabira Forest campaign; (c) explain the crisis of the state in Uganda; (d) discuss the ramifications of civil society movements; and (e) link the empirical findings to the discourse on governing the commons. The engagement with media reports and scholarly work is balanced by background interviews on the functioning of civil society that I conducted in Uganda and neighbouring countries during field trips in five consecutive years starting in 2008.[2]

The Mabira Forest project

In early 2007, the Ugandan government announced that it would degazette and clear one-quarter of Mabira Central Forest Reserve – the largest nature reserve in Central Uganda – and give the land to the Sugar Corporation of Uganda Ltd (SCOUL), jointly owned by a private investor and the Ugandan state, to cultivate sugarcane. Ugandan

---

2   As the Mabira Forest issue is considered sensitive and there is increasing apprehension about a government clamp-down on critical civil society organisations and media, I have not revealed the identity of my interlocutors in civil society circles.

President Yoweri Museveni justified this decision on the grounds that the country needed to expand its agricultural and industrial sectors, create incentives for foreign direct investment and boost the economy.[3] A letter that the president had allegedly written to MPs of his party was leaked to the press, presumably by his own office. In the letter, the authenticity of which the presidency never confirmed or denied, Museveni gave a threefold explanation for the proposed leasing out of Mabira land. First, he argued that granting land to SCOUL would create jobs. Second, he maintained that the success of the country's economy depended on the Ugandan Asian business community, which had been expelled under Idi Amin and the reinstatement of which had been a central concern of his government from the beginning. Third, he claimed that in order for businesses in Uganda to compete with China, India and other developing countries, they had to lower costs and expand. In the case at hand, forest land had to be given away, according to the president, as no other land was available.[4]

Museveni's line of argument follows a neoliberal logic holding that what is good for business is good for the country. There appears to be no place in his thinking for the concerns of local communities, which are so vital for sustainable development centred on the protection of the commons. Baden and Stroup (1977: 235) sum up the tension resulting from the impossibility of quantifying the value of using the commons for non-extractive purposes as follows: "We know, for example, how much people are willing to sacrifice for a thousand board feet of lumber, but how much would they pay for a day's access to a wilderness area?" The Ugandan government's path dependency explains why it is unwilling to consider leaving Mabira Forest alone, for no other reason than preserving an untouched part of nature.

Countering such criticism, the Ugandan government has argued that the part of Mabira Forest being allocated to private concession either does not belong to the natural forest or belongs to a degraded part of it However, the government has not addressed reports indicating that illegal logging is being carried out alongside the logging for which concession has been granted. In 2012, sources on the ground informed that twenty lorry loads of illegally logged timber were being hauled from Mabira on a weekly basis.[5] Even if the extent of illegal logging is hard to verify independently, it is difficult to deny that it is indeed happening. Satellite images of Mabira Forest, taken periodically from 1972 to 2003, show a significant decrease of forest cover in the area (Lung and Schaab 2008: 28). Any further deforestation is likely to irreparably damage an ecosystem already under stress. Deborah Baranga (2007: 2) claims that uncontrolled exploitation and illegal timber extraction pose a major threat to Mabira Forest, which

---

3   Listing infrastructure development, agricultural production and employment as national priorities, the website of the Ugandan presidency cites a number of model projects; however, there is no mention of the government plans for Mabira Forest. See State House of Uganda, online: <http://www.statehouse.go. ug/national-priorities> (21 March 2014).
4   Felix Osike and Mary Karugaba, Why I Support Mabira Give-Away: Museveni, in: *New Vision*, 18 April 2007, online: <www.newvision.co.ug/news/495386-why-i-support-mabira-give-away-%C3%A2-museveni.html> (21 March 2014).
5   Gerald Tenywa, Mabira Forest Destruction Continues, in: *New Vision*, 9 January 2012, online: <www.newvision.co.ug/news/628233-mabira-forest-destruction-continues.html> (21 March 2014).

is why there is a need to investigate the current activities in the reserve and their effect on its conservation status.

In this section, we have seen that the Ugandan government advocates the handover of Mabira forest land to a private company, a market-oriented tactic. In the next section, we will discuss why civil society organisations (CSOs) are campaigning for a state-driven approach to governing the commons, namely the retention of government control over forest land.

The Save Mabira Forest Campaign

The Save Mabira Forest (SMF) campaign has gained international visibility for opposing the Ugandan government and questioning its stance on governing the commons. The decision to allow SCOUL to take over 7,100 hectares of Mabira Forest met with bitter resistance on the part of a cross-section of public institutions, political actors and CSOs. More awkwardly, even the heads of the National Environment Management Agency (NEMA) and the National Forestry Authority (NFA) rejected the government proposals as ecologically imprudent, arguing that the environmental impact of cutting trees in an area more than twenty times the size of Central Park in Manhattan was likely going to be significant (Price,2007). The NFA executive director, and later the entire board, resigned over the Mabira issue, citing political interference.

The SMF campaign soon turned into a mass mobilisation of unprecedented scale, pitting the Ugandan government against a range of CSOs, international donors, the political opposition, the Buganda kingdom and significant segments of civil society. Museveni eventually shelved his plans for Mabira Forest but put the issue back on the political agenda in August 2011, a few months after winning his fourth term in office and cementing his two-and-a-half-decade-long hold on power. As had happened in 2007, a network of civil society groups launched a campaign for the preservation of Mabira Forest. The campaign gathered momentum when young Ugandans started using social networking sites like Facebook and Twitter to organise, among other things, nature walks in the forest, which, at approximately 50 km from Kampala and 20 km from Jinja, is easy to reach, even by public transport. In September 2011, Mahendra Mehta, the head of Mehta Group, was quoted as saying that he was no longer interested in acquiring part of the Mabira Forest for sugarcane growing.[6] Tensions eased, but the calm again proved deceptive.

At a party retreat in January 2013, without prior indication, Museveni announced that he would follow through on his plans for Mabira. The announcement prompted a swift response from the "Save Mabira Crusade", an umbrella group made up of CSOs, local communities, conservation bodies and public-interest lawyers. Beatrice Anywar, an opposition politician who is perceived as the figurehead of the movement, went on

---

6   John Njoroge, "I'm Not Interested in Mabira: Mehta", in: *Daily Monitor*, 3 September 2011, online: <www.monitor.co.ug/News/National/-/688334/1229602/-/bjs08mz/-/index.html> (21 March 2014).

record saying that the government would not be allowed to divert attention from the challenges the country was facing, and the fight for Mabira Forest would continue.[7]

Ugandan researchers and international observers have interpreted the massive show of support for the anti-deforestation campaign as a sign of growing civil society assertiveness in a country with a history of authoritarian regimes and political repression. Bashir Twesigye (2008: 7) expressed the view that the Mabira advocacy campaign reflected increasing environmental awareness and the determination of the Ugandan people to oppose misguided government policies. In line with liberal streams of analysis, Keith Child (2009: 241) called the SMF campaign a "powerful demonstration" of how civil society movements with a limited agenda may transform themselves into platforms that put forward "more radical demands for democratic accountability". Similarly, Aili Tripp (2010: 105) wrote that the response to the cutting down of trees in Mabira Forest was a showcase of how civil society in sub-Saharan Africa had woken up to the challenges that threaten human survival, notably the protection of the environment.

However, the opposition against the Mabira Forest project is no monolithic bloc. Even though it is widely portrayed as the outcome of concerted action against pro-business land use policies, the SMF campaign is composed of a variety of groups whose mandates overlap and whose interests conflict. The first pillar of the SMF campaign consists of a cluster of environmental groups, which argue that the conversion of forest land into a sugarcane plantation will spell environmental disaster for its adverse effects on biodiversity, fresh water supply, soil fertility and carbon reduction, harming ecotourism in the process.[8] Building on a growing movement for the preservation of forests in Africa, the late Nobel Peace Prize laureate Wangari Maathai argued that participatory tree-planting programmes in developing countries were an "important mechanism to support responsible global warming mitigation efforts" (2009: 257). Moreover, Mabira Forest constitutes an important catchment area and its partial deforestation will further diminish fresh water supplies to Lake Kyoga and the Victoria Nile. Lake Victoria, the biggest water reserve in the Great Lakes region, has already seen a steady decline in water levels over the years, contributing to a hazardous concentration of toxic substances, which in turn has jeopardised the survival of the lake's fishing industry. Any further deforestation will also adversely affect biodiversity in Mabira Forest, which, according to a detailed study by Davenport and others (1996: 4), is home to 71 restricted-range species of birds, butterflies and moths. Furthermore, some environmentalists claim

---

[7] Mercy Nalugo and Solomon Arinaitwe, 'Activists Dare Museveni', in: *Daily Monitor*, 15 January 2013, online: <www.monitor.co.ug/News/National/Mabira--Activists-dare-Museveni/688334/1665636/-/item/1/-/g2s0s0/-/index.html> (21 March 2014).

[8] *Chain Reaction: The National Magazine of Friends of the Earth Australia* (2013), 'Ugandan Activists Regroup to Protect Mabira Forest', 117, 9; *National Association of Professional Environmentalists* (2011), Mabira Petition to President Yoweri Kaguta Museveni of Uganda, online: <www.redd-monitor.org/2011/08/31/can-redd-protect-the-mabira-forest-in-uganda> (21 March 2014); Nature Uganda (2013), 'Mabira Forest Should Not Be Sacrificed for Sugar Production', online: <http://natureuganda.org/save_mabira_campaign.php> (21 March 2014).

that cutting down one-fourth of the Mabira Forest will translate into a loss of USD 316 million worth of UN-certified carbon credit.[9]

The SMF campaign has drawn further support from a range of leftist groups, which oppose international investment in agro-industrial business in developing countries on economic and ideological grounds. According to these groups, the idea that business companies adopt strategies that keep society's best interests in mind has been discredited in light of neo-liberal policies that consider community land as a commodity for sale. Samir Amin (2010), a staunch critic of the Washington consensus, asserts that subjecting land to the "law of the market" uproots people and, contrary to the arguments of supporters of privatisation policies, exacerbates poverty. While the use of forest reserve land for agro-industrial purposes does not in itself lead to displacement, it nevertheless forms part of an economic paradigm that comes to its logical conclusion in what Amin calls the "destruction of the peasant societies", which he believes is a major cause of the pauperisation of the Third World. In a study on the impact that the Mabira project has had on poverty alleviation, Zommers and others (2012: 190-192) conclude that before expanding sugarcane production into forest reserves, the Ugandan government will act responsibly only if it carefully evaluates the importance of ecosystem services to local livelihood, which so far it has failed to do. More generally, Mabira activists may draw support from arguments developed by thinkers such as Rob Gray, who argues that corporations are a force against social justice. The logic behind such thinking is that corporations are pursuing the goal of maximising wealth for shareholders, who, as they are becoming increasingly wealthy, oppose the concept of material redistribution, which lies at the heart of social justice (Gray 2013: 162-163). Therefore, for left-leaning anti-poverty campaigners, Mabira is an open-and-shut case.

The third plank on which the Mabira protest rests is composed of a rainbow coalition of watchdog groups that base their criticism on a variety of concerns, including corruption charges. The Advocates Coalition for Development and Environment (ACODE), for instance, laments that the government has failed to invite offers from Mehta's business competitors or call for tender.[10] The waters are further muddied by the fact that the land deal with Mehta Group is far from transparent. There is no information about how the Ugandan exchequer stands to benefit from the proposed transaction. The media is rife with speculation that once the land deal is complete, the government will part with its 30% stake in SCOUL, for a price, leaving in charge Mehta Group, a business conglomerate that operates in four continents and holds assets in excess of USD 400 million.[11] Unsurprisingly, a recent policy briefing listed

---

9   Mubatsi Asinja Habati, 'Mabira: No Storm in Mehta's Tea Cup', in: *The Independent* (Kampala), 26 August – 1 September 2011, 18-20, online: <www.independent.co.ug/news/news-analysis/4550-mabira-no-storm-in-mehtas-tea-cup> (21 March 2014).

10 Mubatsi Asinja Habati, 'Interview: Museveni Shouldn't Be Mehta Spokesman', in: *The Independent* (Kampala), 26 August – 1 September 2011, 8, online: <www.independent.co.ug/column/interview/4554-museveni-shouldnt-be-mehta-spokesman> (21 March 2014).

11 The Mehta Group website shows SCOUL as already being part of its business assets. See Mehta Group, online: <www.mehtagroup.com> (21 March 2014). In 2012, the news broke that a development

the envisaged sale of forest land in Mabira as one of several examples of how the ruling coalition in Uganda is being bought off by big business (Kjær and Katusiimeh, 2012: 27). In terms of social acceptance, it does not help that SCOUL is the least productive of the three major sugar producers in Uganda and reportedly incurring substantial losses.

The fourth tributary to the SMF campaign is made up by supporters of the Kabaka, the king of Buganda, who believes the forest is part of "Buganda land" and should be preserved in its entirety. It is important to recall that Museveni's capture of power in 1986 is largely seen as the result of his alliance with the Buganda movement, which supported his armed struggle originating in Central Uganda, where many Baganda live. Due to disagreements over the question of "federo", at the core of which lies the restoration of dignity and autonomy to the kingdom of Buganda, apart from administration and ownership of land, the relations between President Museveni and Kabaka Ronald Mutebi II were considered to be "no longer as warm as they used to be" (Mukasa Mutibwa, 2008: 251). That was before the Kabaka was prevented from visiting Kayunga district, located in his kingdom, which led to the Buganda riots in 2009, and the destruction, in mysterious circumstances, of the Kasubi tombs, the burial ground of the Kabaka dynasty and a UNESCO world heritage site, in March 2010. After that it has not been possible for this author to find anyone willing to comment openly on the nature of the relationship between the president and the Kabaka of Buganda. In private conversation, however, observers close to the Buganda movement suggest that Museveni might be using the Mabira Forest issue to show the Kabaka his place, which further raises suspicion about the existence of hidden agendas.

In sum, the SMF campaign draws its significance both from an articulation of a rainbow coalition of civil society voices in a public discourse centred on government action, and from serving as an example of a social movement that breaks with the tradition of party movements, from which the current multi-party system in Uganda has developed. A brief overview of the history of engagement with the idea of the state in the postcolonial world, and the concept of civil society within and around it, will help place the SMF campaign on the matrix of political practices in the governance context of sub-Saharan Africa.

State crisis in Uganda

The Mabira Forest agitation is one of only a handful of political campaigns that have been able to attract interest and support from large segments of the Ugandan public over a period of several years. The success of the SMF campaign, as well as its shortcomings, will not be easily understood unless placed in the context of a debate on the state and its decline in sub-Saharan Africa. After its independence in 1962, Uganda witnessed short-lived coalition governments, single-party rule, Idi Amin's tyranny and a series of wars that ended with the takeover of power by Museveni and his National Resistance

---

finance institution had agreed a USD 23 million loan to SCOUL to help boost the company's performance. For details, see: Trade Finance (2012), 'Proparco Agrees Uganda Sugar Loan', 15, 6, 172.

Army in 1986. Some authors have described the Uganda of the 1990s as a country that, unlike the Democratic Republic of the Congo, had pulled itself back from the brink of a "failed state" and managed to break through the logic of violent conflict to initiate processes of "negotiation and rebuilding" (Bayart et al., 1999: 5; Crawford, 2004: 47). Such a reading of Ugandan history tends to downplay the disastrous consequences of the civil war of the 1980s and the significant fallout from the subsequent war in northern Uganda that pitted troops loyal to the government against the Holy Spirit Movement led by Alice Lakwena and, later, the Lord's Resistance Army (LRA) under suspected war criminal Joseph Kony. Moses Khisa (2013: 201) argues that what gave rise to the current conception of the state in Uganda can be traced to the trauma of prolonged tyranny and civil war that resulted, first, in a pronounced urge for minimum stability and personal security among the population at large, and, second, in a strong belief among the ruling elites that militaristic methods of managing society will pay off.

Soon after taking over power, Museveni was faced with a military threat to his leadership and a budget crisis exacerbated by increasing military expenditures. He responded by performing a U-turn from nonaligned rhetoric and, under pressure from the Bretton Woods institutions, embraced neoliberal reforms through structural adjustment programmes. Uganda adopted policies of market liberalisation, privatisation and deregulation, and started to downsize its civil service and roll back the state generally. The implementation of such measures required a political rigidity that contradicted the call for 'liberalisation' in any sense other than economic and flew in the face of civil society's requests for democratic consultation and accountability. An authoritarian streak soon accompanied Uganda's transition to free-market politics (Crawford, 2004: 42; Olukoshi, 2007: 18). Museveni's acceptance of the neoliberal straightjacket imposed by the Washington Consensus made him a regional 'donor darling' and gave him considerable leeway to consolidate his power at the expense of competitive politics. This may well have reinforced his 'personalistic politics' and stifled the emergence of a legitimate opposition strong enough to challenge him in free and fair elections (Hesselbein et al., 2006: 30; Mamdani, 1994: 557). The results are plain to see. The 2006 presidential elections were reduced to a contest between Museveni and his main rival Kizza Besigye. Upon his return to Uganda from exile in 2005, Besigye had first been held on charges of treason and rape, then, when he moved to apply for bail, on charges of terrorism (Oloka-Onyango, 2006: 43). Although Besigye eventually stood in the elections, the impact of the allegations against him probably doused his chances of winning before his campaign could take off.

In the lead-up to presidential elections in 2011, Sabiti Makara (2010: 91) warned that there was little to indicate a shift from the deeply-rooted "reluctance to promote and deepen multiparty democracy" in Uganda. As an example, Makara cited the role of the Electoral Commission, which he said was widely suspected to be catering to the wishes of the ruling party. Others echoed such scepticism about the democratic credentials of the Ugandan polity. Olive Kobusingye (2010: 193) stated that Uganda was committed to "perpetual electioneering". While acknowledging that elections were welcomed with great excitement when the National Resistance Movement came to power, she argued that the sheen of elections had worn off over time. In her view, elections can no longer be considered a means of choosing a leader of the people's choice.[12] Concern over securitisation, de-politicisation and erosion of democratic procedures is routinely expressed in conversations about the state of affairs in Uganda.

Ugandan civil society groups, such as Advocates Coalition for Development and Environment and Human Rights Network Uganda, have been consistent in their criticism of a wide range of government policies. Human Rights Watch (2010, 2011) published a report on intimidation and harassment of the media in Uganda, followed by another on the practice of torture and illegal detention by Uganda's Rapid Response Unit. On the 2011 elections, the European Union Election Observation Mission (2011: 5-7) noted that the electoral process had been "marred by avoidable administrative and logistical failures", leading to the disenfranchisement of an "unacceptable number of Ugandan citizens".[13] Emboldened by the 2011 election results, Museveni started clamping down on the political opposition with renewed vigour. Tellingly, the massive police crackdown on the "walk-to-work" campaign, which the political opposition had organised in Kampala to protest rising living expenses, coincided with the democratic uprising in a variety of capitals in North Africa and West Asia.

Before long, the debate had focused on whether Uganda could be described as a neopatrimonial state, which Paul Williams (2011: 56) has characterised as hybrid, unstable and shot through with streaks of authoritarianism. However, the limitations of the neopatrimonial label, a universal catch-all classification, soon became apparent. State features differ from region to region, and it cannot be said that every state that is hybrid is unstable or that every state that is unstable is authoritarian in nature. Against that background, Erdmann and Engel (2007: 104-105) argue that neopatrimonialism may offer a useful lens through which to conceptualise the state, as long as the definition is not so broad that it loses all meaning. Providing an in-depth analysis of the literature, they consider the "invasion" of informal politics and personal relations into the formal structures of legal-rational reasoning as the core element of the neopatrimonial state. In other words, some features of the formal bureaucratic Weberian state continue to function, while others are being eroded and fall prey to competing networks of informal power. Similarly, Daniel Bach (2012: 35, 44) observes that the concept of neopatrimonial rule has become equated with predatory, anti-developmental and personalised power, while regulated forms of power have been overlooked or side-tracked. It makes sense to view the essence of neopatrimonialism not in the usurping by individuals of power assigned to constitutional organs, but in the mixing of competing layers of decision-making, formal and informal, resulting in erratic functioning of state institutions and

---

12 Olive Kobusingye being the sister of opposition leader Kizza Besigye does not in itself detract from the quality of her analysis.
13 The findings of the mission include violation of the principle of equality of the vote, "inadequate safeguards against fraud" in the drawing up of a national voter register, "distribution of money and gifts by candidates, especially from the ruling party", significantly greater access of candidates of the ruling party to the media, and a lack of "police impartiality".

clashes of power formations with unpredictable outcomes. The way decisions on the Mabira Forest have been made and revoked in a haphazard and incoherent way, without any procedures being followed, fits this definition of neopatrimonialism.

Meanwhile, the launch of structural adjustment programmes devised by Bretton Woods institutions since the 1980s has been accompanied by talk of the informal state, the predatory state, the shadow state or even the vampire state. According to Khisa (2013: 212), Uganda presents an interesting departure from the phenomenon of shadow states that rely on clandestine economy networks amidst collapsing state institutions. Khisa argues that the defining feature of the state in Uganda is donorisation, the result of which is the emergence of a CSO economy fuelled by Western aid and loans. While the state is stripped of many of its core functions, CSOs are being given extensive mandates to implement education, infrastructure, environment protection and health care programmes. Such analysis ties in with left-leaning criticism of the dismantling of the state by free market forces. Achille Mbembe (2001: 74-75) recalls that the "African crisis" of the 1980s originated from the state placing excessive demands on the economy. Based on the argument that recovery from such crisis depended on strengthening free market forces, measures were put in place to restrict state intervention in the economy without introducing safeguards in key sectors such as health, education and protection of the environment. Predictably, the results were not all positive. For example, Uganda's draconian "anti-homosexuality act", which has received strong support from evangelist groups based in the United States, shows that pro-business strategies in line with policies formulated by Bretton Woods institutions do not necessarily translate into a liberal vision for society.[14] The changing dynamics in the interaction of state and civil society actors will be at the centre of the following section.

Ascendency of civil society

One section of the literature believes that the only way to fix the broken state, neopatrimonial or otherwise, is to develop strategies to stop the erosion of state legitimacy, preferably by involving informal CSO coalitions, watchdog groups and informed citizens. Informed citizens and watchdog groups formed by such citizens are regarded as an embattled but important safeguard for democratic institution-building in Uganda, a corrective to policies devised by authoritarian regimes (Kasfir, 1999). Recalling that none of Africa's newly established multi-party regimes have abandoned presidential for parliamentary rule, Nicolas van de Walle (2012: 121) considers the curtailing of presidential prerogatives through mechanisms of vertical and horizontal accountability to essentially be a task incumbent on democratic movements emerging from authoritarian traditions. Broadening the frame of analysis beyond national borders, Andreas Godsäter (2013: 68) asserts that, for the sake of legitimate and effective resource governance, African governments will need to engage with wider

---

14 Sexual Minorities Uganda, a Kampala-based NGO, has documented a sharp rise in violence, threats and discriminatory practices against lesbian, gay, bisexual, transgender and intersex people following the passage of the act in December 2013.

social layers and popular forces within civil society, enhance cooperation at the regional level, and adopt environmental rules and regulations governing cross-border relations. From an international relations perspective, Ulrich Beck (1999: 17) compares civil society movements to a "world party" that places "globality at the heart of political imagination, action and organisation" and appeals "to human values and traditions in every culture and religion". Beck also feels that naming-and shaming campaigns by civil society organisations are promising tools to persuade corporations to comply with international law and corporate social responsibility schemes.

However, mass protest and anti-government agitation are easily confused with democratic resilience and political vision. Explaining the uniformly positive portrayal of African civil society in northern policymaking circles as a product of cultural bias, Thomas Kelley (2011: 993-994) points out that people and institutions in the Global North typically picture African non-governmental organisations (NGOs) as spaces of democratic decision-making that will pass rights-based resolutions advancing "environmental justice, freedom of expression, due process, and the rule of law", when in fact many of these NGOs have visions of a just society diverging radically from those nurtured by actors in northern countries. Taking a similarly sober position on the capacity or willingness of CSOs to advance liberal agendas, Hovil and Okello (2011: 336) remind us that civil society groups, like state agents, are susceptible to usurping authority that they cannot legitimately claim and act as "anticorruption czars", while replicating the "behaviour of despots". Considering CSOs as the last line of defence against state suppression and the guardian angels of constitutional values – irrespective of their sometimes contradictory views and ideological aberrations – makes it all the more difficult to detect where they contradict what they preach and operate on the same lack of internal democracy, transparency and gender equality as the state actors they find reason to criticise.

Mindful of the political economy of civil society activity, another segment of the literature takes a more critical approach and makes a point of analysing the organisational capacity of watchdog groups to live up to their mission statements, measuring rhetoric against performance. Playing out in variations, these observers argue that CSOs in semi-authoritarian sub-Saharan African countries may be well-meaning but are confused about their mandate, alienated from their constituencies, given to believing in the power of just talking, weakened by infighting and coopted by either the state or international donors (Barr et al., 2005: 664-665; Omona and Mukuye, 2013; Opoku-Mensah, 2008: 80-83; Tripp 2010: 30). Shedding light on the structural constraints of civil society activism, Miller and others (2013: 136) have noted that CSOs are permanently trapped between "a desire to enhance community well-being and an inability to shape the context in which to do so". Even where a *contentious* civil society has emerged – "strong, well networked and capable of proposal as well as protest" – independent decision-making is constantly imperilled by a shortage of funds and the need for CSOs to operate in a national context governed by laws and regulations that have a bearing on their activities (ibid. 141-143). This seam of research offers explanations for why civil society movements, particularly in Africa, tend to be eclectic and short-lived; however, it fails to explain why protests erupt when they do and why people give their time and money to campaigns when they have no reassurance that they will receive anything in return.

A third strand of analysis, following a neo-realist line of reasoning, is sceptical of the value of democratic governance and the role of civil society within it. Michael Ignatieff (2005: 69) claims that four decades of "post-colonial misrule" in sub-Saharan Africa have proven that Africans themselves do not know what kind of governance works for them. He adds that the regimes that have made the "best fist of a difficult situation" have been those in countries such as Uganda, which are "neither liberal nor democratic but simply have relatively farsighted and honest, if authoritarian, leadership". Alex Thomson (2010: 232) describes a noticeable trend towards chaos and disintegration of existing power structures as the flipside of civil society ascendancy in the post-colonial African state. This is the context in which we need to place Dambisa Moyo's controversial call for a "decisive benevolent dictator" in aid-dependent Africa, where leaderships demand nothing from the public at large and are not required to give anything in return (Moyo, 2010 [2009]: 42). However, if solutions are sought from centralised decision-making, rather than the building of consensus around diverse voices, civil society groups will hardly be considered as significant, or even useful, players in the larger scheme of things. Buying into this logic, the Ugandan government maintains that CSOs are not to be trusted because they are funded by "the West" and also because they are opposition parties in disguise, bent on defaming the country (Human Rights Watch, 2012: 20).

The next section examines the question of how the racial overtones of the agitation impact the conceptualisation of civil society in Uganda and the framing of the debate on Mabira Forest.

Governing the commons

As discussed earlier, the Mabira Forest movement does not result from a single concern shared by all. Rather, it is fed by a wide range of groups with agendas as complex and multi-layered as Ugandan society itself. Cutting across debates on development, social justice and environmental protection, the Mabira Forest case serves as a magnifying glass under which an array of problems pertaining to resource management come into focus. Whether the SMF campaign is cited as an example of civil society resistance to government folly or interference in sound policymaking depends largely on the criteria used to evaluate the agitation on its merits. Fischlin and Nandorfy (2012: 89) argue that in devising regimes governing the commons, individual rights, such as the right to property, need to be balanced against "community rights"; in other words, the "rights of community commons to exist and be protected". At the heart of such a balancing test lies a re-orientation towards an understanding of community and rights centring on "interests shaped by the most basic practices that guarantee sustainable life", such as food, water, shelter and respect for difference. The conceptual connection of resource governance and community-building explains the importance of addressing the racial overtones of the SMF campaign.

From its early days, the Save Mabira agitation provided cover for free-riders who launched attacks on Ugandan Asians on the rationale that they were to be collectively held responsible for the business activities of the Indian-owned Mehta group, a transnational corporation that holds the majority stake in SCOUL. In response to what came to be known as the "Mabira riots", Museveni declared that his decision to allocate part of the Mabira Forest to SCOUL was non-negotiable. However, the conclusions he drew from the outbreak of violence were unconvincing. Apart from holding a meeting with the Ugandan Asian community in Kampala, in which he reassured them of government protection, Museveni struck a clearly populist chord, blaming the police for allowing the demonstration that had led to the casualties, announcing tax breaks for investors and calling for tougher laws on the media.[15] The organisers of the Mabira protests, on the other hand, claimed their democratic right to assemble freely and peacefully but failed to decisively distance themselves from the violence against Ugandan Asians and draw a line between environmental concern and racism.

The repeated outbreak of violence targeting Ugandan Asians suggests that, under the guise of ecological and social justice concerns, a band of operators are exploiting popular anxieties and employing divisive tactics for political gain. Tensions along ethnic lines had built up gradually under colonial rule and were deliberately exploited by Idi Amin during his reign of terror from 1971 to 1979. As early as 1972, Amin launched an expropriation and expulsion campaign against Asian Ugandans on the grounds that they were "sabotaging Uganda's economy and encouraging corruption" (Manby, 2009: 54, 96). Irreconcilable as his policies were with international human rights standards, it is perhaps important to note that the anti-Asian resentment and the expropriation of their assets and businesses was a safe card to play for Amin as it met with the approval of significant segments of both the Baganda and the increasingly influential Nubi-Muslim trading communities who saw the Asian traders as rivals (Hansen, 2013: 91).

In the 1990s, President Museveni started encouraging foreign investment and, yielding to pressure from donor countries, asked Ugandan Asians to return and repossess their property. The *Economist* wrote in 1995 that Asians (5,000 lived in Uganda at the time, compared to 70,000 before the expulsion, 23,000 of whom were Ugandan citizens) had not lost their image as "cut-throat businessmen", adding that their "influence in Uganda stretched far beyond their numbers" (*The Economist* 1995). The Mehta family, which owns the business conglomerate that carries its name, had been forced to leave the country in the 1970s and returned only in the 1990s to reclaim its property. Meanwhile, Museveni's public remarks about his personal investment priorities have done little to ease ethnic tensions. In an interview with the *New African*, Museveni said that foreign investors were more useful to the country than some of its domestic ones because they created jobs, paid taxes, bought raw materials and paid

---

15 Felix Osike, 'Museveni Assures Asians', in: *New Vision*, 19 April 2007, online: <www.newvision.co.ug/news/495293-museveni-assures-asians.html> (21 March 2014).

for the electricity they used.[16] Such condescension brings back images of the colonial times. Ugandans have not forgotten that it was a hallmark of the colonial state to introduce crops, decide on the colony's trading partners and clear forests "without any consideration to environmental or religious importance" (Mueni wa Muiu, 2010: 1314).

Given the country's record of violence against Ugandan Asians, it is somewhat surprising that academic writing has tended to ignore the campaign's racial undercurrents and the threats they pose for the Ugandan polity as a whole. Mahmood Mamdani (2007), himself a Ugandan of Asian descent, wrote that what had made the leasing of land so explosive was the collusion between an increasingly unaccountable president who treated the country as his private preserve, and a tycoon who claimed to be doing the country a favour while lining his own pockets. Mamdani maintained that the political opposition had taken advantage of the situation but had not created the issue, omitting any mention of actors who might have a vested interest in escalating ethnic tensions in Ugandan society. Bashir Twesigye (2008: 6) stated that protesters had turned on people of Indian origin "to demonstrate their disapproval of the Indian owners of Mehta" as if this was an excuse for the violence that unfolded. Keith Child (2009: 251-253) wrote that the attacks on Ugandan Asians of April 2007 had drawn condemnation from many of the civil society groups that helped organise it, which is why analysis of the cause of the agitation and its consequences should be kept separate. However, if we accept Child's argument that the Mabira land deal confirms increasing domination of the country's economic assets by Indian-controlled companies, it seems hard to disassociate the consequences of the agitation from the ill will towards Ugandan Asians that Child claims is entrenched in Ugandan society. It is perhaps the desire to brand the SMF campaign as a "symbol of civil society efficacy" that makes it so difficult to recognise its racial undercurrents. Our analysis of the SMF campaign shows that while civil society movements address people's concerns in rhetoric, they may in fact contribute to discursive practices that are rooted in prejudice and aimed at divisive politics along ethnic lines. The Save Mabira agitation has potential as a building block for participatory democracy only if it owns up to the acts of injustice and the crimes perpetrated in its name.

Outlook

The Mabira Forest issue could move in one of several directions. One strand of analysis emphasises that, through the results of the 2011 parliamentary elections, a challenge has arisen to Museveni in the form of a "record number" of parliamentarians belonging to the same party as the president but being considerably younger than him (Vokes, 2012: 311-312). The argument goes that this young generation of politicians thrives on local support and has challenged the president on a number of counts, from ministerial appointments and the draft anti-bail Bill (presumably targeting members

---

16 *New African*, President Museveni: "Development Is the Destination", 1 October 2012, 8, online: <www.newafricanmagazine.com/president-museveni-development-is-the-destination> (21 March 2014).

of the opposition and dissidents) to the decision to sacrifice part of Mabira Forest for a sugarcane plantation. The International Crisis Group (2012: 33) considers opposition to the Mabira project – even from MPs belonging to the National Resistance Movement, Museveni's own political party – as one of several promising signs for the preparedness of parliamentary democracy to assert its constitutional powers.

Off the record, however, many analysts admit that they are sceptical about the longevity of the SMF campaign, given its heterogeneity and lack of vision. They predict that the resistance from a cross-section of political dissidents and civil society groups will eventually wane, allowing Museveni and his inner circle to prevail with their plans for Mabira Forest. It has not been lost on observers that Ugandan government rhetoric no longer distinguishes between lawful and unlawful dissent on constitutional grounds, but "loyal and disloyal opposition", as measured by the State House, the seat of the president.[17] Government interference is particularly grave in scenarios where CSOs operate in sensitive areas or pronounce views on large-scale investment projects such as the one planned for Mabira. In a report on the conditions of NGO work in Uganda, Human Rights Watch (2012: 27) observes that organisations carrying out research, advocacy, and citizen education on environmental issues have faced "increasing obstructions" from the government in the form of threats of deregistration, accusations of sabotaging government programmes, and arrest.

There are also indications that government agencies are being streamlined on controversial issues. Neither the National Environment Management Agency nor the National Forestry Authority makes any reference to the Mabira issue on their respective websites, which is curious given that both initially positioned themselves against the leasing out of forest land to SCOUL. It is clear, therefore, that the Ugandan government has adopted a flexible approach to handling the Mabira Forest case, yielding to pressure when it became too strong and pushing for the leasing out of land when it felt that it was in a politically advantageous position to do so and the campaign had started to come undone. However, even if Museveni gives up on his plans for Mabira Forest, the divisive tone used by all stakeholders has introduced a toxic element into the discourse on development that will take time to diminish.

Conclusions

This paper has attempted to show that since the SMF campaign was launched in 2007 in response to plans of the Ugandan government to hand over one-fourth of the forest to a sugar company for cultivation of sugarcane, it has drawn strength from a network of loosely connected civil society groups. Contrary to popular perception, the SMF campaign does not constitute a continuous and sustained movement. Instead, it must be understood as a string of activist spells, each provoked by a perceived need to respond to government initiatives to push the agenda on Mabira.

---

17 The distinction between loyal and disloyal opposition was pointed out to the author in an informal meeting with a high-ranking government official working in the presidential office.

The paper cites evidence indicating that the government's case in support of the Mabira Forest project is weak in terms of substance. The lack of available data on the impact of agro-industrial investment in Mabira is matched by a lack of risk assessment in the planning phase. In light of the documentation gap and the resulting margin of error in assessing the impact of the proposed development project in Mabira Forest, the case for abandoning the plans of clearing one-fourth of the forest seems compelling. Even though a solution has remained elusive, the SMF campaign is a significant achievement, given the fact that President Museveni has used tremendous political capital to bulldoze an array of dissenting voices, not on policy grounds, but by way of declaring a personal "war on sugar".

The paper also challenges the uncritical appraisal of civil society groups in sub-Saharan Africa as democratic checks to neopatrimonial regimes. Although it is popular strategy among activists to paint political controversies with a broad brush, the portrayal of land use issues as a fight between good and evil creates binaries that are easily exploitable for purposes of identity politics. Irrespective of whether the Mabira Forest dispute sees business interests or community concerns prevail, the way in which racial stereotypes were played up in the campaign reveals a disquieting trend towards fragmentation of Ugandan society. In the final analysis, the SMF campaign and its ugly underbelly lend credence to claims for a widening and deepening of civil society engagement, but also to calls for a critical reflection of what drives activism, within local communities and across national borders. For civic activism to become an asset for democratic governance of the commons, however problematic the term, it will need to focus not only on a campaign agenda but also on a vision for an inclusive society.

References

Amin, Samir (2010). 'Millennium Development Goals: A Critique from the South', in: *Pambazuka News*, 498, online: <www.pambazuka.org/en/category/features/67326> (21 March 2014).

Anderson, David M., and Adrian J. Browne (2011), The Politics of Oil in Eastern Africa, in: *Journal of Eastern African Studies*, 5, 2, 369-410.

Bach, Daniel C. (2012), 'Patrimonialism and Neopatrimonialism: Comparative Receptions and Transcriptions', in: Daniel C. Bach and Mamoudou Gazibo (eds), *Neopatrimonialism in Africa and Beyond*, London and New York: Routledge, 25-45.

Baden, John, and Richard Stroup (1977), 'Property Rights, Environmental Quality, and the Management of National Forests', in: Garrett Hardin and John Baden (eds), *Managing the Commons*, San Francisco: W. H. Freeman, 229-240.

Baranga, Deborah (2007), 'Observations on Resource Use in Mabira Forest Reserve, Uganda', in: *African Journal of Ecology*, 45 (Suppl. 1), 2-6.

Barr, Abigail, Marcel Fafchamps and Trudy Owens (2005), 'The Governance of Non-Governmental Organisations in Uganda', in: *World Development*, 33, 4, 657-679.

Bayart, Jean-François, Stephen Ellis and Béatrice Hibou (1999), 'From Kleptocracy to the Felonious State?' in: Jean-François Bayart, Stephen Ellis and Béatrice Hibou (eds), *The Criminalization of the State in Africa*, Oxford: James Currey; Bloomington: Indiana University Press, 1-31.

Beck, Ulrich (1999), *World Risk Society*, Cambridge and Malden: Polity Press.

Child, Keith (2009), 'Civil Society in Uganda: The Struggle to Save the Mabira Forest Reserve', in: *Journal of Eastern African Studies*, 3, 2, 240-258.

Davenport, Tim, Peter Howard and Michael Baltzer (1996), 'Mabira Forest Reserve: Biodiversity Report', Kampala: Government of Uganda, Forest Department.

Erdmann, Gero, and Ulf Engel (2007), 'Neopatrimonialism Reconsidered: Critical Review and Elaboration of an Elusive Concept', in: *Commonwealth & Comparative Politics*, 45, 1, 95-119.

European Union Election Observation Mission (2011), 'Final Report on the Uganda General Elections', online: <www.eueom.eu/files/pressreleases/english/eueom_uganda2011_final_report_en.pdf> (21 March 2014).

Fischlin, Daniel, and Martha Nandorfy (2012), *The Community of Rights – The Rights of Community*, Montreal, New York and London: Black Rose Books.

Godsäter, Andreas (2013), 'Regional Environmental Governance in the Lake Victoria Region: The Role of Civil Society', in: *African Studies*, 72, 1, 64-85.

Gray, Rob (2013), 'Accountability, Sustainability and the World's Largest Corporations: Of CSR, Chimeras, Oxymorons and Tautologies', in: Kathryn Haynes, Alan Murray and Jesse Dillard (eds), *Corporate Social Responsibility: A Research Handbook*, London and New York: Routledge, 151-166.

Hansen, Holger Bernt (2013), 'Uganda in the 1970s: A Decade of Paradoxes and Ambiguities', in: *Journal of Eastern African Studies*, 7, 1, 83-103.

Hesselbein, Gabi, Frederick Golooba-Mutebi and James Putzel (2006), 'Economic and Political Foundations of State-Making in Africa: Understanding State Reconstruction', Crisis States Research Centre Working Papers, 2, London: Crisis States Reseach Centre.

Hovil, Lucy, and Moses Chrispus Okello (2011), 'Editorial Note, in: *International Journal of Transitional Justice*', special issue: *Civil Society, Social Movements and Transitional Justice*, 5, 3, 333-344.

Human Rights Watch (2010), 'A Media Minefield: Increased Threats to Freedom of Expression in Uganda', New York.

Human Rights Watch (2011), 'Violence Instead of Vigilance: Torture and Illegal Detention by Uganda's Rapid Response Unit', New York.

Human Rights Watch (2012), 'Curtailing Criticism: Intimidation and Obstruction of Civi Society in Uganda', New York.

Ignatieff, Michael (2005), 'Human Rights, Power and the State', in: Simon Chesterman, Michael Ignatieff and Ramesh Thakur (eds), *Making States Work: State Failure and the Crisis of Governance*, Tokyo, New York and Paris: United Nations University Press, 59-75.

International Crisis Group (2012), 'Uganda: No Resolution to Growing Tensions', *Africa Report*, 187, Brussels.

Kasfir, Nelson (1999), 'Démocratie de "Mouvement", Légitimité et Pouvoir en Ouganda', in: *Politique Africaine*, 75, 20-42.

Kelley, Thomas (2011), 'Wait! That's Not What We Meant by Civil Society! Questioning the NGO Orthodoxy in West Africa', in: *Brooklyn Journal of International Law*, 36, 3, 993- 1010.

Khisa, Moses (2013), 'The Making of the "Informal State" in Uganda', in: *Africa Development*, 38, 1&2, 191-226.

Kjær, Anne Mette, and Mesharch Katusiimeh (2012), 'Growing But Not Transforming: Fragmented Ruling Coalitions and Economic Developments in Uganda', DIIS Working Papers, 7, Copenhagen: Danish Institute for International Studies.

Kobusingye, Olive (2010), *The Correct Line? Uganda under Museveni*, London: AuthorHouse.

Lung, Tobias, and Gertrud Schaab (2008), 'Land Cover Change for Mabira Forest and Budongo Forest in Uganda: Results of Processing Landsat Satellite Imagery Time Series, 1972-2003', Karlsruhe: Karlsruhe University of Applied Sciences.

Maathai, Wangari (2009), *The Challenge for Africa: A New Vision*, London: William Heinemann.

Makara, Sabiti (2010), 'Deepening Democracy through Multipartyism: The Bumpy Road to Uganda's 2011 Elections', in: *Africa Spectrum*, 45, 2, 81-94.

Mamdani, Mahmood (1994), 'Pluralism and the Right of Association', in: Mahmood Mamdani and Joe Oloka-Onyango (eds), *Uganda: Studies in Living Conditions, Popular Movements, and Constitutionalism*, Kampala: JEP Books, 519-563.

Mamdani, Mahmood (2007), 'The Asian Question Again: A Reflection', in: *Pambazuka News*, 303, online: <www.pambazuka.org/en/category/comment/41273> (21 March 2014).

Manby, Bronwen (2009), *Struggles for Citizenship in Africa*, London and New York: Zed Books.

Mbembe, Achille (2001), *On the Postcolony*, Berkeley, Los Angeles and London: University of California Press.

Miller, Chris, Marilyn Taylor and Joanna Howard (2013), 'Surviving the "Civil Society Dilemma": Critical Factors in Shaping the Behaviour of Non-Governmental Actors', in: Jude Howell (ed.), *Non-Governmental Public Action and Social Justice*, Basingstoke and New York: Palgrave Macmillan, 136-158.

Moyo, Dambisa (2010) [2009], *Dead Aid: Why Aid is Not Working and How There is Another Way for Africa*, London: Penguin Books.

Mukasa Mutibwa, Phares (2008), *The Buganda Factor in Uganda Politics*, Kampala: Fountain Publishers.

Ndulo, Muna (2011), 'From Constitutional Protections to Oversight Mechanisms', in: Chandra Lekha Sriram, Olga Martin-Ortega and Johanna Herman (eds), *Peacebuilding and Rule of Law in Africa: Just Peace?*, London and New York: Routledge, 88-108.

Oloka-Onyango, Joe (2006), 'Criminal Justice, the Courts and Human Rights in Contemporary Uganda: A Perspective Analysis', in: *Makerere Law Journal*, 1, 1, 22-53.

Olukoshi, Adebayo (2007), 'Assessing Africa's New Governance', in: Joe Oloka-Onyango and Nansozi K. Muwanga (eds), *Debating Form and Substance in Africa's New Governance Models*, Kampala: Fountain Publishers, 1-25.

Omona, Julius, and Ronard Mukuye (2013), 'Problems of Credibility of NGOs in Uganda: Implications for Theory and Practice', in: *Voluntas*, 24, 2, 311-334.

Opoku-Mensah, Paul (2008), 'The State of Civil Society in Sub-Saharan Africa', in: V. Finn Heinrich and Lorenzo Fioramonti (eds), *CIVICUS Global Survey of the State of Civil Society*, 2nd volume, Bloomfield: Kumarian Press, 75-90.

Ostrom, Elinor (1990), *Governing the Commons: The Evolution of Institutions for Collective Action*, Cambridge and New York: Cambridge University Press.

Polack, Emily, Lorenzo Cotula and Muriel Côte (2013), *Accountability in Africa's Land Rush: What Role for Legal Empowerment?*, London: International Institute for Environment and Development.

Price, Stuart (2007), 'Storm over Plans to Clear Uganda Rainforest', in: *African Business*, 331, 22.

Risse, Thomas (ed.) (2011), *Governance without a State? Policies and Politics in Areas of Limited Statehood*, New York and Chichester: Columbia University Press.

The Economist (1995), 'A Mixed Welcome for Uganda's Asians', 336, 7922, 42.

Thomson, Alex (2010), *An Introduction to African Politics*, 3rd edition, London and New York: Routledge.

Tripp, Aili Mari (2010), *Museveni's Uganda: Paradoxes of Power in a Hybrid Regime*, Boulder and London: Lynne Rienner Publishers.

Twesigye, Bashir (2008), 'Lessons from Citizen Activism in Uganda: Saving Mabira Forest', in: *SAIIA Occasional Papers*, 7, Johannesburg: South African Institute of International Affairs.

Van de Walle, Nicolas (2012), 'The Path from Neopatrimonialism: Democracy and Clientelism in Africa Today', in: Daniel C. Bach and Mamoudou Gazibo (eds), *Neopatrimonialism in Africa and Beyond*, London and New York: Routledge, 111-123.

Vokes, Richard (2012), 'The Politics of Oil in Uganda', in: *African Affairs*, 111, 443, 303-314.

Wa Muiu, Mueni (2010), 'Colonial and Postcolonial State and Development in Africa', in: *Social Research: An International Quarterly*, 77, 4, 1311-1338.

Williams, Paul, D. (2011), *War and Conflict in Africa*, Cambridge and Malden: Polity Press.

Young, Crawford (2004), 'The End of the Post-Colonial State in Africa?: Reflections on Changing African Political Dynamics', in: *African Affairs*, 103, 23-49.

Zommers, Zinta A., Paul J. Johnson and David W. Macdonald (2012), 'Biofuels Bonanza? Sugarcane Production and Poverty in Villages Surrounding Budongo Forest, Uganda', in: *Journal of Eastern African Studies*, 6, 2, 177-195.

SECTION V
The State and Civil Society

15

Ugandan Civil Society in the Policy Process: Challenging Orthodox Narratives[1]

Karen Brock

Abstract

The author examines here the participation of civil society organisations as actors in the poverty reduction policy process. She notes that the quality and effect of this participation is shaped not only by the preferences of international development actors, but by the historically situated dynamics of politics and power, which mediate the role of state and civil society actors. The article discusses some of the assumptions and contradictions implicit in the application of external narratives about civil society to Uganda, such as its being distinct from the state, 'addressing poverty' or providing 'voice' for 'empowered citizens' and the limited extent to which these hold true, thus revealing a disconnection between rhetorical public statements and political realities.

The article reviews the dynamics of the wide range of spaces in the policy process which are occupied by civil society actors. It suggests that civil society actors are largely reactive to resources offered for a particular range of activities and functions. This in turn limits their capacity to develop autonomous agendas and raises questions about where their accountability lies. At the lower levels, a fundamental shift in the understanding of citizenship would be required, to transform ordinary people into active, engaged participants in the policy process, rather than distanced and excluded clients of an inequitable system of resource distribution controlled by distant, powerful actors.

The author concludes that a challenge faced by the range of development actors in Uganda is to recognise not only the diversity contained within 'civil society', but to acknowledge that the spaces in which CSO participation is enacted frequently limit the possibilities for developing accountability. Designing and implementing policy according to external narratives about poverty reduction produces a disconnection between what is meant to happen and what does happen. The orthodox framing of civil society actors needs to be critically questioned, as many of its key assumptions do not reflect the lived realities of Ugandans.

---

1 Reprinted from K. Brock, R. McGee and J. Gaventa (eds), *Unpacking Policy – Knowledge, Actors and Spaces in Poverty Reduction in Uganda and Nigeria*, Fountain Publishers, Kampala, 2004.

Introduction

The rise of civil society in development narrative and practice is an indicator of broader shifts in the way that development finance is disbursed, administered and evaluated. Current orthodoxy constructs civil society organisations as crucial actors in poverty reduction and policy, transmitting the voices of ordinary people to decision-makers, creating a constituency to ensure efficient, demand-driven service delivery, and holding governments accountable for their actions. Evidence of civil society participation has become a marker of legitimacy for poverty reduction policy processes, particularly since the advent of Poverty Reduction Strategy Papers (PRSP).

Many African scholars, examining both theory and practice, have concluded that there is a severe disconnection between narratives of civil society originating in the North, and the complex histories and realities of states and societies in Africa.[2] As Oloka-Onyango and Barya observe, "accompanying conceptual confusion is the fact that the historical legacy of the notion of civil society in Africa is suspiciously like other alien imports, of both convoluted pedigree and questionable validity."[3]

These two threads of experience, the imported narratives of the role and position of civil society, and the local histories and realities in which civil society is embedded, are essential background to an examination of how civil society actors participate in the poverty reduction policy process in Uganda. The broad contradictions between the two are made more acute by the particularities of Ugandan history and development, and by the unusual uniformity of donor understandings of the role of civil society organisations which is articulated in the Ugandan context.

The violent closure of associational space that took place under Amin and Obote's second regime, and during the civil war, meant that civil society, as well as the state itself and the formal economy, were barely functioning when Museveni gained power in 1986.[4] The Movement system of government, with its rhetorical and structural focus on inclusion and decentralisation, has subsequently shaped a political landscape where the dividing line between state and non-state actors is blurred.[5]

---

[2] Mamdani, M., 1995, 'A Critique of the state and civil society Paradigm in Africanist Studies' in Mamdani, M and Wamba-dia-Wamba eds) *African Studies in social Movements and democracy,* Dakar, CODESRIA Book Series; Oloka-Onyango, J, and Barya, J-J, 1997 'Civil Society and the Political Economy of Foreign Aid in Uganda', *democratisation,* Vol 4(2); Chabal, P. and Daloz, J-P, 1999, *Africa works: Disorder as Political Instrument,* Oxford: James Currey; Lewis, D., 2002, 'Civil society in African contexts: reflections on the usefulness of a concept', *Development and Change,* Vol 33 (4).

[3] Oloka-Onyango, J, and Barya, J-J, 1997, op.cit:115

[4] Himbara, D. and Sultan, D., 1995, 'Reconstructing the Ugandan State and Economy: the challenge of an international Bantustan', *Review of African Political Economy,* Vol 27 (63); Kabwegyere, T., 2000, 'Civil Society and Democratic Transition in Uganda since 1986' in Mugaju, J. and Oloka-Onyango, J, *No-Party Democracy in Uganda, Myths and Realities,* Kampala: Fountain Publishers.

[5] Allen, J., 2002, 'Forming Farmers' Fora: the Enmeshment of State and Civil Society and its Implications for Agricultural Modernisation in Uganda', M.Phil Thesis, mimeo, Brighton: Institute of Development Studies; Lister, S. and Nyamugasira, W., 2003, 'Design contradictions in the "new architecture of aid"? Reflections from Uganda on the roles of civil society organisations', *Development Policy Review,* Vol. 21 (1).

Into this landscape have come the international financial and development institutions, who have wielded extraordinary power in the Ugandan economy and policy process since the early 1990s.[6] The varied, but nonetheless similar, development narratives of institutions like the World Bank, the UNDP and DFID have eased the passage of 'civil society' into common parlance amongst local development actors, partly replacing the collective 'NGOs' which were the focus of the late 80s and early 90s.

Beyond this shift in words, external actors have also catalysed opportunities for the participation of civil society actors in the policy process, often by encouraging government to create invited spaces for participation. The resultant expansion of spaces for participation was contiguous with a sharp growth in the number of civil society organisations since the late 1980s, and has resulted in a dramatic increase in the range and variety of actors who participate in the policy process. The quality and effect of this participation, however, is shaped not only by the preferences of international development actors, but by the historically situated dynamics of politics and power, which mediate the role of state and civil society actors from the centre to the peripheries of Ugandan politics.

This chapter critically examines the participation of civil society organisations as actors in the poverty reduction policy process, at both the centre and the district levels. It begins by discussing some of the broad assumptions and contradictions implicit in the application of external narratives about civil society to Uganda. It continues by examining different perspectives about the role of civil society in the policy process. It then discusses the dynamics of the wide range of spaces in the policy process which are occupied by civil society actors. In conclusion, some areas of challenge for a more accountable, responsive policy process are presented.

Definitions, assumptions and contradictions

In Uganda, largely due to the nature of the state, the arena of civil society is somewhat narrower than in many other African countries. Some civil society organisations, such as trade unions and cooperatives, have either been systematically weakened by or absorbed into the state itself. This has led some to characterise Ugandan civil society as 'weak' or 'underdeveloped'.[7] Nonetheless there is a diverse range of organisations which operate in the arena of civil society, encompassing a wide variety of institutional forms and agendas for action. Notwithstanding such diversity, the written statements put forward by a range of policy actors reveal a common set of assumptions about what civil society consists of, and its role vis-à-vis development, poverty reduction and the state: Attempts to engage 'civil society' in the partnership process present a formidable

---

6   Uganda's position as the 'golden child of the IFIs' is discussed in detail in Dicklitch (Dicklitch, S., 1998, *The Elusive promise of NGOs in Africa: lessons from Uganda*, Basingstoke: Macmillan Press1998), while Himbara and Sultan (op.cit. 1995) characterise Uganda as an 'international Bantustan'.

7   Okuku, J., 2002, *Ethnicity, State Power and the democratisation Process in Uganda*, Uppsala:Nordiska Afrikainstitutet.

challenge (...) but citizens need to be empowered and the 'voiceless' need to be heard in setting development priorities.[8]

> Civil society, including NGOs, has roles both in service-delivery and in contributing to public debate about poverty-reduction. Government cannot control the activities of NGOs.[9]

> Civil society in Uganda is starting to play a more prominent role in raising awareness of rights, undertaking advocacy on behalf of disadvantaged groups and generally holding the Government to account.[10]

> Civil society organisations are [...] important in the analysis and articulation of the critical needs of society [...] as well as addressing poverty, inequity and marginalisation.[11]

Implicit across this range of statements are several key assumptions, the most basic of which is that civil society has, in some sense, an identity with clear boundaries, with CSOs having similar identities and purposes.[12] On the contrary, however, in addition to diversity of form and function, we encountered marked differences in CSO identities between Kampala and the districts.

CSOs in the capital, heavily shaped by direct engagement with international development actors and latterly with the government, conform quite closely to the image of modern, formally constituted institutions and structures - capable of advocacy, service delivery and contributions to public debates - which emerges from the narratives. CSOs at the district level and below, however, while including formally-constituted NGOs, also include local, small-scale self-help organisations, often based on structures of clan and lineage. These structures, usually informal, are frequently vital in local people's efforts to sustain their livelihoods in the absence of services. Many members of such groups stated that there was little point in their attempting to engage a governmental system which they perceived as seldom acting in their interests.

A second fundamental assumption implicit in the documents cited is that civil society is a separate entity from the state. Interviews with civil society actors at the district level and below suggest that this is far from the case, with many actors in local processes of planning and politics having more than one identity, being simultaneously active in government, in civil society, as well as in their geographic and social constituencies. Examples range from the 'Councillor-led CSOs' of Tororo District, where elected officials have founded NGOs to take advantage of contracts arising from the service provision activities of local government[13], to a women's NGO

---

8   'Poverty Eradication Action Plan Volume I Government of Uganda', Ministry of Finance Planning and Economic Development, July 2000:13.
9   'Poverty Eradication Action Plan Volume III Government of Uganda', Ministry of Finance Planning and Economic Development, December 2001:25.
10 DFID, 1999, Country Strategy Paper, p.6.
11 ActionAid, 2001, Uganda Country Strategy Paper, p. 7
12 Of the four documents from which the quotations are drawn, only AAU's Country Strategy Paper continues with a disaggregation of 'civil society' into some of its constituent parts.
13 This finding is resonant with Dicklitch (1998, op.cit) who discovered many civil servants amongst the staff of NGOs in the mid-1990s.

in Bushenyi, founded and headed by a local MP. Allen labels this phenomenon as part of a broader process of 'enmeshment' of state and civil society, which arises partly from the tentacular structure of the Movement state, and notes that there is a tendency amongst development planners who come from outside to assume "that the state and civil society are, or at least should be, distinct."[14]

Many of the functions ascribed to CSOs - particularly that of holding government accountable for its actions - rest on the idea that civil society has a separate identity from the state. The act of holding government accountable also relies on there being adequate political freedom for dissent and criticism of government. The assertion made by the Ministry of Finance in the Poverty Eradication Action Plan, that "government cannot control the activities of NGOs", contributes to the assumption that there is not only a separate identity for civil society actors, but that there exists adequate civil society autonomy for accountability to be exercised. The government's use of its NGO Registration Statute, however, suggests otherwise; as the co-ordinator of a national women's organisation commented, "they often remind us of our registration, which requires us to be non-political, non-partisan, non-everything. So whenever there is a controversy, they tell us we are violating our statute."

Similarly, the visions of civil society as 'addressing poverty', 'undertaking advocacy on behalf of disadvantaged groups,' and providing 'voice' for 'empowered citizens' obscure the political realities of the composition of CSOs, positioning them squarely as representatives of the less powerful. This belies the class identity of CSOs; at both centre and periphery, the leaders and staff of CSOs usually come from a contextually-defined elite. At local levels, elite status is closely related to educational profile, as well to the position of an individual in social and family networks. Similarly, those engaged in CSOs at the centre are also likely to be highly educated, and to be urban-based.

As the observations of the leader of Kampala-based women's CSO observes, elite identities have implications for representation:

> Some of the men criticise us that our arguments are from elitist women, but we answer back that "it is only elitist women who discuss with elitist men..." For example during our land advocacy campaign, we brought some women from the rural areas and they spoke for themselves. Some of them were breaking down in tears as they narrated their stories. But we were criticised for bringing in emotions and the Vice-President said that this was stage-managed.

An important, if underlying, component of elite politics, certainly at the centre, is ethnicity. Many of the leaders of CSOs who have successfully participated in the policy process are from Western Uganda, the ethno-geographic power base of the current regime.[15] As one research respondent observed, "many of these persons may argue that they do not benefit from their ethnicity ... but the silence about ethnicity in Uganda does say a lot about the noise it makes in shaping the local political terrain." Such

---

14 Allen, 2002 op.cit: 50
15 Okuku, 2002 op.cit argues that, despite the inclusive rhetoric of the Movement regime, Uganda is an ethnically-organised, one-party state.

considerations contest the assertion of a simple, representative relationship between 'civil society' and a constituency of unrepresented, unempowered citizens.

Challenging some of the broad assumptions that underpin publicly-stated perspectives on civil society participation thus reveals a disconnection between rhetorical public statements and political realities. This is no surprise; the frequent use in policy of terms with multiple meanings allows room for competing interpretations to emerge.[16] Examining in more detail the dissonance between policy narratives and their interpretation in practice by a range of differently positioned actors creates an opportunity to examine the prospects for an improved quality of civil society participation in the policy process.

Occupying the middle ground between government and external actors?

> Central government to local government is a tug of war, with each protecting their own turf. Maybe civil society can be a middle ground - getting central and local government to declare their processes. Ugandan NGOs used to rely on their larger brothers the international NGOs, but if they are to do advocacy, then we want their considered opinion to provide horizontal accountability. They would be more independent advocates, beyond service delivery, if they had central government as their larger brother.[17]

> Much of the space opened up here [for civil society participation] has been opened because of what the donors say. How far would it have opened up if the donors didn't think it was the best way to do things? What happens if donors stop pressing the government of Uganda to take on participation? What is the likelihood that the government will continue creating the spaces necessary for NGOs to participate?[18]

The extent to which civil society participation is both positioned between and 'manufactured'[19] by government and international development actors, is an important feature of invited spaces and the power dynamics that surround them. Such a positioning results in civil society actors being largely reactive, responsive to resources offered for a particular range of activities and functions. This in turn limits their capacity to develop autonomous agendas and raises questions about where their accountability lies. Simultaneously, however, it does create opportunities for participation which civil society actors can use to articulate their own agendas and pursue actions congruent with them.

The role of international development actors in opening spaces for civil society actors is unquestionable, and has undoubtedly had positive impacts in terms of a more diverse range of actors gaining access to some parts of the policy process. Interviews with

---

16 Brock, K., Cornwall, A. and Gaventa, J., 2001, 'Power, knowledge and political spaces in the framing of poverty policy', IDS Working Paper 143, Brighton: Institute of Development Studies, p11.
17 Interview with Government Official, Ministry of Decentralisation.
18 Interview with Ugandan NGO Director.
19 See Howell and Pearce (Howell, J and Pearce, J, 2001, *Civil society and Development: a critical exploration*, Boulder: Lynne Reiner) on the role of the international development community in 'manufacturing' civil society

a range of international development actors in Kampala show that all of them consider their principal development partner to be the government; this is well illustrated by a broad movement in the system of aid disbursement towards sector wide approaches arid budget support.[20] With such a governmental focus, their relationship with civil society organisations is often framed by the influence that CSOs might have on the state; almost all respondents mentioned that they use some resources to strengthen civil society in order to hold government accountable. Three extracts from interviews with staff of bilateral and multilateral agencies point to some of the constraints to civil society participation implied by this:

> Government has to do its job and the CSOs have also to control the government, both at the district and at the sub-county level. At the centre we have enough good CSOs.

> Donors spot NGOs and think they are very politically correct to support; and they drown them with project funds, but not with funds for recurrent costs - this leads to corruption scandals.

> We have tried to bring in effective and meaningful CSOs - before it was just the Farmers Union [...] The Plan for the Modernisation of Agriculture[21] is open to interpretation - one wants a good critique, but wants to make it constructive, without cramping the space of either the government or of civil society.[22]

These views suggest that the boundaries of invited spaces for civil society participation are drawn partly by the opinions of external actors concerning what is 'good', 'constructive,' 'effective', 'meaningful' or 'politically correct'. While this has clearly strengthened some CSOs, it excludes others. At the centre there may be 'enough' CSOs, but the autonomy they require to 'control' the government is constrained by necessary compliance with external agents. This results in an over-emphasis on the politics of consensus, as opposed to an acknowledgement of a range of interests which may challenge or conflict with these external agendas; this in turn reinforces the tendency, noted earlier, of the interlocking of government and non-governmental actors.

At district level and below, international development actors have less of a visible presence, and formally constituted CSOs are less numerous or vocal than they are at the centre. The response of one Chief Administrative Officer, asked about the role of NGOs in the policy process, is instructive about the relative power of different actors at the district level:

> In principle, CSOs are vocal and speak out, they write papers which can then be discussed. Their views can somehow influence change - but here it is not very significant. The group which is significant is the donors. It is very influential because it has the money. We say it's not fair, because sometimes they don't conceptualise the

---

20 Lister and Nyamugasira, op cit, 2003.
21 The Plan for the Modernisation of Agriculture is the GoU's plan to deliver on one of the four pillars of the PEAP. Amongst other things, it creates 'Farmers' Fora' as structures for farmers to decide their extension priorities.
22 Interviews with staff of international development agencies, Kampala.

real issues behind the problems. Sometimes the policies behind their money are very hurting.

Similar comments from a range of respondents in all three districts reiterate this point: it is access to resources which buys the influence necessary for participation in the policy process to have an impact. Donors, in many senses 'invisible' at the district level because of the current emphasis away from projects and towards budget support, in fact wield considerable power as policy actors at this level, sometimes to the detriment of the CSOs they profess to support.

These findings imply that the progression from "strengthening civil society" to "holding the government to account" contains several assumptions which do not necessarily stand up to rigorous inspection. The idea of a civil society with an autonomous identity and self- defined agendas at either central or district level is questionable, given the resilience of linkages with donors and the lack of alternative sources of funding. This is shown to some extent by the difficulty many CSO respondents described in occupying positions which oppose or criticise dominant narratives of poverty reduction. It is also shown by a lack of critical reflection within civil society, noted by some CSO actors themselves, about its own role and motives.

The lack of an autonomous identity is also, however, inextricably linked to government. While the direct interface between donors and CSOs is principally situated in Kampala, the multiple interfaces between CSOs and government stretch from Kampala to the most isolated rural village, thanks to the LC system. The mechanisms that link CSOs and government are far more diverse and complex than those that link them to international development actors, partly due to the interlinking noted above.

At the centre there is a greater separation of identity between government and civil society actors than at the lower levels. The principal visible mechanism of interaction between central government and CSOs in the policy process is invitation. Since the first revision of the Poverty Eradication Action Plan, government has increasingly issued invitations to civil society to take part in different stages of the policy process. As an interview at the NRM Secretariat testifies, by issuing such invitations, the government enhances its claims that the NRM provides a participatory and consultative political system for Ugandan citizens. When asked about poverty alleviation policy, an NRM respondent went to find a copy of the UPPAP report[23] and said "Have you seen this? There were meetings at the sub-county, at the parish, giving views on how things ought to be done. The PMA is the same - it made wide consultations - even the very constitution itself. People come and they are encouraged to speak."

While this phenomenon of invitation to CSOs is relatively new, it is already the dominant mechanism for their participation in the policy process at the centre, whether in a task force, a budget conference or a sector working group. Only one CSO respondent identified a process of civil society participation instigated from outside government, the case of the Land Act. One outcome of this invitation culture is a

---

23 The UPPAP report in question presents the findings of the first stage of a qualitative research exercise designed to elicit poor people's opinions and understandings of their experience of poverty.

separation between the dynamics involved in getting a seat at the policy table, and those involved in acting on behalf of poor people once this seat has been taken. Getting a place at the table requires tactics of accommodation and amicability, while acting on behalf of poor people may require more adversarial approaches; it cannot be assumed that the former will lead automatically and seamlessly to the latter.

Many CSOs in Kampala seem to be at the level of actively pursuing the single goal of getting their people onto seats in meetings or committees; and reactively responding to any invitation issued to take part in any public forum which might afford profile to the organisation or the issue on which it works. These activities are pursued with apparently little analysis of the impact that they might have: an all-consuming fixation with what might be termed 'the politics of presence' rather than the politics of influence.[24] Some of those more experienced in advocacy use the 'politics of presence' consciously, as one strand of a broader strategy which embraces a range of approaches to representing issues of concern. Oxfam GB/Uganda, for instance, pursues its lobbying work on internal displacement partly by bringing internally displaced people into the same room as decision-makers. A national NGO claims that if it ceased to seek and secure a presence at every table 'people would ask, "Where are the women?", an indication that the 'politics of presence' tactic meets - but fails to challenge - strongly held expectations and understandings that representative democracy amounts to merely getting people of all kinds onto seats.

What are the implications of the invitation culture and the politics of presence? The research found that whether an invitation for civil society participation is delivered depends on the issue at stake. While government is currently inviting participation on many issues that are clearly framed as poverty reduction, other subject areas, some of which lie outside the frame, but have critical influence on the prospects for poverty reduction, do not produce the same invitations. With civil society actors so intensively engaged with government in poverty-framed debates, these issues - which include the impact of the current round of the WTO, and the negotiations surrounding the Poverty Reduction Strategy Credit and the Poverty Reduction Growth Facility - are therefore being subjected to much less public debate than is desirable.[25]

Much of this section has discussed government and international development actors as dominant, 'intrusive' and 'dominating' in relation to civil society. While their power undoubtedly has a part in shaping the spaces in which policy is made, it is not the only influence. Civil society organisations themselves, while their agency may be limited as well as facilitated by other actors with greater access to financial and political resources, make their voices heard and exercise influence through their invited participation. It is to the challenges which arise in exercising opportunities for participation that we now turn.

---

24 The term 'politics of presence' is taken from the work of Phillips (Phillips, A., 1995, *The Politics of Presence*, Oxford: Clarendon Press).
25 Nyamugasira, W. and Rowden, R., 2002, 'New Strategies, Old Loan Conditions: Do the PRSC and PRGF support poverty reduction strategies? The case of Uganda', Kampala and Washington DC: Uganda National NGO Forum and Results Educational Fund.

Along a vertical slice: spatial dynamics of civil society participation

The diversity of CSO activities and identities means that CSOs can occupy a range of spaces in the policy process. The activities that take place in those spaces, and the nature of the spaces themselves, differ between the centre and the district.

At the centre, these activities are frequently labelled 'advocacy', and are often undertaken by one or two individuals, either acting to represent a single CSO with an interest in the policy issue being discussed, or to represent an issue-based CSO network. Members of these networks in turn represent wider constituencies. Some of these constituencies - those of international NGOs - lie in part outside Uganda, others are membership-based, and some have started at the centre and are trying to build decentralised structures at the district level to support their campaigning activities.

At the district level, the activities which take place when CSOs occupy spaces in the policy process are much more likely to be labelled as 'participation in decentralised planning'. Although some CSO actors did report experience of participating in formal political spaces such as the district council, most, if they engage directly with government processes in any capacity, are much more familiar with the arenas in which service delivery is planned and implemented. While the number of invited spaces for engagement in planning and implementation has increased, especially as the decentralised structures of the Poverty Action Fund (PAF) and the Plan for the Modernisation of Agriculture (PMA) have been rolled out, there is a sense of doubt amongst CSOs concerning the impact that their participation might have.

Given the range of spaces on offer for civil society participation in the policy process, it is important to understand what is necessary for the effective occupation of different kinds of space. The nature of spaces is dynamic, and is shaped by the expectations of those who occupy them about what participation consists of, and can or should achieve.[26]

Some civil society actors at the centre see participation as a right; one commented that "there are constitutional powers given to civil society to participate in governance, so civil society derives its power from the Constitution itself." Making this right real takes the form both of invoking rights to create new spaces, and of enlarging or subverting existing ones. Another civil society actor commented that "someone who creates it can say the space starts and ends here'. The opportunities for pushing the boundaries of or further enlarging an existing space depend in part on the power of those who initially created it, and in changing their expectations of what it exists for.

Many note that increased civil society participation has resulted in changing attitudes amongst government actors, which can be exploited to expand space. The opportunity presented to CSOs to participate more actively in setting the agenda for the 2001 Consultative Group meeting was cited as evidence of a change in expectations: "increasingly, as well as asking CS to contribute to analyses of what is the problem, government is asking for contributions towards the solutions." Another

---

26 Brock, Cornwall and Gaventa, op.cit. 2001.

respondent cited the importance of the government's ownership of the UPPAP process in "converting government people to civil society views". In recognising this, both actors noted that they now felt empowered to take issue with government concerning the limits to current invited spaces for participation, in one case feeling able to challenge the Ministry of Finance concerning the timing and nature of the current PEAP revision, which had previously been driven by the timetables of the international financial institutions.

This process of challenging expectations and taking advantage of changing attitudes in order to widen invited spaces may, however, involve expressions of dissent which mean CSOs moving towards the margins of what is deemed legitimate behaviour. One respondent noted:

> when you push too far you get an oppressive response from the state. This comes in various forms, some very personalised — the Permanent Secretary rings our Director and tells him to stop saying what he is saying. Relations between government and civil society are maybe only cordial because we aren't challenging government, we are being yes-people. We need the skills to know how to proceed when push comes to shove.

This account also alerts us to the importance of 'backstage' spaces in the politics of invited participation. It is in these spaces at all levels that decisions are made and political relationships are enacted. They shape what goes on in the invited spaces. In the case of the Plan for the Modernisation of Agriculture, which makes claims to have been elaborated in a consultative way, one international development actor noted that "there is some resentment - CSOs were not at the PMA tea parties. The PMA was done and dusted before it was presented to a workshop." The 'tea parties', exclusive gatherings of the more powerful and their allies, are in this case the spaces in the policy process where the basic decisions about policy direction and structure are made; and civil society actors in this case were not part of that conversation.

CSOs themselves use informal spaces as part of their activities, placing a premium on changing the attitudes of powerful individuals within their own arenas, and their allies. Ugandan Joint Council of Churches, for example, does a great deal of work around the parliamentary process, lobbying and alliance-building. A member of UJCC noted that its effectiveness in this regard is in part due to its being regarded as 'a very respectable CSO', and in part due to the skills and capabilities of the organisation. Others noted that it is essential to access these backstage spaces where possible, as it is often the only way to access the "few people who are not accessible" on whom a "final output" depends. These people seldom enter invited spaces for participation, sending junior staff in their place.

In the districts, the dynamics of effectively participating in invited spaces are very different from the strategies of occupying backstage spaces or taking advantage of shifting attitudes that are found at the centre. This is in large part because of the relative lack of formal invitation, and of the principal functions of CSOs at this level, which are social provision and mutual self-help. Many CSO respondents argued that it is far easier to influence what is in front of you than to undertake the more abstract work of creating broader changes to a 'policy' which is not always clearly articulated. Further, and perhaps most importantly, they pointed out that there is a need for CSOs to follow resources: being sub-contracted to provide services is a crucial source of income.

Engaging in service delivery, however, is much more than a default choice for some CSOs. Several respondents were keen to emphasise that their strength is to have a positive influence on development through good practice in service delivery. One respondent in Lira gave the example of a credit programme which was failing because of the inflexible terms of government management. When it was handed over to an NGO experienced in managing credit programmes, the repayment rate recovered, and the NGO was able to attract additional funding to expand the programme. The respondent saw this as an example of positive change to policy through the action of better practice in implementation.

Further, while several CSOs emphasised that service delivery for them was a positive opportunity, many saw it as a preferable option to engaging in the policy process, which was seen as both corrupt and corrupting. Beyond the fears of what would happen if engagement were to take place, there are also uncertainties derived from 'the habit of non-consultation', which have made CSOs feel sidelined from the policy process. Many are now unsure if they are actually invited to engage, and if so, under what terms and in which spaces. The comments of one CSO worker in Lira illustrate the thoughts of many: "District council meetings are theoretically open to all corners, but CSOs don't even know that their attendance is invited ... If planning meetings take place and other people are sent invitation letters, how can you attend if you have not received a letter? This creates fear in us."

The arena of civil society exists beyond NGOs engaged in service delivery. Looking past the district level to the dynamics of community based organisations (CBOs) pushes orthodox understandings of civil society to its limits, yet it is instructive to those who consider that poor people, as citizens, have a right to be represented in decisions that are made about their lives. Howell and Pearce note that "donors have defined civil society as an arena of formal and modern associations, distinct not only from a venal, inefficient state but also from an amorphous array of informal and primordial associations."[27] The civil society organisations of Ugandan villages, however, are firmly rooted within this amorphous array, tending to be informal, unregistered and arising out of the existing social configurations of kinship and clan. If the challenge of 'representing the grassroots' in the policy process is to be met, learning from the spatial dynamics of this level becomes critical. As Howell concludes, excluding this domain from a discussion of 'civil society' overlooks the fact that "family, tribe and clan-based associations might also be the locus of social and political change."[28] While there is variance and flexibility in the way that different donors approach this domain

---

27 Howell and Pearce, op.cit: p. 17
28 Ibid.

of local civil society, the tendency to overlook it in favour of CSOs with formal and modern structures remains strong.

CBO formation is frequently linked to a local understanding of poverty - women's credit unions as a solution to income poverty, or digging groups as a response to loss of cattle through cattle raiding. A member of a village women's credit group, asked why the group had formed, replied "Enough is enough - we can't go on depending on men, even reaching to the extent of having to ask them for money to buy salt and soap for home use. Women want to be able to sustain their families and themselves. We women have to take charge and without money we can't do that." A sense of 'taking charge' of a situation which is normally beyond control is an important feature of the formation of many CBOs.

One district-based NGO staff member argued that most CBOs rely on their own collective efforts, discussing their own ideas and initiatives for development; it is on the basis of their collective initiative that others come in and support them. This is not, however, the whole story. External stimulus, often in the form of the provision of resources, is commonly a trigger to group formation, as well as a source of support after formation. One CBO in Bushenyi, headed by an educated woman resident in a town, was created specifically in response to an advertisement placed by the Ministry of Health, looking for CBOs to raise awareness about AIDS prevention. As the head of the CBO candidly stated, "It was more for business reasons."

Also in Bushenyi, a representative of the District Farmers' Association pointed out that they actively encourage the formation of 'interest groups' at the parish level - centred around the production of a particular crop - so that farmers can be directed towards a market for their harvest. Such externally-stimulated agriculture-based CBOs are proliferating as the Plan for the Modernisation of Agriculture is more fully implemented, creating Farmers' Fora (FF) at the sub-county level which decide three priorities for crop or livestock production systems which will receive agricultural extension services.

Some CBOs are formed in response to a perceived promise of external resources and are subsequently disappointed. This was particularly common in Tororo, where a women's councillor commented, "Some are from the district, some are from NGOs, some are from the centre - but they are all saying that groups should be formed. But groups have formed and they have got nothing from these people who told them to form groups." This process had resulted in groups becoming demoralised, and was seen by some to represent a culture of dependency which severely reduced the potential for collective action.

While it is difficult to generalise, the most stable and effective CBOs encountered in the course of the study were those which were either the result of indigenous collective action, or based on a culturally-embedded institutional pattern which is adaptable to current circumstances. Perhaps the best example of the latter is the proliferation of neighbourhood digging groups in Lira District. These allow farming households to maximise their labour while they are forced to practise unmechanised agriculture because they have lost most of their cattle to cattle raiders. In this way, a traditional Lango[29] lineage-based institution has been adapted to a contemporary political reality - Karimojong[30] cattle raiding - in a direct attempt to prevent whole communities falling further into poverty and food insecurity. The contrast with the 'empty promise CBOs' of Tororo could not be greater.

Despite these differences between the form and function of CBOs, one thing that most of them hold in common is a feeling that they are disconnected from the activities of the lower local councils (LCs) and that 'poverty reduction' activities, of the kind which they actually practise but do not necessarily label as such, are disconnected from the services and programmes of government. As such, they exist in a space somewhat removed from the LC system, but are nonetheless embedded in local politics and society.[31]

Notably, however, no CBO we encountered was formed to allow ordinary people to pursue from government the entitlements which are their rights as citizens.[32] Early experience with the implementation of the PMA has meant that the local landscape of civil society has become more densely populated with hybrid institutions formed to create privatised, 'demand-driven' service delivery, mandated by central government policy. These could provide different mechanisms through which claims for entitlements could be made by the poor; or they could allow local elites to co-opt the resources for themselves.

Occupying newly-opened spaces on the basis that participation in decisions that affect one's life is a constitutional right requires changing expectations. At the lower levels, a fundamental shift in the understanding of citizenship would be required, to transform ordinary people into active, engaged participants in the policy process, rather than distanced and excluded clients of an inequitable system of resource distribution controlled by distant, powerful actors.

Challenges for representation and voice

As discussed earlier, the challenges for shaping policy processes where civil society participation moves beyond invitation and consultation and towards representative and accountable decision-making processes are played out in many arenas. In each, there are dilemmas for civil society actors, and trade-offs. How can civil society at the centre move from the politics of presence toward the politics of influence? How can accountable processes be achieved when government and civil society overlap? How can civil society actors widen the spaces for autonomy whilst remaining inextricably connected to international development actors and their agendas?

---

29 The majority ethnic group of Lira District.
30 Pastoralists occupying north-eastern Uganda.
31 See Allen (op.cit, 2002) for a comprehensive discussion of early experiences with PMA implementation in Soroti and Kabale.
32 Similarly, although some CSOs - notably the Uganda Debt Network - exist to facilitate the claiming of rights, they do not frame their own activities in terms of the rights and entitlements of citizenship.

The challenge faced by the range of development actors in Uganda is to recognise not only the diversity contained within 'civil society', but to acknowledge that the spaces in which CSO participation is enacted frequently limit the possibilities for developing accountability. Designing and implementing policy according to external narratives about poverty reduction produces a profound disconnection between what is meant to happen and what does happen. Apthorpe suggests that part of the trick of policy discourse is to "present what is intended and then to be done as unavoidably and unobjectionably necessary and correct."[33] The orthodox framing of civil society actors, with the unobjectionable correctness suggested by civil society's central position in development discourse, needs to be critically questioned, on the grounds that many of its key assumptions do not reflect the lived realities of Ugandans.

---

33   Apthorpe, R., 1986, 'Development Policy Discourse', *Public Administration and Development*, Vol 6, p. 382.

16

Relations between Gender-Focused NGOs, Aadvocacy Work, and Government: A Ugandan Case Study[1]

Mary Ssonko Nabacwa

Abstract

Relations between the Ugandan government and NGOs engaged its gender-focused advocacy tend to keep NGOs visibly engaged but do not necessarily alter the status of poor women. These relations manifest themselves in government advising NGO advocacy work; sympathising with the NGOs; co-opting NGOs and individuals; publicising gender issues; and de-legitimising gender-focused NGO activities. The article links these phenomena to the government's wish to appear receptive to the concerns of civil society organisations of which NGOs are a major component. This is important to its image in the international aid community, where it projects itself as generally democratic and supportive of good governance.

Introduction

Relationships are important to NGOs and others involved in gender-based advocacy in Uganda, as they all seek to frame their choices and optimise their political and economic assets. The relationships between NGOs and other players such as the government at all levels form a complex web that helps to enhance their socio-political interests in terms of identity (authenticity), status (public image), and access to resources (financial, technical, etc.). These three factors affect NGO advocacy work and thus the changes that are likely at the grassroots.

Since NGOs are political and economic entities, they tend to negotiate and manoeuvre their way through their external relations in order to protect their interests. In other words, few NGOs are simply passive recipients of aid, or mere implementers of donor or government agendas. Gender-focused NGOs in Uganda, just like government,

---

[1] Reprinted from *Development in Practice*, Vol. 20, Nr 3, May 2010, by kind permission of Routledge; and by permission of the publisher Taylor & Francis Ltd, http://www.tandfonline.com.

carefully and consistently invest in negotiating spaces to express and promote their agendas and to assert their respective interests. Moreover, the complex processes of co-operation and (covert) conflict played out through the web of relationships in which gender-focused NGOs are involved demonstrate that, while power need not be a zero-sum game whereby the winner takes all (Foucault, 1980, 1982; Kabeer, 1999), social relationships are essentially about power.

Power is determined partly by sheer luck, deliberate influence, and observable decision-making over subjective interests, but also by non-observable decision-making, and non-decision making. These factors may include actions (observable and non-observable, overt and covert, conscious or unconscious) to stop, exclude, or suffocate potential challenges to the status quo in terms of the distribution of resources or privileges, excluding other alternatives from the decision-making arena. Such actions can take the form of socially structured and culturally patterned biases in the decision-making system which may be manifested through individual inaction, or through influencing, shaping, or determining people's wishes by controlling their thoughts and desires, for example through mass media and processes of socialisation such as education, training, and learning (Lukes, 1974: 16-20). In other words, power is also about having knowledge, and being able to apply knowledge to one's own benefit, and also therefore about the ability to choose to invoke notions of rationality, rules, resources, profit maximisation, opportunity, co-operation, competition, conflict, and interest - most of which are politico-economic in nature (Cassell, 1993; Kabeer, 1999). This article explores the manifestation of power in the form of relations and actions between NGOs and government, and how this affects the advocacy work of gender-focused NGOs in Uganda.

Government - NGO relationships

NGOs in Uganda have not nurtured their relations with government in strategically visible processes as one might expect, given that they are involved in advocacy to change government policies. Generally these relationships can be classified as relations of fear, confrontation, and manipulation.

Relations of fear

NGOs are afraid to challenge the *status quo,* because to do so may imply that they are questioning the government's effectiveness. This fear might be due to the historical patriarchal principle of household and community governance, in which male leadership should not be challenged, should be in control, and should be recognised as exclusive (Kabeer, 1995; Goetz, 1998). NGO gender advocacy tends to challenge these principles, and this causes tension and conflict, possibly in part owing to the fact that it is seen as a threat to the privileged position of most government leaders, who are men. Moreover, women leaders in government fear to challenge the *status quo* overtly, because they have achieved such positions via the mostly male-dominated electoral colleges (Nabacwa, 2002; Mugisha, 2000; Tripp, 2000; Tamale, 1999; Asiimwe, 2001). Rocking the boat may come at a price. During the 2000 campaigns for land ownership, the Vice President (a woman) challenged the demand for women's co-ownership in the following words:

> ...the issue in contention should be access to land and its productivity and not co-ownership of land. To say that without land we [women] will go nowhere is pushing the women back to the last millennium...and confining them to the hoe... what we should have is education to enable girls to use more of their brains. (*The Monitor*, 7 December 2000)

NGOs could not understand how a woman could challenge efforts to establish a fair land law. The point is that even when women are in government, they tend to adopt patriarchal ways of operating and defend the *status quo*, thus generating a sense of fear among the NGOs.

Relations of confrontation

Gender-focused NGOs tend to see women parliamentarians as people they need, but whom they also view as traitors. So they sometimes regard them as unsupportive of gender concerns. NGOs also complain that the executive arm of government calls on civil society organisations (CSOs) to participate in identifying problems, but then signs memoranda of understanding (MOU) with the World Bank (Lister and Nyamugasira, 2003; Nyamugasira and Rowden, 2002). These MOU contain conditionalities that are difficult to contest for fear of the consequences. Confrontational relations are also observed in the undermining of each other's knowledge. Government technical personnel undermine NGO capacity in policy analysis, while NGOs criticise government personnel concerning the delivery of services, accusing them of being corrupt and bureaucratic.

Relations of manipulation

The relationships between government and NGOs have also been marked on both sides by manipulation, partly influenced by the relationship with donors. Uganda is a major target for the World Bank, and the government is thus placed in a 'symbiotic relationship', a delicate situation. The Bank and IMF need Uganda as a showpiece of their policy success, like a pharmacy wanting to show that its medicines are good. Bratton considers that the state and NGOs, "although uncomfortable bed fellows" in a neo-liberal paradigm, "are destined to cohabit" (Bratton, 1989:585). Both parties are very much aware of the mutual importance of this relationship. As Hearn states: "Donors have found in the government of Uganda an African 'partner' willing to be the 'star pupil' for its latest 'development' paradigm" (Hearn, 2001:50).

The relationship between the government and its major donors might have influenced the common NGO perception that they should complement rather than challenge the government. Rather than critiquing a policy, NGOs tend to agree and participate, being involved rather than stepping back to understand its implications for the men and women at the grassroots. It can hence be said that the NGOs take their neo-liberal role seriously.

It could be argued that donors and government see the role of civil society as providing the service of 'accountability'. Foreign aid is no longer channelled through sector budgets and CSOs act as external monitors ensuring current poverty reduction policies are implemented accountably. (Hearn, 2001:50)

While NGO staff may have advocacy skills, mainly acquired through donor-supported capacity building, not all of them apply these skills to situate their advocacy work. They do their advocacy in an abstract manner, focusing on how things should be (based on modernisation theories), rather than analysing the local situation within Uganda's historical social, economic, and political context. Resources are often the critical factor in understanding how identity and status (or recognition) are sought (or contested), and how relationships and advocacy strategies are negotiated. However, although the relationships are unequal, not all the power lies on one side. In part this is because of the actors' shifting and overlapping identities, not being fixed but depending on the particular stage of the specific lobbying or advocacy activities in question (Foucault, 1982; Kabeer, 1999; Weedon, 1987). The next section further explains the complexity of the relations between NGOs and government, as traced through the reaction of government to NGO advocacy.

Factors that determine the nature of the relations between government and NGOs

There are limitations on the ways in which NGOs can influence government policy-making processes. The inclusion of gender issues in these processes has tended to be due more to the goodwill of those in power, or to the influence of donor pressure, than to the efforts of NGOs. A major drawback is that NGOs seldom occupy a clear position in the policy-making institutions and processes. The government does try to relate to NGOs in a variety of ways, often keeping them visible but unthreatening, because the public image of democracy and good governance makes it necessary for the government to maintain dialogue with civil society and reduce its own transaction costs.

Keep NGOs visible but unthreatening

The government want to keep NGOs ('civil society') engaged and to make the on-going process of engagement visible, without threatening its own identity, status, or access to resources. Being seen to be broadly receptive to the concerns of CSOs in general is important to the government's self-image, which is to be seen as responsive to all sectors of the population, including marginalised sectors such as women. It publicly announces sympathetic policies and undertakes research on gender issues, for example on land and gender-based violence, but in ways that do not necessarily antagonise male voters; even if women form the majority of voters, men are the main decision makers.

Democracy and good governance

Government considers that its international status depends on being seen as generally democratic and supportive of good governance: key conditions for aid (Fowler, 2000;

Goetz, 1998; Hearn, 2001; Abrahamsen, 2000). Its interest in gender issues seems to have more to do with political and economic self-interest than with ideology or a genuine commitment to gender equality. On the one hand, government carefully and skilfully promotes civil society participation in the policy-making process involving gender-focused NGOs through their advocacy work. On the other, it seeks to retain ultimate control over the NGOs' gender agenda, to ensure that it remains unthreatening, which it does by identifying and publicly critiquing the weaknesses in NGO relations with other actors, especially with donors and grassroots communities (Nyamugasira and Lister, 2001).

Public image of government

The government is sensitive about its public image and seeks to recognise gender issues while not offending patriarchal sentiments (Goetz, 1998; Tripp, 1998; Tamale, 1999). While acknowledging that household-level gender inequalities are detrimental to development, it calls on policy technocrats and NGOs to build consensus regarding legislation against such inequalities. The call for consensus arises from the differences among the various social groups - men, women, clans, tribes, religious institutions, NGOs, and the private sector - in their understanding of what constitutes acceptable household gender relations. The government's approach to legislation against gender inequalities, which is mainly to avoid antagonising any specific group, has important implications for the way in which it interacts with gender-focused NGOs. Adhering to 'good governance' principles by being sympathetic to gender advocacy can he rewarded with international recognition and aid. The donors' view of the government affects its access to resources, which can in turn reinforce its national and international status (Abrahamsen, 2000). This does not mean, however, that government will zealously promote changes to the *status quo* in response to NGO advocacy.

Opportunity for dialogue with civil society

The government certainly recognises the need to provide opportunities for dialogue and interaction with 'civil society', especially with NGOs that are considered to represent marginalised social sectors, such as women. It is aware of the close relationships between NGOs and donors (who are also its own donors) and knows that the latter are interested in 'partnership' between the private sector, government, and 'civil society', so that all actors, including 'grassroots' representatives, are involved in policy making (Fowler, 2000: 5; Craig and Porter, 2005; Power, 2003). Inclusion of civil society, even if tokenistic, is critical to the government's policy-making processes and its own access to resources (Pearce, 2000; Hearn, 2001; Nyamugasira and Rowden, 2002; Power, 2003; Abrahamsen, 2000; Craig and Porter, 2005; Tembo, 2003). According to Fowler, partnerships are premised on the assumption that the "state, market and third sector can apparently be persuaded or induced to perform in consort" (Fowler, 2000: 5) - in other words, inclusive neo-liberalism (Craig and Porter 2005) - and on building social capital (Power, 2003). Abugre observes that partnerships are designed to promote local ownership of programmes and policies, ensuring control over donor relationships, and fostering harmony: "partnerships seek to address inclusiveness, complementarity, dialogue and shared responsibility as the basis for managing the multiple relationships among stakeholders in the aid industry" (Abugre1999:2).

Reduce the transaction costs

The transaction costs of responding to NGOs can be reduced in a number of ways, each of which has implications for NGO advocacy work. It is important not to exaggerate the degree to which the government acts in a single, consistent manner. Rather it seeks to juggle various approaches in order to maximise leverage and choices, as well as rewards. While analysed separately for the purpose of this article, in reality these approaches are interlinked with other kinds of action and policy, but they may include any combination of the following elements: (i) Advising NGOs; (ii) Sympathising with gender-focused NGOs; (iii) Co-option of organisations and individuals; (iv) Publicity for gender issues; (v) De-legitimising gender-focused NGO activities.

Government relations with NGOs

Advising NGOs

In its advisory role, government appears to be impartial. For example, an analysis of statements and actions in meetings with NGOs on the Land Rights Campaign showed that government officials advised NGOs on what they needed to do to elicit the support of policy makers and the public to ensure the success of the campaign. The advisory role took three major forms:

a) Advising NGOs to provide more information to the government and supplement the information already available.

b) Directing NGOs to lobby some other official identified as responsible for a specific change. The advice may be presented as 'insider information' disclosed to the NGO.

c) Telling NGOs to elicit more grassroots support for the advocacy campaign in order for their agenda to reflect popular priorities at the local level.

NGOs tend to take the advisory role of government seriously, and it usually influences their work and even their advocacy strategies.

Sympathising with gender-focused NGOs

Another government role is to sympathise with gender-equity issues and the women's cause. This approach is exemplified by government officials taking the opportunity to pledge in public their support for gender equality, women's empowerment, and women's rights. This tactic is more commonly used in public forums or at events such as International Women's Day, or workshops at which government personnel are guests of honour. During such occasions, officials articulate their recognition of the importance of women's increased ownership and control of resources, including land, and agree that this is likely to lead to national development. They also claim that they will include co-ownership of land in the law and that they are working on this issue, However, they rarely make such statements in smaller, private, or policy-related gatherings.

Co-option of organisations and individuals

In co-opting NGOs, government usually opens up dialogue and seeks to bring NGOs and NGO leaders into meetings and technical committees. In part, the aim is to seek much-needed information and ideas on what the government can do to protect and promote the gender interests of women and men (Lister and Nyamugasira, 2003). However, once the government has co-opted NGOs onto its technical committees, it tends to neutralise the critical stance that such NGOs might adopt in relation to the topic at hand. For example, the Uganda Land Alliance is a member of the technical committee on land in the Ministry of Lands. It is thus to an extent bound by the decisions of this committee. Membership of a committee means that decisions are the result of joint efforts of NGOs and government, which obviously makes it more difficult for NGOs to criticise the government, since it appears to recognise the seriousness and importance of their concerns, and to be addressing them. So NGOs become visible but unthreatening actors in the policy-making process. Donors support such committees, because they are an expression of the success of broader policy goals such as partnership and good governance (Abrahamsen, 2000; Power, 2003). It should also be noted that having government and NGOs in partnership provides donors with an efficient and effective mechanism for achieving the same development discourse in the country (Hearn, 2001).

Publicity for gender issues

Historically, government has mainly turned to publicity when under pressure from gender- focused NGOs, especially when these are openly backed by donors. At such times, it will be keen to be seen to be 'doing something' in order to relieve itself of the NGO pressure. The response involves increasing media coverage of what is being done on gender issues, and showing how existing policies are helping development. For example, during the campaign for women's land rights, the government spoke of the importance of women's ownership of land for agriculture as a whole, and for Uganda's overall development. It also set up committees to co-opt NGO representatives to provide technical assistance in handling the issues: for example, the land-rights campaign (Lister and Nyamugasira, 2003). Government publicity includes indications that matters are being sorted out, and that NGOs should therefore not worry.

De-legitimising gender-focused NGO activities

When government falls short of expectations and does not sufficiently integrate NGO concerns into the policy-making process, a common NGO reaction is radical advocacy (Razavi, 1997) or advocacy for transformation (Kabeer, 1999) in which the government is attacked as being patriarchal and undemocratic, and the need for gender transformation is asserted. This failure to respond to their demands can undermine the NGOs' identity and status, since their advocacy will be deemed to have failed. In a lose-lose fashion, a pattern of blame is likely, with each side claiming that the other has let it down. If the government feels threatened by accusations of being unresponsive to NGOs representing "civil society as an antidote to the state" (Van Rooy, 1998), then it may respond by attacking the NGOs and delegitimising their agendas. One way of doing this, is to label the gender–focused NGOs as 'foreign' and 'elitist', thus undermining their identity and status and seeking to de-link them from the broader civil society. It may accuse NGOs of failing as 'representatives of the people', claiming that they are designed for the self-aggrandisement of narrow-minded elites (Pearce, 2000) or even agents of imperialism (Tembo, 2003). For example, in a letter to the Minister of Constitutional Affairs, the President said that he had

> ...caused the Ministry of Gender Affairs in the previous administration (1996-2001) to withdraw the Domestic Relations Bill ...The Bill was trying to copy Western (European-American) ways of life and incorporate them into Ugandan Law and therefore societal practice...Western Societies have completely ruined the family and the society... Therefore those pushing us to copy the West in everything are not helping the human race; certainly they are not helping us. (Museveni, 25 October 2002)

It is important to note that anti-imperialist statements may prompt NGOs, often with donor support, to react by seeking to localise their advocacy agenda in order to counter such accusations by asserting their institutional existence as civil society or the third sector (Van Rooy, 1998). Donor support in such situations may undermine NGOs' claims to be 'grassroots', but the additional resources can enhance their status and identity, as well as their institutional survival. When civil society as a space for action seems to be under threat, some donors will align themselves with gender-focused NGOs, because this can be seen as supporting civil society. Donor alignment with NGOs in such a context constitutes a threat to the government's access to resources and hence its own identity and status.

Implications of NGO-government relations for NGO advocacy work

Government dealings with NGOs variously affect the ways in which NGOs undertake gender advocacy, including the resulting superficiality of their local-level engagement, the adoption of reactionary agendas, and limited understanding and analysis of issues at the grassroots.

Superficial engagement with the grassroots

Government actions affect the ways in which NGOs undertake their advocacy work. In a bid to show that NGOs are 'legitimate' and that their agenda is genuinely popular and grassroots based, local men and women are sought out and encouraged to have their concerns included in the broader NGO agenda. Unfortunately, this process is sometimes marred by superficiality. For example, NGOs carry out one-day awareness training on an advocacy issue such as land rights or gender-based violence, in the hope of eliciting meaningful inputs within a narrow timeframe. The need to account for resources also obliges NGOs to undertake such hasty consultation exercises, and to focus on inputs and outputs rather than outcomes. As a rule, therefore, NGOs focus on measurable and immediate outputs, such as the number of workshops and the number of participants, rather than considering the longer-term impact of their intervention, for instance in terms of lessons learned (Nyamugasira, 2002; Wallace, 2004).

Rather simplistic engagement with grassroots work may also be intended to win government favour by seeming to build broad-based support. Paradoxically, however, this may also appear threatening. Hearn observes of the land co-ownership proposal that "the mobilisation of rural women around the joint co-ownership clause threatened the government" of Uganda (Hearn, 2001: 51). The government prefers to deal with CSOs that confine themselves to the spaces that it sanctions for civil society (Beam, 2001; Nyamugasira and Lister, 2001). Effectively, it prefers to understand civil society as *a noun,* a formal institution, rather than, as NGOs might prefer, in terms of conflictual relations with the state. The donors may not mind either way, as long as their understanding of civil society as a space for action is in line with the good-governance agenda and neo-liberal discourses (Hearn, 2001).

Another interesting insight is the way in which the government manipulates the inter-linkages among the various actors. By either strengthening or destabilising connections among NGOs, donors, and the grassroots, the government can appear more 'populist' than the NGOs. Exerting its influence over NGOs through the advisory, publicity, co-option, and sympathiser roles, the government can thus simultaneously exert its influence, protect its interests, and fulfil donor demands for partnership with civil society in the policy-making process. Overt conflict is avoided wherever possible. Being seen to be working in partnership with civil society, and to be doing something about its demands, is important to government identity, status, and access to donor resources (Beam, 2001).

The critical argument here is that all the actors involved in the gender-advocacy nexus seek to maximise their interests. For the government, this involves balancing a concern about resources with protecting its image as being tolerant of the third sector, and its status as a popular and responsible government. It wants to be seen as guiding a participatory policy-making process without undue donor or NGO influence. However, the whole notion of 'civil society' is undermined when government attacks NGOs and their relations with the grassroots and donors. Second, there seems to be little practical commitment at any level to change the patriarchal *status quo.* For example, as a result of government criticism of land co-ownership as elitist, donors funded the Uganda Land Alliance to popularise the co-ownership campaign, even if one-day workshops could not really change people's beliefs. There has also been a tendency for community leaders to shift the campaigns from a focus on gender equality to other issues, making them people-centred but at the same time relegating gender to second place.

Non-decision making on gender inequality may protect everyone's interests - NGOs, donors, and government. This is most apparent in relation to land rights. By claiming to be sympathetic to the NGOs and encouraging them to publicise their advocacy issues in order to be accepted by parliament, the government deflects NGOs' attention from the real problem, which is its lack of commitment to changing the *status quo.* Not only does this bring a stream of resources to NGOs (in the hope that advocacy can move the policy agenda along), but non-decision making can also be beneficial to official donors who also have their own interests in ensuring that government meets their minimal conditions (such as land privatisation). Such complicity can only disadvantage grassroots women, who have no place in this set of compromises and deals (Hintjens, 1999; Scott 1990).

Adoption of reactionary advocacy agendas
Government non-decision-making tactics usually oblige NGOs to adopt a rather reactionary, or at least narrow, advocacy agenda, rather than a visionary one. They agree, in effect, to reduce the scope of their agenda and confine their analysis to what is thought possible. For example, NGOs focused on the co-ownership clause rather than the wider gendered implications of the Land Act. All that happened in practice was that land became a marketable commodity. Donors, who promote the commodification of land as a mechanism to advance privatisation, similarly play down their stated concerns to tackle gendered inequalities of access to land.

Wittingly or not, by obeying and thus implicitly accepting its advisory and other roles in their advocacy work, NGOs give an influential voice to government. By internalising norms imposed through the notion of 'partnership', NGO relationships with other actors, including donors and the grassroots, are remoulded. This has a major impact on how NGOs set their advocacy agenda. For example, the strategic direction of the NGO agenda on land rights was shaped at critical moments by the government's advisory role. NGOs voluntarily adapted their campaign, anticipating as well as responding to government criticism. The NGOs' acceptance of this role might have been partly shaped by their need to defend their own interests, flatter their providers and protectors, and protect their own identities, while maintaining their status and having continued access to resources. NGOs may also adopt recommendations made by government officials, in the hope that this might lead at least to some of their arguments being accepted. In economic terms, NGOs seem to operate in ways that limit their transaction costs by avoiding severe conflicts with other actors. Relations are not so much wholesomely nourished as drip-fed, and maintained at a 'just enough' level to ensure that they survive. The result is a tendency to lack a long-term focus based on grassroots needs, in favour of ad hoc agendas depending on recent advice from government policy makers and the current likes and dislikes of donors. What defines many gender-focused NGOs is the flexibility of their overall advocacy discourses. By adding their 'flavour' to wider public debates (often through the media), they seek to make visible their involvement in advocacy and the policy process.

Limited scope of understanding and analysis of gender issues
Some of the weaknesses in NGO engagement with the government include the domination of these processes by urban elites and organisations; a limited understanding of deeper gender issues, due to the limited time allocated to both documentary and grassroots analysis; little advance notice of meetings; use of complicated technical language; government initiation of agendas that remain narrow in scope; and an

extractive approach to NGOs on the part of government (Nyamugasira, 2002; Marsden, 2005; Pearce, 2000; Bratton, 1989). Clearly, gender-focused NGOs engaged in advocacy are involved in various indirect ways in the policy process. Having said that, it is difficult to agree with Asiimwe (2001) that NGOs have generally had an influential role in government policy-making processes in any practical sense. All too often the *appearance* of involvement is due to the failure to confront the hegemonic ideology. As Feldman (2003:22) states: "Today the discourse of democracy and popular commitment to decentralisation and good governance works within, rather than counter to, the political space that is dominated by an already established NGO sector". McGee (2002:14) raises similar concerns when she argues that "NGOs and coalitions have been totally unable to influence macroeconomic policy or even engage governments in dialogue about it. In Uganda, as in many other contexts, it seems that NGO efforts to influence government can be described as at best 'information-sharing' or 'consultation exercises'", a view echoed by other recent research (Afrodad, 2002; Hearn, 1999; Nyangabyaki, 2000; Nyamugasira and Rowden, 2002; Lister and Nyamugasira, 2003; ActionAid International USA and ActionAid International Uganda 2004).

Conclusion

The insights of scholars such as Asiimwe (2001) into the success of NGO participation in the policy process can perhaps be better explained by examining the hidden agendas (i.e. the wish for access to resources, status, and identity) rather than the explicit agendas of gender-focused NGOs. It is by having a deeper understanding of their own internal interests that NGO advocacy strategies can be said to be relatively successful in several respects. 'Success' in an environment of extreme resource-scarcity can include the sheer survival of an institution, and maintenance of its complex connections with other organisations. Thus NGOs, like government and donors, are rational institutions that maximise their benefits in their partnerships - thereby *de facto* enhancing the status of official donors, who now parade Uganda as a success story of their good-governance prescriptions for fighting poverty.

References

Abrahamsen, R. (2000). *Disciplining Democracy: Development Discourse and Good Governance in Africa*, London: Zed Books.

Abugre, C. (1999). 'Partners, Collaborators or Patron Clients: Defining Relationships in the Aid Industry', background paper for the Canadian Development Agency, Partnership Branch, Accra: ISODEC.

ActionAid Uganda & ActionAid USA (2004). 'Rethinking Participation: Questions for Civil Society about the Limits of Participation in the PRSPs' (discussion paper), Washington D.C: ActionAid USA. (also available www.actionaidusa.org retrieved 28 February, 2006).

AFRODAD (2002). 'Comparative Analysis of Five African Countries with Completed PRSP (Burkina Faso, Mauritania, Mozambique, Tanzania and Uganda)', available at http// www.afrodad.org/prsp/pdf/synthesis.pdf+ + site: www.afrodad.org+AFRODAD+&hl= (retrieved 1November2005).

Asiimwe, J. (2001). 'One Step Forward Two Steps Back; the Women's Movement and Law Reform in Uganda from 1985-2000', LLM thesis, Washington, DC: Georgetown University Law Center.

Bratton, M. (1989). 'The politics of government NGO relations in Africa', World Development Report 17 (4): 569-87.

Brown, W. (2000). 'Restructuring North-South Relations: ACP-EU development co-operation in a liberal international order', *Review of African Political Economy*, 27 (85): 367—84.

Cassell, P. (1993). *The Giddens Reader*, Basingstoke: Macmillan.

Craig, B. and B. Porter (2005). 'The third way and the third world: poverty reduction anti social inclusion strategies in the rise of "inclusive" liberalism', *Review of International Political Economy*, 12(2): 226-63.

Feldman, S. (2003). 'Paradoxes of institutionalisation: the depoliticisation of Bangladesh NGOs', *Development in Practice*, 13 (1): 5-26.

Foucault, M. (1980). *Power/ Knowledge; Selected Interviews and Other Writings 1972-1977*, C. Gordon (ed.), London: Harvester Wheatsheaf.

Foucault, M. (1982). 'The subject and power, afterword', in D. L. Hubert and P Rabinow (eds.) *Michel Foucault: Beyond Structuralism and Hermeneutics*, Brighton: Harvester Press, pp. 208-26.

Fowler, A. (2000). 'Introduction – Beyond Partnership: Getting Real about NGO Relationships in the Aid System', *IDS Bulletin*, 31(3): 1-13.

Goetz, A. (1998). 'Women in politics and gender equity on policy: South Africa and Uganda', *Review of African Political Economy* 25 (76): 241-62.

Hearn, J. (1999). 'Foreign Political Aid, Democratisation, and Civil Society in Uganda in the 1990's', Working Paper No. 53, Kampala: Centre for Basic Research.

Hearn, J, (2001). 'The uses and abuses of civil society in Africa', *Review of African Political Economy*, 28 (87): 43-53.

Hintjens, H. (1999). 'The Emperor's New Clothes: a moral tale for development experts', *Development in Practice*, 9 (4): 382-95.

Kabeer, N. (1995). *Reversed Realities: Gender Hierarchies in Development Thought* (2nd edn.), London: Verso.

Kabeer, N. (1999). 'Resources, agency and achievement: reflections on the measurement of women's empowerment', *Development and Change*, 30 (3): 435-64.

Lister, S. and W. Nyamugasira (2003). 'Design contradictions in the "New Architecture of Aid"? Reflections from Uganda on the roles of civil society organisations', *Development Policy Review*, 21(1): 93-106.

Lukes, S. (1974). *Power: A Radical View*, London: Macmillan.

Marsden, R. (2005). 'Exploring power relationships, a perspective from Nepal', in L. Groves and R. Hinton (eds.) *Inclusive Aid: Changing, Power and Relationships in International Development,* London; Earthscan pp. 97-107.

McGee, R. (2002). 'Participating in Development', in U. Kothari and M. Minogue (eds.) *Development Theory and Practice: Critical Perspective*, Basingstoke: Palgrave.

Mugisha, M. (2000). 'Gender and Decentralisation; Promoting Women's Participation in Local Councils', available at http://www.fao.org/DOCREP (retrieved 14 December 2005).

Museveni, Y. (2002). 'Views on the reform of domestic relations', Letter to Hon Janat Mukwaya, Minister of Justice and Constitutional Affairs, 2 October, Quote No. PO/17 (unpublished, Ministry of Justice and Constitutional Affairs records).

Nabacwa, S.M. (2002) 'Sisterhood? Advocacy by Gender Focused NGOs and the Reality for Women at the Grassroots of Uganda', Kampala: ActionAid Uganda.

Nyamugasira, W. (2002) 'NGOs and advocacy: how well are the poor represented?', in D. Eade (ed.) *Development and Advocacy,* Oxford: Oxfam GB, pp. 7-22.

Nyamugasira, W. and S. Lister (2001). 'Study on the Involvement of Civil Society in Policy Dialogue and Advocacy Lessons Learnt on their Engagement in Policy Advocacy, and Future Direction', London: Department for International Development.

Nyamugasira, W. and R.Rowden (2002). New Strategies, Old Loan Conditions: Do the New IMF and World Bank Loans Support Countries' Poverty Reduction Strategies? The Case of Uganda, Kampala: Uganda NGO Forum and Results Education Fund.

Pearce, J. (2000). 'Development, NGOs, and civil society: the debate and its future', in D. Eade (ed.) *Development, NGOs and civil Society*, Oxford: Oxfam GB, pp.15-43.

Power, M. (2003). *Rethinking Development Geographies*, London: Routledge.

Razavi, S. (1997). 'Fitting gender into development institutions', *World Development* 25(7):1111-25.

Scott, C. J. (1990). *Domination and the Arts of Resistance, Hidden Transcripts*, New Haven, CT: Yale University Press.

Tamale, S. (1999). *When Hens Begin to Crow: Gender and Parliamentary Politics in Uganda*, Boulder, CO: Westview Press.

Tembo, F. (2003). 'The multi-image development NGO: an agent of the new imperialism?', *Development in Practice,* 13 (5): 527-33.

Tripp, A. (1998). 'Expanding "civil society": women and political space in contemporary Ugandan', *Journal of Commonwealth and Comparative Politics,* 36(2): 84-107.

Tripp, A. (2000). *Women and Politics in Uganda*, Oxford: James Curry.

Van Rooy, A. (1998)'. 'Civil society as idea: an analytical hatstand?', *Civil Society and the Aid Industry: The Politics and Promise*, London: Earthscan, pp. 6-30.

Wallace, T. (2004). 'NGO dilemmas: Trojan horses for global neoliberalism?', *Socialist Register,* 2004 202-19.

Weedon, C. (1987). *Feminist Practice and Poststructuralist Theory*, Oxford: Basil Blackwell.

17

Protecting the Tree or Saving the Forest? A Political Analysis of the Legal Environment for NGOs in Uganda[1]

Arthur Larok

Abstract

It is generally accepted that the legal regime for NGO operations in Uganda, as exemplified by the NGO Act, as amended in 2006 and in 2014, and connected regulations, is restrictive. The reasons for this are, however, less clear, in part because the predominant analysis has focused on the narrow confines of the law itself, rather than on the wider political, social and economic context within which the NGO law is embedded. The unsurprising conclusion has therefore been that Uganda's NGO legal and regulatory regime is draconian and repressive, in comparison to 'international best practice' and 'generally acceptable standards' of NGO legislation elsewhere.

We rather use here as departure point the need to locate the discourse on the legal operating environment for NGOs within the wider political and governance context because the former is a sub-set of the latter. Adopting a historical perspective, we suggest that this legal environment is a consequence of a history of colonial, post-colonial and contemporary State formation anchored around an insatiable quest by the State to control society and actors within it - and NGO legislation is one way to limit the activities of NGOs to politically tolerable levels. It therefore follows that a more enabling legal, regulatory and policy environment for NGO operations must be sought within the larger context. Seeking to salvage the NGO operating space without a corresponding focus on reshaping larger governance and democracy trends is akin to 'protecting a single tree while the forest is being devoured'.

---

[1] This edited paper was originally written in 2008 as part of a fellowship at the International Centre for Non-for-Profit Law, updated in 2011 and appeared in a book on (Dis)Enabling the Public Sphere in Africa by Southern Africa Trust.

Introduction

This paper offers a political analysis of Uganda's current legal and regulatory regime for NGOs, a subject of ongoing analysis and commentary. Unlike mainstream analysis - largely technocratic and apolitical in nature - this paper locates the legal and regulatory regime within broader democratisation and governance trends in the country, in the region and globally. By adopting a political frame for analysis, we directly link the NGO regulatory framework with the nature of Uganda's present ruling regime; a regime that is largely averse to any challenge to its monopoly on political power. Further, the State's attempt to monopolise power has resulted in socio-economic and political choices and policies informed in large part by a narrow State-centric conception of development and the role of other actors. The NGO law is one such manifestation, informed by narrow State objectives, such as the obsession (others say excuse) with security threats, and a desire to control the sector in the wake of its numerical growth and influence on the development scene.

In such circumstances, protagonists keen to see an enabling legal environment for NGOs in Uganda must focus their analysis and action on the political context that shapes legislation generally and that concerning NGOs in particular. We then must interrogate, understand and challenge the State-centric notion that shapes the NGO law, including some common and legitimate concerns about negative trends in the sector.

NGOs and civil society legislation

The term civil society, despite much theorising, remains conceptually fluid, with its utility as an analytical tool varying from country to country. Civil society as a term referring to a range of non-state and not-for-profit organisations is commonly used for similar intents by both State and non-State actors claiming to be part of the development community. But as Chandhoke (2003) cautions, when a variety of dissimilar groups like donors, NGOs and institutions of the State on the one hand and left-leaning liberals, trade unions and social movements on the other subscribe equally to the validity of a single concept of civil society, there is a danger of it becoming flaccid through consensus. Today, various definitions thus vaguely describe civil society as the whole of humanity left once government and for-profit firms are excised, covering all those organisations that fill the spaces between the family, the State and the market. Edwards (2004) notes that faced by many ambiguities, it is tempting to dismiss the concept altogether, but adds that "when subjected to a rigorous critique, the idea of civil society re-emerges to offer significant emancipatory potential, explanatory power and practical support to problem-solving in both established and emerging democracies".

In Uganda, the term civil society is often erroneously equated to NGOs, in part because of their numbers - 7,000 by the end of 2007 and 10,000 by the end of 2010 (though not all are operational at any one time), but these only constitute a set of actors in the civil society space.[2] In this paper, we adapt and use Sarah Michael's definition of NGOs as "independent development actors existing apart from governments and corporations, operating on a non-profit or not-for-profit basis, with an emphasis on voluntarism, and pursuing a mandate of providing development services, undertaking communal development work or advocating on development issues". This definition has a few problems - it forcefully maintains that NGOs are 'independent', when in some cases; there is a strong and even organic relation between NGOs and government. Secondly the definition is loaded with contested terms such as 'development' and 'voluntarism'. With these provisos, the definition generally suits the purpose of this paper, unlike the definition contained in the NGO Act.[3]

A survey of literature on civil society legislation in various countries highlights as frequent starting point instruments that commit states to internationally agreed principles, as defined in the Universal Declaration of Human Rights, the International Covenant on Civil and Political Rights and other internationally agreed frameworks. This unsurprisingly leads to the conclusion that most national civil society legislation, especially in 'emerging' and 'transitional' democracies, as well as in autocratic regimes, fails short of 'international standards'.

The most commonly cited international instruments include the Universal Declaration of Human Rights. Thus, its Article 19 reads: "Everyone has the right to freedom of opinion and expression - this right includes freedom to hold opinions without interference and to seek, receive and impart information and ideas through the media..." and Article 20 stipulates that "Everyone has the right to freedom of peaceful assembly and association. No one may be compelled to belong to an association..." The International Covenant on Civil and Political Rights (ICCPR) is also frequently mentioned. Article 19 reads: "Everyone has the right to freedom of opinion and expression - this right includes freedom to hold opinions without interference and to seek, receive and impart information and ideas through the media..." while Article 22 (3) says "...nothing in this article should authorise States to take legislative measures which would prejudice or to apply the law in such a manner as to prejudice the guarantees provided for in that convention". Several other international rights agreements such as the European Convention for the Protection of Human Rights and Fundamental Freedoms, the African Charter on Human and People's Rights and various national constitutions of sovereign States either build upon or re-affirm these instruments.

Human rights activists and advocates for democracy therefore maintain that it is incumbent for regimes striving to consolidate democracy to acknowledge and protect internationally and regionally binding freedoms of expression, association and peaceful assembly, enshrined in internationally agreed instruments such as those mentioned

---

2 Other actors would ordinarily include Professional Associations (PAs), Trade Unions (TU), Faith-based Organisations (FBOs), Community-based Organisations (CBOs), Social Movements such as women, youth and students, some sections of the media and other groups.

3 "...an organisation established to provide voluntary services, including religious, educational, literary, scientific, social or charitable services to the community or any part of it."

above. Constitutions of many countries (Uganda inclusive) protect such fundamental freedoms.

Calls for an enabling national legislation on civil society are usually inspired by these and other international human, civil and political rights frameworks, as a conducive environment for civil society operations is seen as a product of: the right to associate being clearly protected by law; public interest voluntary associations being given tax advantages; governments not discouraging individuals or corporations from making contributions to the voluntary sector; government-voluntary sector 'partnerships'; the protection in law of the freedoms of expression and advocacy; and the existence and apolitical enforcement of codes of conduct for the voluntary sector, among others (Bebbington and Riddell, 1997: 115-116).

It has been argued that the rise of civil society is not an accident, but a response to local initiative and voluntary action explained in part by the broader socio-economic and political realities of changing times, not least the limits and imperfections of the State and the market (Hulme & Edwards, 1997). Civil society organisations come into being through the initiative of individuals or groups of persons: the national legal and fiscal framework applicable to them should therefore permit and encourage this initiative (Schmidt, 2003). Further, individuals should ordinarily not be required to establish a formal legal entity under civic organisation law in order to exercise fundamental freedoms such as expression, association or peaceful assembly and laws that permit groups to establish themselves as entities with legal personality should therefore reinforce, rather than undermine, these freedoms (OSI, 2004). Proponents of an enabling environment for civil society indeed contend that supporting legislation is both an obligation by States and a human right. It is argued that enabling legislation for civil society encourages pluralism, promotes the respect for the rule of law, democracy, as well as economic efficiency, while addressing public sector and market failures (OSI, 2004: 14).

An operating environment under threat

In spite of the noble rights-based proclamations and benign democracy objectives and expectations listed above, we have witnessed curtailment of space for civil society, restrictions on civil liberties and a general increase in "illiberal democracies" - regimes that, at face value, possess democratic institutions but on closer inspection are governed in an authoritarian manner (Heinrich, 2006: 259). Within just a few years, more than 20 countries have introduced restrictive legislations and regulations aimed at undermining civil society and diminishing the space within which they can operate. Moore (2007:1) writes that in Russia, Peru, Zimbabwe, Sudan [and Uganda] for instance, several amendments to NGO legislation were passed to curtail the freedoms and premises that international rights declarations provide for. He adds that these are not isolated events, but rather part of a regulatory backlash against NGOs and civil society in many parts of the world, which can be viewed as part of a wider offensive on democracy.

A 2008 report by the World Movement for Democracy and the International Centre for Not-for-Profit Law titled 'Defending Civil Society' observes that the ongoing backlash against democracy has been characterised by a pronounced shift from outright repression of democracy, human rights and civil society activists and groups to more subtle governmental efforts to restrict the space in which civil society (especially democracy-oriented groups) operate. While some regimes thus employ standard forms of repression including imprisonment, organisational harassment and disappearances or executions, others revert to more sophisticated measures. These include legal/quasi legal or regulatory and administrative obstacles to discourage or prevent the formation of organisations, purposively creating ambiguities within the legal and regulatory framework or requiring enormous and intricate bureaucratic paperwork for NGOs to register. In Uganda, for instance, the bureaucracy and red tape in the NGO registration process requires support letters from Local Councils 1 and 5, the Resident District Commissioner, sureties and in some cases approval by government ministries. The State can also include erect barriers to restrict an organisation's ability to secure needed resources, such as in Ethiopia where the NGO Law caps the amount of finance a local NGO can mobilise from foreign donors. Other common barriers to a flourishing civil society include arbitrary or discretionary termination/dissolution, stringent oversight and control by the State, challenging CSO credibility and accusing them of importing foreign values, co-opting their leaders or corrupting the NGO sector by creating competition by 'look-alike' (but phoney) NGOs patronised by government, also known as GONGOs.

Why the legal and regulatory backlash against civil society?

As keen observers of the law have remarked, the design and application of the legal and regulatory provisions for NGOs and other civil society organisations must be seen in the broader context of a country's governance system. Democracy, the rule of law and an effective State remain the most important preconditions for a favourable legal environment for such organisations (Heinrich, et al, 2006), as constraints on civil society can spring from a variety of wider political realities. Heinrich (ibid) identifies a number of situations including: a closed economy or a country governed by leaders with autocratic tendencies with a history of human rights violations and abuses, as in China and Zimbabwe; a situation where there is political dissention in the country or a neighbouring country that is perceived as threatening to the incumbent regime or party, situations where there are concerns about religious fundamentalism, as in Egypt, or simply when similar legislation has been introduced elsewhere, amounting to the exchange of worst, rather than best practices.

While the nature of laws and regulations which inhibit civil society activities vary, a set of common rationales for their existence can be discerned. In their negative form, legal provisions can be used to curtail civil society and, in extreme cases, render citizen action for the public good a dangerous activity, leading to harassment, arrest or other adverse consequences (Heinrich). The extent and severity of such State action varies from country to country. In Libya for instance, there is no recognised right to associate. In Saudi Arabia, only organisations established by Royal Decree are allowed to operate, in North Korea any unauthorised assembly is regarded as 'collective disturbance', while in Uganda, any NGO that operates without a permit from government, regardless of its activities, does so illegally and NGOs are not allowed to establish contact with the rural population unless they inform the local authorities of their intention to do so, seven days in advance.

While governments have sought to justify such obstacles as necessary, often couched in counter-terrorism measures, protecting national security, or curbing NGO abuse, such justifications are often suspect. The UN observes that several governments have adopted overly wide-ranging counter-terrorism legislation to clamp down on political opponents, freedom of association, speech and assembly. This ultimately negatively affects civil society work (CGCTC, 2008:4), although NGOs around the world have been actively involved in long-term efforts to address the underlying conditions to the spread of terrorism. On their part, the World Movement for Democracy and the International Centre for Not-for-Profit Law in their 'Defending Civil Society' report, maintain that such State justifications are rationalisations for repression and violation of international laws and conventions to which most States are signatory. While implying that States sometimes have legitimate fears, Moore (2007) also argues that the means to allay them are disproportionately and unjustifiably harsh and overreaching.

While CSOs are often seen as political allies of the State in promoting development, human rights and good governance, they have often been viewed with suspicion because they might be working among marginalised populations or be perceived as supporting political opponents of incumbent governments. In politically challenging environments, governments then perceive civil society as a threat and use the law as a sword to diminish the space in which it operates. As Chandhoke (2003:37-38) observes, civil society goes further than just bringing people together in webs of associational life. It also performs the functions of socialisation and pedagogy. When civil society enables dialogue on the creation, sustenance and expansion of a public discourse on what is desirable for a good and just society, it often becomes a staging ground for mounting a challenge to State-given notions of what is permissible. Arguably, it is this aspect of civil society that threatens the State's monopoly of power (Chandhoke, ibid). Rather than stimulating greater support for a more enabling operating environment for civil society, government then adopts a protective if not highly defensive position.

We can finally note that international law and 'best practices' have been frequently accepted on paper but not translated in practice because of power dynamics, differing cultures, traditions and value systems. It is therefore prudent to examine practical experiences: the next section attempts to do this.

The Uganda context

On paper and in posture, Uganda presents the trappings of a democratic state. A closer examination of the country's democratic credentials however reveals serious deficits and troubling governance trends. In line with the point made earlier that NGO legislation forms a sub-set of wider political and governance contexts, we argue here that it would be foolhardy to expect any enabling legislation for NGOs in Uganda when the wider political environment is not conducive. Drawing from history, we observe that the threat to associational life has been a common feature of successive regimes since the colonial epoch. The current legal atmosphere is then critiqued and the struggle for a more enabling legislation for NGOs presented as a struggle for democracy, rights and self-determination by the NGO sector itself.

Although independent Uganda has experienced manifestations of multiparty and one-party regimes, military dictatorships, 'no-party' democracy, there has not been a sustained difference in real political life between the various political systems, with all having fallen short of truly democratic regimes and being characterised by a struggle by a political elite to capture and control power and by varying degrees of authoritarianism and patronage. Upon ascension to power in 1986, the National Resistance Movement (NRM) however committed to important democratic reforms and a return to constitutional rule. A decade later, it had largely delivered on this promise with important governance fundamentals in place: a landmark Constitution that upholds international human rights commitments, a participatory governance and policy regime and restoration of peace in most parts of Uganda, as well as political and economic turnaround for the country.

In terms of governance, Uganda's effectiveness as a State nevertheless remains mixed. Government has assented to or ratified several international rights conventions and protocols. Domestically, the country boasts of a relatively positive legal and institutional framework for good governance. The 1995 Constitution compares favourably with that of other democratic nations. Chapter Four of the Constitution on the 'Promotion of Fundamental and other Human Rights and Freedoms' for instance states that "every Ugandan citizen has the right to participate in the affairs of government, individually or through representatives...", and that "every Ugandan has the right to participate in peaceful activities to influence the policies of government through civic organisations". The Constitution also commits the State to "...mobilise, organise and empower the Ugandan people to build independent and sustainable foundations for the development of Uganda". The National Objectives and Directive Principles of State Policy stress that "the State shall guarantee and respect the independence of nongovernmental organisations which protect and promote human rights" and add that "civic organisations shall retain their autonomy in the pursuit of their declared objectives".

There are, however, clear discrepancies between Constitutional provisions and practice. Amidst the positive developments are undertones of authoritarianism: the threat to associational life for the most part of the last four decades, though varying in intensity, has for instance remained a lingering feature of successive regimes. After a ban on political party activity for over 20 years, a referendum was held in 2005 to return to multi-partyism but its effective functioning remains a challenge. Quite often, opposition political party activities, especially rallies, are met with police brutality while internal democracy within these parties remains suspect, as manifested in several recent internal crises (UGMP, 2007). The Police Act, though successfully challenged in a constitutional petition, remains in force and empowers the Inspector General of Police to disperse citizen gatherings in excess of 25 people. While the law demands that any procession must only take place only after informing the police, in practice this often translates into seeking permission for assembly. Despite the relative freedom of the press and media in the last two decades, strong State regulation and oversight continue to threaten its freedom. Agencies that express strong political views against the incumbent regime are targeted by State security agencies and several journalists continue to battle cases preferred against, ranging from sedition to inciting ethnic violence. In 2010 government proposed an amendment to the Press and Journalist Act of 1995, a move that has been widely criticised nationally and internationally.

Further, in 2009, an Anti-Homosexuality Bill was introduced as a Private Member's Bill by a Member of Parliament belonging to the NRM party. This also generated widespread condemnation internationally, while opinion was divided locally. While this measure can be seen as in tune with the general cultural dissent with the practice, on closer inspection the proposed legislation is not only about homosexuality, but represents a broader attack on individual freedoms and privacy as argued by the civil society coalition against the Bill: "In sum, the (…) Bill is profoundly unconstitutional… it is a major stumbling block to the development of a vibrant human rights movement in Uganda, and a serious threat to Uganda's developing democratic status…"

As for many other actors in civil society, the relatively positive policy and constitutional framework summarised above has therefore not translated into subsidiary legislation and practice that upholds national and international commitments. Instead, specific legislation, such as the current NGO Act, fall below what is constitutionally guaranteed and accepted in international human rights frameworks or as best practice.

The NGO legal and regulatory regime

The legal regime for NGOs in Uganda, currently defined by the 2014 NGO Act, reflects an enduring control agenda enshrined in previous iterations of the law. The 1989 NGO Act, as amended in 2006,[4] and the 2009 NGO Regulations have a specific history relating to NGOs' dramatic rise and visibility from the mid 80's. In 1986, after capturing State power through a five-year guerrilla war, a then young NRM regime was concerned with security threats to its power base and was therefore cautious of any group in society claiming to be independent. As the number of NGOs quickly grew, ironically on account of the relative peace and democracy ushered in by the NRM, the regime responded by introducing a measure of control - mainly from an administrative and security perspective, rather than a development one (Riddell et al, 1995:194). The 1989 NGO Registration Act created an NGO Registration Board under the authority of the Ministry of Internal Affairs to register and monitor all NGO work, mainly by

---

4   The 2006 NGO Act was repealed and a new one – though substantially similar - promulgated.

attempting to control their access to the local population.[5] The number of NGOs, however, continued to grow and by the year 2000 had reached 3,500, then 5,200 by 2004 and over 7,000 by 2007 (Kwesiga & Namisi, 2006) and 10,000 by 2010 – or a growth averaging 4.2% per annum. Nevertheless, and despite the fears, the NGO sector did not present a direct challenge to the political authority of the State and the full impact of the restrictive elements of the 1989 Act and its attendant Regulations were never realised.

The year 2000, however, marked a major change in the NGO legal regime, when the government drafted a Bill seeking to amend the 1989 NGO Statute, in what was seen by NGOs as a move to further tighten control over them. There was a spontaneous rise of NGO action and campaign in opposition to most aspects of the Bill. Memos, lobby letters and meetings sought to improve the proposed Bill to create a more enabling environment. NGOs challenged the objects of the Bill which were narrowly focused on controlling the sector and conferring much power on the Minister of Internal Affairs. NGOs argued that the proposed Bill was below the minimum standard for regulating civic organisations articulated in the Bill of Rights under the 1995 Constitution. They further argued that the nature of constraints imposed on the formation, registration and operation of NGOs was a clear assault on fundamental rights and freedoms embedded in the Constitution and contended that the new restrictions went beyond what should be allowable and acceptable in a constitutional democracy.

NGOs also criticised the introduction of pre-registration conditions, stating that "an NGO could be denied registration if its objectives are in contravention of the law". They also contested the introduction of a permit system that would be issued periodically to NGOs, without which their operations would be illegal. This, it was argued, would cause uncertainty in the work of NGOs and hamper long-term planning. Finally, NGOs questioned a 'dual liability' provision which stated that, "where an organisation commits an offence … any director or officer of the organisation whose act or omission gave rise to the offence also commits an offence and is liable on conviction". NGOs pointed out the contradiction with the Ugandan Penal Code Act, which states that "a person should not be punished twice under the provisions of any law for the same offense" while other generally acceptable practices provide that "laws governing the establishment of civic organisations as formal legal entities generally establish legal personality for the entity and confer limited liability on it and the individuals associated with it" (OSI, 2004: 21). It was also argued that this provision ignored the standard company law practice where officers or directors of a company are protected under the 'corporate veil', lifted only in exceptional circumstances, such as in cases of fraud.

Despite these concerns and efforts by NGOs, including their drafting in 2004 of an "Alternative NGO Bill", the campaign only succeeded in delaying the law, which became Act in 2006, with little regard to the NGO proposals. The latter petitioned the President, urging him not to assent to the Act as passed by Parliament, but without

---

5   See Regulations 12 (a), NGO Regulations, 1990.

success. What then explains the determined effort by the State to enact the NGO Act, 2006 despite the protests?

Rationalising control-oriented NGO legislation

As argued elsewhere (see Larok, 2008), regardless of NGO action, the Act was bound to be passed in the form that it was, as this was dictated by the wider political context. Several specific reasons can, however, be discerned to reinforce the case made in this paper that the series of legislative reforms resulting in more repressive NGO and civil society laws are by and large part of the backlash against democracy - an argument supported in other analyses (for instance, Moore, 2008; ICNL and WMD, 2008).

Kwesiga & Namisi note in their article, "Issues in NGO Legislation in Uganda", that the advocacy work of some NGOs, especially the anti-corruption campaigns and challenges to State policy and citizen uprisings such as the 'Mabira crusade,'[6] could explain its determination to acquire a high measure of control of the NGO sector. Responding to the citizen uprising opposing the proposed give-away of a forest to a sugarcane investor, a highly placed government official in the Ministry of Internal Affairs commented that 'the mobilisation capacity of civil society took government by surprise and their strength can no longer be taken for granted'.

Secondly, one of the reasons advanced by analysts for the rushed manner with which the NGO law was revised, was linked to NGO governance reports that were critical of national trends. It is for instance known that an Election Monitoring Report on the 2006 presidential elections produced by a consortium of NGOs called the DeMGroup was used by the main opposition political party to challenge the outcome of the 2006 elections, and this did not go well with the regime. Furthermore, the NGOs' campaign in 2004/05 against a proposed Parliament Pensions Scheme caused discomfort with some Members of Parliament who vowed to revenge by passing the NGO Act. Another plausible explanation for the backlash against NGOs in Uganda relates to an external consideration - NGOs' close association with donors that often creates discomfort within the State. NGOs are then seen as avenues for foreign interests on account of their dependence on donor funds. The State seeks to safeguard its legitimacy (Hulme and Edwards, 1997:13), especially if NGOs appear to be a countervailing force and compete for space, funding and appeal to citizens. This has important implications for the State in providing an enabling environment for NGOs or not.

The sector is not beyond reproach

It would, however, not be fair to conclude that the current wave of repressive legislation for NGOs is inspired by political motives alone. Some organisations registered as NGOs have been party to unethical behaviour and have manifested accountability problems.

---

6   The Mabira Crusade was a civic-led demonstration to oppose government's proposed give away of a large portion of a natural tropical rain forest to an investor to grow sugarcane. This was opposed by both CSOs and sections of the political opposition. The peaceful demonstration turned violent, as opposition politicians, according to the media, took a lead role.

In 2005, 15 NGOs were implicated in an embarrassing countrywide corruption scandal concerning the Global Fund for HIV/AIDS, tuberculosis and malaria, leading to a ban on further support by the Fund to Uganda. In 2002 a Ugandan NGO, COWE was shown to have defrauded unsuspecting community members of considerable amounts of money, in a case that led to its deregistration as an NGO (although it continued to operate as a Company Limited by Guarantee). In 2000, a cult registered as an NGO and operating in a remote village in South-Western Uganda persuaded its followers to gather and accept immolation as a faster means to reach heaven. More than 1,000 people perished in the inferno (Kwesiga and Namisi, 2006:87). Most recently several NGOs have faced serious audit queries by donors and a few that have gone through forensic audits have fallen short of expected standards of accountability. In 2019, a serious concern about possible collusion between NGO and donor staff was unearthed in what appears to be a systemic culture that dates back many years.

The government has been fast to draw on these negative instances to justify a more stringent legislation against NGOs. Accurate as these examples are, they are, however, incomparable in scale to the ethical decay and corrupt practices in the public and private sectors, without commensurate State control. Government does in any case not appear too concerned about these deficits, but rather uses them to rationalise its crackdown on civil society and to justify more repressive legislation.

The more NGOs contest the status quo, the more they name and shame corrupt State officials, the higher the risk that they will suffer from a violation of their fundamental rights (Jordan & Tuijl, 2006: 6). Freedom of association and civil society will therefore almost certainly remain under threat. In 2017, for instance, four civil society organisations including ActionAid Uganda, the Great Lakes Institute for Strategic Studies (GLISS) and the Uhuru Institute and Solidarity Uganda were raided and shut down by government on claims that they were involved in illicit activities - their property was confiscated, offices closed and in the case of ActionAid and GLISS, bank accounts frozen. This happened at the height of a move by the ruling party to amend the constitution and remove the age limit for President that was capped at 75 years. These organisations were considered to be key in mobilising national resistance against this move and their shutdown was in part thus connected to a crackdown on dissent.[7] NGOs and other civil society organisations on account of the possibility of their acting as alternative power centres to the State will in all likelihood continue to be perceived as potentially threatening to authoritarian regimes.

Conclusion and lessons for the future

This paper has illustrated the organic link between NGO legislation and the wider political context in which legislation is promulgated, a stronger link than with any campaign for a more enabling legal environment for NGOs. To focus on NGO law

---

[7] https://www.devex.com/news/opinion-our-offices-were-raided-in-uganda-here-s-what-to-do-if-yours-are-too-91288.

without a concomitant engagement with the wider governance trends is akin to trying to protect one tree while the forest is devoured.

Many laws and policies can have a bearing on the work of NGOs and, while a progressive NGO law is important, an overall supportive legal framework is essential. The product of progressive legislation regulating society provides the best opportunity for a conducive operating environment for NGOs in practice. Thus, any supportive NGO law existing alongside draconian provisions, such as the Police Act, the Anti-Terrorism Act, the Interception of Communication Act and proposed Bills such as the Anti-Homosexuality Bill and the Press and Journalist Amendment Bill, cannot meet its intent.

As suggested elsewhere (Larok, 2016), it is therefore important that NGOs keep the focus on the wider perspective, rather than struggle to grow one tree instead of saving the forest or indeed working with others to ensure that the environment is protected. Given the current governance trajectory and the challenges the country faces, civil society needs to 're-politicise' itself without necessarily crossing the thin line of partisanship. This implies overcoming the political fear-factor, being more proactive in challenging injustice, being better socially embedded and relevant to public discourse and challenges and being more accountable to one's constituencies. This demands identification with - and support to - social movements and people's struggles (including actors many may think as 'uncivil society') for entitlements and justice everywhere.

In view of the common threats, there is also a need to think of civil society beyond the limitations of NGOs and connect with other formations, especially trade unions, cooperatives, student movements, business associations, traders and others. It is through engaging collectively – in diversity – and creating a 'Pan Civil Society Platform' that different constituent parts of civil society can secure their own space.

References

Center on Global Counter Terrorism Cooperation (2008). 'The UN Global Counter-Terrorism Strategy: Raising Awareness and Exploring the Role for Civil Society in contributing to its implementation'.

EAC Treaty: The Treaty Establishing the East African Community. Edwards, Michael (2004). Civil Society. UK: Polity Press, 2004.

Government of Uganda (2002). The Anti -Terrorism Act, 2002.

Government of Uganda - The Press and Journalist Act.

Government of Uganda - The Non-governmental Organisations Registration Act, 1989, as amended in 2006.

Heinrich, Finn and Shea, Catherine (2006). 'Assessing the Legal Environment for Civil Society around the World: An Analysis of Status, Trends and Challenges. Global Survey of the State of Civil Society', CIVICUS.

Heinrich, V Finn (Ed), 2007. *Civicus Global Survey of the State and Civil Society.* Vol. 1, USA: Kumarian Press, Inc,

Helmut, Anheier (2004). Civil Society - Measurement, Evaluation, Policy. Helmut Anheier and Civicus, 2004. USA: Earthscan.

ICNL and NED (2008). 'Defending Civil Society: A Report of the World Movement for Democracy'. World Movement for Democracy/ICNL, February 2008.

Irish, Leon, Kushen, Robert and Simon, Karla (2004). 'Guidelines for Laws Affecting Civic Organisations'. Open Society Institute, New York, USA.

Jordan, Lisa and Tuijl Van Peter (2006). 'Rights and Responsibilities in the Political Landscape of NGO Accountability'. In Jordan, L & Tuijl P, (Eds): *NGO Accountability - Politics, Principles and Innovations.* London: Earthscan.

Kwesiga J.B. & Namisi, H. (2006). Issues in Legislation for NGOs in Uganda'. In Jordan, L & Tuijl P, (Eds): *NGO Accountability - Politics, Principles and Innovations.*

Larok, Arthur (2016) 'Re-invigorating Civil Society in Uganda and the Future'.

Michael, Sarah (2004). 'Undermining Development – The Absence of Power among Local NGOs in Africa'. *Africa Issues,* USA & Canada: Indiana University Press.

Moore, David (2008). 'Safeguarding Civil Society in Politically Complex Environments.

NGO Forum and Deniva (2006). 'Narrowing the Space for Civil Society Operations in Uganda - An Analysis of implications of the 2006 NGO Registration [Amendment] Act'.

Riddell, R and Bebbington, A. (1995). 'Heavy Hands, Hidden Hands, Holding Hands? Donors, Intermediary Organisations and Civil Society Organisations'.

Salamon L, et al (2003). 'Global Civil Society – An Overview', The John Hopkins Comparative Non-Profit Sector Project. Center for Civil Society Studies, Institute for Policy Studies, Baltimore, USA: John Hopkins University.

Salamon, Lester, Sokolowski, S. and Associates (2004). *Global Civil Society* (Vol. 2): Dimensions of the Nonprofit Sector. Kumarian Press, Inc.

Schmidt, Linda (2003). 'Public Advocacy – Freedom of Expression and Political Activities'. In *Enabling Civil Society: Practical Aspects of Association. Public Interest Law Initiative*, USA: Columbia Law School.

Tandon, R and Moharty, R (Eds), 2003. *Does Civil Society Matter? Governance in Contemporary India.* New Delhi: Sage Publications.

The NGO QuAM Working Group (2006). 'Our Code of Honour: The NGO Quality Assurance Certification Mechanism, Part 1: What the QuAM is and how it Works'.

UGMP (2007). 'Citizen Mobilisation for Good Governance: The Bumpy Road Ahead', 2007 Annual Governance Report.

18

Developing a 'Civil' Society in Partial Democracies: In/civility and a Critical Public Sphere in Uganda and Singapore[1]

Daniel Hammett,[2] Lucy Jackson[3]

Abstract

The fostering of a critically engaged citizenry and robust civil society are championed as cornerstones of democratisation and development, particularly in partially free or unfree democracies. The role, dispositions and practices expected of both citizens and civil society organisations are often contested, demonstrating differing approaches towards and understandings of public participation in political life and the public sphere. This paper explores the social and normative construction of civility as a tool of governmentality. Drawing upon evidence regarding the role, functioning, and challenges facing civil society in efforts to entrench an open public sphere and engaged citizenry in two partial democracies, Uganda and Singapore, we reflect upon the ways in which such efforts respond to - and are shaped by - the developmental state model, and how discourses of in/civility are deployed to constrain more critical interventions and enactments of citizenship and civil society.

Introduction

Nation-building agendas inherently involve efforts to construct and inculcate expected practices and dispositions of citizenship. Linked to these efforts are policies and practices that determine the availability of - and rules relating to the use of - a (critical) public sphere and the role and functioning of civil society therein. Integral to these practices, key values and behaviours are instilled through practices of governmentality

---

[1] Reprinted by kind permission from Elsevier B.V from *Political Geography*, Vol. 67, November 2018, http://dx.doi.org/10.1016/j.polgeo.2017.08.004.
[2] University of Sheffield, United Kingdom, Corresponding author. E-mail address: d.hammett@sheffield.ac.uk (D. Hammett).
[3] University of Liverpool, United Kingdom.

and expressed through particular vocabularies (Staeheli & Hammett, 2010). Such endeavours are intended to develop and underpin specific, contextually-grounded understandings and manifestations of national identity, 'good' and 'active' citizenship, economic growth, and democratisation. Although typically driven by national governments, these agendas are informed by negotiations of global geopolitical agendas and interventions including agendas for good governance, democratisation and a civilisational geopolitics (Jeffrey, 2008).

Reflecting on the politics of democratisation in Bosnia-Herzegovina, Jeffrey (2008) locates the discourse of civility at the heart of interventionist agendas and efforts to forge a nation within a post-conflict environment. Such practices have historical precedence; from colonial 'civilising missions' to the present, ideals of development and modernisation locate those living outside the laws of the state as uncivilised, in contrast with those citizens who are active and law-abiding participants, and thus deemed as being civilised (Flint, 2009; Scott, 2009; White, 2006). These efforts demonstrate how normative approaches to civility provide for contextually-rooted definitions that form "a set of principles and assumptions relating to social [and political] behaviour set out by elite arbiters" and which underpin a relational dynamic deter-mining and valorising desired political and social behaviours that are situated in opposition to unacceptable or uncivil practices (Jeffrey, 2008, p. 741).

Socio-economic and political conditions, historical experience and memory frame these understandings which are, in turn, expressed through discursive and pedagogical practices including legislation, educational content, political rhetoric and the actions of the institutions of government. Civility, therefore, becomes a tool of governmentality deployed within pedagogies of citizenship and efforts to promote and delineate 'good' citizenship and civil society (Jeffrey & Staeheli, 2015; Pathak, 2013; Pykett, 2010; Scott, 2009). The reception of these ideals, however, provides moments of tension as normative expectations are questioned, adapted or rejected (Hammett, 2008; Jeffrey & Staeheli, 2015). Such moments allow us to think about civility as a "lens for political critique" (Jeffrey, 2008, p. 741). However, whereas Jeffrey (2008: 741) argues that "the question is no longer what does it mean to be civil but rather how do judgements of civility shape political life in any given locality", we examine how contestations of the meanings and judgements of civility intersect as tools of governmentality. Of specific concern is how meanings and adjudications of civility are used to monitor, control and curtail the promotion and development of civil society in hybrid political systems.

International development agencies locate civil society as essential for socio-economic development, a vital space for citizen participation within a critical public sphere, and both a marker and constituent element of the entrenchment of accountable, democratic governance (Freidman, 2010). Good governance and neoliberal development agendas have positioned civil society as a key development partner and funding recipient to promote democratisation and act as a service delivery and development project partner (Rombouts, 2006). Simultaneously, governments seek to manage, co-opt or marginalise civil society to minimise their potentially oppositional and critical nature, with such practices illustrating competing understandings of what civil society 'is' or 'should be', what it 'does' and 'how it does' its function as civil society. Against this backdrop, we pick up on Jeffrey's (2008) provocation and ask whether civil society must be civil in what it does. Some argue that it must, placing civility (and its etymological roots relating to courteousness and good citizenship) and associated public behaviour and progressive social relations at the heart of the concept. However, such an approach risks ignoring dominant power relations and control of the public sphere in determining what is or is not civil. In this article we examine how civility is deployed as a tool of governmentality by states in (de)legitimising which groups are recognised as civil society and the activities and strategies they can use to mobilise, advocate and engage. The article begins with a critical reflection on the nature and purpose of civil society in non-Western socio-political contexts. The next section builds an understanding of the concept of civility and the potential use of this notion as a tool of governmentality. We then detail the empirical underpinning to this paper, outlining the politico-legal contexts of civil society in two hybrid political systems: Singapore and Uganda. Drawing upon interviews with civil society activists we examine how discourses (understood here as a form of power which constitutes knowledge and understanding within a social field) of civility and incivility are deployed as tools of governmentality over civil society, and civil society's responses to these.

Civil society in non-Western contexts

Civil society is positioned as a key space for and of development and democracy within which citizens interact, debate and seek to hold governing elites accountable (Freidman, 2010; Paffenholz & Spurk, 2006; Robinson & Friedman, 2007). Civil society organisations (CSOs) have emerged as vital implementing partners for development projects and interventions, and are viewed by the UNDP as "facilitator, watchdog, catalyst, and policy advocate in implementing national development agendas" (UNDP, 2008, p. 3). In 2015, the UK's Department for International Development distributed roughly 20% of their bi-lateral aid budget through CSOs (DfID, 2016). Despite such privileging, CSOs often face challenges from governments seeking to marginalise their activities and constrain the critical public sphere (Dorman, 2006; Young, 2004).

Critics, however, caution that efforts to promote the role of CSOs in development and democratisation have been used to promote "narrow neoliberal agendas to developing countries, rather than exploring and supporting alternative forms of social democracy" (Hickey, 2002, p. 842; also Volpi, 2011). Others have gone further, questioning the relevance and applicability of Western notions of 'civil society' to non-Western contexts (see discussion in Hammett, 2013), notably in relation to the blurring of boundaries in organisational life with the state, market and family (see Chabal & Daloz, 1999). Meanwhile, De Heredia (2012) suggests African civil society functions as an ambiguous space both supporting and resisting state-building efforts. Despite these reservations, continued impetus for the development of civil society has culminated in a "paradigm of civil society participation" (Rombouts, 2006) and rapid proliferation of CSOs across the global south. This prioritising of civil society for development and democratisation in non-Western contexts means it is vital to understand how these organisations are able to function to promote democratic development (within hybrid political systems wherein multiple forms of overt and covert disciplining power are deployed to curtail the spaces of and activities within the critical public sphere), the limits placed upon them and their responses to these.

In light of these debates, the extent to which CSOs are able to live up to the expected ideal of civil society, as being the "realm in which the promise of democratic participation becomes a reality, ... the organisations that citizens form in order to enjoy a say, and to try and ensure that government responds to their needs and is accountable to them" (Freidman, 2010: 119), warrants critical reflection. Thus, our concern is to think about civil society as a space of governmentality, as both a concept and space shot through with discursive power that frames not only the meaning of civil (society), civility and civilised but also associated practices and dispositions. Such practices are evident in how major development donors define who constitutes civil society and what activities (and involving whom) they will fund (see Staeheli, Marshall, Jeffrey, Nagel, & Hammett, 2014), as well as the myriad ways national governments seek to co-opt or restrict civil society's functioning through both legal acts defining civil society and the use of bureaucratic procedures as tools of governmentality (as are explored below).

These often competing agendas have significant implications for who is recognised as civil society, what they can do, with whom, and how (see Staeheli et al., 2014). Thus, while ideas of civil society are often rooted in ideas of civility and civic duty (often related to ideals of 'good' citizenship (Staeheli & Hammett, 2013)) the partiality and discursive power of these terms means CSOs may act and/or be labelled as acting in ways that are (simultaneously) civil and/or uncivil (Lynch & Crawford, 2011; also; Obadare, 2009). Achieving consensus on 'what' or 'who' is civil society remains challenging, not least given the ways in which practices of governmentality are deployed to produce a politics of contingency intended to impose a view of the expected behaviours, dispositions and practices - the 'civility' of both citizens and civil society - intended to underpin modernisation agendas and Western-style liberal and neoliberal values (Hammett, 2013; Naqvi & Subadevan, 2017; Volpi, 2011).

Civility and civil society

Jeffrey and Staeheli (2015: 481) argue that the promotion of citizenship often emphasises "behaviours [that] are associated with civility". Such efforts seek to promote both a 'civil' society (a set of behaviours and dispositions expected of good citizens (Staeheli & Hammett, 2013) which may be associated with a focus on elements of a 'good society' and associational life grounded in ideas and practices of altruism (Yeung, 2006)) and a 'civil society' (an arena of civic participation). Given that civil society can be "identified with everything from multi-party systems and the rights of citizenship to individual voluntarism and the spirit of community" (Seligman, 1997, p. 5) we need to address the etymology of the term civil/civility and its relationship with civil society.

Within colonial practices, discourses of civility and incivility were used to differentiate civilised settlers from uncivil indigenous populations and justify oppressive policies (Terreni Brown, 2014). Civility emerged as a key discursive tool of governmentality; ordering society and delimiting un/acceptable behaviours linked to a sought-after body politic, and promoting self-government and conditional forms of citizenship (Flint, 2009; Friedman, 2004; Pathak, 2013; Scott, 2009; Turner, 2014). These practices continue to be used to govern citizens and CSOs and inscribe limits to (political) debate (for instance, President Lee Kuan Yew's (2011: 185) "laying down of out-of-bound markers" for media engagements with politics in Singapore).

Within Western political thinking, the notion of civility has been linked to liberal democratic thinking, the centralisation of sovereign power and evolution of expected behaviours of the public (Volpi, 2011; White, 2006). Thus, many approaches to civility draw from the term's linguistic roots (from Old French *civilité* and the Latin *cititatem*, *civitas* and *civilis* and, more recently, in relation to good citizenship or the state and behaviour of being civilised) to frame civility in relation to courteousness behaviour towards others and a sense of identity and commonality beyond kith, kin and other hierarchical social relations (Calhoun, 2000; Davetian, 2009; Volpi, 2011). This etymology, Forni (2002: 12, 14) states, "reminds us that they are also supposed to be good citizens and good neighbours" who "do the right thing by others". Going further we see how expectations of civility extend to the practices and dispositions of 'good citizenship' and carrying out expected 'actions' of citizenship (Calhoun, 2000; Isin, 2008). Balibar (2001) advances this, suggesting civility should be conceptualised as a 'cosmopolitics of human rights', used to (re)build unity and achieve progressive change through political actions for 'antiviolence' aimed at securing emancipation and democratisation from below (Balibar, 2015). Cohen (1992), meanwhile, suggests civil society needs to be understood as including both civil life (non-governmental social life) and civility (defined as actions taken on behalf of other individuals that take the welfare and well-being of others into account). However, as Obadare (2009: 245) outlines, the literal reading has tended to dominate leading to a focus on "civil society 'behaving well' - promoting democracy, civil rights and good governance - as opposed to 'behaving badly'" and "civil society [being] reduced to 'manners', 'distinction', even 'class'" (252). This concern asks us to question the assumption that there is a single 'right thing' to do by others, and to reflect on both the implicit and explicit power structures which determine who defines the meanings and dispositions of civility in the local context.

Thus, the reductive approach outlined above can be seen as a formal rather than substantive engagement, focusing on the 'civilities' of daily life (Boyd, 2006) or the 'anatomy of civility' (Davetian, 2009). This thinking is pervasive, underpinning popular academic engagements including the Johns Hopkins Civility Project, P.M. Forni's (2002) Choosing Civility, and Kent Weeks' (2011) In Search of Civility, as well as government responses to antisocial behaviour (see Bannister & O'Sullivan, 2013; Galdon-Calvell, 2015; Gaskell, 2008). The emphasis in these texts is 'common' or 'everyday' civility as efforts to counter the 'coarsening' of society (Forni, 2002) through reciprocal relations and enactments of "manners, courtesy, politeness, and a general awareness of the rights, wishes, concerns and feelings of others" (Weeks 2011: 6). Similarly, Forni (2002:5) positions civility as a "code of behaviour based on respect, restraint and responsibility" which allows us to connect with others in thoughtful ways. Building on this, Weeks' (2011) argues that deference to others - notably those in power - should also be understood as a component of civility (the resonance of this approach with understandings of differing forms and practices of 'respect' lie beyond the scope of this paper, but see Hammett, 2008). This approach risks providing a framework for engagement which "authorizes certain forms of dialogue at the expense of others and as a mechanism of pacification whereby constraints are placed on dialogue to give voice to the marginalised" (White, 2006, p. 445). Thus, a critical reading of civility highlights its potential power as a tool of governmentality.

Reductive approaches to civility are critiqued as providing a veneer of tolerance and acceptance deployed to manage or govern public(s) behaviour and conduct, rather than to create genuine spaces of/for meaningful interaction (Flint, 2009; Valentine, 2008). Instead, civility may be used as a governmental tool to restrict and prevent critical dissent and discussion, exclude others and maintain social, economic or political privilege (Papacharissi, 2004; Volpi, 2011). Thus, governmentality may be achieved through various mechanisms, including privileging manners and etiquette over heated debate or the strategic deployment of discourses of civility to delegitimise critical voices and curtail the critical public sphere. In such contexts, we witness how "civility has evolved as a vehicle and an effect of power" (White, 2006, p. 446), confining the public sphere to dominant, privileged voices who adhere to the 'rules' of civility (often cast as 'politeness') in public debate (Papacharissi, 2004; but see Jackson and Valentine (2014) on how incivility can close down online debate).

Civility, governmentality and enforcement

Discourses of civility are overtly and covertly deployed as a tool of governmentality to foster particular types and practices of citizenship and civil society. As Jeffrey and Staeheli (2015: 494-5) outline, "concepts of civility may discipline individuals to comport themselves in ways that are conducive to particular social norms". Going further, Scott (2009) argues that notions of civility are formed in the image of power-holders, requiring the adoption and adherence to specific practices, deportments and dispositions as subjects of the state. Civility is thus often prioritised over justice, transparency, debate and accountability. Indeed, Boyd (2006: 864) cautions that civility can be used regressively, as "a conservative or elitist disposition connected with the preservation of inequality and the status quo" (also Jeffrey & Staeheli, 2015). In such situations - where civility is used to foreclose the critical public sphere - questions remain as to whether citizens and civil society should engage in uncivil practices or subvert the 'civil limits' placed upon them?

Various scholars would argue that when the goals of justice and self-respect differ from dominant social conditions it may be necessary to disrupt dominant ideas and norms of civility, over-riding conceptions of civility-as-'law-abidingness' (Calhoun, 2000; Forni, 2002: 166). Thus civility can be seen as a "communicative form of moral conduct" (Calhoun, 2000, p. 260) reliant upon a shared understanding of civil interactions, behaviours and performance. Therefore if a group feels they are denied (the conditions of) civility then the reciprocal obligations to demonstrate the demanded or expected forms of civility may be disputed (see Bannister & O'Sullivan, 2013; Boyd, 2006; Hammett, 2008). Thus, reciprocity is key (Weeks, 2011): I will display civility towards you if you display civility towards me. However, challenges arise from differing conceptions of what is civil (Volpi, 2011), and when civility becomes a hierarchical concept through which elites and power-holders assume and demand civility-as-deference.

These concerns may be particularly pronounced in the global south where Dorman (2006) identifies how post-liberation politics are often beset by tensions between rights and democracy, loyalty and critical political participation. In such contexts, states often curtail the critical public sphere and activities of civil society in order to promote a hegemonic discourse of nationhood, belonging and citizenship. Such conditions may often result in the need to "pay out to dominant groups larger measures of respect, tolerance and considerateness" while disadvantaged groups are marginalised and treated contemptuously "because they [elites] interpret such contempt as civilly displaying the appropriate measure of respect" (Calhoun, 2000:266). Thus, discourses of civility are strategically used to demarcate and marginalise uncivil groupings while being mobilised to justify (uncivil) excesses of power to maintain the status quo (Volpi, 2011: 30; also Altan-Olcay, 2012). In extreme situations, these practices situate any dissenting political debate or activity designed to promote substantive democracy, and governmental transparency and accountability as being uncivil. Thus, while "political contestation is not necessarily inconsistent with civility" (Jeffrey & Staeheli, 2015: 12) limitations to a critical public sphere may result in all such acts being deemed uncivil and embody a lack of formal or substantive civility (Bannister & O'Sullivan, 2013). Therefore, we see how discourses of civility can be deployed as a tool of governmentality to delegitimise civil society and suppress dissent (Boyd, 2006).

Contra to this, Sparks (1997: 75) argues for the importance of 'dissident citizenship' as a set of "oppositional democratic practices that augment or replace institutionalised channels of democratic opposition when those channels are inadequate or unavailable", which may be disruptive but are "creative oppositional practices of citizens who… contest current arrangements of power from the margins of the polity". Similarly, Boyd (2006: 863) argues against the use of discourses of civility as a regressive tool to stifle social change, instead calling for civility to "be understood as democratic, pluralistic and premised on a sense of moral equality" and for recognition of forms of 'uncivil behaviour' as "assertions of freedom and individuality in the face of the objective or disciplining force of urban life" (Boyd, 2006: 870). However, such practices risk being delegitimised for being reflective of 'uncivil society' and labelled as anti-democratic and "discursively exclusionist, undemocratic or violent" (Ruzza, 2009: 87).

The distinction between civil and uncivil society is thus far from clear cut. Obadare (2009: 251; see also De Heredia, 2012; Hammett, 2013) argues we should critically reflect on uncivil society as the activities used to "articulate the discontinuities in the social system, and to create a sort of 'profane' public sphere" in contexts lacking a critical public sphere. This understanding of uncivil society encompasses everyday forms of resistance which may be deemed as uncivil because they "undermine and demythologise hegemonic power and create certain kinds of truth while also contesting the politics of belonging" (Hammett, 2013: 135) and may be met with efforts to strictly curtail and delimit what practices, languages and (forms of) criticism are permitted: witness efforts in Zimbabwe to outlaw derogatory references to cheap, poor-quality Chinese imports as *zhingzhong* (Fontein, 2009) and clamp down on critical depictions of leading politicians (Hammett, 2011), and court cases and extrajudicial pressures against cartoonists in Nigeria and South Africa (Hammett, 2010; Obadare, 2009). In conditions where formal, invited spaces of civil participation are non-viable, marginalised groups may adopt strategic practices of in/civility to create invented, informal spaces of participation as a response to "the otherwise laudable requirement to treat others civilly... plac[ing] a disproportionate burden on groups in society who [then] have to shout or behave in ways that are deemed uncivil in order to be heard" (Boyd, 2006: 873). Going further, Boyd (2006: 874) suggests that it can "add insult to injury to expect groups that are themselves regularly disrespected or ignored to subject themselves to standards of civility. Why should they be obliged to behave with respect and politeness to others when they are regularly treated with contempt and disrespected oftentimes by these very same people?" (Boyd, 2006: 874). The rest of this paper addresses how discourses of civility are encountered as tools of governmentality which strain the relations and practices of civil society. To this end, we draw upon investigations into the practice of in/civility amongst CSOs in Uganda and Singapore.

Researching civil society in Uganda and Singapore

Former British colonies, Singapore and Uganda have endured differing post-colonial state and nation-building projects framed by regional economic and geopolitical concerns and contrasting levels of domestic political stability. They are both marked by hybrid political systems, with a concentration of political power amongst a dominant political party pursuing developmental state ideals while seeking to minimise internal ethnic divisions.

Historical ethnic differences and growing geographical inequalities mark both the Ugandan and Singaporean political landscapes and complicate nation-building efforts. Singapore's efforts to overcome communalistic sentiments and develop a highly cosmopolitan society reflect a complex socio-cultural population which includes historical diasporic populations and high pro-portions of temporary residents and work-permit holders (Kong & Yeoh, 2003: 193). Since independence from Britain (1963) and Malaysia (1965), the Singaporean state has been controlled by the PAP (People's Action Party), allowing the entrenchment of a strong developmental state approach to national unity and development - a development approach subsequently adopted by the Ugandan government. While this model has contributed to tremendous economic development in Singapore, it has enforced a paternalistic narrative of obedience to centrally-dictated national development agendas and strict regulation of political activities.

Uganda's post-colonial political history demonstrates far less stability, characterised by ethnically-rooted conflicts and violent transitions of power. The 1986 ascent to power of the National Revolutionary Movement (NRM) brought a period of greater political stability (at the expense of political plurality through the introduction of a 'no party' political system which, in reality, meant a 'hegemonic party system' (Hickey, 2005: 998) until the reintroduction of multi-party politics in 2006). Throughout this period, the NRM sought to decentralise government and increase local political participation, while at the same time curtailing the political sphere and space for civil society to operate. The civil society sector in Uganda is, therefore, relatively young but rapidly growing, from less than 200 registered NGOs in 1986 there were 12,500 registered NGOs by the end of 2013 (Uganda NGO Forum, 2015: 2).

These practices indicate a historical resistance to critical civil society and efforts to co-opt this sector to support national developmental policies. In Singapore outright resistance to civil society in the 1980s gave way to a strategic co-opting and directing of civil society and active citizens during the 1990s. This policy shift reflected a sense among PAP leaders of the importance of state oversight of this sector to ensure there was a positive "mutually reinforcing relationship between the state and society" with state oversight to prevent "civic organisations [being] plagued by internal disputes. There are deep cultural reasons for this. The separation of powers is not a tradition in Asian society. Without central leadership, many Asian societies do not hold together naturally ..." (George Yeo, Minister for Trade and Industry, 2003).

Speaking in 2004, the then Deputy Prime Minister of Singapore, Lee Hsien Loong, argued for Government to be guided by "the community with regard to morality and decency issues", encouraging civil participation, but cautioning that any criticism which undermined the government would be rebutted (Loong, 2004). This delimiting of the space and role of civil society reflects a longer history of efforts to curtail and co-opt civil society through tight control over acceptable limits to the practices and engagements of civil society in daily and political life, including ordinances to "rein in the early activist tendencies of the trade unions" in 1968, a tightening of control over media freedoms and introduction of 'out of bounds' markers for political topics in popular debate, as well as increase restrictions on the funding and activities of CSOs.

These restrictions are underpinned by three ordinances. The Societies Act (1967) utilises the notion of public order to restrict and control societies and freedom of association by requiring most organisations of more than 10 people to register with - and be approved by - the government; only registered associations may engage in organised political activity, thereby restricting free speech and assembly. The Sedition Act (1985), Public Entertainments and Meetings Act (2001) and Public Order Act (2012) further limit the freedoms of civil society as well as of assembly and speech, justified as necessary to prevent "protest, criticism and expression culminat[ing] in nuisance or something even more serious".[4] These ordinances link ideas of public order to notions of peace, safety and tranquillity - or, put another way, an embodiment of civility-as-public-order, enforced through controls (and punishment) over the generating of loud noise in public places and regulation over the times and places of public discussion. Thus, while Speakers' Corner was established in Hom Ling Park in 2000 as a space allowing greater freedoms of (political) speech and assembly for citizens (but denied to those without this status) within a clearly demarcated space, significant limitations over the use of and extensive surveillance of this space remain in place. The need to pre-register to use this space, as well as continued limits to free speech and assembly under Articles 14(1) (a) and (b) of the Constitution of Singapore in order to protect security and public order have meant many CSOs have criticised Speaker's Corner as an ineffective 'token gesture'.

Thus, despite this (partial) opening up a specific space to permit more freedom of debate, The Societies Act continues to restrict the scope of civil society on the grounds of public order interest. The Act requires all organisations (not already lawfully registered under other statutes) comprising ten or more persons to be registered with and approved by the Registrar of Societies. Affected groupings include those representing or discussing issues relating to clan, ethnicity, nationality, religion, gender and sexuality, political associations, organisations advocating or discussing civil or political rights (including animal, environmental and human rights), and groups discussing issues relating to how Singapore society is governed. This registration and approval process, coupled with continued reporting and monitoring activities, provides the Singaporean government with surveillance and control opportunities, and the ability to limit the existence, focus and activities of civil society organisations. Concomitantly, this means that many CSOs also exercise great care and are strategic in defining their direct aims and objectives, often seeking to tread a fine line between operating within the legal requirements of the Societies Act while continuing to engage in critical debate and to foster a critical public sphere.

At such moments tensions are evident between efforts within CSOs to develop an open space for civil society to engage in critical debate and practice, while the state seeks to retain control and purview over this sector - as George Yeo suggested in 1991, drawing on the Banyan tree as a metaphor, that it remains important for the state 'prune judiciously' in order to maintain control over and shape the development of civil society as civic society (as a manifestation of social life) (discussed in Devan, 2017;vi). This emphasis on civic rather than civil society echoes the linking of (good) citizenship to familial obligations, social capital and national (economic) development,

---

[4] Chee Siok Chin v. Minister for Home Affairs [2005] SGHC 216, [2006] S.L.R. (R.) [Singapore Law Reports (Reissue)] 582, High Court (Singapore).

thus prioritising communal rather than liberal citizenship (Thompson, 2014). These moves embody centralised developmental narratives and provide powerful discourses to determine not only the issues with which civil society can engage, but also the activities and language they can utilise amidst broader efforts to resist increased citizen participation in governance (see Freidman, 2010). Consequently, Singaporean civil society is often located within a social rather than political arena, required to embody civil(ity) as being 'respectful' of laws and norms and 'peaceful' in activities while contributing to economic development goals and efforts to create racial and social harmony (as witnessed in the annual courtesy campaign, introduced in 1979, and focussed on encouraging citizens to be more courteous and to think of others on public transport, in everyday life, and to contribute towards an engaged and harmonious citizenry).

Similar conditions are evident in Uganda, where state oversight of civil society and the public sphere is rooted in restrictive legislation - such as the Public Order Management Act (POMA) (2013) and Non-Governmental Organisation Bill (2015) - as well as practices of state surveillance and extra/judicial harassment of political opponents and civil society activists. As Robinson and Friedman (2007:647) have observed, the Ugandan government has effectively used "constitutional provisions to control freedom of association and expression, inhibiting the functioning of civil society groups". Human Rights Watch (2012) has identified how the civil society landscape in Uganda has been encouraged to develop to support and provide service delivery, while being discouraged and intimidated when seeking to engage with issues of political change, corruption and accountability. This framing of the space for civil society in Uganda is echoed in the opening justification for the Non-Governmental Organisations Act, 2016. When proposed as a Bill in 2015, this was prefaced with a clear view of what role civil society should play in Uganda: "It is well known that the Non-Governmental Organisations sector complements Government service delivery through the provision of services like health, education and water, among others. It has however been noted that the rapid growth of Non-Governmental Organisations has led to subversive methods of work and activities" (2015:1). The preamble to the NGO Act (2016) reiterates this shaping of the civil society landscape by the state when stating that the Act was intended "to strengthen and promote the capacity of Non-Governmental Organisations and their *mutual partnership with Government*" (emphasis added). The content of this legislation, along with the POMA and Anti-Homosexuality Act have been described as "legislations [that] potentially create difficulty for the effective democratic engagement in the country. The government has created a clear systemic architecture for repression" (Chapter Four, 2015: 3) and displaying a "perceivable mistrust by the government towards the activities of NGOs" (Chapter Four, 2015: 3).

The measures outlined in this legislation mark a clear move towards increased state control over civil society but couched within a language of regulation that is worded in vague terms which, activists fear, "open the door to the control and silencing of peaceful government critics and activists" (Chapter Four, 2015: 7). Crucially, the deployment of the concepts of 'public interest', 'public order', 'non-partisan', 'interests of Uganda' and 'dignity of the people of Uganda' are nebulous concepts which, as in Singapore, provide the government with a mechanism through which to police the limits of civility to the topics and practices of popular political engagement. The NGO Act provides the foundations for the mechanisms of surveillance and control to enact these limiting practices. While the requirement for a member of the National NGO Board to have 10 years' experience of security matters was removed between the Bill (2015) and Act (2016), there remains a requirement for internal security officers to sit on both District and Sub-County NGO Monitoring Committees. This presence, coupled with the requirement for NGOs working in a District or Sub-County to submit not only budgets and details on funding but also work-plans to these Committees, provides the state with enhanced mechanisms for oversight and control through the providing, renewing or revoking of NGO permits based upon intelligence gained through these Committees.

Thus, while the NGO Bill (and latterly, Act) was presented as a means to "provide a conducive and enabling environment" for NGOs and civil society (2015:1) the institution of increased and onerous registration requirements, oversight and disciplinary indicates a move towards control and curtailment rather than enablement and support. These mechanisms, and continued reference with legislation towards 'cooperation', 'mutual partnership', 'shared responsibility' and service delivery clearly signpost the expectation that civil society would work to support the government's development plans and policies, rather than functioning as a critical watchdog or operating as a sector independent of the State.

Civil society in both Uganda and Singapore faces multiple challenges, including state control and surveillance, political disengagement amongst citizens and difficulties in empowering communities and mobilising of rights-based discourses, and negotiations over their role (as providers of essential services, as a bridge between citizens and the government, as critical voices seeking to hold the state accountable). To explore how discourses of in/civility are deployed as tools of governmentality over civil society, as well as civil society's responses to these efforts, we draw upon empirical research drawn from interviews with CSO actors and leaders in Uganda (10 interviews) and Singapore (5 interviews) plus observational methods in both countries. Interviews were conducted over a four-month period in 2015. These interviews were conducted in English, transcribed verbatim and analysed using NVivo software to highlight the role of civil society and how CSOs are (un)able to operate in each context and their negotiations of the boundaries of civility. Our discussion and analysis are not intended to present a comparative analysis of the two contexts, rather we draw upon these data to address the normative and social construction of civility as a tool of governmentality as part of agendas towards democratisation, development and a civilisational geopolitics (Jeffrey, 2008).

The linguistic contextuality of the terms civil, civility and civil society (noted above) delimit the argument of this paper. The discussions presented relate solely to

Anglophone usages of these terms as they do not engage with how these concepts are deployed in other languages (for instance, civil society in French is referred to as *société des citoyens*, translated as 'society of citizens'). As our argument is based solely on Anglophone uses of the terms civil, civility and civil society, it cannot be unquestioningly translated or transposed to other languages - including the vernacular languages used in both Singapore and Uganda. The continued privileging of English in both Uganda and Singapore as official languages, and their widespread use in official documents and communications means that it is possible to explore the use of civility as a tool of governmentality in these contexts.

Contesting the role of civil society in Uganda and Singapore

Civil society in Uganda and Singapore faces various challenges in mediating what their role is and should be. In both contexts, CSOs are faced with mediating relations with a disinterested - but simultaneously co-optive state - negotiating strict restrictions on their topics, practices, partners and spaces of engagement, achieving sustainability of funding and resourcing, and facilitating political participation amongst a disengaged public.

In the face of such challenges, many CSOs viewed their role as not simply being a bridge between citizens and the government, but as an agent of education and empowerment and a critical advocate for citizens in an inequitable context,

> representing people out there who don't have their voice, representing people who want to improve their lives and they can't do that on their own. We look at ourselves as a bridge between those who can't say anything to those who can do something about their situation. In this case we are looking at improving the life of the common person (Uganda A).

> Civil society under the most normal of circumstances should be like a bridge between the people and the government ... And I think in Uganda, civil society originally played a facilitation process but more and more is getting into the actual battle ground (Uganda B).

The idea of civil society becoming a 'battle ground' reflected concerns over the introduction of restrictive legislation, perceptions of increased state surveillance and harassment, and continued efforts to delegitimise critical engagements by civil society aimed at promoting transparency and accountability (Boyd, 2006). These concerns underpinned tensions over what civil society should do: activists in both Singapore and Uganda were concerned that government was seeking to control and co-opt civil society while demarcating acceptable boundaries of un/civil practice which depoliticised the terrain of civil society.

This sense of depoliticisation was also linked to pressures on CSOs to focus on service delivery and basic welfare provision (a drift in part linked to the civil society turn within international development policy and clearly indicated in the preamble to the NGO Bill (2015) in Uganda) through both overt and covert practices, including the directing of funding streams, the deployment of out-of-bounds markers surrounding political engagement and transparency, surveillance and intimidation of CSOs and activists, and government legislation. This drift in Uganda has been noted by Human Rights Watch (2012: 1-2), who identify how "government officials at both the national and local levels have deployed an array of tactics to intimidate and obstruct the work of NGOs … Some sectors enjoy significant latitude. For instance, groups focusing on small-scale development or service delivery programmes have relative freedom to operate. These organisations are often promoted by government officials as examples to emulate … [while] those groups that advocate for change while documenting governance failures, mismanagement of public assets, and the ways that government officials profit from foreign investment at the expense of local communities are at the most risk of state interference." Thus, to be civil, civil society is increasingly expected to meet the social, welfare and civic needs of communities, whereas efforts to challenge, question or critique the government - to embody and empower citizens' political needs and rights - are increasingly suppressed and marginalised as being uncivil. Such practices clearly embody an understanding and discursive deployment of the etymology of civil society as a space for 'doing good' rather than a space for political action. Thus, those CSOs mobilising around political issues and rights are castigated and delegitimised as uncivil and acting with incivility, while those working on service provision and welfare support are deemed to be civil. In Singapore this has culminated in civil society being dominated by service delivery focussed organisations,

> We call it voluntary welfare organisation. A lot of these are providing welfare, providing services. These are handsomely funded by the government. I think that very few of these provide advocacy work, they don't look at the issues causing this. If you want to look at the issues and you want to change things at the policy level. If you are doing that then you don't have to solve a problem. But I think a lot of our VWOs are just happy doing philanthropic work and being seen to be helping people which is good but I think that is the gap in our civil society. It's not orientated towards 'let's try to advocate for change' (Singapore B).

This emphasis, in legislation and in practice, directing civil society away from activism and advocacy is indicative of efforts to impose a particular form of civility on to civil society; civility as focused on everyday or quotidian civics and civil behaviour in a reductive manner, in in other words, the routinised habits and expectations of politeness and normative social behaviours.[5] In framing these agendas and spaces, government positions CSOs are both service delivery partners but also implementers of broader policies promoting particular visions of citizenship and nation-hood.

In Singapore we see how "despite its pragmatic adoption of both (neo)liberal and communally oriented policies toward citizenship over the past two decades, the PAP's neo-Confucian principles have long contained a sense of social citizenship emphasizing duty and responsibility toward others" which develops a socially responsible rather than politically active citizenry (Thompson, 2014: 326). There is subsequently the enactment of a specific form of (limited) civility which results in "The interplay between

---

5 For example, see the Singapore kindness movement, as well as Singa the Lion be courteous campaign.

(neo)liberal-individualist and communal values mutually work to deny the obligation (munis) of the social" (Thompson, 2014). As one Singaporean CSO complained, this emphasis on everyday civilities rendered moot the political aspect or terrain of civil society,

> When you talk about civil society it is based on civil and political rights ... there is confusion, there are campaigns for how to brush teeth and flush toilet. Come on, this is not for the state to tell us this, you should learn from your father, but the government coming to teach us how to do this it is not necessary. There is how to be kind to people, they have a kindness movement, come on! It is too far! (Singapore A)

This sense that the political 'teeth' of CSOs had been removed through the shift towards welfare and civic mindedness rather than political participation and engagement meant many CSOs were concerned about the implications of there being limited scope for challenge to the dominant state and ideology. Integral to these concerns was a sense that government policy and practice were intended to pacify citizens rather than engage them in a drive for social and political change (White, 2006). The framing of the allowed - or civil - role and practices of civil society were thus intended to ensure the continued provision of respect and civility towards elites rather than being a reciprocal dynamic, thereby meaning marginalised voices remained side-lined or silenced (Bannister & O'Sullivan, 2013; Boyd 206; Calhoun, 2000). CSOs who called for citizens to be engaged in social and political justice rather than simply accepting the status quo therefore faced challenges from the simultaneous politicisation of civility - in the deployment of a politicised approach to and use of discursive tool for governmentality - and depoliticisation of civil which facilitated the privileging of civility over demands for critical engagement.[6]

Constraining civil society

The space for, and models of, civil society allowed by the Singaporean and Ugandan states are intended to prevent civil society from cracking open the institutions and systems created to maintain authoritarian political power (Boyd, 2006). Instead, both countries have witnessed efforts to undermine civil society in recent years in order to minimise opposition groups in the political sphere. To some extent this exemplifies Boyd (2006) and Jeffrey and Staeheli's (2015) discussions of the use of civil tactics to foreclose a critical public sphere. A key governmental tool in such practices is the deployment of discourses of civil and civility to limit topics and practices of engagement. Thus, we see

---

6   The backdrop of 19th century Singapore is a quintessential product of over-lapping diasporas (Kong & Yeoh, 2003:193). Kong and Yeoh argue that the local born inhabitants have anchored their cultural orientation to imaginary homelands. This has made the process of creating a unified nation even more difficult. Singapore is a highly cosmopolitan society; while each race is urged to maintain and draw sustenance from a carefully contained sense of ethnic and cultural identity, they are also encouraged to develop a larger identity based on secular, non-cultural national values. It is also important to note here that Singapore has a high number of temporary residents and people on work passes. One quarter of Singapore's workforce is comprised of foreign workers. Available data shows that out of a total resident population of over four million, three million are Singapore citizens, 350,000 are permanent residents, and 800,000 are foreign residents on long-term employment or spouse passes (Lyons, 2007: 9).

how "civil society in Singapore is called upon to be civil in all manner of activity ... [they] are urged to be 'respectful' and 'peaceful' and to operate within the bounds of the country's laws and norms. This means keeping in mind the overarching goals of the state, which are to maintain stability and to continue to prioritise economic growth" (Freedman, 2015: np). In practice, this means that CSOs face structural and social constraints on their practice where the idea(l) of civil society is to 'do good' rather than to 'make changes'. This can be seen through the implementation of the Societies Act (1967) and the Sedition Act (1985) in Singapore, and the NGO Act (2016) and Public Order Management Act (POMA) (2013) in Uganda, which use the rhetoric of public order to legitimise restrictions on the acts and practices of CSOs. Underneath the umbrella of 'public order', both governments are able to impose expectations of civility to curtail the public sphere but without overtly prohibiting the civil society sector. Thus, we see how the Singaporean government employs a 'careful management' approach so as to ensure a positive external image while curtailing the power and influence of civil society. On an everyday level, the need to act with civility embodies itself in the requirement to maintain civil relations and positive communication links with the state - including ensuring the state was fully informed of CSO activities - despite concerns that this relationship is largely unidirectional and lacking in genuine reciprocity. These pressures mean CSOs seek to maintain a 'polite distance' and to avoid aggravating state representatives for fear of recrimination. In turn, governments in both countries legitimised the use of surveillance and governmentality to ensure CSOs adhered to the strict parameters of activities and audience, and the securing of relevant permits for events in outdoor, public spaces and indoor, private venues,

> there are certain types of activities that if we want to do then we need to get permits for... we usually stick to the innocuous ones like having a lunch so that is not controversial. We have of course in the past tried to organise Singaporeans and migrant workers to do like solidarity walks - [but] they won't give us a permit ... so when it comes to events we kind of do keep it quite safe because we don't want our migrant workers to get into trouble ... (Singapore C)

These restrictions in Singapore, borne out of the Societies Act (1967), and the threat of arrest and imprisonment for anyone attending an un-permitted event, mean CSOs feel constrained by what they called an 'audit society',

> it's a constant balance that you have to strike between maintaining that relationship with them [the government] but also in a way what they call speaking truth to power ... you kind of learn along the way and you know where the boundaries are ... But these boundaries are often invisible and it also depends on who is the politician who is overseeing the issues (Singapore C).

Similar restrictions are in place in Uganda, where CSOs feel that the ways in which the POMA is enforced means that they are required to inform the police about all 'conversations'. However, creative 'disorganisation' by officials and subsequent failure to issue permits resulted in many CSO-organised events being cancelled. Thus, while

CSOs were required - out of civil and civic duty - to gain permission for events, the lack of reciprocal civility and civil practices curtailed the public sphere.

> The Public Order Management Act basically tells you, you cannot have conversations without informing the police, and at times they put it upon themselves not to respond to you, to ignore your communication. There was a time I was holding an event, but the police refused even to acknowledge receipt of my letter, so what was the evidence that I had actually informed them? (Uganda B)

Additional practices of surveillance (including phone tapping and alleged police-backed break-ins and other forms of harassment) and control over approved funding sources embody uncivil practices deployed by the government to monitor and restrict the civil practices of civil society,

> The Museveni regime has increasingly become dictatorial. Those that speak democracy and such are being silenced, and the NGO Bill is actually an attempt to silence civil society actors ... they want to control what and how civil society speaks ... Because civil society is seen as aligned to the opposition ... they want to adopt a state controlled NGO regulatory framework (Uganda C).

> The type of harassment in the Ugandan case, sometimes it might not even be overt or open, now they can have well organised break-ins that take all of your equipment, they can have restrictions on meetings - you set up a programme but at the last minute you get no permission from the police, they make sure that they make it difficult to operate, they can make it difficult to draw money from the bank ... there is a lot of tapping of phones - I know that my phone is on their list of those the government has interest in ... Then for us to work in the communities, they can begin refusing the local authorities to allow us the space, they find some traditional leaders who then don't allow their people to come to your meetings, those small, small things (Uganda A).

These concerns illustrate how approaches to the control of public space deploy civil and uncivil practices in both formal and informal - or 'hidden' - ways including break-ins to offices, withholding of money, and the arrest or intimidation of CSO actors (Human Rights Watch, 2012). While these actions may be seen as simple power politics by the government, they represent a form of operationalisation of civility-as-governmentality whereby elites use their power to delimit the actions, acts and very practices of CSOs towards their own interests (Calhoun, 2000; Volpi, 2011). The constraints placed on CSOs in both contexts are both civil and un-civil tactics through which CSOs and the public sphere are corralled by the state. Whilst such civil methods of control follow a Foucauldian structure of governance, CSOs navigate and negotiate their positions, demonstrating performative dimensions of strategic opposition and resistance, through acting in civil and uncivil ways to seek change and to act on behalf of the citizenry. Such actions reflect Scott's (2009) discussion of what civil is and the ways in which such discourses are defined and used as tools of control by those in power which are then negotiated and resisted by citizens and civil society.

Civility and incivility: Practising and performing civil society within constrained spheres

Civility is understood in various ways, from formal to substantive, and deployed to differing degrees as a tool of governmentality to facilitate or curtail participation and critical engagement. In both Singapore and Uganda, discourses of civility are deployed as tools of governmentality to restrict how CSOs operate through delimiting what constitute practices of civility and the civil component of civil society and the public sphere. Whilst civility can be used to fore-close a critical public sphere (Jeffrey & Staeheli, 2015) some CSOs enact a sense of quiet power (Allen, 2016), engaging with the un-civil boundaries of civility to respond to uncivil treatment by the state. In such situations CSOs must continually, and fluidly, negotiate the boundary between civil and uncivil to create spaces within which to operate.

Responding to such restrictions, CSOs create networks and alliances - with organisations, citizens, and sympathetic government ministers and civil servants - in order to navigate the imposed restrictions on their activities (Koh & Soon, 2012) and campaign for social change. In Uganda, one CSO strategically invested in developing positive relations with a government department, drawing them in to conversations about the establishment of a major project to ensure Departmental support and that any critical findings would not be unexpected or seen as an attack on the relevant Minister,

> at the national level we work with different government departments mostly about corruption and accountability institutions ... so we come, introduce ourselves, tell them what we do, show them all that we do, what we are for ... so before we even set up the project, the application, we first got the buy-in from the District so that whenever we are bringing up issues they know what to expect, it doesn't spring on them some surprises. So that's one of the strategies (Uganda A).

The formation of a strategic alliance afforded the CSO legitimacy (by acting in certain civil ways towards the government) and thus greater space to operate within. Moreover, this alliance formation as strategy blurs the imposed boundaries of civil and uncivil as it affords a degree of protection while it allows for boundaries of engagement to be pushed.

Such efforts to 'bend' the rules of civility demonstrate a response to both civil and uncivil restraints. In Singapore our respondents explained how they were able to bend but not break the rules, not least in relation to rules regarding public speaking and permits,

> These activities [indoor events] that we organise are an opportunity to give them [migrants] this platform to express themselves so they may not be able to do an outdoor rally ... there is some space for negotiation because the regulations don't say that you can't do an indoor rally. The regulations do say that if you are a foreigner you do need to apply for a permit to speak even if it's an indoor event but this is something which as long as you don't publicise it so widely ... nobody really cares about enforcing it (Singapore C).

> We have a speaker coming soon …. She is speaking in private at our event …. She would not be able to speak at Speakers Corner because she would need a permit (Singapore D).

These concerns reflect the continued limitations on critical public interventions, despite the establishment of Speaker's Corner. The expectations of civility, imposed by placing topics off-limits to civil society, meant CSOs tactically worked at these boundaries in order to 'play civil' and thus reduce the state's interest in them,

> When they want to monitor you it's because they view you as a security threat so as long as you don't get too involved in politics then you are not a threat because when you are involved in politics it means you are threatening the legitimacy of the government, of the ruling party. So it is that which makes you a security threat (Singapore C).

Avoiding overtly political campaigns meant that CSOs were able to promote their central message without attracting too much (negative) attention which would result in further restrictions on their activities. In this sense, CSOs are, too, performing what Weeks (2011) defines as a relationship of reciprocity, whereby CSOs reflect the treatment towards them from the state. On the other hand, CSOs here engage with ideas regarding 'dissident citizenship' (Sparks, 1997); in disrupting hierarchical power structures, even through small acts, CSOs demonstrate that such uncivil behaviour is merely a practice of individual freedoms (Boyd, 2006). CSOs enact 'strategic practices' (Hammett, 2011) to enable continued engagement. However, it was not only the types of campaigns that CSOs strategically involved themselves with, but also how they were able to spread their messages.

Respondents noted the role of traditional and social media to spread campaign messages in ways that avoided - or reduced - state surveillance or which allowed individuals to remain anonymous, and thus avoid state censure,

> On social media we work anonymously and whatever but in direct dialogue yes we are all polite and all the rest of it but even as a campaign we are very careful (Singapore E).

The anonymity afforded by social media was seen as allowing CSO actors to have a split personality, where they could act civil in [face-to-face] meetings with government officials but then respond on social media in potentially uncivil ways. Thus the CSOs perform questionable acts, themselves on the boundary of civility and civil behaviour (Volpi, 2011), using these 'less extreme' uncivil actions to carve out an operating space within a constrained public sphere (Obadare, 2009). CSOs operate on - and negotiate the limits of - boundaries of civility in multiple ways. As one Singaporean CSO commented,

> We have to be civic in our behaviour and it can still be different from being civil society I think … (Singapore E)

Other CSOs commented specifically on their own strategies for surveillance, for example, keeping records of overt and covert surveillance of their organisations, including of government officials who 'watch' them at events and rallies. This ensured

CSOs could respond to specific allegations, but also that they could build a list of those for whom it was vital to perform in civil ways.

In these hybrid-political contexts, with curtailed public spheres, CSOs deploy multiple civil and uncivil practices in strategic response to such constraints. As one participant outlined, these deployments of civil and uncivil practices were vital when negotiating often contentious relationships with the state and citizens,

> On a public platform they say we engage civil society but it is a relationship that is never easy because there are days when we are civil but there are also days when we are actioning angry words ... you have to be realistic ... the relationship between the state and civil society must always be one that is tense, it has to be tension ridden, for the very simple reasons that I will always be telling you that you are not doing enough, you are not doing it fast enough. The day I will stop telling you this is the day I can close up shop and say that the problem has been solved! (Singapore B)

Thus, some CSOs felt the need to act in uncivil ways and to push at the (imposed) boundaries of civility if they were to achieve anything or have government respond to them (Boyd, 2006). The constant negotiation for many CSOs in Singapore and Uganda remained between being uncivil enough in order to challenge the status quo, while remaining civil enough so as to avoid being shut down or subject to harsh/ uncivil treatment from the state. The question here, then, is whether CSOs in partial democracies are behaving in uncivil, uncivilised or uncivilly civil ways to ensure their continued presence.

Discussion: Civility within an uncivil state

The discussions above demonstrate that the distinction between civil and uncivil society are far from clear cut (De Heredia, 2012; Obadare, 2009). The Institute for Civility in Government argues that "civility is about more than just politeness .... It is about dis-agreeing without disrespect ... It is political in the sense that it is a necessary prerequisite for civic action. But it is political, too, in the sense that it is about negotiating interpersonal power such that everyone's voice is heard". We would go further, however, and expect CSOs to operate in the fractures between society and the state, and negotiate the boundaries of civility and incivility to action change in conditions marked by a lack of reciprocal civility or a hierarchical form of civility which serves to entrench inequalities and injustice. In other words, to achieve social change CSOs must often disagree and challenge and that in so doing, their actions may have to be uncivil e if the definition of civility is used as a tool of governmentality to maintain the status quo and prevent dissenting speech.

Two important issues follow. First is the need to recognise how notions of civil, civility, incivility and uncivil are used as discourses of governmentality, and thus how these are used to suppress or marginalise civil society. Second is the need to consider how CSOs respond to the civil and uncivil strategies of the state and the strategic practices of being civilly uncivil in order to push the imposed boundaries on civil society in order to drive progressive change but without causing too much disruption so as to be labelled as illegitimate for being uncivil. The key tension being negotiated in both Singapore and Ugandan civil society is, in part, the reciprocity of civility and the potential for this discourse to be used for progressive and regressive means.

As Boyd (2006: 873) outlines, "the otherwise laudable requirement to treat others civilly may place a disproportionate burden on groups in society who have to shout or behave in ways that are deemed uncivil in order to be heard .... By virtues of the sameness of uniformity it imposes on difference, the claim is that civility excludes or dilutes those voices already most likely to be lost in the conversation". For CSOs to be able to communicate their actions and demands in ways that are respectful of others, thereby operating civilly, they must be provided with the conditions - the public sphere - to do so. In contexts where this arena is constrained, however, they may also need to be uncivil (according a government which deploys a reductionist discourse of civility to maintain power and inequality) to be heard. In so doing, however, they must not dehumanise those that are opposed. Thus, CSOs are often required to be civilly uncivil, commonly in response to the 'dark side' of forms of incivility deployed by governments' to police and educate citizens and promote a particular form of political civility (Volpi, 2011: 828). In certain situations, then, it is unsurprising that CSOs advocating for the voiceless and marginalised seek to engage elites in a language they understand - uncivil behaviour - in order to be heard. Thus, CSOs in (un)civil states may act in terms of self-defence or preservation by strategically negotiating the boundaries between civil, uncivil, and openly hostile actions of the state. To refer back to what one participant argued,

> It is a constant balance that you have to strike between maintaining that relationship with them (the state) but also in a way of speaking truth to power so it is a very delicate balance ... you kind of learn along the way and you know where the boundaries are ... when you overstep them they tell you that you have ... but these boundaries are often invisible ... you can only learn as you go along (Singapore, C).

Conclusion

Civil society is deemed to be increasingly important in promoting development and democracy, meaning it is vital to reflect on how this sector is conceptualised and operates. The practices and policies of national and international institutions - governments and donors - reflect competing concerns regarding the implementation of pedagogies that not only frame the learning of citizenship but also of civil society. These processes inform understandings of what civil society is, what it should do, what is does, and how it does. Recognising the historical precedent for a "constant interpenetrating or straddling" (Chabal and Daloz, 1999: 17) between the state and civil society in Africa, it is unsurprising that we see continued efforts by governments to control and mould civil society more broadly. Not only do such issues present challenges to liberalist pluralist models of civil society, which assume both the space for and ability of citizens to influence government (as noted by Robinson and Friedman (2007)), but they furthermore allow for the deployment of (an often reductive) discourse of 'civility' which provides an effective tool of governmentality over civil society. Whether manifest through legislation, surveillance or other practices, the concept of 'civility' is used to impose a (politically) acceptable version of civil society - and associated beliefs, practices, and areas of work - that contains and curtails the work of civil society.

The practices of civil society organisations in Singapore and Uganda demonstrate everyday responses to and reworkings of the rhetoric of civility and efforts to negotiate the fine line - the 'delicate balance' as one CSO representative called it - between being civil-enough to avoid overly strenuous government intervention and being uncivil-enough to be able to push for change, to act as a voice for marginalised groups and to hold political leaders accountable, what we have termed being 'civilly uncivil'. In this respect CSOs develop a strategy of partial reciprocity (Weeks, 2011), developing a code of respect (Forni, 2002) in response to that which they themselves are afforded. The success of civil society groups in hybrid political systems of negotiating this fine line is vital for the realisation of democratic participation (Freidman, 2010) but also reflects more localised restraints on civil society actors, including a disinterested public. Furthermore, the efforts by civil society to creatively rework the margins of reductive discourses of civility, which are used as a tool of governmentality to exclude and marginalise dissenting voices, demonstrate an awareness of the distinction between civil society and civil society. Flowing from this, is a clear - if implicit - attempt to rework the notion of 'civility', from a reductive and controlling concept deployed in a unidirectional manner, to being an inclusive, reciprocal ideal facilitating participation, accountability and critical citizenship.

Conflict of interest

We, the above mentioned authors, know of no conflict of interest in the conduct of this research nor the submission of this paper. It is not under review by any other journal nor has it been published elsewhere.

Acknowledgements

The authors would like to acknowledge the influence of the You-Citizen project workshop on "Dilemmas of Civil Society" and discussions which prompted ideas incorporated in this paper (European Research Council Advanced Grant 'Youth Citizenship in Divided Societies: Between Cosmopolitanism, Nation, and Civil Society' (ERC295392)). The authors would also like to thank the participants in the "Mobilising and claiming citizenship in constrained public spheres" session at the 2016 AAG Conference and the three anonymous reviewers for their comments on versions of this paper, as well as the Sheffield Institute for International Development for financial support for fieldwork costs.

References

Allen, J. (2016). *Topologies of power: Beyond territory and networks*. London: Routledge.

Altan-Olcay, O. (2012). 'Protest, memory, and the production of "civilized" citizens: Two cases from Turkey and Lebanon'. *Citizenship Studies*, 16(2), 135-151.

Balibar, E. (2001). 'Outlines of a topography of cruelty: Citizenship and civility in the era of global violence'. *Constellations*, 8(1), 15-29.

Balibar, E. (2015). *Violence and Civility: On the limits of political philosophy*. New York: Columbia University Press.

Bannister, J., & O'Sullivan, A. (2013). 'Civility, community cohesion and antisocial Behaviour: Policy and social harmony'. *Journal of Social Policy*, 42, 91-110.

Boyd, R. (2006). *The value of civility? Urban Studies*, 43(5/6), 863-878.

Calhoun, C. (2000). *The virtue of civility. Philosophy and Public Affairs*, 29(3), 251-275.

Chabal, P., & Daloz, J.-P. (1999). *Africa Works: Disorder as political instrument*. Oxford: James Currey.

Chapter Four (2015). 'An analysis of the human rights and constitutional implications of the non-governmental organisations Bill, 2015'.

Cohen, R. (1992). 'Altruism and the evolution of civil society: Embracing the other'. In P. Oliner (Ed.), *Philosophical, psychological, and historical perspectives on altruism* (pp. 104-129). New York: New York University Press.

Davetian, B. (2009). *Civility: A cultural history.* Toronto: University of Toronto Press.

De Heredia, M. (2012). 'Escaping state building: Resistance and civil society in the Democratic Republic of Congo'. *Journal of Intervention and Statebuilding*, 6(1), 75-89.

Devan, J. (2017). 'Civil society: The idea and its ideals'. In C. Soon, & G. Koh (Eds.), *Civil society and the state in Singapore. Singapore*: World Scientific Publishing Europe Ltd (V-xi).

DfID. (2016). 'Civil society partnership review FAQs'. https://www.gov.uk/ government/ publications/civil-society-partnership-review/civil-society-partnership-review-faqs. (Accessed 15 July 2016).

Dorman, S. R. (2006). 'Post-liberation politics in Africa: Examining the political legacy of struggle'. *Third World Quarterly*, 27(6), 1085-1101.

Flint, J. (2009). 'Migrant information packs and the colonisation of civility in the UK'. *Space and Polity*, 13(2), 127-140.

Fontein, J. (2009). 'Anticipating the tsunami: Rumours, planning and the arbitrary state in Zimbabwe'. *Africa*, 79, 369-398.

Forni, P. (2002). *Choosing civility: The twenty-five rules of considerate conduct*. New York: St Martin's Griffin.

Freedman, A. (2015). 'Civil society in Malaysia and Singapore. Middle East Institute LIU post. September 10th, 2015'. Accessed at: http://www.mei.edu/content/ map/civil-societymalaysia-and-singapore.

Freidman, S. (2010). 'Beneath the surface: Civil society and democracy after polok-wane'. In N. Misra-Dexter, & J. February (Eds.), *Testing Democracy: Which way is South Africa Going?* Cape Town (pp. 117-139). IDASA.

Friedman, S. (2004). 'Embodying Civility: Civilizing processes and symbolic citizenship in Southeastern China'. *The Journal of Asian Studies*, 63, 687-718.

Galdon-Calvell, G. (2015). Uncivil cities: Insecurity, policy transfer, tolerance and the case of Barcelona's 'Civility Ordinance'. *Urban Studies*, 1-17.

Gaskell, C. (2008). 'But they just Don't respect us': Young people's experiences of (dis) respected citizenship and the new labour respect agenda'. *Children's Geographies*, 6(3), 223-238.

Hammett, D. (2008). 'The challenge of a perception of 'Un-Entitlement' to citizen-ship in post-apartheid South Africa'. *Political Geography*, 27(6), 652-668.

Hammett, D. (2010). 'Zapiro and Zuma: A symptom of an emerging constitutional crisis in South Africa?' *Political Geography*, 29(2), 88-96.

Hammett, D. (2011). 'Resistance, power and geopolitics in Zimbabwe'. *Area*, 43(2), 202-210.

Hammett, D. (2013). 'Civil society and the politics of belonging in Southern Africa'. In E. Obadare (Ed.), *The handbook of civil society in Africa* (pp. 125-142). London: Springer.

Hickey, S. (2002). 'Transnational NGDOS and participatory forms of rights-based development: Converging with the local politics of citizenship in Cameroon'. *Journal of International Development*, 14(6), 841-857.

Hickey, S. (2005). 'The politics of staying poor: Exploring the political space for poverty reduction in Uganda'. *World Development*, 33(6), 995-1009.

Human Rights Watch. (2012). 'Curtailing Criticism: Intimidation and obstruction of civil society in Uganda'.

Isin, E. (2008). 'Theorising acts of citizenship'. In E. Isin, & G. Nielsen (Eds.), *Acts of citizenship*. London (Zed).

Jackson, L., & Valentine, G. (2014). 'Emotion and politics in a mediated public sphere: Questioning democracy, responsibility and ethics in a computer mediated world'. *Geoforum*, 52, 193-202.

Jeffrey, A. (2008). 'Adjudications of 'civility': Gentrifying civil society'. *Geopolitics*, 13(4), 740-744.

Jeffrey, A., & Staeheli, L. (2015). 'Learning Citizenship: Civility, civil society and the possibilities of citizenship'. In K. Kallio, S. Mills, & T. Skelton (Eds.), *Geography of children and young people* (Vol. 7, pp. 481-496). New York: Springer. Politics, Citizenship and Rights.

Koh, G., & Soon, D. (2012). 'The future of Singapore's civil society'. *Social Space*, 92e98 (Social Space).

Kong, L., & Yeoh, B. (2003). 'Nation, ethnicity, and identity: Singapore and the dynamics and discourses of chinese migration'. In L. Ma, & C. Cartier (Eds.), *The Chinese diaspora: Space, place, mobility, and identity* (pp. 193-219). Lanham: Rowman and Littlefield.

Loong, L. H. (2004). 'Speech by Deputy Prime Minister Lee Hsien Loong at the Harvard Club of Singapore's 35th anniversary dinner–building a civic society'. available here: http://unpan1.un.org/intradoc/groups/public/documents/APCITY/ UNPAN015426.pdf. downloaded 15 May 2017.

Lynch, G., & Crawford, G. (2011). 'Democratisation in Africa 1990-2010: An assessment'. *Democratisation*, 18(2), 275-310.

Lyons, L. (2007). *Dignity overdue: Women's rights activism in support of foreign domestic workers in Singapore*. University of Wollongong.

Naqvi, I., & Subadevan, M. (2017). 'Contesting Urban Citizenship: The Urban Poor's Strategies of State Engagement in Chennai, India'. *International Development Planning Review*, 39(1).

Obadare, E. (2009). The uses of ridicule: Humour, 'infrapolitics' and civil society in Nigeria'. *African Affairs*, 108/431, 241-261.

Paffenholz, T., & Spurk, C. (2006). 'Civil society, civic engagement, and peacebuilding'. *Social Development Papers: Conflict Prevention and Reconstruction*, 36.

Papacharissi, Z. (2004). 'Democracy online: Civility, politeness, and the democratic potential of online political discussion groups'. *New Media & Society*, 6(2), 259-283.

Pathak, P. (2013). 'From new labour to new conservatism: The changing dynamics of citizenship as self-government'. *Citizenship Studies*, 17(1), 61-75.

Pykett, J. (2010). 'Citizenship Education and narratives of pedagogy'. *Citizenship Studies*, 14(6), 621-635.

Robinson, M., & Friedman, S. (2007). 'Civil society, democratisation, and foreign Aid: Civic engagement and public policy in South Africa and Uganda'. *Democratization*, 14(4), 643-668.

Rombouts, H. (2006). 'Civil society participation in fragile states: Critical thoughts on the new development paradigm and its implementation'. Institute of development policy and management. University of Antwerp.

Ruzza, C. (2009). 'Populism and Euroscepticism: Towards uncivil society?' *Policy and Society*, 28, 87-98.

Scott, J. (2009). *The art of not being Governed: An anarchist history of upland Southeast Asia*. New Haven & London: Yale University Press.

Seligman, A. (1997). *The problem of trust*. New Jersey: Princeton University Press.

Sparks, H. (1997). 'Dissident citizenship: Democratic theory, political courage and activist women'. *Hypatia*, 12(4), 74-110.

Staeheli, L., & Hammett, D. (2010). 'Educating the new national Citizen: Education, political subjectivity, and divided societies'. *Citizenship Studies*, 14(6), 667-680.

Staeheli, L., & Hammett, D. (2013). 'For the future of the nation': Citizenship, nation, and education in South Africa'. *Political Geography*, 32, 32-41.

Staeheli, L., Marshall, D., Jeffrey, A., Nagel, C., & Hammett, D. (2014). 'Producing citizenship in divided Societies: Pedagogy, civil society, and the citizenship Industry'. You-Citizen Working Paper 2 http://youcitizen.org/images/Working%20Paper% 202_Producing%20 Citizenship%20in%20Divided%20Societies.pdf.

Terreni Brown, S. (2014). 'Planning for Kampala: Histories of sanitary intervention and in/formal spaces'. *Critical African Studies*, 6(1), 71-90.

Thompson, E. (2014). Immigration, society and modalities of citizenship in Singapore. *Citizenship Studies*, 18(3e4), 315-331.

Turner, J. (2014). 'Testing the liberal subject: (in)security, responsibility and 'selfimprovement' in the UK citizenship test'. *Citizenship Studies*, 18(3e4), 332-348.

Uganda National NGO Forum. (2015). 'A position paper and clause by clause analysis of the NGO Bill 2015'.

UNDP. (2008). 'Partnerships in action: A web-based toolkit on UNDP engagement with civil society'. https://info.undp.org/global/documents/partnerships/2008_ Partnerships_ In_ Action_Toolkit_UNDP_engagement_with_Civil_Society_UNDP. pdf. (Accessed 15 July 2016).

Valentine, G. (2008). 'Living with difference: Reflections on geographies of encounter'. *Progress in Human Geography*, 32(3), 323-337.

Volpi, F. (2011). 'Framing civility in the Middle East: Alternative perspectives on the state and civil society'. *Third World Quarterly*, 32(5), 827-843.

Weeks, K. (2011). *In Search of civility: Confronting incivility on the college campus*. New York: Morgan James.

White, M. (2006). 'An ambivalent civility'. *The Canadian Journal of Sociology*, 31(4), 445- 460.

Yeung, A. (2006). 'In Search of a good Society: Introduction to altruism theories and their links with civil society'. Centre for Civil Society. LSE. Civil Society Working Paper No 25 http://eprints.lse.ac.uk/29078/1/CSWP25.pdf.

Yew, L. K. (2011). *From third world to first*. New York: Harper Collins.

Young, C. (2004). 'The end of the post-colonial state in Africa? Reflections on changing African political dynamics'. *African Affairs*, 103(410), 23-49.

SECTION VI
Resourcing Civil Society's Growth

19

The Impact of Western Management Tools on Ugandan NGOs: Some Contextual Notes[1]

Rosemary Adong

Abstract

This paper attempts to explore recent shifts in development practice in Uganda, as evidenced by the engagement of aid agencies, international NGOs and local NGOs in ever broadening political processes. Away from project delivery, 'development actors' are now seeking new relationships, with an accent on enhanced ownership by the country, organisations and local people. Parallel to this shift has been a focus on particular dimensions of the development process, especially with regard to 'participation', 'partnership', 'lobbying and advocacy' and 'gender' which are all have emerged to inform these new development relationships. Where do these words come from? And how are they interpreted locally? How much is put into practice? The paper reviews these selected themes, using experience of working with a wide range of NGO partners in Uganda, as well as reactions at the Community Development Resource Network, as a local 'capacity-building' organisation.

The new language of aid and poverty reduction implies shifts in control and distribution of power: this requires that a relationship of trust and transparency is allowed to flourish, within and between aid agencies and their partners in Uganda. This also means narrowing the gap between words and actions, a process that can in part happen (in both the North and in Uganda) if we start re-thinking old behaviours, procedures and organisational cultures that have kept us trapped into the old ways of doing things.

Introduction

Recent years have seen major shifts in the policies of most aid agencies in Uganda. Poverty reduction is more than ever the overarching goal and agencies have been

---

[1] This paper was originally prepared as a contribution to "Impact and Implications of Rational Management Tools on NGO Partnership and Practice" a 2003 research project run by Oxford Brooks University (UK) and partners in Uganda and South Africa. The full report arising from this initiative is available from the Community Development Resource Network.

shifting from supporting projects and service delivery to becoming co-players in broader political processes. They are now seeking new relationships, with an accent on enhanced ownership by the country, organisations and local people. Consequently, approaches and requirements such as partnership, participation, gender sensitivity and transparency have emerged to inform this relationship.

This implies shifts in control and distribution of power. However, in practice there is a wide gap between what is said and what is done!

This paper attempts to explore these selected themes, using our experience of working with a wide range of NGO partners in Uganda, as well as our own reaction at the Community Development Resource Network (CDRN), as a local 'capacity-building' organisation.

Participation

The concept of 'participation' has been widely used in the development discourse in Uganda for over 20 years now, but this has mainly been driven by the Western world (international development agencies and/or other donors). This, however, does not mean that participation was alien to Ugandan society: participation has been and will continue to be part of our traditional culture. The West however imposed its own vision of 'participation' without much consideration for local tradition and practice: this puts the sustainability of participation, including scaling up, into question.

The meaning and practice of participation has however also been changing with time- though not necessarily in a linear way. For example, participation was originally equated with the involvement of target beneficiaries in running projects; this was followed by greater involvement of marginalised groups in community life, and more recently the engagement of civil society in local decision-making and wider political processes.

The participation discourse stems from disillusionment with failed development initiatives in Uganda in the 1950s, '60s and '70s, which themselves reflected a colonial and neo-colonial vision on community development that sought to 'modernise' its subjects, and to transfer technologies that would ensure compliance with an external vision of development - as well as transforming these subjects into 'good citizens'- domesticated so to say.

In the '80s, the failure of these 'blueprint' approaches pointed towards the critical role that 'beneficiaries' could play in ensuring the success of development initiatives. For was it not their needs that development initiatives sought to address? Thus beneficiaries began to be 'invited' to participate to have their needs incorporated into projects, so that projects would be appropriate and acceptable. Rapid rural appraisal techniques were introduced into the Uganda participation landscape - as a quick method of gathering information from the poor, using semi-structured interviews, diagrams and other techniques using local materials. The issue of 'project ownership' also gained currency: for projects to work and be sustainable, the community had to have a sense of ownership. As a result, more and more communities were drawn into the entire project cycle. The poor thus began to be recognised as key in the development process.

It is also during this period that role of Uganda's state and government was rethought because they were perceived to have failed in delivering services to ordinary people. The state had to be 'rolled back' so that market mechanisms could be left to promote development. Structural adjustment programmes were instituted as a result of this: as elsewhere in Africa, this entailed reducing government expenditure on service delivery and creating the necessary conditions for the private sector to provide those services. Cost sharing in hospitals, retrenchment of civil servants, demobilisation of soldiers, removals of subsidies on agricultural inputs are but a few examples of this. The poor were now viewed as 'consumers' of development rather than 'beneficiaries': this led to a number of people joining the ranks of the poor and increased the vulnerability of those who were already poor.

NGOs stepped in to fill this vacuum in service delivery, a drive mainly triggered by the donor world through the provision of hefty resources for service delivery, both to international and local NGOs. As a result, many NGO s were formed in Uganda - some for genuine reasons (poverty reduction), others for self-serving economic gains.

With donor support to NGOs came the participation agenda: NGOs were seen as well-equipped to 'operationalise' participation. They were people-centred and their work involved organising the poor into groups and supporting them to address their needs. Further, because of their experiences in using participatory methods, NGOs were generally perceived to be closer and more responsive to communities than governments.

By the 1990s, the meaning and extent of participation deepened further. The poor began to be seen as stakeholders in development and Participatory Rural Appraisal (PRA) methods became widely used to engage with the poor. Participation became an end and not just a means to development.

The widespread use of PRA in Uganda was, however, not only informed by the genuine desire to empower the poor. Some organisations used PRA as a fashion (because every other person was using it), and in a bid to attract resources from donors and to remain relevant on the NGO job market. Some were forced into PRA because it was a donor conditionally - PRA was presented by some donors as if it were a 'magic bullet' or panacea for poverty alleviation. On the other hand, some development workers could not apply PRA because of the nature of their organisation (bureaucratic, top-bottom). Poor quality training also contributed to the limited impact of these approaches, as consultancy firms emerged to engage in the lucrative business of training development workers and often did shoddy jobs. Above all, the technocratic application of PRA by some organisations had its toll on the transformative objective of participatory approaches.

Of late, participation has been extended into the realm of government policy-making and citizenship. Could this arise because donor agencies and some NGOs have come to realise that traditional development projects have offered little in terms of changing the structural causes of poverty and inequality?

How has CDRN positioned itself?

CDRN was initially formed to promote participatory approaches to community development work. Training development workers in PRA was thus our 'core business' We were however concerned by two obstacles: the cost and quality of PRA training and the way in which it was being applied by various organisations (lip service and technocratic application). On the one hand, foreign and expensive consultants were being hired to provide training in PRA within a cultural context that they were not conversant with (issues of cost effectiveness); on the other hand some (money-minded) local consultants offered poor quality training.

CDRN thus introduced a new approach to PRA training in Uganda, based on a rigorous six-week training programme, divided into three modules of two weeks each. Each module covered both the theory and practice of PRA. Field practice took place in selected villages to provide 'hands-on experience' for the participants. The outcome of the six weeks was a community project, which in part compensated the community for time spent during field practice.

This approach enhanced the capacity of development workers (behaviour, attitude and skills) to facilitate community members to participate actively in the development, implementation, monitoring and evaluation of their projects. It also helped communities to better understand their situation and their potential to shape their destiny.

Much as this training contributed to the empowerment of target communities from a micro perspective, it did not promote a fundamental change in the structural causes of poverty and inequality in those communities to any large extent. This in part was attributed to the micro-focus of the training and the tools, which sometimes did not allow for a 'revolutionary' process.

Another core area of CDRN's work is organisational strengthening. The focus is to facilitate local organisations to adopt participatory principles in their thinking, practice, and the way they are organised and behave. Facilitating these organisations to adopt participatory management styles is the principal tenet of this approach. This has helped local organisations become more participatory in the way they organise and manage themselves, as well as becoming more critical in the way they engage with poverty reduction activities.

Partnership

The concept of 'partnership' emerged in Uganda in the 1990s, at the very time when the meaning and extent of participation had deepened. As we noted, the poor started to be seen as stakeholders in development with the right to influence development initiatives - as opposed to being 'mere' beneficiaries. The partnership agenda also emerged as a new language of development aid meant to transform unequal power relations between aid agencies and development organisations not only in Uganda but also in developing countries as a whole. Of particular interest to us has been the relationship between local and international NGOs.

The aims and objectives which international NGOs believe they are fulfilling by working with and through local organisations include strengthening civil society, improving the sustainability of their work by enhancing local structures, encouraging mutual learning through co-operative relationships, and encouraging participatory approaches through local intermediaries. Local organisations are usually felt to be better acquainted with programme/project areas. They usually maintain better relationships with local communities and are more sensitive to local cultures and traditions. Further, the involvement of two or more agencies can increase the power and creativity of the work at hand.

In principle, partnership is supposed to foster the empowerment of the weak, and to promote accountability, transparency and ownership of development processes. In practice, however, it is often the opposite because aid agencies with funds normally carry the day: conditions are imposed (although empowerment is preached), accountability is demanded (although aid agencies are rarely accountable to local organisations themselves), ownership is much talked about (although these agencies heavily influence local policy!)

With the changing environment of development aid, many international organisations active in Uganda have moved from service delivery to facilitating local organisations to deliver services to their constituencies. They include ActionAid, CARE, Save the Children and ACORD to mention but a few. Support to local NGOs involves funds and other forms of capacity-building, such as management support and other forms of organisation development and training. In principle, the relationship between local and international NGOs is based on authentic partnership – a type of collegial equality.

Partly as a result, many local Ugandan development organisations have become 'mirrors' of their international partners, both in terms of thinking and practice. Some of them have become unfocused in the process and are largely seen as instruments for implementing the agenda of donors or international NGOs; others have lost their original purpose of existence. This points to the fact that INGOs are failing to let go of their operational agenda: is this why there is a push on their side to make local NGOs do exactly what they used to do themselves?

Further "down the aid chain", community-based organisations (CBOs) and small groups are also feeling the pinch through local NGOs who espouse the agenda of their donors. To give an example, a small group we recently worked with was encouraged by an international NGO to become a CBO to implement the former's agenda of constructing schools and health units, run literacy classes and promote sustainable agriculture. When asked why they exist, this CBO realised that they had lost their initial vision and were implementing someone else's programme.

Secondly, the unequal relationship that exists between international and local NGOs in Uganda is deepened because many local NGOs view themselves as "children of international NGOs" since their existence depends on them (money, capacity-building). This parent-child relationship prevents local organisations from growing into purposeful and self-determined entities. It appears that little is being done by INGOs to address this problem. INGOs need for instance to explore whether it is possible for them to be capacity-builders and donors simultaneously and still be effective - or whether they should only do one at a time.

Thirdly, many international NGOs have limited trust and confidence in local NGOs, in addition to expecting too much from them. This manifests itself through the stringent conditions imposed on local organisations (reporting and proposal formats, accountability mechanisms, composition of the board/educational background...), even on those that are located in the most remote parts of the country. In addition, follow-up visits are rarely used to provide adequate back-stopping support: instead, some local organisations view them as fault-finding missions. Some local NGOs have viewed field visits by their donors as interfering with their work and belittling them in front of their target group. This is especially evident with international NGO staffs that were once field based.

Fourthly, many international NGOs in Uganda are competing with local NGOs in the field of capacity-building. Instead of positioning themselves strategically to build the capacity of local, indigenous organisations that are themselves involved in capacity-building, they are threatening their very existence and 'poach' capable staff from the local NGO sector, thanks to the better terms and conditions of service they are able to offer.

Despite the ideals and aspirations of those seeking to form partnership, the problems encountered in forming equitable and effective partnerships therefore remain considerable, to the point where the usefulness of the concept is being seriously questioned, highlighting both value incompatibilities and practical constraints (governance and management, financial management, reporting and communication)

How has CDRN positioned itself?

CDRN believes that authentic partnership (understood as a mutually enabling, interdependent interaction with shared intentions) is crucial because relations of such quality between national and international NGOs would contribute to the 'social capital' which enables civil society deal better deal with states and markets at all levels of their operations. Partnership is a process of permanent negotiation, which demands acknowledgement of and respect for differences, as well as a strong belief in the need to reach specific agreements based on the higher concern of achieving maximum impact on poverty reduction. These views have informed CDRN's engagement with its international and local partners. CDRN also supports its local partners to develop 'authentic' partnership with Northern NGOs and government.

CDRN has itself entered into a strategic partnership with a few international NGOs, to foster synergy and complementarity. ActionAid is thus providing institutional support to CDRN, and CDRN is building the capacity of ActionAid partners. CARE and CDRN are involved in a joint research venture (with, importantly, funding from both institutions). CORDAID has funded CDRN to undertake a capacity building project for CBOs in Eastern Uganda - at the same time as CDRN is building the capacity of a few CORDAID partners. CDRN's partnership with MS is yet evolving - but is likely to take two forms- capacity-building to CDRN and a joint venture in the field of policy advocacy and gender. Although CDRN has also tried to develop a partnership with SNV, this appears not to be taking off, possibly because the two organisations do not see how they can complement each other's efforts, although they are all participating in the same arena.

CDRN's successes and challenges with partnership have highlighted two issues: in the first place, compatibility of values and mission is the most important criterion for developing and managing a partnership; where these are incompatible, the relationship becomes unequal and turbulent. Secondly, partnership should be built on equality of commitment with recognition that the contributions each partner makes to the relationship will be different but is afforded equal respect. Choosing to enter a partnership should be a process of mutual selection, without any exploitative hidden agenda.

As a member of the Transform network, CDRN has been engaging with donors to improve their relationship with Southern NGOs. Transform is an international network made up of 6 African training institutions plus a unit in the UK. A three-pronged approach is being used by CDRN to improve partnership between southern and Northern NGOs: (i) Strengthening the capacity of Southern NGOs to become self-determined, purposeful and strategic in engaging with their northern counterparts; (2) Lobbying Northern NGOs for a policy environment that promotes authentic partnership; (3) Cultivating a relationship of trust, confidentiality and equal partnership with southern NGOs (CDRN and local NGOs/Transform partners).

When requested by an international NGO to support the capacity of local NGOs, CDRN thus attempts to use this opportunity to engage with the international NGO as well as with the relevant local partner NGOs.

Experience has shown that problems of partnership must be tackled at several different levels. There are many practical ways to strengthen partnerships but basic assumptions, attitudes and behaviour need to be tackled as well.

To be effective in redressing the inequities and imbalances created by a world becoming quickly global, CDRN will need to form alliances (by joining or facilitating their formation) within and beyond the aid system which are equitable and mutually empowering. These coalitions can act as mediators for CSOs when negotiating partnership issues.

Lobbying and advocacy

Liberal capitalism, as the dominant mode of social organisation, currently defines the development context and indeed influences development theory and practices the world over. Development and aid transfers have thus come to be dominated by a 'New Policy Agenda', which is driven by beliefs organised around the twin poles of neo-liberal economics and liberal democratic theory. Markets and private initiatives are seen as the most effective and efficient mechanisms for achieving economic growth and providing services to people. Within this framework, civil society organisations are considered vehicles for democratisation, acting as a counter-weight to state power by opening up channels of communication and participation. Aid to civil society organisations is thus a way of operationalising the New Policy's economic and social goals.

This perception has not spared Ugandan civil society: here too, if civil society is seen as a necessary counter-balance for good governance, and efficient, demand-driven service delivery, then it has a role to play in the policy process. Lobbying and advocacy are thus now widely accepted by donors, civil society and government institutions as a means of ensuring greater transparency and accountability. Yet in practice much of what is done could be considered as shallow.

This assumption about civil society's role originates outside Uganda: while the growth of Civil Society is partly due to the change of government in 1986, it must also be seen as the result of a donor-driven agenda. Bilateral and multilateral donors, convinced that the assumption mentioned above is essentially correct, have invested time and other resources into CSOs, in their belief that through supporting civil society, a "vibrant, multi-form political system" would emerge.

Such a belief, some of whose roots can be found within the international development community, has also informed funding strategies and many CSOs are thus 'forced' to take on a role in tune with this dominant assumption if they are to survive. This is happening against the backdrop of the prevalent local notions about civil society, which are rather different. These are indeed based on a perception of civil society as a mostly neutral body that can create mutually beneficial linkages, such as with Government, of a non-confrontational nature.

The tension between these two views gives rise to an identity crisis amongst CSOs. Which role should they play, at a time when their survival greatly relies on external resources and their participation in decision-making relies on invitation?

Given donor power on civil society actors, some CSOs have tried to adapt to these pressures, for instance by having flexible strategic plans to fit donor talk.

As a result of donor pressure, CSOs engagement in advocacy is also still centred in Kampala. District-level CSOs have mixed feelings about participating in advocacy work: some feel that contributing to policy making is a corrupting process, which they do not want to be part of. Others feel that, much as they want to participate, they are never invited, and that if they invited themselves, they would be ignored.

Lack of capacity of CSOs to engage in policy advocacy is a major bottleneck. Many district CSOs do not understand how policy gets made and how government operates. And many do not have a critical view of poverty, beyond its material dimensions (food, shelter, clothing and health).

Many civil society organisations are thus comfortable with service delivery because they feel that it is there that they can influence the quality of service provision and promote good practice rather than to engage in abstract policy issues. More importantly, CSOs view subcontracting as a crucial source of income for their survival. How does one raise resources from government and at the same time hold it accountable? Engaging in policy advocacy would undermine this crucial source of income.

Subcontracting of CSOs to deliver services on behalf of government is also a role that has been prescribed for them by some donors/international development organisations. Many CSOs that do not have concrete pro-poor values, and the capacity to influence contracts (to suit their agenda), are being turned into business organisations whose interest is in profit maximisation rather than poverty reduction. Many district-based CSOs appear to be falling into this trap.

There is thus considerable debate about the role of the expanding CSO sector. While the World Bank believes that civil society organisations have the ability to substitute for weak public sector capacity, opponents of this view question the place of CSOs in the New Policy Agenda, both in terms of taking on service provision and in assuming a democratising role for good governance. They point to the growing financial dependency of CSOs and to less diversity in CSO roles and functions. This is reinforced by the discourse of the market but challenged on the other hand by participatory approaches which can open up state-society-market relations.

How has CDRN positioned itself in this context?

To address some of the challenges above, CDRN has re-defined its mandate to include mobilising and triggering civil society to re-think its role in the light of the current development context and challenges. CDRN's focus is to stimulate civil society to influence policy processes that are key to poverty reduction in Uganda.

CDRN understands advocacy as a political process that involves the coordinated efforts of people in changing existing practices, ideas, and distribution of power and resources that exclude disadvantaged groups. Advocacy therefore deals with specific aspects of policymaking and the values and behaviours that perpetuate exclusion and subordination. It is about causing a fundamental change in society, and therefore includes changing specific decisions that affect people's lives and changing the way decision-making happens into a more inclusive and democratic process.

CDRN's advocacy agenda targets different layers of civil society in Uganda, which includes CBOs, NGOs, and civil society (as a sector).

We believe that CBOs are poor people's organisations which, if promoted and strengthened, could contribute to a deep-seated change in the landscape of poverty in Uganda. For this to happen, the recognition of CBOs as a necessary instrument in the fight against poverty is crucial, to allow for their active participation in the poverty reduction policy-making. CDRN is involved in three different initiatives to promote these issues. Research has been undertaken to understand the CBO sector in Uganda and the environmental challenges that hinder it from achieving its goals – the outcome of this research is being used to promote the status and recognition of CBOs in Uganda. Finally, many development interventions focus on CBOs with the assumption that: "Find the groups and you have found the poor", or that groups comprise of the poorest of the poor - or at least represent the interests of the poorest (This is CDRN's perspective as well). Research is currently being undertaken to clarify this assumption - the outcome will be used for advocacy purposes.

CDRN is also implementing a project aimed at promoting collaborative and accountability mechanisms for CBOs and local government in Nakasongola and Lira districts. This project promotes a rights-based approach that encourages female and male participants to realise their rights to participation in decision-making, accountability, access to information and demand for them.

CDRN's new vision for the CBO sector in Uganda is to facilitate the emergence of a Centre for Public Participation. This centre will deepen the quality and practice of participation and promote citizen centred and social justice advocacy in Uganda.

Our NGO advocacy agenda focuses on capacity-building and improving the relationship between local NGOs and Northern NGOs and governments. The capacity of local NGOs is built so that they can understand their role better and engage constructively with government in the policy process.

In addition, CDRN in collaboration with CARE, is currently involved in a research project "Biting the hand that feeds you" to assess the effect of sub-contracting of local organisation (by government) on their autonomy and performance. The outcome of this initiative will be used for advocacy and lobbying purposes.

Lastly, our civil society advocacy agenda seeks to engage more strategically with the impact of global capitalism on civil society (and its poverty reduction endeavours) in Uganda. Although this idea is still young and requires further development on CDRN's part, it tries to work through and with several Networks and coalitions within the country and the region.

Gender

Gender analysis has become widely accepted as an essential part of development thinking and practice. The major development actors, such as the UN agencies, the European Union and bilateral funders such as DFID and DANIDA, include mandatory frameworks to check that gender is considered in all projects they support.

In addition to donor agencies being the force behind gender in Uganda - through conditionalities - the dominant political ideology of the Movement Government has created a healthy environment for gender to thrive. This includes a national gender policy to guide the integration of gender concerns and affirmative action for women in the political and educational spheres. This strategy has improved the status of women in Uganda to some extent. A handful of women are now participating actively in the political and economic arena. Many girls have joined higher institutions of learning on an affirmative action ticket.

Many people, especially men, however, see government's interest in women as a strategic trick to amass political capital. The support that the movement government rallies mainly comes from women, although a few women are beginning to question the 'so-called benefits' that they have garnered from this government.

In many ways, civil society organisations have embraced gender as a development issue. This is usually operationalised in terms of ensuring that women do not get left out of the development process. Development policy is now fully gender balanced, rather than being male biased, as was the case in the past.

A closer look at development policy in Uganda, however, shows that gender issues have been co-opted and internalised into mainstream development activity rather than allowing them to fundamentally challenge ideas and institutions. Consequently, gender mainstreaming has become a technocratic endeavour (gender balance) informed by the desire to maintain the status quo, an indication that gender analysis is losing its transformatory intention and potential.

Many development agencies furthermore view gender oppression in isolation of other forms of oppression such as ethnicity, class, age and region. Yet these different forms of oppression are intricately linked: they are all informed and perpetuated by the quest for power over others and one form of oppression cannot be removed without the other. In addition, gender oppression cuts across all other forms of oppression, implying that many poor women suffer from 'multiple oppression'.

As a result, many organisations in Uganda appear to be "practicing gender at face value". In practice they hide behind jargon (gender blind, gender sensitive, gender responsive etc.) without a genuine desire for change. A closer look at their work shows just how little gender considerations inform what they do. This arises because the very language of gender is seen to be a Western obligation, a neo-colonial imposition on organisations and communities where other priorities and understandings of gender differences and gender roles in fact prevail. This causes outright resistance in people, especially men, who will learn the new language of gender, or reject it, but they will not change. The Western approach to gender thus appears to have been designed without a critical understanding of local institutions, norms and values.

Such resistance to change also occurs because the root cause of women's subordination is seen as caused by men and masculinity. Yet men also have multiple gender roles: changes in men's ability and desire to fulfil these roles pose challenges for men as well as women. In Uganda, more often than not, men's concerns are not the focus of gender analysis: they are not supported to appreciate that gender sensitive work would be beneficial to them as well.

In addition, local organisations construct their gender knowledge from various sources: government, church, Western world and local community. Each of these sources reflects its an ideology and worldview. Because development workers are in constant interaction with these different sources of gender knowledge, they become ideologically and conceptually confused and find it difficult to engage constructively with gender in their work.

How has CDRN positioned itself?

Recognising that gender and other forms of inequality are the major causes of poverty in Uganda, CDRN has made a deliberate move to position itself strategically to address this concern. To measure up to this, we have had to build our own capacity in the field of gender. This has included a 'gender awakening' process for the whole organisation, training staff, developing a gender policy, and mainstreaming gender in the organisational structure, programmes, values and culture. This re-awakening process has allowed CDRN to broaden its gender agenda to include diversity and social justice issues. We are also a member of several gender networks (for learning and to share our perspectives).

CDRN's capacity building work with local NGOs and CBOs is also implemented with a gender perspective since we believe that Development – Gender sensitivity = Underdevelopment. Our partner organisations are thus supported to develop gender sensitive worldviews and values.

We are currently steering a new initiative, having been selected to lead and coordinate the "Africanisation of gender thinking and practice" a project of the Transform Network. The purpose of the project is to develop an approach to gender that is rooted in the local cultural context. This project will employ three strategies: (i) Research to identify tools and frameworks that are relevant to African women and men; (ii) Lobbying and advocating for a policy environment that allows this African approach to flourish; and (iii) Capacity building of local organisations to operationalise this approach.

Within this context, we plan to develop a gender-training package based on the principles of popular education, geared towards a radical approach to challenging sexism, gender and other forms of oppression. This training aims at reclaiming the transformatory potential that gender analysis appears to be currently loosing.

Conclusion

The new language of aid and poverty reduction implies shifts in control and distribution of power, with more ownership by partner countries, local organisations and citizens. This however, requires that a relationship of trust and transparency is allowed to flourish, within and between aid agencies and their partners in Uganda.

This means narrowing the gap between words and actions. A 'reduction process' that can in part happen (in both the North and in Uganda) if we start re-thinking old behaviours, procedures and organisational cultures that have kept us trapped into the old ways of doing things.

20

The Financial Sustainability of Ugandan NGOs: Are we no Better than Government?[1]

Silvia Angey, Christina Nilsson

Abstract

Local NGOs are increasingly being required by donors and supporters to show that they are not only accountable, but also financially sustainable. As a concept, financial sustainability has however been developed in the business sector and exported to an NGO setting without adequately defining it and discussing the extent of its applicability in this new setting.

Among Ugandan NGOs, financial sustainability is seen as an integral part of the overall sustainability of the organisation. It does not entail being totally independent from external donor funding, but rather to diversify the organisation's income sources and manage the resources soundly to enable the NGO's continued existence and relevance to its beneficiaries.

The NGOs interviewed combine attempts directed at generating both external and internal income and they diversify their financial resources mainly through broadening and refining their donor base, negotiating good terms with donors, income-generating activities, local fundraising, consultancy work, engaging in micro-finance, building international connections and constituting money reserves. NGOs have showed an ability to attain at least a certain degree of financial sustainability by having a clear and shared vision, a stable and competent leadership, proper structures and systems in place, running the organisation with a business-like approach and using local and international connections to secure support. The current type of fundraising training was generally not seen as useful.

Ugandan NGOs still face a number of internal and external challenges in their pursuit of financial sustainability. Internal challenges include setting up a specific function for resource mobilisation, not allowing attempts to generate their own income to steer the organisation away from its social agenda, and working together to carry out joint

---

[1] This is a slightly abridged version of a paper published by the Community Development Resource Network in November 2004.

activities. Some of the major challenges of an external nature affecting the NGOs' attempts to pursue financial sustainability include the NGO Registration Statute, which stipulates that NGOs are non-profit making organisations and individual philanthropic behaviour that is not developed. Finally, donor policies and priorities are often inconsistent and sometimes even contradictory: while donors require NGOs to be financially sustainable, they are often unwilling to support initiatives that are directed at generating income for these organisations.

Introduction

In recent years, the issue of financial sustainability has been high on the agenda of most indigenous NGOs[2] in Uganda and has for instance been a concern in many visioning workshops. This quest for sustainability reflects rapid growth in the sector, as well as changes in the donor environment.

When the current National Resistance Movement government came to power in 1986, Uganda experienced relative peace in most parts of the country. However, the collapse of the state, which this regime inherited, coupled with vast demands for relief, reconstruction and rehabilitation, meant that the government did not have the capacity to deliver services. The opportunity to complement the role of government in service delivery coupled with abundant donor funding encouraged people to build various types of voluntary organisations. The number of NGOs has thus grown from 160 registered NGOs in 1986 to 4,700 in 2003, with most of this growth accounted for by local organisations (Tulya-Muhika 2002; Barr et al 2003).

This growth has taken place in a context where external donor funding has not only been abundant, but where the availability of this funding was never really questioned, leading many NGOs to become very dependent on such financial sources. As much as 80% of NGO funding in Uganda thus comes from external sources (Barr et al 2003) and it is not uncommon to find a local NGO dependent on one or two donors for its entire budget. With increased competition as a consequence of the growing number of local NGOs, with the change in funding mechanism from individual NGO projects to basket funding through government, and with donors becoming more strategic in their relationships (leading to supporting fewer local development organisations), NGOs are, however, now faced with a reality where dependence on one or a few donors could threaten their very existence.

Although the concept of financial sustainability in an NGO context is not clearly defined (reflecting the nature of NGOs and the type of work they engage in), a number of NGOs are actively attempting to reduce their dependency on donor funding and pursue financial sustainability. While the opportunities for doing so are somewhat limited in Uganda (given the youthful character – and therefore lack of experience – of most NGOs, given the lack of a substantial middle class as an alternative source of local fundraising, and given the prominence of donors), some attempts are being made

---

2   This research is confined to NGOs, defined as voluntary, non-profit development organisations driven by a value system, with recognised governance structures and community programmes.

in this direction and this research attempts to examine and reflect on some of these attempts.

Objectives and methodology

Intensified competition for donor funding among Ugandan NGOs, the dependence of many on donor funding and subsequently their lack of autonomy, leading them to uncritically adopt donor agenda, makes a study of the ways in which NGOs have attempted to become financially sustainable both timely and important. Our research aims at:

- Understanding the concept of financial sustainability in an NGO context and how it is perceived by Ugandan NGOs.
- Exploring innovative ways, in view of the local context, in which local NGOs have tackled donor dependence and attempted to become financially sustainable.
- Examining what factors have contributed to success, what the 'boundaries' of this success are, and the extent to which such success stories are replicable.

It is also hoped that this report will inspire local NGOs to pursue financial sustainability and learn from the success and failures of the NGOs interviewed.

Our methodology centred on semi-structured interviews with a cross-section of NGOs, government officials, donors and corporate funders. Where needed, this information was triangulated to ensure the accuracy of data collected.

The focus of the study was on local NGOs and those we interviewed are mainly large, well-established organisations within the Uganda NGO sector. Their selection was based on success stories known to the research team. A few NGOs were also selected to illustrate a failure to successfully maintain their fundraising levels, despite their long period of existence, and thus provide information on the difficulties faced when pursuing financial sustainability. Nineteen NGO leaders were interviewed both rural (four) and urban-based NGOs (fifteen). These thus do not constitute a representative sample but hopefully provide us with lessons from which other NGOs can learn. The criteria for selecting the NGOs included their ability to: diversify income sources; engage in income generating activities (IGAs); successfully negotiate terms with donors; fundraise locally from the public and the private sector; engage in private consultancy work; and develop financial strategies and practices relating to the long-term vision of the organisation.

Three officials were interviewed from the Ministry of Finance, Planning & Economic Development, the Ministry of Local Government and the Office of the Prime Minister. The latter was selected because it is the arm of government that coordinates NGO activities in conjunction with the NGO Board. The Ministry of Local Government through the Local Government Act is responsible for local governance issues in districts where NGOs are being requested by donors to seek funding support and contracts from Local Government. In the Ministry of Finance, the Tax Policy Department was selected to provide insights into whether the current tax policy encourages a philanthropic culture and if not what appropriate taxation policy would encourage giving.

Three donors, Cordaid, Danida and DFID, were interviewed to determine what role they have played in supporting or hindering NGOs to become financially sustainable. The selection of the donors was based on their substantial interest in supporting NGO work in Uganda.

One local corporate funder, Nile Bank, and one international corporate funder, Mobile Telephone Network (MTN) was interviewed. MTN has supported an NGO to provide low cost housing and Nile Bank has provided support to disabled children. The corporations were selected to provide a perspective on what motivates private sector to support NGOs.

Our report is divided into six sections. First the concept of financial sustainability in an NGO context is discussed in view of the available literature. We then move on to examine how Ugandan NGOs understand financial sustainability in their context and why they consider financial sustainability important. The issues addressed in the two following sections relate to the way NGOs have pursued financial sustainability and what factors have contributed to financial sustainability. Finally, before concluding remarks, the challenges facing NGOs in pursuing financial sustainability are discussed.

Financial sustainability in an NGO context – a brief literature review

Vincent & Campell (1989) assert that most NGOs and development associations in the South work on the principle that they should be promoting and supporting the self-reliant efforts of local communities to take charge of their own development. Financial self-sufficiency is therefore an important concept in development today and many pay lip-service to its importance. But the reality is that Southern NGOs are largely, if not entirely, dependent on external aid from the North.

The notion of financial sustainability originated in the business sector in the North and has increasingly been applied to civil society by the donor community, at a time when Treasuries have greater demands for aid funding accountability and donors have become disillusioned with the results and effectiveness of projects (Wallace, 2004). Financial sustainability appears to be an example of a concept that is exported to other countries, though not necessarily with much regard for the values and context in which it was developed and applied.

Kruse et al (1997) show that several studies to examine the sustainability of projects undertaken in developing countries tend to suggest quite a strong contrast, if not contradiction, between increasing demands by donors that funds only be provided if projects are likely to achieve financial sustainability at least in the medium to long term, and the evidence that many, if not most, projects have little chance of being financially sustainable. Further, financial sustainability is less likely to occur where a majority of project beneficiaries are very poor: the poorer the beneficiaries are, the less the likelihood that an implementing organisation will recoup a large share of recurrent project costs. If donors continue to put a strong emphasis on financial sustainability, this may thus increase pressure on the NGOs to veer away from helping the poorest groups. The study undertaken by Kruse et al indicates that to encourage NGOs to maintain, or even expand, their poverty focus, it is important to take account of the discrepancies between demands and practice and to rethink the concept of financial sustainability in an NGO context.

A number of authors have attempted to conceptualise financial sustainability in an NGO context. Commercial Markets Strategies (2004) defines NGO sustainability as an organisation's ability to improve its institutional capacity to continue its activities among target populations over an extended period of time, to maximise impact by providing quality services and products, and to develop diversified sources of institutional and financial support. Other authors link financial sustainability with the NGO's power to access and control its resource base (Bhat et al, 1999) and internal management (Beijuka, 1996). Financial sustainability requires sound financial planning and management, including cost-efficient management systems, and commitment from the management is essential to plan and manage financial resource mobilisation plans and strategies. The management should carry out IGAs without jeopardising the NGO mission and fully understand how business and the market place work. However, the services that the target group requires should be given priority over a too business-like an attitude. Finally, management should be convinced that the long-term viability of the organisation depends on increased financial self-reliance, indicated by providing quality service to the target group in the absence of donor support.

In an assessment of the financial sustainability of Nigerian NGOs, Hare (2004) argues that a number of internal NGO capacities are needed to achieve financial sustainability, defined as an organisation's capacity to sustain its institutional structure and production of benefits for its intended client population *after* the cessation of donor technical, managerial and financial support. Hare found that viable NGOs, compared to unsustainable ones, were more likely to have had international funds for start-up capital, were more likely to be older, tended to change leaders less often and were more likely to monitor their efficiency. They also tended to have trained accountants or bookkeepers, recording their revenues and expenses, monitoring their cash flow and having regular external audits. In addition, they were more likely to promote their services and tended to earn most of their income from fees for services. Further, they were more likely to benefit from services provided through networks or umbrella organisations such as bulk purchasing of supplies, thus benefiting from economies of scale.

Instead of narrowing financial sustainability to an internal affair, Norton (1996) proposes to look at it more broadly. He contends that external funding to an NGO should be seen as an investment in a development process, rather than a subsidy for work done. This happens when the organisation uses funds to build income generation activity in the community, so that people will have more resources to invest in their own future and to building institutions and other capital investments in the community, which give community control over resources and an ability to generate income.

What the above implies is that financial sustainability involves the ability of an organisation to sustain itself financially to meet its goal beyond a project/programme portfolio, the ability to raise its own income and having a high degree of latitude in negotiating[3] with its supporters. NGO sustainability therefore goes beyond its financial sustainability per se to include power to access and control the resource base as a whole. Sustainability is thus multifaceted and includes aspects of leadership, management, promotion/marketing and community participation.

Financial sustainability in a Ugandan NGO context

The NGO sector in Uganda is young but rapidly growing, with growth often driven by external factors such as decentralisation, other government initiatives and donor funding. De Coninck (2004) argues that:

> This makes for a youthful, vibrant sector but it also highlights some of the weaknesses associated with formative years: dependence on founder members, lack of focus and questionable stability. The NGO sector is an extremely diverse sector driven by both a social and an 'economic advancement' agenda. In a poor country like Uganda, employment access and security are often paramount and working in an NGO represents for many a source of employment rather than a contribution to relieve poverty 'out there'. Many NGOs thus appear to be preoccupied with accountability to their donors and their own self-perpetuation, rather than with accountability to their would-be constituencies (De Coninck, 2004).

A study of the funding sources in the Ugandan NGO sector shows extreme variation in the level NGO funding and differences in funding sources for large and small NGOs[4] (Barr et al 2003). At the aggregate level, most NGO funding comes from international NGOs, bilateral donors and local government, but it is a handful of large NGOs that attract most of the funding while small NGOs tend to depend on non-grant income. In this sense, the Ugandan NGO sector is an offshoot of international charity and the mode of operation of Ugandan NGOs largely reflects the agenda and concerns of international charitable organisations. The average NGO generates some funds from members and individual donations but at aggregate levels these amounts are very small. Donations received from non-members and profits from fundraising events also account for a very small share of NGO funding and there is little solicitation from the general public. One third of the surveyed NGOs own a business, the profit from which is used to finance its charitable activities. The types of business run by Ugandan NGOs are extremely varied, but mostly concern farming, canteens, and retail trade. A small proportion also rent out land and buildings.

Studies of Ugandan NGOs thus show that they belong to a young and rapidly expanding sector heavily dependent on founder members and external funding

---

3   Being able to take its own decisions, have power and control over its destiny.
4   The study does not clarify the criteria for large and small NGOs but notes: "The average total number of staff members and volunteers is 129. This figure masks large disparities among NGOs, however. Three sampled NGOs alone account for three quarters of the manpower resources of the sample as a whole, indicating considerable concentration in the sector. The median of 18 staff members and volunteers is much smaller than the average but is still non-negligible..."

sources. Many NGOs are however engaged in income generating initiatives, indicating an attempt to become less dependent on external funding. Before we examine these attempts in depth, however, we first look at how Ugandan NGOs understand financial sustainability in their context.

How do Ugandan NGOs understand financial sustainability?

The NGOs interviewed for this research broadly offered three definitions of what financial sustainability means in their context:

a) *The financial situation of the organisation*
The ability to continuously generate income, having internal income to avoid dependency on one or two external funding sources and utilising raised funds efficiently. This notion of financial sustainability supports the argument made by Vincent & Campell (1989) that financial self-sufficiency has become part and parcel of the development agenda.

b) *The social aspect of the NGO*
In line with Bhat et al (1999) who link financial sustainability to the NGO's power to control its resource base, many informants argued that an organisation could be considered sustainable when it has the ability to keep itself moving, when it is relevant, when it makes a difference and when it is in charge of its own direction. Financial sustainability was here considered an integrated part of overall organisational sustainability.

c) *An ability to diversify the organisation's income sources*
In stark contrast to both Hare's (2004) and Beijuka's (1996) definition of a sustainable NGO as one that continues its existence without donor support, the vast majority of the informants argued that Ugandan NGOs cannot become financially sustainable if this means being totally independent from external donor funding. This has to do with the nature of the work, such as working with issues of poverty and HIV/AIDS, and the limited possibilities of raising funds or membership fees from the public, given general poverty levels in the country and the lack of a substantial middle class as an alternative source of local fundraising.

Several informants also added that NGOs are by definition non-profit making. They should therefore not be expected to be self-sustained or go for profit. NGOs focusing on generating their own income risk becoming too focused on making a profit and thus lose their identity and mission. All the NGOs were conscious that pursuing financial sustainability should not be prioritised to the extent that the organisation risks turning into a small business and thereby lose sight of its social agenda. Most informants also noted that for donor agencies to demand that Southern NGOs be financially sustainable seems unwarranted as the latter themselves rely on one or a few sources of funding and even the Ugandan government is heavily dependent on donor funding (currently representing half the budget resources). The NGOs interviewed yet felt it important to seriously consider the issue of financial sustainability and how this can practically be obtained. This discussion, however, needs to be considered in the context in which local NGOs operate.

Although most respondents did not consider it feasible to be totally independent of external donor funding, they did note that generating one's own income is important because it allows the organisation to pursue its own priorities. Rather than carrying out an activity or project simply because this falls within a donor's priority, it was seen as crucial that an NGO be able to set its own agenda and carry out programmes that meet the needs of the beneficiaries as stipulated by its mission. Being financially viable was thus seen to provide an NGO with the necessary freedom to plan and carry out its activities.

All our respondents perceived financial sustainability as an important part of the overall sustainability of the organisation because finances sustain the organisation's programmes, maintain its human resources and all other assets. A number of respondents compared lack of financial resources to a vehicle without fuel. Financial sustainability also protects the organisation's independence, which is a basis for action and credibility. It gives confidence and legitimacy as a strong and reliable NGO. This also leads to staff retention, and thus organisational stability, growth and professionalism.

Where organisations have attempted to be financially sustainable, this has generally yielded positive effects. Being perceived as financially sound was cited as beneficial to the organisation's reputation and image among the general public, government, private sector, donors, and local and international NGOs. Both corporate companies interviewed stressed that the NGOs they support must be financially sound and therefore not dependent on their support. Financial sustainability can thus be self-reinforcing: a positive reputation and image as financially sustainable makes an NGO attractive to funders and this enhances its ability to gain more support, both in breadth (getting more supporters) and depth (the current supporters providing more money). A quarter of the respondents also noted that an organisation with a healthy financial resource base is often in a position to ask funders for co-funding for programmes, an easier task than having to ask for core cost funding, and this seems to be perceived as positive by funders.

It was also reported that an organisation in such a position gains confidence and the power to negotiate terms with their funders. The latter, especially donors and government, look at the organisation as equal partner and colleague, they are willing to listen to such organisations for ideas and use them as reference points for other less independent organisations. Funders have also been referring potential donors to organisations whom they consider financially sustainable. Again this indicates the self-reinforcing nature of financial sustainability.

The road to financial sustainability

Ugandan NGOs have various experiences in trying to ensure a diversified or broadened economic base. All the interviewed NGOs pursue an array of initiatives and strategies to improve externally and internally generated income. The research findings showed no clear differences in the way the rural- and urban-based or research and non-research organisations pursue financial sustainability and the factors contributing to this. In the following sections the issue of rural- vs. urban-based and research vs. non-research NGOs is therefore not dwelled upon.

In the following section, we explore nine ways in which the NGOs interviewed have pursued financial sustainability.

(a) ***Broadening and refining the donor base***

All respondents have tried to diversify their funding base as they recognise that being dependent on one or two donors is very precarious should a donor decide to stop funding. Broadening the donor base by having different donors funding specific components of the organisation's programme is one of the main ways in which the respondents have been able to enhance their NGO's financial sustainability. Their ability to do so was linked to planning not only for programmes but for resource mobilisation as well.

Some organisations that have reached a stage where they attract many donors have decided to refine their donor base by setting a limit on the number of donors to have at a time. It was noted that donor maintenance requires much time and energy and putting a ceiling on donor numbers at a time allows for effective management of donor relations, including timely reporting. Another advantage is the ability to zero down on 'quality donors' who provide substantial funding, who are flexible and have minimum reporting requirements. Another way is to set a limit to the percentage, e.g. 20%, of total income, that originates from one donor, thus enabling the NGO to maintain its autonomy and avoid dependence.

(b) ***Negotiation terms with donors***

All the respondents have negotiated long-term funding (two to three years), although two organisations negotiated for five to 10-year support. Seven out of the nineteen NGOs interviewed have managed to convince their core funders to support their strategic plan and to rely on the annual audit for accountability. A strong sentiment against project support in favour of strategic plan support was voiced. This could lead to predictable funding flows, hence providing the NGO with leverage to concentrate on implementing its plan.

Two-thirds of the organisations interviewed managed to convince their funders to convert balances on programme funds to assist them to purchase office premises, although donors have repeatedly questioned the justification for such investments. In the Ugandan context, having one's own premises is seen as an important pillar of financial sustainability. It provides an organisation with a permanent address and when supporters visit they gain confidence. While one informant explained that "having your own premises alone is not enough, you need to put systems in place to ensure a consistent cash flow", another noted that "having your own premises means to have a place to meet even if money runs out".

In the Ugandan NGO sector, most organisations struggle to meet different reporting demands from their various donors. This is considered a waste of resources that could have been spent on improving the situation of the beneficiaries. Three of the NGOs mentioned that they had managed to persuade some of their donors to have coordinated reporting. The success of an organisation like LABE to negotiate better terms with their donors can at least partly be attributed to the fact that the leadership has clarity of the organisation's direction and vision and has been able to share this vision with staff and supporters. As an organisation, LABE is consciously "thinking big", i.e. not from project to project, but in terms of programmes and expansion possibilities. With an expressed desire to focus as much time and energy as possible on programme work, LABE has managed to convince their donors of the need for coordination of different reporting demands, which otherwise are time consuming and expensive.

(c) *Income Generating Activities (IGAs)*
When financial sustainability in the local context is mentioned, it is often IGAs that come to mind. All the NGOs interviewed are indeed involved in some kind of IGA and 15 of the 19 respondents highlighted the sale of their services as a means of generating income. This gave them independence, challenged them to provide quality services and was also noted to have been used to salvage organisations when donors pulled out. Income from the sale of services was seen as important and most respondents felt this is the way to go, although the proceeds cannot fully support the core costs of an NGO. The demand for providing such services is however so high, especially from government, donors and international NGOs, that it is not uncommon that organisations take on work indiscriminately even when it does not fall within their mandate. Consequently, a few informants noted that IGAs need to be properly managed to prevent a situation where the staff are focused on looking for contracts, rather than meeting the organisation's social obligation.

Besides selling their services, a number of NGOs were involved in other types of IGAs, including training centres, hostels, model farms, dairies, wood lots and radio stations. These types of IGAs, characteristically, were separate income generating projects set up to support the organisation's overall programme. Another characteristic was that the proceeds from such projects often do not contribute significantly to the running costs of the organisation, although they are often sufficient to sustain the IGAs themselves.

SOCADIDO's extensive engagement in IGAs is attributed to a number of factors. The leadership has been willing to experiment, take risks and find innovative ways to supplement programmes focusing on social work with IGAs. At the same time, the leaders are conscious that the IGAs must complement rather than compromise the social agenda of the organisation. SOCADIDO entered into all the IGAs through starting them within existing programmes and developing them from there, as it was not possible to get donors to fund such initiatives on their own. But before starting an IGA, it made sure to do its groundwork by e.g. visiting other organisations with experience in a similar activity. Where SOCADIDO did not have the skills to undertake such work, consultants were hired to make thorough assessments of the feasibility of the planned initiatives both in terms of the needs and interests of SOCADIDO's beneficiaries, as well as in terms of income generation.

(d) *Local fundraising*

NGO attempts to fundraise from the local public have not yielded much funding but those who have ventured into this believe that it has enhanced their organisation's image by exposing people to its work. The respondents who tried local fundraising succeeded where the issue is specific, such as raising money from community leaders and people living in Kampala to buy books for community schools in West Nile. Success was also registered where the issues touch the heart and arouse personal sentiments, such as palliative care for cancer patients, disabled children and AIDS orphans.

In the rural areas, income from district authorities through contracts for service provision is also looked at as a source of local fundraising, together with community contributions in kind and cash.

USDC is one of the NGOs in Uganda heavily involved in local fundraising as a way of generating income. Although USDC is engaged in a type of work that touches the heart, and thus attracts support, it has seriously taken up the challenge of local fundraising, with even its organisational structure designed to accommodate local fundraising. USDC has managed to attract people to its Board who can assist in local fundraising either through their experience or connections. USDC also has an office in England to assist with fundraising and generating new ideas to attract support from the UK.

Very few NGOs have, however, been successful in getting support through corporate fundraising. Some NGOs approach this sector with requests for sponsoring an event. In cases where the corporate sector agrees, this is usually when an opportunity to advertise is considered beneficial to the company. Four NGOs mentioned that they had been successful in securing support for their social programmes over an extended period of time from such sources. Where appeal letters have been sent to businesses, the NGOs rarely receive any positive response but the respondents felt that it gave them an opportunity to penetrate the private sector. Some members from the corporate sector have also committed themselves to pay monthly or annually for specific activities of certain NGOs.

While very few NGOs are successful in mobilising support from the private sector, many corporations have defined their area of interest. NGOs must therefore make an effort to know what areas of interest ta company supports before sending a proposal, which must be focused, with a clearly defined benefit for the target group. Corporate focus on NGOs that are not dependent on corporations' support for organisational survival also calls for the NGOs to argue for the sustainability of the project or activity that is proposed for support.

(e) *Setting up private consultancy companies*

It has been noted that all the NGOs interviewed provide services for a fee. Three NGOs have however taken this service work a step further by setting up, or being in the process of establishing, a private consultancy company. The decision to set up a separate entity to undertake consultancy work was taken by management in recognition of the problematic nature of intermingling consultancy assignments, as required by the market, with the main work of the NGO. In this way, the consultancy business is an independent entity with a purely business motive run by its own Board.

The experiences of the NGOs interviewed show that engagement in consultancy work needs careful thinking through, as well as policies and structures, to avoid a situation where staff get too engaged in consultancy at the expense of other organisational work. Since consultancy work is often not part of the NGO's social agenda, to prevent the needs of the beneficiaries from being compromised, there is also a need to ensure that any profit from consultancy work is used for supporting programme activities or for organisational strengthening rather than personal enrichment.

(f) *Setting up a Micro-Finance Institution (MFI)*
Of the 19 NGOs interviewed, three have set up MFIs as a means of meeting a social need and for generating income. These MFIs, the respondents reported, are self-sustaining as interest charged on the loans is adequate to cover administrative costs. One respondent mentioned that proceeds from the MFI are used to finance some of their other activities. Respondents also pointed out that regulation of MFIs by Bank of Uganda since 2001 has placed difficult requirements which affect the performance of those MFIs that collect and intermediate savings from their clients, although MFIs that lend money raised from grants and other sources (rather than savings from clients) are not affected by the new regulations.

Experiences from both organisations show that money generated from MFI is limited: the MFI can sustain itself but is not providing substantial income for the organisations' programme work. However, micro-financing is seen as an important activity because the goal behind MFI is to assist the target group in becoming financially sustainable and such financing mechanism thus addresses the NGOs' social agenda.

(g) *International connections*
Three of the large urban-based NGOs interviewed have an office, a trust or a charity registered in Europe. These establishments are mainly for the purpose of assisting the local NGO in fundraising but at times they also help by giving advice and guidance in particular situations.

In all three cases, the assistance of overseas groups, organisations or individuals has been made possible by the founders' or patron's connections abroad. In two NGOs, the founders are of European origin, thus enabling them to take advantage of their networks in their home and neighbouring countries to secure support. For local NGOs currently without such international connections a point of departure could however be to attend international conferences and events where like-minded organisations and individuals can be approached and prospective connections nurtured.

(h) *Money reserves*

One third of the NGOs interviewed have established different types of funds, including reserve, trust, development and endowment funds. The purpose of the funds varies: to ensure that the organisation can pay for its core costs for a specified amount of time in case donors pull out; to make publications which they then sell, or to provide for future vehicle and assets replacement.

Methods used by NGOs to set up such reserves also vary: setting money aside from the use of vehicles, selling the organisation's services such as consultancy work and trainings, setting aside e.g. 10% of the total assets purchased in a year and transferring part of the organisation's surplus from the yearly budget to a fund.

(i) *Optimal use of resources*

Other creative means through which NGOs have tried to broaden their financial resource base include charging each programme for the use of resources within the organisation such as vehicles, photocopiers, computers, staff time and renting rooms to programmes. One respondent noted that the NGO as a whole must be seen as responsible for sound financial management, i.e. management, the financial manager and staff must have skills in financial management and be held accountable for being consumption- and cost reduction- conscious.

Financial sustainability – What does it take?

Securing a broad and sustainable financial resource base is a difficult task and the success of initiatives taken in this direction depend on a variety of factors, related both to internal organisational requirements and to external circumstances. We explore in this section seven factors that have enabled the NGOs interviewed to diversify their income sources. These should, however, not be considered as a complete list of requirements that an NGO has to fulfil in order to be financially sustainable.

(a) *A clear and shared vision*

A clear and shared vision in the organisation was seen as paramount in enhancing financial sustainability in an NGO. This enables an organisation to be relevant as it continually evaluates itself and stays focused. In addition, it projects a leading image that can attract resources.

(b) *Leadership*

A chief executive who can inspire and share the vision with the rest of the organisation and its supporters was considered paramount. Constant communication from the chief executive to the staff, the Board and supporters was seen as the engine for sharing the vision. The chief executive should have a professional approach, have integrity, be willing to take calculated risks and run the organisation in a business-like manner.[5] Respondents argued that donors, government, NGOs and the public gain confidence in a leader who exudes these qualities and therefore tend to trust

---

5 This was interpreted by our respondents as professionalism, cost consciousness, an ability to scan the environment and seize opportunities, yet stay focused on the NGO's vision.

such an organisation with resources. Respondents also stressed the role of the Board[6] for ensuring the financial sustainability. A Board which is forward-looking and supportive to management, adding value and whose members are well known instils trust in the NGO, hence increasing its funding. Some respondents pointed out the importance of having Board members of NGOs coming not only from civil society, but also from the private sector. This was seen not only as helping to fundraise from the private sector but also to bring in business experiences to running an NGO. One NGO has also brought government servants to its Board to understand the way government works and get first-hand information on developments in official circles.

All our respondents cited continuity of figureheads, especially the chief executive and the Board, and a smooth transition of leadership as important in enhancing financial sustainability. With the exception of one organisation, all the other NGOs have a strong presence of founder members either as chief executive or on the Board. Half of the respondents noted that their founder executive director was still holding the position of executive director. Although the respondents recognised the potentially problematic nature of a continuous strong presence of founding members within an NGO,[7] founder members were seen to be crucial in terms of holding the organisation's values at heart and sharing them with new entrants. In five of the organisations, the founders were in the process of handing over their position to new directors who were nurtured within the organisation. A carefully planned transition to new leadership was considered vital for continuing linkages with the organisation's donors and other supporters through established personal contacts and relations. It was also seen as providing the new director with confidence and the power to negotiate with authority derived from experience rather than from a pleading position.

These findings indicate that good leadership is a mix of interrelated aspects; a leader with a strong vision and an ability to project this vision, continuity in the leadership, as well as supportive and knowledgeable staff, Board and supporters. In organisations where the leadership is less strong, the NGO can easily find itself in a position where its movements are constrained because the leadership is unable to project a clear vision or has to be accommodative of various interests. One of the respondents explained why their organisation has only ventured into a few profit making activities: "We have to be cautious, otherwise our donors will say that we are now doing business and even our members would ask why we are doing business since we are non-profit."

(c) *Structures and systems*

The importance of having structures and systems that allow the organisation to operate professionally was stressed by respondents as a key factor to ensure financial sustainability. Structures include having a supportive and knowledgeable Board,

---

6   In case of church-based NGOs, support from the Bishop was mentioned as crucial in pursuing financial sustainability.

7   Especially if founder members are not willing to share power and are dependent on the organisation's resources for their survival rather than enriching the organisation with their experiences and connections.

a director who exercises inspirational leadership, active members, clearly defined roles and responsibilities and adequate human resources to meet the needs of the organisation.

Stress was also put on having economically viable structures, which are lean and accommodative of changing circumstances and which ensure the right balance between expenditure on administration and on programme delivery. Becoming financially sustainable requires a financial management system geared towards handling money and costs effectively and implemented by well-trained and motivated technical and financial staff. Having a competent accountant who is able to ensure fulfilment of financial demands from donors was also mentioned as a prerequisite for financial effectiveness. Proper financial management was noted as instilling trust in donors and in some cases even increasing donor funding. Other respondents added the importance of having a proper management system for organisational resources, such as vehicles, and monetising staff time spent on specific activities for the purpose of cost management. Finally, respondents stressed the importance of honest and timely reporting to donors. Not being afraid to admit mistakes and not painting a glossy picture but rather providing an analysis of lessons learned is thus considered paramount. As one respondent noted "donors actually prefer to deal with sincere people".

(d) *NGOs run with a business attitude*
One third of the respondents stated that running their organisations using a business-like approach has contributed to their success, especially in broadening their resource base. Having a business attitude towards NGO management means being entrepreneurial, scanning the environment for opportunities and responding in a timely fashion so that the organisation remains relevant. One NGO also found it useful to hire a consultant with a business background to support a process, which the organisation felt it needed to propel itself forward.

These two examples illustrate that a leader with a business approach is not enough for an NGO to successfully venture into profit generating activities. The leader has to be accompanied by a supportive team, including staff, members and Board, as well as structures and systems that ensure that the activities are planned and managed diligently.

(e) *Patrons*
In 3 of the organisations interviewed, patrons played an important role in their financial sustainability, although in different ways. In one organisation the patron is the First Lady of Uganda, who uses her position and wide contacts to publicise the organisation's work and raise resources for the organisation.

In another NGO working with issues of HIV/AIDS, the founder of the organisation is now its patron and she uses her public recognition for her contribution within the area of HIV/AIDS to advocate for and promote this issue and the work of the NGO. The patron in the third organisation is from the corporate sector and was at the time of appointment Chairman of the Uganda Manufacturers' Association.

The organisation is using the patron to sponsor some of their activities as well as getting some of the members of the patron's association to support the organisation. This includes building houses for the treatment of cancer patients and sponsoring charity walks, all of which have increased the organisation's profile.

(f) **Donor support**

One third of our respondents acknowledged the contribution to financial sustainability made by donors who support programmes or strategic plans rather than projects. Supporting an organisation's strategic plan was seen as a sign of a donor supporting the development of the NGO without interfering unduly with its direction and control. Two thirds of the respondents also pointed out the importance of having donors with an equal partnership attitude, who are understanding and appreciate that long-term support to development activities is important.

(g) *Are fundraising trainings and workshops useful?*

Only four of the respondents had attended a fundraising training while the rest claimed to have learnt fundraising on the job. Fundraising training was generally perceived as a fairly new phenomenon and its usefulness questioned. One respondent noted that no single training can prepare one for the skills needed because fundraising is mainly a personality issue. To convince supporters and fundraise effectively, it was argued, one needs to draw on your experiences in life and be passionate and knowledgeable about one's work. One respondent also stressed the usefulness of a degree of charm and the ability to 'massage' supporters. This includes timely and honest reporting, effective utilisation of any resources one is entrusted with and nurturing a personal relationship with supporters.

Fundraising training may thus provide participants with tools but it is not likely to provide the 'x-factor' that makes a fundraiser successful. A successful fundraiser rather seems to possess a mix of skills, experience, passion and a strong personality.

Challenges facing NGOs in pursuing financial sustainability

Although several NGOs are consciously and rigorously pursuing financial sustainability, Ugandan NGOs are still faced with a number of constraints and challenges. We now discuss these challenges, which are both of an internal and external nature.

(a) *Organisational challenges*

Only four of the NGOs interviewed have set up a specific fundraising function with full autonomy to mobilise resources and with funds allocated to implement fundraising activities. Most NGOs in Uganda indeed do not set aside resources for resource mobilisation in terms of specialised staff/function, staff training and a budget allocation. The reasons for this could include the small size of many NGOs, limited resources and skills, as well as a perception of fundraising as 'an-every-(wo)man's-job' and therefore not a specialised skill that consciously needs to be nurtured. It is thus common to see staff and Board members go for fundraising training only when an opportunity occurs or when there is a financial crisis, without linking the training strategically to the NGO's plans and functions.

Another reason for the absence of fundraising functions within Ugandan NGOs could be the dependence of most of the NGOs interviewed on founder members and/or executive directors for fundraising. In addition, some leaders are running their organisations tightly and do not give much space for others when it comes to decision-making. This can result in limited specialisation in resource mobilisation and dependency on an experienced individual, a vulnerable situation should the person leave the NGO.

NGOs further face the challenge of striking a balance between time spent on furthering their social agenda and time spent on generating their own income. Four of the organisations interviewed found themselves in a situation where staff got more involved in consultancy work than project activities. Two organisations experienced losing, rather than making, money from engaging in IGAs or consultancy work and in two organisations the activities only generated enough money to sustain these very activities. Such situations occur when the rate charged per day is, for instance, not adequate to cover the staff time spent on the activity, when more than one staff is involved when only one is provided for or when time required for the activity is understated but commitments are made, i.e. the proceeds from the IGA do not cover the costs. Initiatives directed at generating own income thus require careful planning and reviewing the market opportunities realistically, backed up by clear organisational policies and priorities to avoid the organisation veering off its mission.

Two of the government officials and one NGO respondent argued that Ugandan NGOs also face difficulties in terms of mobilising resources, especially from the public and the government, because the sector in general has an image problem in the eye of many Ugandans. Easy access to donor funding has resulted in a number of 'briefcase NGOs', organisations existing only on paper, while some NGOs are set up for personal benefit rather than for the right cause, and thus change their vision with the flow of funding. Unfortunately, such NGOs can easily create a credibility problem for the wider sector and can deter potential supporters from providing support to genuine NGOs. It was, however, noted that NGOs that will stand the test of time are those that have carved a strong identity through their work and those who have a distinctive focus over a period of time.

(b) *Learning and sharing*
Another challenge facing local NGOs is that of learning and sharing experiences with each other. Most of the NGOs interviewed stated that there is little sharing or conscious replication of their financial sustainability initiatives, except for the purchase of office premises. The only collaboration between NGOs in the area of financial sustainability mentioned was that some NGOs share their list of donors with others and help them initiate contact with these donors. None of the more successful NGOs, however, went out of their way to share their experiences, suc*cesses or failures, with other organisations.*

(c) *Merger/ joint planning and networking*

One avenue that has been little explored by Ugandan NGOs is that of merging and carrying out joint planning or activities to attract large resources and lessen the burden of reporting demands. This might be as a consequence of the lack of culture of sharing experiences and lessons learnt between NGOs. Such initiatives may also be hindered by lack of trust between the NGOs, believing that the lead agency would reap all the benefits. One of the respondents, however, pointed out a successful programme for support to farmers in which three local NGOs came together and have benefited in terms of increased resources, increased knowledge from sharing and improved image.

Networking is another avenue that could be further exploited. Donors such as Danida and DFID pointed out that the trend in the donor community is towards donor coordination, which could mean that individual NGOs will find it increasingly difficult to receive funding from many different donors. The Head of Programmes in Danida also noted that it has a preference for supporting good concepts that are beneficial to a number of organisations rather than just one, e.g. through network cooperation. The philosophy behind such a network approach is that it creates support, cooperation, synergy and relationships between the member organisations. It is important, though, that internal policies, roles and responsibilities are clearly defined in such networks to avoid a situation where an unequal relationship between member organisations emerges.

(d) *Legal framework*

Half of the NGOs, especially those heavily involved in advocacy work, mentioned the precarious situation of the controversial revision of the law regulating NGO operations, the 2000 NGO Amendment Bill, as a challenge. The government has been reviewing this legislation with stricter provisions, which affects the right of NGOs to associate. The NGOs feel that some of these provisions are a threat to their very existence.

Another area of the legal framework that is seen as affecting the ability to pursue financial sustainability, especially in terms of business ventures, is the NGO Registration Statute 1989. This states that NGOs are non-profit making organisations and therefore engaging in a profit-making activity can be contravening this law. Should 'non-profit' however be looked at so rigidly? It could be argued that the concern should rather be how this profit is used. The NGOs engaged in IGAs, such as training centres and demonstration farms, argued that the reason for venturing into these activities was their direct benefits for beneficiaries and that the profit would be ploughed back into the organisation's programmes, again to their beneficiaries' advantage.

All our respondents felt that government had a role to play in promoting the financial sustainability of NGOs, both at policy and operational levels. At the policy level, the government was considered responsible for creating a conducive environment for NGOs to operate as partners in development and for providing information on relevant policies to NGOs. At the operational level, it was argued that government should provide resources, access to resources and tax exemptions where necessary. The current tax law came under scrutiny because tax exemptions for NGOs who are genuinely supplementing government efforts in development are not provided for, especially when purchasing equipment and vehicles for programmes.

All our respondents also felt that taxes make NGO work expensive and some suggested that mechanisms for screening genuine NGOs to be tax exempted could be instituted by government. It was noted that the current income tax law provides tax exemption for a few international organisations mentioned in the law schedule. Local NGOs perceive this as favouring international organisations which are better resourced and increasing the vulnerability of local NGOs through higher operating costs. Some NGOs delivering services at the district level also noted that they are charged holding tax, which is levied on their income, while international NGOs is not charged tax for similar work. This makes local NGOs less competitive when they bid for service provision for government, hence affecting their financial sustainability.

While the NGOs pointed out areas in the legal framework which could be improved to assist them in pursuing financial sustainability, there are, however, provisions in the law which are not currently being fully exploited. Section 35 in the Income Tax Act provides private sector and private people with a 5% tax deduction when giving donations for charitable causes. Despite this provision, a philanthropic culture does not much exist in Uganda, unlike in e.g. the US and the UK, and it could be worthwhile for NGOs to make a joint effort and explore ways of encouraging such a culture by making the public aware of the provision for tax deduction on donations.

(e) *Donor policies and priorities*
Respondents mentioned frequently changing donor policies which affect the financial sustainability of NGOs as another challenge. One respondent noted: "Donor policies change so fast that by the time you complete writing a proposal, another change is brought to your attention". At the same time, there is increased competition among Ugandan NGOs. Yet the need is growing – the percentage of those living below the poverty line is now 39% compared to 35% two years ago, famine is reoccurring and HIV/AIDS affects every layer of society – while it is evident that the government does not have the capacity to provide all the services needed.

The change by donors to basket funding for development support and encouraging NGOs to get funding from the districts affects the independence of NGOs. Two NGOs drew attention to the problematic nature of this way of accessing funds by explaining that they have had to withdraw from competing for government funds because officials expected kickbacks. Thus, in some cases, the competitiveness of the individual NGO is not considered.

One third of the respondents explicitly stated that the demand for financial sustainability comes from donors, although the legitimacy of such a demand was questioned. The issue of whether donor agencies themselves are sustainable was raised and respondents questioned whether such agencies are truly interested in seeing Southern NGOs becoming financially sustainable, since the funding needs of Southern NGOs are the very reason for donors' existence. Donors ask NGOs to produce a Business Plan[8] while they are often unwilling to fund money-generating projects. Financial sustainability is therefore seen as a buzzword used by donors with a contradictory mindset: on one hand, they demand financial sustainability but on the other, they are unwilling to support initiatives that can generate money.

Conclusion

Our research findings show that the perception of financial sustainability among Ugandan NGOs is two-faceted. On one hand, a financially sustainable NGO is seen as one that has diversified income sources, manages financial resources soundly, has a financial sustainability plan, raises its own money either internally or through local fundraising, owns its own premises and is able to co-finance its social activities. On the other hand, a positive impact of the NGO's work, a strong vision and a good image are also seen as determining factors for a financially sustainable NGO. In other words, financial sustainability involves an NGO's ability to define a relevant mission, to follow sound management practices and to develop diversified sources of income that assure continuity of quality activities and services and coverage of target populations. It thus becomes clear that financial sustainability cannot be separated from wider organisational sustainability issues.

All the NGOs interviewed pursue financial sustainability through diversification of income sources and through sound financial management that help ensure the continued existence of the organisation. The NGOs combine attempts directed at generating both external and internal income and the way they diversify their economic resource base is mainly through broadening and refining their donor base, negotiating good terms with donors, IGAs, local fundraising, consultancy work, MFIs, international connections and money reserves.

The aim of Ugandan NGOs is not to move totally away from external donor funding, but rather to be in a position where the organisation can retain a degree of independence to pursue its own agenda. None of the NGOs saw it as feasible to consider financial sustainability in terms of being independent of external donor funding. Our research thus indicates that the concept of financial sustainability as being self-reliant and independent from external funding (as it is perceived in a business setting and imported to the NGO sector) is illusory. Considering the environment in which the NGOs are operating, it also seems unlikely that NGOs will be able to raise enough funds to support their programmes through the Ugandan society: the government is heavily supported by donors to fund its budget, individual philanthropic behaviour is not developed and the country's narrow economic base limits the private sector's

---

8   Also referred to as Sustainability Plan, Self-sufficiency Plan and Financial Strategy Paper.

ability to support NGOs. Furthermore, NGOs are often predominantly staffed by social workers who do not have the capacity to plan and/or carry out profit making activities.

Besides struggling to comply with a concept that is not well defined or thought through in an NGO context, Ugandan NGOs also find it hard to conceptualise financial sustainability in their setting because of the strong image of NGOs as non-profit organisations. Yet our reality is that all the NGOs interviewed aim at obtaining a degree of independence from external donor funding and they are all in one way or the other involved in activities that are geared towards generating own income. Donors add to the confusion by demanding financial sustainability without having defined what it means and how it can be obtained. Thus, to assist local NGOs in becoming financially sustainable, there donors need to be more consistent in their funding priorities to create a degree of stability and to be willing to back up their demand for financial sustainability by supporting income generating efforts.

This implies that the future challenge for both NGOs and donors is to rethink the notion of NGOs as strictly non-profit to accommodate the need to diversify income sources. What then becomes crucial is how the income generating activities assist to fulfil the NGO's social agenda and mission and how the profit is used. Mechanisms must thus be put in place to ensure that the profit is used on programme or organisational activities, rather than enriching persons within the organisation, and that the income generating initiatives do no divert the organisation from its original philosophy. Experiences from some of the NGOs interviewed show that organisations are, in fact, able to design their income-generating activities in such a way that they benefit the target group or enable the organisation to use the profit to engage in more project or programme activities.

From our sample of respondents, there was no indication that the location of the NGO, i.e. rural- or urban-based, has any influence on the ability to pursue financial sustainability. It did become clear, however, that those NGOs that are relatively successful in terms of securing financial sustainability portrayed a number of common traits. These include: continuity and therefore stability in the leadership (which gives supporters confidence in the organisation); visionary, creative and innovate thinking and the consistency to carry out the vision, although in most cases the organisation's founder seems to be the one carrying the organisation forward. A supportive structure within the organisation, including the Board and staff, and the leaders possessing knowledge that is processed and used to create opportunities for the organisation is also important. Finally, the NGO must have a strong image and linkages that are used both to assist in fundraising and to promote its work. What appeared from the findings, though, is that the current type of fundraising training is not considered useful. Rather, what is needed is a forum where NGOs can share experiences and learn from each other.

The experiences of local NGOs in Uganda in pursuing financial sustainability thus provide some important lessons for other NGOs struggling to gain financial sustainability.

References

Barya, J. (2000). "The state of Civil Society in Uganda: An analysis of the legal and Politico-Economic Aspects" Working paper No. 58, Kampala: Centre for Basic Research.

Barr, J., Fafchamps, M. and Owens, T. (2003). "Non-Governmental Organisations in Uganda", Department of Economics, Oxford University: Centre for the Study of African Economies.

Beijuka, J. (1996). "NGOs and Resource Mobilisation: A study of the state of local resource mobilisation amongst DENIVA member organisations" DENIVA Studies Series No 3 July 1996.

Bhat, M., Cheria, A. and Edwin (1999). "Life goes on... sustainability of community development programmes and withdrawal of NGO support; an inquiry into expectations and imlications" The Center for Innovations in Voluntary Action [CIVA].

Brock, K., M'Gee, R. and Gaventa, J. (eds) (2004). *Unpacking policy: poverty reduction in Nigeria and Uganda* Kampala: Fountain Publishers.

CDRN (2002) Annual report.

De Coninck, J. (2004). "The political part is [best] left to the politicians: supporting the implementation of the PEAP – Change Analysis in Uganda: Civil Society". A report prepared for DFID Uganda.

Hare, L. (2004). "Nigerian NGO Sustainability Assessment: Findings and Recommendations on NGO financial sustainability". Initiatives/JSI Research & Training Institute (website article).

Kruse, S., Kyllönen, T., Ojanperä, S., Riddell, R. and Vielajus, J. (1997). "Searching for Impact methods: NGO Evaluation synthesis study". A report prepared for the OECD/ DAC Expert Group on Evaluation.

Munene, J. (2003). "The interrelationship between Non-governmental Orgnisations and Target communities: A case study of Kiambu, Machakos, Thika and Kajiado Districts" Iceberg Africa and Transform UK.

Norton, M. (1996). "The Non-Profit Sector in India", London: Charities Aid Foundation International.

Riddell, R., Gariyo, Z. and Mwesigye, H. (1998). "Review of National Policy on Non-Governmental Organisations for Uganda". Kampala.

The Non-Governmental Organisations Registration Statue, 1989 (under amendment) The Republic of Uganda.

Tulya-Muhika, S. (2002). "Uganda NGO sector Study - Notes for presentation of preliminary findings" [Hotel Equatoria, Wednesday 23 October 2002].

Vincent, F. and Campbell, P. (1989). "Towards Greater Financial Autonomy: A Manual on Financing Strategies and Techniques for Development NGOs and Community Organisations" Geneva: Development Innovations and Networks.

Wallace, T. (2004). "The Impact of Rational Management Tolls on NGO Partnership and Practice".

21

The Current Aid Architecture: Challenges for Civil Society Organisations in Uganda

John De Coninck[1]

Abstract

Civil society organisations (CSOs) active in Uganda are often very dependent on donor support. Understanding the current aid architecture, its changing nature, its limitations and the opportunities that arise therefore assumes much importance to these organisations, their supporters and observers.

This short paper examines the context of current debates on the aid architecture in Uganda, then moves on to discuss the challenges, including a set-up that reduces risk-taking, choice and diversity within civil society, reflecting the existence of an 'aid chain' that distributes and codifies power to its various participants. It is also a set-up informed by a vision of change that suits relatively simple recipes, especially politically-neutral 'projects' and donor-driven vision of development. This results in NGOs increasingly being contract-, rather than vision-driven, at the expense of sense of independent identity, its cohesion and its local ownership.

The author however points out the opportunities existing with the current set-up too, including the 'aid industry's' own internal logic of survival and self-preservation, the opportunities offered by the growing industrial and service sectors, and their attendant 'middle classes'. Paradoxically, the general drive to reduce transaction costs also in itself provides an opportunity for CSOs, through credible, collective proposals, leading towards increasing autonomy for the sector.

To conclude, the author points to the need to ensure that local analyses are developed, that they inform civil society priorities and that civil society is not turned into a sub-contractor for donor agencies, at the expense of accountability towards its own constituencies and the nurturing of 'political activism'. Donors, on their part, need to be encouraged to embrace diversity and move away from the usual Kampala-based

---

[1] Part of this paper was initially presented at a reflection event organised by the Civil Society Capacity-building Programme in September 2007.

'NGO culprits'. Long-term strengthening of civil society for democratic engagement is needed, not short-term project-oriented opportunism.

The 'recipients': CSOs in Uganda

Civil society organisations (CSOs) active in Uganda are often very dependent on donor support. Understanding the current aid architecture, its changing nature, its limitations and the opportunities that arise therefore assumes much importance to these organisations, their supporters and observers.

What characteristics of CSOs are relevant to an examination of the aid architecture and the challenges and prospects it presents? Four features can usefully be kept in mind to inform the discussion.

The first, and perhaps most obvious, is that 'CSOs' are very diverse and that their numbers are growing. So-called "NGOs" represent only a tiny fraction of the CSOs in the country. Community-based organisations and other types of CSOs are far more numerous (with, for instance more than half the Ugandan population, according to a recent survey, belonging to a religious group). The proportion is even higher for CBOs, service committees, PTAs. etc. The sector is also growing – there are now almost 8,000 registered NGOs alone and these command a large personnel complement: one estimate puts the number of staff working for NGOs at 240,000 in 2003.[2] Partly as a result, the voice of civil society is more loudly heard on some issues, including human rights, policy priorities, basic needs and people's marginalisation than ever before. Such growth and variety has a direct bearing on our analysis of the way aid support is defined and managed in Uganda.

Thus, and secondly, while dependence on donors is much in evidence, it is a minority (but dominant) group of NGOs that have direct access to such sources. According to one survey, 86% of NGOs' income comes from institutional donors,[3] although income from the corporate sector, while tiny, is growing. And so is sub-contracting, especially from district local governments. One of the last comprehensive analyses of NGOs in Uganda notes that just under one-quarter of those surveyed had ever been paid to provide a service, 40% by another NGO or 25% by Government. One-third owned a business to finance charitable activities, although revenues in volume terms were still dwarfed by donor funds. Dependence on donor funding (in part a knock-on effect from the Government's own dependence on external finance) has meant that fundraising has become a major activity for many CSOs. When donors sneeze, NGOs catch a cold!

The way CSOs relate to the state is also an important characteristic to consider: NGOs often tend to define themselves as service providers and their relationship with the state is essentially non-confrontational. One reason for this stems from recent trends in donor funding modalities: as sub-contracting from Government grows as a source of

---

2   See De Coninck/Kayuki, 'CIVICUS overview report', 2006.
3   Barr et al (2003): 'Non-governmental organisations in Uganda, A report to the Government of Uganda', Oxford, Centre for the study of African economies, Oxford University, p. 29.

income for NGOs, it becomes more difficult to question the provider. The environment in which CSOs operate is also of relevance here: it has recently been described as *rather disabling* for civil society.[4] This reflects a legal framework characterised by cumbersome, even oppressive registration procedures and the Government's ambivalent attitude on what constitutes allowable advocacy activities for CSOs. This 'tightening up' also highlights the blurred boundaries between the state, the private sector and civil society. CSOs are difficult to define, given these uncertain boundaries and the diversity of the sector – when does an NGO stop being one and becomes a business, for instance?

Finally, and possibly in part as a result of the above, NGOs are currently undergoing a period of lack of confidence in the eyes of the public, as the many stories of lack of accountability in the press, and the new NGO registration Act (partly) reflect. Some Ugandans increasingly question whether CSOs 'represent the poor'. Issues of ownership and internal governance have also been raised to question the legitimacy of NGOs (much more than is the case for CBOs and other CSOs). There is even a danger of the voice of civil society becoming increasingly considered as irrelevant and tainted in policy circles. Nevertheless, Ugandans still keep NGOs in high regard, especially when they have a physical presence in the community.[5]

The 'providers': Evolution of funding for CSOs in Uganda

A quick overview of the evolution of funding mechanisms also helps us to understand where we currently stand. In the 1960s and 1970s, whatever resources were made available to NGOs were from foreign private donors, with some limited local fundraising, mostly from the Asian-dominated business community. Governments were conspicuous by their absence in CSO funding. An example: OXFAM funding to a number of local charities during this period.

From the mid-1980s, new entrants appeared on the local funding scene: international NGOs (INGOs) and Northern Governments became important actors: the former with their emergency work in Karamoja and the Luweero Triangle, the latter to co-finance the work of INGOs. NGOs later moved from relief to becoming operational in development work – an area of specialty for INGOs which adopted the strategy of development zones or areas, often in the process displacing rudimentary government services where they worked.

More recently, with decentralisation, budget support and the Paris declaration[6], major changes have occurred (or are about to occur). To date, an important new feature for CSOs is sub-contracting of NGOs by Government, especially at the local level, (the other side of the 'budget support' coin which, as we have noted, has introduced a

---

4   CIVICUS/DENIVA: 'Civil Society in Uganda: at the crossroads?', Civil Society Index Report for Uganda, 2006.
5   Cf. Barr, (2003); World Values survey.
6   In 2005, the High Level Conference held in Paris proposed the reformulation of international aid policies, stressing "country ownership", aid effectiveness", "aid coordination and joint agenda", as major principles.

structural contradiction in their advocacy and accountability work),[7] and an emphasis on donor coordination and harmonisation.

Another recent development is the emphasis on 'partnerships': these define many funding relationships, especially along an 'aid chain' that brings together northern governments and multilateral agencies, INGOS, local NGOS, CBOs and the eventual beneficiaries into a web of interactions.

Current challenges arising from the 'aid architecture'

CSOs in Uganda are financially and programmatically supported by donors through a number of different channels, including agreements with affiliates and sponsors outside Uganda, funding through INGOs (which in turn may receive support from bilateral and/or multilateral agencies), sub-granting from INGOs in country, and in-country donor funding mechanisms.

These are defined as partnerships, said to be characterised by 'flexibility and autonomy', but the reality – as lived by Ugandan CSOs, is primarily one of growing conditionalities, as recent research[8] has amply shown. What are these conditions and what are their consequences?

Conditions exist at several levels, a first being that a donor's or government's priorities and plans increasingly dictate the agenda of the CSOs receiving funds. A CSO, for instance, rather than putting in a 'proposal, has to fit 'into' the strategic plans of those 'above' in a funding chain. In terms of the actual contents of specific programmes, actors in the chain are therefore most often expected to fit blueprints, not to market their own ideas. There are many examples of this: international calls for proposals that have to fit pre-determined priorities; gender issues being a must, or advocacy work, or 'participation' itself.

Because of this, the recipient CSO also has to fit within donor prescriptions of civil society's role in our country (as a consequence, for instance, of donors' increased emphasis on budget support): a good example here is the fact that local NGOs are comfortable in their role of service delivery; whereas "holding government to account" (a theme for many current funding modalities) is a more alien, externally imposed agenda. This can lead to an identity crisis for local development organisations.

Beyond this, are more profound consequences. One is that we can now better understand why questions are being raised on the lack of accountability by CSOs to their members or constituencies. The current funding modalities indeed foster certain forms of responsibility and often unhealthy competition. There is usually sole upward accountability to donors: thus, an NGO must claim 'success' to its donors, to whom it is accountable (rather than to the local population it claims to work for, or with); there are onerous reporting requirements; and there is much mistrust (in part because NGOs must compete for funding).

---

7   See 'Biting the hand that feeds you?', CDRN/CARE, 2005.
8   See Wallace, T, 'The Aid Chain', ITDG Press, Rugby, 2007.

There also appears to be a narrowing of choices for NGOs seeking support in Uganda. This, to a great extent, stems for the constant pressure in the aid chain to reduce 'transaction costs': face-to-face contacts are expensive, so NGOs have learnt to deal with paper-driven bureaucracies, and 'basket funds' are the names of the few doors they now often have to knock on.[9] Harmonisation concerns by donors leads to more pooled funding, more standardisation of planning and reporting, and also to a 'flock mentality'. It reduces risk-taking, innovation, choice and diversity in civil society (but not funding volumes). Local ownership of multi-donor funds can be problematic, especially where donors continue to 'pull the strings', a situation that arises where donor expectations are not sufficiently harmonised and when the growing number of such funds remain largely confined to medium-term programmes. These instruments also rely much on calls for proposals as selection mechanism, and have increased recourse to intermediary agents (INGOs, commercial firms) as pressure mounts to disburse larger amounts of funds at least cost. At the same time, capacity-building is then recognised as essential for accountability and effectiveness. Although such funds can result in greater efficiency (e.g. single reporting format for CSOs, less duplication, etc.), some donors in Uganda already find these funding mechanisms too numerous.

Behind these challenges, lie deeper issues, that can guide our analysis. One is that the aid chain distributes and codifies power to its various participants. INGOs for instance have recently become more powerful, as essential go-betweens, able to respond to calls for proposals, whose preparation costs exclude local CSOs. Similarly, while this may not be the intention, there is some evidence that budget support can create a 'donor compact'; and that negotiations between donors and government often exclude CSOs at the crucial stages. It is therefore important for Ugandan CSOs to wear 'power analysis lenses'.

Secondly, we need to remember that aid delivery mechanisms are informed by a vision of change that suits relatively simple recipes, especially 'projects'. Change has become controllable, predictable, linear, fit for our computers and logframes – quite distant from the realities of development with all its intricacies, unpredictability and 'messiness.' The poverty discourse is in itself largely conditioned by the adoption of messages that, given government's and NGOs' dependence on foreign funding, have quickly become akin to conditionality and have resulted in a *de facto* donor monopoly on ideas underpinning an accepted vision of development and development policy-making. So NGOs no longer have to think too much about 'development': they increasingly appear to be contract-, rather than vision-driven.

The lure of contracts can lead to a civil society focusing on service delivery and sub-contracting from government and others, at the expense of its sense of independent identity, its cohesion and its local ownership. 'Projects' have become the usual vehicles for development work (the many relief, rehabilitation and reconstruction funds belong here). Projects often encapsulate a mechanistic vision of development, devoid of political

---

9   Current funds include: the Legal aid basket fund, Support to Deepening Democracy Programme (DDP), HIV/AIDS basket fund, and Local Government association basket fund, among others.

content (although firmly informed by implicit neo-liberalism). But does this really fit with the realities of human and social development, a process of struggles, winners and losers? Fragmentation is a consequence of this project-dominated landscape: if NGOs are often heavily networked into each other, rarely are the boundaries of other civil society sub-sectors crossed. Trade Unions, for instance, seldom appear on NGO radar screens. Further, communication between civil society actors within a sub-sector remains poor: in part, this reflects uneven access to means of communication (the 'digital divide' between urban-based NGOs and their rural counterparts), as well as the prevailing competitive spirit and scramble for donor attention. Most projects are therefore implemented separately, not as part of a broader strategy for a sector.

We must finally note that the aid chain is a simple representation of a complex reality: in fact there are several aid chains in existence simultaneously, all with their own actors, ideas about development and rules of the game. Actors compete with each other and attempt to put their mark on processes or parts of processes: there is a struggle for ownership, for recognition. Progress in donor coordination should also be seen in this light. Further, the aid chains, their actors, relationships and contexts are not static: this fluidity and complexity needs to be monitored and understood, quite a challenge, especially for local CSOs.

Opportunities

So far, challenges have captured our attention. What are the opportunities that arise from current trends?

First, we can usefully remember that donors depend on donating: while the proportion of funding available to civil society in relation to total aid envelopes in Uganda is tiny, there is an opportunity in the likelihood that this total will rise in the coming years. The 'aid industry' has its own internal logic of survival and self-preservation. Sound programme ideas are likely to continue receiving an ear, if not necessarily concrete support. Donors, in particular, increasingly recognise that capacity-building and a healthy civil society infrastructure are essential for accountability and effectiveness.

Second, we must recognise that there is very little solicitation from the general public in Uganda. Very few NGOs are successful in mobilising support from the private sector, outside the 'standard' donations by multi-national corporations to high profile causes. Growing industrial and service sectors, and their attendant 'middle classes' offer opportunities too.

Limited success in local fundraising may partly be due to the crisis of confidence mentioned above. It is imperative that CSOs are seen by the public, Government and donors to be cleaning up their act. The opportunity here is that the NGO Quality Assurance Mechanism (QuAM) has been developed. It must swiftly be put into practice, by NGOs acting independently, and/or by NGO district networks, and/or through the leadership of DENIVA and the National NGO Forum. Further, we recall that most CSOs are not NGOs: there is much energy and legitimacy among other

CSOs, another opportunity for all of us to build on. So, while trends point towards less direct donor involvement, this needs to be compensated by stronger mechanisms for accountability, a results focus and transparency. This can be achieved through a more sustained dialogue by the parties involved, more explicit performance criteria, more support to weaker entrants and provisions for innovation and risk taking. Working on this would allow donors to increasingly take up the challenge of funding initiatives where ownership issues take precedence over efficiency issues (e.g. alignment to CSOs systems not vice-versa, mitigated donor dependence; increased independence of the sector, increased accountability to its own constituency).

The general drive to reduce transaction costs also in itself provides an opportunity for CSOs: if we are credible, work together and have sound proposals, this can help us mount a drive towards increasing autonomy and, therefore, help donors reduce their supervisory tasks and other transaction costs. Networks, coalitions and alliances are starting to make a mark. By making sure that these networks meet our aspirations and are accountable, we can build on the opportunities for collective action at the reduced cost that they provide. We can also support and document those positive donor funding experiences we have come across, those that allow for a measure of flexibility to respond to changing circumstances, those that have delivered high-quality capacity-building, those that have been willing to address sector-wide issues, and those that have fostered dialogue rather than control.

Conclusion: The power of argument

The need for an active civil society in Uganda is as valid today as it has ever been. By making the argument powerfully, we can tap into opportunities that arise from a global realisation that an effective civil society is an essential instrument for democratisation. A few final points lend themselves to taking this logic further.

One is that support mechanisms need to ensure that local analyses are developed, that they inform civil society priorities and that civil society is not turned into a sub-contractor for donor agencies, at the expense of accountability towards its own constituencies. We need to start developing these alternatives.

Secondly, the desire to amalgamate a wide variety of CSOs under the label 'civil society' must not mask very large differences in intent and characteristics. In particular, faith-based and community-based organisations need to be considered in their specificity, given their prevalence and potential foundations of social movements. Donors need to be encouraged to embrace diversity and move away from the usual Kampala-based 'NGO culprits'. We need to propose scenarios that guarantee the autonomy and independence of the sector; promotes collaboration amongst CSOs; increases their membership base and popular support, and increases the linkages between national and district organisations.

Third, we need to propose how 'political activism' can be nurtured, without creating dependency and other problems associated with the aid chain. Can faith-based organisations be supported, for instance, to find renewed inspiration in the churches' history of 'activist' political involvement in Uganda?

Finally, let us therefore press for longer-term, home-grown, wider perspectives. As CSOs are expected to deliver project-related outputs, wider issues lose prominence whereas, in a fluid environment, CSOs need to be attuned to changing circumstances to be able to produce credible social projects. While civil society leaders are becoming increasingly aware of the need to reflect on issues such as civil society identity, legitimacy, and accountability, this remains a considerable challenge. Long-term strengthening of civil society for democratic engagement is needed, not short-term project-oriented opportunism.

SECTION VII
Conclusions

22

Uganda's Civil Society – Where do we go from here?

Arthur Larok

Where we begun

This volume intended to shed light on Uganda's civil society, its evolution, relationship with the State and contribution to the country's development. Whatever aspect of its existence is examined - whether its diversity and relationships, the values (or absence thereof) that drive it in theory and practice, its impact and resourcing - this volume demonstrates the relevance of the enduring notion of civil society in Uganda. Overall, as Michael Edwards asserts, when subjected to a rigorous critique, the notion of civil society constantly re-emerges to offer significant emancipatory potential, explanatory power and practical support to problem-solving in both established and emerging democracies.[1] Indeed, whether seen from its associational, normative or public deliberation analytical perspectives, Uganda's civil society has and continues to play an important role in the country's socioeconomic and political trajectory. As argued here, it could nevertheless be more relevant and effective if it re-invented itself and adapted to, facilitated and supported more authentic people's struggles for socioeconomic and political justice, rather than remaining a predominantly project-driven sector. New crises and challenges, such as the climate crisis and the global pandemics that transcend nation states further highlight the need for constant adaptation.

Several questions, however, remain underexplored in this volume and should inform future publications of this nature. We outline some of these questions at the end of the chapter, which also seeks to analyse the key trends likely to shape the future of the country's civil society and to examine critical issues in nurturing a more effective sector.

Re-affirming the notion of civil society

While this collection of essays focuses on Uganda's civil society (rather than civil society in Uganda), a precise definition of 'civil society' remains difficult to ascertain, as any such definition will inevitably depend on the context to which it is applied.

---

1   Edwards, Michael (2004): Civil Society, Lonod: Polity.

But clarity we must seek, especially when trying to forecast the future of the sector. When Prof Oloka suggested in a 2017 review that after 30 years of operation in its current configuration, there is need for stock taking and asked "what is the essential *raison d'etre* of civil society"[2], he adopted an expansive definition as "the full range of voluntary associations and movements that operate outside the market, the State and primary affiliations, *and that specifically orient themselves to shaping the public sphere.*"[3]

Given the changing contexts and therefore roles of civil society throughout the world, it is therefore essential to recognise it as encompassing far more than a sector dominated by the NGO community, to include an ever wider and vibrant range of organised and unorganised groups[4]. In this volume, we have drawn cases from a variety of organisations - religious and faith-based, traditional cultural institutions, NGOs in their diversity, women's organisations, community associations and environmental groups.

Factors likely to shape the future of Uganda's civil society

> ... the context for civil society is changing: economic and geopolitical power is shifting away from Europe and North America, technology is disrupting traditional funding models and dramatically shifting social engagement, and political pressures are restricting the space for civil society activities in many countries...all these shifts pose challenges, create opportunity and require rapid adaptation...[5]

Global and historical conditionings

As De Coninck observes in chapter 3, the growth and evolution of Uganda's civil society is often driven by external factors, mainly government initiatives and donor funding. From a global and historical perspective, two developments[6] have shaped the agenda of contemporary civil society and especially of the NGO sub-group. First was the large-scale reduction in public expenditure during the structural adjustment era, occasioned in part by the perceived failure of top-down development initiatives. CSOs became 'development darlings' because of their perceived ability to connect with beneficiaries and their innovations in working with people at the margins. Second, was the subsequent 're-governmentisation' of aid, accompanied by the language of human rights, participation and strengthening of civil society. Civil society was then touted as a countervailing power against local and national governments. Meanwhile,

---

2   Cited in Larok, Arthur (2016): 'Re-invigorating civil society in Uganda: An agenda for the future' - *an unpublished paper presented at a DGF Partners Conference, November 2016.*
3   Heller, Patrick (2013), "Challenges and Opportunities: Civil Society in a Globalizing World," UNDP Human Development Report Office 2 Occasional Paper 2013/06 at p.2 http://hdr.undp.org/sites/default/files/hdro_1306_heller.pdf>.
4   World Economic Forum (World Scenarios Series) on the future role of civil society, http://www3.weforum.org/docs/WEF_FutureRoleCivilSociety_Report_2013.pdf.
5   WEF, World Scenarios, ibid.
6   See Bunks. N, Hulme and Edward, NGOs, States, and Donors Revisited: Still too close for Comfort? World Development, 2015 Vol 66, Issue C, 707-718.

the rapid growth of CSOs had mirrored the re-engagement in Uganda of international donors and institutions, following the decade of military dictatorship of the 1970s, the Obote II government and the short-lived rule of the military junta that overthrew his government in 1985. The embrace by the Museveni government of the structural adjustment programmes in the second half of the 80s saw an upsurge of donor supported programmes that contributed to civil society growth, particularly of international NGOs. With the 1993 decentralisation policy, the 1995 Constitution and the 1997 Local Government Act, the context was also set for the rise of advocacy oriented CSOs.

The changing character of the State

The character of the Ugandan State continues to evolve from one that was cautiously open to the direct and active participation of civil society in the policy process between 1997 and 2004, to the current different manifestations of control. The referendum that led to the official return of multiparty politics, rather than open more civic and political space, instead heightened its restrictive nature, with several laws introduced or amended after the multiparty elections in 2006. Previously heralded as critical to furthering democratisation in a no-party era,[7] civil society was henceforth viewed with increased suspicion. This led to the emergence of civil society groups that designed more politically-oriented programmes. Voices within civil society itself became more critical of 'NGOism' and an appeal for greater mobilisation of citizens to participate in the political process through initiatives such as the citizens', women's and youth manifestoes.

This resulted in an attempt to create a movement for political accountability, driven by activist leaders as opposed to those who favoured conformism. Unsurprisingly, a 2018 report[8] revealed that State hostility towards civil society activities was considered a prominent threat by civil society respondents across the country, with 84% reporting being subject to State control through interference, sanctions and surveillance. Another important dimension of the state-civil society relations has reflected a context of increased global corporate power and challenges to national sovereignty. The hidden power of corporates, the transnational character of globalisation and the resurgence of imperialism now affects what the Ugandan State can or cannot do, sometimes within its sovereign boundaries as the country's increasing indebtedness jeopardises its control of national assets. The future iteration of Uganda's civil society will likely therefore continue to be informed by both State capacity and its breakdown.

Resourcing and funding for civil society

The nature, source and type of funding will also determine the trajectory of Uganda's civil society, especially the dominant sub-group of NGOs. The survival of most NGOs and their activities, which often includes support to citizens' struggles and sub-granting

---

7   See Kabwegyere Tarsis – "Civil Society and Uganda's transition since 1986" in Mugaju, Justus and Oloka- Onyango (Eds) *No Party Democracy in Uganda: Myths and Realities*. Kampala: Fountain Publishers.
8   Uganda National NGO Forum - 2018 State of Civil Society Report.

to community-based organisations, is heavily tied to donor funding. In the last decade several have closed or reduced their operations because of loss of donor funding, either on account of changing donor priorities, cut-throat competition with other organisations or internal governance and management problems such as corruption, conflict of interest and mismanagement of funds. The character of Uganda's civil society therefore remains heavily influenced by donor conditions and practices, many of them patronising when determining permissible activities, results, and relationships with the State[9]. With conventional donors, especially bilateral agencies, increasingly redirecting their involvement to serve national interests, mainly commercial than 'aid', more funding restrictions for civil society are likely to emerge.

CSOs unable to exit single-donor dependence will progressively wither into oblivion or involuntary accept 'mission creeps' as part of their survival tactics, while those able to diversify their funding portfolio stand a chance to remain more faithful to their mission and more relevant to the changing expectation of society.

Technology and the future of civil society

The interplay of technology, geopolitics and markets have created immense opportunities and pressures - they have spurred the creation of millions of CSOs around the world and have given rise to exciting models of citizens' expression both on- and off-line. The technology-enabled power of the millennial generation to influence is growing in rapid and interconnected ways.[10] In Uganda, increased Internet penetration and ownership of smart phones has meant that information is more accessible and flows more rapidly than ever before. The traditional role of civil society as provider of information through resource centres will become less relevant as ordinary people access information in a variety of ways - radio, social media sites (and rumours). While technology is inspiring greater online campaigning and mobilisation, it is also creating a false sense of fulfilment among civil society actors who are often content to participate in online petitions whose consequence and impact is rarely measured beyond the numbers of comments, as opposed to actual face-to-face organising.

Simultaneously, as civil society becomes more dependent on technology whose access is now seen as a right, this can also facilitate State control and crackdown through Internet shutdowns, as was the case during the 2016 elections. Critiques are also emerging concerning technology undermining privacy and being used as a tool for control rather than freedom. Technology can thus be a force for progress or one that makes civil society irrelevant, depending on how it embraces and uses it.

'Traditional' civil society and the emergence of new movements and popular struggles

The future of Uganda's civil society is also likely to be the influenced by the rise of popular movements and struggles that deploy different approaches then those currently

---

9   See, Arthur Larok, Resourcing Democracy Promotion Efforts - A Letter to DGF Donors, September 2018.
10 WEF, World Scenarios, ibid.

in use by mainstream civil society. In the article, 'Uganda's new civic activism - beyond egos and logos'[11], this author argues that, as traditional civil society space is shrinking due to repressive legislation and with a government delegitimising CSOs as agents of foreign powers and cultures, emerging movements and activists are creating their own, less constrained spaces. While traditional NGOs yearn to be invited to the next budget conference, parliamentary hearing, or are willing to pay large sums to appear on prime TV and radio, emerging activists forge their own path. The new movements and popular struggles differ from conventional CSOs, whose missions and programmes tend to creep toward donor priorities. They also set themselves apart from some co-opted traditional groups such as trade unions, cooperatives, and student or women's movements, whose existence tends to depend on State favours or other forms of patronage. They are much less dependent on high-cost events and are more driven by their leaders' imagination. While 'traditional' civic groups are often locked into an unproductive and consumptive culture of per diems, transport refunds and endless reports, emerging movements are masters of their own time with less bureaucracy and fewer time-wasting ventures. Rather than perfecting internal systems, they prioritise improvisation - an ethos of building the boat as it sails.[12]

As Nicola Bunks and others observe, "we are [...] at a point in the NGO debate, at which serious questions are being raised about the ability of NGOs to meet their long-term goals of social justice and transformation at a time when the development sector is narrowly focusing on short-term results and value for money."[13] New challenges of a transnational nature such the Covid-19 pandemic have also raised questions about how Uganda's civil society is ready to adapt or 'repurpose', especially when governments use such pandemics to re-assert control and authority. The future of Uganda's civil society and its legitimacy will thus ultimately reflect the causes it espouses, rather than any endorsement by the State or by donors.

Will Uganda's civil society rise to the occasion?

To overcome some of the challenges described above and seize opportunities - including turning crisis into impetus for change - Uganda's civil society must address several important issues that present serious structural as well as self-imposed challenges.

The first concerns the weak roots of the majority of CSOs in society and amongst the public. Marina Ottaway[14] used the word 'trusteeships' to describe the assumed mandate of CSOs that are rarely as embedded as they ought to be in the societies and communities they work in. As is often asked, how many people would rise to take any action if a CSO was shut down by government? Clearly, many organisations

---

11 https://carnegieendowment.org/2017/07/24/uganda-s-new-civic-activism-beyond-egos-and-logos-pub-71600.
12 Ibid.
13 Nicola Bunks, David Hulme and Michael Edwards - NGOs, States, and Donors Revisited: Still too close for Comfort?
14 See Marina Ottaway and Thomas Carothers - Funding Virtue: Civil Society Aid and Democracy Promotion

would fail the public support test. This reflects the rising tide of technocracy that has swept through the aid industry and has driven NGOs to become clients working on a limited range of agenda, mainly biased towards service delivery and democracy promotion instead of deep-rooted transformation of politics, social relations, markets and technology.[15] If civil society is to re-assert itself and become more relevant improve its relevance, it must therefore better relate with the population, lest it increasingly alienates itself from the real world. Uganda's civil society's engagement and identification with societal challenges will determine the extent of public responsiveness to the causes it espouses. There is thus an urgent need to re-politicise civil society by overcoming the political fear-factor, by being more proactive in challenging injustice, by being more socially embedded and relevant to public discourse and challenges and by being more accountable 'downwards'. Civil society also ought to identify with and support social movements and people's struggles (including actors many may think of as 'uncivil society') for entitlements and justice everywhere.

The second challenge to overcome relates to a knowledge and intellectual crisis. Two or so decades ago, some organisations were dedicated to building knowledge about civil society's work. Several articles in this volume have been drawn from past work undertaken by agencies such as the Community Development and Resource Network (CDRN), the Development Network of Indigenous Voluntary Associations (DENIVA) and the Centre for Basic Research (CBR). While these organisations are still in existence, their output on civil society knowledge research is now negligible. Beyond the often donor-driven evaluations and project baselines, quarterly and annual reports produced by CSOs, much deeper and robust action and knowledge research is required. Uganda's civil society must regularly learn, unlearn and relearn if it is to adapt and renew.

Important questions for deeper interrogation include the ability of the sector to overcome the internal abuse of power and privilege which negatively impact on the sector's positioning. There is a need to better understand weakening internal governance and the erosion of values that hitherto inspired social justice intentions. Another question relates to the evolving notion of the State, its sovereignty and accountability: will an increasingly indebted State be able to protect its citizens' interests? If not, shall we witness a growing resistance to foreign investments and control, further complicating the relationship between Sate and civil society? Finally, despite several half-hearted attempts, there is no robust inquiry as to the empirical value and contribution of Uganda's civil society to socioeconomic and political change, be it through campaigning and advocacy, defence of human rights or humanitarian and livelihoods interventions. Most of the available data is sparse, anecdotal and lacks the expected rigour.

The country's civil society will in the foreseeable future remain dependent on donors and foreign funding and, as already mentioned, this translates into considerable donor influence over it. The business model that is the lifeblood of most of Uganda's civil society organisations is one in which funding is sought from foreign sources rather than

---

15 Bunks et al, op.cit.

domestically generated. The structure many organisations adopt is largely dependent on donors, without which they would cease to exist, as many such experiences have shown. However, much could change in civil society, including donor relations with a more honest dialogue, beyond the current 'shadow boxing'. There appears to be a deep-seated mutual mistrust but, rather than openly discuss relationship challenges, the tendency is to remain politically correct at the dialogue table, including at the frequent donor conferences, where discussions are technocratic, rather than political or ideological. Critical areas of dialogue should include a debate about what constitutes results from donor-funded progammes, the impact of funding on civil society - State relations, the undue influence of donors on civil society activities (making them appear as donor appendages), and the sensitive issue of donor-civil society collusion to divert funds. Tensions between civil society and donors, unsurprisingly affect state-civil society relations, with the latter often using donor dependency to deligitimise civil society.

The fourth challenge relates to leadership and the issues associated with it, including the value base that drives the sector. As Uganda's civil society is increasingly driven to become more 'professional', it also becomes more corporatised, with many professionals joining the sector because of the employment opportunity it provides rather than the causes it espouses. A leadership development programme, such as was run by Uganda Rural Development and Training (URDT) in the 1980s and 90s that focused on the value base and vision to drive the sector is essential. Another leadership issue concerns the endemic problem of the 'founder syndrome', where founding leaders never transition and sometimes run civil society organisations as private family enterprises, thus compromising organisational systems. Leadership longevity has also made it difficult for many organisations to continue at the same level of performance when leaders exit. Several vibrant organisations in Uganda's civil society have struggled to outlive long-serving leaders. Uganda's civil society, as many other sectors, needs deliberate transition and succession planning.[16]

A fifth challenge relates to corporate governance. NGO leaders are frequently part of management in one organisation and on the board of another. While this commitment to self-governance within the sector is important, it sometimes presents accountability challenges and undermines the independence of governing boards and their ability to exercise effective oversight 'over their friends'. Without an effective board that acts professionally and independently to provide oversight on management, compromises and friendship considerations become dominant in governance, thus weakening effectiveness.

Choices at the crossroads

Uganda's civil society is thus at a crossroads. Faced with internal contradictions that threaten to unravel its coherence as a collective; confronted by a tough external environment dominated by a fast-changing donor funding terrain and an increasingly aggressive State bent on greater control of the public sphere; and presented with the

---

16 Larok (2016), op.cit.

opportunity in the rise of more organic people's struggles for social justice, Uganda's civil society could choose from being co-opted by the State or donors, slowly becoming irrelevant and self-censored, or it could find creative ways of resisting and extending the boundaries of civic activism. These possibilities will ultimately depend on the individual and collective leadership of the sector to drive it in any or all three of the options below.

The first is to remain at the crossroads and get consumed by a self-serving bureaucratic character, face extinction or become irrelevant to social struggles. This option reflects the sector's conditioning to survive, rather than to thrive. And will depend on whether sector leaders are able to effectively respond to the multiple but interconnected holes that it finds itself in.[17] The second is a faster shrinking of the sector, especially the vocal NGO sub-group, driven largely by a combination of key exogenous factors: donor funding shifts, State clampdown or a combination of both. Already, several vibrant and critical CSOs at national and sub-national levels are facing closure or considerable reduction of their activities due to loss of funding. This may be because of changed donor priorities or internal accountability problems as outlined in the article by Larok in chapter 10. An increasingly authoritarian State will continue to exercise even greater control at a time of vulnerability for the sector and use the excuse of internal accountability deficits to further constrict civic space.

The third possibility is more hopeful and envisages a civil society able to re-invent itself, re-politicise its work and connect with more organic people's struggles for social justice in the country. Uganda, as elsewhere across the world, is witnessing a resurgence of activism in non-formal spaces, driven by those that face injustices, be it land-grabs, threats to the ecosystem and people's livelihoods or resistance against political repression. This is mainly propelled by young people across the country - musicians, performing artists and other activists. As argued elsewhere,[18] mainstream civil society in Uganda "must re-imagine its role and learn new, adaptive, and creative ways of working". It must unlearn its obsession with log frames and other buzz concepts instilled by donors. In an unpublished article, Leonard Okello[19] outlines three actions essential for civil society's future existence - what he terms "biting the bullet" - which entails rethinking operating models (from being implementers of donor projects to facilitators of movements and citizen membership organisations); ideological re-orientation to social justice values and organising principles; and generating local revenue through (among others) social enterprises to reduce dependence on donors.

Civil Society must also spell out more clearly how it believes change can happen - through theories of change and critical pathways to reform. And it must relearn the ethos and value of solidarity and collective action rather than getting caught up in

---

17 See more in a letter from across the border written by Arthur Larok to civil society in leaders in Uganda in 2018 - https://uganda.actionaid.org/sites/uganda/files/leading_us_out_of_the_holes_by_arthur_larok.pdf.
18 https://carnegieendowment.org/2017/07/24/uganda-s-new-civic-activism-beyond-egos-and-logos-pub-71600.
19 Okello, Leonard (2016): Confronting the elephant in the room - An unpublished paper presented at *a DGF Partners' Conference in November 2016.*

the cutthroat competition among NGOs that celebrates brands and logos rather than substantive change. While the past may have been largely shaped by exogenous factors, the future of Uganda's civil society will be shaped by the kind of leaders it will deploy. Uganda's civil society leaders must be at the forefront of boldly engaging with and driving reform to overcome the numerous internal challenges the sector faces, mobilise collective thought, creative imagination and new knowledge to turn external crisis into opportunity, to learn and adapt to change.

Index

abortion rights 16
academic engagements 343
accounting agencies 208
Acholi
    sub-region 252, 259, 264
    tradition 264
Acholi Education Initiative (AEI) 266
Acholi Religious Leaders Peace Initiative (ARLPI) 252, 259, 261-264, 266, 268
Acol-pii camp 261
advocacy work/advocacy activities 4, 5, 173, 256, 312, 313, 315-317, 319, 321, 334, 352, 375, 397, 404, 405
affirmative action 71, 77, 160, 377
agricultural
    extension 59, 60, 72, 209, 309
    production 44, 59, 249, 255, 277
    training 249
agro-industrial business 280
Akabway, Steven 17
alliance-building 307
Amin, Idi 23-25, 45, 49, 51, 54, 85, 119, 150, 151, 171, 173, 207, 257, 277, 280, 281, 287, 298
anti-corruption campaign(s) 213
Anti-Homosexuality Bill, 2009 228, 332, 336
antiretroviral
    therapy 231, 232
    treatment 224, 225, 233
Asian
    community(ies) 151, 287
    interests 150
    societies 347
authoritarian
    regime(s) 25, 422
    state 220
autocratic rule 35
Bahati, David 228
behaviour change 223
Besigye, Kiiza 227, 282, 283
Bigombe, Betty 259-261
black market 151, 152
budget allocation 395
Buganda
    kingdom 115, 142, 150, 278
    land 281
    monarch 150. See Buganda kingdom
    monarchy 55
    riots, 2009 281
Buganda Agreement, 1900 141
Bwogi, James 54
capacity-building 8, 164, 165, 168, 169, 183, 184, 200, 368, 369, 372-374, 377, 406-408
capital intensive businesses 247
carbon reduction 279
casual labouring 69, 74, 76
Catholic
    action 115-117, 122, 125
    Church 3, 92, 106, 109, 111-113, 116, 118, 121, 122, 125, 126, 128, 129, 131, 251, 259-262
    doctrine 125
    interests 117, 125
    lay organisations 126
charitable
    activities 385, 403
child abuse 16
Christian Democratic Party 116, 117. See DP
church
    -based organisations 122
    -linked organisations 151
    -related organisation 187
    -run hospitals 223
civic
    community 26
    duty 342, 355
    organisations 41, 331, 333, 347
civil
    behaviour 352, 357
    participation 346, 347
civilisational geopolitics 340, 350
civil society 1-9, 13-16, 18-23, 26, 31-43, 47, 53-57, 59, 80, 96, 99, 100, 106, 107, 108-114, 121-123, 126-131, 134-136, 139, 147, 149-155, 157, 158, 160-163, 165-167, 170-172, 174, 181, 205-211, 213, 214, 219-221, 223, 224, 226-233, 240, 250, 251-256, 259-264, 266-269, 275, 276, 278, 279, 281-286, 288-290, 297-312, 314-316, 319, 320, 326-329, 330, 332, 334-336, 339, 340-360, 369, 372, 373, 375-378, 383, 393, 402-409, 413-421
    activism 7, 227, 285

420

Civil Society Organisations (CSOs) 59, 60, 153, 157-160, 162, 164, 165, 170-172, 174, 206, 208-211, 231, 250-253, 255, 256, 259, 261-265, 267, 268, 278, 284-286, 289-301, 303-310, 314, 315, 320, 330, 334, 341-343, 346-348, 350-360, 374-376, 402-409, 414-418, 420
Cold War 47, 52
   politics 47
collective
   agricultural labour 65
   efforts 221, 309
   interests 206
   rights 132-135, 139
colonial order 5, 141, 149
command economy 154
commercial agriculture 64
Common Man's Charter, 1969 150
communal
   development 327
   gain 168
   movements 132, 133
community
   associations 79
   contributions 390
   development 159, 187, 369, 371
   -driven development 100
   initiatives 27
   interests 83, 87
   life 369
   mandate 198
   participation 23, 29, 32, 135, 161, 385
   well-being 285
Community Action Programme (CAP) 72
community-based
   AIDS groups 222
   organisation(s) 100
   services 225
Community-Based Organisations (CBOs) 90
competitive politics 282
conflict mediation 264
confrontational relations 314
consolidated democracies 253
constitutional
   powers 289, 306
   values 285
Co-operative and Peasant Societies Act, 1970 45
Co-operative Societies Ordinance, 1946 43
Corporate Social Responsibility 243
cosmetic change 159, 201
credibility gap 174
credit management 247
cultural
   bias 285

diversity 134, 173
institutions 4, 141, 173, 414
pressures 182
purity 135
rights 133, 135
sites 136, 137
traits 167
democratic
   governance 3, 35, 36, 79-82, 84, 99, 100, 121, 156, 194, 251, 286, 290, 340
   participation 38, 342, 360
   rule 110, 131
   struggles 252
Democratic Party (DP) 114-122
de-racialised state 43
development
   aid 371, 372
   initiatives 88, 369, 371, 414
   institutions 299
   partners 77, 90, 157, 159, 178
   planners 301
   policy(ies) 5, 147, 148, 150-152, 159, 172, 351, 378, 406
digital sub-wallet(s) 245
disempowered citizenry 9
dissident citizenship 345, 357
divine king 168
domestic
   conflicts 18
   violence 16
donor
   agencies 106, 152, 208, 370, 377, 386, 399, 402, 408
   compact 406
   conference(s) 222
   dependency 419
   -driven agenda 375
   environment 158, 381
   funding 159
   organisations 91, 93
   pressure 188, 233, 315, 375
   relations 168, 388, 419
double taxation 209
drug abuse 245
early marriages 246
economic
   assets 288, 312
   development 155, 156, 300, 382
   empowerment 247, 266
   exchange 140
   growth 148, 340, 354, 375
   war, 1972 49
electoral politics 21
electronic media 55

elite status 301
endowment funds 392
entrepreneurial
   aspirations 242
   growth 246
   skills 247
environmental
   awareness 279
   destruction 162
   disaster 279
   justice 285
   protection 286
essential services 350
ethnic
   affiliates 167
   based associations 252
   divisions 28, 256, 346
export-oriented economy 148, 150, 170
extended family(ies) 30, 64, 69, 75, 167, 174, 181, 182, 184, 188, 199
external
   agendas 76, 303
   stimulus 309
faith-based
   organisations 9, 96, 98, 164, 179, 180, 187, 206, 221, 251, 255, 408
Faith-based
   groups 68
family
   groups 62, 64, 65, 71
   lineage 63
   migration 134
   obligations 188, 197
   politics 16, 18
financial
   demands 394
   education 239, 242, 246-248
   empowerment 244
   illiteracy 240
   institutions 240, 242-244, 307
   landscape 242
   management 143, 373, 392, 394, 399
   planning 244, 384
   resources 241, 380, 387, 399
   self-sufficiency 383
   services 7, 239-244, 246, 249
   support 27, 117, 171, 181, 219, 360, 384
   sustainability 380
fishing industry 279
food security 143, 249, 266
foreign direct investment 277
freedom of expression 40, 285
free-market politics 282
'fundamental change' 109, 257, 371, 376

funeral insurance 248
gender
   balance 378
   equality 240, 285, 316, 317, 320
   -equity 317
   -focused NGOs 4, 312, 313, 316, 317, 319, 321, 322
   inequality 239, 246, 247, 320
   knowledge 378
   norms 184, 245
   oppression 378
   responsive 378
   roles 167, 188, 378
   sensitive 202, 378, 379
   sensitivity 379
   subordination 16
gender-based
   advocacy 312
   violence 240, 315, 319
global
   compacts 2
   pandemics 413
   warming 279
good governance 2, 4, 5, 8, 35, 132, 133, 147, 208, 255, 312, 315, 316, 318, 322, 330, 331, 340, 343, 375, 376
government
   legislation 143, 352
governmental corruption 213
group communication 93
guerrilla war, 1980–85 119, 152, 256, 257, 332
health care programmes 284
health insurance 239, 248
hegemonic state 148
HIV/AIDS pandemic 186
Holy Spirit Movement 282
homophobic sentiment 229
homosexuality 228, 229, 332, 336, 349
Household Dialogue 245
human
   resources 195, 387, 394
   society 109
   suffering 260
   survival 279
   values 285
human change/personal change 165, 169, 180, 196
humanitarian assistance 251
human rights 7, 9, 19, 20, 35, 36, 41, 54, 55, 59, 112, 114, 158, 208, 229, 250, 251-254, 256, 258, 259, 264, 276, 287, 329, 330-332, 343, 348, 403, 414, 418
   abuses 251, 258
   organisations 19, 35, 36, 41, 229, 251, 256

identity
    crisis 375, 405
    politics 7, 275, 290
illegal logging 277
illiberal democracies 328
income
    generating activities 8, 68, 69, 240, 382, 400
    generation 65
    poverty 309
income generating
    activities (IGAs) 246, 247, 382, 384, 389, 396, 397, 399
    groups 61
independent identity 8, 402, 406
indigenous knowledge 134
individual
    freedoms 332, 357
    rights 43, 135, 136, 139, 286
informal rules 63
infrastructural rehabilitation 31
institutional
    arrangements 14, 27, 138
    capacity 384
    constraints 208
    landscape 157
institutionalised crimes 25
intellectual crisis 418
interest-free loans 247
intergovernmental
    agencies 250, 252
    organisations 232
internal
    democracy 39, 41, 91, 285, 332
    disputes 347
    ethnic divisions 346
    interests 322
international
    charitable organisations 385
    development actors 297, 299, 300, 302-305, 310
    donors 89, 90, 95, 99, 221, 231, 255, 278, 285, 415
    economy 148
    investment 280
    policies 2
    rights agreements 327
International Monetary Fund (IMF) 50, 51, 150, 152, 314
interpersonal
    networks 225
    power 358
inter-personal skills 166, 177
Islamic fundamentalism 259
Kaleeba, Noerine 224-226, 233, 238

Kasubi tombs 281
Katabira, Elly (Dr) 224, 225, 238
Katana, Milly 226, 227, 230, 238
Kihangire, Cypriano (Bishop) 260
Kiryapawo, Kageni Loi 18
Kony, Joseph 260, 282
Kyoga, Lake 279
Lakwena, Alice 282
land-rights campaign(s) 318
Latek, Odong (Brig.) 260
leadership
    behaviour 164-166, 187, 190, 193, 198
    crisis 197
    development 164-166, 168, 169, 198, 202, 419
liberal
    capitalism 374
    citizenship 349
    democracy 38
loan
    capital 240
    interest 240
local
    fundraising 8, 380, 381, 386, 390, 399, 404, 407
    governance 134, 163, 382
    government(s) 25, 133, 139, 158, 160, 212, 382, 406, 415
    health care 29
    institutions 81, 82, 133, 378
    intermediaries 372
    public 390
local councils (LCs) 161, 310
local council system 18, 112
Lord's Resistance Army (LRA) 206, 258, 259, 260-269, 282
'Lukiiko' (Buganda parliament) 18, 135, 138, 139, 143
Luwero Triangle 46
Maathai, Wangari 21, 279
Mabira
    activists 280
    advocacy campaign 279
Mabira Forest 7, 275-281, 284, 286-290
    agitation 281
    campaign 7, 275, 276
    project 276, 279, 290
'mailo' land system (Buganda) 141
market
    -based economies 207
    liberalisation 282
mass demonstrations 20
Mayanja, Abu 54

media
    control 5
    council 55
    freedoms 347
Mehta Group 278, 280
micro-insurance products 248, 249
migrant labourers 63
military
    demobilisation 208
    dictatorship(s) 415
millennial generation 416
mobile banking 244
moral
    conduct 345
    reform 109
Mulago Hospital 224
Mulondo, Besweri 140
multicultural entities 137
multilateral agencies 251, 252, 303, 405
multiparty
    democracy 38, 282
    politics 160, 415
Museveni, Janet 228
Museveni, Kaguta Yoweri 17, 22, 25, 38, 87, 112, 119, 121, 136, 140, 152, 153, 163, 220-223, 226-229, 230-233, 251, 256-258, 260-262, 277-283, 287-290, 298, 319, 355, 415
Mutebi II Ronald, Kabaka 281
mutual
    mistrust 419
    partnership 349, 350
    solidarity 177
national
    assets 415
    integration 251, 256
    interests 416
    unity 162, 347
National Institute of Journalists of Uganda (NIJU) 55
National Organisation of Trade Unions (NOTU) 47, 49, 53
National Resistance Movement (NRM) 22-25, 34-36, 38, 40, 46, 51, 53-56, 112-114, 119, 120, 121, 125-128, 130, 131, 133, 140, 143, 152-155, 157, 158, 162, 171, 173, 207, 227, 304, 331, 332, 347
nation-building projects 346
Nekyon, Adoko 45
neo-liberal agenda 56, 207
Nkore kingdom 141
non-governmental organisations (NGOs) 36, 250, 252, 285
    Act, 2016 349
    Bill, 2015 349

non-grant income 385
non-party politics 114
non-state actors 2, 276, 298
Obote, Milton 23, 44, 45, 50, 51, 85, 119, 120, 133, 150, 152, 154, 222, 256, 257, 298, 415
Odama, John Baptist (Archibishop) 268
Okello, Angelo (Lt. Col.) 260
Okello, Bazilio (Gen.) 25
Okello, Tito (Gen.) 24, 257
Oloka-Onyango, Joe 35, 37-40, 45, 49, 130, 140, 153, 282, 298
one-party
    regimes 331
    state 119, 301
operational agenda 372
organisational
    challenges 395
    change 165, 169, 180, 181, 183, 196
    culture 166, 167, 186
    learning 191, 192, 199
    sustainability 3, 386, 399
palliative care 390
participatory
    development 61, 161, 163
    leadership 124, 187, 189, 193
partisan politics 4, 132, 140, 142, 227
partnership(s) 6-8, 156, 219-221, 226-233, 240, 243, 244, 255, 266, 299, 316, 318, 320, 321, 349, 350, 368, 369, 371-374, 395
peacebuilding activities 250-252, 266, 268, 269
peace education 264
peasant co-operatives 34, 36, 42
personal
    humility 166
    savings 241
    security 112, 282
    traits 166, 191
policy
    advocacy 170, 374-376
    -based lending 208
    priorities 403
political
    accountability 415
    activism 149, 171, 256, 268, 402, 408
    actors 22, 278
    agenda 251, 258, 259, 268, 269, 278
    associations 19, 348
    capital 290, 377
    change(s) 3, 106-108, 111, 126, 174, 308, 349, 353, 418
    civility 359
    commitment 10, 221
    culture 14, 31, 219, 232
    economy 35, 40, 298

engagement(s) 350, 352
identity 114, 116
instability 153, 251
institutions 41
legitimacy 138
mobilisation 20, 111-114, 126, 221
needs 352
opposition 140, 227, 278, 283, 288, 334
order 16
parties 5, 19, 21, 37-39, 44, 53, 99, 113, 114, 120, 121, 149, 157, 158, 161, 171, 206, 207
prisoners 20
realities 37, 38, 173, 297, 301, 302, 328, 329
reform(s) 33, 109-111
repression 279, 420
resources 305
rights 327
space 13, 14, 21, 30, 32, 33, 39, 42, 155, 226, 322, 415
stability 132, 134, 346, 347
struggle 30
transitions 19, 112
political mobilisation 20, 111-114, 126, 221
polygamous households 245
poverty
  eradication 2, 62
  reduction 4, 7, 35, 59-62, 73, 147, 148, 155, 159, 160, 162, 170, 255, 297-299, 304, 305, 310, 311, 315, 368, 370, 371, 373, 376, 377, 379
Poverty Action Fund (PAF) 306
poverty alleviation 36, 41, 47, 56, 76, 208, 280, 304, 370
print media 55, 144
professional
  ability(ies) 185
  will 166
psychological support 265
psycho-social
  insecurity 201
  needs 68
public
  debates 113, 300, 321
  fora 18
  humiliation 17
  image 312, 315, 316
  interventions 357
  life 15, 155, 156
  resources 151, 161
  space 355
  sphere 13-16, 18, 20, 26, 32, 111, 122, 124, 125, 129, 131, 135, 339, 340-342, 344, 345, 346, 348, 349, 353-357, 359, 414, 419
  transport 278, 349
  vetting 212
public order 347, 348, 350, 354
  Act, 2012 348
  interest 348
public-private
  dichotomy 20
  split 14
reciprocal relations 344
reintegration rites 265
religious
  identities 113, 115, 120-122, 126
  mobilisation 112, 126, 128, 129
  organisations 30, 109, 110, 113, 129, 130, 220, 251, 261
  pluralism 115
Resistance Council structure 153
resource mobilisation 133, 143, 380, 384, 388, 395, 396
Rodriguez, Carlos (Fr.) 262, 268
rotational
  credit groups 61
  digging groups 65
  savings 65
rule of law 54, 251, 285, 328, 329
Save Mabira Forest (SMF) 276, 278
savings accumulation 247
security threats 326, 332
Sedition Act, 1985 348, 354
selective justice 209
self
  -awareness 5, 147, 157, 168
  -confidence 123, 192, 196, 197, 201, 247
  -employment 174
  -governance 133, 211, 419
self-help
  groups 21, 58, 61, 64-66, 70, 76, 123, 250, 255, 266
  initiatives 23
  projects 124, 135
sensational media 53
service delivery 2, 3, 7, 34, 59, 60, 81, 149, 153, 155, 160, 170-172, 208-210, 224, 226, 227, 229, 256, 298, 300, 302, 306, 308, 310, 340, 349-352, 369, 370, 372, 375, 376, 381, 405, 406, 418
sex trade 245
sexual
  abuse 25
  behaviour 222
  exploitation 246
  harassment 16, 25

networks 222
norms 222
partners 222
slavery 259
shared
　identity 135
　responsibility 317, 350
Small Christian Communities (SCCs) 122-125
social
　achievement 157, 171
　agenda(s) 172, 184, 194, 380, 386, 389, 391, 396, 400
　approval 196, 197
　behaviours 340, 352
　change 14, 26, 32, 110, 161, 345, 356, 358
　class(es) 182
　cleavages 26
　cohesion 253
　configuration 27
　construction 350
　democracy 341
　disorder 135
　environment 2
　exclusion 61, 69, 74, 77, 82, 246
　expectations 6, 164, 185, 196
　fund 240, 247, 248
　gaps 81
　harmony 349
　hierarchies 98
　identity 116
　inequality 16
　insurance schemes 248
　integration 252
　justice 2, 7, 43, 111, 275, 280, 286, 287, 377, 379, 417, 418, 420
　media 357, 416
　networking 278
　norms 244, 245, 344
　obligation 389
　order 135
　organisations 106-109, 127, 129
　power 106-109, 114, 126, 129, 131
　protection 241
　support groups 62
　transformation 137
　welfare 7
　work 389
social capital 3, 6, 79-84, 87-89, 91, 93, 95-101, 207, 225, 241, 316, 348, 373
　formation 99, 101
social movements 123, 140, 207, 326, 336, 408, 418
　alliances 140
social service(s) 149, 153

societal pressures 25, 179
socio-cultural
　population 346
　rules 63
socio-political interests 312
soil fertility 279
spiritual dimension 167, 177, 178, 191
Ssemogerere, Paul 117, 262
staff development 176
state
　-civil society 219, 220, 233, 415, 419
　-inspired violence 26
　institutions 3, 6, 209
　-society-market relations 376
　surveillance 349, 351, 357
subsistence farming 170
Sudan People's Liberation Army (SPLA) 259
sugarcane production 280
sustainable agriculture 93, 372
tax advantages 328
titular head 143
trade unions 3, 9, 20, 34, 36, 37, 38, 41, 47, 48, 49, 50, 51, 52, 53, 56, 83, 149, 150, 151, 154, 171, 206, 207, 252, 255, 299, 326, 336, 347, 417
　ordinance, 1952 48
traditional
　authority(ies) 133, 135, 136, 137, 141, 252
　cleansing rituals 265
　cultural practices 143
　healers 70
　institutions 133, 135, 136, 137, 138, 139, 140, 141, 142, 143, 144, 250, 267
　justice rituals 267
　leaders 132-144, 168, 260, 265, 355
　rituals 265, 267
transformational change 181, 193
transitional democracies 327
transnational networks 232
Tripp, Mari Alli 2, 3, 13, 17, 22, 40, 42, 106, 279, 285, 313, 316
Uganda Journalists Association (UJA) 54, 56
Uganda National Congress (UNC) 115
Uganda Patriotic Movement (UPM) 119
Uganda People's Congress (UPC) 44, 49, 50, 54, 116-119, 140
Universal Declaration of Human Rights 327
universal suffrage 139
value
　-based social project 10
　chain development 239, 242
vernacular languages 351
Victoria, Lake 279

Village Savings and Loan Associations (VSLAs) 7, 240-243, 247, 249
vulnerable households 247, 248
walk-to-work campaign 283
women-headed households 69
World Bank 23, 35, 51, 81, 82, 88, 89, 100, 150, 152-156, 249, 253, 299, 314, 376

World Health Organisation (WHO) 222
World War II 48, 52, 171
youth
    employability 246, 247
    migration 245
    organisations 37, 38
    skilling 245, 246